# ECONOMICS: Principles of Income, Prices, and Growth

R. MURRAY HAVENS
Professor of Economics, University of Alabama

JOHN S. HENDERSON
Professor of Economics, Georgia State College

DALE L. CRAMER
Professor of Economics, University of Alabama

# ECONOMICS: Principles of Income, Prices, and Growth

The Macmillan Company, New York
Collier-Macmillan Limited, London

First Printing

Experimental edition © copyright 1963 by
R. Murray Havens, John S. Henderson, and Dale L. Cramer.

Library of Congress catalog card number: 66–16704

**The Macmillan Company, New York**

**Collier-Macmillan Canada, Ltd., Toronto, Ontario**

Printed in the United States of America

To Catherine, Anne, and Jeana

# Preface

This is a textbook designed for a beginning course in principles of economics. It was written because the authors felt that existing texts failed to meet certain needs. In our annual search for the best teaching materials we found that the more popular texts have become encyclopedias of economic information. Crammed with institutional and factual material, as well as the principles they are billed as presenting, some of these constitute excellent syntheses of the body of economic doctrine. But the time spent in study of factual material left too few class periods for thorough presentation of basic principles within the usual two-semester course.

As we considered the problem, it became evident to us that much of the material in these texts duplicated topics in other courses taken by the student. This duplication is particularly evident in the case of students in colleges of business administration who examine commercial institutions and practices intensively in many other courses. Therefore, we decided to write a basic text on economic theory that would reduce to a minimum the duplication of subject matter covered in other courses, but would contain just sufficient institutional and factual material to give relevance and life. As a result, this is a somewhat shorter book than most, but it goes even more deeply into the treatment of basic theory. For students who do not have the assumed background, supplementary assignments may be made in a book of readings.

We also felt strongly that the theory presented should be directed toward the solution of economic problems. As one of the most vital of these, economic growth comes in for particular attention. This topic is not disposed of merely by adding a chapter at the end of the book. Rather, it is woven into the theoretical discussion at many points through the text in order to provide repeated exposure to the topic from a number of viewpoints and in different contexts. For example, basic ideas on growth are presented in Chapter 1; the significance of the microeconomic concept of equilibrium of the industry for analysis of growth is treated in Chapter 16; the relationship of distribution of income to growth is analyzed in Chapter 22; and the final development of growth models is treated in Chapters 28 and 29. The result, we believe, is a theory that is considerably more dynamic in spirit than most. Such other current topics as the gold problem, international trade, and the United States balance of payments problem are treated in some detail within the framework of basic economic theory.

A particularly difficult problem for the teacher is presented by classes composed of students with diverse abilities and backgrounds. Some pupils can follow detailed theoretical arguments, whereas others blanch at the sight of a diagram, let alone an equation. No one textual discussion is going to be sufficient to meet the needs of all types of students. Our solution is to provide what we consider to be the essential topics in the text proper. Then, in places where the needs of more advanced students seem to call for further details or analysis, we have provided additional material in an appendix at the end of the chapter. Such material can be used to stretch the abilities of advanced students, while providing the instructor with a more precise basis for certain of the arguments used in the text.

Because the theory of value and distribution is so basic, some mention of our approach seems desirable. In the section on value we have tried to place oligopoly and monopolistic competition at the center of our analysis. The purely competitive model, with product prices determined by the free action of the market, seems unrealistic to the business student who has just studied calculation of costs and the addition of a markup in setting prices. For this student Chapter 15, "Price Policy of the Firm," will be a more understandable theory of the determination of prices than the much simpler purely competitive explanation. The liberal arts student will also find a challenge in the rigor of an analysis that avoids reliance upon excessively simple and unrealistic assumptions. The competitive market model is used in the introductory chapters to show how the economy would function under ideal conditions, but in the value theory section it is treated as a special case.

In distribution theory the traditional shares of wages, interest, rent, and profit are each treated separately. Although it is difficult to write satisfactory theory in such an unsettled area of analysis, we have tried to present in each case a definite theory as opposed to an institutional treatment or a statement of a number of conflicting ideas. Although reliance is placed upon a carefully developed marginal productivity analysis, several significant modifications of the usual textbook treatment increase the utility of the analytical tools in practical application. For example, in Chapter 19 stress upon the inelasticity of the demand-and-supply curves for labor under certain conditions enables the student to understand better the role of collective bargaining and its limitations. In the following chapter careful analysis of the elasticity of demand and supply of investment funds aids the student in his comprehension of the role of the banking system in determining interest rates.

As a further step in the direction of realism, we have recognized the growing importance of the international sector of the economy. Rather than treat it as a stepchild by assigning it special treatment in a single chapter, we treat international economics as an integral part of the functioning of the entire economy. As an example, in Chapter 25 a traditional treatment of exports and imports is presented and then fitted into the framework of income analysis to reveal the effects of trade on economic activity. Because international trade is recognized as an important determinant of economic activity, and because trade presents some very real problems, we feel that the student should be equipped with more than a passing knowledge of the balance of payments problem. For this reason we introduce and explain measures that would restore equilibrium, noting the effects of these measures on the functioning of the domestic economy. Foreign trade is also considered in the discussion of growth theory.

Although nominally a first edition, this text might well be designated a third. Originally it was brought out in a multilith edition used in the principles course at the University of Alabama by more than 2,000 students. This version was considerably revised and used once again in the principles course the following year. Finally, the text was revised once again, and the current text represents the third formulation of the basic material. At every stage we have benefited from the criticisms of reviewers provided by The Macmillan Company, from the reactions of students, and from the suggestions of colleagues. As a result of this preliminary testing and revision, we believe we have worked out a more satisfactory version of our basic idea of a compact, realistic textbook on economic theory with particular emphasis on growth.

R. M. H.
J. S. H.
D. L. C.

# Contents

## PART 1 The Background of Economics

## PART 2
## National Income, Prices, and Economic Change

## PART 3 Money and Economic Control



## PART 4 The Pricing of Consumer Goods and Services

# PART 6 International Trade

## PART 7 Economic Growth

PART

# 1

# The Background of Economics

This part describes the basic factors that underlie the operation of a mixed capitalistic system. The functioning of an economic system under dynamic conditions is discussed. The role of government in making our system work is revealed.

CHAPTER

1

# The Background of Economics: Scarcity, Diminishing Returns, and Growth

**What Is Economics?** In order to get into the subject we may start by defining economics. Taking a rather literal point of view, we may guess that economics has to do with economizing, with acting in an economical manner. From this we may conjure up a vision of the prudent and frugal housewife, carefully administering the household funds to secure the best food and clothing for the family. Then we can extend this idea to society as a whole, assigning to the economic system the role of economizer. Actually, this approach comes very close to the mark, because economics has a great deal to do with social problems that involve economizing. But perhaps we might do best by being more specific.

At bottom economics is concerned with the satisfaction of human wants. Presently we will develop the notion that these wants are unlimited in amount. This statement applies to the individual and, even more strongly, to society as a whole. Owing to the indefinite extent of wants and the limited productive power of any society it is necessary to make choices. Ideally, the choices are made with a view to producing the collection of the goods that will best satisfy wants. This is economizing, considered from the social viewpoint. We may summarize these ideas with the following definition: *Economics is the social study that deals with the organization of productive resources for the satisfaction of human wants.*

As we have suggested, production requires the organization of resources. The nature of this organization is not self-evident and will require considerable attention.

## THE BASIC ECONOMIC PROBLEM: SCARCITY

The economist concerns himself with the process by which human wants are satisfied through productive activity. As he gets into the subject it soon becomes evident that the ability of any system to produce goods is limited and that human wants are unlimited. This leads to a consideration of the problem of scarcity, to be considered in the following pages. We start by considering the nature of wants.

**The Character of Human Wants: Insatiability.** One striking property of human wants is their insatiability. To begin with, the variety of wants is almost endless, ranging from the simplest needs for food, clothing, and shelter to the most refined cultural desires satisfied in music, art, and the dance. Moreover, wants continuously evolve; as one set of wants is satisfied, further and more elaborate wants arise. Consider the evolution of the American diet. In earlier days the fare was rather a basic one centering on bread, meat, and vegetables. As incomes rose the emphasis shifted to dairy products, including milk and eggs. Then fresh fruit in sizable amount was added to the list. Today ordinary foods are supplemented by tablets containing various vitamins and minerals. Thus our diet is far more varied and complete now than it was a hundred years ago.

In a dynamic society the evolution of wants is stimulated by changes in technology. A case in point is found in the history of the automobile. At one time the car was a reasonably simple mechanism. Indeed, this was the attraction of Henry Ford's Model T, so popular in the early 1920's. As a result of developments in technology the automobile has become a mechanical marvel, with devices that shift gears automatically, raise and depress headlight beams, and otherwise take the effort out of driving. A car may be equipped with radio, air conditioner, and a set of push buttons to raise and lower windows. Work is in progress on automatic braking and steering mechanisms as well as radically different motors, such as the gas turbine engine. For the most part such innovations have been well received, and once accepted, are required by consumers in future models. Thus the march of technology leads to the discovery and satisfaction of many latent human wants.

**The Character of Human Wants: Their Social Nature.** A factor that reinforces the evolution of wants is their social character. Often our enjoyment of something is enhanced through the effect it produces on neighbors and associates. We like to impress them with our ability to procure the good things of life. In part, our choice of a car and a house, for example, is determined by what others already have and by our desire to surpass others in some respect. Some see in this phenomenon a desire for "status" or position in the eyes of the community; the objects themselves are "status symbols," which represent attainment of a certain standing in the community. In short, we identify, and expect others likewise to identify, possession and use of certain things with position in society. Such an attitude provides an outside force raising our standards of living and our wants.



The discussion of human wants leads naturally to the question of how they are to be satisfied. Clearly, these needs must be satisfied by production.

**The Problem of Production.** In order to satisfy human wants useful things must be created. For convenience in discussion let us define *production* as *"the creation of utilities"* (useful goods and services). Production is carried on with the aid of resources or factors of production, which consist of the various agents that are combined in the creation of things. By long convention economists classify resources under four headings: land, labor, capital, and entrepreneurship. These are generally called the factors of production.

To the economist land is roughly synonymous with natural resources, and it includes mines, oil wells, and forests as well as land used in agriculture or as sites for the construction of buildings. Only resources that can be put to fruitful use under current conditions are included. Labor refers to any human effort directed to producing goods and services, but excludes recreational activities no matter how strenuous, as well as misdirected activity that yields no fruitful result. Capital consists of material things produced by man that are used in production. The category includes not only buildings, machinery, and tools but also the inventories, goods in process, and other stocks of goods necessary to a continuous flow of production to the buyer. Although measured in money and purchased with money borrowed from savers or banks, capital consists strictly of goods. Finally, entrepreneurship is used by the economist to denote the activity of organizing the factors so as to form an enterprise or business, bearing the risks and making crucial decisions. In the modern corporation the entrepreneur is a mixture of the board of directors, stockholders, and top management.

At any point of time these factors are all strictly limited in amount. Although one or more may respond to some stimulus, the quantity of each that is available cannot be increased indefinitely. For example, consider the supply of labor. In 1961 the labor force amounted to a bit over 74 million persons. During the six years prior to 1961 the labor force increased by about 0.9 million per year; this amounts to an increase of a shade more than 1 per cent annually. In the absence of some strong impulse, such as mobilization for war, the labor force is not subject to much variation in the short run. In fact, economists do not believe that a rise in wages alone will provide any significant increase in the labor force or hours worked. Consequently, barring a national emergency, the labor force is limited in amount. Much the same can be said of land and capital. As a result, economists often assume that the factors of production are fixed in amount in the short run. This statement is doubtless a fairly accurate one under normal conditions.

By the same sort of argument we may assert that the factors will expand in amount through time only at a limited rate. Thus the additions to the labor force per year cannot be increased or decreased very much from the normal trend mentioned previously. Over time, therefore, each of the factors increases only at a limited rate per year.

**Scarcity.** If resources are limited in amount, production is necessarily limited also. After all, production is carried on by these resources and grows in only two ways: (1) an increase in the amounts of the factors, (2) increased efficiency in the use of factors—that is, in methods of production. Because the amounts of the factors are limited, we turn to the second consideration. Could we, if the need arose, bring forward some new technique that would raise production quickly? Generally, the answer is no. Consider the reasons.

If a technique is to be introduced now, it must already be known. If known already and capable of increasing production, it should have been introduced by now. Thus it seems unreasonable to assume the existence of any such technique. True, in case of emergency some untested methods may be tried, but such testing involves time and expense. Moreover, the untried method may ultimately be rejected. Therefore, we must conclude that production techniques are not subject to significant change at a given moment.

With limited factor supplies and fixed techniques at a given moment the output that can be produced is also limited. On the other hand human wants are unlimited in amount; no fixed quantity of goods will ever satisfy all wants. The relation between limited resources and techniques, on the one hand, and of unlimited wants, on the other, creates a situation known as scarcity. Let us define *scarcity* as the *"limitation on productive resources and techniques making it impossible to provide sufficient output to satisfy all wants."* A cumbersome definition, perhaps, but one that covers the relevant points.

**Scarcity of Output and Resources.** The scarcity of output is a result of our unlimited wants for output combined with a limited amount of available output. This output is limited, given the technique, by the amounts of resources; these amounts are fixed, as explained earlier. On the other side, the unlimited wants for output generate unlimited wants for the resources with which to supply them. When the unlimited wants for resources are combined with the limited amounts available, the result is scarcity of resources. Thus scarcity of output has its counterpart in a scarcity of resources.

Economists regard scarcity as the most basic and stubborn of all economic problems. Because it is inherent in the nature of the human situation, it claims our first attention. Let us here make an aside. In the United States and certain other countries great progress has been made in raising output and meeting the most intense human wants. Possibly as we approach the solution of these basic needs, some secondary problems may join scarcity at the center of the stage. For example, economic instability, the proper use of increased income and leisure, or a more equitable distribution of income may come to rival scarcity as the main economic problem in the future—possibly. It now appears, however, that the United States must apply its talents and resources to conquering scarcity abroad before this day will come.

**The Effects of Scarcity.** In our economy, as elsewhere, scarcity exists. Even with the full use of our resources, all wants are not satisfied. We now come to an important effect of scarcity which we may call *the law of scarcity: In a fully employed economy production of one item can be increased only by a decrease in the production of some other item or items.* Why? To begin with, we assume that all resources are taken up in producing needed goods, wants being unlimited. If society decides that it wants more rockets now, it must turn more resources from the production of something else—say, automobiles. If the resources are withdrawn, automobile production must drop. Therefore, the increase in rocket output is bought only at the expense of a decline in automobile production.

To give quantitative expression to this idea economists use a concept known as the *transformation curve, or production frontier, which expresses the combinations of goods obtainable in a full employment economy.*[1] Assume that two goods—rockets and automobiles—are produced in the economy. We may list some of the possible combinations in tabular form.

Such a table has a number of characteristics; let us note only two. First, any combination of the two goods chosen requires use of all the available factors. Thus full employment exists. Second, a movement from one combination to another implies that the economy gives up some of one good as it acquires more of a second. This is a result of the fact that the increase in automobiles, for example, is

[1] P. A. Samuelson was apparently first to employ the transformation curve in this connection. See his *Economics, An Introductory Analysis* (5th ed.; New York: McGraw-Hill Book Company, 1961), pp. 19–24. The curve was used at a much earlier date in other connections by Vilfredo Pareto in his *Manuel d'Economie Politique* (Paris: Giard, 1927).

made possible by a transfer of resources that were being used in making rockets.

Let us now transfer the information in Table 1–1 into the graph of Figure 1–1. Note how each combination in Table 1–1 plots into a point in Figure 1–1. Connecting the points with a smooth curve we arrive at the production frontier of Figure 1–1. Notice that the production frontier divides the whole region into the two shaded areas: (1) an underproduction region, marked by less-than-full employment, (2) an unattainable region beyond the production frontier. In the first region some resources are not being used, and production is not as high as it might be. Consider point *X*, denoting the production of 5 million automobiles and 3,000 rockets. Greater production than this

**TABLE 1–1**
**Production Frontier Table**

| Automobiles | Rockets | Combination |
|---|---|---|
| 10 | 1 | A |
| 9 | 4 | B |
| 8 | 6 | C |
| 7 | 7 | D |
| 5 | 8 | E |
| 2 | 9 | F |

can be attained by putting unused factors to work producing rockets and expanding their output to 8,000 while continuing to produce 5 million automobiles. This is the limit; the production frontier.

It is impossible for an economy to move beyond the production frontier at any moment. Consider a point such as *Y*, requiring production of 7,000 rockets and 10 million cars. If all resources are put into use to produce, say, combination *D*, the economy can provide 7,000 rockets and 7 million cars. It will then be 3 million cars short of its goal. Why? There simply are not enough resources available to do the job. What about eliminating "waste"? With the given method of production assumed there is always a certain lack of efficiency, but this condition is inherent in the existing state of knowledge and method of organizing production. In fact, this "waste" is really just the name for the limited scope of human experience and ability; it is not something that can be made to vanish at a stroke. Therefore, we cannot move above and beyond the production frontier to *Y* right away by eliminating something called "waste," "duplication," "inefficiency," or any other like name for our limited production capabilities.

**Shape of the Production Frontier.** As depicted in Figure 1–1 the production frontier is bowed away from the origin. If society makes a decision to produce more autos, it gives up some rockets.

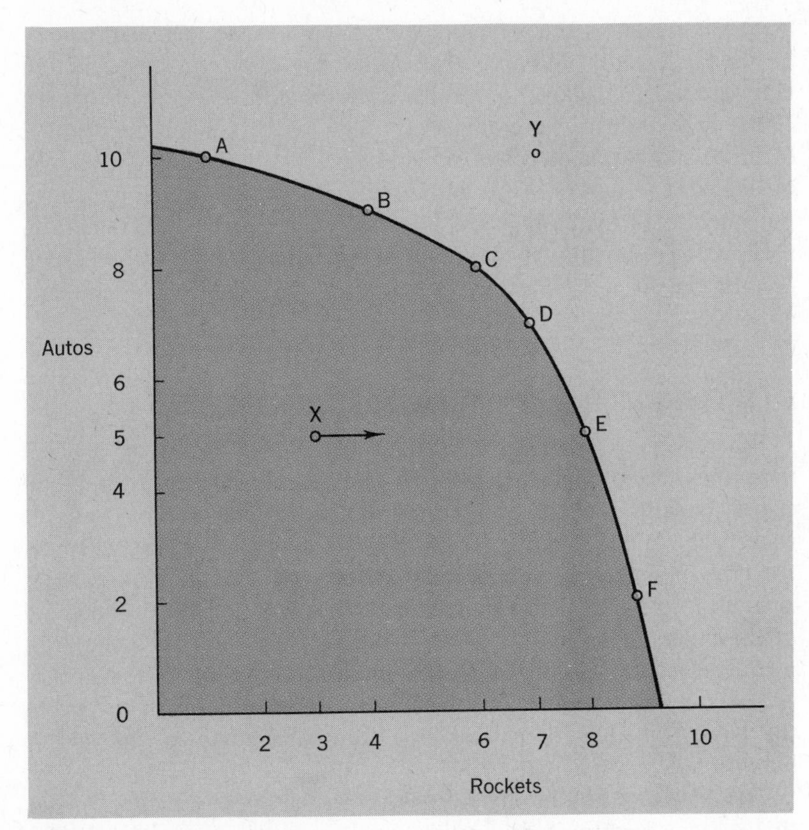


**Figure 1–1.** The production frontier.

The more autos it produces, however, the greater is the sacrifice of rockets to secure one more auto. Why?

First, resources are partly specialized. To be sure, some resources can be shifted readily from one industry to another. For instance, steel enters into the production both of autos and rockets, and the allocation between the two fields can be altered without much difficulty. Also certain types of labor can about as easily assist in rocket as in automobile assembly. On the other hand, certain resources or factors are rather specialized or have a tendency to be "fixed" or "sunk" in their current uses. The machinery and equipment used to produce the shell or engine of a rocket is probably not convertible to automobile production, and vice versa. Likewise, certain types of skilled labor used in rocket manufacture cannot be used to great advantage in auto production. As auto production expands it runs into increasing resistance because it cannot obtain from the rocket industry increases in certain specialized factors.

Second, the inability to expand the amounts of certain of the factors implies that other factors whose supplies are increased cannot be used efficiently. Suppose that additional steel and unspecialized labor are made available to the auto industry at the expense of rockets. If the auto industry is cramped for lack of certain needed capital facilities and various types of skilled labor, it will make inefficient use of the extra resources. Thus automobile production can be expanded but only at an increasing cost in terms of resources and, therefore, rockets. The difficulty encountered in expanding output when certain factors are fixed is considered below in the context of economic growth.

## DIMINISHING RETURNS AND GROWTH

Whereas output is limited by fixed supplies of factors at a given time, these factors increase *through time,* causing the transformation curve to shift outward and permitting greater production both of rockets and autos. If all the factors of production increase on schedule, the growth spoken of will occur. On the other hand, suppose there is some factor that fails to increase or lags well behind the increase of the others. Then the question is posed: What will be the growth picture when certain of the factors increase while others remain approximately constant? This brings us to the consideration of one of the basic principles of economics, often referred to as *the law of diminishing returns.*

**The Law of Diminishing Returns.** In the above situation we see that certain factors of production may be fixed or specialized. The fixed factors used in a given industry cannot readily be shifted to another. For example, railroad locomotives are not useful to the trucking industry, nor are trucks very useful to railroads. A railroad engineer is not necessarily an adequate truck driver, and vice versa. From the viewpoint of a given industry, or perhaps a firm, a good part of the capital, as well as a part of the labor, takes a very specialized form. Tied in with these fixed factors will be certain quantities of land. Taken together they make up what is called *the fixed factor.*

With this background we are ready to discuss the principle of diminishing returns. This concept describes the variation of output as units of a variable factor are applied to a fixed factor in a well-defined situation. Let us begin with the example of a farm with a certain number of acres, say 1,000, given fertility, and other characteristics. In addition, the owner has a certain array of tractors, cultivators, plows, and other equipment. All this represents the fixed factor. Now suppose the owner applies succesive "doses" of labor and some appropriate combination of seed, fertilizer, and other chemicals to the land.

At first, the output (for example, corn) should show a marked jump with each new dose. *After a certain number of doses is applied, however, the use of one more dose will add less product than did the preceding dose. This marks the stage of diminishing returns* (in the application of a variable to a fixed factor). Once diminishing returns have set in, the same principle continues to operate, causing each dose to add successively less to output than the preceding one.

The cause of diminishing returns lies in the presence of a fixed factor. More intensive cultivation of a given plot of land brings greater output. As the additional doses are added, however, each dose is able to make less and less effective use of the fixed factor. Additional labor must compete with existing labor for the use of the same tractors and tools, thus lessening efficiency. Each additional application of labor, equipment, and raw materials is made onto land already given prior treatment. Naturally, the additional cultivation of the same soil yields successively smaller additions to the total product.

Now consider an imaginary numerical illustration of this situation. First, we list the successive doses of the variable factor. Then, we include a column headed "Fixed Factor." The quantity is listed as 10 units; however, the important thing is not the number itself but the constancy of this amount.

Next we list the total product or output in terms of bushels. At

**TABLE 1-2**
**Numerical Illustration of Diminishing Returns**

| Variable Factor (Doses of Labor and Raw Materials) | Fixed Factor (Units of Land and Capital) | Total Product (Output of Corn, Bushels) | Marginal Product (Bushels) | Average Product (Bushels) |
|---|---|---|---|---|
| 0 | 10 | 0 | | — |
| 1 | 10 | 8 | 8 | 8 |
| 2 | 10 | 20 | 12 | 10 |
| 3 | 10 | 30 | 10 | 10 |
| 4 | 10 | 38 | 8 | 9½ |
| 5 | 10 | 45 | 7 | 9 |
| 6 | 10 | 51 | 6 | 8½ |
| 7 | 10 | 56 | 5 | 8 |
| 8 | 10 | 60 | 4 | 7½ |

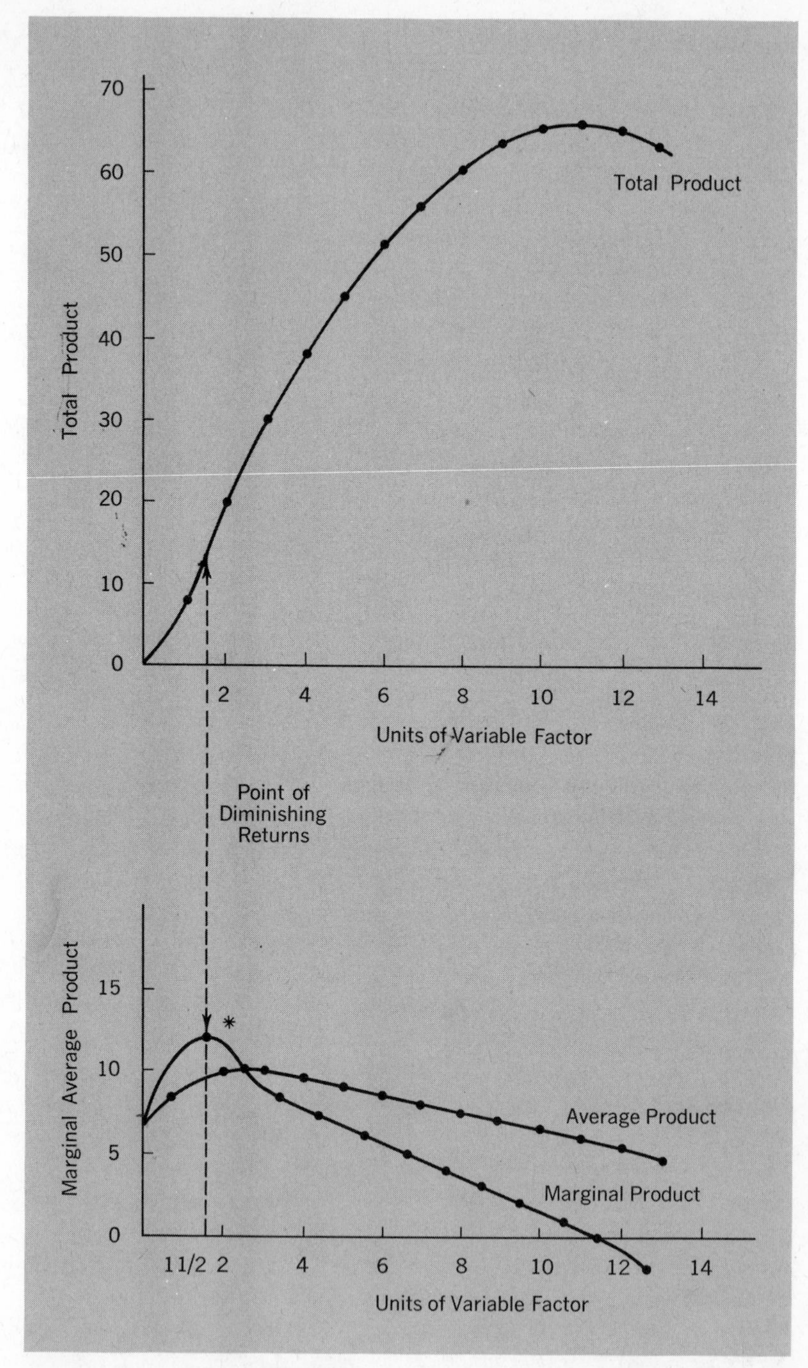


**Figure 1–2.** The product curves: total product, average product, and marginal product.

this point we must define two new terms, marginal product and average product. *Marginal product* is the additional product resulting from the addition of one more unit of the variable factor. *Average product* is the total product divided by the number of units of the variable factor—that is, it is product per unit of the variable factor.

Let us now delve into the table to illustrate these concepts. If four units of the variable factor are applied, total product is 38, whereas if five are applied, the total jumps to 45. The addition to output is $7 = 45 - 38$ and results from adding the fifth unit of the factor. The figure 7 is the number of bushels added by application of the fifth dose of the variable factor. Because the 7 in question is the difference between total products of 38 and 45, it is properly listed on a line falling between these two amounts. Evidently, the marginal products consist of successive differences in the total product column when the variable factor is increased one unit at a time.

The average product is found simply by taking the total product, say 45, and dividing by the corresponding number of units of the variable factor, 5, giving an average product: $45/5 = 9$. This figure 9 represents the average number of bushels produced by 5 units of the variable factor.

As the earlier italicized statement indicates, diminishing returns is a decline in the added product resulting from one more dose of the variable factor. Now this added product is what we have called the marginal product. Looking into the marginal product column, we see that the marginal product first rises from 8 to 12, but then drops to 10 with the application of the third unit. This marks the stage of diminishing returns. Notice that the output of corn is increasing from 20 to 30, as seen in the third column; diminishing returns does *not* indicate a decline in total product. Actually, *diminishing returns sets in when total product begins to increase at a decreasing rate.*

In Figure 1–2 we exhibit the plot of the total, marginal, and average product curves. The vertical line at 1½ units of the variable factor denotes the beginning of the stage of diminishing returns. The star by the marginal product curve just beyond the peak designates declining marginal product or diminishing returns. Note that the total product curve is just passing its steepest point and is beginning to rise a little more slowly.

Notice from the figure that the average product is still rising at the point of diminishing returns. In fact, as long as the marginal product is higher than the average product the average product continues to rise. Eventually, in the course of diminishing returns, marginal product declines to equality with average product. Here average product is at its peak. Beyond this point marginal product falls below average product, and average product begins to decline.

If the variable factor continues to be applied, marginal product may eventually reach zero. Then total product reaches its maximum point and declines. In this event the application of doses has been so intense as actually to decrease production. Of course, this is very uneconomical, and production will never be carried on in the range of declining total product except by miscalculation.

The law of diminishing returns is important because of its widespread influence. It operates sometimes in an entire economy when some particular factor, like capital, becomes fixed, as during certain stages of World War II. It operates in industries where equipment and labor may be specialized, as we indicated in the discussion of the transformation curve. Often it applies to a particular firm possessing certain factors that can neither be readily expanded nor contracted. Our numerical example illustrates this case. Presently, we shall refer to this law in connection with a theory of growth.

In the discussion just ended we have been dealing with the situation at a given moment of time. Suppose we now take a longer view. Let a certain amount of time elapse in which the factors can grow and techniques improve. Then the level of output will increase through time, thus modifying the situation. Just what is to be expected from the progress of the economy? Let us consider this question in some detail.

**Progress and the Law of Scarcity.** If the factors of production increase in amount and production techniques improve, increased output will result. This can be interpreted as an outward shift of the production frontier, making possible the production of more of everything. Suppose in a given year the economy finds itself at point $D_1$ in Figure 1–3. If more rockets are wanted right away, they can be procured only by giving up automobiles. This is accomplished by moving from $D_1$ to $E_1$ on the production frontier, a change that illustrates the law of scarcity.

If a certain amount of time elapses in which the added rockets can be produced, a different situation develops. During the interval techniques may improve, while the labor supply and quantity of capital increase; concurrently, new raw materials sources may turn up. As a result of these improvements in productive power the production frontier shifts away from the origin to the new position $F_2$. Starting with combination $D_1$, the economy can move to $D_2$ after the lapse of a certain time interval. Such a movement implies that more rockets along with more automobiles can be procured with the passage of time. This states a principle very different from the law of scarcity. We may summarize it as follows.

**The Principle of Growth.** *In a growing economy, with the passage of time more of one good may be obtained together with more other goods.* This implies that the various items wanted by society may be

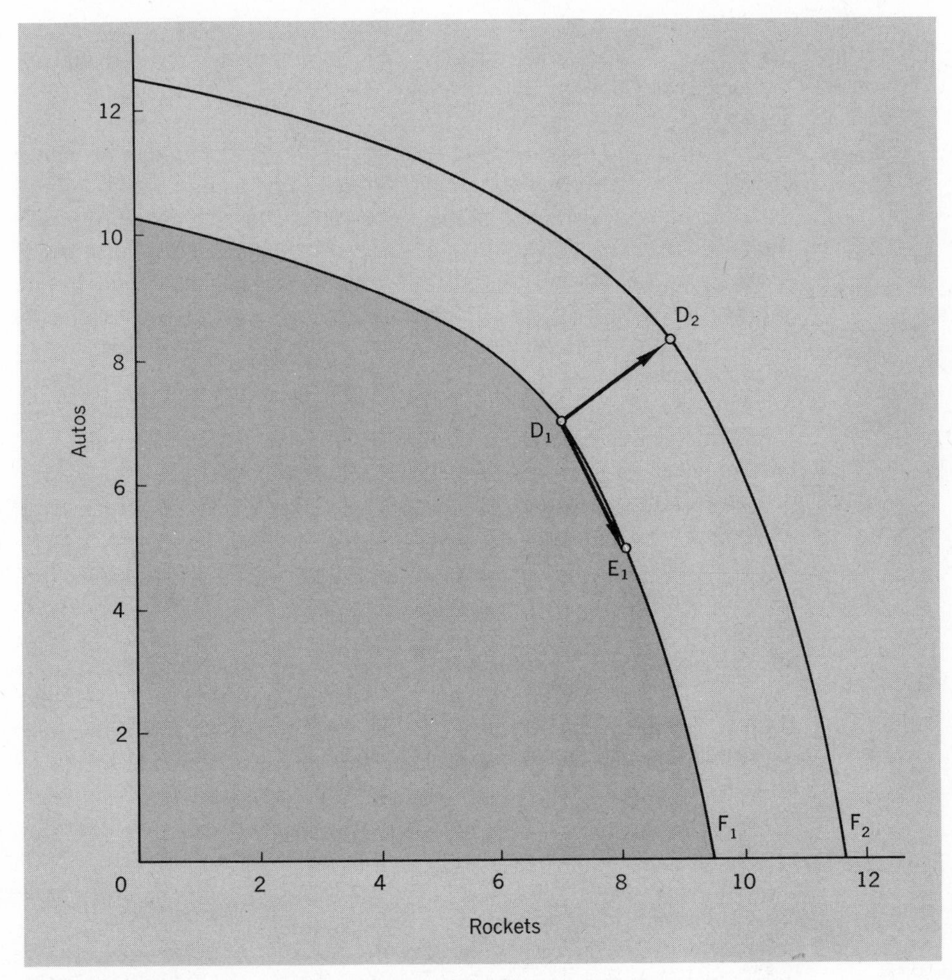


**Figure 1–3.** Effects of an outward shift in the production frontier.

complementary; more of each can be had. In the short run the items are strictly competitive; having more of one requires giving up some of the others. Does this mean that progress repeals the law of scarcity? No; that law operated under the conditions assumed in its statement, namely, fixity of techniques and resources. However, progress allows us to get around the effects of the law of scarcity in the long run with the aid of expanding techniques and resources.

**Progress and the Existence of Scarcity.** We have just seen that progress permits society to avoid the effects of the law of scarcity. What about scarcity itself: can this condition be eliminated by progress? As society progresses, and output increases, can wants be fulfilled ever more completely until we all reach a point of "bliss" in which all earthly pleasures are satisfied? Probably not. Because wants evolve through time, and because our wants are social and change in step with those of others, these wants have no set limit. In the unceasing race between output and wants there is little doubt that the latter will always win.

Perhaps some milestones in the satisfaction of wants can be established. What these markers are to be does not seem clear to economists at present. For example, if one could define the group of goods called necessities, the attainment of such a standard for all citizens would mark a boundary line in economic development and in the elimination of scarcity. For many people today a car, television set, high-protein diet, cigarettes, and similar items are "necessities." Life without these things would be inconceivable. It is not clear, then, how such a milestone could be found. So, for the time being, we will assume that scarcity is inevitable and that even progress cannot allay its bite in a way we can clearly explain.

**Diminishing Returns and Progress.** In the early part of the nineteenth century two famous economists, T. R. Malthus and David Ricardo, developed an account of growth making use of the principle of diminishing returns. Roughly the argument ran like this:

In an advanced industrial country like England the best techniques are known. Therefore, any but rather slow change in this basic influence can be ignored. Moreover, the entire land area is limited. As society develops, the territory occupied by a country will be settled, the resources will be identified, and industry will develop to utilize the resources. As time passes, and population grows along with capital, successive doses of labor and capital will be applied to a relatively fixed supply of land. Eventually, the point of diminishing returns will be reached. By resorting to inferior grades of land—less fertile agricultural land, mines with thinner seams, more poorly situated store sites—the operation of the law may be slowed but not stopped. Inevitably, the outcome of growing capital and labor with limited land is declining marginal and average product, which implies that real income per laborer declines.

The theory develops other consequences that we will not discuss here, such as (1) rising rents, (2) the ultimate cessation of population growth, (3) the fall of real wages (purchasing power of the money wage) to a minimum called subsistence, and (4) the cessation in the growth of capital. For our purposes the important thing is that the trend in economic development, under the assumed conditions, is toward lower per capita incomes. So gloomy are the implications of this classical analysis by Ricardo and Malthus that economics was long called "the dismal science."

How well did Malthus and Ricardo fare as prophets? Have the advanced, fully occupied Western countries been marked by steadily declining per capita incomes, as predicted? Not at all. Over the long run, there has been a steady rise in per capita incomes. To take one example, consider the development in the United States over the past 60 years. As estimated by John W. Kendrick,[2] output per capita in the period 1889–93—that is, around 1890—was $424, measured in dollars having the purchasing power of 1929. By 1955 output per capita had risen to $1,396, again in 1929 dollars. Thus in six and a half decades output per capita more than trebled. Clearly, in the United States the predicted result fails to conform to the facts. Likewise, in other advanced Western countries there has been an upward trend contrary to the prediction. This calls for some explanation.

## PROGRESS IN THE UNITED STATES

We see that the gloomy predictions of Malthus and Ricardo have not been fulfilled in the United States. This leads us to ask where the classical analysis went wrong and how this country has managed to sustain continued economic progress. It seems appropriate to consider growth in the quantity and quality of the factors or resources used in production, together with the trend in technology, if that can be measured. Together, these elements should help to measure the change in productive power and therefore in output. A word of caution is necessary. We are interested primarily in the lot of the individual and, accordingly, in the improvement of individual living standards. In turn, this leads us to consider changes in output per capita rather than those in total output.

**Trends in Land or Natural Resource Supplies.** As the classical economists saw it, the main barrier to progress lay in the comparatively fixed supply of land. Because agriculture was the main type of economic activity in their day, this led them to consider the limited supply of agricultural land in existence. Nowadays, with industry, service, and trade accounting for 95 per cent of output, a more important hindrance to growth consists in limitations on supplies of raw materials such as iron, oil, and lumber. We could speculate in abstract terms on the matter, but we will bypass such a discussion in favor of a brief consideration of certain facts.

One indication of the availability of raw materials is found by studying the trend in their prices. Between the periods 1900–04 and 1957 raw material prices rose 24 per cent more than prices of finished products.[3] This situation indicates something of an increasing scarcity

[2] *Productivity Trends: Capital and Labor,* Occasional Paper No. 53 (New York: National Bureau of Economic Research, 1956).
[3] *Economic Report of the President* (Washington, D.C.: U.S. Government Printing Office, 1962), p. 134.

of raw materials and substantiates to a degree the assumptions of Ricardo and Malthus. During the same span of time, however, efficiency in the use of raw materials has increased steadily. Consider this briefly.

First, we must note that a suitable measure of the output produced by the economy goes by the name of the real Net National Product, or real *NNP*. In Figure 1–4 we have plotted real *NNP* per unit of raw material input on the vertical axis against time on the horizontal. Considering 1929 as a *base period,* or reference point, for our series of data, we assign an index value of 100 to this year. In years when efficiency is less than in 1929 the index is less than 100 and in other years above 100. Note finally that we are using what is known as a

**Figure 1–4.** Real *NNP* per unit of raw material input.

Source: John W. Kendrick, **Productivity Trends in the United States** (Princeton, N.J.: Princeton University Press, 1961), p. 95, Table 16.

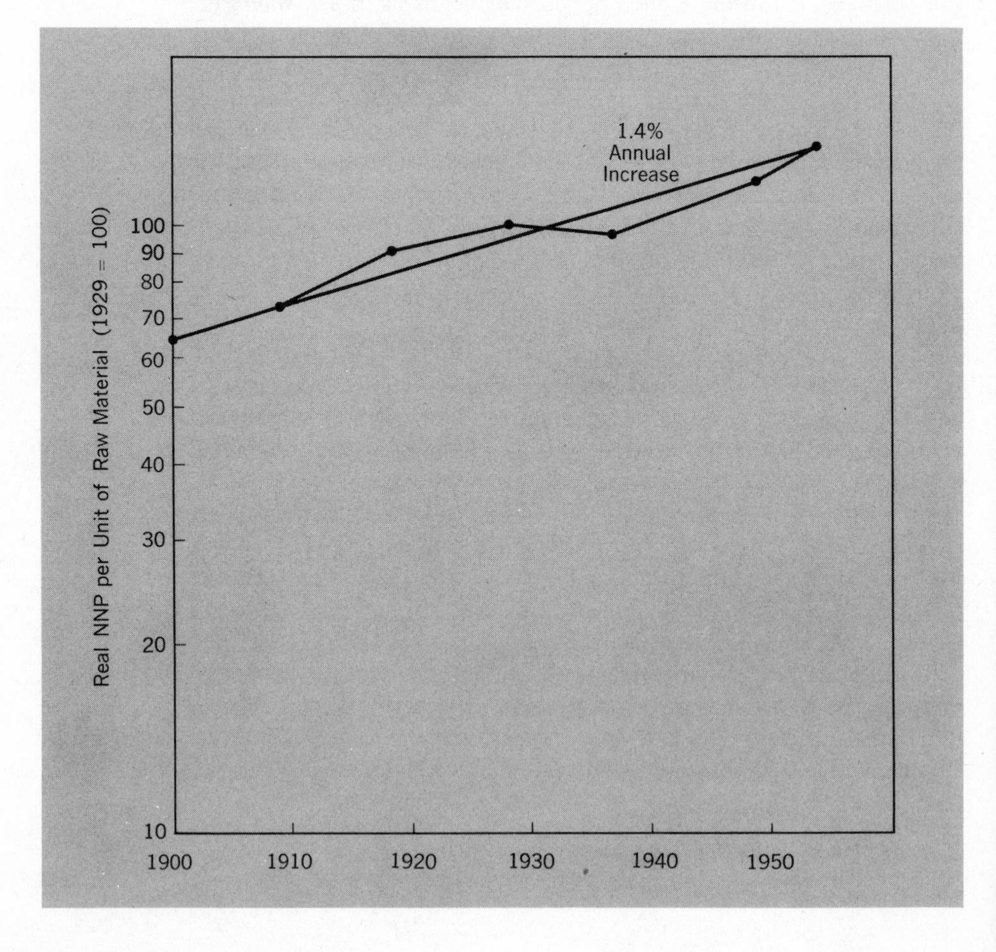

semilogarithmic chart. On the horizontal axis, here measuring time, an arithmetic scale is used in which equal distances represent equal amounts (equal periods of time). On the vertical axis, giving an index of real *NNP* per unit of raw materials, a logarithmic scale is used in which equal distances represent equal percentage changes. Thus the distances from 10 to 20, from 20 to 40, and from 40 to 80 are all equal. Test this for yourself.



Now for the facts. In 1900 real *NNP* per unit of raw material was 63.7 compared to the base value of 100 in 1929 and to 130 in 1952. The straight-line trend inserted in the figure indicates an improvement of about 1.4 per cent annually. No doubt the factor of technological change is the main cause of this gain. Further, the increased efficiency

**Figure 1–5.** Fraction of the labor force made up of chemists and engineers, 1890–1950.

Source: See Table 1–3.

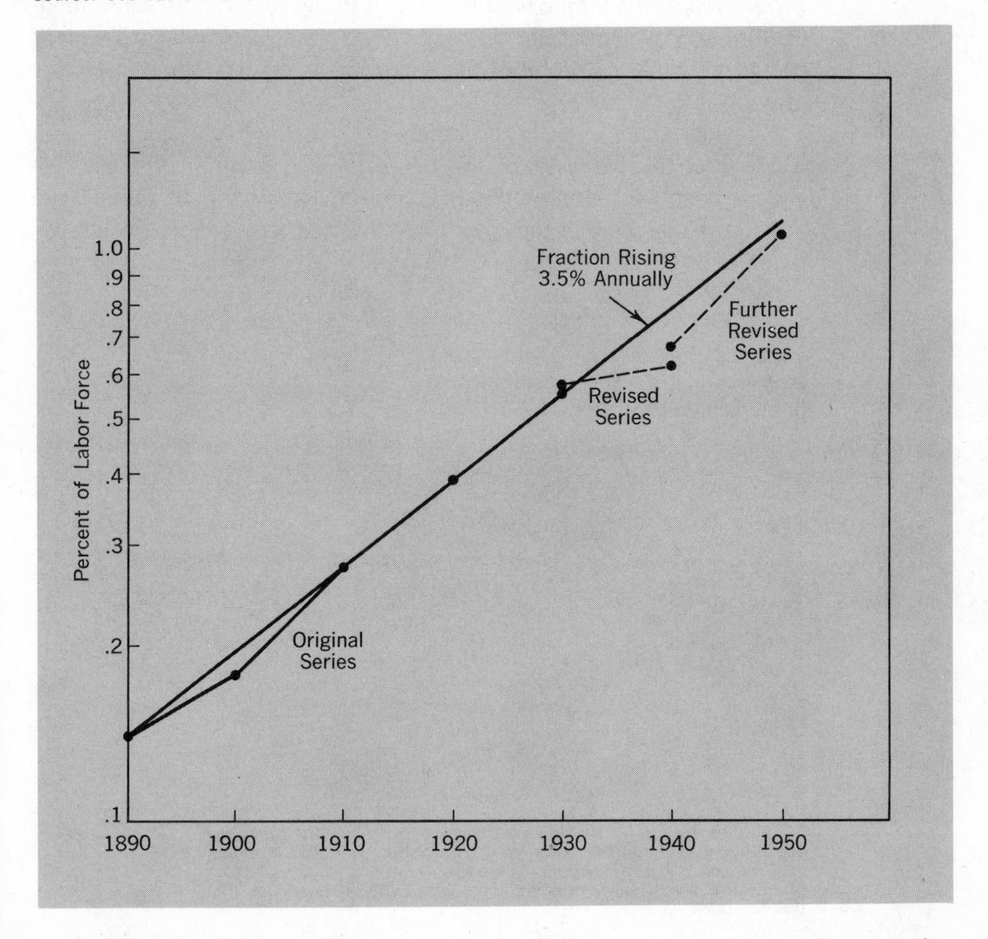

of raw material use makes possible a corresponding growth in output. This does not mean that it permits any desired growth rate, just some corresponding rate.

In addition to increased efficiency in the use of materials larger total supplies make possible increased output. Thus the unit cost of electric power generated by nuclear-powered reactors is dropping to levels that are now nearly competitive with the output of steam plants. When a competitive point is reached, our usable energy supplies will expand very greatly. Similar results are being accomplished through the use of plastics and synthetic fibers. Chemistry opens up a whole new world of possible resources not envisioned in the theories of Malthus and Ricardo.

**Quality of the Labor Supply.** One of the most dramatic changes now taking place in modern society is the revolution in education. Education is being extended to the mass of the people, and a larger proportion of the public is being trained in the sciences. Because modern industry is geared more than ever before to technological change permitting material progress, this tendency is important in considering growth.

Consider the growth in the numbers of chemists and engineers. In Table 1–3 the per cent of the labor force consisting of these two groups is shown, along with their absolute numbers. In Figure 1–5 (p. 19) the per cent of the labor force that consists of these two groups is plotted against time on semilogarithmic paper. What do the figures show?

**TABLE 1-3***
**Distribution of Engineers and Chemists in the Labor Force, 1890–1950**

| | Number of Thousands | Per Cent of Labor Force |
|---|---|---|
| 1890 | 33 | 0.14 |
| 1900 | 52 | 0.18 |
| 1910 | 105 | 0.28 |
| 1920 | 169 | 0.40 |
| 1930 | 273 | 0.56 |
| 1930 | 277 | 0.58 |
| 1940 | 338 | 0.63 |
| 1940 | 363 | 0.68 |
| 1950 | 636 | 1.08 |

* Source: David M. Blank and George J. Stigler, **The Demand and Supply of Scientific Personnel** (New York: National Bureau of Economic Research, 1957), Tables B–1 and B–2, pp. 144–157. Changes in statistical methods or divergent estimates account for the overlaps.

In 1890 the number of chemists and engineers combined amounted to about 0.14 of 1 per cent of the labor force. Forty years later, in 1930, the fraction had quadrupled to 0.56 of 1 per cent. In the graph we drew a line between these corresponding points and extended it to the terminal date of 1950. Despite two successive revisions in computation methods the data seem to conform pretty well to this line. By 1950 the per cent had risen to 1.08, or better than 1 per cent. Thus more than one person in a hundred had acquired a high degree of technical and scientific knowledge by this time. The trend represented by the straight line indicates that the fraction of such personnel in the labor force has been rising at the rate of about 3.5 per cent annually. This is just one indication of the ways in which our reservoir of practical skills is filling up at a steady rate.

Another and broader evidence of improvement in the human factor is found by considering the figures on enrollment in colleges and universities. Absolute numbers are meaningless, a fact that leads us to compare enrollments with college age population. The best comparison that the available statistics seem to afford is the ratio between resident enrollment in colleges and universities and the population of college age, from 18 to 21 years. Let us call this *the enrollment ratio.* About 55 per cent of the enrollment consists of people in this age bracket, and the bulk of the remainder are older. A rise in this ratio indicates that a larger fraction of the population is receiving education at the college level.

In the academic year 1869–70 the enrollment ratio was only 1.68 per cent, but this figure rose to 4.01 per cent in 1899–1900 and to a surprising 36.75 per cent in 1957–58. In Figure 1–6 the enrollment ratio is plotted against time, at ten-year intervals, on semilogarithmic paper. The free-hand trend line is broken at 1899–1900 for a better fit. Apparently the enrollment ratio increased at a faster rate after this time with no immediate signs of slowing down.[4]

The trends in numbers of scientists and in college enrollment are symptomatic of a widening and deepening of the educational process. The fact that increasing emphasis is being placed on scientific training may reflect the usefulness of this type of study in raising output. One of the encouraging things about broadened and deepened education is that there is no set limit to its extent or its effects.

**Increase in the Stock of Capital.** From a negative point of view the accumulation of extra capital is not very helpful if it simply keeps

[4] Between 1869–70 and 1899–1900 the ratio rose at the rate of about 2.9 per cent annually; from the latter date to 1957–58, at a rate of 3.8 to 3.9 per cent annually. To illustrate, in 1905–06 the enrollment ratio was around 5 per cent. In 1906–07 the expected value was about 5.2 per cent (or 5 + 3.8% of 5 = 5.19, but *not* 8.8% = 5% + 3.8%).

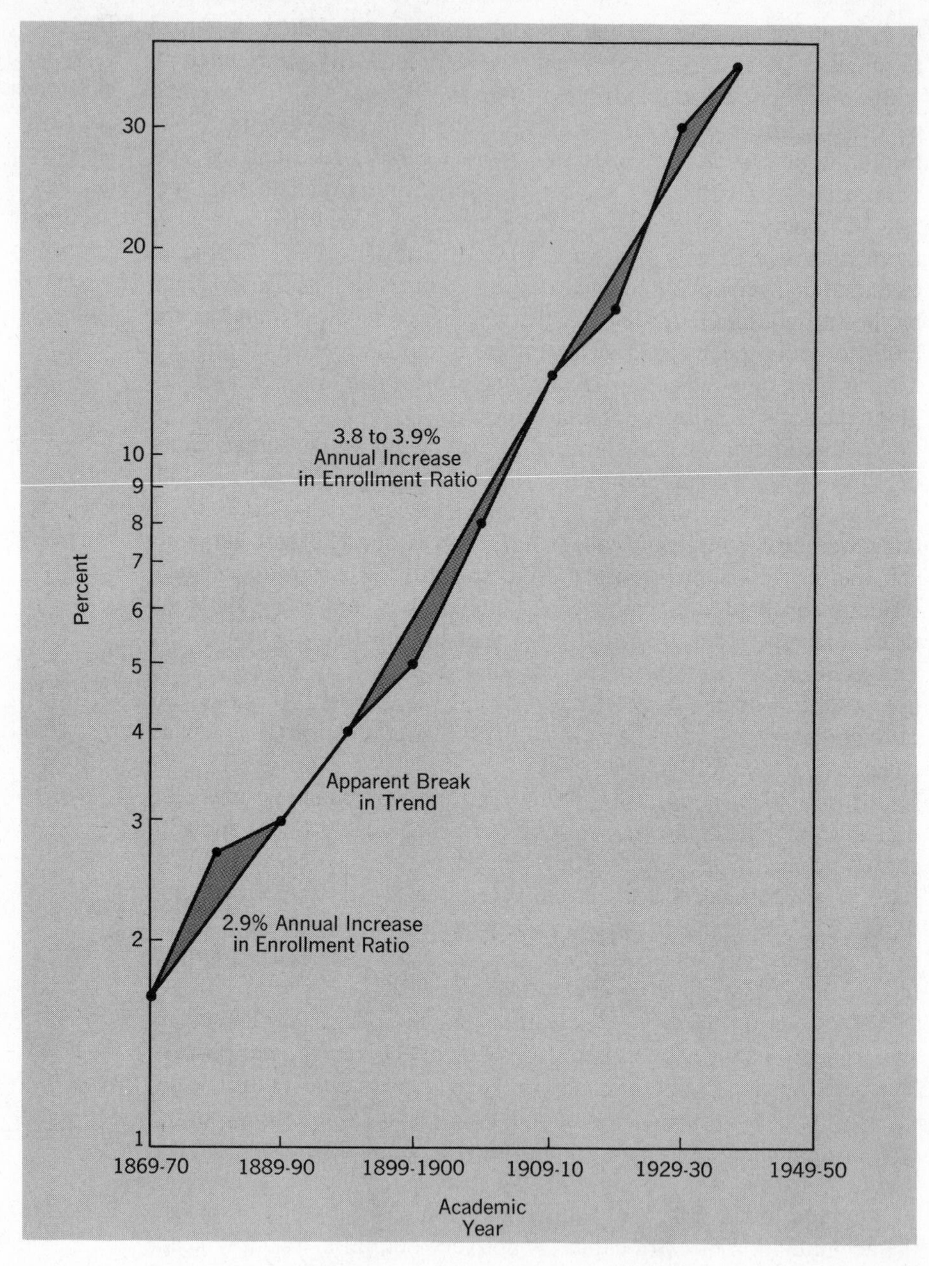


**Figure 1–6.** Enrollment in colleges and universities: total resident degree students expressed as a per cent of the population aged 18–21 (those of college age).

Source: **Statistics of Higher Education, 1957–58,** Biennial Survey of Education in the U.S., 1956–58, U.S. Department of Health, Education, and Welfare (Washington, D.C.: U.S. Government Printing Office, 1962), p. 7, Table 3.

pace with a rising population. In Egypt, for example, the completion of the Aswan High Dam will permit irrigation of great areas of desert with a resultant increase in usable farmland. Yet students of this area doubt whether the corresponding increase in crops will do more than feed the rising population of that country. In contrast to a stalemate of this kind what we hope for is a situation in which sufficient means are forthcoming to meet the needs of a growing population *and* to provide the typical person with a rising standard of living.



In order to focus attention on this possibility we will consider the relationship between the rise in the input of capital per capita and the corresponding rise in the output of the economy. (The conjunction of the terms *capital* and *per capita* is awkward but unavoidable.) The output of the economy is referred to as real Net National Product, real *NNP,* for short. Instead of dealing with amounts we will work with percentage increases per capita in order to put the data within a growth framework.

Table 1–4 exhibits the relationship between the percentage growth in capital input per capita and the corresponding percentage growth in real *NNP* per capita. The data is given by decades or shorter time periods since 1889 and is plotted against midpoints of corresponding time periods in Figure 1–7. Over the entire period real *NNP* per capita has risen at an average annual rate of 2 per cent, whereas capital input per capita has risen by 1.2 per cent on the average. Looking at the diagram, we see that the percentage growth in *NNP* per capita varies in the same direction as the percentage growth in the input of capital per capita. What moral can we draw from this association?

**TABLE 1–4***
**Real *NNP* per Capita and Capital Input per Capita, 1889–1957, Average Annual Percentage Rates of Change**

| | Real *NNP* per Capita | Capital Input per Capita |
|---|---|---|
| 1889–1899 | 2.6 | 2.4 |
| 1899–1909 | 2.3 | 1.7 |
| 1909–1919 | 2.3 | 1.7 |
| 1919–1929 | 1.6 | 1.2 |
| 1929–1937 | −0.5 | −1.3 |
| 1937–1948 | 3.2 | 0.5 |
| 1948–1953 | 3.0 | 2.5 |
| 1953–1957 | 0.4 | 1.4 |
| 1889–1957 | 2.0 | 1.2 |

* Source: John W. Kendrick, **Productivity Trends in the United States** (Princeton, N.J.: Princeton University Press, 1961), pp. 84–85, Tables 8 and 9. This is a study of the National Bureau of Economic Research.

Clearly, this data suggests that a rising input of capital per capita is essential to a high rate of growth of output. The basic reasons for this condition are two. Partly, the increased capital is needed to provide labor with additional tools for production. In addition, the demand for additional capital raises incomes, which keeps the economy in high gear. Working together, these influences result in prosperity when the input of capital is moving ahead rapidly. We must note, though, that the willingness of the population to work is also a factor

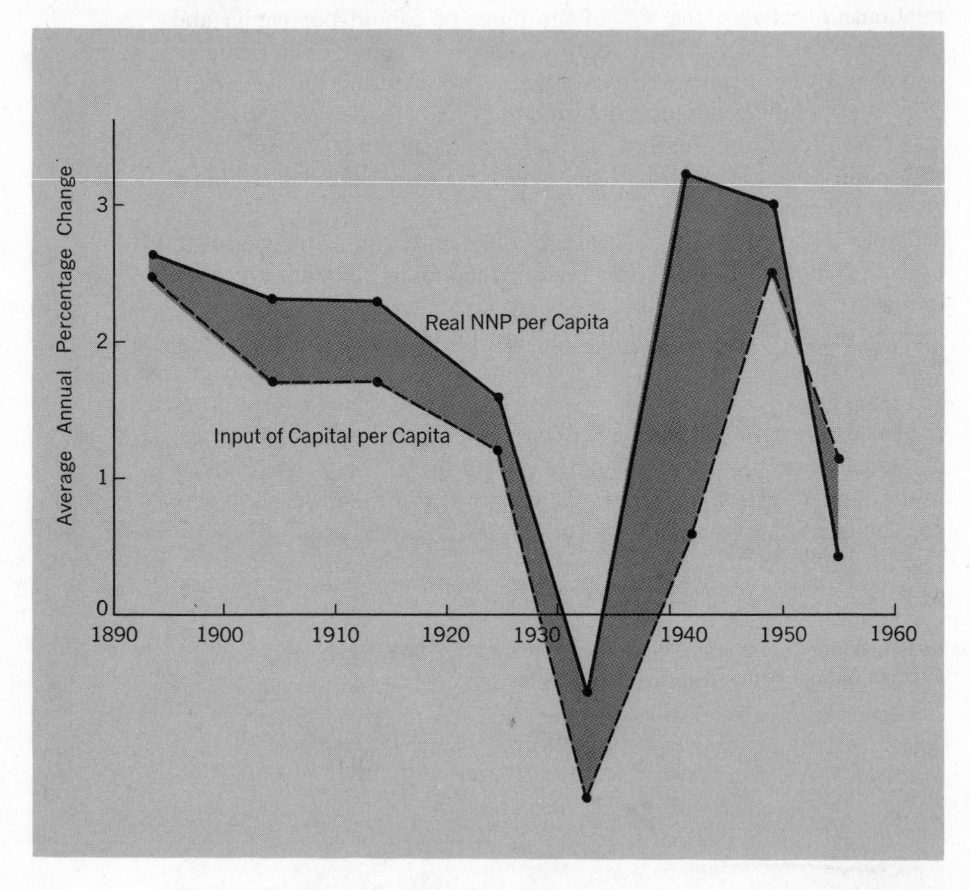


**Figure 1–7.** Annual percentage changes in real *NNP* per capita and input of capital per capita.

Source: See Table 1–4.

in the situation. The sharp fall in the rate of growth in real *NNP* per capita in the period 1953–57 seems to have been caused by the decline that took place in labor input per capita. (We will not explore this development here.) Insistence by the public on a rapid decline in

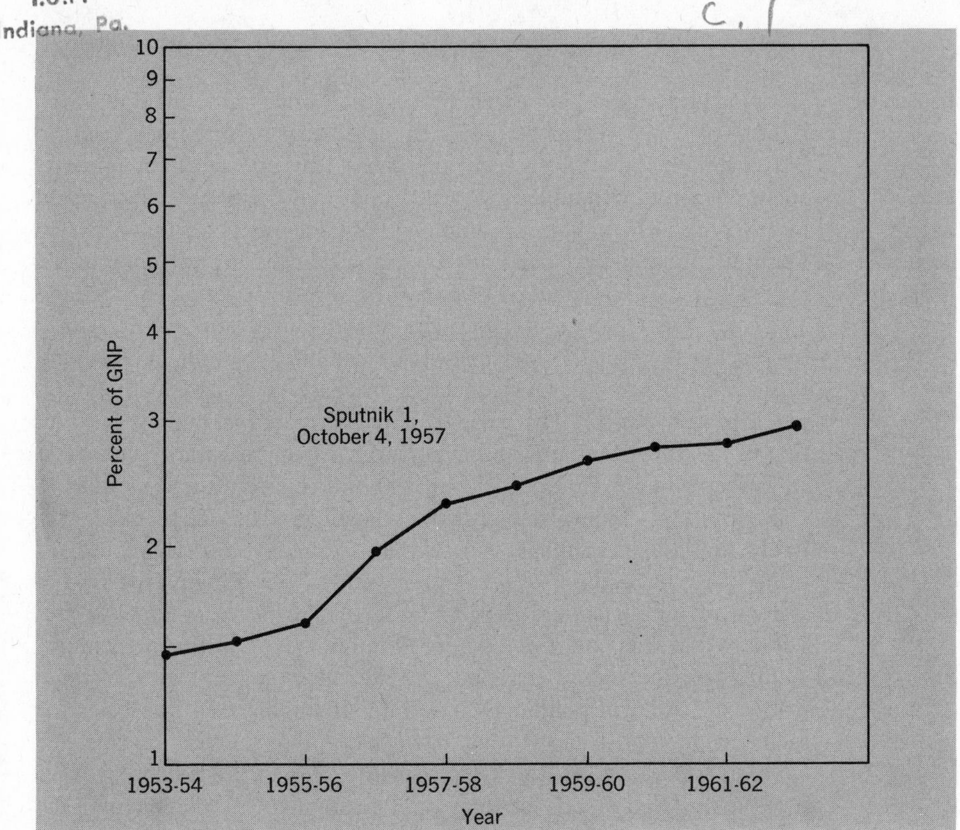


**Figure 1–8.** Per cent of *GNP* spent on research and development.

Source: National Science Foundation, **10th Annual Report, 1960,** p. 141, and **Statistical Abstract of the United States** (Washington, D.C.: U.S. Government Printing Office, 1963), p. 543, for Research and Develomment expenditures. For *GNP* see **Survey of Current Business,** U.S. Department of Commerce, July, 1963, p. 14. Because most research money is counted on a fiscal year basis, *GNP* was reduced to an approximately similar basis by averaging *GNP*s for the pairs of years indicated.

hours of labor or an increase in the amount of unemployment will sharply reduce the measurable rate of growth.

**Technology.** It is easy to talk about improvements in technology but difficult to describe this tendency in quantitative terms. In the discussion of raw materials we showed how increased output per unit of raw material input is now obtained. This indicates indirectly one aspect of the progress of technology. For a measurement of the overall growth of technology we will make the drastic assumption that this variable is related to expenditure on research and development. In Figure 1–8 we have plotted research and development expenditure as a per cent of the gross output of the economy, referred to as Gross National Product, or *GNP*. The expenditures, abbreviated *R* and *D*, are divided into three main categories—universities, private business, and the Federal government.

In the period 1953–54 expenditures for *R* and *D* amounted to $5.15 billion, or 1.4 per cent of *GNP*. By 1962 expenditures had risen to $16.4 billion, or 2.88 per cent of *GNP*. Thus the per cent of *GNP* spent on *R* and *D* doubled over the period. Of the $16.4 billion spent in 1962–63, $11 billion, or about 70 per cent was contributed by the Federal government. Note from the graph that the biggest jump in the percentage of *GNP* spent on *R* and *D* occurred between 1955–56 and 1957–58. On October 4, 1957, the Soviet Union amazed the world by placing in orbit the first man-made satellite, Sputnik I. No doubt this event helped to spark the large increase in *R* and *D* that took place in this period. This suspicion is partly borne out by the fact that of the $10.9 billion *R* and *D* performed (not necessarily financed) by industry in 1961, about 37 per cent was in aircraft and missiles.

From 1957–58 on, the growth is more gradual. It seems rather likely that the percentage will continue to grow, for technology is quite likely to be the key to our economic future. Finally, the rate of growth of output should depend more on the per cent of *GNP* devoted to research and development than on a trend in this percentage. A high fraction should generate a rapid rate of technological change; a low one, a correspondingly slow rate. If this be true, the basis for faster technological growth has been laid within the past decade.

**Past Trends and Outlook for Growth.** In the preceding pages we have considered trends bearing on the amounts of the factors, the efficiency in use of the factor or its qualitative improvement, and the probable change in technology. These tend to undercut the classical economists, assumption that land and resources are constant. Also they indicate long-run trends making for an increase in the quantity and quality of the factors. Finally, judging by the increased research and development expenditures, the outlook for rapid technological change is bright. All-in-all prospects are excellent for a continuation of steady growth in per capita incomes, the best simple measure of progress. This is not to say that poverty will disappear right away. But the prospects for improved living standards look good.

**Summary.** Economics is the social study that deals with the organization of productive resources for the satisfaction of human wants. As a result of the evolution of wants, their social nature, and latent needs being brought to light by technological change, wants tend to be insatiable. In order to satisfy these wants an economic system must exist that will produce and distribute output.

The basic problem of economics is scarcity, a condition arising from the unlimited number of human wants combined with the limited amounts of goods or resources that can help to satisfy them. Productive resources are classified under four headings—land, labor, capital, and entrepreneurship. In a fully employed economy the law of scarcity prevails, implying that more of one good can only be attained by giving up some of another. This is expressed by a production frontier showing the various possible combinations of two goods that can be obtained with the available quantity of resources.



With the passage of time it may be possible to increase the available factors or resources, causing an outward shift in the production frontier. In such a growing economy more of one good may be obtained together with more of other goods. This may happen provided that all resources can be increased. However, Malthus and Ricardo pointed out that a limitation on land or natural resources necessarily limits growth. They used the principle of diminishing returns to show that output increases by a smaller and smaller amount as labor and capital increase with a fixed amount of land. Their prediction was that the economy would ultimately tend to a static level with little or no growth.

This prediction was found to be false for the United States and other Western countries. Per capita incomes have risen over the long run at a constant percentage rate. Contrary to the expectations of Malthus and Ricardo, the effective supply of resources is growing steadily. The efficiency in the use of raw materials is growing, and new types of resources are being developed as technology advances. Improvement in the human factor through education and rising capital per capita are conducive to the same result. Finally, the doubling in the percentage of *GNP* devoted to research and development in less than a decade points toward even more rapid improvements in technology in the future. Prospects for continued growth appear to be good.

## QUESTIONS

1. What is economics?
2. Very briefly, why is it necessary for society to make choices in the goods and services it uses?
3. In what sense is it reasonable to say that human wants are "insatiable," or unlimited in amount? Illustrate from your own experience.
4. "If it were not for the law of diminishing returns, all the food in the world could be produced in a flower pot." Evaluate.
5. If goods and services are as scarce as they are supposed to be, why is it that we always seem to have a surplus of farm products? (If you get stumped on this, ask your instructor.)
6. Why does the production frontier slope downward from left to right? What does this fact have to do with scarcity?
7. The production frontier is believed to be bowed away from the origin. Why does it have this shape rather than that of a straight line descending from left to right?

8. Technological change does not follow automatically from expenditures on research and development. Why, then, are these expenditures used as a measure of *R* and *D*?
9. In what way do *R* and *D* affect the production frontier or transformation curve?
10. What is the relevance of the increasing level of education, both technical and general, to the rate of economic growth?
11. What is believed to happen to the production frontier through time?

CHAPTER

2

# Pure Capitalism and the Market System

## INTRODUCTION

As we saw in the first chapter, the basic and inescapable problem of economic life is scarcity. Faced with a lack of sufficient output to satisfy all our wants, we try to raise per capita output by increasing other factors relative to labor and by improving technology. However, wants evolve as per capita incomes increase and emulation ("keeping up with the Joneses") causes the wants of people to rise in step. Therefore, increasing per capita incomes lead in the direction of a fuller and more varied life but not one in which all wants are satisfied.

## THE CONCEPT OF AN ECONOMIC SYSTEM

To meet the problem of scarcity, of satisfying unlimited wants with limited means, society must find a way of organizing resources. Even Robinson Crusoe, cast away on his desert island, had to organize his resources and time in order to survive. So today we organize ourselves into a sort of machine with which we turn out the things needed by society.

Let us think of an economic system as the set of arrangements by which society makes use of its resources in the production of output to satisfy human wants. Clearly, the system is not the same thing as the resources, the people, and the items produced. Rather, it is the *method* by which these are organized into a functioning unit. Among the systems that have actually been used are the manorial system, or large self-sufficient farms characteristic of the Middle Ages; capitalism, or the private enterprise system characteristic of the early nineteenth century; communism, or government ownership and control of the productive organization characteristic of Russia and China today; and mixed capitalism, or capitalism modified by government intervention, which is the type characteristic of the economies of the West.

**Common Features of Present-day Systems.** There are only two major systems in use today: communism, found in Russia or China, and mixed capitalism, characteristic of the United States. There are other systems in the backward countries, but these do not set the pace. It is an interesting fact that communism and our system of mixed capitalism have important elements in common. Let us comment briefly on each of these.

**Heavy Use of Capital.** Modern economic systems are marked by a heavy and growing use of capital. Consider that part of capital which corresponds to what we ordinarily call machinery and equipment, namely, producers' durable equipment. In the United States this category of capital increased from $61.5 billion in 1945 to $128 billion in 1956, measured in dollars having constant purchasing power.[1] This represents an increase of over 100 per cent in only 11 years.

Our transportation and public utility industries have long provided examples of heavy use of capital. American Telephone and Telegraph alone had assets of $14.5 billion at the end of 1960; the bulk of these assets consisted of capital in one form or another. A further example is found in the generation of electricity; hydroelectric dams, steam turbines, generators, and transmission lines involve enormous expenditures.

In manufacturing industry the trend is toward automated plants marked by increased use of machinery. Such increased complexity and sophistication in the factory involve increasing outlays for capital. But perhaps the most surprising developments, at least in the United States, have taken place in the field of agriculture. Where once the farmer's main investment lay in his barns, fences, and the simple tools for tilling the soil, the present-day farm is commonly marked by the presence of a multiplicity of complicated machines.

Perhaps the best symbol of increased investment devoted to agriculture is the fact that crops are "dusted" by airplane to control

[1] *Producers' durable equipment* is a term defined and used by the Department of Commerce. Data from *Historical Statistics of the United States,* Bureau of the Census (Washington, D.C.: U.S. Government Printing Office, 1960), p. 152. The capital is measured in terms of dollars having the purchasing power of the period 1947–49. This is accomplished by adjusting the actual dollar values by a *price index,* which measures price changes between the period 1947–49 and the years in question.

insects. Increased power being used in production is indicated by the following facts. The value of machinery and motor vehicles per farm worker increased from about $363 in 1940 to about $1,395 in 1960, measured in 1947–49 dollars.[2] Such an increase implies that this item is about 3.85 times what it was only two decades ago. No wonder American farming is so productive that we are threatened perennially with surpluses of many commodities.

**Specialization, Exchange, and Use of Money.** To find a suitable contrast with today's economy we must go back to the Middle Ages. With the dissolution of the Roman Empire, the system of roads, of law, of protection for the traveler—all tended to disappear. In time, the main economic unit became the manor, a basically self-sufficient agricultural establishment, supported by handicrafts. Exchange between different geographical areas was quite difficult overland, because roads were poor, robbers numerous and unchecked, and tolls exorbitant. Travel by ship, though easier, was beset with perils. Lacking navigational aids, employing sailing craft inadequate to withstand storms, preyed on by pirates, the mariner led a precarious existence. All-in-all, traveling to exchange goods was hardly worth the risk. No wonder the payoff of a successful trip was so fabulous that we still speak of "our ship coming in"; the great scarcity of goods made possible the extraction of a very high price.

In contrast with the self-sufficient manor, modern economic society is marked by exchange. Consider your morning cup of coffee. Here we have coffee from Brazil and sugar from Cuba, Mexico, or Hawaii served in a cup and saucer from Japan or Europe. Obviously, we must pay for these items by sending the respective countries our own products—mostly manufactured goods of one kind or another. As a matter of fact, each item we import is usually a specialty of the country sending it. We buy it because the country in question produces an item that is either high in quality, low in price, or both.

In our specialized economy each person tends to produce, or help to produce, a single item. This is obviously true of such professions as law, medicine, the ministry, and teaching. It is also true in manufacturing, where an individual works on an assembly line producing a particular item: an automobile, a TV set, or a washing machine. Now this raises a question. How do the specialized workers, producing only one thing, manage to acquire all the other things with which to satisfy their wants? Obviously, by exchanging their goods

[2] *Economic Report of the President* (Washington, D.C.: U.S. Government Printing Office, 1961), Table B–11, p. 100. These figures are not given directly in the table, but are derived by applying the proportion of farm production assets represented by machinery and motor vehicles to total production assets per farm worker.

for those turned out by other specialized workers. Yet swapping of goods for other goods does not occur in our society, because such barter turns out to be an involved process. Consider this point briefly.

Under a barter system an individual with a surplus of a given item must acquire needed goods by direct exchange. Suppose he is a weaver with a supply of woolen cloth and wants some bread. First he must locate one or more bakers. Among these he must find one who needs some cloth and who is willing therefore to exchange bread for cloth. To summarize, the hungry weaver must find a baker who needs cloth. The required condition is sometimes referred to as a *double coincidence* of wants and supplies, because the weaver wanting bread must find a baker needing cloth. Clearly, this would be a difficult condition to fulfill, and the weaver would probably have to do a good deal of looking.

**Money.** By the use of money society avoids this and other difficulties met in barter. When the weaver comes to market, he simply puts his cloth on sale at a price expressed in money. With this money he can buy the bread and other items that he needs. Because money serves here as the medium or go-between that facilitates the exchange of cloth for other items, it is often called a *medium of exchange*. Money also has other important characteristics that we will consider in Chapter 8.

**Modern Economies Are Geared to Change.** Returning to the Middle Ages, we see there a good example of extremely slow change. In fact, the story of *Sleeping Beauty* illustrates this idea. In the year 900 a person might well have slept 100 years, awakened, and found the circumstances of everyday life not much changed. Today, a popular form of novel is to write of a period in the future and to comment on how different things will be then. In the novel *1984* George Orwell writes of a tremendous change (not improvement) that comes over England in the space of three decades.[3] Nowadays, people expect change to take place rapidly. They accept it—even anticipate and welcome it.

Although this feature of present-day society is not institutional in character, it is basic. It affects Russians just as it does us. They look to exploits in space technology, whereas we savor these same exploits as well as enjoy the ever-changing forms of consumer goods. Such an attitude is extremely favorable to material progress. Old customs, traditions, and habits of thought are brushed aside to make way for change, especially material change. To mention just one item, consider the effects being brought about by the new interstate highway system. This road network provides extremely fast, safe transporta-

[3] George Orwell, *1984* (New York: Harcourt, Brace & World, Inc., 1949).

tion between distant points. However, to build this system long-established interests of businesses along the old routes had to be set aside. In spite of these incidental losses no really serious opposition has appeared to challenge the system. Progress is king.



## CAPITALISM AS AN ECONOMIC SYSTEM

As we have already stated or implied the United States is marked by capitalism modified by a considerable degree of government influence. Basically, though, we adhere to capitalism. For the sake of simplicity let us start our description of the American economy by a discussion of pure capitalism. Such a system has never existed, but it might serve as a useful basis for discussion.

**Motivation.** To get the needed jobs done in any economic system some sort of incentive or motivation is required. To take a simple example, how do you persuade people to get out of bed in the morning and go to work? Although some people simply enjoy work, thus providing their own motivation, most others need an additional stimulus. Under capitalism the basic motive is self-interest operating through a price mechanism; to persuade people to do a job you must make it worthwhile to them by offering a monetary incentive in the form of a price or return, such as wages, interest, or the like.

Adam Smith, the founder of modern economics, argued that self-interest was the most reliable of all motives. He said that it is time to be suspicious when someone in business offers to do you a service out of pure altruism. Perhaps this is true; it is certainly correct that we are ordinarily reluctant to ask a favor but feel justified in appealing to a person's self-interest. In any event, pure capitalism rests firmly on an appeal to self-interest, on compensation for services rendered.

Other systems make appeals to different motives. In Russia the masses are exhorted to work in order to "build socialism"; an appeal is made to give unselfishly for the benefit of society. Along with this goes some use of the self-interest principle, but the latter is not fully accepted as an incentive *in principle*. In a theocratic society people act in accordance with the laws of God, interpreted through a body of priests. Under the manorial system, associated with feudalism, which characterized the Middle Ages, custom and status decreed a certain behavior on the part of the individual; thus his class—lord, priest, freeman, serf—determined his consumption pattern. In the satellite countries of Eastern Europe, held in bondage to Russia, the factors of fear and coercion necessarily play an important role. The wall erected between East and West Berlin by the Communists stands as a monument to the role of coercion in their society. So every economic system must provide a basic system of motivation—something that makes the wheels go 'round. Later we shall tie in motivation with the necessary economic function of distribution.

**Institutions of Capitalism.** Perhaps the most basic institution of capitalism is *private property,* the right of the individual to hold wealth, to use it as he wishes, and to dispose of any income that results from its employment. Actually, because of the increasing complexity of our society, the privateness of property cannot be clearly and simply defined. Who holds the wealth, disposes of the associated income, and makes use of this income in a corporation? Clearly, the stockholders play a limited role, decisions being made primarily by the president, other executives, and board of directors. In the individual proprietorship a simpler situation prevails; here private property is more absolute and less diffused. In our modern interdependent world the scope for purely private use of resources steadily shrinks, because so many people are affected by a given action. Firms cannot dump wastes into the nearest river or noxious fumes into the air in all cases, because *others' rights are affected.* As society grows in complexity, it becomes more and more difficult to separate the private property of the individual from the social context.

In a substantial measure, however, individuals and firms can dispose of property and wealth. They can buy and sell property and receive and spend income resulting from its use. Although the government exerts an influence on the disposition of property, as through taxation, the fact is that much freedom to use wealth and enjoy its fruits does exist.

**Freedom of Contract.** An almost equally important institution of capitalism is freedom of contract. Under this principle individuals are free to buy and sell goods and services, to organize a business with a view to production and sale. Here there emerges an important aspect of capitalism. Spurred on by the motive of self-interest, individuals are permitted and encouraged to undertake production and various other tasks of an economic system. When people refer to the scope for individual initiative in production, they often use the phrase *free enterprise.* Not to be overlooked, as well, is the very important ability of consumers to choose the goods they wish to buy without government restrictions, such as rationing. Because consumer choices help to direct the flow of production, this aspect of freedom of contract is sometimes called *consumer sovereignty.*

Insofar as property is involved in contracts the institution of private property implies freedom of contract. The opportunity to own property is associated with the right to use it. An important feature of the use of property is the ability freely to buy, sell, or rent it. In turn, this implies that freedom of contract exists with respect to this property. However, the right to buy or sell services is also involved in freedom of contract, which therefore covers a broader area than private property.

Both private property and freedom of contract are indispensable to capitalism. Moreover, they are related, because the ability to buy and sell is necessary to the full use of property. Mixed capitalistic systems such as ours place certain restrictions on freedom of contract. For example, a property owner cannot build a store in a zoned residential district. Some systems, while retaining many aspects of capitalism, as did the fascism of Nazi Germany, have placed severe restriction on freedom of contract and therefore on the uses of property. But private property nominally existed.

Under pure socialism,[4] presently existing only in the communist countries, all productive land and capital are appropriated by the state, and private property ceases to exist. It seems natural that freedom of contract should also be abolished, the productive apparatus being run by the state. Keep in mind, though, that the productive apparatus could be owned by the state and leased out to private individuals for use. In the United States the government often leases timberlands to private individuals. So free enterprise with all property publicly owned is a curious but seemingly unimportant possibility.

**Capitalism, Self-Interest, and Competition.** Under capitalism self-interest motivates people to carry out production and other socially needed activities. However, there is a matter that needs examination here. Can we be sure that the actions of private individuals seeking their self-interest will necessarily result in public good? Not necessarily. If I play poker with the boys and win $100, it does not follow that everyone will be better off. Actually, the possible pleasure of gambling aside, my gain is their loss. More to the point, if a businessman by one method or another secures a monopoly in a given line, he can raise the price and enjoy a fat profit. Such a high price is probably not in the public interest, especially if the item is consumed by poor as well as rich. This brings us to the role of competition.

Some sort of restriction on the exercise of self-interest is implied under pure capitalism. To begin with, we assume that people are

[4] The discussion refers to pure socialism in the sense of *complete* socialism. We might have partial socialism or mixed socialism, in which specific industries were nationalized. In England, for example, the railroad industry is owned and run by the state. This indicates that there is a range of possibilities lying between pure capitalism and pure socialism. Note that in England, France, and Sweden, which have a number of nationalized industries, or more socialism mixed with the capitalism, democratic governments are firmly established.

rational. If so, in pursuing self-interest they will not undertake any acts that will yield an immediate advantage but later work to their own disadvantage. For example, just after World War II the automobile companies failed to raise their prices to the extent warranted by demand. In 1945–46 a recent-vintage old car sometimes sold for more than a new one to a person on the waiting list. This self-restraint was rational, being in the companies' own long-run self-interest. For this reason such actions fall under the heading of *enlightened self-interest.*

Assuming that people act according to enlightened self-interest, how can the system guarantee the delivery of ample output at reasonable prices? Clearly, a force is needed to temper the action of self-interest, to retain the motive but to restrict the reward. The answer lies mainly in competition. If there are a number of firms turning out the same product, and selling to the same body of customers, each will be forced by competition to limit his price. As a result, the desired product will become available on more reasonable terms than if offered by a monopolist. The curious fact is that the more vigorous the search for profit, the less that profit will tend to be and the lower the price. In such a situation the pursuit of private gain leads to public good. For this reason competition is an essential ingredient of a properly functioning capitalistic system.

## HOW CAPITALISM FUNCTIONS: THE MARKET SYSTEM

Consider now the way in which capitalism functions to make use of its resources in the production of output to satisfy human wants. There are a good many links in the chain connecting production with the ultimate satisfaction of human wants. At this juncture we will take an overall look at the workings of the system. Having done this in the present chapter, we will be in a better position to appreciate just what an economic system can expect to accomplish, a topic that will occupy our attention in the following chapter.

**The Function of Markets.** Markets may be divided into two categories, product markets and factor markets. In the former case the producer is the seller and the individual is the buyer of products. With factor markets the reverse is true; the producer is the buyer of factor services and the individual is the seller or owner who offers them.

Markets are places where the producer and household meet to effect the exchange of goods and services. More specifically, though, buyers may come into a market with needs for certain quantities of an item; sellers enter with certain amounts to offer. If a market is to be effective, it must synchronize the quantities desired by potential buyers and the quantities offered by sellers. In other words, a market should equate the quantity supplied with quantity demanded. Merely putting buyers and sellers in contact with each other is not enough. Some way to influence the quantity demanded and the quantity supplied, and thereby to equate them, must be found. The price of the item exerts such an influence. Consequently, it is the function of the market to equate quantity supplied with quantity demanded and thus clear the market by setting an appropriate price.

**The Operation of Markets.** To illustrate the operation of markets let us consider a case in which there is a high degree of competition among buyers and sellers: the product is homogeneous in quality; there is perfect information about the item being exchanged—its quantity and price; there are many buyers and sellers none of whom is important enough to influence the market price on his own; and perfect mobility of the item exchanged exists within the market area (thus assuming that the item can be moved immediately and without cost from one place to another). Although this very pure form of competition is an abstraction only infrequently approached in practice, the case is simple in character and illustrates neatly some important characteristics of markets. The industry in which this type of situation most nearly prevails today is agriculture.

An example of competitive exchange is found in the wheat market. Wheat is divided into grades or varieties according to certain characteristics and is regarded as homogeneous within each grade. Exchange occurs, say, in the wheat pit in Chicago, which is one of the main American markets. Here prices are set by the bids and offers of those who supply and demand the commodity.

## DEMAND AND SUPPLY

**Meaning of Demand.** Let us inquire now what meaning we should attach to the word *demand*. Sometimes *demand* is taken to mean "desire" or "want." This is clearly not a useful concept; my desire for a yacht will have no practical result, because the item is beyond my means. Only when backed up by purchasing power can a desire be effective. Thus actual willingness to buy, to pay money for the item, is the critical point.

Another possible usage is to refer to demand as a certain quantity the buyer wishes to purchase. For example, a person might say that he had a demand for 5 apples. Yet such a statement is almost certainly incomplete. If the price of apples were $1 apiece, the item would be out of reach, and the person would have no demand in this sense. Clearly, the quantity demanded must be associated with a price; in the above case the person doubtless had in mind a given price, say 6 cents. Then he may say: my demand for apples is 5 at a price of 6 cents.

Even this statement, although informative, is not as complete as it might be. Suppose the price is 8 cents; then we are left high and dry, with no information as to what the buyer will do. Clearly, we need to extend the information given, to find out how much the buyer will purchase at other prices. This leads to a definition of demand that meets these specifications. *Demand is the schedule of amounts of a good that the buyer will seek to purchase at a corresponding schedule of prices.* Let us fill out a hypothetical schedule for John Doe. Note that we have filled it out for just 5 possible prices. In practice, we will be able to obtain only a limited amount of information about demand. So this is not unrealistic. In theory, however, there certainly could be other prices and corresponding quantities; the ones listed are merely representative. The name given to the information in the table is the demand schedule of John Doe for apples.

**TABLE 2-1**
**John Doe's Demand Schedule for Apples**

| Price (¢) | Quantity Bought (per Month) |
|---|---|
| 10 | 0 |
| 8 | 2 |
| 6 | 6 |
| 4 | 12 |
| 2 | 20 |

**Demand Schedule and Demand Curve.** To obtain a better picture of demand we may plot the information in this schedule on a graph. On the horizontal axis we measure the quantity of apples; on the vertical axis, the price. Plotting price against quantity gives a set of 5 points. Although we actually have no further information, we can interpolate or fill in the spaces by drawing a smooth curve through the points. This gives rise to the curve shown in Figure 2–1. Actually, this curve is closer to what economists think of as demand than is the schedule, because it represents an estimate of all possibilities within a given price range. Roughly speaking, either the demand curve or schedule is what we mean by demand.

**Individual and Market Demand.** Now we are not primarily interested in one person's demand but in the demand of the whole group of buyers. Therefore, some method of adding together the various demands of all individuals for the same good is necessary. This happens to be rather easy to accomplish in theory, because in

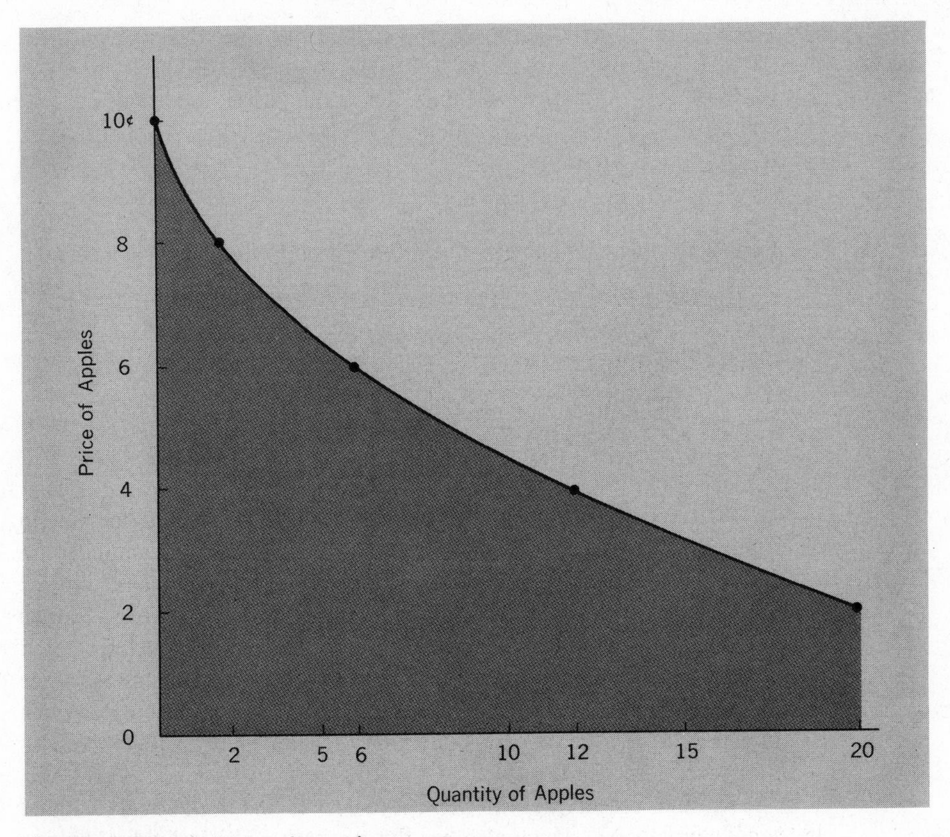


**Figure 2–1.** Demand curve for apples.

a perfect market all buyers face exactly the same price. Therefore, we can assume the price to be the same for each buyer, with only the amounts bought being subject to variation. Then to represent the demands of, say, three people only one price list would be needed to go with the three quantity lists, one for each buyer. Suppose we take the same price list for apples as the one given earlier in Table 2–1. We combine this with quantity lists for three people. This yields a combined schedule, as shown in Table 2–2. Now we would like to find the total demand of these three people.

To find the total demand we add the quantities buyers wish to purchase at every level of price. At a price of 6 cents buyers *A, B,* and *C* demand 6, 3, and 1 apples, respectively. The total, $10 = 6 + 3 + 1$, is recorded in the last column. At a price of 6 cents, then, the total quantity demanded is 10. Similarly, we find the total amount demanded at each price. Finally, the first and last columns constitute the total demand schedule of these three buyers.

To find the market demand schedule we simply extend this method.

We list in columns like *A, B,* and *C* of Table 2–2 the quantities demanded by each customer at each separate price. Adding them all up gives a "total quantity" column. Then the price and total quantity columns form the market demand schedule. Only the arithmetic would pose a problem.

**TABLE 2-2**
**Demand Schedule for Apples—Quantities Bought by Consumers A, B, and C**

| Price (¢) | A | B | C | Total |
|---|---|---|---|---|
| 10 | 0 | 1 | 0 | 1 |
| 8 | 2 | 1 | 0 | 3 |
| 6 | 6 | 3 | 1 | 10 |
| 4 | 12 | 4 | 5 | 21 |
| 2 | 20 | 7 | 10 | 37 |

**The Law of Demand.** By examining Table 2–1 and its plot in Figure 2–1, we can discern a tendency for quantity demanded to increase as the price falls. At a price of 8 cents John Doe buys 2 apples per month, but at 6 cents he buys 6. Graphically, this is shown by the tendency of the demand curve to slope downward from left to right. The tendency for quantity purchased to increase as the price falls is known as the *law of demand.* It applies with even greater force to market than to individual demand schedules. Consider some of the reasons for the law.

The first reason lies in the character of the individual demand schedule or curve, which also has this property. The individual buying a larger quantity is clearly willing to do so only if the price is lower. This indicates that the desirability of the commodity and the willingness to pay for a large quantity somehow decline as the quantity increases. At bottom, this goes back to the diminishing usefulness of additional quantities of anything. One pair of shoes is extremely necessary, and we would pay dearly rather than go without. A second pair is extremely useful as an alternate; but the convenience it affords is far lower. The third, fourth, and so on, may each have its use, but the need that each successive pair satisfies tends to diminish in intensity. Economists refer to this as the *principle of diminishing marginal utility.* Because the utility of successive pairs of shoes declines rather steadily, we are willing to pay less and less for additional amounts. Thus the price declines as the amount consumed increases, giving the law of demand.

In addition to the law of diminishing utility, applying to every individual and causing his demand curve to slope downward from left to right, there is another factor. As the price of the item falls, more customers enter the market. There are two reasons for this:

(1) differences in tastes, and (2) differences in incomes. Some people do not care a great deal for apples and will buy them only when the price drops. As the price falls, additional buyers enter the market who did not care enough about apples to buy at the higher price. Then differences in incomes play a role in that a lower-income family will not be able to buy an article at a high price. As the price is lowered, the article comes into a range in which it can be bought. This tendency has been observed in connection with most durable consumer goods. Only when the price is cut to fairly low levels does the article achieve mass-consumption levels.

The tendency for more customers to enter with declining price is illustrated in Table 2–2. At a price of 10 cents only customer *B* will buy. As the price falls to 8 cents customer *A* enters the market, and at 6 cents customer *C* also enters. Clearly, the broadening of the market by lowering the price reinforces the increased purchases of individuals already in the market.

**Changes in Demand.** The law of demand states that there is a relationship between the price of a commodity and the quantity purchased such that the quantity purchased increases as the price falls; this law is illustrated by the downward-sloping demand curve. However, we know that there are a number of other factors that affect the amount of the item purchased. These are variables other than the price of the item, such as incomes, prices of other products, tastes, and population. Consider very briefly how these operate.

An increase in consumer incomes will enable people to buy more of the commodity at a given price. For example, rising incomes will enable consumers to buy more boats, automatic dishwashers, or other durable items that they lack. Also a rise in the price of a competing product will induce a person to buy more of a given item. If orange juice rises in price, people can switch to tea or hot chocolate. If a favorable change in tastes occurs, brought about possibly by new information or advertising, people may buy more of the commodity. Sales of liver increased greatly when the dietary value of the iron and vitamins it contains was recognized. Finally, a growth of population tends to cause an increase in the demand for such items as housing, clothes, and food. All these changes are the result of variations in magnitudes other than the price of the commodity.

**Changes in Demand and Law of Demand.** By definition, *a change in demand is an increase or decrease in the quantity purchased at a given price*. Suppose we take the market demand schedule of Table 2–2 and plot it. Of course, this is our law of demand. Now suppose there is a general increase in incomes. Then, given the price (of apples), there will be an increase in the quantity purchased. Naturally, this increase will occur at every level of price. At 6 cents, for example, the quantity purchased increases from 10 to 20. Why? Well, not because price has dropped but because incomes have increased, price remaining the same. The change is indicated in Table 2–3 and Figure 2–2. This change is referred to as an *increase in demand*. The cause is a change in incomes or some variable other than price. It shows up as a movement to the right of the demand curve.

**TABLE 2–3**
**Increase in Demand**

| Price (¢) | Quantity Purchased | New Quantity Purchased |
|---|---|---|
| 10 | 1 | 11 |
| 8 | 3 | 13 |
| 6 | 10 | 20 |
| 4 | 21 | 31 |
| 2 | 37 | 47 |

Perhaps more confusion arises over the distinction between the *law of demand and changes in demand* than any other topic in economics. Keep in mind that the standard causal factor influencing quantity purchased is price; the causal influence is built into or revealed by the demand curve or the demand schedule. The relationship is also called the law of demand. When some variable other than price changes, the relation of quantity to price also changes, so that *a change in demand is said to occur.*

Consider the distinction as pictured in Figure 2–2. Suppose the price of apples is 6 cents, a quantity of 10 being bought. Now *other things remaining the same,* a decline in price to 4 cents will occasion an increase in the purchase of apples from 10 to 21. This illustrates the operation of the law of demand; only one demand curve $D_1$ exists, and there is no shift in demand to be considered.

Suppose now that the price of apples *remains constant* at a level of 6 cents. In these circumstances incomes increase and people expand their purchases of apples despite the constant price. This change in demand is in sharp contrast with the first case, where the law of demand operates to increase quantity purchased with no change in demand (as originally defined). The student should try to master this distinction; it represents the contrast between the effects of price variation, shown by the demand curve, and the effects of other changes shown by shifts in the curve.

**Supply.** We can now repeat for supply most of what we have said about demand. By definition, *supply is the schedule of amounts of a good that the seller will offer for sale at a corresponding schedule of prices.* Again, there is a distinction between individual and market

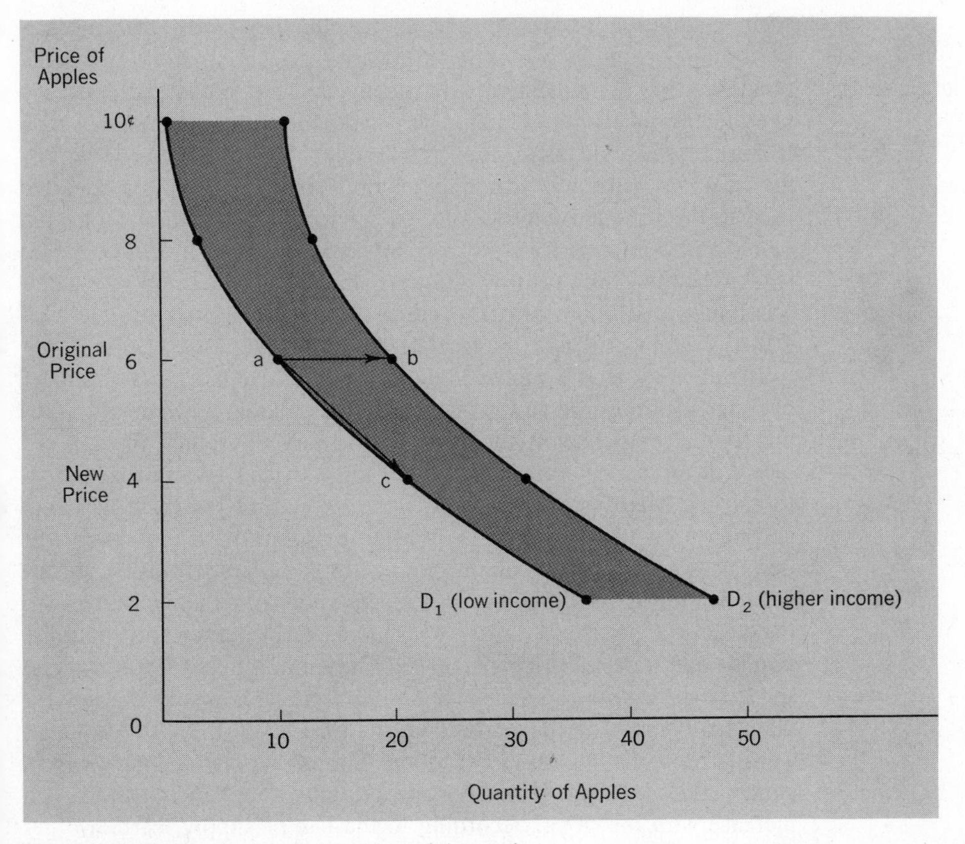


**Figure 2–2.** Change in demand and law of demand.

supply. To secure the latter we add up the individual supply schedules in the way described for demand. We can also plot supply curves from supply schedules in the accustomed way.

Is there a *law of supply?* Under conditions of competition, as presently assumed, and subject to a minor exception,[5] the answer is yes. The law of supply states that the quantity offered by sellers increases with the price. We cannot justify the law fully until production costs have been studied, but we will discuss here an important case.

Economists, in dealing with price behavior, are primarily concerned

[5] The exception occurs in the long run with what economists call "external economies." Here the costs per unit of an individual firm decline as the output of other firms increase. The development of an industry may necessitate the construction of roads into a new area. As the output of the industry expands and more roads are built to facilitate the work of the industry, transportation costs decline for every firm in the industry. See also Alfred Marshall, *Principles of Economics* (8th ed.; New York: Macmillan Company, 1920), p. 441.

with a situation known as the short run. This term designates a period long enough to permit output to vary, yet so short that land, plant, and equipment cannot be changed. This statement defines a fixed factor consisting of land, plant, and equipment. At the same time it implies the existence of such variable factors as labor and raw material. As output is expanded, more labor and raw material are used in the productive process, together with a fixed amount of land, plant, and equipment. As we explained in Chapter 1, this situation leads to diminishing returns. Output per unit of labor and raw material tends to decline; also the added output (marginal product) of doses of labor and raw material tends to decline. (See Table 1–2.)

If the productivity (measured by average and marginal product) of doses of labor and raw material declines, the cost of bringing output to market increases concurrently. In short, the failure of the fixed factor to increase makes it more and more expensive to bring output to market. There is a close tie between the cost of producing an item and the price at which sellers will offer it. Naturally, if the cost of the item rises as a result of diminishing returns, sellers will ask a higher price for the item. Summing up, in the short run the presence of a fixed factor causes cost to rise with increases in output and therefore implies that a rise in price is necessary to tempt sellers to produce and sell a larger output. Somewhat different arguments justify the law for other time periods used in economic analysis.

Finally, a distinction between the law of supply and changes in supply must be observed. Although quantity supplied is assumed to increase with the price, according to the law of supply, certain other factors may cause the supply curve to shift. Among such factors are changes in the prices of productive services (such as wages of labor) that affect cost of production and supply price, variations in taxes, improved methods of production, or changes in prices of other products that could direct resources away from or toward the item in question.

Let us define an increase in supply as the willingness of sellers to offer a larger quantity of an item at the same price. Such a change is illustrated in Figure 2–3. An increase in supply is marked by a movement to the right of the supply curve. At a given price *OR,* the quantity offered increases by the amount *AB*. Of course, a decrease in supply is shown by a movement to the left.

**Price Determination.** It is now time to put together the twin elements of supply and demand. Imagine a large arena peopled with buyers and sellers of an item; this is the market. Here the buyers and sellers meet to decide on a quantity that will be supplied by sellers and demanded by buyers. Moreover, the price at which the item is to be sold must be determined. To interpret what goes on in this situation we need the relevant supply-and-demand information. Let us add to the new market demand schedule of Table 2–3, columns 1 and 3, a supply schedule, all as shown in Table 2–4.

If the price were to be set at 6 cents to begin with, equilibrium would exist, for the quantity demanded would amount to 20, which equals exactly the quantity supplied of 20. Therefore, a price of 6 cents would exactly clear the market; buyers and sellers would go

**TABLE 2–4**
**Supply Of and Demand For Apples**

| Price (¢) | Quantity Demanded | Quantity Supplied | Situation |
|---|---|---|---|
| 10 | 11 | 30 | Excess supply—price falls |
| 8 | 13 | 26 | Excess supply—price falls |
| 6 | 20 | 20 | Equilibrium—no change |
| 4 | 31 | 13 | Excess demand—price rises |
| 2 | 47 | 4 | Excess demand—price rises |

**Figure 2–3.** An increase in supply.

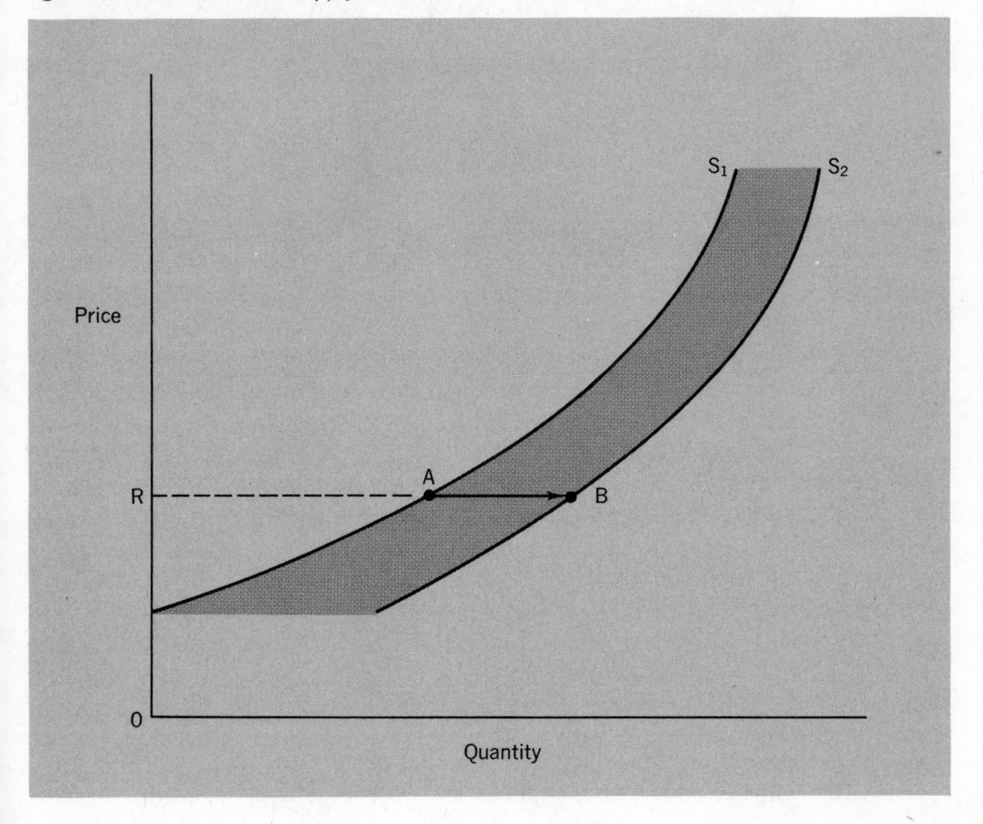

away satisfied. But what if the price is above or below 6 cents at the start? We will argue that the price must tend to move toward this same equilibrium price of 6 cents that clears the market.

Suppose that a price of 8 cents is announced in the market. Such a price generates a quantity supplied of 26 and a quantity demanded of 13, as seen in Table 2–4. In Figure 2–4, which is the plot of the table, this excess supply is revealed in the heavily shaded area above the equilibrium point *E*. Such an excess supply presents a problem

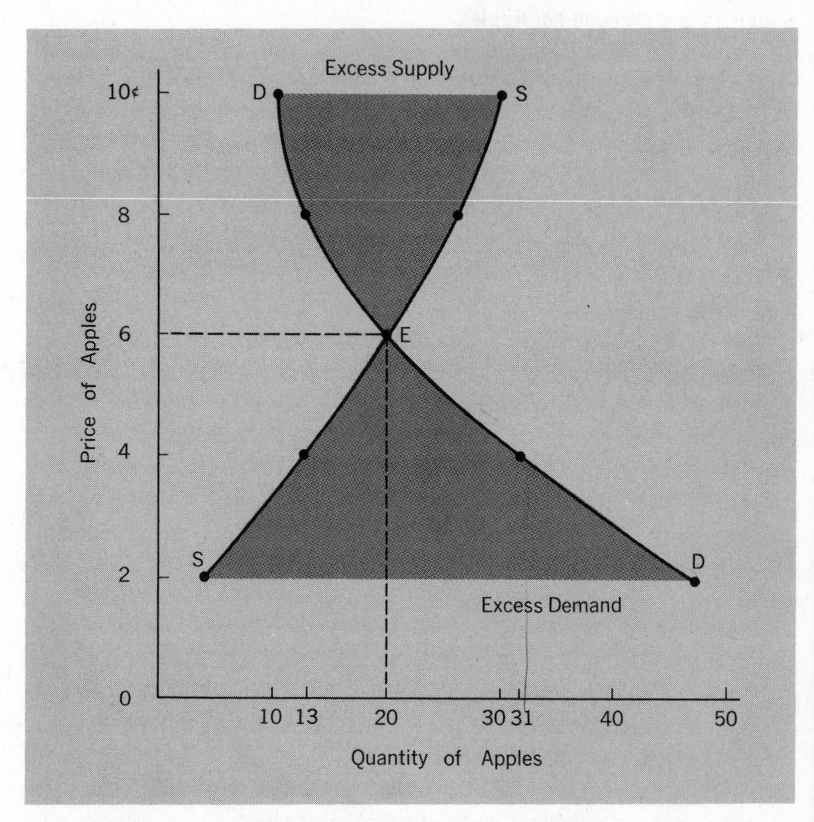


**Figure 2–4.** Price determination by supply and demand.

for sellers; it means that they are unable to sell part of the output they are producing. To get rid of this excess some venturesome seller will cut price, causing buyers to flock to him. In order to meet competition other sellers will also cut their price. Eventually, all sellers must offer the product at a reduced price. Thus the price would tend to fall from 8 cents toward a lower level. The decline would continue as long as excess supply exists and the price remains above 6 cents. On the other hand, suppose the price is initially set below 6 cents, say at 4 cents. Then the quantity demanded is 31, compared to a quantity supplied of 13. Evidently, there is an excess demand of 18 (= 31 − 13); buyers are not able to acquire all of the commodity they want at this price. Rather than accept the small quantity offered, some buyer will doubtless offer a higher price in the hope of securing a larger share of the good being offered. As he easily gets priority in virtue of his higher bid, other buyers will follow suit. Eventually, only a buyer offering the higher price will be able to buy the good. As long as excess demand is present, as in the price range below 6 cents, upward pressure on price will exist. The lower, shaded area in the diagram represents excess demand, a range in which price tends to rise.

**Conclusion.** A price *above* the equilibrium value of 6 cents will set up an excess supply, which will tend to force a *fall* in price; a price *below* the equilibrium value will set up an excess demand, which will tend to force a rise in price. Only at 6 cents, where quantity supplied is matched to quantity demanded, will the price tend to remain unchanged. Therefore, *the equilibrium price is one that equates quantity supplied and quantity demanded; if the law of demand and the law of supply prevail, price will tend toward the equilibrium.*

**The Role of Competition.** In the purely competitive market described above the interaction of buyers and sellers leads to the determination of quantity exchanged and price of the item. No individual buyer or seller can affect this price but must accept it as a given fact resulting from market conditions. The responsibility for high or low prices rests on the impersonal forces of supply and demand expressed through exchange in the market. Thus no one person can be blamed if prices are too high or too low.

In the mutual adjustment of supply and demand, competition plays the leading role. If the amount demanded exceeds the amount supplied so that the item is in short supply, the competition of buyers for the limited quantity forces the price up. If the amount supplied exceeds the quantity demanded so that an excess quantity is being supplied, the competition of sellers for the limited number of buyers prompts them to cut prices. Evidently, it is the mutual competition of buyers that keeps prices up and the mutual competition of sellers that keeps them down. Taken all together competition forces price and quantity to certain definite values.

## MARKETS AS A WHOLE

In our discussion of markets above we dealt with setting the amounts and prices of individual items by supply and demand. Each item, its price and quantity, is one part of the overall economic structure. At this point we may pass on to a consideration of the way in which the individual items fit into such an overall pattern. One convenient way of doing this is to take a bird's-eye view of the economy by considering the flow of income and production in the economy.

**The Circular Flow of Income.** In our society there are two basic economic units: the producer and the consumer. The producer has two main activities—the hiring and organizing of the factors of production and the channeling of the resulting output to the buyer. In hiring the factors of land, labor, and capital (with the aid of management or entrepreneurship) the producer necessarily pays out corresponding rewards to these factors. Rent goes to land, wages to labor, interest to capital, and profit to management or entrepreneurship. All of this constitutes the flow of money income, and it goes to the owners of the several factors.

By the use of the factors the firm produces a stream of output. It hopes to find a sale for this product and, thereby, to acquire funds with which to pay the factors for their services.

For the sake of simplicity let us imagine a society in which people consume all their income (and save nothing). Then the recipients of income and the buyers of output are one and the same. Also by virtue of the factors people provide they receive income that they spend in purchasing goods and services. The income people receive, then, is passed back to the producers. All this indicates a certain interdependence between producer and buyer (income recipient), which may be summarized in a so-called *circular flow chart.* See Figure 2–5.

Starting with the producer, we see a flow line at the bottom from the producer, indicating such income payments as rent, wages, and so on, going to the income recipient (the buyer). The sum of all these payments, known as the *national income,* corresponds to a flow of factors, indicated by a flow line just below this, from the owner of the factors who is also the income recipient. Also there is a flow line at the top from producer to buyer, indicating the passage of output. In return, there is a flow of expenditure, as indicated by the flow line, from the buyer to the producer. Let us use the word *expenditure* to mean the total sum of money that all buyers spend on goods and services in a year. The expression *aggregate demand* is used as a synonym, because the total expenditure of society on output may be regarded as an expression of its aggregate or total demand for goods.

**Expenditure Depends on Income.** The circular flow chart shows the close relationship between income and expenditure. Under our assumptions the relationship is very simple: people spend on output

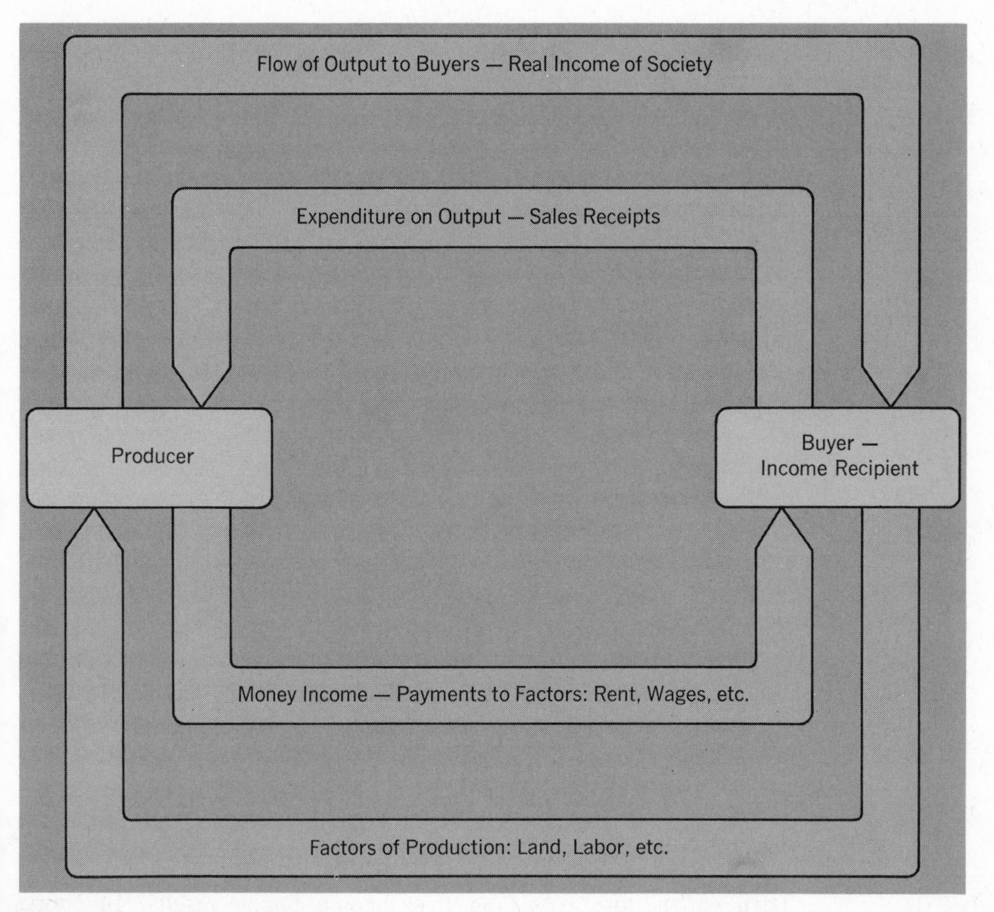


**Figure 2–5.** Circular flow chart.

all they receive as income. With low incomes people spend correspondingly little; with high incomes, correspondingly much. Even when this assumption is relaxed, the relationship between income and expenditure remains. Statistical data indicate that expenditure on output varies directly with national income. Consequently, high-level expenditure absolutely requires high incomes. Similarly, low incomes are associated with low expenditure.

**Production and Expenditure Depend on Each Other.** Let's show first how production influences expenditure. In order to produce goods firms must hire appropriate amounts of the factors of production, which must be paid corresponding rewards. The income earned by the factors accrues to the owners of the factors. As we indicated above, these owners are themselves spending units. Thus production generates income which is ultimately available to spending units.

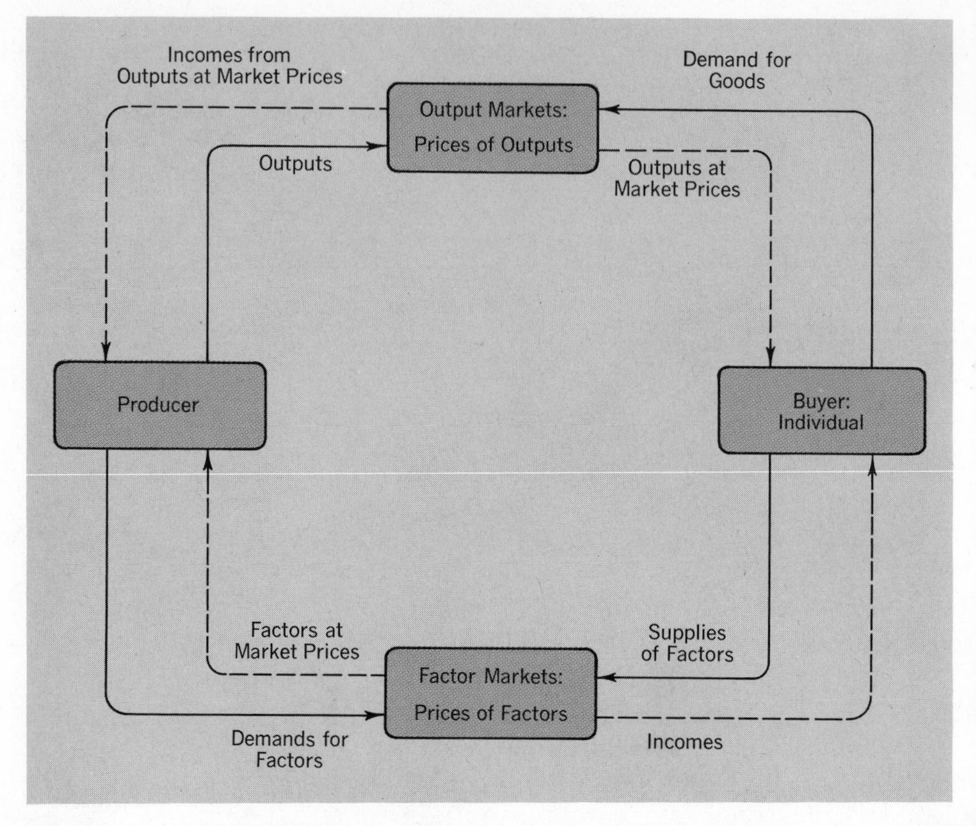


**Figure 2–6.** Markets and the circular flow.

Then expenditure based on this income finally results. In short, production strongly influences expenditure.

Now let's turn this process around. Expenditure on output tends to be met by corresponding production. Producers base their production on the amount they can profitably sell. Hence production is based on expenditure. We have now completed a full circle. Production determines income and thus influences expenditure. On the other hand expenditure determines production. Is this circular reasoning? No! But we need to put the elements together to show a precise stopping point for the two mutually dependent elements of production and buying. We will sketch this solution in the paragraph below headed "How Aggregate Output Is Determined: The Market for Output As a Whole."

**Product and Factor Markets.** The circular flow concept sheds light on the relation between product and factor markets. We see two activities going on here: the exchange of output for money and the exchange of factor services for money. By revamping our circular flow chart somewhat we may bring this out in greater detail, as in Figure 2–6.



In the lower part of the diagram an arrow drawn from the producer toward the buyer (individual) shows the demand for factors. This arrow ends at the factor markets, where the demand is to be exercised. Here factor prices are formed by this demand in connection with the supply of factors coming from the individual. When the factors are properly priced, they go to the firm. Likewise, the prices of the factors represent incomes to the factors and to the people who own them. Clearly, factor markets constitute the main focal point of the lower part of this circular flow.

Similarly, output from the producer meets demand from the buyers, thus forming output prices. The priced output goes to the buyer. Also the receipts (or income), representing the priced output, go to the producer. Again, the market represents a key point in the upper part of this circular flow process. Actually, the circular flow mechanism is a simple device for showing how the two basic types of markets are interrelated.

## HOW AGGREGATE OUTPUT IS DETERMINED: THE MARKET FOR OUTPUT AS A WHOLE

In the earlier part of this chapter we studied the determination of individual quantities and prices by supply and demand. We found that the quantity of an item supplied tends to equal the corresponding amount demanded. Price is the factor that brings these two magnitudes into equality. Is it feasible to apply a similar technique to the entire economy? If so, we can speak about the equality of total amount produced and total amount demanded under the influence of price. Let us consider briefly why this kind of analysis does *not* seem to be workable and then outline a similar method that is.

The notion of an equilibrium of supply and demand depends on the law of demand and the law of supply. Let's check the law of demand and see whether it applies to all output. Suppose the prices of all outputs dropped exactly 10 per cent. If everything else remained the same, this price cut would be exactly like giving the buyer 10 per cent more income with which to buy goods. On the basis of this the buyer could purchase more goods, and thus the law of demand seems to operate. But how likely is this to happen?

The seller hires factors on the assumption that a certain price will prevail on the product he is selling. Unless the prices of factors drop along with the prices of products, the producer cannot afford to hire quantities of the factors as great as before. If the prices of products are to drop 10 per cent, it seems all too likely that the prices of factors, especially wages, must drop also, possibly by 10 per cent. But incomes are derived from the sale of factors to the producer. If prices of factors are cut 10 per cent, incomes will immediately fall to the same extent. The result is that the consumer experiences a decline of 10 per cent in his income combined with a 10-per-cent drop in the prices he pays. Clearly, his ability to buy is about the same as it was to begin with. As a result, his purchases will remain about the same as they were before the decline in prices, so that the law of demand fails.

This argument seems to have led us up a blind alley. Must we abandon the hope of analyzing the market for output as a whole? Certainly some change in the argument is required. Fortunately, an alternative approach has been suggested by part of our discussion. We noticed that a cut in output prices of 10 per cent with incomes constant would be equivalent to a 10-per-cent increase in income. We had to reject this situation as highly unlikely. But why not consider the effects of changes in the level of income? In fact, the level of income may be the factor that controls aggregate demand, because, as we mentioned in our discussion of the circular flow, the public spends more on output as incomes rise.

Let us begin by showing that the money income of society measures output or real income. When producing a given level of output producers hire certain quantities of the factors. In turn, these factors are paid money incomes. The owners of the factors—namely, the public—receive in this way an income identical with the cost of the factors. By definition this cost constitutes a sum sufficient to pay for the factors and therefore to buy the output. So our first step leads us to the conclusion that the money income of society, the cost of the factors, is exactly sufficient to buy the output of those factors. Therefore, we can speak of the income of society as consisting either of its money income or the output it will buy.

We can look at this matter from a slightly different point of view. The collection of goods produced by society is its real income. After all, you cannot eat dollar bills or drive them to work. Only the goods and services that society turns out can be used. Therefore, we can think of the output of society as its real income. As we explained above, this real income can be measured in money.

From experience we know that our own expenditure on output depends on our income. Statistical evidence shows this to be true for society as well. In line with this let us assume that the amount the public spends on output depends on the level of real income. For present purposes let us express this expenditure in real terms, in terms of output rather than money. Then we can compare the amount the public wants to buy with the amount produced and supplied. Clearly, the amount produced (aggregate supply) must equal the amount bought (aggregate demand) in order to provide balance or equilibrium in the economy.

Let us assume that the public buys some output even with no income. After all, a person must live regardless of his income. By consuming stored-up capital the public can spend more than its income for a while. Then we assume that people spend two thirds of all additional income in buying output; the rest they save. In Table 2–5 we show an assumed relationship between real national income (aggregate supply) and expenditure on output (aggregate demand).

**TABLE 2-5**
**Equilibrium Level of Output or Real National Income**

| Real National Income: Aggregate Supply | Expenditure on Output: Aggregate Demand | |
|---|---|---|
| 0 | 200 | Demand exceeds supply |
| 300 | 400 | Demand exceeds supply |
| 600 | 600 | Equilibrium output or real income |
| 900 | 800 | Supply exceeds demand |
| 1,200 | 1,000 | Supply exceeds demand |

We assume that the numbers listed in the table are expressed in hundreds of billions of dollars but represent output, dollar for dollar. Notice that aggregate demand equals aggregate supply only at 600. This is the equilibrium amount produced (or supplied) and demanded. At a lower level of real income demand exceeds supply, and at a higher level supply exceeds demand. So the level of real income established tends to be 600 (billion dollars).

Expressing this graphically presents a bit of a problem. To forestall this we will do something artificial but not incorrect. Rewrite the above table, as shown in Table 2–6. We have made up one column for real income and a separate one for aggregate supply, as well as one for aggregate demand. Of course, we know that aggregate supply is exactly the same thing as real income. But let us judge this device by its fruits.

Using the data of Table 2–6, we plot the value of aggregate supply on the *Y*, or vertical, axis against real income on the *X*, or horizontal, axis, as shown in Figure 2–7. This gives five points represented by small circles. Connecting these points we get the aggregate supply line. (Note that it is a straight line through the origin, making a 45-degree angle with the *X* axis.) Similarly, we plot the value of aggregate demand on the $Y$ axis against real national income on the $X$ axis. This gives five points represented by small $x$'s. Connecting these we get the aggregate demand line.

At point $E$, where the two curves cross, aggregate supply equals aggregate demand, and equilibrium in the market for output is realized. Then output, or real national income, is adjusted to the level

**TABLE 2–6**
**Equilibrium Level of Output or Real Income (A Rearrangement of Table 2–5)**

| Real National Income (on X axis) | Aggregate Supply (on Y axis) | Aggregate Demand, Expenditure (on Y axis) | |
|---|---|---|---|
| 0 | 0 | 200 | |
| 300 | 300 | 400 | |
| 600 | 600 | 600 | Equilibrium; aggregate supply equals aggregate demand |
| 900 | 900 | 800 | |
| 1,200 | 1,200 | 1,000 | |

$600 billion, at which total output of this amount is taken off the market by purchases. Like the interaction of supply and demand for an individual item under the influence of price, the above process illustrates a phase of the market system. We see once again how outputs, aggregate as well as individual, are set in the market.

**Summary.** An economic system is the set of arrangements by which society makes use of its resources in the production of output to satisfy human wants. All present-day systems are marked by the presence of the following characteristics: heavy use of capital; specialization, exchange, and use of money; gearing of modern economies to change. Pure capitalism is marked by the institutions of private property and freedom of contract. Private property refers to the right granted to the individual to use property as he wishes and to receive the income that results from its employment. Such rights are bound to be limited by the necessity of avoiding injury or loss to others through the use of property. Freedom of contract refers to the freedom of individuals in the purchase and sale of goods and services, organizing of businesses, and the choice of occupation. Involved in freedom of contract are the elements of free enterprise, or the right of individuals to start and manage their own businesses, and consumer sovereignty, or the exercise of free consumer choice and its influence on production decisions. Competition among buyers and sellers, motivated by enlightened self-interest, is the factor that converts these individual actions into a pattern that benefits the public.



Capitalism carries out the functions it is expected to perform through the market system. In markets the quantities of goods and services supplied are brought into equality with those demanded. When dealing with an individual good or service we identify supply and demand as schedules that relate a series of prices to corresponding quantities. There is a law of demand that states that more of any good will be purchased as the price falls, and a law of supply that states that more of any good will be supplied as the price rises. Supply

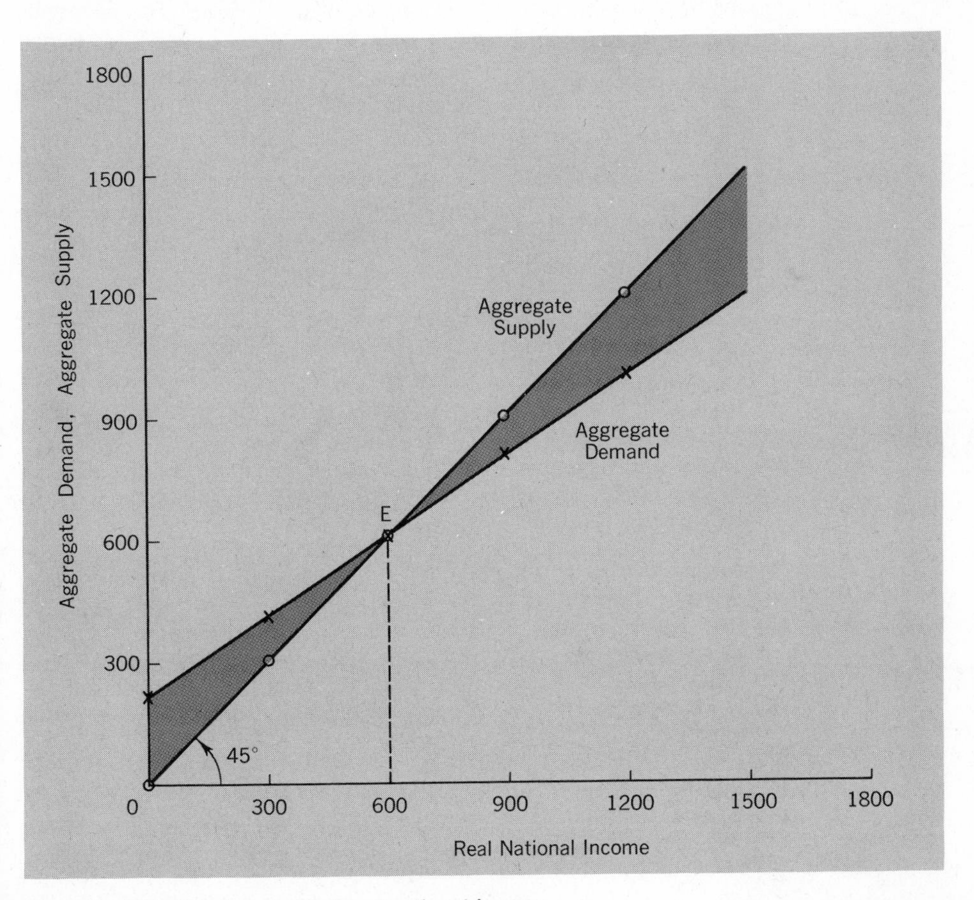


**Figure 2–7.** Equilibrium level of real national income.

and demand interact to determine an equilibrium price at which the quantity supplied is exactly equal to the quantity demanded. This common quantity is the equilibrium quantity exchanged. Graphically, equilibrium price and quantity are found at the point where the supply and demand curves intersect.

Having explained the determination of individual quantities of goods and services we turn our attention to the behavior of the economic system as a whole. Of primary interest is the process by which the overall level of output is determined. As background we consider the relationship between producers and spenders. Producers turn out goods and services that go to individuals in return for expenditure on this output. Also individuals furnish the necessary factors of production in return for income that serves to reward the factors. This set of relationships is known as the circular flow of income.

This brings us to the market for output as a whole. The aggregate demand for output can be thought of as the total sum spent on that output. Similarly, aggregate supply can be thought of as the sum of money producers must receive for a given level of output. This may be referred to as cost of output, because it must be used to pay for the services of the factors. In turn, it also equals the income of society, being the amount that the factors earn for their part in production. When aggregate demand equals aggregate supply, the level of output as a whole is determined.

## QUESTIONS

1. What is an economic system? Name several types of economic systems of past and present.
2. Why is specialization linked to exchange and the use of money?
3. List the basic features common to all economies.
4. What factors are (or were) presumed to motivate the members of society under capitalism, socialism, feudalism, and theocracy, respectively?
5. Why is a vigorous competition essential to capitalism?
6. What is a market? What are the characteristics of a highly competitive market?
7. Discuss the various meanings that may be attached to the word *demand,* including the correct one.
8. What, briefly, is the law of demand, and what is the basis of the law?
9. Draw a circular flow chart freehand, labeling all parts. Explain the interaction of the various parts.
10. Draw a supply-and-demand graph freehand, labeling all parts fully. Explain how equilibrium price is established.
11. Why is real national income referred to as aggregate supply?
12. Why does the equality of expenditure and real national income represent an equilibrium?

CHAPTER

# 3

# The Operations of a Growing Economy

## FUNCTIONS OF AN ECONOMIC SYSTEM

We are all more or less aware that our economic system performs its functions rather effectively. In the United States almost anyone seeking work can usually find a suitable job and thereby earn an income. Moreover, this income is very generally sufficient to afford an adequate supply of necessities, in view of the moderate prices that prevail on such items. All this occurs without a great deal of fanfare and without detailed direction from the government. These facts lead us to inquire just what our system is supposed to do and how it manages to do it.

**Basic Problems Faced by Any Economic System.** Any economic system must solve certain basic problems: (1) setting the amounts of the various outputs; (2) determining the amounts of resources used; and (3) distributing the outputs. Capitalism handles these matters through the operation of the market system, as described in the previous chapter. Here we want to develop at length the behavior of the system in performing these tasks.

**Setting Outputs.** By setting the amounts of certain outputs at zero and others at positive amounts, the economy chooses what kinds of goods it will produce. As a result of man's ingenuity there are always far more types of goods available than it is feasible to produce. For this reason certain items are replaced by others as changes in consumer tastes or technology take effect. Some classic examples of this process are found in the replacement of the horse and buggy by the automobile and the straight by the safety razor. Once the items to be produced have been determined, the way is open for a decision on exactly how much of each one to produce.

It is very useful for the purpose of studying the behavior of the economy to make a distinction between individual and aggregate output. Thus the economy must decide how many apples, radios, pencils, and whatever else to produce. In addition to the decision on amounts of individual outputs, there arises the question of what the total output of the economy is to be. Of course, the whole must equal the sum of the parts. Still it is very enlightening to study this question independently because of its inherent importance. The total output of the economy, often called national income, is a measure of the activity and vitality of the system. More than any other fact, the size of aggregate output determines the well-being of the members of society.

**Determining Amounts of Resources.** As we have already noted a number of times, it is convenient to group resources or factors of production into four categories: land, labor, capital, and entrepreneurship or management. The specific characteristics of these four factors need not concern us at this point. In any given firm or industry a decision must be made on how much of each factor to use. Similarly, the overall level of resource use, that is, the cost of all the factors used to produce total output or the national income, must be determined.

In dealing with this problem it is necessary to touch on three matters: techniques of production, the provision of necessary resources, and the allocation of resources. Techniques of production may be defined as the ways in which factors of production are combined in order to produce output. To a large extent techniques depend on the current state of scientific knowledge and so are beyond immediate control. At the moment of writing, the process of nuclear fusion, which provides the power of the hydrogen bomb, cannot be harnessed to provide power for peaceful uses. On the other hand steam plants, using coal as fuel, can generate electric power economically. The state of technique that dictates use of the latter process influences the choice of resources or factors. Thus for our energy source we use coal instead of uranium; for capital equipment, steam power plants in contrast to currently undetermined nuclear power systems. At a given moment the technique of production may be regarded as a given factor greatly influencing the ways in which factors are used.

Suppose we are given the kind of good to be produced, the amount of it, and the technique of production. A good deal can be said about the amount of a specific factor to be used. If an automobile firm produces 1 million automobiles in a given year, then 5 million tires will be needed. Doubtless the labor requirements could be determined too within fairly narrow limits. Once the needed amounts of resources have been determined the system must provide them. Thus 5 million tires must be secured for the corresponding automobiles. For this to occur a suitable incentive to the production of this number of tires must be created. Under capitalism price serves as an incentive, so that the problem is solved by determining a price high enough to induce the production of the desired number of tires.

Our last step is to allocate resources properly among competing uses. At any given time various industries compete for the use of resources. Thus steel is used in automobiles, home appliances, and construction, among other things. With a limited quantity available the total must be rationed out among these uses. In fact, steel may be regarded as a scarce item that must be parceled out among competing ends, the total of which are unlimited in amount. This is very close to the general problem we are here considering, namely, setting the amounts of resources to be used. The general problem, however, includes the problem of setting the overall level of resource use, and is, therefore, somewhat broader in scope.

**Distribution of Output.** When the desired output of society has been produced, it becomes necessary to distribute this output to appropriate recipients. The recipients of the output will be determined partly by institutional factors varying with the type of economic system. Under pure capitalism the institution of private property permits individuals to receive income from property, specifically land and capital. Also the bulk of all output flows into private hands, because the role of government in economic affairs is sharply limited. By way of contrast socialism is marked by public ownership of the "means of production," land and capital. For this reason no rents and interest are paid to individuals. Finally, the government has the power to retain as much of the flow of output as it wishes for investment in capital facilities or defense.

## THE OPERATION OF A CAPITALISTIC SYSTEM

**Capitalistic Economy As a Mechanism.** In a capitalistic economy producers have a choice as to what goods they want to produce and in what quantity. Consumers have a similar freedom in reaching decisions on what they buy. Considering the fact that there are millions of producers and many millions of consumers it is rather remarkable that the actions and decisions of these many individuals lead to satisfactory results. In fact, we know that all the usual functions of an economy are performed under our system. Everyone gets fed, clothed, and housed, and most receive a share of the finer things of life. How so?

It appears that the capitalistic system operates as a kind of mechanism to solve the three functions of an economy. The decisions of the various parties are coordinated by this mechanism in a way that leads to production of suitable outputs, the setting of corresponding quantities of resources, and the distribution of the outputs to the members of society. Now the most important characteristic of the mechanism is that it is automatic. No political authority is required to plan the operation of the system. In fact, the automatic, self-adjusting character of capitalism, its ability to function without centralized government authority, is one of its chief attractions.

In the next few pages we will give a preview of the functioning of an economic system under pure capitalism. Actually, the description will be very idealized and simplified. In practice, the automatic mechanism may break down or prove to be inadequate. In such a case our society may find it desirable to correct or shore up some phase of the system. This leads to government intervention in the economy and a movement away from pure capitalism to a mixed system. Here the basic mechanism is left intact but is braced or strengthened by government action at certain points.

**The Market System and Setting of Outputs.** The output of any individual good is determined under a competitive capitalistic system by supply and demand. Thus the output of wheat of a specific grade is determined in the market by the interplay of buyers and sellers. To begin with, individual wants serve as the basis for a buyer's demand schedule. By adding up the individual demand schedules for the product in question we arrive at the market schedule. Likewise, the firm or producing unit has an individual supply curve based on conditions of production and costs. Adding up the supply schedules of the different firms gives rise to the market supply schedule. When the forces of supply and demand interact, as in a competitive market, they determine a certain quantity produced and purchased at a corresponding price. Graphically, this outcome is shown by the price and quantity found at the intersection of the market demand-and-supply curves. Here the quantity determined is the output of this item and is associated with a corresponding price. The collection of all such individual outputs constitutes the composition of output, as well as its level, and is associated with the corresponding set of prices. Thus prices are instrumental in bringing about the setting of outputs of individual items.

The overall level of output is determined by aggregate demand and aggregate supply. Recall that aggregate demand is the total sum of money spent on all output. Similarly, aggregate supply is the sum of money that is just sufficient to get producers to set the current level of output; it is sufficient because it will just induce the factors to put forth their current efforts in production. Aggregate supply is also the cost of output and the national income. When aggregate supply equals aggregate demand, producers receive exactly what is necessary to produce the current level of output. Consequently they continue this level of output, thus determining overall output and total expenditure, which equals the national income. Thus the market mechanism again solves the problem of amounts to produce by facilitating an equality of supply and demand. In this case the mechanism operates through the medium of changes in total output, which must move to a level at which aggregate demand equals aggregate supply.

One question that this discussion raises is whether the market system described in its various aspects is feasible or workable. Will the different parts of the system adjust to one another so as to provide the necessary solutions, the outputs and prices? As we see the system in actual operation, it is clear from its smooth functioning that the answer is yes. One reason for this workability lies in the alternative plans expressed in the demand-and-supply schedules or curves. If something in the situation changes, a shift from one plan to another can be effected; more or less can be bought or sold. Here the influence that sets off the change in plans is a rise or fall in price. To summarize, the forces of supply and demand adjust to one another because of the alternative plans that they express and that price serves to coordinate.

**Setting Amounts of Resources.** The required amounts of resources are related to corresponding outputs. Suppose that there is a demand for a given product, say houses. In order to produce houses certain quantities of lumber are required. However, there are other products made from wood, such as furniture and paper. Therefore it is necessary to add up the total amount of lumber required to provide for all the uses. Suppose that the total amount needed is determined. How is this quantity to be provided? This is the question of *provision of resources.*

Briefly, the market system solves this problem by putting an appropriate price on the resource, lumber. Such a price is supposed to stimulate lumber producers to bring forward for sale the needed amount. If the amount offered is insufficient, the price of lumber tends to rise. In turn, the higher price serves as an incentive to the producers to supply a larger quantity. By a movement of price to the proper level exactly the right inducement will be provided for the amount of lumber needed.

Once the appropriate quantity has been provided there arises the necessity of dividing this amount among the several uses. Thus there is the question of how much lumber is to go into housing, furniture, and paper, respectively. This is the question of *allocation of resources* among competing uses. Again, this question is decided by price: the resources are allocated to uses by competitive bidding. Only those uses that can afford to pay the competitive price for lumber will receive an allocation. Also the more lumber a given use can absorb at the going price, the larger its allocation will tend to be. In order to make allocation effective the price of lumber must be raised high enough to exclude some potential users. Otherwise, the quantity demanded would exceed the amount available. Generally speaking, the price of lumber is too high in the United States to make it available as a fuel for heating houses. Thus the price put on lumber all but excludes this use.

Essentially, the question of provision of a resource is one of supplying the necessary quantity. The problem itself finds concrete expression in the supply curve for the resource. Similarly, the allocation of resources deals with the fact that price is associated with a limited demand for the resource on the part of each producer. Of course, the sum of the individual demands is the market quantity demanded at this price. The collection of all market quantities demanded in relation to the corresponding price is the market demand schedule for the factor. In short, this demand curve implies an allocation of the resource between users at each price, the allocating agent being price itself. To summarize, the functions of provision and allocation of resources are summed up in their supply-and-demand curves. A solution is provided by the interaction of these forces in the market.

**Techniques and Use of Resources.** A technique of production

**Figure 3–1.** Relation between product and factor markets.

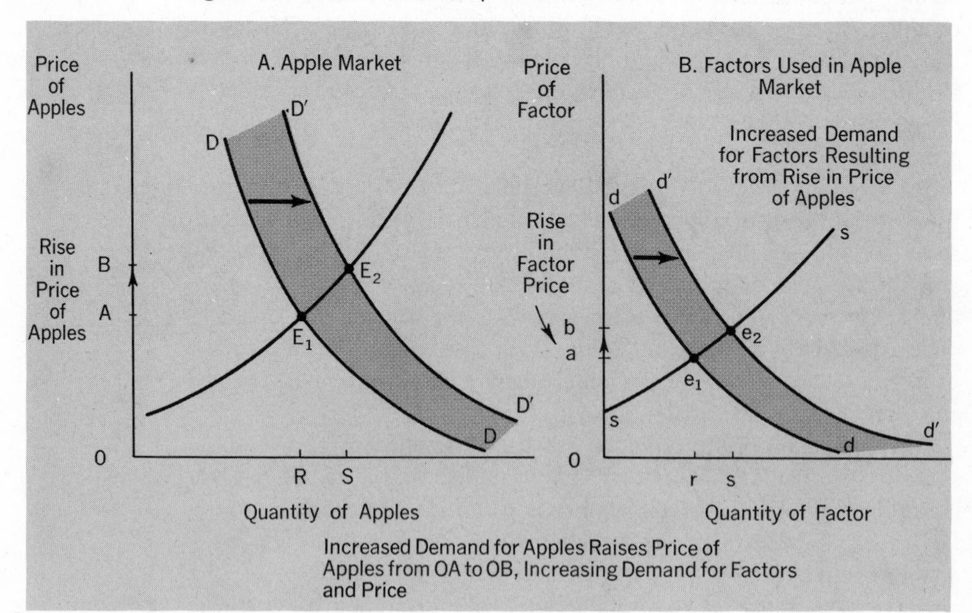

is the way in which factors are combined to produce a given product. Clearly, the market system cannot of itself provide any technical knowledge that does not already exist. However, the pattern of prices can be influential in deciding which of several techniques of production should be adopted. This kind of decision is commonly faced when a choice exists between extensive use of labor with a moderate amount of capital and a moderate use of labor with a large quantity of capital. For example, cotton can be hand-picked with only the most negligible use of capital. On the other hand, given large, fairly level tracts of land, mechanical cotton pickers can be used that require very little labor to operate. Consider how a choice is reached in such a case.

The pattern of factor prices is influential in arriving at a decision on the appropriate technique, or factor combination. If labor is rather abundant, its wage low, and if a scarcity of capital exists such that interest rates and other costs of capital use are high, the scales may tip in favor of hand-picking. If labor is scarce and wages high, and capital is abundant and costs of borrowing low, the mechanical cotton pickers may be employed. In fact, the increasing scarcity of the necessary grade of labor and the rising wage rates combined with improved productivity of machines and moderate costs have led to a steady trend toward the mechanical cotton picker. In this movement the market system has played a definite role.

**The Relation Between Outputs and Factors.** Basically, the relationship between outputs and factors is dual in nature. On the one hand, certain quantities of the factors are required to produce a given output. On the other hand, the demand for the factors is derived purely and simply from the demand for the final product. From this reciprocal relationship a number of things follow.

Suppose the demand for a final product, such as apples, increases, and the price of apples rises. As a result of the higher price of apples in conjunction with the increased demand, applegrowers will find it profitable to increase bids for the land and labor used in their line of work. Next, the demands for these productive services rise, their prices rise, and larger quantities are attracted into this business. Thus the ultimate effect of an increase in demand for apples is an increased allocation of factors to apple production and a rise in the factor prices in question. This process is illustrated in Figure 3–1.

**Overall Level of Resource Use.** Lastly, we must consider how the general level of resource use in the economy is determined. The employment of labor provides a good measure of resource use, since the use of every factor or resource is associated with that of labor. The problem, then, may be put in these terms: How is the overall level of employment in the economy determined?

To answer this question we may note first that employment depends on the amount being produced, and this depends on the aggregate demand for output. When the demand for all output is high, producers will take on a great deal of labor (and other factors). This happens during prosperity. When the demand for output is low, employment will be small, as during depression. In summary, then, the overall level of resource use, meaning especially the employment of labor, depends directly on aggregate demand for output.

**Distribution of Output.** In a pure capitalistic system rewards are assigned to people on the basis of the factors they own and the prices of these factors. Suppose John Doe is a carpenter who has capital of $10,000. To find this person's income we must find the wages of carpenters and the interest on capital. Now there are markets for carpenters and for capital in which these prices are determined by demand and supply. Suppose the carpenter's wage is $3.00, an amount set by supply and demand. Likewise, the interest rate is set at 6 per cent in the market for funds. Then it is easy to find his income.

**TABLE 3-1**
**John Doe's Income**

| Type of Factor | Price of Factor | Amount Provided Yearly | Yearly Income |
|---|---|---|---|
| Carpenter's labor | $3 per hour | 2,000 hours | $6,000 |
| Capital | 6% | $10.000 | 600 |
| Total | | | $6,600 |

First, a table is set up recording in separate columns the type of factors, the price of each factor, the amount of each factor provided yearly, and the income from each factor. We record the prices of labor and capital in the second column, and the amounts of labor and capital in the third. If the carpenter works 50 weeks a year 5 days a week on an 8-hour day, his yearly work load is 2,000 hours. This is recorded in the third column. Now the yearly income of John Doe from labor is the product of his hourly wage of $3.00 and the work load of 3,000 hours, namely $6,000. Likewise, the interest income is the interest rate of 6 per cent times the amount of capital provided of $10,000, which amounts to $600. Adding these together we arrive at John Doe's total income of $6,600. These calculations are arranged in Table 3–1.

Therefore an individual's income is determined by (1) the prices of the factors, resulting from the demand for, and supply of, each such factor, and (2) the amounts of the factors owned by one person. For society as a whole the income paid depends on the total amount produced. We speak of this income as being *distributed* when it is passed out to the owners of the factors. This distribution of income is based on (1) the prices of the factors, and (2) the distribution of quantities of the factors among the members of society. By the second point we mean this: the available quantities of factors of production are owned by the members of society, and the pattern of ownership determines, in part, the pattern of incomes received. John Doe can claim a certain part of the supplies of labor and capital. In virtue of this ownership and the prices of the factors he can claim a certain income.

Actually, the process of distribution is not completed with the determination of money incomes. Money is prized because it is a means of commanding goods and services. So to complete this discussion we need to ask how incomes are translated into a flow of goods and services.

When the individual receives his money income, he has at his disposal a means of acquiring the goods and services that make up his *real income*. He goes into the market for goods and services and buys these items at prices set by supply and demand. Given his money income, the collection of goods he will wish to buy depends on the level and pattern of prices. Therefore his actual reward, what he can and will buy, depends on the prices of outputs.

We can conclude very briefly. Given the pattern of resource ownership, the distribution of output (real income) depends on the prices of factor services and on the prices of outputs. Clearly, there is a double dependence of the distribution of rewards on prices.

## THE OPERATION OF A PROGRESSIVE ECONOMY

Let us consider, successively, some of the changes likely to take place in a dynamic economy and how they affect the performance of the system in performing its functions.

**Changes in Demand.** One of the marks of a progressive economy is rising per capita income. Such a tendency will cause the demands for most items to increase through time. Let us assume that the conditions of supply remain substantially unchanged. Consider the impact of this change in conditions under a system of competitive capitalism. As pictured in Figure 3–2 the demand curve shifts from $D_1$ to $D_2$. In the original situation equilibrium is found at $E_1$, with a price $OA_1$ and a quantity $OB_1$. The increase in demand changes the equilibrium point from $E_1$ to $E_2$, the price from $OA_1$ to $OA_2$, and the quantity produced from $OB_1$ to $OB_2$.

Let us remark on several features of this situation. First, the increase in demand has actually resulted in an increase in the quantity produced. In general, a system of competitive capitalism is responsive

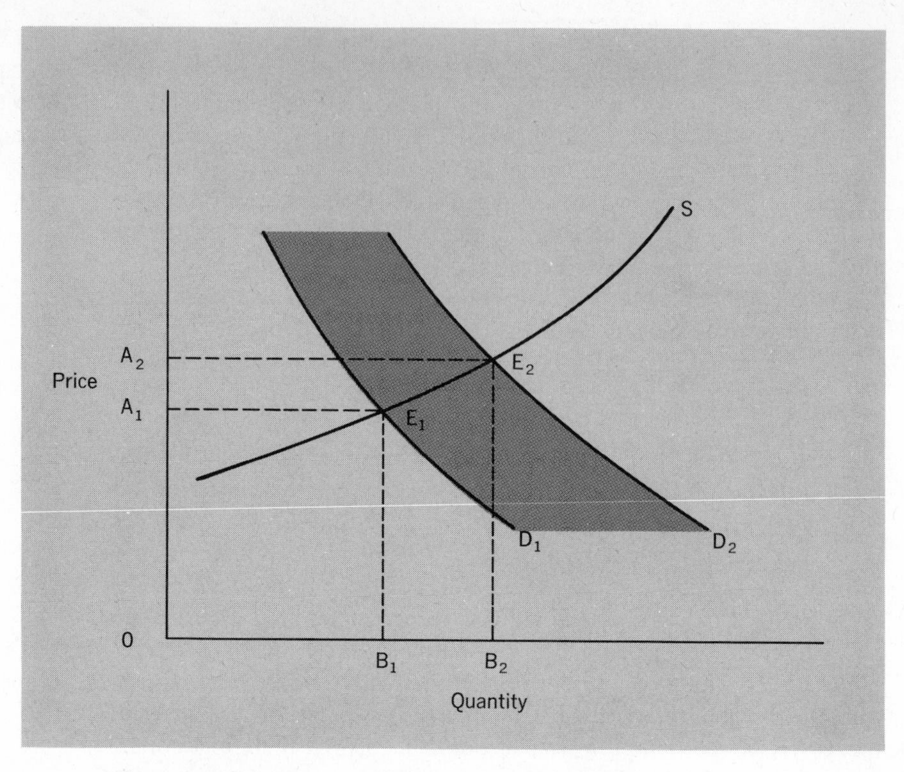


**Figure 3–2.** The effects of increasing demand.

to changes in the demand for particular items and tends to turn out more of the item. Second, if the supply does not increase along with demand, the item becomes scarcer and the price rises. Scarcity is the relationship between the wants for the item and the quantity available to satisfy them. Under capitalism scarcity is measured by price, and here the wants that buyers are able to express have increased relative to the quantity available to satisfy those wants. In consequence, the price rises, indicating that this item is now scarcer relative to other things. As far as the function of setting outputs, the system responds by setting a larger output and a higher price; the latter indicates an increased scarcity of the item, a smaller availability relative to need expressed through demand.

**Changes in Supply.** Suppose that an increase in the amounts of the factors of production or an improvement in the technique of production leads to an increase in supply. Assume that the demand remains the same. As shown in Figure 3–3, the increase in supply appears as a movement to the right of the supply curve, an increase in the quantity offered at each price. The result of this is that the quantity produced increases from $OB_1$ to $OB_2$, and the price drops from

$OA_1$ to $OA_2$. The response of the system to greater availability of the item is an increased quantity and a reduction in scarcity. In the particular case of farm products prices have fallen so low through time as to lower farm incomes and precipitate government intervention.



**Changes in Supply and Demand.** It is very likely that, as society progresses and per capita income rises, demand will increase. At the same time improved techniques and greater supplies of factors

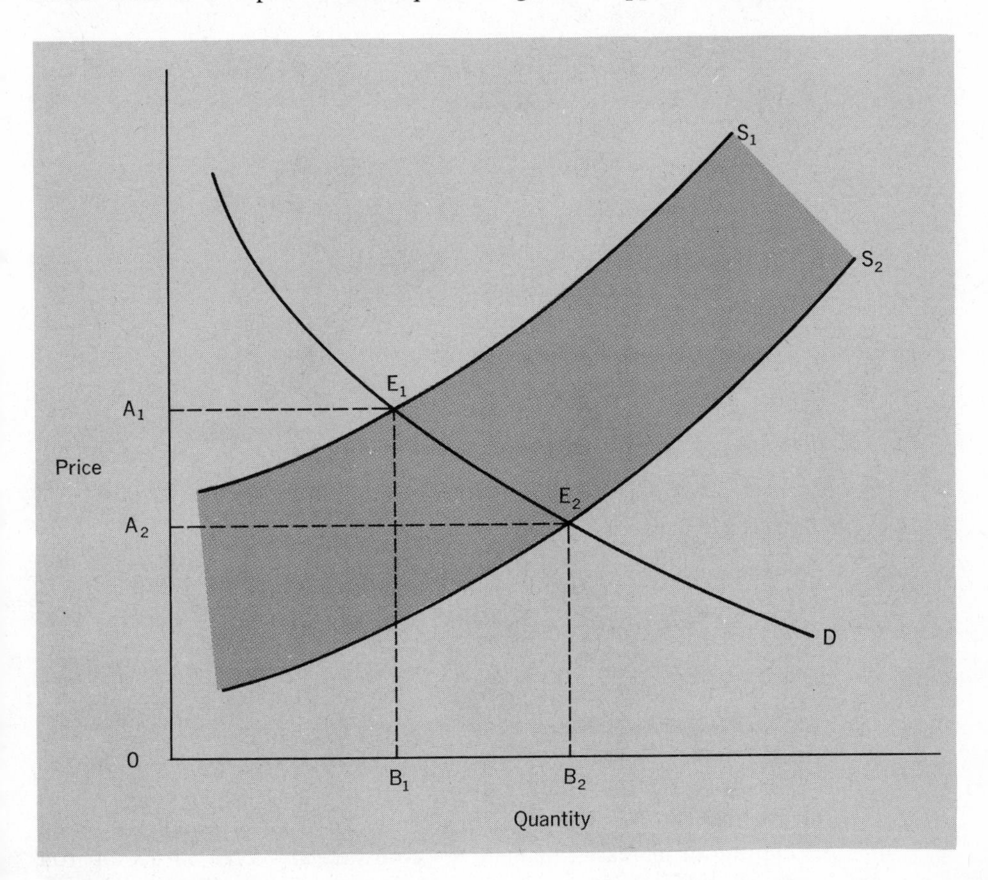


**Figure 3–3.** The effects of increasing supply.

are likely to increase supply. If these two influences have about the same strength, the quantity produced will increase twice (once for demand, once for supply), and price will remain about the same. In Figure 3–4 the price remains the same, at $OA$, while quantity increases from $OB_1$ to $OB_2$. If through time demand increases faster than supply, the price will rise; if the reverse, price will fall.

The same discussion can be applied to the factors of production. The amounts of the factors used, their prices, and their scarcities

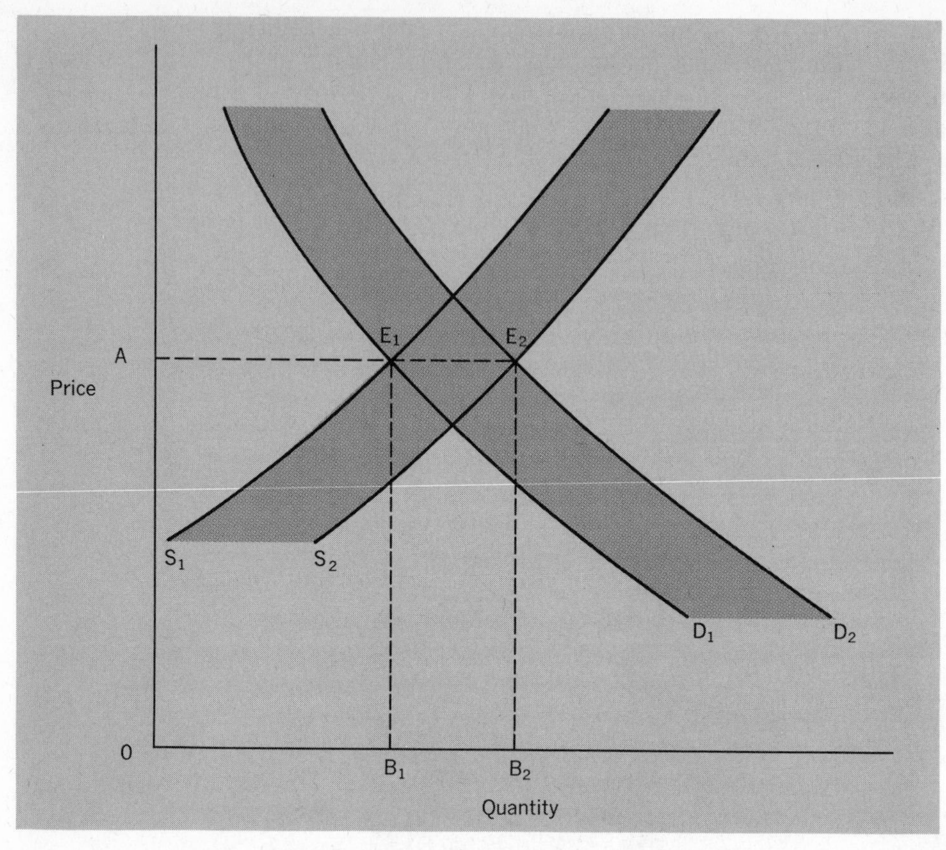


**Figure 3–4.** Effects of increasing supply and demand.

respond to changes in the demands for and supplies of these factors, as we have indicated above for outputs. There is one additional aspect of the matter; namely, that the demand for a factor, such as iron ore, depends on the demand for the final product, steel (or automobiles). If the demand for steel rises, this causes not merely a higher price of steel but an increased demand for iron ore, an increased use of iron ore, and a rise in its price. Thus the amounts of the factors used respond to changes in the demand for the product using that factor. We illustrated this case above in Figure 3–1 and the accompanying discussion.

Finally, the distribution of income or output depends on the prices of the factors. Any increase in the demand for a factor tends to raise the price of that factor. In turn, a rising price for the factor implies that the owner of that factor receives a higher income. Thus, if the demand for gasoline increases, leading to an increased demand for oil, this raises the price of oil and increases the incomes of the owners of oil wells. In short, the demand for final products influences the distribution of income received by the members of society. In a progressive society the demands for natural resources, such as oil, may increase faster than supply, causing the owners of these resources to gain increased incomes.

One of the biggest problems of adjustment in a growing society has to do with aggregate output and employment. Changes in technology may occur that replace labor with machines. This frees a certain amount of labor for work elsewhere in the economy. Unless an additional demand for goods or services appears now in the economy there may be no call for the unemployed workers. In this event unemployment will develop in the economy. We can secure a partial picture of this in Figure 3–5. Originally, equilibrium prevails at *E*, with output *OA*. Now automation displaces a certain number of workers. If these workers were put to work elsewhere in the economy,

**Figure 3–5.** Effects of automation.

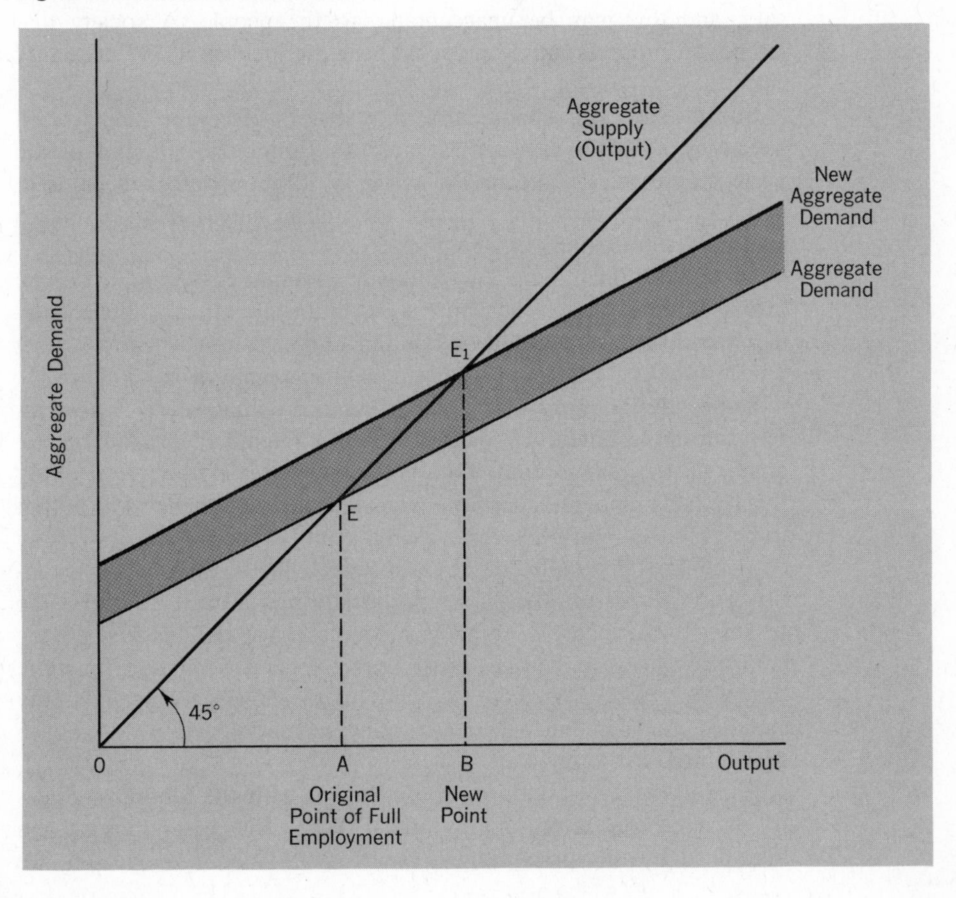

they could increase production to *OB*. This would happen, however, only if aggregate demand increases to the position indicated by the higher line. Such an additional demand for goods will require employment of these workers, and output will, indeed, increase to *OB*.

Let us note that a given society may not want progress badly enough to sustain the many resulting strains and costs. Consider the problem of technological change discussed above. New techniques or automation displace workers from one job, and time is required before they can be reabsorbed in another. Furthermore, the worker may have to be retrained in the new jobs that are constantly opening up. Another cost is found in the destruction of businesses that produce outmoded items or that otherwise cannot adjust themselves to changing economic conditions. A further cost consists in the necessity for holding down present consumption in order to invest part of present income for growth. Some societies simply may be unwilling to pay such a price, preferring instead to consume just about the entire national income. In some countries population control may be necessary, and this may be unacceptable to the people. A society that intends to progress must resolve to bear the incidental and necessary costs.

**Summary.** This chapter first describes the basic problems faced by any economic system. These are (1) setting the amounts of the various outputs; (2) setting the amounts of the resources to be used; and (3) distributing the outputs. Capitalism solves these problems through the operation of the market system.

Setting the quantity of any individual output is accomplished by setting price at that level which equates the quantities supplied and demanded. The overall level of output or real national income is set at a level where aggregate supply equals aggregate demand.

Setting the amounts of resources is more complicated. It involves the state of technique by means of which factors of production are combined to create output. To a large extent this element is given by the available amount of scientific knowledge. Given the level of output to be produced and the technique, the need for the resource is largely determined. Then the resource must be provided in the proper quantity, and for this to take place appropriate prices must be set on the resource as an incentive. Finally, resources must be allocated among competing uses, and prices must be set to carry out this function. When the price of a resource moves to the level at which quantity supplied equals quantity demanded, the appropriate quantity has been determined.

Finally, the distribution of output begins with the setting of prices on resources or factors of production. When the prices thus set are multiplied by the quantities of resources provided by a person, we get the personal income of that individual. With the aid of this income the individual buys outputs, his choices depending on the prices. When the combinations bought by each person are known, the process of distribution is complete, because the entire output will have been distributed to the members of society.

In a progressive economy demands or supplies may change and thus alter the results of the system. If the demand for a good increases as a result, say, of a rise in per capita income, and supply remains unchanged, the price will rise. This indicates the increasing scarcity of the item under the pressure of demand. If supply increases as a result of improving techniques, and demand remains the same, reduced price and scarcity of the item result. If demand and supply increase to the same extent, the price will remain the same. In the market for goods as a whole technological progress may present a problem if the demand for all goods fails to rise and create employment opportunities for workers displaced by new methods. We may note finally that not all societies are prepared to bear the various costs incidental to economic progress.

## QUESTIONS

1. What are the three main problems faced by any economic society?
2. A decision to produce or not to produce certain items is an important problem faced by society. Which of the three basic problems includes this? Explain.
3. Why is it necessary to provide for necessary resources? Aren't these resources already available in any event?
4. What is the meaning of a comparison between a capitalistic system and a mechanism or machine?
5. In recent years there has been a good deal of discussion about national goals. Does a pure capitalistic system have national goals? If so, how and by whom are these goals defined?
6. It has been found that the provision of resources cannot be handled in the usual way in such fields as defense and education. Why?
7. Iron and steel used to be the most common materials for the manufacture of toys in the United States. Why are iron and steel being replaced by other materials for this purpose in spite of greatly increased steel production?
8. In what way does the price system help choose the right technique of production in wheat farming (extensive farming with a lot of automatic machinery)?
9. How is the output of a particular good or service determined under a capitalistic system?
10. The problem of provision of resources finds a specific form in what tool of economic analysis?
11. In what sense is the purchase of consumer goods by individuals a part of the process known as *distribution?*
12. What effects do increasing demands for products have on the problem of providing resources relatively fixed in supply, and how is an answer to this worked out under capitalism?

CHAPTER

4

# Government and the Economy

## GOVERNMENT AND PURE CAPITALISM

**Role of Government.** In a pure capitalistic system economic activity is carried on by private firms and households. Self-interest, limited by competition and operating through the market system, solves the basic economic problems. As long as the system operates effectively in carrying out its functions, it will probably be continued in the United States and similar societies.

At the same time government has a role in this system. It watches the operation of the competitive system and acts to enforce ethical rules of conduct. Government's part has been likened to that of a referee in a game of sport; the referee is there, not to participate, but to ensure conformity to the rules of the game. So the government should see to it that contracts are honored, that products are correctly labeled and advertised, and that fair play prevails generally.

Apart from this there is little for government to do, following the doctrine: "That government is best which governs least." However, private industry cannot successfully carry on certain types of business for profit. Such industries, when necessary for the welfare of society, are turned over to government. Examples are defense, education, and such internal improvements as airports. Accordingly, government plays a supporting role in providing unprofitable but socially necessary goods and services.

**Laissez-Faire.** Under pure capitalism a laissez-faire philosophy is said to prevail. Literally, this means that government lets people do as they wish. Left to themselves, but spurred on by self-interest, individuals will carry on the necessary economic functions. Supply and demand will automatically interact to provide the goods and services needed by society. In short, the market system will operate to perform all necessary functions.

## THE END OF PURE CAPITALISM

**Who Killed Cock Robin?** In the United States the philosophy of pure capitalism prevailed for a number of decades. Then came developments that undermined its set of beliefs.

**Combinations and Unions.** In the last quarter of the nineteenth century a change in the American economy got under way that is still continuing. This change may be called the combination movement, and represents a tendency for business firms to increase in size and power. Originally, the growth occurred by combination of existing firms, but later it took on a variety of forms. Such a tendency threatens the competitive character of the economy and thereby weakens its ability to operate effectively. One manifestation of this degeneration is seen in the tendency toward rigid pricing practices in those industries marked by a small number of competing firms. In turn, fewness of firms leads to instability in the level of output. There is also the possibility that some firm will attain a monopoly of a particular product and, as a result, raise the price of the product to an undue extent. Such a policy changes the distribution of income in society in favor of those who own and control the monopoly. If this tendency were to continue unchecked it would threaten the competitive property of our system, which is one of its principal supports.

Following this combination tendency in business has come a corresponding organization of labor. Originally, this movement was necessary to balance the strength of large-scale enterprise. Today, the AFL-CIO confederation, comprising a total strength of about 16 million laborers, dwarfs any single business enterprise or combination of them. Clearly, this organization of labor represents a further distinct step away from a competitive price system. And it compounds the problem of combinations or monopoly in business.

**The Great Depression.** After the United States recovered from the immediate effects of World War I, it enjoyed for most of the 1920's a high level of prosperity. Then in 1929 the prosperity was succeeded by a recession that carried the country to a lower economic level each year until 1932. At the deepest part of the trough in 1932 and 1933 one person in four was totally unemployed, and output was 30 per cent below the 1929 peak. Although a substantial recovery from this trough occurred in the succeeding years, full employment and production were not attained in the 1930's. In fact, it was not until the mobilization for World War II was well under way in 1942 that the country pulled out of the depression. So severe and lengthy was this period of economic distress that it precipitated some fundamental changes in economic thinking.

**Trouble in Agriculture.** When the depression struck in 1929, prices in general began to fall. This is to be expected in a period of reduced demand and lowered economic activity. However, the fall in farm prices was particularly severe, and the subsequent recovery was unsatisfactory. In fact, the problem of low farm prices continues to be a major economic concern for this country.

The causes of this problem are deeply rooted and lie in both the supply and demand sides of the market. With rapidly improving technology supply forged ahead, but demand lagged, being attracted into other channels. Under such conditions prices inevitably fall with attendant distress to the small farmer, who has been unable to cut costs sufficiently. Along with the rigidity and high level of certain industrial prices the weakness of farm prices indicates a partial failure of the price system.

**The War, Foreign Aid, and Defense.** Next came the aftermath of World War II. During that struggle the national debt increased manyfold, reaching a point where it exceeded Net National Product. In 1946 the Federal debt was $260 billion compared to a *NNP* of $200 billion. Such a huge debt necessitated large interest payments; the $4.8-billion interest payments on the debt exceeded the *total Federal budget* of $4.6 billion in 1933. Furthermore, the huge debt had to be refinanced; as old issues matured, new ones had to be issued. It was, and still is, generally agreed that the debt could not be repaid for fear of depressing effects on the economy. Here was a problem, debt management, that had long been handled by the British but was largely new to us.

Finally, there came the postwar emergence of the United States into a different world situation. After the war only this country possessed the strength and the will to raise prostrate Europe to her feet. To provide the necessities of life for the stricken areas, to supply essential raw materials, to rebuild the transportation facilities and factories—all required a major involvement in the affairs of foreign powers. With the passage of time it has become only too evident that events call for us as a nation to invest a certain part of our output in foreign countries, with or without promise of return.

Moreover, at this time the free world is faced with a frank and brutal challenge to its way of life. Like Proteus, this challenge takes on a bewildering variety of forms. On the one hand we are faced with naked, unashamed military aggression to be exercised whenever the USSR or China deem it feasible. On the other hand, we see an attempt to penetrate uncommitted areas by propaganda, paid agitators, diplomacy, and economic aid. This effort is vigorous, well conceived, and rather well financed. To counter this threat the United States, as the main economic bastion of the free world, is committed to taking appropriate military and foreign aid measures. Inevitably, this involves large expenditures and a considerable amount of effort. From all signs now apparent this country will be oscillating around a path somewhere between peace and war for the indefinite future. To the degree that our defense is involved the Federal government must take a hand in the economic process.

**The Rise of Social Conscience.** As companion to these great events and especially the great depression has come a changing social attitude. Under pure capitalism each man was responsible for his own destiny and welfare. If some individual ran afoul of the workings of the system to his distress, private charitable agencies, such as churches, were available to minister to his needs. For the support of these institutions the individual, guided by his own conscience, was responsible. Therefore private conscience, operating to support such charity, was presumed to be sufficient.

In the nineteen thirties, with the partial breakdown of the system on which it was based, private charity failed to meet the public need. As unemployment spread to include one person in four, the resulting distress, so plainly evident for all to see, stirred the consciences of almost everyone. In order to guide the sympathies and potential efforts of the public a systematic organization was required. At this juncture government appeared to be the proper focus of efforts to relieve human distress. In short, social conscience gave a sanction to government for the relief of human distress on a large scale.

**Government and Mixed Capitalism.** As the historical events in question suggest, certain defects have appeared in the workings of pure capitalism. Out of these developments has come a realization that the market system of capitalism needs to be supported and supplemented by government action. Let us consider briefly the points at which government is supposed to take action in our society as well as the concrete results of any such action.

**Role of Government.** In our system at present government may be said to take action on three fronts. First, it is expected to preserve the workings of capitalism by presiding over and helping to maintain vigorous competition. Second, it must supplement and modify the price system by providing for the production or use of certain socially needed items, by smoothing out the distribution of income, and by correcting particular errors in the price system. Third, it is expected to take action to push the economy toward full employment and a satisfactory rate of economic growth. Consider briefly each of these in turn.

**Presiding Over and Maintaining Competition.** From the time Adam Smith first explained the meaning of capitalism back in 1775 it has been understood that government established the legal basis for this system. By providing for private property and freedom of contract as workable concepts under the law, government makes capitalism possible. By seeing to it that competition is fair—products are correctly labeled and advertised by sellers, relevant information is available to buyers and sellers, and market dealings are free from fraud and deception—government assists in the smooth operation of the system. Perhaps the most significant and difficult task in this area lies in the maintenance of competition. Consider briefly how this has been approached.

**Maintenance of Competition.** As the combination movement got under way public concern grew to such a point that a basic law, the Sherman Act, was passed in 1890. This law declared that "Every contract, combination, or conspiracy in restraint of trade . . . is hereby declared to be illegal." The provisions of this law were supplemented by the Clayton Act and the Federal Trade Commission Act, both of 1914. Subsequent developments in this area have hinged around efforts of the government to limit the tendency for firms to acquire large market shares and thus attain a position of oligopoly where there are few sellers, or a simple monopoly. As the government detects what it regards as a violation, it may bring action in the courts under one of these laws. Ultimately, the important cases go up to the Supreme Court, which decides on the validity of the government's charge against the company in question.

The government, operating through the Antitrust Division of the Justice Department, has enjoyed varying success in its efforts to preserve competition. For example, it achieved a stunning success in its case against John D. Rockefeller's Standard Oil Company. As a result of this action Standard Oil was dissolved into a number of constituent firms: Standard Oil of New Jersey, Standard Oil of Indiana, and so on. Even so, the first of these today is one of the largest manufacturing firms in the United States. On the other hand the government suffered a severe reverse in a case brought against United States Steel (1920). In denying the program of the government to break up the company the Supreme Court stated that the law "does not make mere size . . . or the existence of unexerted power an offense." Thus no clear pattern of success or failure emerges from the antitrust actions of the government.

There have been a number of conflicting currents in the competitive situation in the past hundred years. However, no one disputes the following tendencies. Despite the antitrust laws cited above, firms have continued to grow in size, to merge, and to achieve significant market shares along with limited numbers of other sellers. Today, there is scarcely a manufacturing industry that can be called competitive in the sense that there are large numbers of competing firms selling an identical product. Only in agriculture and the service industries do large numbers of sellers still prevail. Nor are pricing problems absent in these areas. As a result of this regression from competition, government increasingly intervenes to protect the public from the possible misuse of private power.

**Supplementing and Modifying the Price System: Government Production.** Ever since capitalism emerged as a well-defined system it has been understood that government would be charged with producing certain items. Such things as defense, education, the development of transportation facilities, and the maintenance of internal order can scarcely be handled by private individuals on a profit-seeking basis. With the passage of time an increasing fraction of total output is produced by government. Consider briefly some facts on this matter.

**TABLE 4–1***
**Employment in Government Compared to Total Employment (Millions)**

| Year | Total Employment | Employment in Government (Federal, State, and Local) | Employment in Government As Per Cent of Total |
|---|---|---|---|
| 1929 | 47,890 | 3,065 | 6.4 |
| 1942 | 57,720 | 5,483 | 9.5 |
| 1947 | 59,616 | 5,474 | 9.2 |
| 1952 | 64,628 | 6,609 | 10.2 |
| 1956 | 67,565 | 7,277 | 10.8 |
| 1957 | 67,808 | 7,616 | 11.2 |
| 1958 | 66,603 | 7,839 | 11.8 |
| 1959 | 68,133 | 8,083 | 11.9 |
| 1960 | 68,907 | 8,353 | 12.1 |
| 1961 | 69,368 | 8,594 | 12.4 |
| 1962 | 70,673 | 8,890 | 12.6 |
| 1963 | 71,546 | 8,199 | 12.9 |
| 1964 | 73,095 | 9,501 | 13.0 |

* The series from 1947 on is based on a revised definition. Also from 1961 on, the data includes Alaska and Hawaii. Figures include the armed forces. Source: **Economic Report of the President,** 1965 (Washington, D.C.: U.S. Government Printing Office, 1965), Tables B–21, p. 214; B–26, p. 220. Total employment is obtained by adding the armed forces column to the Civilian Employment total.

Government output cannot easily be measured, but an indication is given by the number of workers employed by the government. Comparing this data with total employment in Table 4–1, we see that the fraction has risen a great deal since 1929. In fact, a bit more than one eighth of the labor force (13 per cent) was employed by government in 1964, compared to about half of this, or 6.4 per cent, in 1929. This trend indicates the great increase in the fraction of output produced by government. At the same time it also shows that government production still amounts to a fairly small part of the total for the economy.

**Government Consumption.** What government produces it generally makes available as services to the economy. Thus the services of military personnel constitute part of government production. Here the production consists of services that contribute to the defense of the country. Again, police and fire protection consist of services rendered to the public that are classified as government production. Tied in with government production, mainly consisting in the provision of services, are government purchases of output. Clearly, national defense requires more than the recruitment and training of soldiers and civilian personnel. It also involves the purchase of a good deal of output to equip the armed forces. Very likely this output is produced by private firms. Consequently, government purchases can be expected to include some privately produced output along with the services the government itself provides. In short, government purchases of output serve to buy the government production (consisting mainly of services) and some private output that renders it more useful.

In our society expenditures determine what is to be produced. To the extent that government spends money on output, decisions about production tend to be socialized. This gives rise to collective decisions concerning production and the use of output, where the decisions are achieved by political means. As our society becomes richer and our immediate individual needs are satisfied, there seem to arise more complex wants that are most easily satisfied by collective purchase of output through the government. Consider the trend in government purchases of output, compared to total purchases (Gross National Product). As Table 4–2 reveals, the fraction of total spending attributable to government has risen from 8.1 per cent in 1929 to 20.7 per cent in 1964.

Clearly, collective decisions about what is to be produced, carried out through government purchases, play an important role in our economy. What is the primary cause of the increasing importance of government in our economy? Very simply it is: *increasing defense needs*. Between 1929 and 1964 expenditures on national defense jumped from less than 1 per cent of total spending in the economy to about 11 per cent. This rise accounts for nearly all (about 80 per cent) of the jump in the fraction of total spending accounted for by government. With the increasing urbanization of the economy, and its growing complexity, further social needs are bound to arise that

**TABLE 4-2***
**Government Spending and Total Spending on Output (Billions of Dollars)**

| Year | Government Spending | Total Spending (Gross National Product) | Government Spending as a Per Cent of Total Spending |
|---|---|---|---|
| 1929 | 8.5 | 104.4 | 8.1 |
| 1940 | 14.1 | 100.6 | 14.0 |
| 1954 | 75.3 | 363.1 | 20.7 |
| 1955 | 75.6 | 397.5 | 19.0 |
| 1956 | 79.0 | 419.2 | 18.8 |
| 1957 | 86.5 | 442.8 | 19.5 |
| 1958 | 93.5 | 444.5 | 21.0 |
| 1959 | 97.2 | 482.7 | 20.1 |
| 1960 | 99.6 | 502.6 | 19.8 |
| 1961 | 108.0 | 518.7 | 20.8 |
| 1962 | 116.3 | 556.2 | 20.9 |
| 1963 | 122.6 | 583.9 | 21.0 |
| 1964 | 128.7 | 622.3 | 20.7 |

* Source: **Economic Report of the President,** 1965 (Washington, D.C.: U.S. Government Printing Office, 1965), Table B-1, p. 189.

may require an even further increase in the fraction spent by government. Just how far the tendency will or should go is hard to determine. Actually, in our democratic society it will depend on the wishes of the public as expressed through political means.

**Redistribution of Income.** Under pure capitalism the income a person receives depends on the factors he owns and the prices of these factors. Given this income, the individual can buy outputs that will meet his needs. Ultimately, then, a person's ability to acquire output depends on the value of the factors (including his labor) that he possesses. With the rise of social conscience in the United States has come a disposition to change the existing distribution of income through government action. Although this is the richest country in the world, there are still many people who are in comparative want. Establishment of a tax system bearing more heavily on the rich than on the poor and subsequent use of these taxes to provide services going mainly to the poor makes it possible to change the distribution of outputs received.

It is not easy to estimate the effects of taxation on the distribution of income. Thus income taxes clearly tend to be paid by the individual on whom they are levied, but the same is not true of sales taxes. Consider the gasoline tax. Although the tax is nominally paid by the seller to the government, it may be passed on to the purchaser by raising the price of gasoline. But be careful. The seller may be afraid to raise the price by the full amount of the tax, because this action might lead to an excessive loss in the quantity purchased. When the seller has this expectation, the price he sets is too low to allow him to recover all of the tax. At this point we admit that it cannot be said exactly how much of the tax is borne by seller and buyer, respectively. In general, the exact distribution of the tax burden cannot be determined.

On the other hand, the distribution of government benefits cannot be estimated exactly either. Whereas "aid to the blind" affords gains roughly measured by payments to the recipient, defense measures yield little direct advantage to any part of the public. Despite these difficulties, attempts have been made to measure the taxes paid and benefits received by people in various income classes. Such an estimate is summarized in Figure 4–1. It shows that at very low income levels the benefits much exceed taxes, whereas at high levels taxes exceed benefits. Somewhere in the middle, in the \$3,000–\$5,000 range of income, a balance of taxes and benefits is found. All-in-all this chart indicates a substantial redistribution effect from government taxing and spending.

**Correcting Errors in the Market System.** It is generally agreed that the market system fails to perform its functions perfectly. In determining the output of a particular commodity to be produced the price at this point of equilibrium represents two things: (1) the supply price of the seller; (2) the demand price of the buyer. Consider now the supply price.

Insofar as there is a cost of producing the item this cost should be reflected in the seller's supply price. If the equilibrium price just covers this cost, then the happy situation is reached where society is securing all of the item possible at the market price. However, in certain cases the seller's supply price underestimates the true social cost. Suppose a factory turns out a product at a relatively low cost but lets go a large volume of waste products into nearby streams and fouls the air with noxious fumes. Here is a true social cost that does not enter into the market price of the product. Because the product sells at a low price, as a result, its sale and production tend to be encouraged. Thus the fact that social cost is concealed, and does not enter into product price, leads to an unduly large production of this item. In turn, this situation implies an improper allocation of resources, because too much of this item is being produced at the expense of other, more socially desirable outputs.

On the other side the value or usefulness of an item should be measured by the buyer's demand price. Ordinarily, this is the case, but sometimes a particular item yields advantages or disadvantages to others. Thus the planting of a fine lawn or painting of a house may

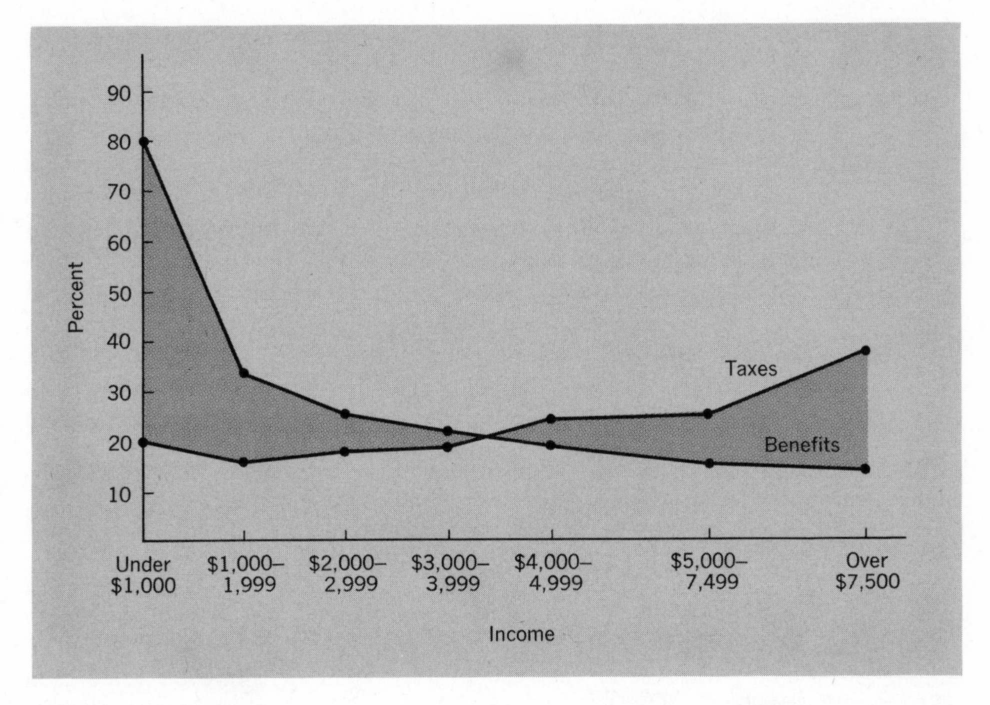


**Figure 4–1.** Tax burden, receipt of government benefits as per cent of income, 1946–47.*

* John H. Adler, "The Fiscal System, the Distribution of Income, and Public Welfare," Ch. 8 in **Fiscal Policies and the American Economy,** ed. Kenyon E. Poole (Englewood Cliffs, N.J.: Prentice-Hall, Inc., 1951), pp. 382, 388. Data combined as in G. L. Bach, **Economics: An Introduction to Analysis and Policy** (3rd ed.; Englewood Cliffs, N.J.: Prentice-Hall Inc., 1960), p. 645.

yield benefits not merely to the owners but to all the inhabitants of the neighborhood.

The Federal government recognizes that certain items afford social benefits and provides subsidies to particular industries on this account. In view of the transportation problems of a large country such as ours this industry has long received special favors. Part of the initial cost of building railroads to the west was borne by providing land grants and other assistance, and automobile and water transportation have been favored by government-financed road building and waterway improvements. The actions taken by the government to modify or supplement the price system are fairly extensive.

**Helping to Maintain Full Employment.** As a result of the great depression of the 1930's, a general concensus was reached that government must act to prevent any major decline in economic activity. Next to the defense of the country this ranks as one of the greatest responsibilities of the Federal government. So important is this function that we will devote a separate chapter to it. Here we merely note the importance of this relatively new function of government.

**Outlook for Capitalism.** As our discussion indicates, government is assuming an increasingly important role in the working of the economy. From all the signs it appears that the scope of government activity will continue to grow. In fact, outright socialism presents itself as an alternative to a system of mixed capitalism. Socialist or socialist-minded parties have come to power at certain times in various democratic countries, notably Great Britain and Sweden. None of these countries has adopted such a system, although their economies contain somewhat more governmental influence than does ours. Nor does it seem likely at present that socialism will ever be adopted in the United States. Despite this fact, it will be instructive to examine a distinct alternative to our present system.

## SOCIALISM AND COMMUNISM: ALTERNATIVE SYSTEMS

**Background.** The discussion of alternative economic systems is made difficult by the fact that many other elements—political, social, and moral—enter into the problem. Let us, however, refer to a system marked by government ownership of capital or productive facilities, combined with a totalitarian political system, as *communism*. We could elaborate on the atheism or the atmosphere of repression that are to be found in this system, but will not pause here to do so. The USSR and Red China constitute the main examples of communistic countries.

On the other hand, we may refer to a system marked by government ownership of productive facilities, combined with a political democracy, as *socialism*. Here one would expect to find the usual freedoms present in the countries of Western Europe and the United States. In Great Britain the British Labor Party under the leadership of Clement Attlee made moves in this direction following World War II. At no time did the actions taken appear to pose a threat to freedom. In the discussion that follows we will take up the socialist, rather than the communist, system as a possible alternative to capitalism. Communism is too repugnant in its noneconomic aspects to receive serious consideration.

**Institutions of Socialism.** The primary objective of socialism is to nationalize "the means of production." Although this action leads to state ownership of the land and capital used in production, it does not preclude the existence of private property, such as personal effects, automobiles, and the like. The private ownership of homes falls in the doubtful category. In any event, factories, farms, mines, and offices would all be owned by the state.

If the state owns the farms and factories, it follows that it will also run them. Or does it? We can imagine the state owning an oil field. In order to assure its exploitation it could offer areas of land for lease to the highest bidder, or to any bidder meeting fixed specifications. Private enterprise could then undertake to exploit the oil field for profit. Or suppose the automobile industry were nationalized. The government could lease out the capital equipment and facilities to private firms for specified periods of time. Provided the incentives were great enough, there seems little doubt that this would work. However, it is not socialism.

Under a socialized system the nationalized industry is run, as well as owned, by the state. Accordingly, the ability of businessmen to make use of resources for gain vanishes. In short, private enterprise ceases to exist, being replaced by state operation of the means of production. Presently, we will discuss the reasons for coupling state ownership with operation.

Suppose that the state acquired ownership and control of the productive apparatus but avoided operating responsibilities. Doubtless this plan could be accomplished by a system of decentralized, semi-private cooperatives, municipal enterprises, and local boards.[1] No limitation would have to be placed on the purchases of the consumer. Such a system is beyond the scope of this discussion, for it is now generally understood that socialism includes the idea of centralized planning of production by the state. Once government accepts this responsibility it must see to it that production is coordinated with consumption. Such coordination can scarcely be exercised without controls on consumption. In turn, this leads to rationing or other controls placed on the free choice of output by the members of society. Moreover, it also implies that output is not planned purely to correspond to individual consumer wants. Thus consumer sovereignty is diminished, if not entirely lost.

Summarizing, socialism is characterized by (1) public ownership of (productive) land and capital, (2) public operation of productive enterprises, and (3) centralized planning by the state. The first condition essentially abolishes private property in relation to the economic system. The second abolishes the free enterprise element of freedom of contract, and the second and third together severely limit the role of freedom of choice by the consumer.

## TRANSITION TO SOCIALISM

There are one or two confusing points concerning the possible transition from capitalism to socialism. According to Karl Marx, founder of "scientific socialism" and the spiritual father of modern commu-

[1] A. C. Pigou, *Socialism Versus Capitalism* (London: Macmillan Company, 1938), pp. 6–8.

nism, socialism would be achieved by the rising of the proletariat or working class. This event comes about in the following way, according to Marx. Under capitalism all people will drift either upward into the bourgeosie, which owns and operates the productive apparatus, or downward into the proletariat. With the passage of time the condition of the working class will become worse and worse. Finally, the proletariat will rise against their oppressors, the bourgeosie, and forcibly expropriate the means of production (land and capital). There will follow the disappearance of the bourgeosie and the merging of everyone into the proletariat. Then the state, acting through and for the proletariat, will operate the productive apparatus.

The preceding paragraph gives a thumbnail sketch of Marx's version of the appearance of socialism. A key point for the present discussion is that the capitalists are simply to be expropriated, relieved of their property without compensation. (They are said to have come by this property unfairly.) Clearly, incomes arising from property would cease under this dispensation. However, this development is not the only conceivable one. Even admitting Marx's contention that a revolution will inevitably occur at some future date, the transition might occur sooner by another method, perhaps by a political decision arrived at through democratic means. Consider briefly a problem or two that would be involved for a socialist party that had come to power under our system.

Under what conditions would the productive apparatus be transferred from owners to the state? Obviously, one method would be to expropriate the desired property without compensation. Such a solution, arrived at by democratic political means, hardly seems likely. This solution definitely seems to be associated with the violent overthrow of the capitalist system and the replacement of a democratic with a totalitarian government. An alternative would be to offer compensation to the owners. At this point a fundamental issue arises. Is society going to allow the receipt of interest or rent from the ownership of property? If so, the owners could be given a government bond promising payment of interest and redemption of principal at a future date. The ex-capitalist then retains a claim to income derived from property. If not, a lump sum payment could be made in compensation.

Without being dogmatic it seems fair to say that most socialists associate the payment of interest and rent with inequality in the distribution of income. Perhaps the principal thing that motivates the socialist is dissatisfaction with a widely unequal or unfair distribution of income. Accordingly, the socialist is likely to frown on or flatly oppose the payment of interest. The strict Marxian, for example, would abolish interest. At any rate here is a vital issue. In the United

States corporate profits, rental income, and interest income amounted to $92 billion in 1960, or 20 per cent of Net National Product. If we would determine the part of proprietor's income attributable to property, the figure would be even higher. Conversion of private into public property with compensation would either substantially preserve or eliminate this share, depending on whether payment of interest is or is not allowed.

## OPERATION OF A SOCIALIST SYSTEM

**Setting Outputs.** In a capitalistic society the setting of outputs is carried out by the summation of individual decisions or desires. The summed up decisions, based on individual estimates, are expressed in supply-and-demand curves. Then the quantity determined by the intersection of the supply-and-demand curves represents the output for the item in question. Under socialism outputs are determined by a central authority or planning board; perhaps it would be more accurate to say, by a collection of planning boards pointing up to one supreme or coordinating board at the top. What is important here is the centralization of the power to make decisions in the hands of a few. Such a small body of men may set goals that differ radically from the sum of the desires of the individual members of society. For example, national power or prestige may be accepted as a primary objective of the economy, thus conditioning the general pattern of outputs at the start.

**Setting Amounts of Resources.** Under a capitalistic system setting the use of resources is carried out through the market system. Serving as a coordinating device for individual decisions, the system constitutes a means of determining appropriate techniques of production and for providing and allocating resources. Under socialism, with the outputs to be produced having been set collectively, the planning board at the top must make a master plan for the coordination of all economic activity. In so doing it must allocate resources between different firms and industries to meet the defined production goals. This necessarily involves a comprehensive organization of men and physical resources. It is not our purpose here to say just how it is done, but we may comment that it involves making explicit decisions concerning the use of resources.

**Distribution.** Finally, there is the question of how output is to be distributed. Let us note first some points at which socialism differs from capitalism. Because the physical apparatus of production, including land and capital, has been nationalized, no payment of rent or interest to these factors is required or even appropriate. Thus the distribution of income can be boiled down to making wage or transfer payments to individuals. Next, rewards are not necessarily based on productive contribution, which is presumably the case under capitalism. Indeed, the typical socialist rule is "From each according to his ability, to each according to his need." Where this is followed, socialism departs completely from the capitalist method of paying returns according to the productivity of the factors owned, whether human or nonhuman. In practice, however, the Soviet Union pays wages that vary directly with estimates of the productivity or social contribution of the individual involved.

Under pure capitalism the overwhelming bulk of the production is carried out by private business firms. Even under our mixed capitalistic system over 85 per cent of production, as measured by employment of labor, is carried on by private firms. Almost all output or income, therefore, originates in the private sector. Under pure socialism, however, the situation is reversed. Almost all output and income originates from state enterprises. Under capitalism the private enterprise will tend to make available this income to the factors of production with the exception of funds recovered in the form of taxes by government and some retained corporate earnings. In contrast, the socialist enterprise is not compelled to pay out as income the money it receives from the sale of the product to, say, labor. As much as seems desirable can be reserved by the state to provide capital goods, defense items, or other social uses of output. Of course, what is paid out as income to labor can be partly recovered in taxes. As we see, the socialist enterprise and, therefore, the government is in a position to control directly the portion of the Net National Product that is paid to individuals.

**Distribution and Incentives Under Socialism.** Under capitalism there is a close association between the distributive shares paid to individuals and incentives to economic activity. In fact, each such payment serves as an inducement to put some factor to work at a particular point in the economic system: the factor may be labor or it may be one of the others, such as land or capital. Because the members of society are assumed to be susceptible to the profit motive or the motive of self-interest, these stimuli supposedly lead to the performance of the needed economic functions. From our everyday experience of the capitalistic system in well-developed economies we must agree that the incentives are effective under normal conditions.

Now the socialist state does not rely solely on an appeal to self-interest or the profit motive to provide an incentive. Instead the state may try to touch on the altruistic tendencies in people, to release their desires to serve others, and to forward the interests of the state as a whole. Also, the resources of land and capital having passed into the hands of the state, no rewards need to be paid to private owners.

Suppose, however, that industry were socialized by a political decision. In order to promote acceptance of its policy the government might exchange interest bearing government bonds for the property being nationalized. Such a solution implies that the payment would continue, possibly for an indefinite period. Because socialists, and especially Marxists, regard the payment of interest as unjustified, the solution mentioned involves a moral or ethical issue. Clearly, the person who wants to socialize by peaceful means must face both the issue of persuading people to part with their property and the ethical question whether compensation involving the payment of interest is proper.

## EVALUATION OF SOCIALISM

It is virtually impossible to say anything concrete concerning the behavior of a socialist society. In the realm of theory we can note the reliance on a system directed from above. Also we can foresee the probable effects on the distribution of income arising from state ownership of the means of production.[2] In fact, we need empirical evidence comparing the operation of capitalistic with socialist economies under like circumstances. Yet comparisons are made difficult by the fact that the two main socialist countries, Russia and China, were relatively underdeveloped when they converted their economies to socialism. In short, the gap between the communist and Western capitalistic economies is hard to appraise and discuss. Furthermore, because information from the socialist countries is both fragmentary and of doubtful accuracy, we cannot really trust our conclusions. However, we may consider one or two points.

First, it is evident from previous discussions that increasing resources and capital per head together with improving technology are the keys to rising per capita income. With reference to the latter it

[2] In abstract theory a socialist society would be one with rather equal incomes determined by the state. In a mixed capitalistic society reliance is placed on taxation to equalize incomes in response to demands for social justice. The rich bear higher tax burdens than the poor. In the United States the tax system appears to have a moderately leveling influence. (See Figure 4–1.)

In the Soviet Union, in the latter part of the 1940's and the year 1950, two things seemed clear about the tax system. First, the average percentage of income taxed was higher than in the United States. Whereas the tax rate appeared to exceed 40 per cent in the Soviet Union in the late forties and in 1950, it was apparently no more than 31 per cent in the United States in 1949. Second, the reliance on indirect taxes was greater, probably two thirds or more of the total being raised in this way. Such taxes tend to be "regressive"—that is, take a larger percentage of the poor man's income than of the rich man's. Therefore taxes are apparently not a significant leveling influence on incomes in the Soviet Union. See F. D. Holzman, "The Burden of Soviet Taxation," *American Economic Review* (September 1953), pp. 548–571.

appears that the Russians enjoy a lead in space technology and are virtually on a par in nuclear weapons. Both areas of study rest on a deep foundation, indicating Russian achievements in science. In addition, it appears that the Russians are investing a larger fraction of their national income in capital equipment than we are.[3] This suggests the possibility that their capital per head may grow faster than ours. Finally, the Russians would appear to have greater possibilities for new resource discoveries than we do, because their immense land mass comprises a sixth of the world's land surface.

How has the Soviet economy performed in the last few years? Let us begin with a comparison of Soviet and United States Gross National Products for 1962. In this year the total production of the USSR measured in dollars, their Gross National Product, is estimated to have been $256.3 billion, or 46 per cent of the $551.8-billion figure for the United States. Briefly, their economy turned out less than half of our production. In per capita terms the difference is even greater, their *GNP* per capita being $1,158 or a bit over 38 per cent of our $3,004 figure. Per capita *GNP* is regarded by economists as a better indicator of welfare than *GNP,* as we emphasized in Chapter 1 (although we used *NNP* per capita there). The spread between the United States and Soviet values indicates that the Soviet Union will have to grow faster for a long time to equalize the per capita incomes.

**TABLE 4–3***
**Comparative Percentage Growth Rates of Gross National Product**

| Country | Aggregate | | Per Capita | |
|---|---|---|---|---|
| | Average Rate 1950–58 | Average Rate 1958–62 | Average Rate 1950–58 | Average Rate 1958–62 |
| United Kingdom | 2.4 | 2.8 | 1.9 | 2.0 |
| United States | 2.9 | 4.3 | 1.2 | 2.5 |
| USSR | 6.8 | 4.6 | 5.0 | 2.8 |
| Western Germany | 7.6 | 6.2 | 6.4 | 4.9 |

* Source: Estimates of S. H. Cohn in **Annual Economic Indicators in the USSR.** See footnote 3.

[3] It is estimated that Russia is investing about 25 per cent of its total output (Gross National Product) as compared to our 20 per cent. "A comparison of Soviet and United States National Product," Morris Bornstein, in *Comparisons of the United States and Soviet Economies, Part II* (Washington, D.C.: U.S. Government Printing Office, 1959), p. 380. Fixed capital investment in 1962 was computed by S. H. Cohn as being about 16 per cent of *GNP* in the United States and 33 per cent in the USSR in *Annual Economic Indicators for the USSR* (Washington, D.C.: U.S. Government Printing Office, 1964), Table VIII–5, p. 96.

Now for the growth pattern. To get a balanced picture we include besides the United States and the Soviet Union a low-growth-rate industrial power, the United Kingdom, and a high-growth-rate power, Western Germany. In the period 1950–58 the USSR enjoyed a high growth rate, comparable to, but not as great as, Western Germany. In the period 1958–62 something has gone wrong in the agricultural sector, which has resulted in a sharp decline in the Soviet growth rate. For this period their growth rate exceeds ours by only a slight margin.

It is not clear just how we can expect growth rates to behave in the future. It seems likely that the Soviet economy will grow at a rate below that of the earlier period but perhaps higher than the later one. Probably they will grow at much the same rate as Western Europe and a bit faster than ours. Keep in mind that the *GNP* of the United States in 1962 about equaled the *GNP* of the USSR combined with that of the United Kingdom, Western Germany, France, and Italy. Accordingly, there may be more immediate scope for development in these areas than in the United States.

**The Soviet Union: A Postscript.** In 1938 two well-known economists, Oskar Lange and Fred M. Taylor, joined hands to produce a book bearing the title *On the Economic Theory of Socialism.*[4] Lange, originally from Poland, came to the United States in the late thirties and while writing and teaching at the University of Chicago rose to be one of the world's leading mathematical economists. Lange returned to Poland after World War II, and has held high positions in that government ever since. The coauthor, Fred M. Taylor, was honored for his writing and teaching when he was named President of the American Economic Association in 1928. Lange is a socialist, and Taylor holds more orthodox views.

These men suggested that socialism, although marked by state ownership of the "means of production," might utilize a market (or price) system. Instead of forcing the production and consumption of each item to conform to a fixed quantity given in a master plan, they suggested, it would be preferable for a socialist system to allow for some interaction between consumer demand and the quantity produced. Prices and quantities would be set on a trial-and-error basis. If there was an excess supply, the price could be cut or production adjusted. If a shortage appeared, the reverse policy would be followed. Eventually, a balance between production and consumption at given prices would be reached. Reliance on rationing and other direct controls to arrive at preplanned outputs would be dropped. In effect, the proposal suggested that socialism combine public ownership of the means of production with a flexible market system.

[4] B. E. Lippincott (ed.) (Minneapolis: University of Minnesota Press, 1938).

According to recent reports (*Time,* February 12, 1965, pp. 23–29) experimentation with such a system is now taking place in Russia at the suggestion of certain Soviet economists, including one Evsei Liberman. Whether the book mentioned above had any influence on this development is not indicated in the source. At any rate, the experiment, which began in the last year or two of Krushchev's regime, has been described by *Time* in the following terms:

> Two clothing factories—Moscow's Bolshevichka and Gorky's Mayak—were cut loose to negotiate prices and sell their suits and dresses directly to 22 retail stores. The stores told the two factories what kinds of goods the consumers wanted and the factories were judged by the profits made on what goods were actually sold.

According to *Time's* report the results were extremely gratifying to Soviet authorities. As a result, and we quote again from *Time:*

> Kosygin announced that in gradual stages the new system would be spread throughout the whole of the consumer-goods industry. Last month the first 400 clothing and shoe firms scattered across Russia were authorized for the changeover—together, significantly, with 78 of their raw-material suppliers, who also had to be freed from the restrictions of the planners if the Kremlin really meant business in the reforms. Kosygin went even farther, asserting that eventually the reforms would be extended to all of Soviet industry.

As further described in the *Time* account, prices would be set on the factors, including an interest rate on capital. Profits would be the criterion of a plant's efficiency rather than consistency in meeting output quotas. The development is described in the source as an effort to meet economic problems evidenced by the recent reduction in the Soviet growth rate. If such a change is actually carried out, it will represent a giant stride from the concept of a totally planned economy toward a free, consumer-oriented market system. As such, we will welcome it as a relaxation and liberalization of the previously regimented Soviet system.

**Summary.** Under pure capitalism the primary role of government is to assure fairness in the competition of such economic units as firms. Events such as the combination movement in business and labor, the great depression of the 1930's, maladjustment in agriculture, World War II, and the rise of social conscience led to increased governmental activity. In addition to actions directed to the maintenance of competition, government supplements and modifies the market system by the following actions. First, government production, primarily in the form of direct services, has increased in the past few years, but still amounts to a small part of the total. Second, government purchases of output have increased to the point where this category amounts to 21 per cent of total spending. Third, unevenness in this distribution of income has been attacked by taxes and transfer payments designed to correct this situation. Fourth, errors of the market system in estimating costs and benefits have been corrected by taxes and subsidies. Fifth, government intervenes in the economic process with a view to the maintenance of full employment.

Socialism, an alternative system, is marked by state ownership of the "means of production," or productive land and capital with a democratic political system. It is generally agreed that this is accompanied by government operation of enterprises and centralized planning. In planning a transition to socialism the question arises whether the acquisition of the needed property is to come about through expropriation or peacefully through purchase. In the latter case there arises a further question whether a return on bonds used to acquire the property ought to be paid.

Under socialism both the outputs to be produced and the production requirements are determined in accordance with a detailed economic plan. In theory, distribution is made in accordance with need rather than productivity. In practice, however, incentive wages based on productivity are actually paid in the USSR, even though they subscribe to the above idea.

We can compare the relative performance in the postwar period of the American mixed capitalistic and the Russian communistic systems. In the period 1950–58 the economy of the USSR grew quite a bit more rapidly than that of the United States. However, the Soviet growth rate dropped off sharply in the 1958–62 period, whereas ours increased, thus narrowing the gap to minor proportions. Only if the Soviet Union attains something like the former relationship can it hope to overtake the United States.

## QUESTIONS

1. Why is government's role under pure capitalism likened to that of a referee in a game of sport?
2. Under the rules of pure capitalism certain industries may be turned over to government, when necessary for the welfare of society. What are examples of these?
3. Under what assumptions can the statement "That government is best which governs least" be reasonably applied to the case of pure capitalism?
4. What is "laissez-faire?" Who killed Cock Robin—that is, laissez-faire?
5. What did the great depression (1929–37) suggest about the functioning of pure capitalism?
6. What is the primary cause of the increasing government role in our society?
7. What are the antitrust laws? What is their purpose? How are they enforced?

8. Trace briefly, with percentage figures, the trends in government production and government spending on output since 1929. Give reasons for these trends.
9. What appear to be the effects of government spending and taxing on the distribution of income (Figure 4–1)?
10. What is a social cost? Give a number of examples. Why do social costs lead to an improper allocation of resources?
11. Describe how a socialist system might attempt to solve the three basic economic problems. What experimentation is now going on in the USSR?
12. Compare recent trends in growth rates in the United States, the USSR, Western Germany, and the United Kingdom.

PART

# 2

# National Income, Prices, and Economic Change

An explanation of the idea of national income and how it is calculated and an explanation of the forces explaining the level of national income and the causes of its changes. The study of price-level determination as well as inflation is followed by the study of fluctuations in national income, employment, and general economic activity.

CHAPTER

5

# National Income Concepts and Measurement

In the present state of the world the behavior of our economy has come in for close scrutiny. With the spread of information and education has come the desire for improved economic status by the bulk of the population. At the same time the communist countries have by their rapid growth sounded a sharp economic challenge to the Free World. As a result, we are interested in finding ways to measure the power and productiveness of our economy.

## MEASURING THE ECONOMY'S PERFORMANCE—NATIONAL PRODUCT OR INCOME

In measuring the performance of an economy interest centers on the output of the system. How great a quantity of goods and services can the economy provide? At the same time certain other indexes do have relevance. For example, a measure of the employment of labor indicates the success experienced by an economy in making use of its resources. On this basis the American economy would have received low marks in the 1930's, when unemployment was extensive; it would have a good record in the decade following World War II, when unemployment was consistently low.

Because we are more interested in the result than in the effort, output necessarily takes precedence over input. Therefore, the standard indicator of an economy's overall behavior is its overall output of goods and services. In the present chapter we shall attempt to explain in detail the various concepts used in measuring this flow of ouput.

**Basic Concepts.** The flow of output produced by an economy is the best measure of its performance. To describe this flow in general we use the term *national income*. Because the flow of newly produced goods and services constitutes the real income of society, the above term is appropriate. Later, more narrowly defined concepts will be introduced and used, in particular one known as *Net National Product, NNP.*

Now that we wish to discuss the flow of output as an aggregate, how are we to measure it? This flow consists of a variety of different items—apples, haircuts, automobiles—that are not directly commensurable. Only by expressing these items in terms of a common unit can the product be added into a total. Such a unit is money; by expressing these items in monetary terms and adding them up we can arrive at a money measure of the flow of output. Consider now the ways in which a measure expressed in money may be assigned to each commodity.

First, we may use the market price of a commodity as its measure

**Figure 5–1.** Circular flow of income—restated.

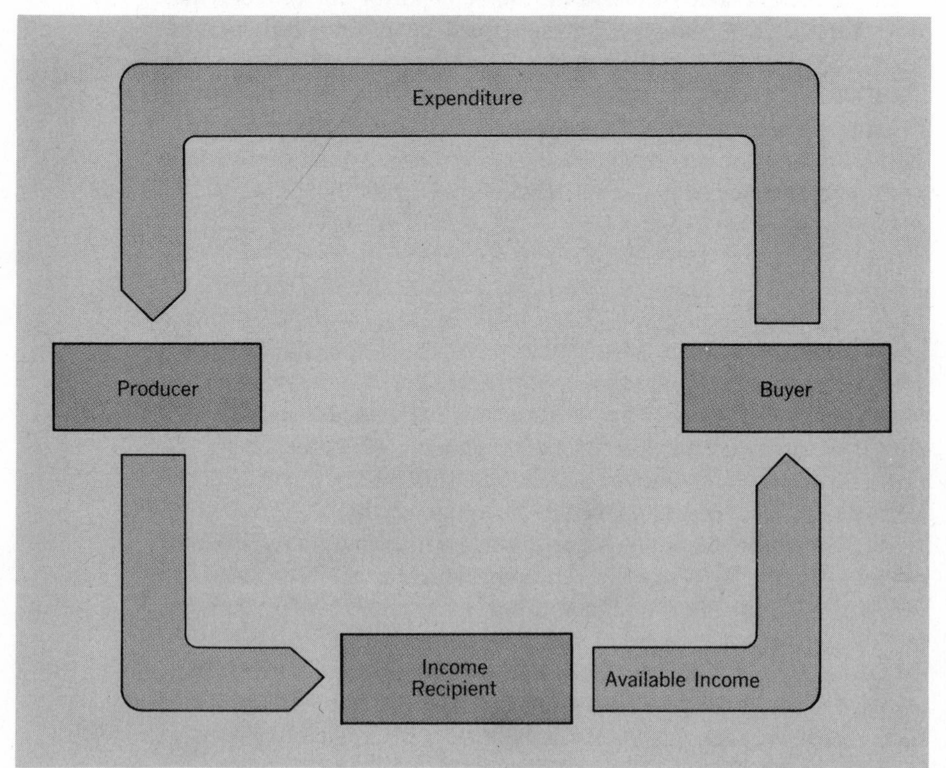

in terms of money. By expressing the entire collection in terms of the prices paid for them we arrive at the total spending of the economy on this flow of output. Therefore, the output may be valued at market prices and estimated, accordingly, by total spending on output.

Second, we may use the cost of the commodity as its money measure. By expressing the collection of outputs in terms of cost we arrive at total cost of output as the measure of that flow. What is to be included in cost? In a pure capitalistic system only factor cost would be included, but in our mixed system we may add indirect business taxes levied on the sale of the product. According to whether we wish to emphasize gross or net output we may include or exclude depreciation charges for the wearing out of capital.

To clear the way for discussion let us lay down several rather broad definitions. *Total spending* is the outlay of society in purchasing the flow of newly produced goods and services. *Cost of output* is the sum of money that producers must earn as a condition of sustaining the flow of output. *Income* is the sum of money earned by society as a result of producing the current flow of output. Now these definitions take on more specific meaning as we attach qualifications of one sort or another.

## THE CIRCULAR FLOW OF ECONOMIC LIFE

Let us divide up the participants in economic activity according to the role they play. First, we must consider the producer, because he incurs cost in creating output and receives the spending on it. Second, we must consider the spender who, by purchasing the flow of output, generates the expenditure that serves to measure output. Third, we must consider the income recipient because he provides funds to the spender; that is, income serves as a source of taxes that support government spending; again, income is the origin of the saving that leads to investment spending; and, finally, income provides funds necessary for personal consumption. Each participant—producer, spender, and income recipient—marks a stage in the flow of income.

**Expenditure.** Let us begin the circuit of the income flow with the buyer. In return for a flow of goods and services from the producer, the buyer spends a sum of money that passes to the producer in receipts. This is shown in Figure 5–1 by the broad arrow labeled "Expenditure" going from buyer to producer.

**Cost Equals Income.** As the producer receives this sum, he must allocate it among the various costs. He must defray the factor costs of wages, interest, and rent. In addition, he is liable for the payment of indirect business taxes that are levied on the sale of output and that become government income. (If gross output is considered, depreciation passes to business firms as income or proceeds used to buy replacements.) If all this does not absorb the expenditure, the remainder can be allotted to profit. Consequently, all expenditures on output are resolved into costs: factor costs, industry profit, and nonfactor costs (including indirect business taxes). Both of these elements constitute income—wages, interest, rent, and profit being factor income going to the owners, and such nonfactor costs as indirect business taxes becoming income to the government. So expenditure is resolved into income.

**From Income to Available Income.** At this stage the money is in the hands of income recipients. Before the income can be spent, however, it must pass into the hands of buyers. Consider the portion of national income made up by corporate profits. Of this, a part passes to individual stockholders as dividends, but part is paid to the government in taxes, and part is retained for use by the corporation. Thus the corporation's income is made available to individuals, government, and the corporation itself for possible spending.

Again, the government siphons off social insurance payments and corporation and individual income taxes and makes transfer payments before it is in a position to buy goods and services. Finally, individuals pay various taxes before they are in a position to purchase output. With part of aftertax income individuals acquire balances in savings accounts, securities, insurance, and other objects of individual saving. In turn, this sets up a flow of funds available to business firms who wish to invest in the purchase of new capital goods. Combined with corporate saving, individual saving makes an aggregate flow of funds available to businessmen who wish to buy capital goods.

**Closing the Circle.** After income passes into the hands of recipients it must be allocated to uses. When this has been done the funds must all be channeled to buyers. In the last analysis the funds end up being used by individuals for consumption, by government for buying social goods and services, and by investing firms for the purchase of capital. Thus in the figure the broad arrow labeled "Available Income" has passed to the buyer, who can now spend it. Thus we return to our starting point.

Note that income made available to buyers is exactly the sum spent on output. This is true because all expenditure on output is resolved into income and becomes available for use. Does this mean that all available income will subsequently be spent? No. The equality has reference to exactly one trip around the circular flow circuit. We postpone consideration of what buyers do on the next circuit—whether they spend more or less than they received.

**Summary of Circular Flow.** The flow of product and income is divided into two parts: (1) an *upper loop,* expenditure on output, measuring the value of output, and (2) a *lower loop,* cost of output, which becomes income. It is convenient to break up the flow of income (cost) in the lower loop into two stages: (1) translation of expenditure into costs or income passing to recipients; (2) the allocation of income of the recipients (its resolution into available income that buyers can use to purchase output). The upper and lower loops are equal. Let us entitle this common value of expenditure and cost of output "Net National Product."

Schematically, we can represent the equality of upper-loop expenditure on output and lower-loop cost of output by an equation or table. The equation states that:

$$\text{Expenditure on Output} = \text{Cost of Output} \begin{cases} \text{the income generated} \\ \text{by the production} \\ \text{of the output.} \end{cases}$$

This equation can be represented in somewhat greater detail by means of a table.

**TABLE 5-1**
**The Expenditure and Cost Approaches to *NNP***

| Expenditure, Value of Output | | Cost | | Income |
|---|---|---|---|---|
| | | | | Factor costs |
| Consumption of individuals | | | | Wages |
| Net investment by business | = | *NNP* | = | Interest |
| Purchases of goods and services by government | | | | Rent |
| | | | | Profit |
| | | | | Nonfactor costs |
| | | | | Indirect business taxes |

As we have already indicated, the costs constitute income, or sums desired from the sale of output, and subsequently become available for spending on further output.

We are now in a position to consider the concept of national income (*NNP*) in more detail. Consider the problem of trying to determine or measure the size of the national product.

## ESTIMATING NATIONAL PRODUCT

**Scope of National Product.** What is to be included in the national product? Clearly, national product should include all newly produced goods and services. Various kinds of trades and exchanges of existing goods, not done with a view to earning a living, are excluded. If you own a capital asset, such as a piece of land or a share of stock, that you bought at a price of $1,000 and resell a year later at $1,500, your gain of $500 is counted as a *capital gain* rather than as income.

From a purely practical viewpoint it is only feasible to include items whose quantity and price can be estimated. Thus although housewives perform useful services in cooking, making clothes, and other tasks, these cannot be calculated in amount or value, and so are omitted from the estimates. Again, the allocation of potential working time to leisure is a feature of advanced societies. Because leisure represents an alternative to output in such societies, it would be desirable to measure it along with output as an indicator of the performance of society. However, difficulties of measurement alone preclude the inclusion of leisure time in national product.

To sum it up, the national product includes newly produced goods and services that come onto the market for sale or that otherwise have a well-defined amount and value.

**Estimation—General Concept.** First, we require estimates of the quantities of all goods and services produced in the economy during the year. Then the prices at which these outputs are to be valued is sought. Multiplying each quantity by its price (or value) gives a sum of money representing the contribution of the good to the value of output. To illustrate, suppose two dozen apples are sold at 60 cents a dozen and three dozen oranges sold at 50 cents a dozen. Then the value of output is: two dozen apples at 60 cents plus three dozen oranges at 50 cents equals $1.20 plus $1.50 which equals $2.70. These calculations can be arranged in the form of a table.

**TABLE 5-2**
**Calculation of the Value of Output**

| Commodity | Quantity Sold | Price (¢) | Value of Output |
|---|---|---|---|
| Oranges | 2 dozen | 60 | $1.20 |
| Apples | 3 dozen | 50 | 1.50 |
| | | | $2.70 * |

* Multiply the quantity sold by the price to get value of output for each commodity, as shown in the last column. Add up the items in the "Value of Output" column to get the total value of output.

**Double Counting.** Basically, this technique is quite simple, but a problem soon arises in applying it. Thus, on first considering the matter, it seems that the quantity of every good and service produced should be entered in the calculation. Such a technique would be faulty, however, as the following example indicates. Consider the following newly produced items: cotton, cotton cloth, shirts at wholesale, shirts at retail. Clearly, these items duplicate one another, each item entering into the production of the next item in the list. If we enter each of these items into a table like the one above, and add up the values, we will have overestimated seriously the usable flow of product. How is this difficulty to be surmounted?

**Value Added Method.** Either of two methods will provide the desired answer. First, we may count the value added in the stage of production in question. This amounts to the sale value of the output at this stage less purchases from other firms. For example, suppose shirts at wholesale sell for $2.00 and the price of cloth entering into a shirt is $1.10. Subtracting the $1.10 of purchases from $2.00 of sales gives 90 cents as the value added in making a shirt. By adding this 90 cents to the contribution at every other stage in shirt production we arrive at the value of output.

The sense of this approach can be shown in Table 5–3. To add the price of the cotton to that of the cloth entering into a shirt, and add this to the wholesale price of the shirt, and this to the retail price, would mean nothing. Furthermore, it would be a great overstatement of the productive activity being measured. To secure value of output we start with the value of the cotton, 60 cents. Then we subtract the price of cotton, 60 cents, from that of the cloth produced, $1.10, to secure the value added at the second stage, $1.10 – $.60 = $.50. Proceeding in this way we find value added in each of four stages. Summing the value added at each stage—cotton, cotton cloth, shirts at wholesale, shirts at retail—we find the value of the output to be $3.00. This is shown in the third column of the table.

**Final Product Method.** If the value of the national product is to be found in this way, each stage of production must be considered separately. Table 5–3 suggests another, shorter method, however. It turned out that the sum of the value added in all stages was $3.00; but this proves to be exactly the same as the price of shirts at retail.

**TABLE 5-3**
**Calculation of Value Added**

| Good | Price of Good | Value Added in Stage = Price – Price in Last Stage |
|---|---|---|
| Cotton | $0.60 | $0.60 |
| Cloth | 1.10 | 0.50 |
| Shirts at wholesale | 2.00 | 0.90 |
| Shirts at retail | 3.00 | 1.00 |
| Sum | means nothing | 3.00 |

What else could it be? The final sale price of the shirt must include the productive contribution of every stage up to this point. And this suggests an alternative way of calculating national product. Just add up the values of all items sold for the last time. By doing this we could virtually skip all consideration of the earlier stages of production.

In fact, the final product approach is the method actually used by the Department of Commerce in computing national product. However, the value-added method is available as a means of checking on the accuracy of the final-product method.

**Changes in Prices.** One of the problems in using value of output as the measure of national product is that it is expressed in terms of money. Unlike the measuring units used in the physical sciences—yards, days, pounds—the dollar has no fixed value. What $1 would buy in 1941 cost a little more than $2 in 1963. So the dollar itself is smaller in terms of what it will buy—in fact, less than half of its 1941 value. If comparisons of national product are to reflect the flow of output, something must be done to adjust for changes in the price level. Only by eliminating price change from the figures will we find a measure of the performance of the economy.

**Meaning and Use of a Price Index.** In 1954 the value of output, as measured by the *Gross National Product* of the Department of Commerce, was $363 billion, and it had risen to $585 billion in 1963. What a large increase this seems to be—about 61 per cent in only nine years! As we might suspect, however, prices rose in those years—by about 18.7 per cent. This leaves us wondering what the answer would be if we took out the price change, so that the increased Gross National Product reflected only a rise in output. To accomplish this it is necessary to find a *price index* or measure of the price rise. Then the index is used to *deflate* the data on *GNP*—that is, to eliminate the price change.

A price index measures the relationship between the price level of a given year and that of a base year. A base year is one characterized by economic behavior of a sort that provides a good yardstick for comparison with other years. In the base year a price index has a value of 100. Interpreted, this means that prices in the base year are 100 per cent of themselves or that they are equal (obviously) to those of the base year. If the price index in a subsequent year is 120, this means that prices are at a level equal to 120 per cent of the base year figure. Or it means that prices are 20 per cent higher in the given than in the base year.

Essentially, a price index is a percentage, with the excess above 100 to be taken as the percentage increase above the base-period value. Now the index can be changed to a proportion, if desired, so that 100 becomes 1 and 120 becomes 1.2. Then a value of 1.2, say, means that prices in a given year are 1.2 times as great as those of the base year; or, prices of the given year are .2, or one fifth higher than those of the base year. When used to deflate national income for price change, price indexes are used as a proportion with a base value of 1.

Let us assume that a price index has been prepared for the two years. Making use of these index numbers of prices, as shown in Table 5–4, we eliminate price change from Gross National Product. After this adjustment has been made we find that Gross National Product is still $363 billion in 1954 but only $493 billion in 1963. If 1954 is the *base year* for the index, we take the price level of this year as normal and leave the prices unchanged. This being the case, the 1954 figure remains the same. Because prices rose from 100 to 118.7 in 1963, a downward revision in *GNP* must be effected to deflate for the price change. This reduces the figure from $585 to $493 billion. Now the jump in income (from $363 billion to $585 billion) looks considerably less impressive. It indicates an increase in output of only 36 per cent instead of 61 per cent.

**TABLE 5-4**
**Deflating *GNP* with a Price Index**

| Year | Gross National Product (1) | Price Index (2) | Real *GNP* (with 1954 Prices) (3) |
|---|---|---|---|
| 1954 | $363 | 100 | $\frac{\$363}{100} \times 100 = \$363$ |
| 1963 | 585 | 118.7 | $\frac{\$585}{118.7} \times 100 = \$493$ |

Deflate *GNP* by dividing *GNP* (with current prices), column (1), by price index, column (2), and multiplying by 100, as in column (3).

By deflating national income estimates over time we secure a series of values reflecting variations in output. In Figure 5–2 are plotted values of Gross National Product (a measure of national income) in current prices and in prices of 1954, the base year. Observation reveals clearly that *GNP* in current prices rises much faster and fluctuates more as a result of its inclusion of price change than does deflated *GNP*. In measuring economic growth it is desirable to use deflated values, because the desired thing is a rise in output. The same process of removing price change can be applied to other measures of national income, such as the Net National Product.

**Comparisons of Countries.** It is often useful for purposes of governmental planning to compare output in one country with that

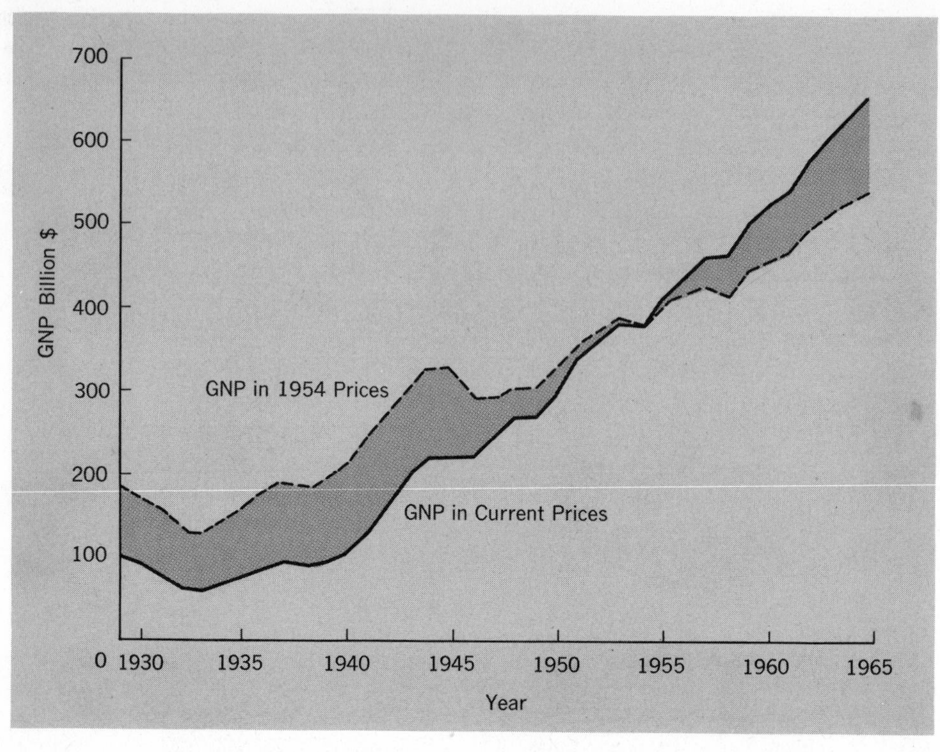


**Figure 5–2.** *GNP* in current prices and in 1954 prices, compared.

in another. Today, it is pertinent to compare the outputs of the United States and Russia. Yet the operation involves certain difficulties, because prices of items are different in the two countries. In making the comparisons of value of output, should the prices obtaining in Russia or those in the United States be used? Neither. Rather, it would be desirable to take the prices as indicated by the exchange of goods in international trade. Because many items, such as services, are not traded, this method is not always available. Consequently, it is probably necessary to take an average of the prices as the value of the commodity for the purpose of making a comparison. In any event, the comparison depends quite heavily on the somewhat arbitrary choice of prices. Consequently, some system that is not entirely perfect must be used.

There are three sorts of methods to be used. First, use the prices prevailing in the United States. Second, use the prices prevailing in the foreign country. Third, use an average of the two prices. In concept the first and second methods are alike but have opposite biases. The third gives a compromise answer that avoids the extremes, but is hard to interpret. Let us illustrate with a hypothetical example.

In Argentina steaks are cheap and bicycles expensive, let us say. In the United States the opposite is true. Let us ignore currency problems and assume that the dollar is the unit of currency in both countries. Suppose prime steaks cost 25 cents a pound in Argentina and bicycles $200, whereas steaks cost $1.50 a pound in the United States and bicycles $50. Suppose the Argentinian consumes 400 pounds of beef and 1 bicycle, whereas the citizen of the United States buys 100 pounds of beef and 4 bicycles. To compare the value of these outputs we may use first the Argentine prices, then the United States prices, giving the following table.

**TABLE 5-5**
**Comparisons of *NNP* in Two Countries**

| | U.S. | | | Argentina | | |
|---|---|---|---|---|---|---|
| | | Value | | | Value | |
| | Consumption | U.S. Prices | Argentine Prices | Consumption | U.S. Prices | Argentine Prices |
| Steak | 100 lb. | $150 | $ 25 | 400 lb. | $600 | $100 |
| Bicycles | 4 | 200 | 800 | 1 | 50 | 200 |
| Net National Product | | $350 | $825 | | $650 | $300 |

Notice that when United States prices are used, Argentina shows the larger *NNP* but that when Argentine prices are used, the United States comes out ahead. Why? This happens because the high-consumption Argentine item is steak, which is scarcer and commands a higher price in the United States. If we use United States prices, Argentina shows a high *NNP* value, because the large output of beef is multiplied by the high United States price. If we use Argentine prices, the United States shows a high *NNP* value, because the (relatively) large output of bicycles is multiplied by the high Argentine price.

If some sort of average price is used, the *NNP* values are more nearly equal. This is the best approach, because the item of which the most is produced in a given country is likely to be cheap there but expensive abroad. The weighting of this item (or items) will be decisive in determining *NNP*. It is better for purposes of comparison to weight this item by a price neither high nor low—namely, by a compromise figure. Try the following problem. Work out the two *NNP* values at prices that are simple arithmetic averages of the two prices and compare the results with those already obtained.

**Components of Value of Output.** The value of output is the money value of all goods and services produced in the economy. In turn, this is measured by the expenditure of buyers on these goods and services. As we have already indicated, there are three classes of buyers: individuals who wish to consume, government, and investing firms. Let us consider successively the corresponding classes of expenditure: consumption, government expenditure, and investment.

**Consumption.** *Consumption is the outlay on goods and services that yield direct satisfaction to the buyer.* It consists of expenditure on such items as food, clothing, shelter, medical expenses, automobiles, and consumer durables. By far the largest of the three basic types of spending, consumption expenditure, in 1963 was estimated as $373 billion out of a Net National Product of $533 billion, or roughly 70 per cent. Consumption is not designed to measure the current use of output, only the current purchases. For example, an automobile purchased in 1963 at $3,000 adds a like amount to consumption. Although the car still yields services in 1964, when no car is bought, nothing is included for consumption in this year.

**Investment.** *Investment is the outlay on newly produced capital goods.* To be perfectly definite let us note that *capital goods consist of produced goods used for further production,* and that *production is the creation of utilities,* or want satisfying goods and services. Among the goods included are such items as machinery, factory construction, commercial construction, and additions to stocks of goods (inventories) held by business firms. A seemingly debatable item, residential construction, is also included. Because this is shelter, why is it not included in personal consumption? Consider this argument. If an individual buys a house with a view to renting it out, he certainly expects a set of future returns (utilities) to flow in over time. In short, this constitutes investment in a capital good, a house, which is used for further production, the provision of housing services for the occupants. By the same argument a person who buys a house with a view to using it himself expects it to provide a stream of housing services he will enjoy. In short, the purchase of a newly produced house is regarded as investment.

**Gross and Net Investment.** In the treatment emphasized here we are concerned with what is known as net investment. *Net investment* consists of the total flow of capital goods demanded less the quantity required to replace the amount currently wearing out or otherwise consumed. Let us refer to *the total flow of newly produced capital goods as gross investment.* Obviously, net investment is equal to gross investment less depreciation and other using up of capital.

As a rule the gross investment in capital is much larger than depreciation. The net investment remaining represents an increase in the stock of capital—more machinery, buildings, stocks of goods, and houses. In a progressive society, with a growing labor force, improving techniques, and rising living standards, it is normal to have substantial net investment. Recently, this has amounted to about 7 per cent of Net National Product. During bad times, however, producers cut back sharply on purchases of capital, failing even to replace capital equipment. For example, in the five-year period 1931–35 depreciation outweighed total production of capital goods. At the times when this occurs, the capital equipment of society runs down.

What was the meaning of the situation prevailing in 1932? At that time $7.6 billion in capital goods was needed merely to replace the capital equipment wearing out. Because only $.9 billion of new capital goods were produced, a $6.7-billion deficit developed. In failing to produce this capital, society was allowing its capital stock to run down by a like amount; it was consuming its capital in the amount of $6.7 billion.

**TABLE 5-6**
**Gross and Net Investment in Relation to Business Conditions**

| Year | Business Condition | Gross Private Domestic Investment (Billions of Dollars) | Depreciation (Billions of Dollars) | Net Private Domestic Investment (Billion of Dollars) | Capital Stock |
|---|---|---|---|---|---|
| 1929: | good times | 16.2 | 8.6 | 7.6 | growing |
| 1932: | bad times | 0.9 | 7.6 | −6.7 | shrinking |
| 1959: | good times | 72.0 | 40.5 | 31.5 | growing |

**Domestic and Foreign Investment.** Almost all of investment consists in private domestic investment, but part consists in what is called *net foreign investment*. Roughly, this equals the amount by which foreign spending on American goods and services exceeds our spending on foreign goods and services. Because we are trying to measure domestic production by expenditure on this output, and because foreign demand generates output, foreign spending must be added to the other elements of spending. On the other hand, only that part of total spending that is applied to domestic goods generates domestic production. Consequently, we must subtract from total spending the expenditure on foreign goods. Evidently, just the excess of foreign spending here over our spending abroad should be added to the total.

Let us note several points, one of terminology. Foreign spending on our goods leads to exports of these goods; conversely, our spending on foreign goods leads to imports of those goods. Clearly, the excess of foreign spending on our goods over our spending on foreign goods equals the excess of our exports over our imports. Briefly, net foreign investment equals net exports of goods.

Next, net foreign investment can be negative. If we import more than we export and net exports are negative, then net foreign investment is negative. In 1959, for example, we imported \$0.8 billion more than we exported, giving rise to net foreign investment of −\$0.8 billion. Because this item is a difference it is rarely of significant size, usually equaling \$2 or \$3 billion. For example, in 1962 net foreign investment was \$3.3 billion.

Finally, why is this item referred to as investment? If we export more goods than we import, foreigners owe us the difference. Then we may acquire with this difference some claim on foreigners, such as foreign securities or short-term notes. In effect, these are claims on the capital goods (or other wealth) of these countries. As such, the difference represents an increase in the capital equipment belonging to us.

**Government Purchases of Goods and Services.** This item consists of the expenditure of all levels of government—Federal, state, and local—on goods and services. It entirely excludes transfer payments by governments that do not reflect current output transactions. Because transfer payments amounted to about 25 per cent of total government spending in (the calendar year) 1962, it is clear that government purchases are quite a bit smaller than the total budget of government. If the student should notice a wide disparity between government purchases and the budget, he may attribute the difference to transfers.

To summarize, total expenditure on output, *NNP,* is the sum of consumption, investment, and government expenditure on output.

## COST OR INCOME APPROACH TO INCOME CALCULATION

In the previous discussion we adopted the upper-loop, value-of-output or expenditure, approach to Net National Product calculation. If we know the total expenditure on output, *NNP,* then we have a sum to be distributed to income recipients. Let us recall our definition of income as the sum of money earned by society as a result of producing the current flow of output. Now the sums to be distributed fall into two categories: (1) factor costs (incomes); (2) nonfactor costs (incomes)—for example, indirect business taxes. (If we are considering Gross National Product, *GNP,* an additional flow of expenditure has to be allocated, because then part of investment expenditure is used for replacement. Consequently, another nonfactor cost (income) must be added, namely depreciation.)

In order to find *NNP* we may use the cost or income approach. First, we may add up the various income shares, consisting of items like wages, interest, rent. Then we add such nonfactor costs as indirect business taxes (and depreciation, if investment is gross instead of net). The sum of factor and nonfactor costs gives *NNP*. Now this approach gives more reliable results than the upper-loop approach. Reason? Net investment figures for the upper-loop approach are unreliable, because the estimates of depreciation are subject to wide error. The lower-loop method is free from this defect.

In the first chapter we described the four factors of production: land, labor, capital, and entrepreneurship. Since then we have spoken of the respective returns to these factors, namely rent, wages, interest, and profit. For various reasons business firms, from whose records we secure our data, use a different set of definitions of these incomes. Although wages are defined in much the same way, interest is construed very narrowly as the return on money borrowed at a fixed rate—for example, bond interest. Rent refers primarily to the return on real estate, consisting of land as well as capital rented along with the land. The profit of the firm is the excess of sales receipts over costs. As the economist sees it, business profit covers what he regards as interest on the capital contributed by the owner as well as profit to the entrepreneur. In the discussion below, the classification follows business usage, because the data is provided on this basis.

**Wages.** As recorded in the national income accounts, this item goes under the heading *compensation of employees.* Under this heading the main item is *wages and salaries,* which means ordinary wages and salaries plus commissions, tips, and payments in kind. A second item called *supplements to wages and salaries* includes *other labor income,* meaning such things as employer contributions to private pension, health and welfare funds, and employer contributions for social insurance.

**Rental Income of Persons.** This includes such items as earnings from rental of real property, imputed rent of those who own their own homes, and returns on natural resources.

**Net Interest.** This refers to interest flowing to persons from private businesses. Government interest payments are excluded. In fact, *NNP* is defined to include in factor incomes only those payments arising from current productive services. The bulk of government debt is that of the Federal government, and was almost entirely incurred during World Wars I and II. In contrast with private borrowing, the money provided by this debt was used to finance pay of soldiers or the purchase of military equipment, leaving behind no capital equipment. Consequently, the debt corresponds to no capital or tangible asset, and the interest on the debt cannot be attributed to the productivity of capital. Consequently, this interest is omitted from the sums counted here.

**TABLE 5–7**
**Expenditure and Cost Approaches to Net National Product, 1964 (Preliminary Estimate)**

| Expenditure | | | Costs (Income) | | |
|---|---|---|---|---|---|
| Personal consumption expenditure | | 399.3 | Factor costs | | |
| | | | Compensation of employees | | 361.7 |
| Net investment, consisting of: | | | Rental income of persons | | 12.4 |
| Gross private domestic investment | 87.8 | | Net interest | | 26.8 |
| less | | | Proprietor's income | | 52.0 |
| Capital consumption allowances | 53.4 | | | | |
| equals | | | Corporate profits (including inventory valuation adjustment) | | 57.0 |
| Private domestic investment | 34.4 | | | | |
| and | | | (a) Dividends | 19.8 | |
| Net foreign investment | 7.0 | | (b) Profits tax liability | 25.6 | |
| Total net investment | 41.4 | 41.4 | (c) Retained earnings | 11.8 | |
| | | | (d) Inventory valuation adjustment | −0.2 | |
| Government purchases of goods and services | | 128.6 | (a) + (b) + (c) + (d) = total above | | |
| | | | Nonfactor cost | | |
| | | | Indirect business taxes (and minor items) | | 59.4 |
| Net National Product | | 569.3 | | | 569.3 |

**Income of Unincorporated Enterprises.** What economists call profit cannot be distinguished clearly from other returns. Thus, proprietorships, partnerships, and cooperatives earn incomes that amount, in part, to profit, but also include other types of income—for example, some wages, interest, and rent.

**Corporate Profit.** Again, this item does not consist entirely of what economists call profit. Rather it is the income left after paying certain costs defined by the accountant. However, it certainly includes all profits earned by corporations. Such earnings consist of corporate profits adjusted for inventory change, and differ from private estimates by a different handling of inventory valuation. The sum is allocated into three parts: corporation income tax going to the government, dividend payments going to stockholders, and retained corporate earnings, or what remains after the other two payments have been made. The latter sums are used to expand the facilities of the firm.

**Indirect Business Taxes.** This item consists mainly of sales taxes that business firms pay to the government. Though not a factor cost, this item must be paid to the government, and consequently is a cost of providing the current level of output. Also it can be regarded as income to the government.

**Expenditure and Cost Approaches Compared.** By adding up the factor and nonfactor costs we achieve the lower-loop estimate of *NNP;* this is a measure of the income available for use by the economy. In a similar way we may add up the expenditure items to secure the upper-loop estimate. Theoretically, these are the same, because expenditure is resolved into cost; if into nothing else, then into profit. However, because the two are derived from different sets of information, there arises a *statistical discrepancy,* or error arising from faults in data estimation. This comparison for 1964 is shown in Table 5–7.

This table summarizes the elements in the upper and lower loops—the expenditure and cost approaches to national income. It also points to the accounting equality of the two. Later, we shall take a different viewpoint and adopt definitions (especially of profit) under which they are not necessarily equal.

**Summary.** The best measure of economic activity is thought to be the overall output of society. In describing this generally we use the expression *national income;* to add precision we most often use a specific measure called *Net National Product.* Such a measure must be expressed in terms of the common denominator of money. Expressed in terms of the circular flow, *NNP* can be thought of as (1) the value of output, or what buyers spend on that output; and (2) the cost of output, or what producers must receive so that the earnings of the factors will be adequate, and the claims of government for indirect taxes may be met. It is argued that the value of output, the upper loop of the circular flow, is equal to the cost of output, the lower loop.

In calculating national income the simplest approach is to measure the upper loop or value of output. Care must be exercised to avoid double counting. According to the use being made of the data it may or may not be desirable to iron out changes in the value of money by means of a price index. Net National Product can usefully be broken down into spending components: consumption; investment, including net foreign investment; and government purchases.

In approaching income calculation by the cost approach, Net National Product is built up from the shares going to certain factors, such as wages, or income going to certain groups, such as unincorporated enterprises. By adding up the several shares together with indirect business taxes we arrive at a cost measure of Net National Product. This cost estimate is equal to the value of spending on output.

## QUESTIONS

1. How is the performance of an economic system best measured? What is an alternative?
2. How do we measure the total flow of output when it is composed of a great many incommensurable items?
3. Summarize the steps in the circular flow.
4. Explain the equality of the expenditure (value of output) and cost (income) approaches to the measurement of *NNP*.
5. How does the problem of double counting arise in calculating the national product? Outline the value-added and final-product methods of solving this problem.
6. Why do changing prices introduce a problem in the calculation of the national product? How can this problem be handled?
7. Which prices are used in making comparisons of national product between the United States and, say, the USSR—ours or theirs? Explain.
8. List the components of the value of output (expenditure), and explain carefully the nature of each.
9. Discuss briefly the normal pattern of relationships among gross investment, depreciation, and net investment. What is the pattern in a deep depression year like 1932?
10. What distinction is drawn between government expenditures on goods and services and the entire budget or outlay of government?
11. Summarize briefly the cost approach to the calculation of Net National Product. List and identify the various elements actually entering into the statistical calculations of the cost of output.

**12.** Define the terms *Gross National Product, Net National Product,* and *National Income,* and describe their relationships. See Appendix.

# Appendix

## DEPARTMENT OF COMMERCE ESTIMATES OF NATIONAL INCOME

The Department of Commerce works up and presents periodic estimates of national income. Because there are a number of complicating practical circumstances, it is not surprising that they provide not one but several measures. Let us consider these and the ways in which they are derived.

**Gross National Product.** By definition, Gross National Product is the sale value of output at market prices plus government output at factor cost. In finding this measure the Department calculates the money value of all final products at average market prices during the year and adds to this value the expenditure of government on output. Because transfer payments involve no purchase of output, they are excluded. It may seem puzzling that private output is valued at market prices, whereas government output is valued at cost. Government output receives this treatment because (1) there is no estimate available at market prices; and (2) government is in business to render services at costs to be defrayed by taxes.

**Net National Product.** At first glance it appears that *GNP* is just what we need. However, the figure thus attained does not measure the usual concept of *income as that flow of output that can be used by society in any desired way.* In fact, a large part, about 8 per cent, of *GNP* is used to replace machinery that is wearing out and needs to be replaced in the current year. Suppose all of *GNP* were to be consumed; no part of output would be available to replace capital now wearing out. As a result, the stock of capital would decline. If consumption equaled *GNP* every year, all capital would be used up, not replaced, and the economic system as we know it would cease. Clearly, all *GNP* cannot be used by society, part necessarily being set aside for consumption of capital. For example, in 1959, with a *GNP* of $482 billion Gross Private Domestic Investment was $72 billion. Out of this about $41 billion in capital consumption allowances was set aside to replace capital used up during the year. This leaves $31 billion to expand the capital facilities of society.

Unfortunately, the estimates of capital consumption are very inexact. To a considerable extent this lack of precision arises from variations in methods of depreciating capital; accountants take different views on how much capital has been used up during the year. Attempts are made to give consistency to the accounting methods at the Department of Commerce by making statistical adjustments. However, this is an inadequate remedy, and the Department does not even print a figure labeled "Net Investment." To find this estimate you must subtract capital consumption allowances from Gross Private Domestic Investment and add Net Foreign Investment.

Summarizing, *Net National Product is found by subtracting capital consumption allowances from GNP.* This gives a measure of value of output net of the wearing out of capital.

**National Income.** By moving from *GNP* to *NNP* we find an estimate of the monetary value of available output produced during the year. However, it does not measure the flow of factor incomes (costs), because indirect business taxes are included. Consequently, the Department of Commerce gives us a measure of factor income, *National Income, which is equal to Net National Product less indirect business taxes and other minor adjustments.*

Unfortunately, none of the three measures of income indicates the usable income of private individuals. As a transitional figure, the Department calculates a measure of income that differs from take-home pay only in that it includes personal taxes; this measure is called *Personal Income.* In order to secure income received by individuals it is necessary to take out sums *earned* by the factors *but not received by* the individuals. All of corporate profit is earned by the factors, this being an accounting category of income, but only dividends are actually paid to individuals. Consequently, we may first deduct corporate profit and later add in dividends in order to find Personal Income. Another deduction from National Income is made by government in the form of social security taxes. These sums go into a social security fund rather than into the pockets of individuals.

Next, it is necessary to add *sums not earned but paid to individuals, known as transfer payments.* Almost all of this consists of government transfers—such items as veterans benefits and aid to the blind. The sums do not correspond to the current productive effort of the recipient. Because the payments come from the income stream, they are said to be "transfers" from people who do earn the sums but who relinquish them, mainly as a result of taxes.[1] There is also a small

[1] Along with this are classed government interest payments. The bulk of the debt on which interest is paid was incurred during war, leaving no capital to the government to earn the interest charges. Consequently, the interest charges, though not earned by factors, must be taken from the income stream and paid to individuals.

sum transferred from business firms to individuals, known as *business transfer payments*. Then, as mentioned above, we add dividends.

Summarizing all this in the form of a brief table, we get:

*National Income*
— *Corporate income and excess profit taxes*
— *Retained corporate earnings*
— *Social insurance payments*
+ *Transfer payments (including government interest)*
= *Personal Income.*

**Disposable Personal Income.** To find the income that individuals can actually use it is necessary only to deduct personal taxes, principally the personal federal income tax. Hence *Disposable Personal Income* is simply *Personal Income less personal taxes.*

We can now summarize these results in the form of a table and diagram.

**TABLE 5-8**
**Income Concepts of Department of Commerce for 1964 (Preliminary Estimate—in billions of dollars)**

| | |
|---|---|
| Gross National Product | 622.6 |
| − Capital consumption allowances | 53.4 |
| = Net National Product | 569.2 |
| − Indirect business taxes and other adjustments | 59.4 |
| = National income | 509.8 |
| − Corporate profits and inventory val. adj. | 57.0 |
| −Contributions for social insurance | 28.7 |
| + Dividends | 19.8 |
| + Transfers (and interest on government bonds) | 47.4 |
| = Personal Income | 491.3 |
| − Personal taxes | 59.5 |
| = Disposable Personal Income | 431.8 |
| − Consumption | 399.3 |
| = Personal saving | 32.5 |

In Figure 5–3 the same arrangement is shown schematically. To illustrate the complex change from National Income to Personal Income a special sequence of blocks is provided.

## USES OF NATIONAL INCOME MEASURES

Out of this collection of concepts we ought to be able to find one that is best for subsequent use. Unfortunately, careful consideration of the different measures indicates that no one measure is ideal. Let us run down the list and check off the merits and demerits of each so as to give it a suitable role in subsequent discussion.

*Gross National Product*

*Good Points*

*Measures total flow of output available in the short run.* For short periods capital may be used up in order to provide output for other purposes. During wars countries allow their railroads and housing to run down, using the resources released for war purposes.

*Bad Points*

Because capital cannot be continually used up, *it is a poor measure of product available in the long run.*

**Figure 5–3.** Relation of GNP to other income concepts—1964.

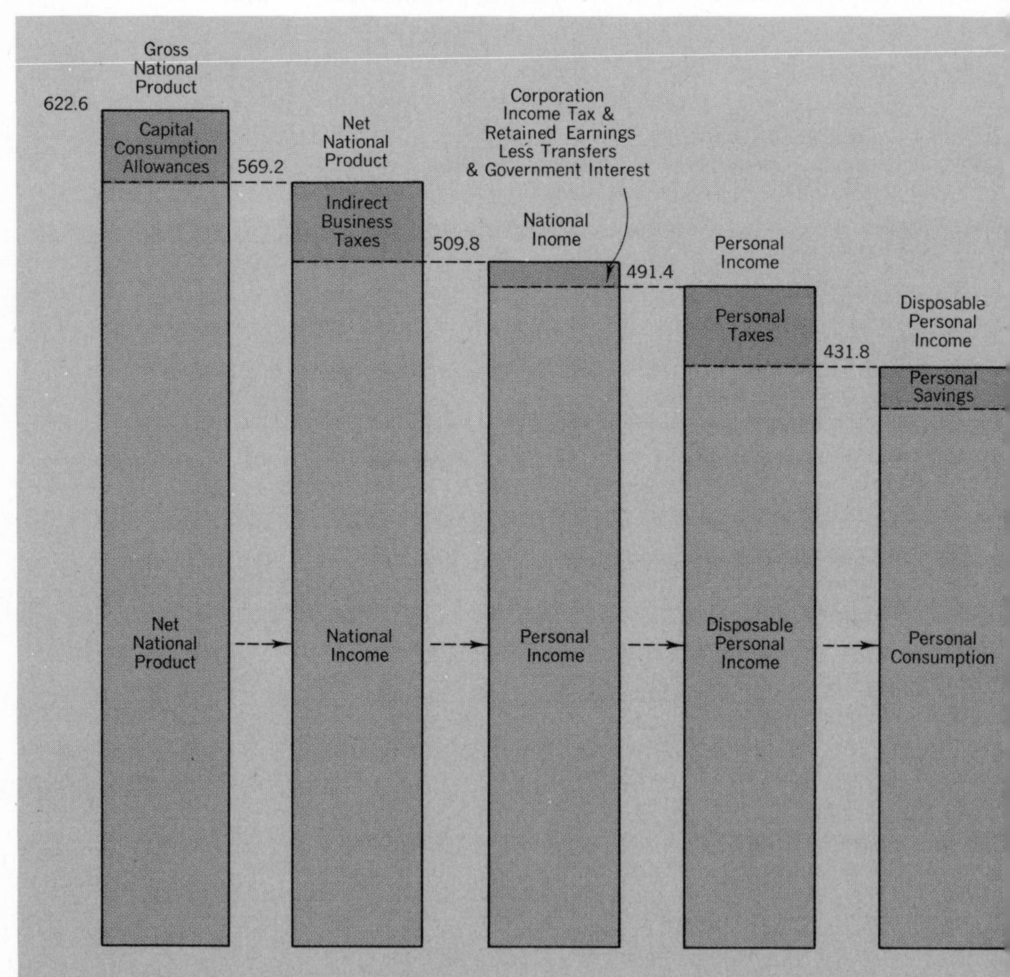

*Net National Product*

*Good Points*

*Measures total flow of output available in the long run.* One of the best bases for estimating overall productive power.

*Bad Points*

1. *Fails to measure factor income,* because it includes indirect business taxes.
2. If factor cost is the measure of what output is worth, *NNP* is the wrong measure; it includes an element, indirect business taxes, that does not represent factor cost and so exceeds factor cost of output.

*National Income*

*Good Points*

1. *Measures factor incomes*—wages, interest, rent, and profit.
2. *Provides a factor cost measure of the flow of product.*

*Bad Points*

Fails to measure what people can and do actually spend.

*Personal Income*

A transitional measure.

*Disposable Personal Income*

*Good Points*

*Provides a basis for estimating consumption and saving.*

*Bad Points*

Neglects the role played by corporations and government in the income flow.

# CHAPTER 6

## Income Determination, Basic Concepts

As we examine recent history one fact reveals itself rather clearly: our economy does not always provide the highest possible level of output. During the decade 1931–40, unemployment ranged from 14 to 25 per cent. To interpret these figures it is necessary to keep in mind that workers are constantly changing jobs. Such movement implies that at least 3 or 4 per cent of the labor force will be unemployed, if a healthy mobility is to be preserved. Adjusting for this circumstance, we find that unavoidable, persistent unemployment of 10 to 21 per cent prevailed for the decade mentioned. During the same period this country experienced a shocking loss in production: real *GNP* fell 44 per cent between 1929 and 1933. Furthermore, output did not reach the 1929 peak until 1941. More than a decade of stagnation occurred.

In other periods our economy has been marked by relatively full employment. During the 12-year period 1946–57, unemployment stayed below 6 per cent at all times. Deflated *GNP* grew or remained steady in each successive year but one, 1954, and the following year was marked by a sharp rise in output. At the same time the price level rose or remained steady in each year of the period. This behavior affords a contrast with the comparatively steady price level prevailing between 1931 and 1940.

This contrasting behavior of the economy raises a question. Is the performance of the economy susceptible to explanation? Fortunately, as a result of pioneering work by a good many economists we can answer yes. One of the pioneers in this area of economic thought was an English economist, John Maynard Keynes. Working with the concept of national inome, he developed the notion of an aggregate equilibrium of the economy. In such an equilibrium the various forces operating combine to determine a given level of national income. Such an idea contributed a great deal to the understanding of how the economy operates. Most of the remainder of this chapter will be devoted to a discussion of this idea.

## THE NOTION OF EQUILIBRIUM

In an earlier section we encountered the idea that supply and demand tend to reach an equilibrium. Such an equilibrium is a state of balance in which the quantity supplied is exactly equal to quantity demanded. Now we are ready to extend this idea to the realm of total output. Let us say that the economy is in aggregate equilibrium when the aggregate quantity of goods supplied is exactly equal to the aggregate quantity demanded. If this definition is to hold up, suitable definitions for *aggregate supply and aggregate demand* must be found. Let us identify aggregate supply with the lower loop of the circular flow, and give the following definition. *Aggregate supply is the sum of money whose receipt insures continuation of the given level of output.* Also we may identify aggregate demand with the upper loop. *Aggregate demand is the sum of money that buyers are willing to spend for the given level of output.*

Recalling the discussion of national income measurement we may interpret these definitions in terms of *NNP*. Thus lower-loop *NNP* represents the sum of factor costs and indirect taxes; payment of these elements is necessary if factors are to be hired, the government paid off, and output thereby maintained. Such a sum of money can be regarded both as cost of output and income. Consequently, lower-loop *NNP* is a cost measure of aggregate supply. Keep in mind that the sum of money is related to physical output, being a money measure of it. Therefore we take lower-loop *NNP* as a measure of output expressed in terms of money.

**Equilibrium.** Aggregate demand is identified with upper-loop *NNP,* total expenditure on output. When total expenditure on output just equals cost of output—upper-loop *NNP* equals lower-loop *NNP,* or aggregate supply equals aggregate demand—equilibrium prevails and output remains steady. Before examining this question more deeply let us consider the elements making up aggregate demand.

## CONSUMPTION

Most important of the components of expenditure is consumption. Consider the size of the elements entering into *NNP* in 1964 as shown in Table 6–1. We observe that consumption amounted to more than

70 per cent of *NNP* in 1964, with government purchases running a poor second, at about 23 per cent. Because this is a study of aggregates, we are not going to be concerned with a breakdown of consumption expenditure into parts.

**The Consumption Function.** In 1936, in his work *The General Theory of Employment, Interest, and Money,* J. M. Keynes advanced the hypothesis that consumption spending was a function of national income, or *NNP*. To be more direct, he said that the level of consumption depends on *NNP;* there is a schedule or curve relating consumption to the level of *NNP*. By the present time a substantial

**TABLE 6–1**
**Composition of *NNP* for U.S. in 1964 (Preliminary Figures)**

| | Consumption | Net Private Domestic Investment | Net Foreign Investment | Government Purchases | *NNP* |
|---|---|---|---|---|---|
| Amount (billions of dollars) | 399.3 | 34.4 | 7.0 | 128.6 | 569.3 |
| Per cent | 70.14 | 6.04 | 1.23 | 22.59 | 100.0 |

body of knowledge has been brought to bear on this subject. It tends to verify the assertion made by Keynes, and we are justified in taking this as an accepted fact.

**Some Evidence.** Suppose we consider the period 1953–64; it is dangerous to take too long a period, because economic conditions may change generally. As we indicated in the chapter covering national income concepts, *Disposable Personal Income* (*DPI*), which gives the public's take-home pay, is the one most closely related to consumption. Plotting consumption against *DPI* (both adjusted or deflated for price change), we get a set of 12 points in Figure 6–1, each representing the consumption-income combination for a given year. We then draw a line freehand through the middle of the points. We see that such a line represents extremely well the general tendency of the points. Therefore, we may assume that this or some very similar line represents a relationship between deflated consumption and deflated Disposable Personal Income.

## BACKGROUND FACTORS AFFECTING CONSUMPTION

Such evidence as we have just given reinforces our belief in the existence of a consumption function; consumption variations appear to be explained almost entirely by income changes in the 1953–63

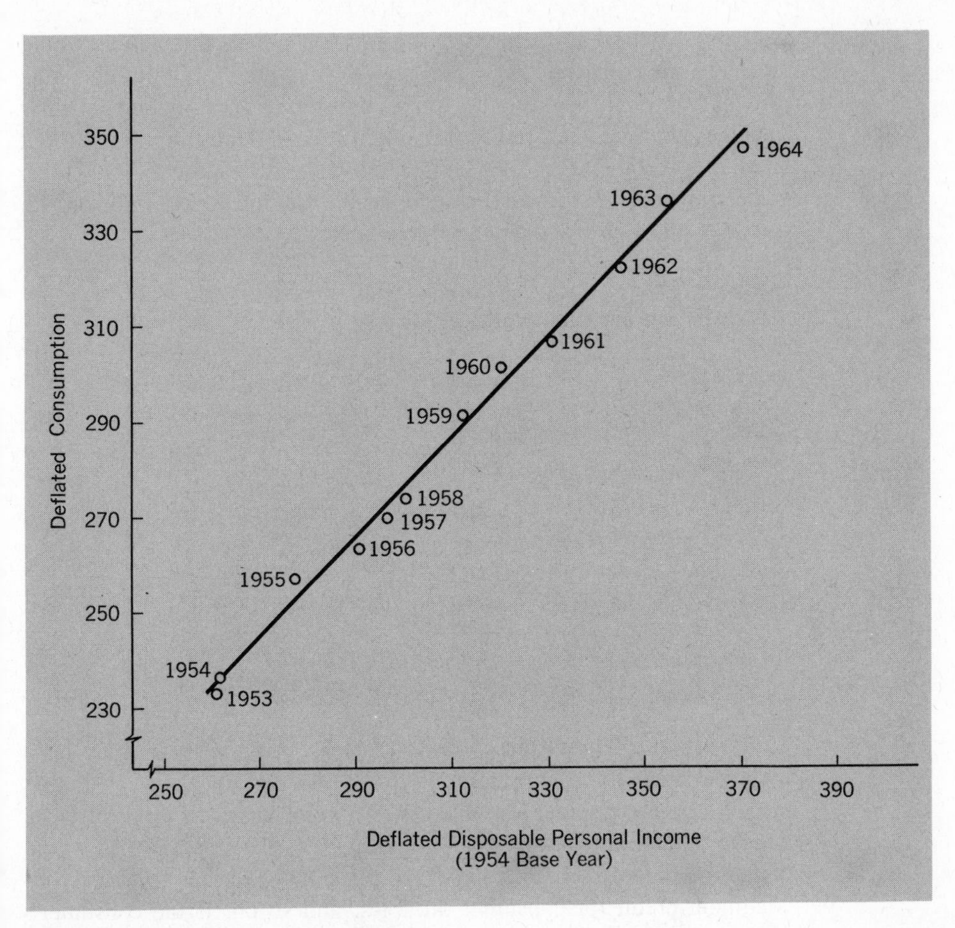


**Figure 6–1.** Consumption line—1953–64.

period. However, it is clear that there are a number of factors that ought to exert some influence on consumption. Some of these may be in the nature of constants, whereas others may change over time.

**Distribution of Income.** The evidence tends to indicate that as individuals move into higher income brackets, they consume a considerably smaller fraction of *DPI* and save a larger fraction. A survey conducted in 1956–57 by the Bureau of Labor Statistics showed that at an income of about $4,400 the typical family consumed virtually its entire income. On the other hand, a household earning $13,300 a year consumed only 77 per cent of its income. Lastly, we note that at incomes below $4,400 families apparently consumed more than their incomes. Suppose that something happens to change the distribution of a *given* income in favor of the lower incomes. Perhaps the government plugs a number of tax loopholes for the rich and cuts income tax rates in the lower brackets. In effect, this action would take income from the "rich" and give to the "poor" without changing the income level. Because the "poor" consume larger fractions of their incomes than do the "rich," this ought to raise consumption without changing income. Thus, the consumption line of Figure 6–1 ought to shift upward. The reverse should hold true for a redistribution in favor of the rich by reversing this process.

**TABLE 6-2**
**Family Income and Consumption, 1950**

| Average Income (dollars) | Average Consumption (dollars) | Per Cent of Income Consumed |
|---|---|---|
| 651 | 1,683 | 258.5 |
| 1,629 | 1,924 | 118.1 |
| 2,564 | 2,795 | 109.0 |
| 3,487 | 3,573 | 102.5 |
| 4,454 | 4,408 | 99.0 |
| 5,434 | 5,262 | 96.8 |
| 6,603 | 6,187 | 93.7 |
| 8,394 | 7,161 | 85.3 |
| 13,292 | 10,342 | 77.8 |

**Assets and Liabilities of Consumers.** If we were to draw up a balance sheet for a consumer, it would list certain assets: a house, a car, other consumer durables; such financial assets as insurance, stocks and bonds, and a bank account. On the other side it would list some debts, such as a mortgage on a house, notes for a car, installment credit for consumer durables, and so on. If the consumer's assets are a good bit larger than his liabilities, so that his net worth is large, he is in good shape. If his assets consist largely of cash or items quickly convertible into cash, he is in a still better situation. At least he is in a position to expand his purchases at his own pleasure.

During World War II the public acquired $45 billion in United States Savings Bonds. These can readily be converted into cash at the nearest bank. Consequently, they constitute a very liquid asset. With such a liquid asset almost burning a hole in the public's pockets it is not surprising that postwar consumption exceeded the predicted level. By this we mean that extension of prewar trends based on the change in income alone did not account for the postwar consumption boom. No doubt possession of these assets contributed at once to the boom and the error in forecasting.

**Prices.** Some economists claim that the absolute level of prices exerts an influence on consumer spending. They argue that very low prices will imply a high purchasing power of the individual's bank account. With a large *effective* bank account the individual would be prompted (as in the case of the possessors of savings bonds) to increase consumption. However, prices are sticky; in the great depression following 1929 they fell little more than 20 per cent. Consequently, we cannot expect a significant influence from this source.

Let us consider instead the influence of a given rate of price increase—of inflation—on consumption. Such a discussion has relevance because consumer prices have risen by 1.5 per cent or more in 13 of the last 20 years. In nine of the 15 postwar years the same has been true. What effect does such inflation have on consumption spending?

It is not possible to state wtih any assurance the effect of inflation on consumption. However, it probably increases consumption for a number of reasons. First, it lowers the effective rate of interest unless the money rate is raised. People may borrow money in order to consume; later they may pay off the loan in depreciated money. Second, rising prices cause the values of some consumer assets to increase; among these are houses, land, and securities. Such increases may be of the purely nominal variety that result from inflation. However, people are quick to recognize the increased value of their own assets and slow to identify a rise in the general price level. Consequently, the inflation creates a feeling of having gained owing to this *money illusion,* or failure to recognize the rise in the general price level. Third, holding liquid assets such as a bank balance now involves a double loss—the failure to collect interest and the fall in the purchasing power of money as prices rise. Consequently, people are less prone to hold cash, and may decide instead to consume.

**Population.** Among factors leading to consumption, increased population growth is one of the more obvious. When a new child arrives, it simply must be fed, clothed, housed, and educated. Even though income remains the same, heavy pressure exists to expand consumption. Now one of the more striking phenomena of the postwar world has been the acceleration of population growth, and the continuance of growth at a high rate. As long as this condition prevails, consumption out of a given income should be high.

**Interest.** It used to be thought that a high interest rate would induce income recipients to postpone consumption and to save instead. Interest was thought to be a payment necessary for the reduction of consumption and encouragement of saving. Nowadays this view is at a discount. Few economists attribute a significant direct influence of interest rates on consumption.

**Social Attitudes Toward Consumption.** In some societies a favorable attitude exists to high-level consumption; in others, saving is encouraged, which implies low consumption. During the nineteenth century the prevailing social view favored thrift and relatively low consumption. Today the social attitude strongly favors high consumption—a man is judged in large part by his material possessions:

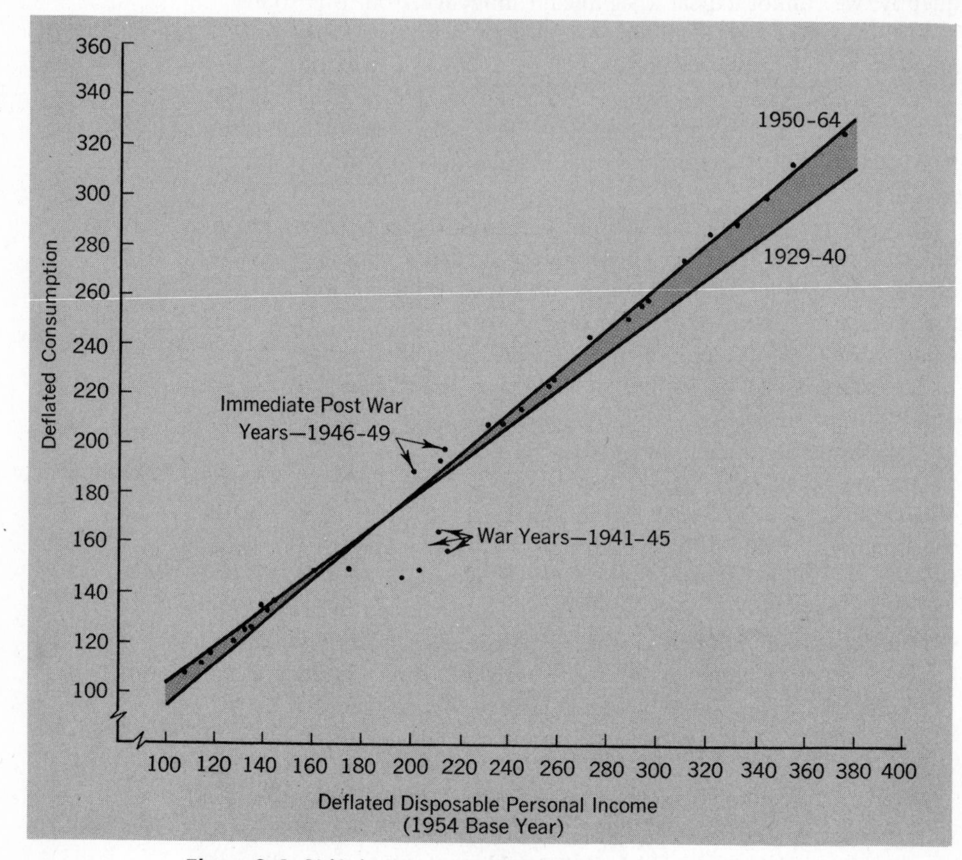


**Figure 6–2.** Shift in the consumption line.

his house, car, boat, appliances, and other good things of life. It is doubtful that such an attitude can undergo rapid change.

## SHIFTS IN THE CONSUMPTION FUNCTION

The relation between consumption and *DPI* will undergo change if and when one of the background factors changes significantly. Consider the situation as it existed in 1940. At that time only the data for

1929–40 was available. Based on the deflated data for these years it is possible to find a consumption line. In Figure 6–2 the consumption-*DPI* data is plotted for the years 1929 through 1964. The 1929–40 and the 1950–64 points are indicated simply by dots, the other points by arrows also. Drawing a line freehand to fit the 1929–40 data, we see the situation as it appeared immediately prior to World War II. The extension of this line to higher values of income (always a dangerous procedure) is also shown.

During the war consumption values were depressed by lack of availability of goods, especially durables, and the patriotic pressure to save and "invest" in government bonds. Consequently, the war data were clearly unusable as a guide to consumption at higher incomes and under changed conditions. In forecasting postwar economic conditions some investigators made use of such a line as the one we have given for the 1929–40 period. Its extension falls well below the postwar data, as inspection shows. At any rate investigators following this procedure were led to predict serious postwar unemployment. Of course, this prediction proved to be quite inaccurate, employment having maintained a high level for a dozen years after the war. Yet the original line fitted the data available very closely.

Comparing the 1929–40 line with a freehand line related to 1950–64 data, we see that the latter is both higher and steeper. At current income levels consumption out of a given income is greater, and consumption out of any *extra* income is also greater. Clearly, the consumption behavior of the economy varies due to changes in underlying conditions, and here is an example. Because we have omitted the experience of 1946–49 right after the war, we cannot attribute the change to pent-up demand. Surely that tendency largely exhausted itself in this four-year period.

Perhaps higher consumption is the result of (1) rising population, (2) the increased capital assets of consumers, especially savings bonds, and (3) an almost uninterrupted inflation and its tendency to raise spending. In any event these or other background factors were surely operating to change consumption patterns.

## CONSUMPTION AND *NNP*

It is more convenient to relate consumption to *NNP* than to *DPI* in later discussion. We may regard the relation of *DPI* to consumption as the basic behavior pattern. In addition, however, the relation between *DPI* and *NNP* may change; if this happens the relation between consumption and *NNP* will vary. Consider how this may occur.

## TAXES, TRANSFERS, AND THE RELATION OF CONSUMPTION TO *NNP*

**Corporation Income Taxes.** About half (50 per cent) of all corporate income in good times is absorbed by Federal tax. If this rate were to be decreased, more net profit would be left to the corporation. Insofar as the corporation pays out extra dividends from profit, *DPI* would thereby be increased. In turn, consumption would increase. Thus a cut in the corporation income tax might increase consumption out of a given *NNP*.

**Government Transfer Payments.** These items are not included in *NNP*. A large increase in transfers with no change in *NNP* would result in an increase in *DPI* and thereby in consumption. If interest rates on government bonds rise, *DPI* would again be increased with no change in *NNP*, and consumption would increase.

**Personal Income Taxes.** An increase in the tax rate would lower *DPI* out of a given *NNP*. In turn, this would lower consumption out of the given level of *NNP*.

**Disposition of Corporate Income.** In good times, when earning substantial profits, corporations may pay out 40 to 60 per cent of

**Figure 6–3.** Consumption related to *NNP* (billons of current dollars), 1929–64.

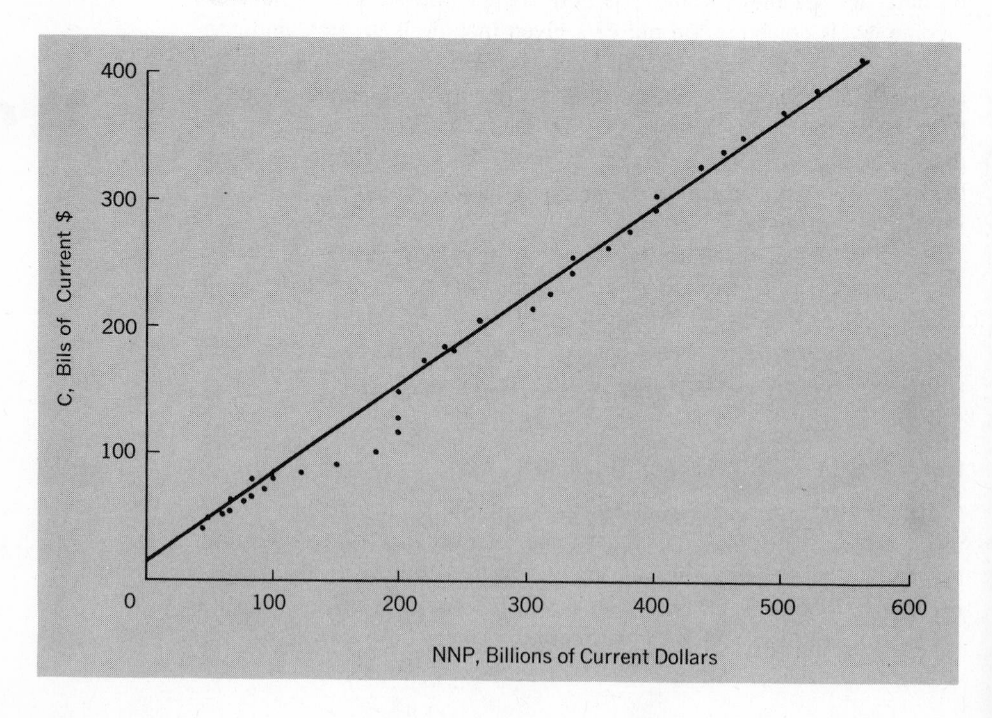

their net profits after taxes. During the depression of 1930–38 when net profits were quite low, dividends exceeded net profits. If a change in this pattern should occur, it would alter the relation of *DPI* to *NNP*. Paying out all corporate earnings in good times would have the effect of increasing *DPI* about 3 per cent; the reverse would be true, approximately, if none were paid. In turn, these changes would affect the relation of consumption to *NNP*.

The effect of relating consumption to *NNP* instead of to Disposable Personal Income is to flatten out the curve considerably. In Figure 6–3 we have plotted consumption against *NNP*, both being given in current dollars—that is, not adjusted for price change. Then a straight line that seemed to fit the points was drawn by commonsense; or rather, the closest convenient line was drawn that could be embodied in a simple numerical table. This is actually the basis for the information in Table 6–3. It also serves as the model for all the standard consumption lines and tables given later.

**Consumption and *NNP*.** Let us now write down an imaginary consumption–*NNP* table.

**TABLE 6-3***
**Relation of C and *NNP***

| *NNP* | C | *NNP* − C = S + T |
|---|---|---|
| 0 | 15 | −15 |
| 60 | 55 | 5 |
| 120 | 95 | 25 |
| 180 | 135 | 45 |
| 240 | 175 | 65 |
| 300 | 215 | 85 |
| 360 | 255 | 105 |
| 420 | 295 | 125 |
| 480 | 335 | 145 |

* This table is an idealization of the experience of the American economy since 1929. It corresponds to the solid line in Figure 6–3, which fits fairly well the actual data shown by dots.

We have also calculated a column entitled $S+T$, or saving plus taxes. The "saving" includes individual and corporate saving, the latter being retained corporate earnings. The "taxes" refer to the excess of indirect taxes, corporation income taxes, personal taxes, and social security taxes over transfers including interest on government bonds.

In the upper part of Figure 6–4 we have plotted consumption on the vertical axis against *NNP* on the horizontal axis, using the figures of Table 6–3. In order to interpret this line we need to note several

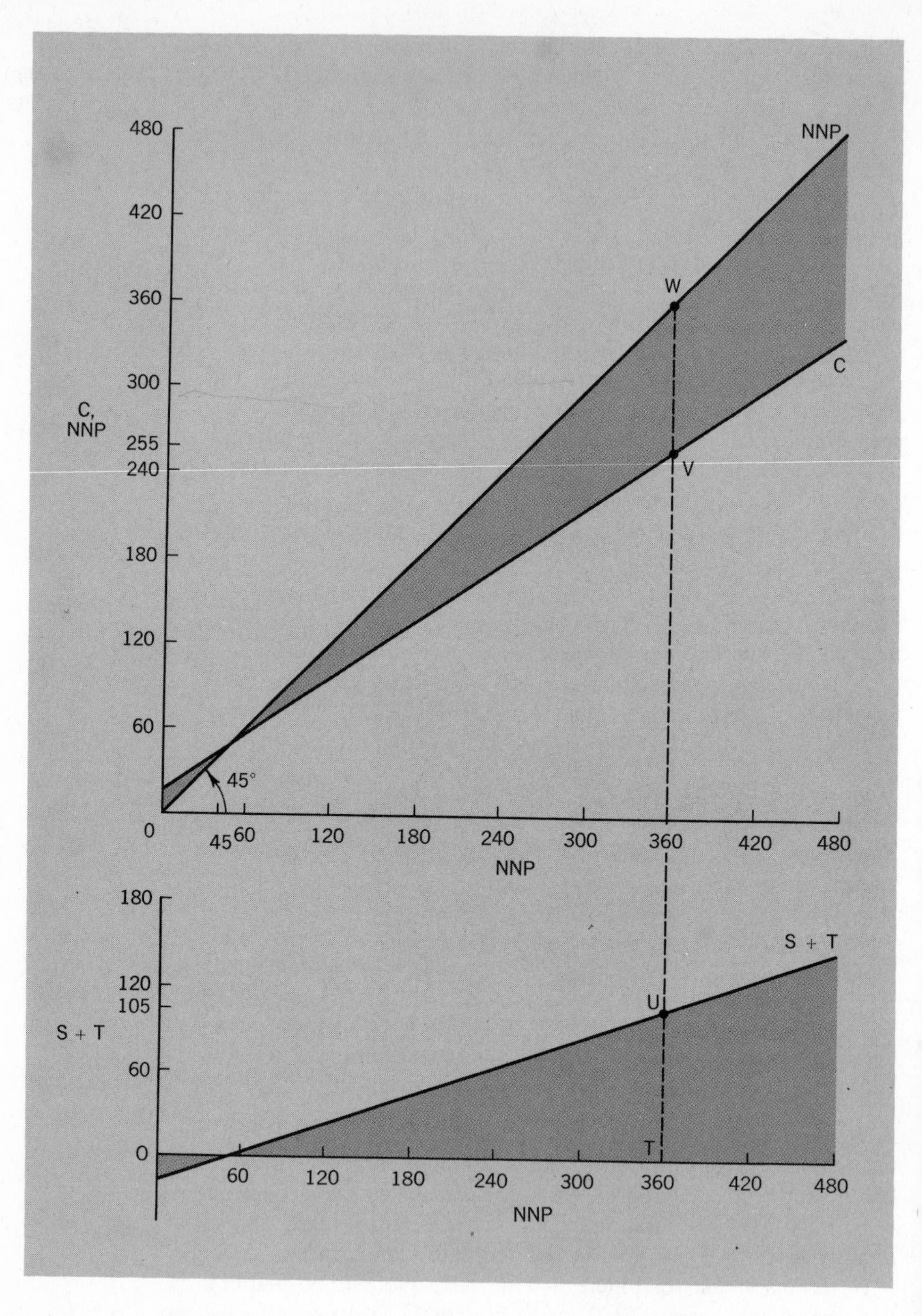


**Figure 6–4.** Consumption and saving plus taxes in relation to *NNP*.

further points. First, *NNP* consists of three parts: consumption, saving, and taxes (less transfers). For analytical purposes it is handy to divide the allocation of *NNP* into (1) consumption spending, and (2) the drains from the income flow not spent on output, namely saving and taxes (less transfers). Because *NNP* = consumption plus saving plus taxes (less transfers), we may write an allocation equation for *NNP*: $NNP = C + S + T$, where obvious abbreviations are used. In general, the drains—*S* and *T*—are grouped together.

As we examine the data in Table 6–3 we see that consumption exceeds *NNP* at very low levels of *NNP*, so that saving and taxes are negative. As *NNP* increases, a point is soon reached at which *NNP* exceeds consumption, so that a margin is left for saving and taxes. If we had the *C* line alone in the upper part of Figure 6–4, it would be difficult to judge the relation between *C* and *NNP* from the diagram alone. It would be convenient to be able to measure *NNP* vertically and thereby to compare it directly with *C* along the vertical axis. To do so we plot *NNP* values *against themselves*. Referring to Table 6–3 we plot 60 along the vertical axis against 60 on the horizontal, 120 against 120, and so forth. This process generates a line passing through the origin and making a 45-degree angle with the *NNP* (horizontal) axis. We label this the *NNP* line, because any point on the line yields the same numerical value on the vertical axis that it does on the *NNP* axis. Point *W* defines a value of 360 along the vertical axis as well as the *NNP* value it defines for the horizontal axis. *Thus the NNP line gives a measure of NNP along the vertical axis.*

With this measure of *NNP* along the vertical axis we can compare *C* and *NNP*. Note first that the vertical distance from the *NNP* axis to the *C* line represents consumption. For example, at $360 income consumption is $255. Then the vertical distance from the consumption line to the *NNP* line, $VW = \$105$, is saving and taxes. In virtue of the allocation equation

$$NNP - C = S + T, \tag{1}$$

or the part of *NNP* not allocated to consumption is devoted to saving and taxes. In the diagram this difference is the vertical distance *VW* between the *NNP* and *C* lines at *W* and *V*, respectively. The saving and taxes element is shaded to mark it off from consumption. Note that when *NNP* recedes below 45, saving and taxes are negative; the public consumes more than *NNP*. At incomes above 45, *NNP* rises above consumption.

Immediately below this figure we have plotted the $S + T$ line against *NNP*. Note that the shaded areas in the two diagrams correspond exactly. The only difference is that the base for saving and taxes is now the *NNP* axis instead of the *C* line, as in the upper diagram. Note that $TU = VW = \$105 = S + T$ at an *NNP* of $360. For certain purposes the $S + T$ line alone is useful.

## INVESTMENT

Let us now consider the second component of total spending, investment. This consists of two parts: (1) private domestic investment, and (2) net foreign investment, the excess of exports over imports. The second category is numerically small, and we will not devote consideration to it at this juncture. Let us consider mainly the private domestic investment. In the Department of Commerce data, this figure is given gross—that is, it includes expenditure on capital goods that simply replace those used up during the current year. To find the net figure we must subtract the figures on "capital consumption allowances" from the gross figure.

It would be helpful if investment were a function of *NNP* in the same way we have found to be true for consumption. Let us try out a little data to see how this hypothesis holds up. Our choice of data is governed by what is available. In Figure 6–5 we have plotted deflated gross private domestic investment against deflated *GNP* (net figures deflated are not available). The period chosen corresponds in time with the consumption data used earlier. Do we find here a neat pattern of points suggesting a simple straight-line relationship? Well, not exactly. There is some evidence of an upward trend in both investment and *GNP* through time. Thus we have drawn freehand a line rather closely fitting the dots for 1953, 1954, 1960, 1962, 1963, and 1964. In short, the line drawn represents a trend to which these six years conform fairly well.

There is another side to the picture, however. For the period 1951–61, the 11 dots divide themselves into two groups, representing, respectively, high investment and low investment. In the years 1952, 1953, 1954, and 1958 investment was "low," being scattered around a level just under $50 billion ($49.75 billion in the figure). In the other seven years of the 11-year period investment was "high," the dots being scattered around a level of $60 billion. This suggests that the level of investment is not closely related to *GNP* in a short period of time; instead, investment appears to depend on forces *other than GNP*. (Note that the upward trend asserted itself in the period 1962–64.)

Let us summarize this discussion by noting first that there seems to be an upward trend. However, within a limited period of time, such as a decade, the trend seems to be of minor importance. The important fact seems to be that investment changes independently of *GNP*.

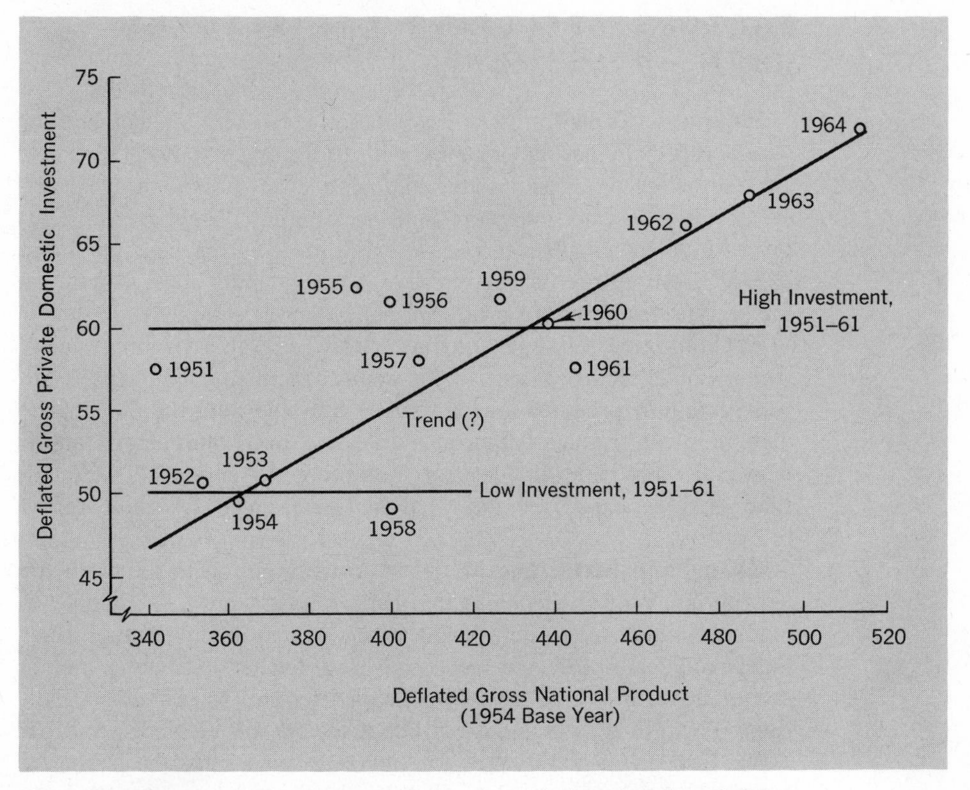


**Figure 6–5.** Relation between gross private domestic investment and Gross National Product, deflated, 1951–64.

In short, we cannot comfortably rely on a close relationship between investment and *GNP*.

## FACTORS DETERMINING INVESTMENT

Disappointed in our quest for a simple relation of investment to *NNP*, we turn to other factors affecting investment. Consider first the basic motivation for purchasing capital goods. When a businessman acquires capital, he does so in the expectation of receiving thereby a stream of future returns. Such returns must serve to provide a reserve for depreciation over the life of the machine and to pay interest on the invested capital. Of these two elements, the set of returns and the costs offset thereby, the returns are more uncertain, dynamic, and therefore more important. What are the factors making for a favorable relation of expected returns to costs? Clearly, the basic factor required is the anticipation of a growing set of future returns from capital.

## FACTORS AFFECTING THE RETURNS FROM INVESTMENT

**Population Growth.** When population is growing, the demand for goods, especially consumer items, will also grow. The need for food, clothing, shelter, consumer durables, and even automobiles will increase. At the same time more housing is required. Altogether, it requires little imagination to see that this involves the need for more capital goods to produce the desired output. Under these conditions the returns from capital producing such output should grow.

**Technological Change and Innovation.** In an expanding society technological change is one of the central factors. If innovations are providing new products that are more desirable than the old, if new machines can produce output at a unit cost lower than before, and if new and more efficient ways of marketing the product are found, then invested capital should yield an increasingly favorable set of returns.

**Changes in Tastes and Social Attitudes.** In order to permit the appropriate growth of demand, consumer tastes must be capable of continuous change. As new products become feasible, consumer tastes must evolve so as to make such goods desirable. If a society is unduly conservative, it will be unable to adapt its tastes to changing conditions. Then the growth and evolution of society will be hindered. What would have happened by now to American society had the public refused to accept automobiles? Clearly, this would have thwarted the revolution in our transportation system wrought by the automobile.

In addition to the growth factors that spark the rise in future returns there are factors that play a general background role.

**Business Psychology.** First, there is the general frame of mind of businessmen—their optimism or pessimism concerning the outcome of business ventures. In the decade of the thirties the anticipations were generally pessimistic; large returns from investment were not expected, and great ventures were therefore not attempted. On the contrary the postwar decade, 1946–55, was marked generally by optimism; businessmen felt they could make profits and did not hesitate to invest their money. In the prewar period investment was quite low; in the postwar, it boomed.

Second, there is the social attitude toward business. If the social attitude toward profit making is unfavorable, businessmen will be prone to hold back on investment. Such was the case, apparently, in the nineteen thirties, when the New Deal reform legislation was being enacted. In the postwar decade the atmosphere has been far more favorable. This has doubtless contributed to the rapid investment of capital that has been occurring.

**Government and Business.** Perhaps the most obvious influence of government is through the taxation of returns. To the extent that government taxes the returns from capital it thereby holds down the incentive to invest.

If private business feels that government is seeking an expansion of its role as producer, that it will socialize many aspects of production, then it will be reluctant to invest in the face of such an attitude toward business. On the other hand, if business feels that government will "invest" in ways complementary to private enterprise, investment is stimulated correspondingly. Thus the anticipation that government plans to expand the system of public roads or other utilities helpful to business will encourage expansion.

**Summary of Factors Affecting Returns from Investment.** The returns from investment depend on general forces making for growth, on business psychology, and on the relation of business to government. A change in any one of these factors could cause a change in expected returns from capital that might alter investment decisions.

## FACTORS AFFECTING THE COST OF INVESTMENT

**The Interest Rate.** In deciding whether or not to invest, the businessman is going to weigh expected returns against costs of capital. If interest rates are low, capital costs will also be low and investment will be encouraged. Of course, the reverse is true with high interest rates.

**Cost of Capital and Depreciation.** Factors tending to extend the life of machinery or to lower its cost will reduce depreciation. Such factors might include technological improvements in the machine itself or tax provisions more favorable to writing off machinery and other capital.

Both of the above *cost* factors enter into decisions to invest. Being somewhat less dynamic, generally, than those pertaining to the expected *returns,* they necessarily play a somewhat subsidiary role. Actually, we stress here the changes in expectations concerning future returns that cause corresponding changes in the level of investment. Let us treat investment for the time being as *autonomous,* or self-governing, and not dependent on the current level of national income. However, it may alter in response to changes in expectations concerning the relation of returns to costs. For these reasons we picture investment in the way shown in Figure 6–6, as a horizontal line parallel to the *NNP* curve—not changing with *NNP* but capable of shifting downward, as shown, or upward in response to changes in expectations.

## GOVERNMENT SPENDING ON OUTPUT

Broadly speaking, government spending is undertaken to provide services required by the public. Profit expectations do not guide the plans for spending, and such spending is not, therefore, subject to fluctuation from this source. In fact, we shall regard government spending as a constant. It is regarded not merely as independent of income but of those outside dynamic factors causing fluctuations in the level of investment.

## INCOME DETERMINATION

We are now in a position to ask how the level of *NNP* is determined. Does this magnitude tend toward some definite value, or is it a random variable like rainfall? As our basic framework for this analysis we take the concepts of supply and demand in an aggregate sense. Let us think of aggregate supply as the sum of money that will cover exactly the cost of output. Now, of course, any sum of money will cover the cost of *some* output. So we mean to associate the supply with a sum of money costs and a corresponding level of output. In speak-

**Figure 6–6.** Investment patterns suggested by Figure 6–5.

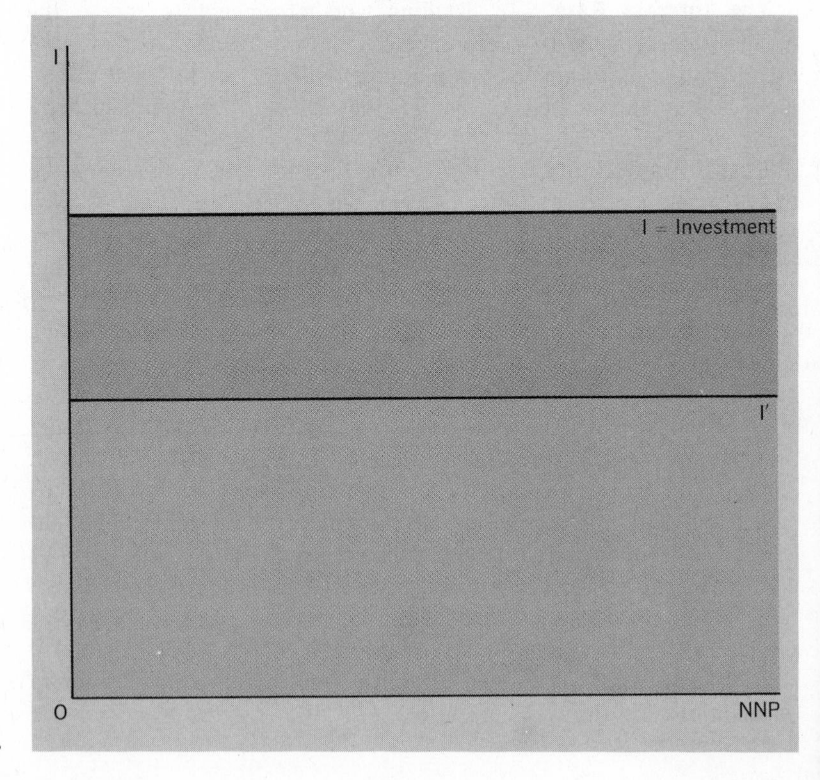

ing of supply, then, we refer to the sum of costs that will motivate the production of a given level of output.

By aggregate demand we mean the sum of money spent on the given level of output with its corresponding level of costs. Thus every level of costs of output (supply) entails some corresponding level of aggregate demand or expenditure on output. Now the level of expenditure generated by a given level of costs is not necessarily equal to the costs; demand is not always equal to supply, and therein lies a story.

Recall our concept of the circular flow. The upper loop represents expenditure on output—consumption plus investment plus government spending—and the lower loop represents the cost of the corresponding output. If the expenditure on output exceeds the cost of output, demand exceeds supply, and supply or cost of output will expand. Production will increase, more factors will be hired, and income increases. As a result income recipients will have more money to spend, and expenditure on output (demand) will rise. Evidently, an excess of demand, upper-loop *NNP,* over supply, lower-loop *NNP,* will cause a speed-up in the circular flow. Now consider certain details.

## GRAPHIC REPRESENTATION OF EQUILIBRIUM LEVEL OF INCOME

**Aggregate Demand.** As explained earlier, demand consists of three elements: consumption ($C$), net investment ($I$), including net foreign investment, and government spending on output ($G$).[1] Adding these three we arrive at total demand, which may be expressed by the equation

$$\text{Aggregate demand} = \text{upper-loop } NNP = C + I + G.$$

Now we have assumed that $I$ and $G$ are independent of *NNP* but that $C$ varies with *NNP*. To represent this graphically in Figure 6–7 we superimpose on the $C$ line of Figure 6–4 an $I$ of 40 and a $G$ of 85. Thus the $C + I$ line gives the variable amount of consumption spending plus a constant investment of 40. In turn, a constant amount of government spending on output of 85 is superimposed onto both of these elements, giving the $C + I + G$ line. This gives aggregate demand or total spending on output or upper-loop *NNP,* call it by any one of the three, at any corresponding level of income (cost of output, lower-loop *NNP*).

**Aggregate Supply.** As previously defined, this is the sum of money that exactly motivates the production of the current level of

[1] In a later chapter foreign trade and investment will come in for special consideration.

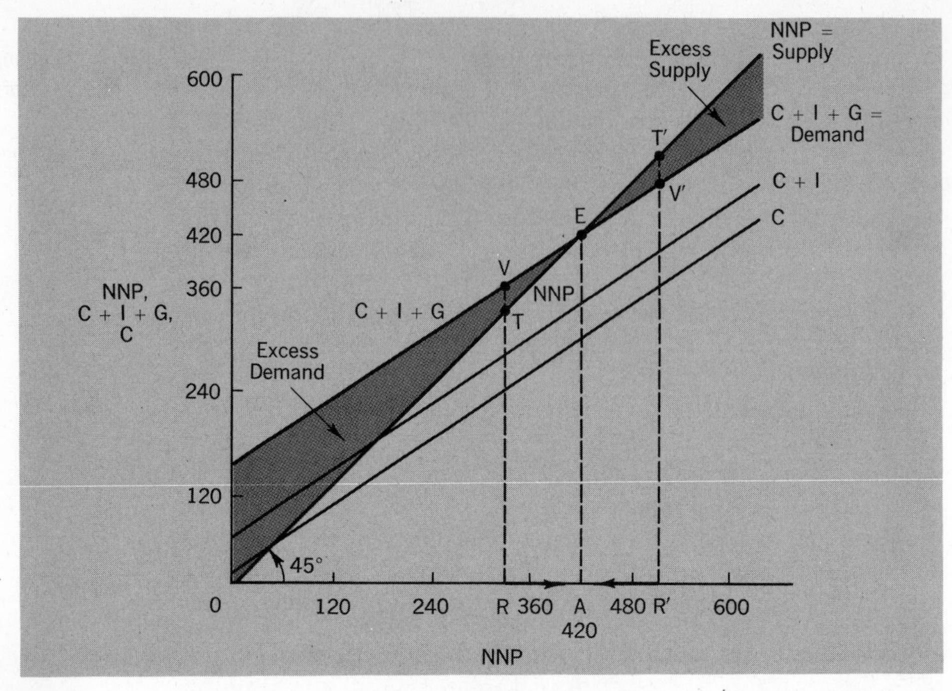


**Figure 6–7.** Determination of *NNP* by demand, C + I + G, and supply (lower-loop), *NNP*.

output. In short, this is the cost of output, or lower-loop *NNP,* or simply income. For the sake of simplicity we now adopt a basic usage. We shall refer to lower-loop *NNP* simply as *NNP,* and upper-loop *NNP* as $C+I+G$, or total spending.

Because we are measuring (lower-loop) *NNP* along the horizontal axis, we need to find a way to compare it with total spending. As before, we use a 45-degree line, labeled *NNP* = Supply, to effect the comparison.

From a simple economic viewpoint the point of equilibrium or balance is one at which supply equals demand. In the figure, a point of equality is found at point *E* where the *NNP* = Supply line intersects the $C+I+G$ = Demand line. At the *E* point the Demand = $C+I+G$ amounts to *AE,* or 420. At the same time *NNP* = Supply amounts to $OA = AE$, or 420. This implies that the receipt of 420 in *NNP* (income) suffices to generate a demand of 420. This demand represents a sum of money that just suffices to cover the incomes (costs) necessary to provide that level of output. Equilibrium then exists, because the output is just taken from the market in a transaction precisely satisfactory to both sides, buyers and sellers. We can illustrate this process also by Table 6–4, which is simply Table 6–3

**TABLE 6-4**
**Income Determination**

| | Excess Demand | Supply—Cost of Output | Consumption | Drain from Income Stream | Injections in Income Stream | Demand (Expenditure on Output) | Behavior of *NNP* |
|---|---|---|---|---|---|---|---|
| | $(C + I + G) - NNP$ | $NNP$ | $C$ | $S + T$ | $I + G$ * | $C + I + G$ | |
| | 140 | 0 | 15 | −15 | 125 | 140 | Grows |
| | 120 | 60 | 55 | 5 | 125 | 180 | Grows |
| | 100 | 120 | 95 | 25 | 125 | 220 | Grows |
| | 80 | 180 | 135 | 45 | 125 | 260 | Grows |
| | 60 | 240 | 175 | 65 | 125 | 300 | Grows |
| | 40 | 300 | 215 | 85 | 125 | 340 | Grows |
| | 20 | 360 | 255 | 105 | 125 | 380 | Grows |
| | 0 | 420 | 295 | 125 | 125 | 420 | Equilibrium |
| Excess supply | −20 | 480 | 335 | 145 | 125 | 460 | Shrinks |
| | −40 | 540 | 375 | 165 | 125 | 500 | Shrinks |
| | −60 | 600 | 415 | 185 | 125 | 540 | Shrinks |

* $I = 40$, $G = 85$; each is constant for the period under consideration.

with some new columns. Note that only at an *NNP* of 420 is *NNP* equal to $C+I+G$, or aggregate supply equal to aggregate demand.

**Disequilibrium.** It is clear from both the table and diagram that there is only one point of equilibrium, and here supply equals demand. Good! But is there anything that requires *NNP* to move to the level of equilibrium? If not, the equilibrium point represents merely an ideal attained only by accident. If there is a tendency in the economy to move toward equilibrium, then we can speak of equilibrium *NNP* as the most likely value of *NNP*.

Suppose demand, $C+I+G$, exceeds the supply, *NNP*. Speaking in a simple manner, we may say that demand exceeds supply. Let us refer to the difference as *excess demand*. To the extent that excess demand exists, businessmen will find themselves under pressure to speed up production. They will have to fill orders from shrinking stocks and try to hire on more factors to meet the excess demand. As they hire more factors and increase output, *NNP* will increase. Therefore, *excess demand leads to increased NNP*.

We can reason more precisely, if necessary. An excess of $C+I+G$ over *NNP* implies that the public is willing to spend more on the current output level $(C+I+G)$ than is necessary to induce businessmen to produce this output, (lower-loop) *NNP*. Such a margin implies that it will be profitable for businessmen to increase output with a view to meeting the excess demand. In turn, this leads to an increased *NNP* as new factors are hired and production increased.

If demand falls short of supply, excess demand is negative and excess supply is present. With stocks piling up because they are unable to sell the current level of output, businessmen will cut back output, lay off factors, and reduce *NNP*. Thus, *excess supply leads to reduced NNP*. We can also interpret this more precisely along the lines of the preceding paragraph.

**Graphic Interpretation.** We can follow through this interpretation in Figure 6–7. At a level of *NNP* equal to $OA = AE$, or 420, demand $(C+I+G) =$ supply $(NNP)$. If this level of *NNP* exists, the market is cleared and no change in *NNP* will occur.

Suppose *NNP* happens to be at the lower level *OR*. At this point supply (*NNP*) is $OR = RT$, whereas demand $(C+I+G)$ is *RV*. Consequently, there is *excess demand* of *TV*. As we have explained, an excess demand prompts businessmen to expand *NNP* to meet demand. As this happens *NNP* increases from *OR* toward *OA*, as indicated on the *NNP* axis by an arrow.

In contrast, assume that *NNP* happens to be at a level above the equilibrium value, falling at $OR'$. Then supply (*NNP*) is $OR' = R'T'$, whereas demand $(C+I+G)$ is $R'V'$. Because $R'T'$ exceeds $R'V'$, supply ($NNP$) exceeds demand ($C+I+G$) in the amount $V'T'$. In short, an *excess supply* of $V'T'$ exists. Facing overproduction, businessmen begin to cut back production, lay off workers, and generally take actions that lead to a decline in $NNP$ (supply) from $OR'$ toward $OA$. This is indicated by an arrow on the base line from $R'$ extending toward $A$.

The conclusion to be drawn is simply that $NNP$ always gravitates toward the equilibrium value. If $NNP$ falls to the left of the value $OA$, excess demand exists, indicated by the shaded area between the $C+I+G$ and the $NNP$ lines. Then $NNP$ rises. If $NNP$ falls to the right of $OA$, excess supply exists and $NNP$ falls. Hence *NNP always tends to gravitate toward and remain at a level at which NNP equals* $C+I+G$.

## AN ALTERNATIVE INTERPRETATION OF EQUILIBRIUM—AN ASIDE

It is possible to look at this equilibrium in a slightly different way. Note that in equilibrium

$$NNP = C+I+G\,. \tag{2}$$

Subtracting $C$ from both sides we find that $NNP - C = I+G$. But we already know that lower-loop $NNP$ is allocated into three parts: consumption, saving, and taxes, so that $NNP = C+S+T$. Substituting this into the equation we get

$$S+T = I+G. \tag{3}$$

In words this says that equilibrium is marked by the equality of saving and taxes, on the one hand, and investment and government spending, on the other. The basic reasoning is exactly the same.

The truth of the correspondence between Equations (2) and (3) can be readily verified from Table 6–4. However, it is even easier to see the correspondence on a graph, as in Figure 6–8. In the following diagrams $S+T$ is shown as the vertical distance between $C$ and $NNP$. At the same time $I+G$ is shown as the vertical distance between $C$ and $C+I+G$. In the lower diagram $I+G$ and $S+T$ are plotted separately instead of as distances between $C$ and $C+I+G$, $C$ and $NNP$. In each case the height of $I+G$ just equals the height of $S+T$ at an income $OA$. Equilibrium of supply and demand implies that $S+T = I+G$, and representing this as the equilibrium simply stresses another aspect of the situation.

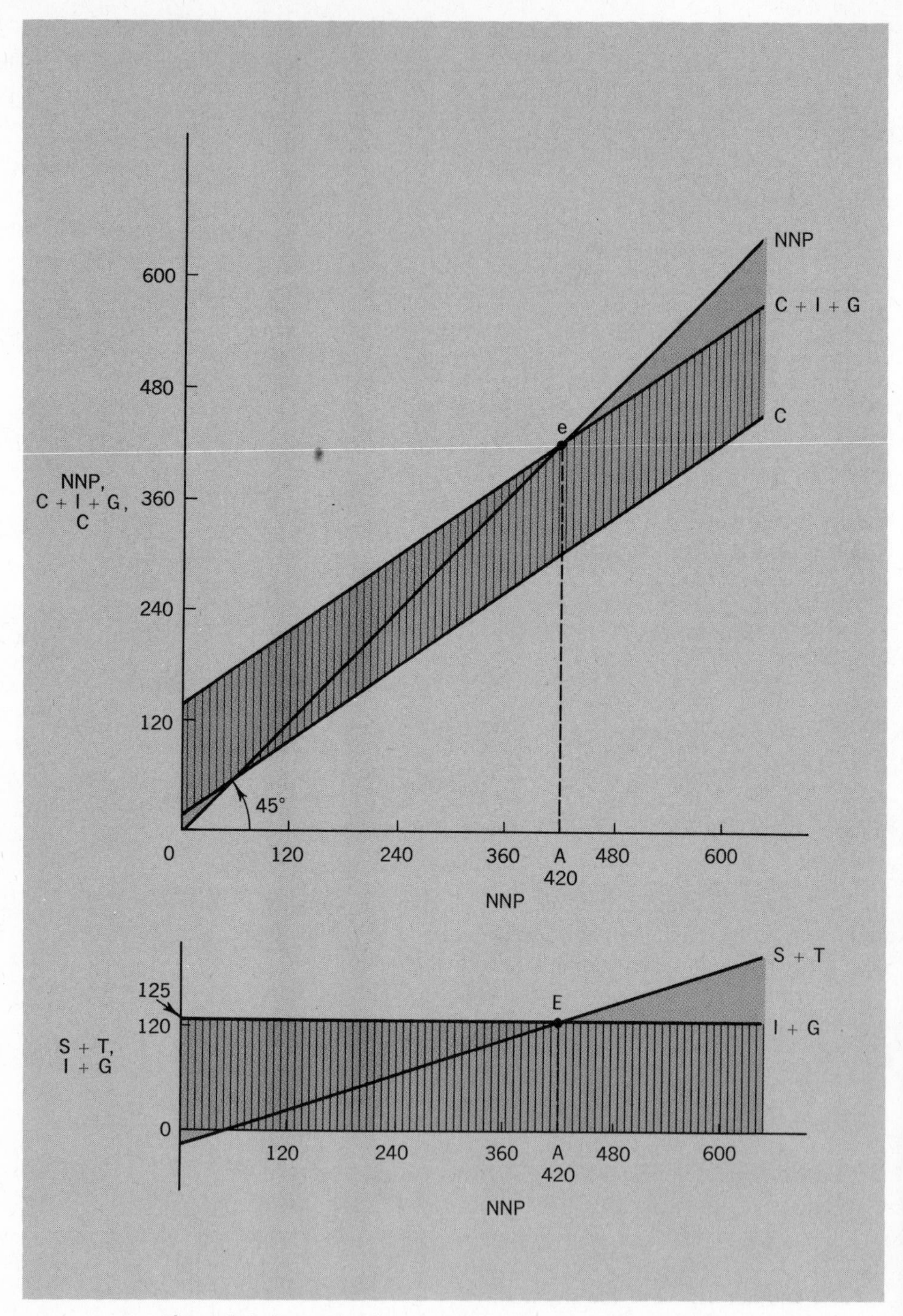


**Figure 6–8.** Determination of *NNP* by equality I+G and S+T.

## AN INTERPRETATION OF DISEQUILIBRIUM

Returning to the thread of our analysis, we must consider a rather baffling question. Why and how does demand, $C + I + G$, exceed supply, *NNP?* In other words, how does upper-loop *NNP* (spending) exceed lower-loop *NNP* (cost of output)? There are several points to be covered. First, there is the purely accounting aspect of the matter: upper- and lower-loop *NNP* should be the same. Second, there is the issue of how spending can exceed income. Consider these in the same order.

**Difference in Upper- and Lower-Loop *NNP*—Accounting.** First, let us note that upper-loop *NNP* (spending) is always resolved into lower-loop *NNP* (cost of output or income). However, there is a different aspect of the matter. A given level of income, lower-loop *NNP,* generates planned spending, $C + I + G$, which is not necessarily of the same magnitude. When we speak of $C + I + G$ as being unequal to lower-loop *NNP,* we are referring to the divergence of *planned* spending from cost of output, lower-loop *NNP*. Much misplaced ingenuity is spent in reconciling the divergence between the *planned* $C + I + G$ and *NNP* and the accounting equality of *recorded* $C + I + G$ and lower-loop *NNP*. Because the planned $C + I + G$ as a function of *NNP* merely represents a *willingness* to spend money on output at given levels of *NNP,* it is not a separately observed phenomenon. Consequently, we must frankly say that $C + I + G$ (in relation to *NNP*) cannot be observed simultaneously with lower-loop *NNP* (except in equilibrium). However, the equality or difference of these two variables is the driving force behind changes in *NNP*.

**Difference in Upper- and Lower-Loop *NNP*—Economics.** We have seen that upper-loop *NNP,* planned $C + I + G$, cannot be observed as having a value different from lower-loop *NNP*. In turn, this is true because upper-loop $C + I + G$, as actually recorded, is taken as resolved into lower-loop *NNP*. However, this does not preclude a difference between planned $C + I + G$ and lower-loop *NNP*. But one question remains: How can society spend more on output than it receives as income?

Let us dispose of a few patent errors. Spending cannot exceed income by borrowing from savers. For example, suppose John Doe borrows $100 from Richard Roe out of the latter's saving with a view to overspending. If John Doe spends his entire income and the borrowed $100, he surely overspends. But what about the two individuals taken together? Insofar as Richard Roe provided the funds by saving out of his income his spending was reduced to the same extent. While John Doe was overspending, Richard Roe was saving correspondingly. Hence the two cannot jointly overspend in this way any more than two people can live by taking in each other's washing.

Another baneful idea that turns up in this connection is the concept of spending out of "past saving." Because the analysis is concerned with present action, it is desirable to wipe the slate of the past clean. We have no way of knowing the results of "past saving," but we are aware of the current situation. So let us speak in terms of alternatives *now* available.

If the excess demand does not come from borrowing the savings of others or "past savings" (a meaningless term), what is its source? Suppose the individual has an idle cash balance in the bank.[2] By using his income and drawing on his bank balance as well, he can spend more than his income. Also he may spend more than his income by securing credit from a business firm or another consumer. But how is the business firm to pay the cost of production, if it receives no immediate return from the sale of output? Obviously, it must make use of another source of funds. One such source of funds is a bank balance possessed by the firm that can be tapped to pay the factors. Similarly, one consumer may borrow from another who taps his balance to make the loan. In this way the joint consumption of the two may exceed joint income.

It is pretty obvious that there are very narrow limits to this process, because consumers and firms normally want to maintain certain balances. If these balances are dipped into, they may lose their proper relationship to income. Is there any other source of free funds? Yes. The individual or firm may borrow money from a bank. As we will explain in a subsequent chapter, banks create new money in the form of bank deposits as they make loans. By borrowing money from banks the public may spend in excess of current income.

To summarize, excess demand is associated with the creation of new money or the use of idle balances. By a similar argument, income that exceeds spending is directed to increasing the idle part of bank balances and paying off bank loans. In Chapter 10 we will show that such a process destroys money by reducing both loans and deposits.

**Circular Flow and the Banks.** The process of expansion and contraction of income can be illustrated by a circular flow chart, such as Figure 6–9. We start as the firm pays out cost or income of 420. In turn, this becomes resolved into available income, ready for spend-

[2] The reader might ask whether the idle cash balance referred to is not the result of "past saving." Not necessarily. An individual may have accomplished no saving up to the time in question. He may then obtain an unsecured loan from a bank and deposit the proceeds. The existence of a monetary asset of this kind does not announce its origin.

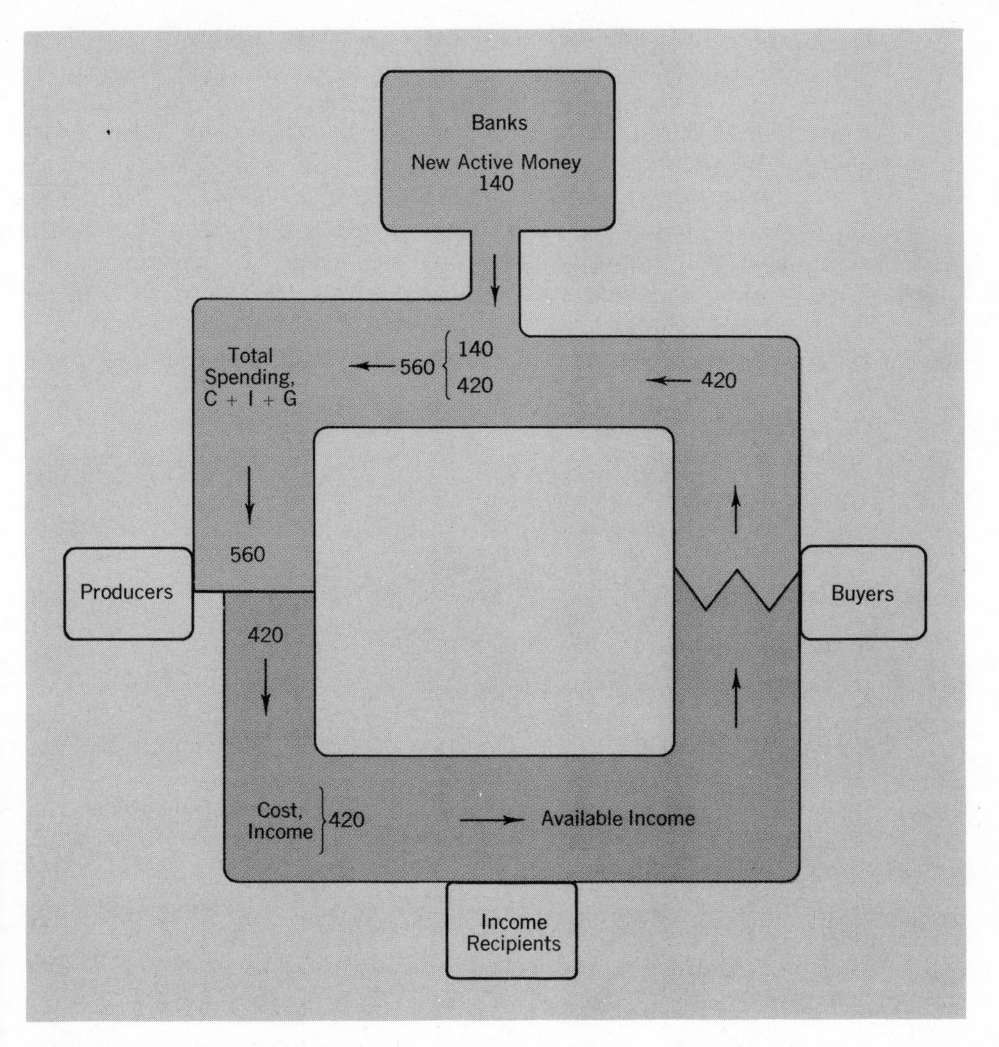


**Figure 6–9.** The circular flow, banks, and expansion of *NNP*.

ing. Suppose spenders wish to spend more than income. They may tap the banks for 140 in new money (idle balances and newly created bank deposits). By combining these resources they spend a total of 560, which generates upper-loop *NNP* of a like amount. In turn, this comes into the firm and is resolved into cost and income. Clearly, income has risen by 140 with the aid of the new money from the banks.

An excess supply and declining income is also related to the banks. Something must be done with the excess of income, lower-loop *NNP,* over spending. Income recipients have several alternatives. One is to add to their idle balances. Another is to pay off bank debts; in so doing they reduce bank deposits to the same extent as the loans retired, a proposition to be demonstrated in Chapter 10. Again this process can be pictured by a circular flow chart, as in Figure 6–10.

We start the circular flow with 560 cost or income. This passes around to spenders, but they want to spend only 420, and the remainder passes out of circulation into idle balances or loan retirement, thus destroying money. By "idle money" we mean money not used to carry out the flow of income. This does not preclude its use for other purposes.

**Review.** Excess demand, the excess of spending over cost of out-

**Figure 6–10.** The circular flow, banks, and contraction of *NNP*.

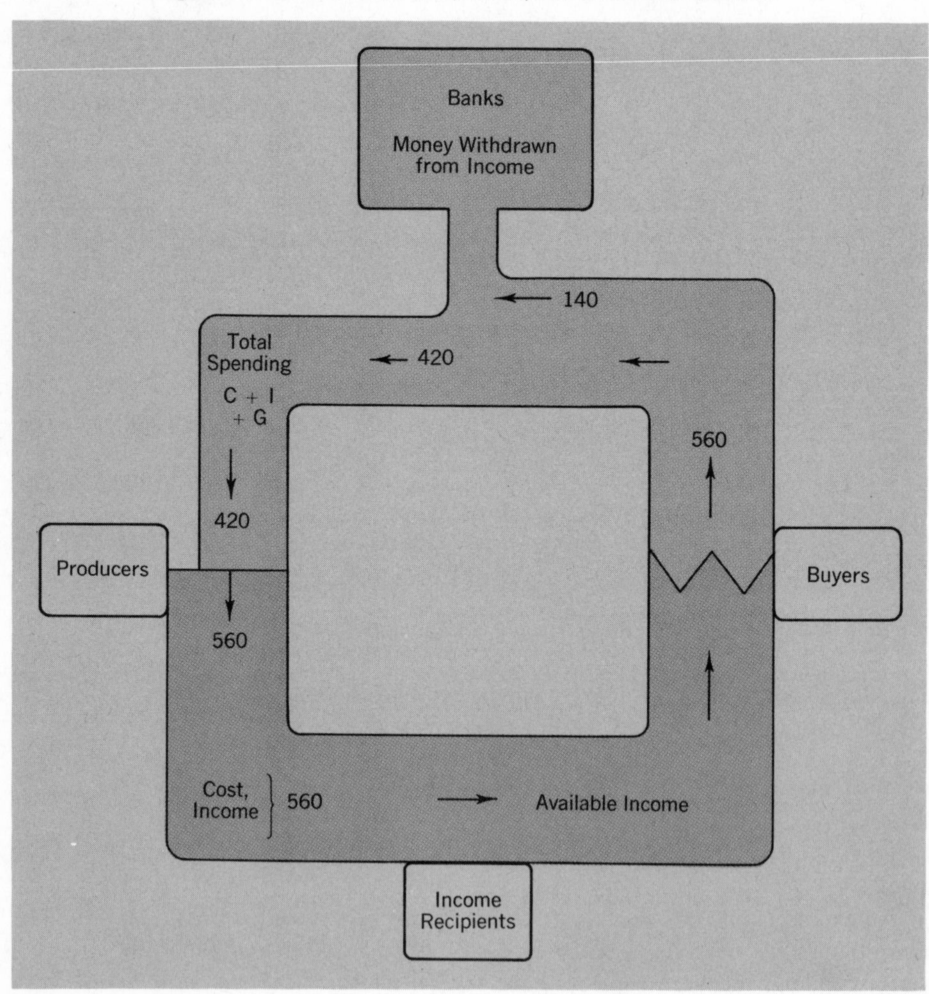

put (income), is made possible by new money from the banks. The latter consists of a flow out of idle balances or the creation of bank deposits. In turn, this flow of funds generates increased *NNP*. On the other hand, excess supply, the excess of costs (income) over spending, implies a flow of income into idle balances or the repayment of bank loans. Either course of action takes money out of active circulation and leads to reduced *NNP*.

In Figure 6–7, where the excess demand and supply areas are shown, the new money element is easily represented. The excess demand area represents money flowing into the income stream from the banks. On the other hand the excess supply area represents money flowing out of the income stream to the banks and out of active use. This explanation supplements and in no way replaces the explanation of equilibrium as a point of equality between supply and demand.

**Summary.** National income interpreted as Net National Product tends to reach an equilibrium marked by the equality of upper-loop *NNP,* total spending on output, and lower-loop *NNP,* output at cost. Such an equality is interpreted as the equilibrium of aggregate demand and aggregate supply. The main component underlying demand is consumption spending; this is shown to be functionally related to *NNP,* the relation being called either the consumption function, schedule, or line. The relationship of consumption to other factors is also considered. Like consumption, the sum of saving plus taxes is also functionally related to *NNP;* this follows, because the three together are equal to *NNP*.

Investment spending is believed to be largely autonomous; in the short run it depends on factors outside the ordinary economic variables, such as business psychology, population growth, and technological change. For this reason it is treated as an independent variable, not dependent on *NNP,* subject to unpredictable changes flowing from the outside factors that primarily determine its value. There does seem to be a long-run relationship between investment and *NNP*. Government spending is treated as a magnitude whose amount is fixed by an outside political decision and not sensitive to changes in *NNP*.

Equilibrium, or a stable level of *NNP,* is described graphically in two ways. The equality of a $C + I + G$ line with a 45-degree *NNP* line designates the level of *NNP* at which upper- and lower-loop *NNP* are equal; total spending equals cost of output. Roughly speaking, we identify $C + I + G$ with aggregate demand, and the 45-degree line, showing *NNP,* with aggregate supply. If $C + I + G$ exceeds *NNP,* aggregate demand exceeds aggregate supply; total spending by the public exceeds necessary factor payments. Under these conditions *NNP* must increase. If $C + I + G$ falls short of *NNP, NNP* must decrease for the opposite reasons. Hence the equality of $C+I+G$ and *NNP* marks an equilibrium of aggregate demand and aggregate supply. Any departure of *NNP* from the equilibrium quantity at which this holds true leads to a return to this value. The equality of $C+I+G$ and *NNP* is found to be equivalent to the equality of $I+G$ and $S+T$.

It is shown that an excess of $C+I+G$ over *NNP* involves recourse to the banking system to finance the extra spending. As we will show later, the banks can create additional money used to finance the excess spending in question. Thus the banking system is an important accessory in an excess of $C+I+G$ over *NNP* and the subsequent expansion of *NNP*. Much the same holds true of a deficiency and a corresponding contraction.

## QUESTIONS

1. Define the terms *aggregate supply* and *aggregate demand*. Explain how these terms may be used to show an economy in aggregative equilibrium.
2. What is the approximate composition of *NNP* in percentage terms, broken down by expenditure components? What per cent is used for consumption, and so on?
3. Give a brief definition of the consumption function. State some evidence favoring the idea of a consumption function for the period 1951–64.
4. What is the character of the shift in the consumption line shown in Figure 6–2? What are some of the reasons for the shift?
5. Draw freehand two graphs: in the first, draw in the 45-degree or *NNP* line and a consumption line relating *C* to *NNP;* in the second, directly below the first, draw $S+T$ in relation to *NNP*. Discuss the various lines (three in number), and discuss their mutual relations.
6. How is the relation between investment and *NNP* pictured in diagrams, as a rule? (Figure 6–6.) Why is the relationship drawn in this way? (Figure 6–5 and discussion.)
7. Why is government spending regarded as a constant in our discussion? In what way is this different from investment behavior, when investment is regarded as autonomous?
8. Explain in words alone the equilibrium of *NNP,* regarded as a relationship between supply and demand. How is this tied in with the twin concepts of cost and level of expenditure?
9. Explain the relationship: aggregate demand = upper-loop *NNP* = $C+I+G$.
10. Explain the relationship: Supply = cost = *NNP* (45-degree line).
11. Why is the intersection of the $C+I+G$ and *NNP* (45-degree) lines regarded as an equilibrium point?
12. In terms of the basic diagram—for example, Figure 6–7—a level of *NNP* below the equilibrium point cannot be maintained and gives way to a larger value. Why?

13. A value of $NNP$ above the equilibrium is also not maintainable and gives way to a smaller value. Why?
14. Interpret the equality between $C + I + G$ and $NNP$ as an equality between $I + G$ and $S + T$.
15. In what sense is $C + I + G$ always equal to (lower-loop) $NNP$? In what sense may it differ and why?
16. How is it possible for spending $(C + I + G)$ to exceed income $(NNP)$, using as examples the spending of families? What are the true sources of such overspending?
17. How is excess demand ($C + I + G$ greater than $NNP$) shown in a circular flow chart? Excess supply?

CHAPTER

7

# Income Determination, Continued

The preceding chapter brought out the basic notion that the level of *NNP* tends toward a definite equilibrium value. At this point aggregate demand, or total spending on output represented by $C + I + G$, is exactly equal to aggregate supply, or total cost, which we entitle simply *NNP*. Thus in equilibrium the total output produced is cleared from the market by total demand at a specific level of *NNP*. Well and good! Now we need to apply this apparatus to various things going on in the world about us. First, we would like to explain changes in the level of *NNP* with the aid of this apparatus. Then we need to prepare the way for the study of some closely related phenomena: the problem of inflation and the impact of government on the level of *NNP*. For these purposes certain additional refinements and concepts will be introduced.

## THE MULTIPLIER

As we have just explained in considerable detail, *NNP* tends toward an equilibrium value under given conditions. Thus economic forces seem to be pushing economic activity toward a given, fixed value. Because economic activity is marked by continual ups and downs, this account raises a question about the pertinence of the foregoing theory. How does this approach account for the frequent ups and downs in production and employment that mark our system? Briefly, the main cause of income variations is found in the variability of investment. Let us consider this point briefly.

**Variability of Investment.** The main factor that governs investment is the set of future returns expected to flow in from capital goods purchased. In turn, these expectations rest on a set of growth factors and such volatile things as business psychology, tastes, and social attitudes. As we indicated earlier, in Figure 6–5 and the surrounding discussion, the investment level varied considerably in the 1951–64 period. Insofar as changes in the level of investment occur, the result will be corresponding changes in total spending and in equilibrium *NNP*.

**Changes in Consumption and Government Spending.** Either consumption or government spending change from time to time. However, significant shifts in the consumption line are hard to discern. The evidence points to a significant upward shift between the prewar period 1929–40 and the period 1951–64. Such shifts will cause variations in the level of *NNP,* just as will changes in investment, but are far less frequent. Government spending decisions are politically inspired, and political forces change from time to time. Consequently, government spending may change. However, inspection of the record shows that, in fact, such spending is quite stable except in times of war or economic collapse. This leaves only investment as the magnitude likely to vary significantly in the short run. Such changes are to be expected with considerable frequency, the record indicates.

**Effect of Investment Changes on Income.** Suppose an improvement in expected returns causes a rise in the level of investment. What is the effect of this change on *NNP?* Clearly, the change will promote an increase in *NNP,* but this interpretation is inadequate. What we really want to know is this: By what amount does *NNP* rise when investment ($I$) rises by a given amount, say 1 (billion dollars)?

First, consider a numerical illustration that gives the flavor of the answer. Suppose investment increases by 20 in an initial situation marked by the equilibrium of $C + I + G$ and *NNP*. First, the increased investment implies the existence of excess demand, because $C + I + G$ was equal to *NNP* at the outset. To meet extra demand, producers increase supply (lower-loop *NNP*) and in the act generate not only additional output but additional income with which to buy goods. With the payment of additional income buyers will seek to consume more, and $C + I + G$ will increase further. Evidently, there is an interaction between rising spending and rising income that can be resolved only if a point of equality is found at a higher *NNP*.

To make the analysis more specific we need to know how much spending will rise with additional income (*NNP*). Recall that both I and G are thought to be independent of income, whereas C depends on income. Now let us denote the increase in consumption generated by a $1 rise in *NNP* (income) by the term *marginal propensity to consume* ($MPC$). Using abbreviations, this expression can be written

$$MPC = \Delta C/\Delta NNP\,, \tag{1}$$

where $\Delta C$ is the increase in consumption generated by an increase in $NNP$ equal to $\Delta NNP$. (The symbol $\Delta$ is a Greek letter corresponding to $D$. Its presence before a quantity like $C$ indicates a change in that quantity.) If consumption increases by 40 as $NNP$ rises by 60, $MPC = 40/60 = 2/3$. Considering the data over the past 30 years, this number is approximately the correct one.

Now, returning to the analysis, $C + I + G$ is 20 above $NNP$, both are increasing as a result of the excess demand, and we hope that a sufficient increase in $NNP$ will afford equilibrium. Suppose $NNP$ increases by exactly 60; then $C$ will increase by exactly $2/3$ of this, because $MPC$ is $2/3$. Clearly, this will lead to an increase in $C$ of $2/3(60) = 40$. Combining the increase in consumption of 40 with the initial increase in investment of 20, and no change in governmental spending, we find $C + I + G$ to have risen by 60. But this exactly suffices to buy the additional output of 60 generated by the like increase in $NNP$. Thus the market is cleared by a rise of 60 in $NNP$. If $I$ continues to be 20 above the old level, $NNP$ will continue to be in equilibrium at a level 60 higher than before.

**Definition of the Multiplier.** We can see that the rise of 20 in $I$ led to a rise of 60 in $NNP$. Accordingly, we can say that the ratio $60/20 = 3$ represents the rise in $NNP$ per unit rise in $I$. Following the usage of John Maynard Keynes, we can express this notion formally by the following definition. *The multiplier is the number of dollars NNP (income) will rise when I rises by one dollar.* In the present case the ratio is 3; for every dollar rise in $I$, $NNP$ rises by 3. It is customary to express this ratio by the letter $K$.

The leverage aspect of the multiplier has great importance. In the American economy the multplier seems to be about 3 in value. When investment increases by $1 billion, income increases by $3 billion. If the increase were 1 to 1 the fluctuation of investment would possess little interest, because there would be no spreading of effects. Very briefly, the significance of the multplier lies in (1) the known instability of investment, and (2) the way in which this relationship causes the disturbance of investment to multiply its effect threefold.

**Illustrations.** Using the graphic approach of earlier pages, we can illustrate the action of the multiplier. In Figure 7–1 equilibrium is shown at point $e$, where $C + I + G$ equals $NNP$ or, in the lower figure, at $E$ where $S + T = I + G$. Thus an income $Oa$ in the upper or $OA$ in the lower diagram represents the initial equilibrium income. Now $I$ increases to $I'$, causing the $C + I + G$ line to shift to position $C + I' + G$ in the upper diagram and $I + G$ to shift to position $I' + G$

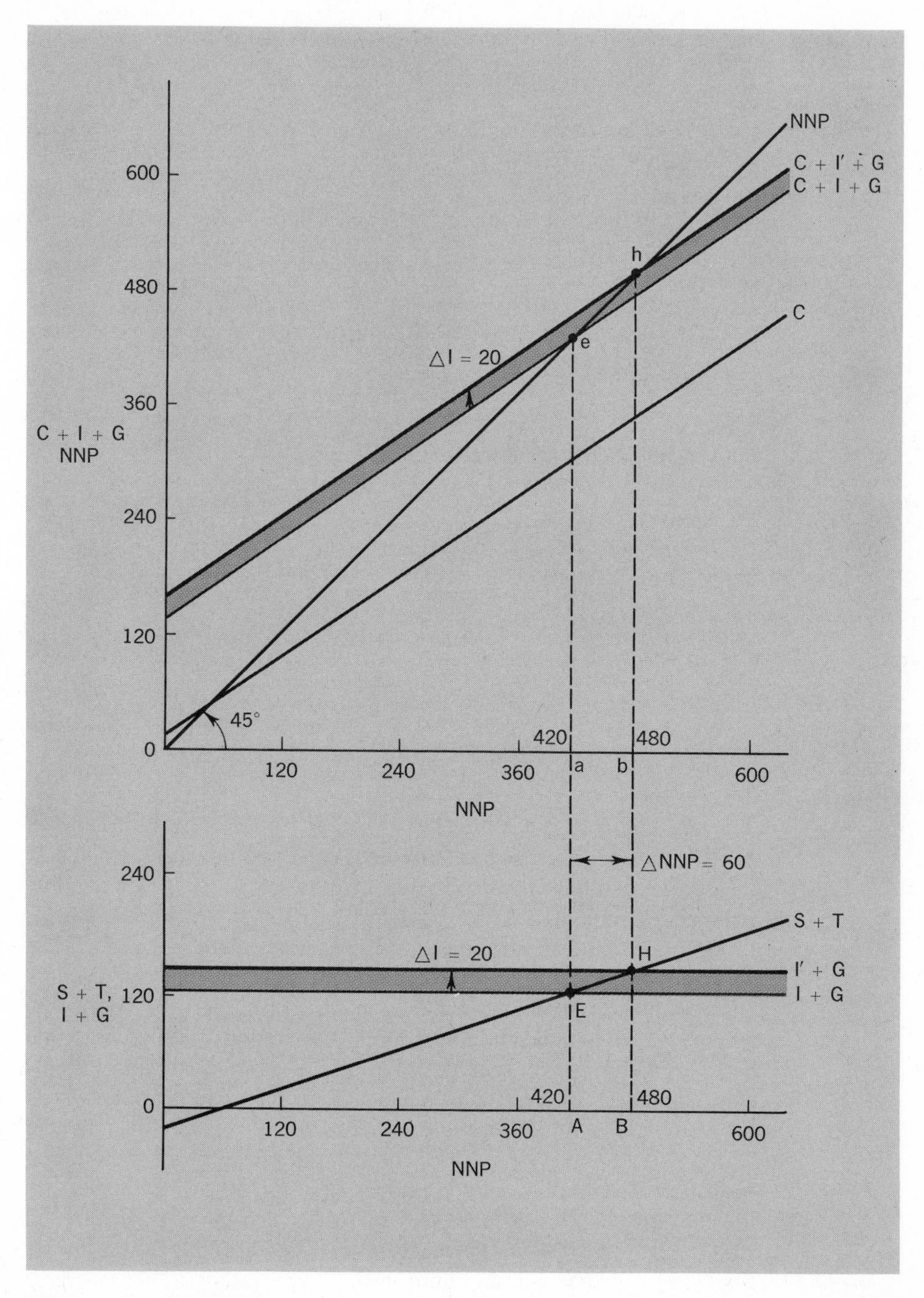


**Figure 7–1.** Expansion of *NNP* as a result of increasing investment operating through the multiplier.

in the lower diagram. In either case the level of *NNP* increases in order to retain equilibrium. In the upper diagram $C + I' + G$ reaches equilibrium with *NNP* at point *h*, giving a new income of *Ob* (an increase of *ab*). In the lower diagram $I' + G$ intersects $S + T$ at point *H*, giving an income *OB* (an increase of *AB*).

Exactly the same principle can be seen at work in Table 7–1. An original equilibrium is found at an *NNP* of 420, but the rise in $I' + G$ $(C + I' + G)$ upsets this equilibrium. For example, $C + I' + G$ is now 440 compared to the *NNP* of 420, implying an excess demand of 20. As *NNP* expands by 60, $C + I' + G$ expands by 40, which, together with the initial excess demand of 20, causes $C + I' + G$ to equal *NNP* at 480.

**TABLE 7–1**
**A Numerical Illustration of the Multiplier**

| | *NNP* | C | S + T | I + G | C + I + G | I′ + G | C + I′ + G |
|---|---|---|---|---|---|---|---|
| | 0 | 15 | −15 | 125 | 140 | 145 | 160 |
| | 60 | 55 | 5 | 125 | 180 | 145 | 200 |
| | 120 | 95 | 25 | 125 | 220 | 145 | 240 |
| | 180 | 135 | 45 | 125 | 260 | 145 | 280 |
| | 240 | 175 | 65 | 125 | 300 | 145 | 320 |
| | 300 | 215 | 85 | 125 | 340 | 145 | 360 |
| | 360 | 255 | 105 | 125 | 380 | 145 | 400 |
| Original equilibrium | 420 | 295 | 125 | 125 | 420 | 145 | 440 |
| New equilibrium | 480 | 335 | 145 | 125 | 460 | 145 | 480 |

**Basic Logic of the Multiplier.** Let us try to interpret the rise of *NNP* logically. In particular, why does *NNP* rise 3 times as much as *I* (that is, by 60 as compared to an increase of 20 in *I*)? To simplify numbers, assume that *I* rises by 1 instead of 20. As *I* increases by 1, producers expand production and hire factors, thereby raising factor cost and income by 1 in the process of producing to meet demand. On this first "round" the lower-loop *NNP* increases by 1. As the income passes around the lower loop, it is resolved into income that becomes available to spenders. On our present assumptions, only consumers wish to increase purchases. With the extra income (*NNP*) of 1 they spend $\frac{2}{3}$ on consumption. In turn, this increase in $C + I + G$ (upper-loop *NNP*) generates additional production, hiring of factors, and so on, resulting ultimately in higher cost of output and income. In short, lower-loop *NNP* increases also by $\frac{2}{3}$ on the second round. By a similar argument, spending increases by $\frac{2}{3}$ of this or $(\frac{2}{3})(\frac{2}{3}) = (\frac{2}{3})^2$ on the third round, generating a like increase in *NNP*.

As we continue trips around the income circle these successive income increases continue to be generated indefinitely. Thus the total increase in $NNP$ takes the form of a series with an indefinitely large number of terms:

$$\Delta NNP = 1 + (2/3) + (2/3)^2 + (2/3)^3 + \ldots . \quad \textbf{(2)}$$

Has a series of this sort any value, or as mathematicians are wont to say, any *limit?* Fortunately, the answer is yes. The sum in question is equal to 3. Why? We will not attempt a real answer here. Rather, let us simply state that the series on the right is known as an "infinite geometric progression with a common ratio between successive terms of r = ⅔." Such a series can be proved to have a value given by the following equation:

$$\frac{1}{1-r} = 1 + r + r^2 + r^3 + \ldots . \quad \textbf{(3)}$$

In the present example $r$ represents $MPC = \Delta C/\Delta NNP = 2/3$. Also the increase in the level of investment is given as 1; this generates the term 1 in the series. Returning to our definition of the multiplier as the number of dollars $NNP$ will rise when $I$ rises by 1, we can summarize the results of this phase of study by the equation for the multiplier:

$$K = \frac{\Delta NNP}{\Delta I} = \frac{1}{1 - MPC} \cdot \quad \textbf{(4)}$$

In the above example $MPC = 2/3$, and we may calculate the multiplier as

$$K = \frac{1}{1 - 2/3} = \frac{1}{1/3} = 3\,, \quad \textbf{(5)}$$

as we have maintained all along.

To fortify the numerical result let us construct a table that indicates the results of following out such a series.

**TABLE 7–2**
**An Illustration of the Multiplier**

| Rounds | Increase in *NNP* in the Round | Total Increase in *NNP* |
|---|---|---|
| 1 | 1 | 1 |
| 2 | ⅔ | 1 + ⅔ = 1.67 |
| 3 | $(2/3)^2 = 0.44$ | 2.11 |
| 4 | $(2/3)^3 = 0.30$ | 2.41 |
| 5 | $(2/3)^4 = 0.20$ | 2.61 |
| 6 | $(2/3)^5 = 0.13$ | 2.74 |
| 7 | $(2/3)^6 = 0.09$ | 2.83 |
| 8 | $(2/3)^7 = 0.06$ | 2.89 |
| 9 | $(2/3)^8 = 0.04$ | 2.93 |
| 10 | $(2/3)^9 = 0.03$ | 2.96 |

Notice that the increase in investment is 1, which occurred at the start. Government spending is constant, no change taking place. Because the change in upper-loop *NNP* is 3, *I* increases by 1 and *G* by zero, *C* must have increased by exactly 2.

After 10 rounds have occurred the rise in *NNP* has approximately the value indicated by the multplier, 2.96 being approximately equal to 3. Only after an indefinite number of rounds will this last little bit be added. The case is something like the growing circles forming in a lake after a rock is thrown in. After a while the widening circle is indiscernible, even though it presumably continues indefinitely.

**Summary of Multiplier.** Of the three components of total spending, investment is the one most capable of spontaneous change. When autonomous changes of this kind occur, *NNP* rises by a multiple of the investment change. In the United States this multiple is roughly equal to 3. Owing to this leverage effect variations in the level of investment are magnified into much larger fluctuations in *NNP*. Changes in *G* and shifts in the consumption function also produce an amplified effect through the multiplier. However, because such changes are less common, they are assigned a less important role in the discussion.

## EQUILIBRIUM *NNP* AND FULL-EMPLOYMENT *NNP*

In the foregoing discussion we have indicated the existence of a definite equilibrium value of *NNP*. When a difference between the actual and equilibrium levels of *NNP* exists, excess demand or supply are present, and a movement of *NNP* to the equilibrium level occurs. If the level of investment changes, a new equilibrium *NNP* will be defined, and *NNP* will seek the revised value. If *NNP* seeks a certain defined level, is this level one that affords full employment to the factors of production? Put another way, is the equilibrium *NNP* the maximum *NNP* that can be produced by society? The answer is "not necessarily." To explain this in detail is a substantial task, and here we can only outline the surface features of the argument.

**Full-Employment *NNP*.** Let us define full-employment *NNP* as the level that is associated with the full use of all resources. Now certain of the factors are said to be *fixed* at any particular moment; such factors can be neither increased nor decreased in amount, and their use in a particular activity tends to be fixed for short periods of time. Most land and capital is counted in the category of fixed factors, though some capital in the form of stocks of goods is capable of variation and possibly some land.



On the other hand, some of the factors are variable at a particular moment; such factors can be increased or decreased in amount in a short period. Labor is generally counted bodily in this category. Although a few classes of laborers stay employed at all levels of output, most will find their use contingent on the amount of activity.

Clearly, a factor that is fixed in its use regardless of the level of output must be regarded as tied up or employed at all times. On the other hand, factors whose use varies with output undergo a variation in employment. Consequently, the factor that is either less than fully or fully employed is labor, in the main. This is a rather obvious point, but one that requires mention.

As lower-loop *NNP* increases, employment rises until all available labor seeking work has found it. The lower-loop *NNP* corresponding to full employment may be entitled *full-employment NNP*. At a particular moment this *NNP* has a fixed value, such as $600 billion. With the passage of time and growth in productive capacity, as well as other changes, full-employment *NNP* will tend to grow.

For a number of reasons a good deal of discussion in the area of determination of *NNP* and changes therein hinge around the above concept. First, the attainment of full employment, other things being equal, is a highly desirable goal for the economy. Operation of the economy short of this point indicates that resources have been left unemployed with a corresponding loss of output. In human terms it indicates that individuals are suffering from unemployment or reduced incomes. Second, the behavior of the economy begins to change radically as this point is attained. At lower levels of *NNP* variations in *NNP* and employment are closely correlated. As *NNP* rises, employment rises; as *NNP* falls, employment falls. As *NNP* approaches and passes the full-employment point, however, employment increases slow down and, finally, cease. In fact, prices begin to rise as this point is reached, so that *NNP* and the price level become more closely related. In the next chapter we will consider the effects on prices of rising *NNP* at full employment.

**Underemployment Equilibrium.** Let us illustrate the notion that the equilibrium of the economy falls at a point that is not the same as the point of full employment. First, we assume that the value of full-employment *NNP* is known and amounts to $600 billion. We mark this point on the (lower-loop) *NNP* axis by the letter $F$ in Figure 7–2. Then the $C + I + G$ curve intersects the *NNP* line at $E$, giving the equilibrium value of *NNP* at $A$ on the horizontal axis. This is the value of *NNP* at which aggregate demand, $C + I + G$, equals aggregate supply, lower-loop *NNP*, and at which the market is cleared. The fact that the equilibrium income level is $OA$, which is less than $OF$, indicates that the economy is in *underemployment equilibrium*.

This situation tends to occur when demand, $C + I + G$, is too low.

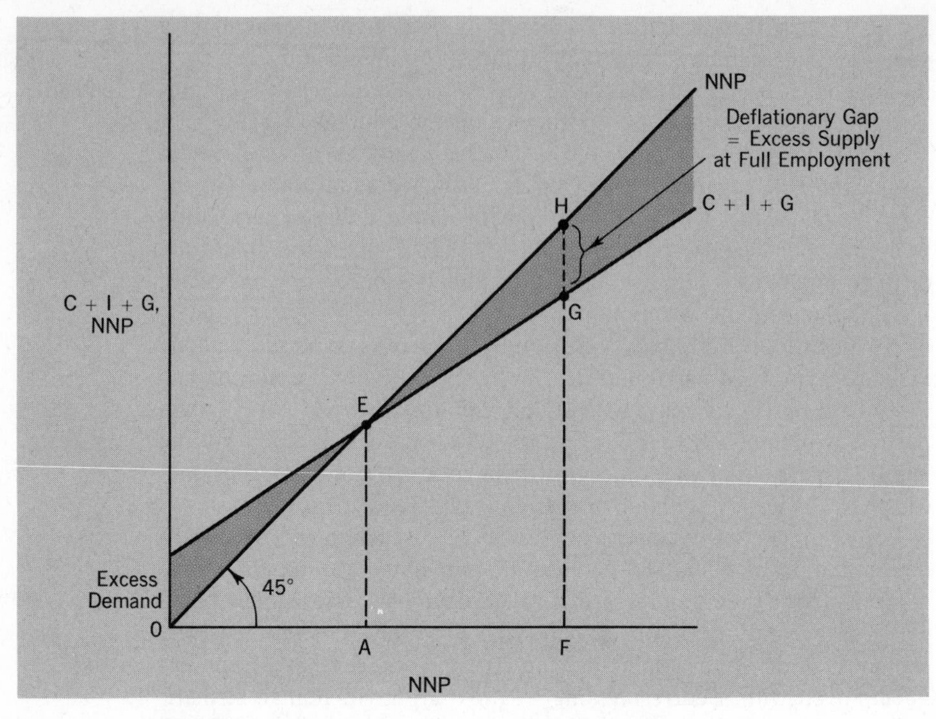


**Figure 7–2.** Underemployment equilibrium of *NNP*.

The natural response one has on encountering this possibility is to ask, "What can be done about it?" In turn, this leads us to consider the possibility of government intervention designed to correct the unemployment. We will not consider the general philosophy of government intervention here. But it is probably clear by now that the effects of various kinds of government policies should be considered. We will, therefore, examine the effects of some of these.

## GOVERNMENT AND INCOME

In the preceding chapter we discussed the determination of *NNP*, incorporating the effects of government taxing and spending. If there is a change in government policy regarding taxes or spending, there will be some repercussions. Briefly, let us consider how such changes take place, as well as the effects they produce.

## TAXES, CONSUMPTION, AND THE MULTIPLIER

**A Tax Increase.** Suppose the government raises tax rates on individual incomes at all levels. At any given level of *NNP* there will be smaller Disposable Personal Income, because income taxes constitute one of the main deductions from *NNP* in securing Disposable Personal Income. With a given *NNP* and smaller Disposable Personal Income there will be reduced consumption expenditure. As we saw in the preceding chapter, any increase in Disposable Personal Income tends to be accompanied by increased consumption spending. By the same token a reduction in *DPI* will lead to reduced consumption. Therefore, at any level of *NNP* an increase in individual income taxes tends to lower the consumption line.

If the tax increase is proportional in all brackets, it will yield a greater absolute amount at high than at low levels of *NNP*. At high levels of *NNP, DPI* would drop more in absolute amount, because the tax take would be larger. For the same reason the absolute reduction in consumption would be greater at high levels of *NNP*. In short, a uniform tax increase would reduce consumption progressively more in absolute amount at higher levels of *NNP*. Ideally, the change might look as it does in Figure 7–3.

**Figure 7–3.** Effect of tax increase on the consumption line.

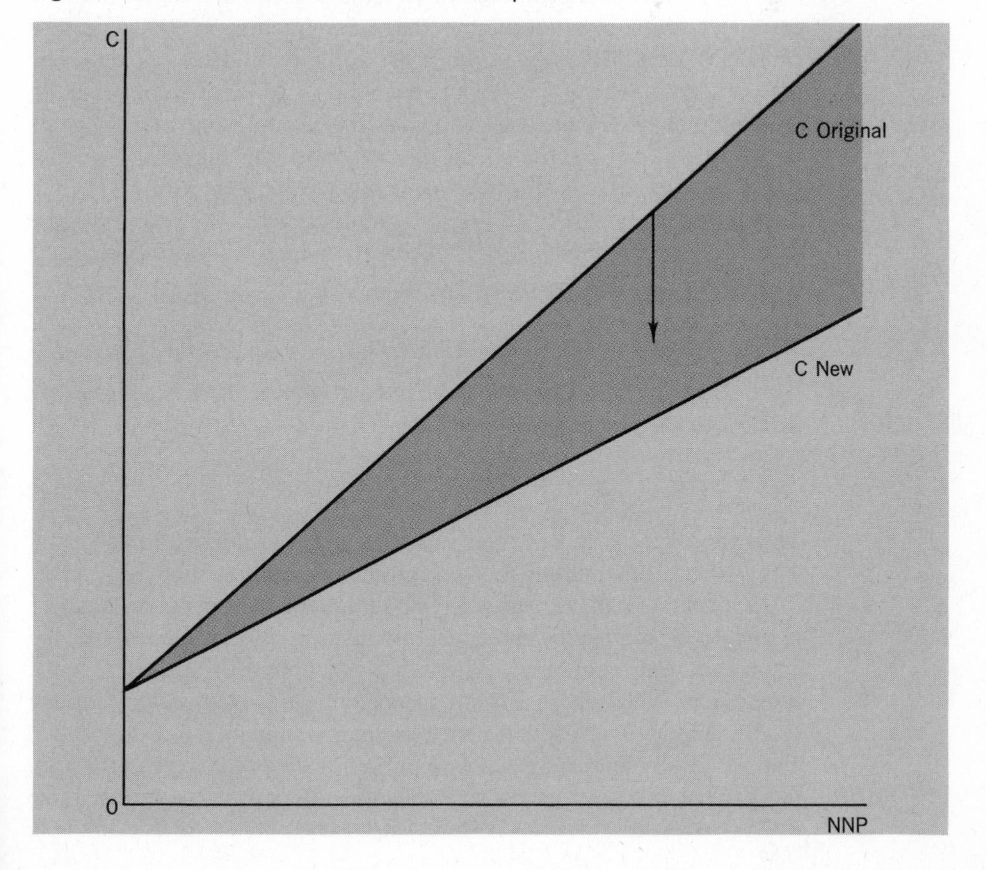

**Decline in MPC.** Considering Figure 7–3 we see that the consumption line is both lowered and flattened by an increase in the tax rates. Because the *C* line is flattened, consumption rises more slowly as *NNP* increases. Because $MPC = \Delta C/\Delta NNP$ shows the relation between the change in *C* and the change in *NNP,* the slower rise in *C* implies a drop in $\Delta C$ (with a given increase in *NNP* equal to $\Delta NNP$) and a reduction in *MPC*. Let us illustrate this by an example.

Assume that, to begin with, no difference exists between *NNP* and *DPI,* and that subsequently a 30-per-cent tax is introduced. Also assume that people consume about $9/10$ of all additional *DPI,* which is approximately the case, in fact. To begin with, then, $MPC = \Delta C/\Delta NNP = \Delta C/\Delta DPI = 9/10$. Because *NNP* is the same as *DPI,* *MPC* is $9/10$ at the outset. Now the 30-per-cent tax is introduced. If *NNP* increases by 10, taxes increase by 3 ($= 30$ per cent $\cdot\ 10$), leaving 7 in *DPI*. Of this $9/10$ or 6.3 ($= 9/10 \cdot 7$) is consumed. Thus the $MPC = \Delta C/\Delta NNP = .63$. Evidently, the *MPC* has dropped from 0.9 to 0.63 as a result of the tax increase.

The commonsense of this is clear. An increase in the tax rate means that less of an increase in *NNP* is passed back as *DPI* to the consumer. Although consuming the same fraction of *DPI,* he also consumes a smaller amount, when the additional *DPI* is cut down by the presence of extra taxes. Thus the ratio of additional consumption to additional *NNP* declines. In short, the tax bite out of *NNP* cuts the additional consumption that the consumer can make.

**Decline of the Multiplier with Increased Tax Rates.** If tax rates increase and *MPC* declines, the multiplier will also fall. Suppose that *MPC* is originally $3/4$. The corresponding value of the multiplier is

$$K = \frac{1}{1 - 3/4} = \frac{1}{1/4} = 4\,. \qquad \textbf{(6)}$$

Now tax rates increase and, as explained above, *MPC* declines, say from $3/4$ to $2/3$. The new multiplier is

$$K = \frac{1}{1 - 2/3} = \frac{1}{1/3} = 3\,. \qquad \textbf{(7)}$$

Thus the increase in tax rates has caused the multiplier to fall from 4 to 3. Does this matter? Let us consider this point briefly.

As explained in the opening paragraph of this chapter, changes in the level of investment constitute the primary cause of income change in our economy. Whereas consumption is a fairly stable function of *NNP* and government spending changes slowly through time, excepting wars, investment can change suddenly and drastically. The cause of such changes lies in variations in profit expectations on the part of businessmen. The changes in investment spending affect

*NNP* through the multiplier. If the multiplier is large, say 5, a $10-billion change in investment is translated into a $50-billion (= $10 billion × 5) change in *NNP*. Reduce the multiplier to 3 by increased tax rates, and the change declines to only $30 billion (= $10 billion × 3). Therefore increased tax rates that reduce the multiplier tend to reduce the susceptibility of the economy to changes in *NNP*.

## EFFECTS OF CHANGES IN GOVERNMENT SPENDING AND TAXES ON *NNP*

**An Increase in Government Spending.** It is plausible to assume that government spending does not change automatically as a result of changes in *NNP*. Rather this component of spending is an outcome of a political decision. At certain intervals, annually in the case of the Federal budget, the amount of government spending is adjusted upward or downward. Suppose government spending is increased. What is the effect on *NNP?* Actually, such an increase affects *NNP* through the multiplier in the same way as a change in investment. With a multiplier of about 3 in our economy, an increase of $1 billion ought to bring about a rise of about $3 billion of *NNP*.

This may be illustrated graphically, as in Figure 7–4. To begin with, equilibrium is found at *E,* where $C + I + G = NNP$ (aggregate demand equals aggregate supply). At this point *NNP* is equal to *OA*. As government spending *G* changes to $G + \Delta G$, the $C + I + G$ line shifts upward to the position shown by $C + I + G + \Delta G$. As a result, the equilibrium point shifts to *E′*, and the level of *NNP* increases from *OA* to *OB*. In summary, an increase in government spending, $\Delta G = RS$, leads to a corresponding increase in *NNP* equal to *AB*.

**A Cut in Taxes.** We have already explained that an increase in tax rates lowers and flattens the *C* line. Conversely, a cut in tax rates raises and steepens the *C* line. In Figure 7–5 such a change in the *C* line from *C* to *C′* is shown. Both *I* and *G* remain constant. Consequently, we combine them into a total $I + G$ and add this sum to the *C* and *C′* curves. Again, the equilibrium changes from *E* to *E′* and the level of *NNP* from *OA* to *OB*.

**Comparison of Increased Government Spending and Tax Cuts.** Clearly, *NNP* will increase either as a result of increased government spending or as a result of a tax cut. Which method is more effective? We must postpone a full discussion of this until we reach the chapter on fiscal policy. Note, however, that an increase in government spending is usually thought of as an increase in dollar amounts, whereas a tax cut is usually considered as a percentage cut in rates. We can attempt to reduce a tax cut to a uniform cut at any level of *NNP*. This case is not discussed above.

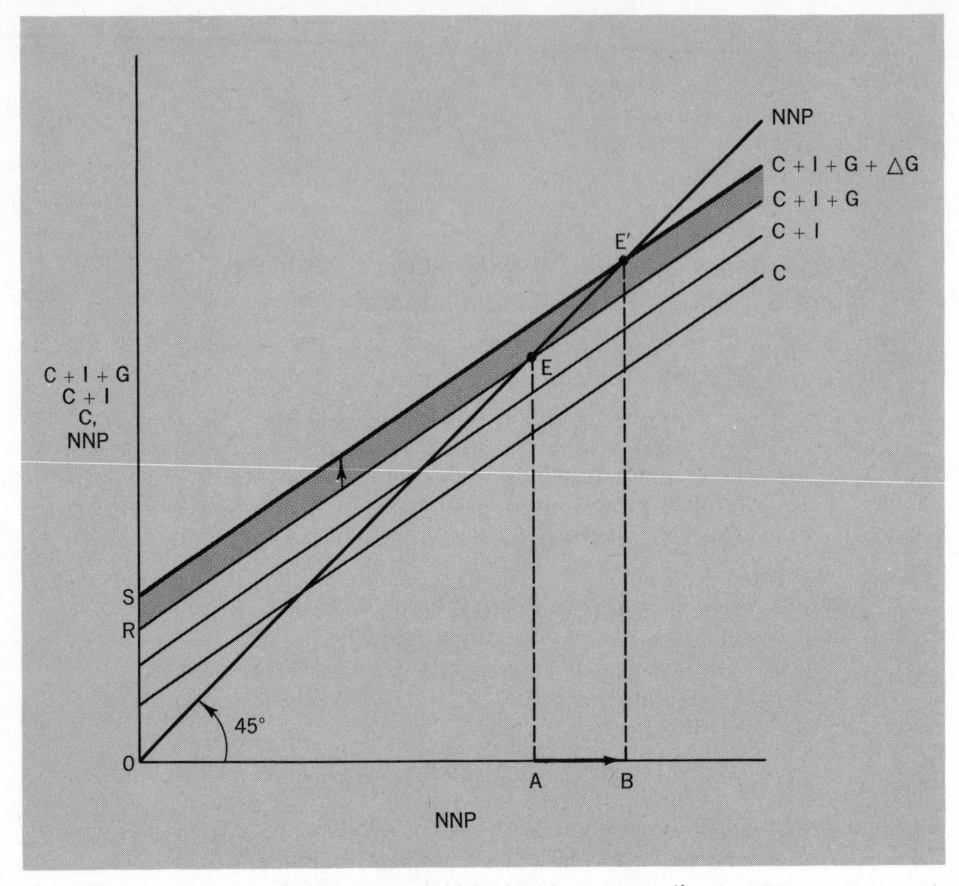


**Figure 7–4.** Effect of increase in government spending on *NNP*.

In this case a $1 cut in individual income taxes should increase *DPI* by a corresponding amount. In the American economy individuals spend roughly 93 cents of an extra dollar of *DPI* on consumption. Thus the direct impact of a $1 tax cut would tend to be an increase in consumption of about 93 cents at any given level of *NNP*. Thus the *C* line would rise uniformly by about 93 cents. With a multiplier of about 3 this would lead to an increase in *NNP* of about $2.79, or roughly $2.8. Speaking very roughly, then, a tax cut of $1 would produce an increase of about $2.8, whereas an increase in government spending of $1 would produce an increase of about $3 (= $1 × 3). In short, a cut in individual income taxes produces a slightly smaller effect than an increase in government spending of equal amount.

**Summary.** Investment is inherently variable, because it depends on unstable expectations about the set of future returns that capital goods are supposed to yield. When independent changes in investment occur, the level of *NNP* tends to change in the same direction. Moreover, the increment of *NNP* is generally about 3 times the original increase in investment. The ratio of the increased *NNP* to the original change in investment can be written in the form of an equation: $K = 1/(1-MPC)$, where $K$ stands for the multiplier (about 3 or a bit less) and *MPC* for the marginal propensity to consume. The multiplier process builds up its effect on *NNP* first through the direct impact of investment on production and *NNP,* then through derived effects on consumption.

*Full-employment NNP* refers to that value of *NNP* at which all usable resources, especially labor, are being used to produce output. When *NNP* begins to approach this level, prices tend to rise, and output reaches an upper limit. If $C + I + G$ falls short of *NNP* at full-employment *NNP,* a deflationary gap is said to exist. Under these conditions *NNP* contracts to a lower level, at which it tends to stabilize. Such a position is referred to as an underemployment equilibrium.

Government, by imposing taxes on incomes, tends to lower and

**Figure 7–5.** Effect of tax cut on *NNP*.

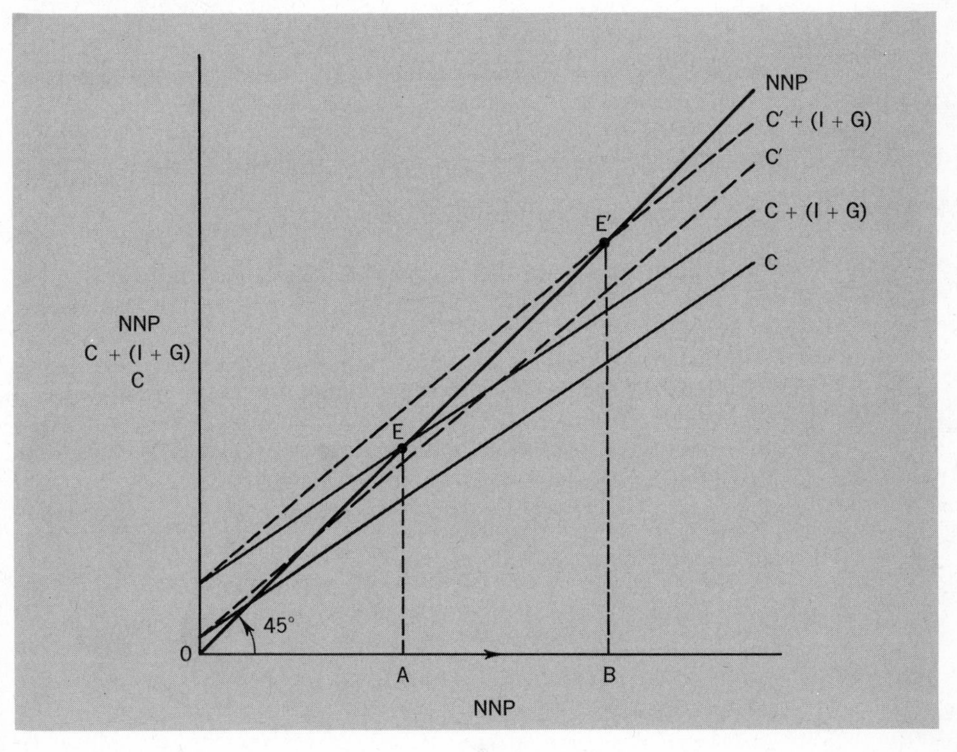

reduce the inclination of the consumption line. The greater flatness of the consumption line arises because of the tax bite that reduces the part of *NNP* that is translated into *DPI* and then into consumption expenditure. This amounts to saying the *MPC* declines as the tax bite increases. With the reduced *MPC* comes a lower value of the multiplier and a reduced responsiveness of *NNP* to independent changes in investment. To summarize, tax increases tend to reduce fluctuations in *NNP* arising from changes in investment.

Government may raise *NNP* by increasing government spending without changing tax rates. Operating through the multiplier, $1 of such spending tends to increase *NNP* by about $3, as indicated by the approximate value of the multiplier. Also a uniform cut in individual income taxes will increase *NNP* by about 0.93 of this, or 2.8 times the amount of the cut. Thus the multiplier effect is slightly reduced, because consumers spend only about 0.93 of additional take-home pay.

## QUESTIONS

1. What is the main cause of changes in *NNP?* Explain.
2. What is the likelihood of changes in consumption or government spending, as compared with investment?
3. What is the marginal propensity to consume? Why is its value believed to be less than 1?
4. Define the multiplier verbally. Give the formula for the multiplier, and illustrate the computation of its value with an *MPC* of 0.6. With an *MPC* of 0.5.
5. Considering the multiplier as a series, calculate the value of the series after the first 10 rounds, when *MPC* is 0.6, and compare with the value found by the formula in question 4.
6. What is full-employment *NNP?* Is full-employment *NNP* the same as equilibrium *NNP?* Explain. What is underemployment equilibrium?
7. What is the meaning of a deflationary gap, and what are the results?
8. What is the effect of a rise in individual income taxes on the relation between consumption and *NNP?* If the tax cut is an across-the-board, percentage increase, is the effect uniform at all levels of income? Explain.
9. What is the effect of such a tax increase on *MPC* out of *NNP?* What effect does the tax increase have on the multiplier?
10. An increase in tax rates reduces the susceptibility of the economy to changes in *NNP*. Explain.
11. What is the effect of an increase in government spending on *NNP?*

CHAPTER

8

# Money, Income, and the Price Level

In Chapters 6 and 7 we dealt with the factors determining the level of *NNP* and those causing that level to vary. Although it is evident that a rise in *NNP* reflects changes in outputs and prices, we have not attempted so far to distinguish between the two sorts of changes. To do this we need to identify the factors that determine the price level and thus distinguish price from output variations. By doing this we will round out the theory of income (*NNP*) determination with an analysis of the forces determining the level of prices.

The variable related to prices in the most obvious way is the supply of money. Because money serves as a medium of exchange, outputs are purchased at certain prices with the aid of money. By reason of its direct connection with prices in the exchange process the money supply is a good starting point in the study of price-determining factors. In what follows we discuss the nature of money and a few basic facts concerning the money supply in the United States. This puts us in a position to examine the relationship of the money supply to prices. With the subject thus thoroughly opened up we proceed to discuss the price level from other points of view.

## INTRODUCTION TO MONEY

**The Functions of Money.** The use of money is essential in a market economy where most output is bought and sold. In such an economy the producer often specializes in the creation of a single item. By selling this item at a price in the market the producer acquires the means with which to buy what he needs and wants. When used in this way money is referred to as a *medium of exchange,* or as an agent that facilitates the purchase and sale of goods and services.

A second major function of money is to serve as a *standard of values.* In a society marked by specialization and exchange there is a need for simplifying calculations. If barter prevailed, every individual would be forced to deal with the rate of exchange of his item for all others. Besides, he would have to consider all the indirect exchanges of items by means of which he could obtain a given item. Money affords a shortcut through this tangle of relationships. When the value of every item is expressed in terms of money, the need for calculating a multitude of exchange rates drops away. Every item has its value expressed in money, rather than in terms of the other items it will serve to purchase.

In another direction the function of standard of value is useful. Whenever there arises a need to add up items that are basically different, the common unit of money will help. When we wish to compute the quantity of all goods and services produced in the economy during the year (Net National Product) or the assets owned by a firm or all physical assets that exist in the economy (the national wealth), a common denominator is needed. Money serves this need.

Sometimes goods are bought from the seller without immediate payment from the buyer. Among the examples of this process are consumer credit, home mortgages, and corporate debt represented by bonds. In all these cases some arrangement must be made by the purchaser of the item to settle the debt. Money used in this way serves as a *standard for deferred payments;* this is one aspect of the standard of value function.

As a final point, people wish to acquire funds with which they can secure goods at their pleasure. Ultimately, they will want to acquire useful things. Until the proper time comes, however, they might want to keep command over goods in the form of money. This gives the individual an option on the time at which he wishes to acquire goods and services in exchange for the services he has rendered. Here the medium of exchange function is extended over time. When considered in this capacity, money is called a *store of value,* and the desire on the part of the public for money to be used for this purpose is referred to as *liquidity preference.* When business is slow or people fear that goods and securities cannot be sold on short notice except at a loss, they will develop a preference for holding money. If inflation develops and the purchasing power of money declines through time, money becomes a poorer store of value and also a poorer medium of exchange. This situation leads people to complete their exchanges by converting their cash into goods or securities.

In the light of this discussion let us try to define money. We might assert that money is anything that performs the functions of money. Out of context this definition is meaningless and apparently circular in its logic. An alternative is to define money in frequently employed terms of the medium of exchange function, as follows: *Money is anything generally acceptable in exchange for goods and services.* Although incomplete, this definition does emphasize the most important of money's functions.

**Forms of Money in the United States: Currency and Coin.** When we refer to money in everyday speech, we usually mean *currency* and *coin*. Starting with coin, we have fractional coins: the penny, nickel, dime, quarter, fifty-cent piece, and the silver dollar. Although all of these coins have a substantial content of valuable metal, none has the property that the constitutent metal is equal to the monetary value stamped on the face. Suppose that in 1962 we had melted down a silver dollar (an illegal practice) and separated out the 361¼ grains of fine silver it contains. Because this amounts to just about ¾ of an ounce, and because the New York price of silver averaged $1.084 an ounce in 1962, the silver content could have been sold for about 82 cents in that year. So the silver dollar was worth more as money than as a commodity. This has consistently been the case with silver dollars and, up until recently, all our other coins. All coins are issued and otherwise managed by the United States Treasury.

Then we have currency, or paper money. Perhaps most familiar to us is the silver certificate issued by the Treasury in one- and five-dollar denominations. If we look at a piece of this money, say the $1 bill, we see written on its face the statement "This certifies that there is on deposit in the Treasury of the United States of America one dollar in silver payable to the bearer on demand." If the owner of the bill goes to the Treasury and asks for this silver, he will receive a silver dollar. As we have just pointed out, the value of the metallic content is somewhat less than a dollar. Again, the value of the silver certificate is clearly not derived from the silver for which it can be exchanged.

Although there are numerous other kinds of currency outstanding in small amounts, the principal remaining one is the *Federal Reserve note*. This currency is issued in all the usual denominations, from $1 up, by the Federal Reserve Banks.[1] Although Federal Reserve notes are backed by gold, this fact is not helpful to the ordinary citizen. Actually, the ordinary person cannot get hold of this gold, which is

[1] In a later chapter we will discuss the Federal Reserve System, consisting basically of 12 privately owned but governmentally influenced Federal Reserve Banks.

held in the form of gold bars in Fort Knox and other government depositories. True, one can exchange Federal Reserve notes for silver certificates, silver dollars, or fractional money, but as we know, this would represent no improvement. In fact, this form of money, like the others already mentioned, is basically *fiat money*. Thus it is currency issued by or with the approval of government and which derives its value from its official standing in performing the usual functions of money.

**Another Basic Form of Money: Bank Deposits.** Suppose John Doe has $10,000 in a checking account at the First National Bank. Then we would probably say that he "has a lot of money." For one thing he can write a check on his account, present it to the bank, and obtain thereby some currency and coin. Then he certainly has some money. But he can do more. Suppose he decides to buy a new tire for his car and enters the appropriate store. After he selects the needed tire, he pulls out his wallet to pay for the tire and finds it empty. What then? The chances are he simply arranges with the salesman to pay by check. Here a check is used directly to buy goods.

Can we now say that checks are money? Not exactly. Money is defined as anything generally acceptable in exchange for goods and services. Although John Doe's check was accepted by the tire store, it does not follow that it would be elsewhere. Here the difficulty is that a number of conditions must be met before the check becomes acceptable: (1) the signature on the check must belong to the signer; (2) there must be an account in that name; and (3) the balance in the account must cover the amount of the check. Thus the check itself is subject to so many conditions that it is not to be regarded as money. Instead the bank deposit in question is taken to be money, because it is used to buy goods and services and to perform the other functions of money. In short, bank deposits are counted as money, but checks are not.

**Importance of Different Forms of Money.** The relative importance of the different forms of money is measured primarily by the value of the transaction performed. As measured in these terms, bank deposits are much the most important, performing about 90 per cent of all transactions. In fact, discussions about changes in the quantity of money revolve around bank deposits and the banking system. As a second indicator we have the quantities of the several forms of money. Again, bank deposits are far and away the largest in amount, with about $124.7 billions compared to $39.3 billion currency and coin (including some currency held by banks). Of the latter sum about $34.1 billion consists of Federal Reserve notes and roughly $5.2 billion of Treasury coin and silver certificates. About $5 billion of the $39.3 of currency, however, is held by the banks. All this is summarized in Table 8–1.

**Money and Income.** Let us turn our attention to the way money enters into the exchange process. By this means we may get some helpful clues about the relation of money to income. We start with what is known as the *equation of exchange*.

**Value of Sales.** The equation of exchange is founded on the fact that every purchase or sale can be regarded from two points of view. The first involves the quantity of the item exchanged and the price of that item. Multiplied together, the quantity exchanged and the price give the value of the transaction. Letting $p$ stand for price and $q$ for quantity, $p \cdot q$ stands for the money value of the transaction. Suppose we concentrate only on exchanges involving *newly produced goods and services* entering into the *national income* (Net National Product). If we add up the values of all such transactions

**TABLE 8-1**
**Money Supply in the United States, November 30, 1964 (Billions of Dollars)**

| | | | |
|---|---|---|---|
| Currency Outside Treasury and Federal Reserve Banks | | | |
| Federal Reserve notes | | 34.1 | |
| Treasury currency | | | |
| silver certificates | 1.4 | | |
| standard silver dollars | 0.5 | | |
| other coin | 2.9 | | |
| other | 0.4 | | |
| Total | 5.2 | 5.2 | |
| Total currency | | 39.3 | |
| − currency held by banks | | 5.0 | |
| = currency held by public | | 34.3 | 34.3 |
| + demand deposits | | | 124.7 |
| Total currency and demands deposits | | | 159.0 |

for a year we arrive at the level of *NNP*. In short, *NNP* is the money value of all the output produced during the year. Symbolically, we can write

$$NNP = p_1q_1 + p_2q_2 + \cdots + p_nq_n, \quad (1)$$

where $p_1q_1$ is the value of the first transaction, $p_2q_2$ of the second, and $p_nq_n$ of the last.

It is customary to write this sum in the condensed form $P \cdot Q$, where $P$ is an index number of prices and $Q$ is an index number of quantity. The index number of price measures the average price, and the index number of quantity measures the total quantity exchanged. Both are measured against a base time period regarded as normal. In brief, we write

$$NNP = P \cdot Q, \quad (2)$$

taking $P \cdot Q$ as the measure of the value of goods sold (relative to a base period), where $P$ is an index number of price and $Q$ of quantity exchanged.

**Money Work.** The other side of the equation stems from the fact that sales are accomplished with the aid of money. (Remember that we include in the definition of money not only currency and coin but also bank deposits utilized by checks.) By measuring the amount and activity of money we can arrive at another measure of $NNP$ exactly equal to the first.

Suppose the level of $NNP$ was $450 billion, whereas the money supply was $150 billion. Obviously, this amount of money will not buy $450 billion worth of goods, if used only once. However, if this same quantity could be used three times, it would buy the entire $NNP$ of $450 billion. Let us define *the income velocity of money as the number of times the money supply must turn over to give the NNP.* This amounts to saying that the following equation defines $V$:

$$NNP = M \cdot V, \tag{3}$$

where $M$ is the money supply and $V$ is the velocity of money.

Setting equal these two expressions for $NNP$, we get the equation

$$P \cdot Q = M \cdot V.$$

By definition, $P \cdot Q$ is $NNP$, and $V$ is defined to make $M \cdot V$ equal to $NNP$, or $P \cdot Q$. Accordingly, this is an equation by definition of $V$.

**Use of Equation of Exchange.** It would be very pleasant to say that this equation *explains* something. Actually, it merely serves to define $V$ and does nothing else. However, it does group together certain factors related to the price level. We may divide through the above equation by $Q$ to put the equation in the form

$$P = \frac{M \cdot V}{Q}. \tag{4}$$

This equation indicates that the price level tends to increase with the quantity of money, provided that $V$ and $Q$ remain constant. Also the price level tends to decrease with increased output $Q$, other factors constant. Actually, it would be handy if $V$ were constant. Then we could analyze price changes in terms of changes in the money supply and output. However, the evidence indicates that this is not the case, velocity changing rather widely from time to time.

**Relation of Equation to Income Analysis.** Since $NNP = M \cdot V$, there is an obvious relationship between $NNP$, $M$, and $V$. By drawing an income graph we can illustrate the meaning of this relation for a certain case.

**An Expansion.** To begin with, suppose the economy to be in equilibrium, with $C + I + G = NNP$, as at point $A$ in Figure 8–1.

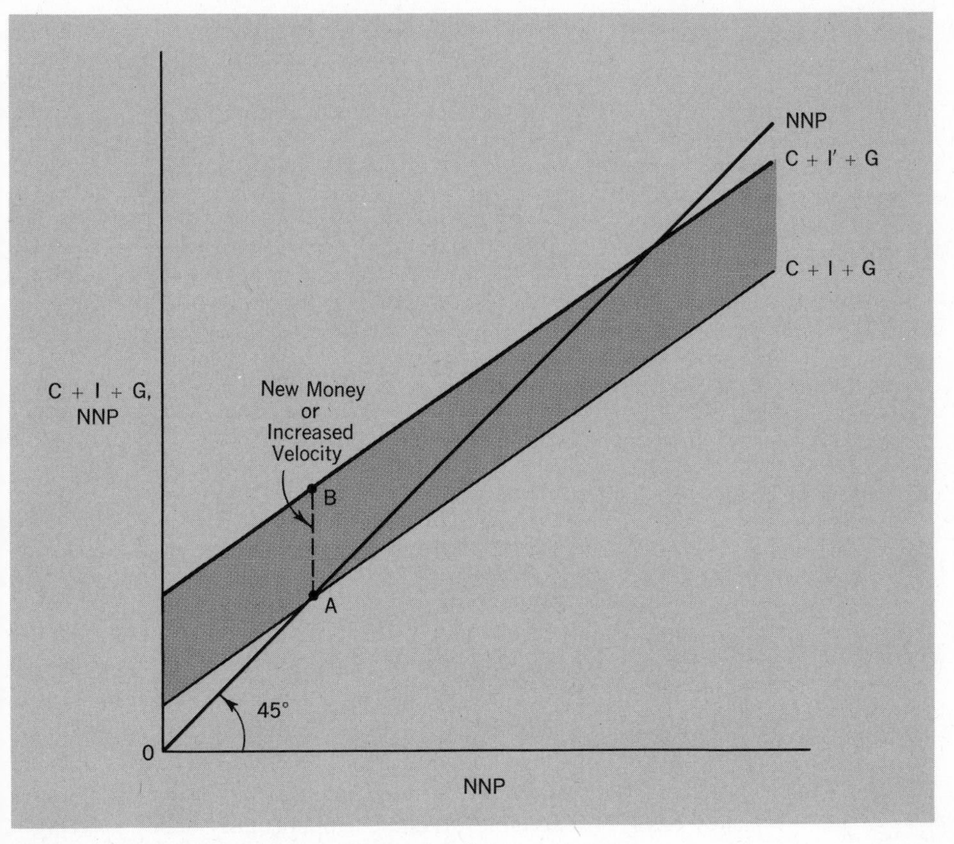


**Figure 8–1.** Relation of changing *NNP* to *M* and *V*.

At this juncture (lower-loop) *NNP* is completely taken up in buying goods—consumption, investment, and government output. Now businessmen decide they want to invest additional sums in new capital equipment resulting in an upward shift of the $C + I + G$ line. Keep in mind that no income is available to finance these needs. Where is the money to come from then? It does no good to say that businessmen will "borrow" the money, because all the available income is now tied up in buying goods. Evidently, no new borrowing from people who lend out of income is possible. Some new source of funds must be found.

First, let us dispose of the government. Broadly speaking, government does not qualify as a lender. Although the government could assume this function, it normally does not, and another source must be found. What about insurance companies, savings and loan associations, and like institutions? Such firms channel the savings of individuals only into investment or into the purchase of government bonds to finance government spending. But this flow is now all taken up by the economy. Subject to a very general exception to be mentioned, these institutions cannot help at this juncture. Finally, corporations also fail to qualify, because their current funds are absorbed in dividends, taxes to government, and current investment. Again, there is an exception to be mentioned.

At this point we have eliminated all likely sources of funds but one—the money and banking system. As we will explain in Chapter 10, banks can create new loans (bank deposits), if they have excess reserves. Suppose a businessman seeking funds for investments is granted such a loan. He can draw on the reservoir of new money, represented by the loan, to buy the capital goods he wants. In Figure 8–1 the gap $AB$ of demand, $C + I' + G$, over available output ($NNP$) may be financed by *new* bank credit.

As the new money comes into circulation, supplementing existing demand, pressure is applied on all sellers to supply a larger volume of output. If they have abundant excess capacity, they will meet the demand largely with increased output, and prices will not rise very much. If output is approaching capacity, however, costs will be rising sharply, and firms will advance prices considerably to choke off the excess demand. At this stage the increase in output will be small.

There is an additional possibility for financing expansion. This is the drawing down of idle bank balances. Manufacturing corporations, financial institutions, and individuals hold balances in banks. Not all of these are strictly required for immediate use, but are held on a contingency basis. If a suitable investment opportunity arises, offering a high enough return, holders of these idle balances may release them for investment purposes. Now this action does not increase the quantity of money. Rather it transfers money from idleness to use, and therefore increases the velocity of money $V$.

To summarize, an increase in $NNP$ must be accompanied by an increase in the money supply or a rise in velocity. The latter implies a transfer of funds from idle to active balances, from money held idle to money used to buy goods. Now prices tend to rise slightly if excess capacity exists, but will rise sharply if little excess capacity is present.

**How Changes in the Money Supply Affect *NNP*.** From the equation of exchange $NNP = M \cdot V$, we know that if $M$ increases *while $V$ is constant* $NNP$ will increase. In fact, $NNP$ is directly proportional to $M$ under this assumption. Actually, $V$ exhibits wide fluctuation, rendering this interpretation virtually worthless. Therefore another approach is required.

**Money, the Interest Rate, and Total Spending.** Here we anticipate some matters taken up in the chapter entitled "Interest—Income Share of Capital." Suppose the government and the banks increase the supply of money available for lending. Such an increase in funds will tend to lower the rate of interest; because the new supply of money competes with alternative sources of funds for borrowing, such as personal and corporate saving, the resulting pressure forces down the interest rate. To a great extent the increased supply of money for borrowing purposes comes from banks that make loans available at lower rates.

Consider briefly the effect on total spending, taking consumption, government spending, and investment, in that order. From what evidence is available consumption spending seems to depend primarily on the net income of consumers. Although a lower interest rate would reduce the cost of articles bought on time payments, the difference is probably not noticeable to consumers. Consequently, the influence is likely to be small. Government spending on output is determined by certain needs of the public based on a political decision. Often, as in the case of certain defense projects, cost is a secondary consideration. In a few cases of long-term capital outlays for public works, such as courthouses, school buildings, highways, bridges, and the like, interest is a major factor in cost. Here a cut in the rate might cause an increase in spending. On the whole, the effect is probably small.

Finally, we come to investment expenditure of business firms on newly produced capital goods. Businesses acquire capital goods only after weighing carefully the prospective annual returns against the annual costs. Now the costs include two main elements, annual depreciation of the capital and the annual interest cost. The longer the life of the capital equipment, the smaller is the annual depreciation charge and the larger is the annual interest cost. When the business firm considers a long-term investment in, say, a new building, the interest cost is probably going to be a significant factor. For this reason we may say that the lower the interest rate, the greater will be the demand by business firms for funds for investment.

We may now formalize this discussion by asserting that the demand for investment funds to be spent on capital depends on the rate of interest. We may include in this total any similar government investment projects influenced by interest. The relationship may be represented by a demand curve for investment funds sloping downward from left to right. On the vertical axis the rate of interest is shown, on the horizontal, the sum of money businessmen wish to borrow and invest. We may call this the investment-demand curve.

Suppose the rate of interest is *OA* in Figure 8–2. Such a rate will prompt businessmen to invest an amount *OB*, as indicated by the dashed line below *E* on the demand curve. If the government and the banks make available additional money for lending at lower rates, the

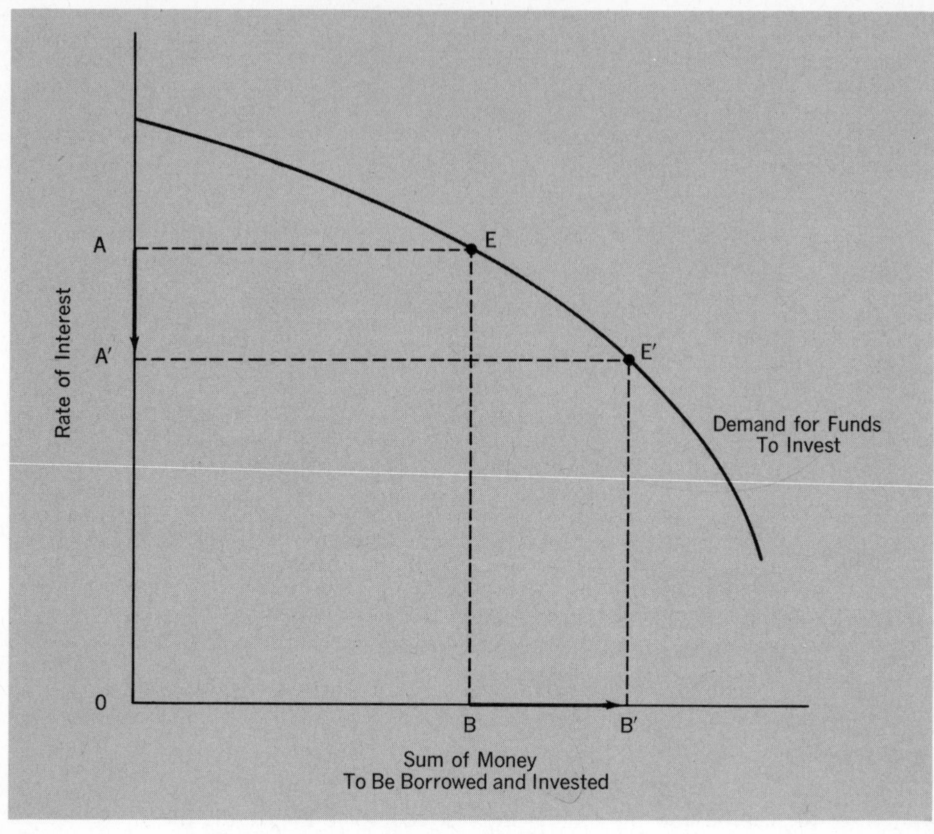


**Figure 8–2.** Demand for investment funds.

interest rate will fall, say, from $OA$ to $OA'$. At this lower rate it will pay businessmen to expand the amount they borrow and invest from $OB$ to $OB'$. This is shown by the shift from $E$ to $E'$ along the investment-demand curve at the lower interest rate.

Let us now summarize all our ideas in this section in one simple statement. *An increase in the supply of money results in a lower interest rate, which increases the amount businessmen wish to spend on investment.* What about the effect on *NNP?* The theory of the multiplier gives the answer. To illustrate this, assume the following to be true: (1) the supply of money is increased, lowering the interest rate and causing investment to increase by $2.5 billion; (2) the multiplier is 3. Clearly, the increase in spending on investment is going to bring about additional rounds of spending on consumption, leading to additional *NNP*. Ultimately, *NNP* will rise by a total equal to 3 times the $2.5-billion increase in spending on investment, or a total of $7.5 billion. Thus we can complete the above italicized statement

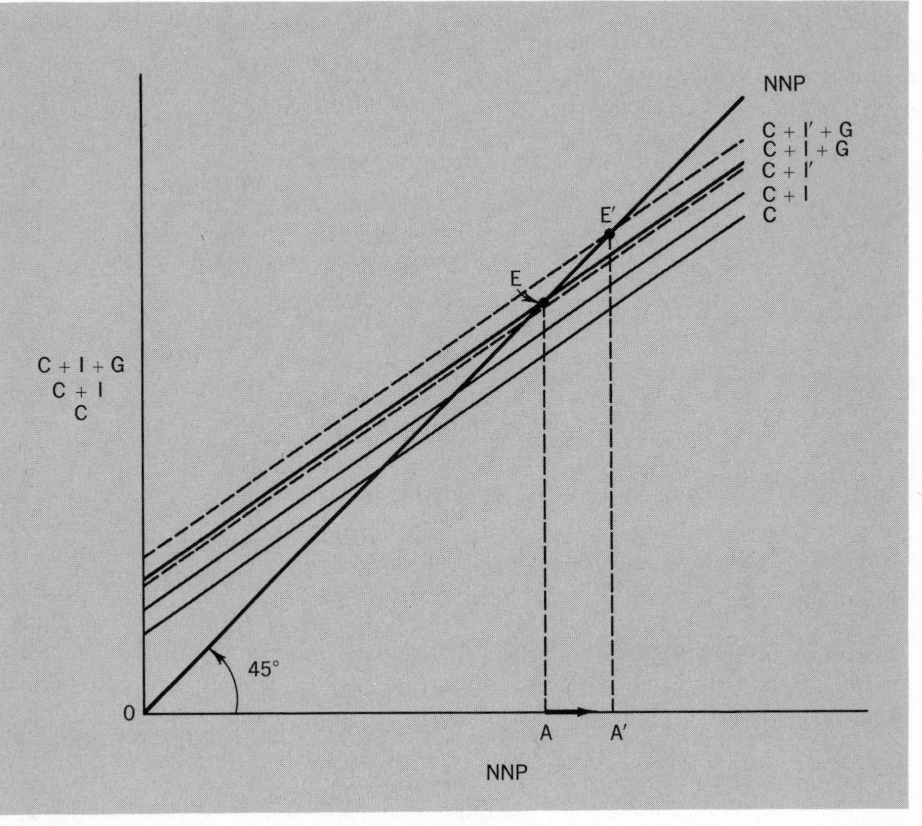


**Figure 8–3.** Effect of increased investment on *NNP*.

with this observation: *Additional investment spending then exerts a leverage effect on NNP as additional consumption spending takes place.*

The effects may be summarized by a total spending diagram. In Figure 8–3 the original level of *NNP* is found at *E*, where $C + I + G$ crosses the *NNP* line. This leads to a level of *NNP* equal to *OA*. As the new money supply is created, the rate of interest drops and investment increases. This leaves the *C* line unchanged, but raises the $C + I$ and $C + I + G$ lines to the dashed positions, $C + I'$ and $C + I' + G$. A new equilibrium is established at *E′*, giving rise to a larger *NNP* of *OA′*.

**Summary and Prospect.** We have now shown how the supply of money is tied in with changes in *NNP* from two points of view. First, any increase in *NNP* requires either an increase in *M* or *V* or both. Such a change can proceed from various causes: an upward shift in the consumption line (unlikely), an increase in government spending on output, or an increase in investment spending for a variety of reasons (a frequent occurrence). Thus an increase in money supply or velocity is necessary to carry out the resulting increase in *NNP*. Second, an increase in *M* through the medium of additional bank loans and lower interest rates leads to additional investment and rising *NNP*. Here money functions as a cause of the change in *NNP* rather than as a mere accommodating element, as in the first case.

From the discussion, it is apparent that the money supply is closely related to changes in *NNP*. Recall, too, that *NNP* can be thought of as the sum of the values of all outputs produced in the economy. Therefore, as *NNP* increases, there will be an increase in outputs and prices. Thus the money supply is related to prices and outputs—that is, to *NNP*. In what follows we will emphasize the relation of prices to *NNP* with no specific reference to the money supply.

We shall approach the problem of the price level from several points of view. First, we describe the forces that determine the level of prices at a given moment of time. Such an approach is essentially static or stationary; that is, it gives a picture of events, in this case the price level, resulting from the action of a given set of economic conditions. This picture is essentially accurate when the economy is operating below the so-called full-employment level. If all factors—labor, land or natural resources, capital facilities, and entrepreneurship or managerial abilities—are being rather completely utilized, full employment is said to exist. As a practical matter a small margin of slack—3 to 5 per cent in terms of unemployed resources—is allowed for. Hence the full-employment level is used to mean a situation in which from 95 to 97 per cent of all resources are being used. This adjustment is necessary, because in a world with many changes taking place it is rare indeed to find all factors in use. Our first discussion below, entitled "Price-Level Determination," deals with the level of prices when the economy is operating *below* full employment.

We also discuss a second case. When the economy approaches full employment, as defined by the above discussion, pressure on prices and a more or less continual rise in prices tends to begin. A self-reinforcing, continued rise in prices may be called *inflation* or an *inflationary process*. In this discussion a case is taken up that traces inflation to a high level of demand.

## PRICE-LEVEL DETERMINATION

In an earlier chapter we discussed the concepts of demand and supply. Let us pick out the concept of supply for consideration here. Assume that we have a way to add up the supply curves for all the different outputs in the economy. Then we will get a relationship between the level of output, designated $Q = NNP$, deflated, and the level of prices. Each of these is, of course, an index number. Then the relationship, when graphed, would look something like the solid curve labeled $P$ in the lower part of Figure 8–4.

The curve in question may be interpreted as an aggregate-supply curve relating output to the price level. It assumes that (1) the level of wages is constant, (2) the quantity of capital is approximately constant (this is actually true only for a short period of time), (3) an appropriate and fixed way has been found to add up the supply curves of all the outputs, (4) competition prevails in the market, and (5) the economy has not achieved full-employment *NNP*.

Now let us combine this with an income-determination diagram. In the latter *NNP* is "deflated" for price changes and so represents output. Then the data available shows a pattern such that the consumption function is a straight line cutting the vertical axis slightly above the origin. (Recall Figure 6–1.)

The data indicate no definite behavior pattern for investment in relation to *NNP*. If output should expand, the price of capital goods would tend to rise, thus increasing the cost of capital. At the same time the increased output implies greater consumption demand and tends to raise the expected returns from the use of capital. Let us assume that these two tendencies offset one another in the sense that investment in real terms remains constant.

A similar description fits the case of government spending. At the outset government appropriations are fixed. If output expands and prices rise, the quantity of service that government could render would diminish. However, with additional output and income the government tax take will automatically increase. We assume that rather than curtail services Congress will appropriate more funds, an action made easy by increased receipts. Therefore we assume that spending on output by government in real terms remains the same. We now proceed to illustrate the determination of the output and price levels.

In the upper part of Figure 8–4 aggregate demand equals aggregate supply, $C + I + G = NNP$, at point $E$. In turn, this determines deflated *NNP* or output as $Oa$. Dropping a line down to the lower diagram, we note that an intersection with the supply curve is found at $e$. Finally, drawing a dashed line over to the left, we arrive at the price level $OB$.

If demand increases, and the $C + I + G$ line shifts upward, deflated *NNP* will increase and the price level will rise. Obviously, as demand increases, prices will rise slowly at first. Later, prices will rise more rapidly as output approaches capacity. Then any increase in demand will cause a rise in prices with little or no change in output. Actually, as *NNP* approaches capacity, a dynamic inflation process

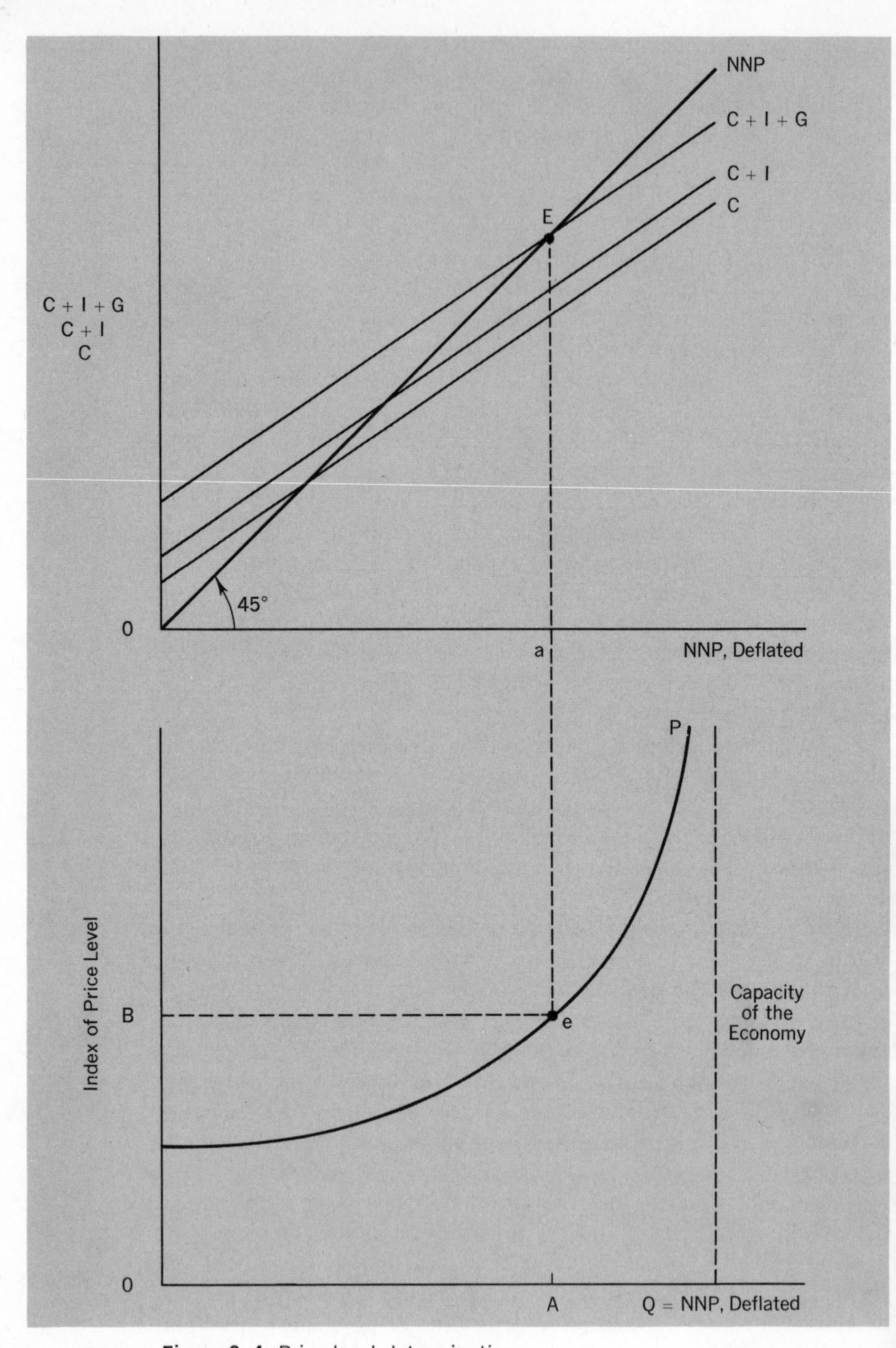


**Figure 8–4.** Price-level determination.

tends to set in. This cannot be shown by the preceding diagram or reasoning. In the chapter proper we will discuss the general concept of inflation. For those who want a more precise account we lay out a model in graphical form in the appendix to the chapter.

## PRICE INFLATION CAUSED BY STRONG DEMAND

One basic cause of inflation consists in the presence of a very high level of demand. As long as the existing demand can be met with corresponding supply from existing productive facilities, and at existing prices, no problem arises. When demand becomes great enough, however, all the factors that can readily be found are put to work, and full employment is achieved. The output produced with full employment of the factors, as measured by the costs of the factors—necessary wages, interest, rents, and profits—is entitled full-employment *NNP*. When aggregate demand, $C+I+G$, is precisely equal to full-employment *NNP*, all factors are employed and the economy produces the largest possible output.

Now suppose an autonomous increase in demand, $C+I+G$, occurs. Then a situation arises in which demand, $C+I+G$, exceeds the maximum supply or output of the economy, full-employment *NNP*. In Figure 8–5 full-employment *NNP* is given as $OF = FA$. Aggregate demand has become so great as to exceed this figure, being $FB$ as compared with $FA$. The excess of $C+I+G$ over full-employment *NNP*, of demand over maximum output, is known as *the inflationary gap* and is represented here by the excess of $FB$ over $FA$ or $AB$. This distance is labeled in the figure.

When an inflationary gap exists, the public wants to spend more money on output than business firms can supply at existing prices. This leads to bidding on the part of buyers for the existing output, and prices tend to rise, presumably in proportion to the relationship between aggregate demand, $C+I+G$, and aggregate supply, full-employment *NNP*. Thus it seems reasonable to assume that prices of output would rise in the proportion $BF/AF = 8/7$. Then all the demand of the public is actually expended on output, but at advanced prices.

We will now carry forward the argument without detailed references to the figure. Let us assume that everything spent on output becomes factor income, either wages, interest, rent, or profit. Exactly how does this come about here? Well, the demand exceeds the supply, as evidenced by the presence of the inflationary gap. In order to meet the excess demand, business firms seek to hire additional factors of production. However, all factors available for use have already been put to work, because full employment exists. Accordingly, firms must bid higher for the use of factors in order to attract them away from the firms currently using them. Therefore factor prices rise. How much? If we assume that firms use all their receipts to bid for factors, these factor prices must rise in proportion to the excess of demand over supply. Clearly, none of the added demand for factors results in the hiring of added factors for the economy, because the factors are already at work. Therefore we conclude that factor prices must rise in the same proportion as output prices.

At this stage the existence of an inflationary gap has forced up product prices. The larger receipts of business firms lead them to bid more vigorously for factors. As a result, factor prices also rise (in proportion, we have argued). Here we must introduce an additional and critical assumption. The monetary authorities must begin to provide an additional supply of money to finance the larger dollar volume of transactions. Assume that they provide an additional

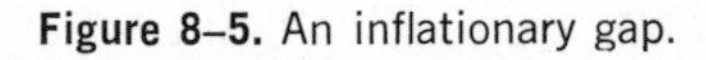

**Figure 8–5.** An inflationary gap.

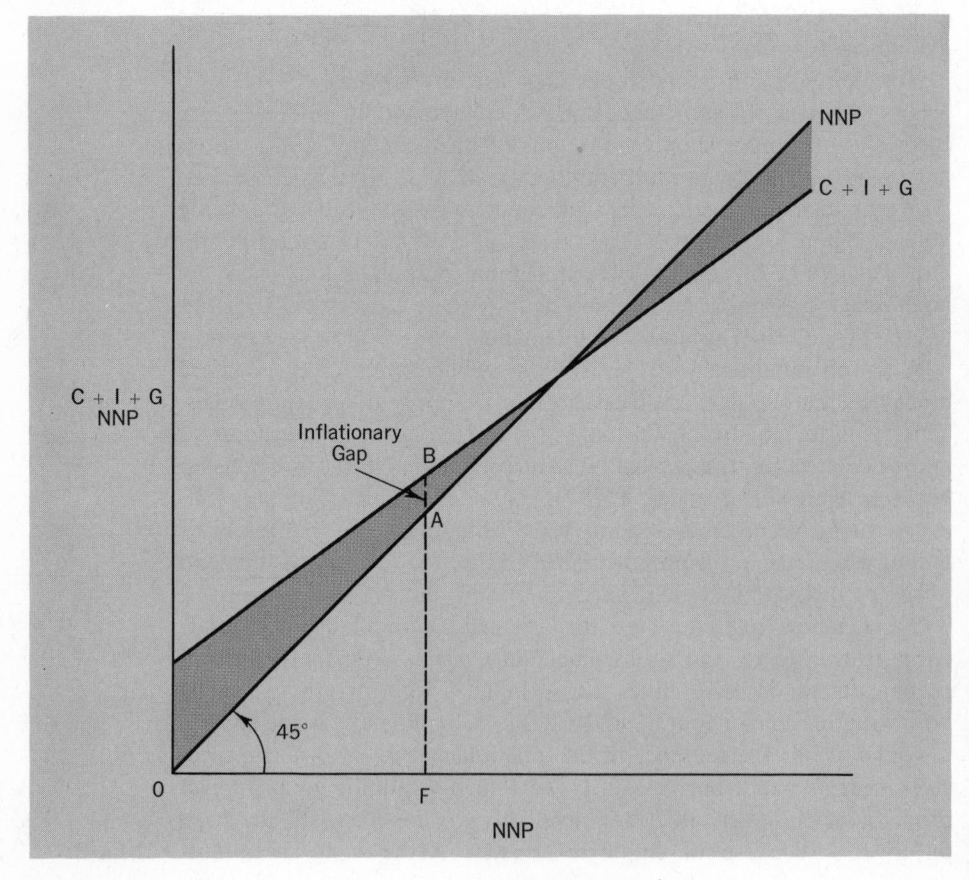

amount proportional to the larger dollar value of transactions—that is, to the increased level of *NNP*. Then the public can handle the larger volume of business without difficulty. Now let us assess the situation at this stage.

Output prices have gone up in a given proportion, *BF/AF* in Figure 8–5. Factor prices and incomes have gone up in the same proportion. By assumption, the quantity of money has been increased to finance the larger volume of transactions, again in this same proportion. Consider the situation from the viewpoint of the spender. His income (*NNP*) has risen. Prices of outputs have risen in the same proportion, and he has a larger stock of cash in the bank. Then he is in the same real situation as he was at the start. His larger income and greater cash balance stand in exactly the same relationship to prices as they did originally.

This indicates that buyers will want to purchase the same collection of goods and services they did before incomes and prices rose. As we recall, the demand originally exceeded the maximum available supply, a condition manifested by an inflationary gap. This situation is now repeated, though incomes (*NNP*), output and factor prices, and the money supply have all moved up a notch. Again, an inflationary gap appears, with corresponding effects. Thus the inflationary gap forces up product prices, leading to higher factor prices and *NNP*, resulting in still higher demand, and so on. This represents an inflationary spiral that takes place step by step as long as the assumed conditions persist.

**Summary of Demand Induced Inflation.** If demand, or $C+I+G$, rises sufficiently, the aggregate supply that matches it will be the largest possible, namely, full-employment *NNP*. No inflation is involved according to this discussion in producing this output. Now (1) we assume $C+I+G$ increases autonomously, causing an inflationary gap, an excess of $C+I+G$ over full-employment *NNP;* (2) this excess demand causes output prices to be bid up in proportion to the inflationary gap, there being no extra output to be had; (3) firms bid for factors to meet the excess demand (= the inflationary gap), and factor prices (wages, and so on) rise in the same proportion as output prices; (4) as a result of the rising factor prices, with constant amounts of the factors, incomes also rise and in the same proportion; (5) we *assume* that the monetary system creates an additional amount of money proportional to the extra income; (6) incomes, prices, and the stock of money all having increased in proportion, spenders raise their spending still further in proportion to the advanced income, repeating the situation in (1) but at a higher level of *NNP* and $C+I+G$. Step (6) is the first step of a new cycle.

**Cost Factors in Inflation.** The analysis above suggests, perhaps, that demand is the devil that inspires inflation. This is not necessarily the case. The inflationary spiral arises from a persistent spread between the *NNP* line and a $C + I + G$ line that shifts upward with the increase in *NNP*. Any steady upward push on costs that is met by rising prices of products leads to an upward price spiral. The mechanics of the spiral are much the same.

**Inflation with Underemployment.** In this analysis we suggest that inflation may begin at the point of full employment. Thus prices will tend to be stable, so this analysis goes, as long as there is slack in the economy. Facts have begun to accumulate showing that inflation may begin when substantial unemployment is present. This is accounted for partly by the structural character of unemployment. Certain classes of labor, particularly the unskilled, tend to have high unemployment levels when other groups are rather fully employed. The expansion of output may be virtually impossible without more skilled labor or other resources. Consequently, rising prices of output, skilled labor, and other resources may commence with substantial unemployment among the unskilled or other special groups.

**Summary.** This chapter begins with a description of the various forms of money in the United States. At this point the predominant importance of bank deposits as money is indicated. Next, the relation of the money supply to the level of *NNP* is indicated. This is done by means of the equation of exchange: $NNP = P \cdot Q = M \cdot V$, where $P$, $Q$, $M$, and $V$ represent index numbers of the price level, output produced, quantity of money, and velocity, respectively. Any increase in *NNP* is shown to require an increase either in $M$ or $V$ or both. Next the analysis shows that an increase in the money supply lowers interest rates, and increases investment, and thereby the level of *NNP*. As *NNP* rises, outputs and prices increase, the latter predominating as full employment is approached.

The final section of the chapter is devoted to price-level determination. First, the determination of the price level below full-employment *NNP* is shown to depend on the added-up supply curves on the one hand and the level of *NNP* determined by total demand ($C + I + G$) and total supply (*NNP*) on the other. As full employment is reached, inflation follows any further increase in demand. At the point of full employment both output and employment reach a peak level that cannot be exceeded. Further increases in $C + I + G$ and *NNP* imply increases in output and factor prices.

An excess of $C + I + G$ over *NNP* at full-employment *NNP*, the inflationary gap, causes a rise in output prices. As business firms bid for factors with which to satisfy the extra demand they raise factor prices (for example, wages) and therefore incomes. If the money supply increases in proportion, as we assume, output prices, money incomes, and the supply of cash have all risen in proportion. Hence the buyer is in the same real situation as before but with a higher base income. Hence $C + I + G$ rises above *NNP* again, in the same proportion as existed at the beginning. Thus the spiral continues.

Cost factors can also initiate inflation by causing a spread between $C + I + G$ and *NNP*, operating on the latter. Finally, inflation can commence at less-than-full employment.

## QUESTIONS

1. Why is the study of money a good starting point for the discussion of overall price determination?
2. List and briefly explain the meaning of the several functions of money.
3. What is money? Are checks money? Are bank deposits money? Why?
4. Write down the equation of exchange, define the terms, and explain the equality of the two sides.
5. How does the equation of exchange contribute to an explanation of price?
6. Using the standard analysis of income (*NNP*) determination, explain how money gets into circulation and how it affects prices.
7. Discuss the above process of price change in terms of the equation of exchange.
8. Explain how an increase in the supply of money affects interest and, through interest, the several components of total spending.
9. How does the multiplier enter into this process?
10. What is the origin of the relationship between the price level and deflated *NNP*, shown in the lower part of Figure 8–4 (the curve labeled *P*)?
11. Why is the upper diagram in Figure 8–4, determining deflated *NNP*, necessary to the determination of the price level?
12. What is an inflationary gap?
13. Why is a rise in product prices at full employment succeeded by a rise in factor prices?
14. Summarize the steps in demand-induced inflation.

# Appendix

## A MODEL OF PRICE INFLATION

In the discussion of static price and output (*NNP*) determination we showed aggregate demand, $C + I + G$, and aggregate supply, *NNP*, in deflated form. Because we are now going to deal with inflation, a price phenomenon, it will be a good idea to change over to money quantities. On the horizontal axis we measure *NNP* regarded as the sum of factor payments. Therefore this axis measures $NNP = P_f \cdot Q_f$, where $P_f$ is an index number of factor prices and $Q_f$ is an index number of quantities of factors employed. On the vertical axis we measure expenditure on output, $C + I + G = P \cdot Q$, where $P$ is an index of the prices of outputs and $Q$ is an index of the quantities of outputs.

**Use of Index Numbers.** Let us explain the idea of an index number by means of an illustration, using employment of labor as the item being measured. An index of employment could (theoretically) range from 0 up to 100 per cent or 1. Assume that the labor force is 120 million and that employment is 0. Then the index of employment would be $Q_f = 0/120 = 0$. If 96 million were employed, the index would be $Q_f = 96/120 = 0.8$, or 80 per cent. If 120 million were employed, the index would be $Q_f = 120/120 = 1$, or 100 per cent. This is as high as the index can go in this particular case, because the number employed could not exceed the labor force. Thus the situation represented by employment of 132, leading to an index of $Q_f = 132/120 = 1.1$, or 110 per cent, is impossible. This confirms the idea that the index must vary between 0 and 1. We will use the proportional rather than the percentage form in the discussion.

***NNP* Scale.** In the diagram we are going to consider, $NNP = P_f \cdot Q_f$ is plotted along the horizontal axis. Both $P_f$ and $Q_f$ are interpreted as index numbers. $P_f$ measures the level of factor prices: wages, interest, rent, and profit. As we have just shown, $Q_f$ ranges in value from 0, when no factors are employed, up to 1, when all factors are at work. $P_f$, the price index for factors, could be as low as 0, but has no upper limit whatever. Starting from a low value of *NNP,* both $P_f$ and $Q_f$ rise with NNP. However, as full employment is reached, $Q_f = 1$, its maximum value, and this variable can increase no more. As *NNP* increases further, only $P_f$ can increase, $Q_f$ remaining constant at the maximum value of 1 (representing full employment).

This leads to the following relationships:

| | |
|---|---|
| Up to full employment: | $NNP = P_f \cdot Q_f$<br>$Q_f = 0$ or greater, but is less than 1. |
| At full employment and beyond: | $NNP = P_f \cdot Q_f = P_f \cdot 1 = P_f$<br>$Q_f = 1$ at all times. |

Consider these relationships as they show up on the horizontal axis of our national income graph. We omit the vertical axis and all curves in Figure 8–6.

Up to the full-employment point *F,* our horizontal scale simply equals *NNP* ($= P_f \cdot Q_f$). At the full-employment *NNP* of *F,* $Q_f$ assumes the value of 1 and $NNP = P_f \cdot Q_f = P_f \cdot 1 = P_f$. Thus at full employment and beyond $NNP$ can be interpreted purely as a *price index for the factors of production.* We have arranged this information along the $NNP$ scale.

**C + I + G Scale.** Much the same kind of argument can be applied to the vertical axis of our income-determination diagram. This vertical axis represents primarily total spending on output, $C + I + G$. Of course, this total spending is the value of all output, so that $C + I + G = P \cdot Q$, where $P$ is taken to mean an index of output prices and $Q$ an index of amount of output. Now the amount of output could be as little as zero if no factors were employed. As employment of factors increases $Q$ rises until full employment is reached. According to the argument of Chapter 1, the production frontier is reached. No matter how great $C + I + G$ becomes $Q$ cannot increase

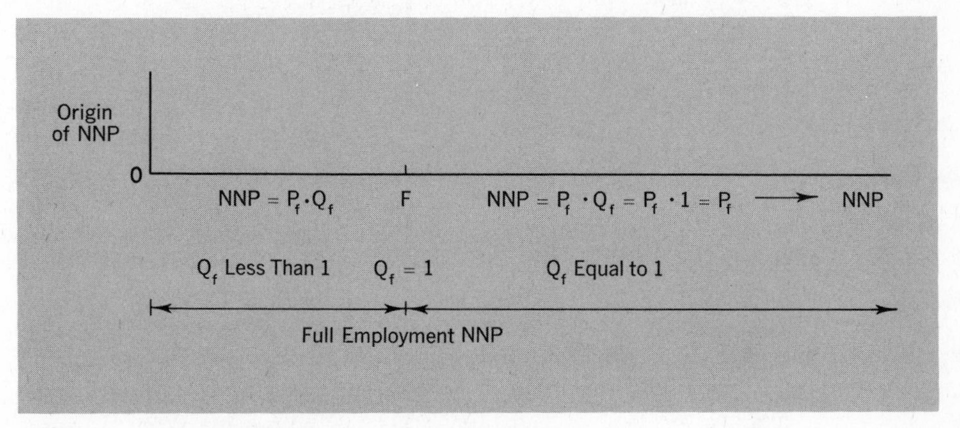


**Figure 8–6.** Details of *NNP* axis for analysis of inflation.

further. Consequently, a maximum output is reached at full employment. Let us make this the base for an index number of output $Q$. Then actual output, considered as an index must be less than 1 below a certain level of $C + I + G$, corresponding to full employment and 1 at higher levels.

Let us interpret the meaning of $Q$. Suppose $Q = 0.8$. Then we would say that output is about $8/10$ (or 80 per cent) of the capacity of the economy. If $Q = 1$, we would say that the economy is operating at 100 per cent of capacity; the factors are fully employed, and the economy is turning out the largest possible output. A value $Q = 1.2$ would imply that the economy is operating at 120 per cent of capacity, or that it is producing 20 per cent more than the capacity level. This is impossible. Therefore, $Q$, as interpreted here, must have a value ranging between 0 (no production) and 1 (capacity).

We can summarize the results of this discussion in much the same way as for the horizontal scale.

| | |
|---|---|
| Up to full employment: | $C + I + G = P \cdot Q$<br>$Q$ varies between 0 and 1. |
| At full employment and beyond: | $C + I + G = P \cdot Q =$<br>$P \cdot 1 = P$.<br>$Q = 1$ at all times. |

We may also line up these relationships as they appear on the vertical axis of our national-income graph. We omit the horizontal axis and all curves in Figure 8–7. We see that beyond *f*, the point representing

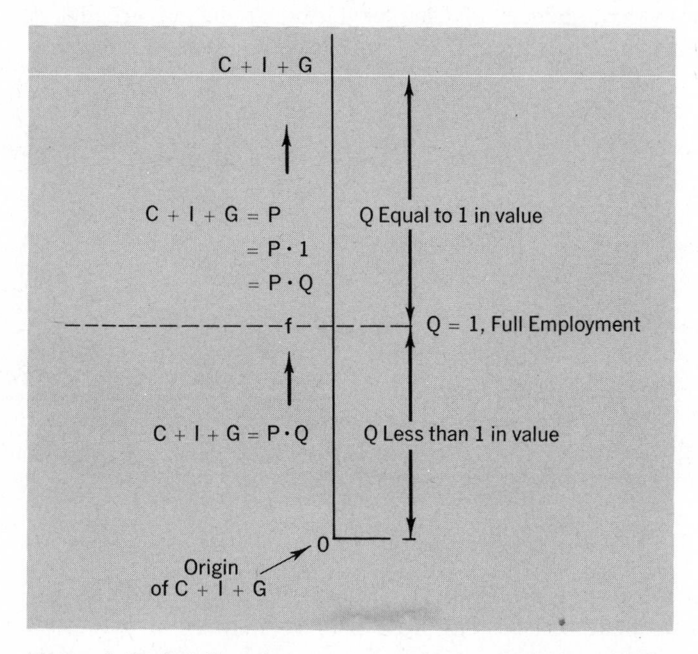


**Figure 8–7.** Details of $C + I + G$ axis for analysis of inflation.

full employment, the vertical scale measures *P*, the price level of output. This arises from the fact that $C + I + G = P$.

**Purpose of Definitions.** A good bit of thought is required to master these definitions, but they bear excellent fruit. Our purpose is to find a way to measure price changes at or beyond full employment. Notice how the definitions used above help in this respect. Along the horizontal axis *NNP* becomes strictly a measure of factor price $P_f$ at and beyond full employment. Similarly, along the vertical axis $C + I + G$ becomes a measure of output prices *P* at and beyond full employment. By this approach we join in one graph the theory of income determination with that of price change or inflation. Finally, a word of caution. The symbol $P_f$ measures the prices of the factors, wages, and so on, and not of products. This should be obvious, because *NNP* measures factor cost, and $P_f$ is the price component of cost.

**Assumptions.** Below the point of full-employment, money wages are assumed to be rigid, because the presence of unemployed workers prevents wages from being raised. On the other hand, unions strongly resist wage cuts. As the economy reaches full employment, wages begin to rise, because the damper of unemployed workers is removed. Also wages amount to about 70 per cent of factor cost so that this element dominates the index of factor cost, $P_f$. Also we assume that the monetary authorities make available enough new money to keep the rate of interest constant. Of course, this implies that they take no effective action to halt inflation. Much the same result is achieved if, as has been the case during recent price rises, society makes more efficient use of the same money supply.

Finally, we assume that there is a time lag in the circular flow. Expenditure of one period generates corresponding *NNP* in the *next* period. This assumption permits us to show a particular way in which inflation develops through time, but it is not a necessary condition for the inflation itself.

**An Inflationary Process, Illustrated.** Suppose that an equilibrium level of *NNP* has been determined where aggregate demand, $C + I + G$, is equal to aggregate supply, *NNP*. In Figure 8–8 this is shown at point *H*, which corresponds to full-employment *NNP*, shown at *F*. Note that the index of employment is at a peak, so that $Q_f = 1$. Also corresponding to *H* on the vertical axis is point *f*, at which output is at a peak, denoted by the fact that $Q = 1$. Beyond *F* on the horizontal axis $NNP = P_f$, and the horizontal axis measures *factor* price. Also above *f* on the vertical axis $C + I + G = P$, and the vertical axis measures output price.

Now suppose that an autonomous change in total spending occurs, represented by a shift of the $C + I + G$ curve to the position indicated by $C + I + G_1$. This could be the result of improved expectations, causing an increase of investment, or by a new and sizable program of government spending. The immediate effect of this is to cause spending to increase from *FH* to *FI* at an *NNP* of *FH* (or *OF*). Now to illustrate more concretely let's assume that $FI = 1\frac{1}{3}$ *NNP* at an *NNP* of *FH* (or *OF*).

The fact that $C + I + G$ is a multiple, equal to $1\frac{1}{3}$, of *NNP* proves to be a persistent feature of the new situation. To represent this relationship at other levels of *NNP* we draw a dashed line from the origin $O$ through $I$. This line has the characteristic everywhere that $C+I+G$, at points like $I$, $K$, and $M$ is $1\frac{1}{3}$ times the $NNP$ at the corresponding points $H$, $J$, and $L$ on the $NNP$ line.

Now back to the situation after $C+I+G$ increased, raising $C+I+G$ to $FI$, which is now $1\frac{1}{3}$ $FH$, where $FH$ is $NNP$. The immediate impact is to raise output prices by $HI$, because, as we may note from the figure, vertical movements above $f$ indicate output price increases. As spending increases by $HI$, businessmen feel the impact of increased demand and try to hire more factors of production. In so doing they bid up the prices of factors without increasing the quantity, because full employment of factors already prevails. As the entire increase in spending $HI$ is resolved into additional $NNP$, $NNP$ and, consequently, $P_f$ increase by the (same) amount $IJ$. You may check the fact that $IJ$ represents a factor price increase from the consideration that $I$ and the corresponding point $F$ represent the full-employment point at which the $NNP$ scale measures $P_f$. Summarizing,

**Figure 8–8.** An inflationary process.

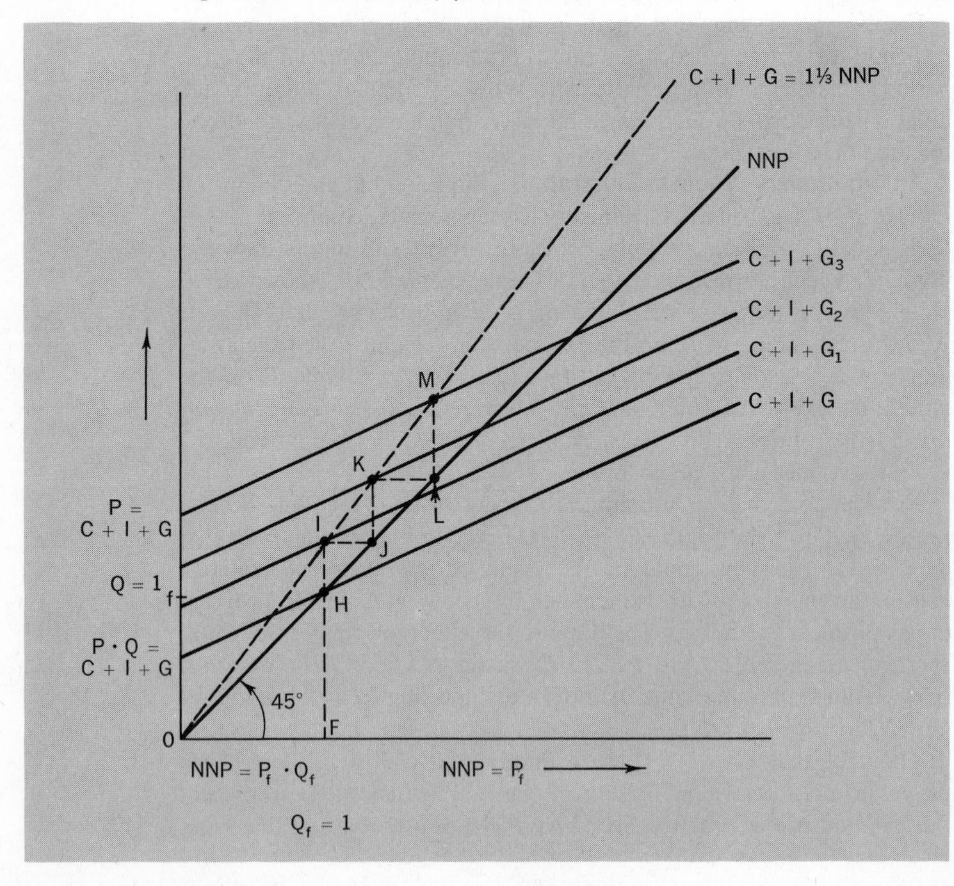

*HI* represents an increase in product price *P*, *IJ* an increase in factor price $P_f$.

Now we are ready for the next turn of the screw of inflation. The increase in product price *HI* and factor price *IJ* has been made possible by an increase in the money supply (or an increased efficiency of use—that is, increased velocity of money). Now suppose that product prices, factor prices, and the supply of money all increase in the same proportion, as here takes place between *H* and *J*. The buyer finds that his income has gone up in a certain proportion, here ⅓, due to the rise in the prices of the factors he owns. At the same time the prices of goods have gone up ⅓ and likewise the stock of money he has. Then he is in no better and no worse position in regard to buying goods than before. He will want to buy the same collection of goods as before; so this will require him to increase his expenditure by ⅓, which is possible on the basis of his extra income. Therefore $C + I + G$ rises to *K* at an *NNP* corresponding to *J*. Here, again, $C + I + G = 1\frac{1}{3}$ *NNP*.

Now let us assess the situation. The insistence by the buyer on the original relationship, $C + I + G = 1\frac{1}{3}$ *NNP*, after *NNP* increased, implies that the $C + I + G$ curve must shift from the position shown by $C + I + G_1$ to that shown by $C + I + G_2$. The new $C + I + G$ is at *K* compared to *NNP* at *J*. The same proportion between spending and *NNP* is true at the second position as at the first. However, prices have increased by ⅓, both output prices *P* and factor prices $P_f$. Now try to reason out the next sequence from *K* to *L* to *M*.

One situation may prove confusing to the student, and we may as well comment on it here and now. The situation starts with an equilibrium of aggregate supply and aggregate demand at *H*. Then $C + I + G$ rises so that a gap *HI* exists between *NNP* (supply) and $C + I + G$ (demand) at full employment. This margin is known as *the inflationary gap*. Once this gap appears, under the assumed conditions, equilibrium is never achieved again; the points of intersection of the $C + I + G$ and the *NNP* curves do not represent points toward which the economy tends to move. This situation is something distinctly new in this analysis. It emphasizes a *dynamic* tendency inherent in the situation that predominates over a static tendency toward equilibrium.

The cause of the dynamic behavior is that once demand ($C + I + G$) exceeds supply (*NNP*) the very gap in question causes both $C + I + G$ and *NNP* to increase. Thus the gap tends to be maintained as *NNP* ($= P_f$) engages in a futile chase after $C + I + G$ ($= P$), alternately catching up and falling behind, as the successive increases in *NNP* and $C + I + G$ occur. Thus the achievement of full employment generates conditions in which any increase in demand can set off an inflationary spiral.

In the situation pictured the successive steps of the inflationary process are large in size, each representing a ⅓ increase in prices. In the United States, however, inflation has taken place typically at a much smaller rate, about 2 per cent annually; but the analysis used above is still applicable to this slower rate of inflation.

CHAPTER 9

# Business Cycles and Economic Change

A look at the facts of economic life will soon convince the reader that ours is a world of constant economic change. Consider just a few incidents of recent history. In 1929 an economic boom culminated in an orgy of speculation on the stock exchange and a subsequent collapse. Following this there ensued a deep and protracted depression. In 1936 a promising recovery was interrupted by a severe slump in 1937. Only the onset of World War II brought us out of this depression and up to full employment of resources. During the war a high level of economic activity prevailed, followed by a very slight reconversion problem in 1946. In 1949 and 1950 the first postwar recession occurred, an event followed by recovery and continued prosperity until 1954, which marked a new but mild recession. Recovery followed and activity resumed at a high level. Then a dip in 1958 occurred, followed by a partial recovery in early 1960. This was followed by another dip in 1961 and a recovery in 1962.

To indicate these movements we have graphed in Figure 9–1 the percentage of the labor force employed. About the maximum number that is employed under normal conditions is 96 per cent. Why not 100 per cent? Because in a healthy and growing economy workers are constantly shifting employment in search of better opportunities. Such mobility of labor is a sign of a healthy, growing economy. On our graph we have drawn in at 96 per cent a line labeled "Full Employment." If employment rises much above this level, the economy is in an artificially high state of activity. If it is below this level, it is in a depressed condition.

By following this chart we can see that employment is subject to continual ups and downs that are due to some set of causes. Nor are these fluctuations confined to recent history. Other data indicate that fluctuations of this kind have been occurring for over a hundred years.

**Types of Economic Fluctuations.** In dealing with the very practical problem of measuring cycles economic statisticians have come up with some distinctions about the various types of observed variations in economic activity. First, there are *seasonal* variations in economic activity; fuels do their best business in the winter, ice in the summer. Second, there are *cyclical* movements in economic activity. These are systematic up-and-down variations that appear to follow a definite pattern. Third, there are *trends* in economic activity. For a particular indicator of activity, such as *NNP,* there is some sort of persistent tendency to growth or decline. Essentially, this is a long-run tendency that is rather constant in its nature. Finally, there are *random* variations (also called irregular, erratic, stochastic) in economic life. Such events have no definable pattern, but are essentially isolated phenomena having an influence on the economy at the time of their occurrence alone. For example, a strike, a spell of unusually cold weather, or a military incident could be random in character.

**Figure 9–1.** Employment as a per cent of labor force: 1929–64.

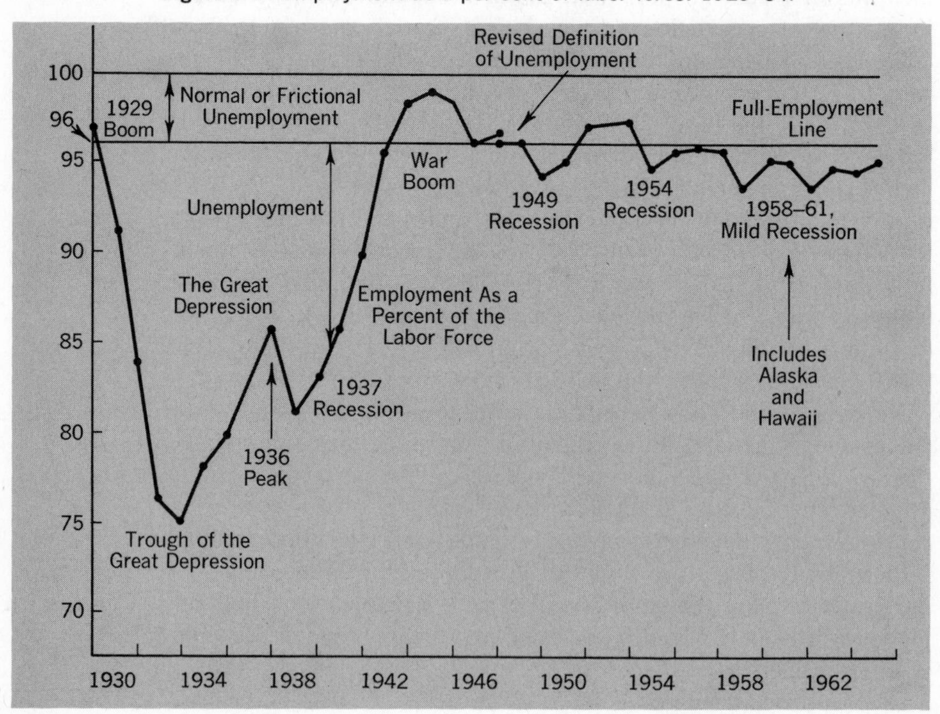

**Interpretation of Economic Data.** In trying to reach an understanding of changes in business activity economists try to eliminate the seasonal and random influences as being of secondary importance. Moreover, it used to be the practice to find trends and eliminate thereby this influence, leaving only cyclical events to consider. Nowadays the tendency is to recognize the interdependence of the two. In a period of rapid growth cycles may be very slight or almost indiscernible. We see this in much of the postwar period. In a period of slow growth or stagnation cycles may be much more distinct. In this chapter we will concentrate on the nature of cycles.

## THE PRINCIPLE OF ACCELERATION AND BUSINESS CYCLES

**General Comments.** *The business cycle is a persistent alternation of high and low periods of economic activity.* Students of the cycle distinguish four successive phases of the cycle: *prosperity, recession, depression, and recovery.* Unless some event of a *random* nature intervenes it is the sense of business-cycle analysis that a succession of separate cycles occurs, each marked by the phases just named. Later we will give a description of the typical phenomena occurring during the various phases.

**National-Income Analysis.** In our study of national income we pointed to investment as the unstable component of total spending. Operating through the multiplier, variation in the level of investment produces an amplified effect on *NNP*. If investment declines by $10 billion, *NNP* will decline by about 3 times this, or $30 billion. The reverse holds true for an increase. Will such fluctuations in the level of investment account for business cycles? Probably not.

A business cycle is a systematic evolution from high to low activity and back again to high activity. This fluctuation is marked by a certain regularity of timing and sequence of events. Occasional ups and downs of investment caused by a variation in expectations will not explain the systematic character of cycles. Consequently, the tools of income analysis must be supplemented, if investment fluctuations are to be given a prominent role in cycle theory.

**Principle of Acceleration.** Most economists are now agreed that changes in the level of investment demand play a fundamental role in cycles. In the attempt to provide a systematic explanation of these fluctuations a number of authors have developed the concept known as the *acceleration principle*. Briefly, this concept relates changes in the level of investment to changes in demand. Consider the general tenor of the argument.

Consumer goods and services consist of items that yield direct satisfaction to the buyer. On the contrary, capital goods consist of items designed to be of use in further production. U.S. Steel does not construct blast furnaces because they look good or give the manager a sense of power. It constructs them to produce pig iron that will enter into steel products destined for final sale. Thus the blast furnace is bought in the expectation that it will yield returns when the final product is sold to the buyer. Going backward from the final product, say an automobile, to the pig iron and blast furnace, we may say that the demand for blast furnaces is derived from the demand for automobiles and other finished products embodying steel. Therefore, we say that the demand for blast furnaces is a *derived demand*—derived from the demand for the final product.

Investment consists in the demand for newly produced capital goods. By the above argument investment depends on the demand for the final product produced with the aid of these capital goods. If the demand for final products increases, new capital will be required to produce the necessary items; investment will occur. Thus investment depends on the *increase* in the demand for the final product, particularly consumption. *The principle of acceleration thus states that the level of investment depends on the increase in the amount of consumption (or final demand).* We will extend these remarks below.

To illustrate this concept let us resort to a simple numerical example, as given in Table 9–1. Let the quantities consumed in a succession of time periods be given autonomously, as shown in column (2). Although this assumption is quite arbitrary, it is necessary in order to permit a simple interpretation of the acceleration principle. More-

**TABLE 9–1**
**Illustration of the Acceleration Principle**

| (1) Period | (2) C Consumption | (3) $\Delta C$ Change in Consumption | (4) $I = 2 \cdot \Delta C$ Net Investment | (5) Replacement | (6) = (4) + (5) Gross Investment | (7) Capital Stock |
|---|---|---|---|---|---|---|
| Zero | 10 | — | — | — | — | 20 |
| One | 10 | 0 | 0 | 4 | 4 | 20 |
| Two | 12 | 2 | 4 | 4 | 8 | 24 |
| Three | 15 | 3 | 6 | 4 | 10 | 30 |
| Four | 18 | 3 | 6 | 4 | 10 | 36 |
| Five | 20 | 2* | 4* | 4 | 8* | 40 |
| Six | 21 | 1 | 2 | 4 | 6 | 42 |
| Seven | 21 | 0 | 0 | 8 | 8 | 42 |

* Consumption increasing at a decreasing rate; $\Delta C$ declines. As a result, net and gross investment fall.

over, we will tie in consumption to *NNP* in a moment. In column (3) we have listed the change in consumption, written $\Delta C$. Every unit increase in consumption is assumed to require 2 units of additional capital. Consequently, net investment $I$ is equal to twice the increase in consumption $\Delta C$; $I = 2 \cdot \Delta C$. To begin with, the stock of capital is so adjusted that there are 2 units of capital goods for every unit of consumption; letting $CS$ stand for capital stock, $CS = 2 \cdot C$. Let us refer to the ratio of 2 units of capital to every unit of consumption goods as *the acceleration coefficient.*

Let us assume that the life of a unit of capital is five years. With an initial capital stock of 20 units, 4 wear out each year and have to be replaced. Gross investment is the sum of net investment and replacement. In periods One through Six gross and net investment differ by a constant amount of 4 equal to the replacement needs.

Examining the table, we see that in periods Three and Four consumption is increasing at a rate of 3 per period, and net investment assumes the high level of 6 ($= 3 \times 2$). Between periods Four and Five consumption only rises by 2, resulting in a *decline* in net investment to 4 ($= 2 \times 2$). Thus a decline in the rate of increase of consumption ($\Delta C$) from $\Delta C = 3$ to $\Delta C = 2$ causes the level of net investment ($I$) to decline from 6 to 4. Note that consumption is rising at the same time that investment falls. But it is not the rise in consumption that is important. Rather it is the fact that consumption increases more slowly that causes investment to fall. When consumption levels off, as between periods Six and Seven, net investment falls to 0.

In Figure 9–2 consumption and net investment are plotted against the time period. Notice that investment reaches a peak at the steepest part of the $C$ curve. When $C$ rises fastest, the need for construction (for example) is greatest, and investment ($I$) reaches a peak. As $C$ begins to *increase at a decreasing rate,* $I$ falls. Note that by the time $C$ reaches a peak $I$ is 0. Don't think that $I$ peaks when $C$ peaks. This would be an awfully trivial sort of idea, not requiring much explanation.

The common sense of this example can be explained. It is not the *level* of consumption that determines the need for new plant and equipment. It is the *rise in the level* of consumption. When consumption increases most rapidly, the greatest need to expand plant occurs; investment is greatest. When consumption, while increasing, rises more slowly, a smaller amount of new plant is required to meet a smaller increase in demand. Thus investment is geared to the growth of demand and not to its level.

Notice that gross investment picks up in period Seven. By this time the increased investment of period Two is wearing out and needs

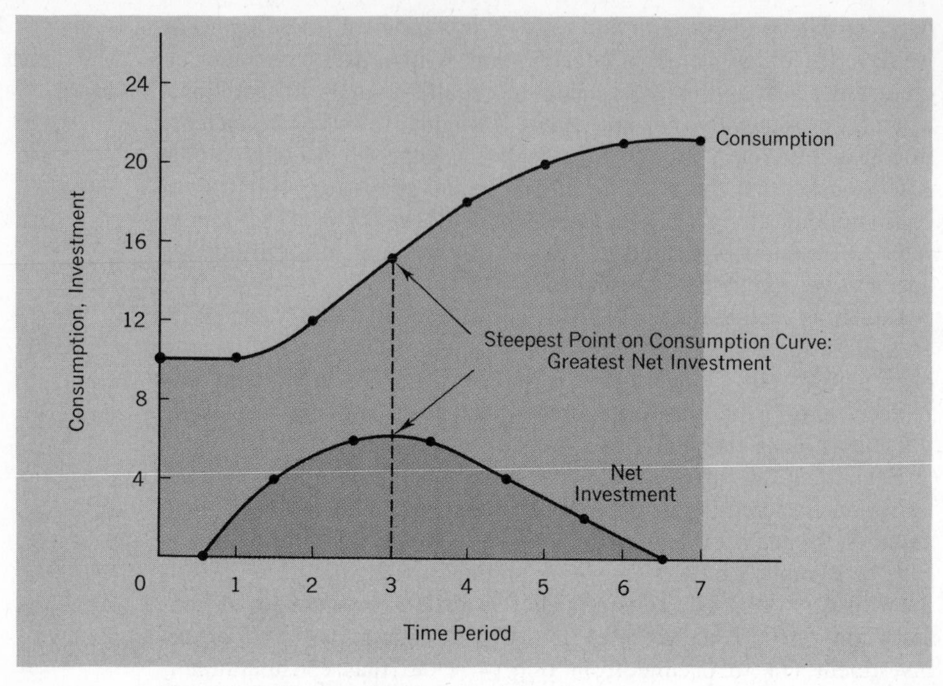


**Figure 9–2.** The acceleration principle.

replacement. Such replacement may, as in this numerical example, have a substantial influence on gross investment and on employment and income.

**Acceleration Principle and National-Income Analysis.** As far as it goes, the acceleration principle is quite helpful. In particular, it is illuminating as an explanation of the turn from prosperity to recession. The seeds of recession are sown in the recovery and prosperity periods. As long as consumption growth continues steady, the investment level is maintained. When that point is reached at which consumption begins to rise more slowly, investment declines. As investment declines, the multiplier takes effect, checking the rise in consumption and replacing it by a fall. As this occurs, investment virtually collapses, because consumption is, by now, decreasing and no further capital construction is necessary.

Although this discussion is extremely suggestive, it does not really assure us that a cycle will actually occur as a result. At this point we may tie in the acceleration principle with the ordinary income analysis. Then we can see what happens. The result is a so-called *model* of the cycle; it does not pretend to reveal all relevant features of the cycle, only certain outstanding factors in the problem. Such a model, in numerical form, is considered in the appendix to this chapter. It shows in some detail that the acceleration principle combined with the preceding income analysis is sufficient to account for systematic ups and downs of *NNP*. Let us summarize how the scheme operates.

Assume that an upswing is under way; then *NNP* is rising. In turn, this leads to a rise in consumption, and this increase generates a corresponding volume of investment. As long as income and consumption are increasing at a constant rate, investment is sustained at a constant level. Whenever the rate of increase of consumption begins to slacken (consumption rising, but at a slower rate), net investment will tend to decline. Construction of new capital depends on the growth in the demand for consumer goods. When this growth slackens, so does the construction of new capital decline in absolute terms. This is the acceleration principle.

When investment declines the growth of *NNP* is reduced, because investment, added to consumption and government spending, makes up *NNP*. A reduction in one part, investment, reduces the growth in the total attributable to another part, consumption. As *NNP* rises still more slowly, investment declines further as a result. Eventually, the fall of investment becomes large enough to offset the rise in consumption; the latter had already begun to rise more slowly. When this happens, *NNP* will decline in absolute amount, and investment will then fall sharply. In turn, *NNP* will fall by several times the decline in investment by the principle of the multiplier.

How do we know that a point will always come when *NNP* and consumption will begin to increase more slowly and thus precipitate a decline in investment? The answer is we don't. However, with the right assumptions about the size of the marginal propensity to consume and acceleration coefficient (the number of dollars of investment prompted by a $1 rise in consumption) the expansion leads inevitably to a decline.

The same process works to reverse a decline in *NNP*. When *NNP* declines, producers need less capital to meet the existing level of demand. In fact, they find that they have excess capacity. Because this is uneconomical, they do not replace all the capital that is wearing out, let alone make additions to their capital stock. Therefore gross investment falls and net investment becomes negative, as producers seek to cut down on their excess capacity. If, at some point in the recession, consumption begins to decline more slowly, less excess capacity develops. By the same token more of the capital wearing out tends to be replaced, and gross investment increases. This stimulus further checks the decline in consumption, causing replacements to be increased further. Eventually, gross investment rises sufficiently to reverse the downward movement in *NNP*. Then *NNP* begins to rise and the upward phase of the cycle gets underway.

## OTHER FACTORS IN CYCLES

**Evaluation.** Is this description of economic fluctuations satisfactory? To begin with it must be said that it gets around the following difficulty in accounting for cycles. The majority of economists feel that investment, being the most unstable part of the demand for goods, must be the central element in an explanation of cycles. Now we know that investment is low in bad times, when *NNP* is low, and high in good times, when *NNP* is high. Yet this fact itself does not help us very much, because we are trying to explain ups and downs in *NNP*. If the investment level is the *effect* of the level of *NNP*, then we are still left with the problem of explaining fluctuations in *NNP*. If the investment level is the *cause* of the level of *NNP*, then we have a further, equally difficult problem: Why is investment low or high? The acceleration principle shows that investment will fall at a time when *NNP* and consumption are still increasing, though at decreasing rates. Therefore it gets around the above dilemma of cause and effect.

On the liability side there are some factors that make the account seem unrealistic. (1) Although the acceleration principle may be operative on the upswing, it does not work with the same power on the downswing. A decline in consumption requires investment to be a negative quantity of a certain size. By assumption (net) investment is proportional to the change in consumption. If consumption drops, this implies investment is negative or that the capital stock shrinks accordingly. But there are limits to this process that are met where firms not only fail to add to their capital equipment but do not replace existing equipment. Investment is negative to the extent that the capital stock is allowed to run down. (Let us ignore here the possible drawing down of inventory.) However, this sets a limit to the decline in investment not included in the model. Although we may modify the account by taking note of this factor, the model then loses its original simplicity.

(2) If *NNP* gets well below the full-employment level, the acceleration principle will cease to act for an increase in *NNP*. As long as considerable excess capacity exists, an increase in *NNP* and demand will have little effect on capital investment. After all, firms can already produce more than the demand. Even an increase in demand should not cause much change in the level of investment.

In addition to these positive criticisms of the acceleration principle is the fact that the foregoing account omits a number of important factors, among them, innovations and inventions as determinants of investment and monetary factors in cycles. Consider these two elements very briefly.



**Innovations.** Economic activity in certain historical periods has been strongly influenced by the development of new industries. In the late 1880's and the decade of the 1890's railroad construction was prominent in the boom and subsequent relapse. In the boom of the 1920's the automotive industry and its sister activities, petroleum and highway construction, were quite prominent. Referring to cases such as these, the late Professor Joseph Schumpeter argued that innovations and inventions leading to the rise of new industries are the principal cause of business cycles. Whether they are the cause or not, it seems safe to say that such developments do strongly influence the course of cycles.

**Monetary Factors.** In our description of cycles we noted that depressions are generally marked by low or falling rates of interest. Often, money for a profitable venture is not hard to obtain. On the other hand, many boom periods appear to be marked by high and rising interest rates and a definite tightness of money; credit is hard to obtain on reasonable terms. We may leave aside the obvious financial crises, such as the panic of 1907 or the stock market crash of 1929. These appear to be surface phenomena. Digging a little deeper, the tendency of tight money to inhibit investment appears to be the thing to watch. In depression the easy availability of money permits expansionary forces, such as innovation, to take effect with the greatest possible ease. In prosperity the increasing tightness of money, which often develops in the later stages, helps to precipitate and intensify the downturn.

**General Description of the Cycle.** In the light of these criticisms we may present a modified description of the cycle.

**Depression.** Suppose the economy is in a depression. Considerable excess capacity exists. Credit is easy, and interest rates are low. Now something must happen to work off the excess capital. If the depression is very deep, disinvestment (failure to replace capital) is taking place, and this will begin to reduce the excess. But this would take an inordinately long time. Sooner or later innovations or improvements in products and techniques of production will occur. In turn, this will set up an increased need for capital equipment, causing investment to rise. Because an increase of $1 of investment causes *NNP* to rise by about $3, according to the multiplier, the aforementioned rise of investment causes a multiple increase in *NNP*. As a result the economy begins to move out of the depression.

**Recovery.** By now the rise in activity is well under way. If the level of *NNP* attained is fairly high, demand will be pressing on capacity in some lines of activity. In these fields the rising demand will stimulate an additional need for capital goods, and investment will begin to pick up in line with the acceleration principle. There will then follow a further increase in *NNP* that will cause a rise in consumer demand. In fact, the acceleration principle, depending on increases in consumption taking effect on investment, and the multiplier, depending on the effects of increases in investment on *NNP* and consumption, begin to interact in a cumulative manner. By this interaction the level of *NNP* is pushed upward to prosperity levels.

During this sequence of events rising demand is financed out of idle balances or the creation of new bank money. At this stage banks have plenty of reserves and have fewer loans out than they like. As a result they are willing to lend money at low rates to any respectable borrower. Thus the ease of borrowing money facilitates the rise in demand, and particularly that of investment.

**Prosperity.** As *NNP* continues to rise, more and more businesses encounter the limit of capacity. The rising consumption stimulates even more investment than when this condition was limited to a few areas. Consequently, *NNP* may continue to rise for a time. However, a combination of factors now begin to militate against continuation of very high levels of *NNP*. First, the rise in *NNP* may begin to slacken because the expansive force of the acceleration principle and the multiplier, working together, are insufficient to continue the growth indefinitely. If this happens, and *NNP* begins to *rise at a slower rate,* the acceleration principle will cause net investment to *fall*. Then recession will commence as the effects of declining investment are accentuated by the multiplier, operating in reverse.

Second, it is possible that the interaction of the multiplier and accelerator is extremely strong and carries the economy up to a full-employment level that limits any further rise in *NNP* and consumption. When the slower rise in consumption becomes evident, the acceleration principle leads to a decline in investment. Again, this leads to a recession as the effects of declining investment on *NNP,* consumption, and, through the accelerator, investment begin to be experienced.

Third, the recovery period may well have been set off by an innovation of some kind. By now the capital necessary for the innovation may well have been produced in large part. Any remaining investment will be steadily diminishing in amount. Insofar as it was a factor in the recovery and prosperity period, the innovation will, by its weakening effect, contribute to a recession.

Fourth, during the recovery and prosperity periods, the banks have been engaged in extending loans to businessmen for construction of new capital equipment. Also they may have contributed to the construction of buildings and houses as well as consumer credit. All of this may have facilitated achievement of the prosperous condition of the economy. However, there are certain limits to the creation of money and credit. By the time prosperity is well advanced, credit may well be rather tight. Interest rates are very likely rising, and bankers are giving prospective borrowers a much more careful scrutiny than before. All of this tends to put something of a damper on spending.

**Recession.** The joint impact of the acceleration principle, taking effect as the level of consumption begins to increase more slowly, combined with the dying away of the effects of the innovation and tighter credit reverses the upward trend of *NNP*. Because the multiplier and accelerator interact also in a downward direction, *NNP*, consumption, and investment tend to decline. It is entirely possible also that interest rates may continue to rise as the cumulative effect of lowered reserves and the excesses of recent prosperity begin to be felt. With diminishing opportunities for investment businessmen will tend to pay off old loans out of earnings. Banks will not easily renew loans, and the quantity of money and credit will be falling.

Certain factors tend to set limits to the decline. In the first place gross investment cannot fall below zero except by consuming or reducing inventories, and this is a process that cannot last very long. Consequently, the effect of declining consumption in reducing investment is sharply limited. Once investment has declined to a low level it will not decrease further, and the depressing effects of declining consumption will work themselves out. In short, the stage would be set for an underemployment equilibrium of the type described in Chapter 7.

A further limitation on the fall consists in the increase in funds available for lending. As the banks liquidate loans during the recession and replenish reserves, they eventually reach a position where they are ready to increase their lending. At this stage the borrower finds low rates and a cordial reception at the bank.

At this juncture excess capacity exists, money is cheap, demand is low, and business is dull. Let us mention the fact that such a situation may, by the interaction of the multiplier and accelerator, lead back to prosperity. See the model discussed in the appendix to the chapter. This is especially likely if the forces leading to recession were weak. In the opposite case we are in for a period of depression. This brings us full circle to our starting point.

**Conclusion.** The arguments presented seem adequate to account for cycles of economic activity. Whether they are precisely the forces that do, in fact, cause cycles is another matter. This is, indeed, an intricate subject. The reader is well advised to think of this discussion simply as a sketch of the operation of the forces that many economists believe to have a causative impact on business cycles.

**Summary.** A study of the facts of economic life indicates that economic activity is subject to ups and downs. Such changes may be classified in four groups: seasonal, cyclical, trend, and random flucuations. In the discussion of this chapter we concern ourselves with the cyclical element, leading to regular, persistent pulsations in economic activity. Every cycle is to a degree unique but is characterized generally by four phases: prosperity, recession, depression, and recovery. The depression phase may be missing if growth forces are strong.

One of the important phenomena characterizing business cycles is that fluctuations in investment are attributed to changes in consumption requiring additions to or subtractions from the stock of capital. According to this principle, the downturn of the cycle from the prosperity phase probably occurs when consumption begins to rise at a slower rate. Such a decline in the *rate of increase* of consumption leads to an absolute decline in investment. In turn, the decline in investment precipitates a fall in *NNP* through the multiplier. By combining the acceleration principle systematically with the earlier analysis of determination of *NNP* we arrive at a *model* that exhibits, roughly, the same kind of fluctuations we observe in practice.

Such a model is somewhat unrealistic, because capital does not shrink in recessions in the way suggested by the acceleration principle. Also it ignores the influence of innovations leading to increases in investment that provide a substantial stimulus to expansion at times. Finally, the influence of such monetary factors as the expansion and contraction of bank credit is ignored. If we take account of these factors, a model can be constructed that suggests more strongly the possibility of prolonged recessions and incorporates the essential dynamics of innovation.

## QUESTIONS

1. State and justify to the best of your ability the concept of full employment as used in the text.
2. List and define the several types of economic fluctuations. Which of these are most important?
3. What is a business cycle? Name the phases of the cycle. Describe each phase.
4. What is the acceleration coefficient? What is the acceleration principle?
5. What is the critical point in the upswing of a cycle at which a downswing (supposedly) becomes inevitable? Explain.
6. Why is the instability of investment and the resulting enlarged instability of *NNP* (as a result of the multiplier) an inadequtae basis for the explanation of business cycles?
7. How does the acceleration principle get around the difficulty mentioned in question 6?
8. List some limitations or drawbacks to the acceleration principle and its use in an explanation of business cycles.
9. How do innovations and the monetary factor contribute to an explanation of business cycles?

10. What is the basic factor holding down the economy in a depression, and what factors serve to overcome it?
11. List four factors contributing to a downturn, as the prosperity phase is reached.
12. What factors set limits to the decline in *NNP?*

# Appendix

## NUMERICAL MODEL OF THE CYCLE

In this model we use all the apparatus of the usual *NNP,* or income determination. To this we add the acceleration principle. These elements enter into the make-up of Table 9–2. Because *NNP* takes on an erratic sequence of values, the resulting consumption levels shown in the consumption ($C$) column are rather scattered. In short, the first two columns are actually similar to, but apparently different from, the usual consumption-*NNP* schedule. Actually, consumption is assumed to equal $9 + \frac{1}{2}$ *NNP;* the 9 is consumption spending at zero *NNP,* and the $\frac{1}{2}$ *NNP* represents the increase in consumption as *NNP* rises. This $\frac{1}{2}$ represents the marginal propensity to consume.[1]

Also we assume 11 to be the value of autonomous investment spending. Adding this amount to consumption as shown in column (3), we get column (4), which is headed $C + I_a$, or total spending in our usual income analysis (ignoring government spending or counting it in $I_a$ for simplicity). Taking the differences in $C$ (or $C + I_a$, because $I_a$ is constant), we get the change in consumption $\Delta C$. Induced investment $I_i$ is equal to exactly twice the change in consumption—$I_i = 2 \cdot \Delta C$—as shown in column (6). This is the acceleration principle. Then total spending $C + I_a + I_i$ is the sum of column (4), $C + I_a$, and column (6), $I_i$. We now assume that upper-loop *NNP,* or total spending $= C + I_a + I_i$, generates corresponding upper-loop *NNP* (production) in the following period.

In order to start a sequence of *NNP*s it is necessary to begin with two arbitrary values. Here they are given by the values 16 and 24 in periods 1 and 2. With the aid of these values, two corresponding levels of consumption can be determined—that is, 17 and 21. The increase in consumption, $\Delta C = 21 - 17 = 4$, can be determined and $I_i = 2 \times 4 = 8$ found by the acceleration principle. Then induced investment $I_i$ can be added to $C + I_a$ to give total spending $C + I_a + I_i = 40$ in the last column for period 2. Because spending in one period generates production and income in the next, the *NNP* of period 3

[1] The value $\frac{1}{2}$ rather than the more realistic one of $\frac{2}{3}$ is chosen, because the table and graph are more easily worked out with this value.

**TABLE 9-2**
**Acceleration Principle and Changes in *NNP***

| (1) | (2) $NNP$* | (3) $C$† | (4) $C+I_a$‡ | (5) $\Delta C$** | (6) $I_i$†† | (7) $C+I_a+I_i$‡‡ |
|---|---|---|---|---|---|---|
| 1 | 16*** | 17 | 28 | | | |
| 2 | 24*** | 21 | 32 | 4 | 8 | 40 |
| 3 | 40 | 29 | 40 | 8 | 16 | 56 |
| 4 | 56 | 37 | 48 | 8 | 16 | 64 |
| 5 | 64 | 41 | 52 | 4 | 8 | 60 |
| 6 | 60 | 39 | 50 | −2 | − 4 | 46 |
| 7 | 46 | 32 | 43 | −7 | −14 | 29 |
| 8 | 29 | 23½ | 34½ | −8½ | −17 | 17½ |
| 9 | 17½ | 17¾ | 28¾ | −5¾ | −11½ | 17¼ |
| 10 | 17¼ | 17⅝ | 28⅝ | −0⅛ | − 0¼ | 28⅜ |
| 11 | 28⅜ | | | | | |

* $C+I_a+I_i$ of one period determines $NNP$ of next.
† $C=9+\frac{1}{2}NNP$; with zero $NNP$ consumption is 9, and because the marginal propensity to consume, $\Delta C/\Delta NNP$ is ½, we add ½ $NNP$ to 9 for total consumption $C$.
‡ $I_a=11$, which is normal investment. If we add $C$ and $I_a$, we get $9+\frac{1}{2}NNP+11=20+\frac{1}{2}NNP$.
** $\Delta C$ is the change in $C$ between rows. Because $C+I_a$ is $C$ plus a constant, $\Delta C=\Delta(C+I_a)$.
†† $I_i=2\cdot\Delta C$. With an acceleration coefficient of 2 induced investment is 2 times the change in $C$.
‡‡ Sum of columns (4) and (6).
*** Arbitrary, assumed value.

takes on the value 40, just mentioned. From here on the sequence proceeds as indicated.

## DIAGRAMMATIC INTERPRETATION

The numerical model just given can be interpreted by means of the conventional diagram showing determination of *NNP*. This can be modified in such a way as to show the above fluctuations in *NNP*. It will be instructive to compare this dynamic interpretation of the diagram with the static one of *NNP* determination.

In the upper part of Figure 9–3 we lay off *NNP* along the horizontal axis and spending along the vertical. The $C+I_a$ line is plotted against *NNP*. Here the $C$ line is omitted for simplicity; changes in $C$, $\Delta C=\Delta(C+I_a)$, can be measured along $C+I_a$, because $I_a$ is constant. The 45-degree *NNP* line is drawn in as usual. An equilibrium value of *NNP* equal to 40 is shown at *c*. Here $C+I_a=NNP$, and if *NNP* were to be fixed here for two successive periods, it would stay there indefinitely. Only because changes in *NNP* occur do the changes in $C$ occur that set off $I_i$ and disturb the equilibrium. Once started, however, this particular sequence of values of *NNP* will continue to oscillate indefinitely.

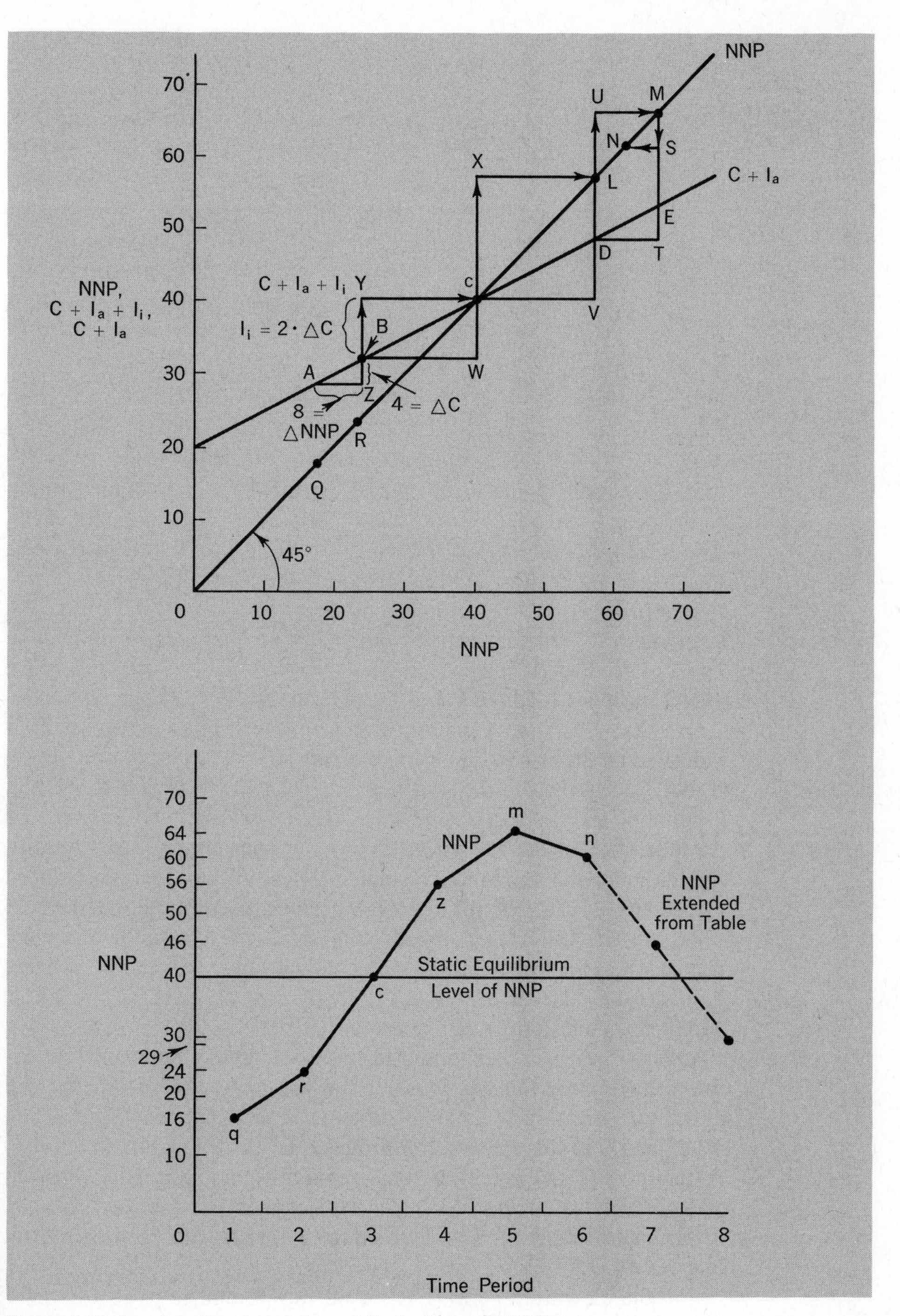


**Figure 9–3.** Acceleration principle and fluctuations in *NNP*.

The initial values of income, 16 and 24, lie below the static equilibrium level of *NNP,* which is 40. An *NNP* of 16 generates a $C + I_a$ shown at *A*. The increase in *NNP* of 8 is shown as distance *AZ*. In turn, this increase in *NNP* causes a rise in $C + I_a$ of $ZB = 4$; actually, this is the increase in consumption $\Delta C$, because $I_a$ is constant and ½ of all additional *NNP* is consumed, so that $\Delta C = \frac{1}{2}\Delta NNP = \frac{1}{2}(8) = 4$. With an acceleration coefficient of 2, induced investment will equal twice the jump in *C*, or $I_i = 2 \cdot \Delta C$. Therefore, using a compass, we mark off *ZB* twice in a vertical direction from *B,* ending at *Y*. Induced investment is thus *BY* by construction. When this sum is added to other spending, the result is total spending at *Y*. Point *B* defines consumption plus autonomous investment; adding induced investment of *BY* defines total spending of $C + I_a + I_i$ at *Y*.

At this juncture we have defined total spending, or upper-loop *NNP,* at *Y,* of 40. This subsequently generates corresponding lower-loop *NNP* (supply and income) at *c*. By accident this is static equilibrium income where $C + I_a = NNP$; but *NNP* does not stop here. The increase of 16 in *NNP,* from 24 to 40, generates an increase in *C* along $C + I_a$ of *Wc*. Again, laying off *Wc* twice in a vertical direction above *c* to take account of induced investment, we secure total spending at *X*. In turn, upper-loop *NNP* at *X* generates lower-loop *NNP* at *L*. Proceeding in this way, we can lay out the successive values of upper-loop *NNP* and the subsequent, equal values of lower-loop *NNP*. Thus we generate a sequence of values whose path is indicated by the arrows following the path.

Why does the upward movement, which carries *NNP* past *c,* eventually reverse itself at *M* and start downward? To answer this we must look at the successive changes in consumption, $\Delta C$; for this is what holds the key to the unstable element in the situation, induced investment $I_i$. At first, the successive jumps in consumption increase (*Wc* exceeds *ZB*), then remain the same ($Wc = VD$), and then decrease (*TE* is less than *VD*). In line with this, induced investment first increases (from *BY* to *cX*), then stays constant ($cX = DU$), and then declines (from *DU to ES*).

Clearly, when consumption begins to increase more slowly, induced investment falls. If consumption increases by less than the fall of induced investment, total spending falls. This happens at *M*. Then *NNP* falls, and the acceleration principle begins to operate in reverse. In the model being used here consumption cannot continue to rise at a faster and faster rate. When the rate of increase slackens, induced investment declines, and the downturn in *NNP* occurs then or shortly afterward.

On the downturn will *NNP* slow down and stop at *c,* where $C + I_a = NNP$? No. The changes in consumption and induced investment prevent this. As a matter of fact, *NNP* shoots back past *c* (40) until it reaches a low point and then begins to rise again. Nor will equilibrium ever be reached in this case. *NNP* will oscillate above and below the equilibrium point indefinitely. The general appearance of the cycle is shown in the lower part of Figure 9–3. We note a rise to a peak, and a subsequent decline; ultimately, a recovery will set in. This pattern is repeated indefinitely.

**Evaluation.** Is this description of economic fluctuations satisfactory? Not entirely. We may list one or two ways in which it may seem unrealistic. (1) Although the acceleration principle may work on the upswing, it does not work as well on the downswing. A decline in consumption requires induced investment to be a negative quantity of a certain size. But investment has a lower limit; this is found where firms not only fail to add to their capital equipment but do not replace existing equipment. Investment is negative to the extent that the capital stock is allowed to run down. (Let us ignore here the possible drawing down of inventory.) However, this sets a limit to the decline in investment not included in the model. Although we may modify the account by taking note of this factor, the model then loses its original simplicity. (2) If *NNP* gets well below the full-employment level, the acceleration principle will cease to act. As long as considerable excess capacity exists, an increase in *NNP* and demand will have little effect on capital investment. After all, firms can already produce more than the demand. Even an increase in demand should not cause much change in the level of investment.

**Conclusion.** For variations of fairly small size in a growing economy this explanation seems pretty satisfactory. It is the really large fluctuations, that bring into question the use of the acceleration principle, that give trouble.

PART

# 3

# *Money and Economic Control*

Following a discussion of the nature of money, the structure of the banking system, and the Federal Reserve System, this section deals with the control of the money supply by the Federal Reserve System in the interests of economic stability. Attention is also given to the role of the Treasury in stabilizing economic activity through changes in government taxes and spending.

CHAPTER

10

# The Banks and the Creation of Money

In Chapter 2 we explained the importance of the role of money in an exchange economy, discussed the functions of money, and stated its definition. Then we detailed the various forms of money, their relative importance, and the agencies by which they are created. On November 30, 1964, the total money supply was $159.0 billion, consisting of $34.3 billion in currency and coin and $124.7 billion of demand deposits. Approximately 15 per cent of the currency and coin is supplied by the Treasury, and the remaining 85 per cent by the banking system in the form of Federal Reserve notes. Clearly, the banking system accounts for most of the money supply. In this chapter we will be concerned primarily with bank deposits and how they are created. As a necessary preliminary we consider briefly the institutional structure of the banking system.

## STRUCTURE OF THE BANKING SYSTEM

Because a bank acts as a custodian of people's money, it occupies a special position of trust in the eyes of the public. For this reason banks are subject to close attention from the government. Thus, in order to start a bank it is necessary to obtain a charter from some branch of the government; banks are classified as state or national according to whether they are chartered by the State or Federal government. National banks automatically belong to the Federal Reserve System, whereas state banks may join by meeting certain standard requirements. National banks are subject to inspection by the United States Comptroller of the Currency.

The following facts provide relevant information about our banking structure. There are about 13,500 commercial banks in the United States (13,434 on June 30, 1962). Of these, 4,500 were national banks, and 1,568 were member state banks of the Federal Reserve System, giving a total of 6,068, or roughly 6,000 member banks. The rest, a bit more than half, are nonmember state banks. However, member banks claimed over 84 per cent of demand deposits; nonmembers less than 16 per cent. Furthermore, the large banks are members, whereas small ones are state nonmember banks for the most part. In short, member banks of the Federal Reserve System predominate over nonmembers.

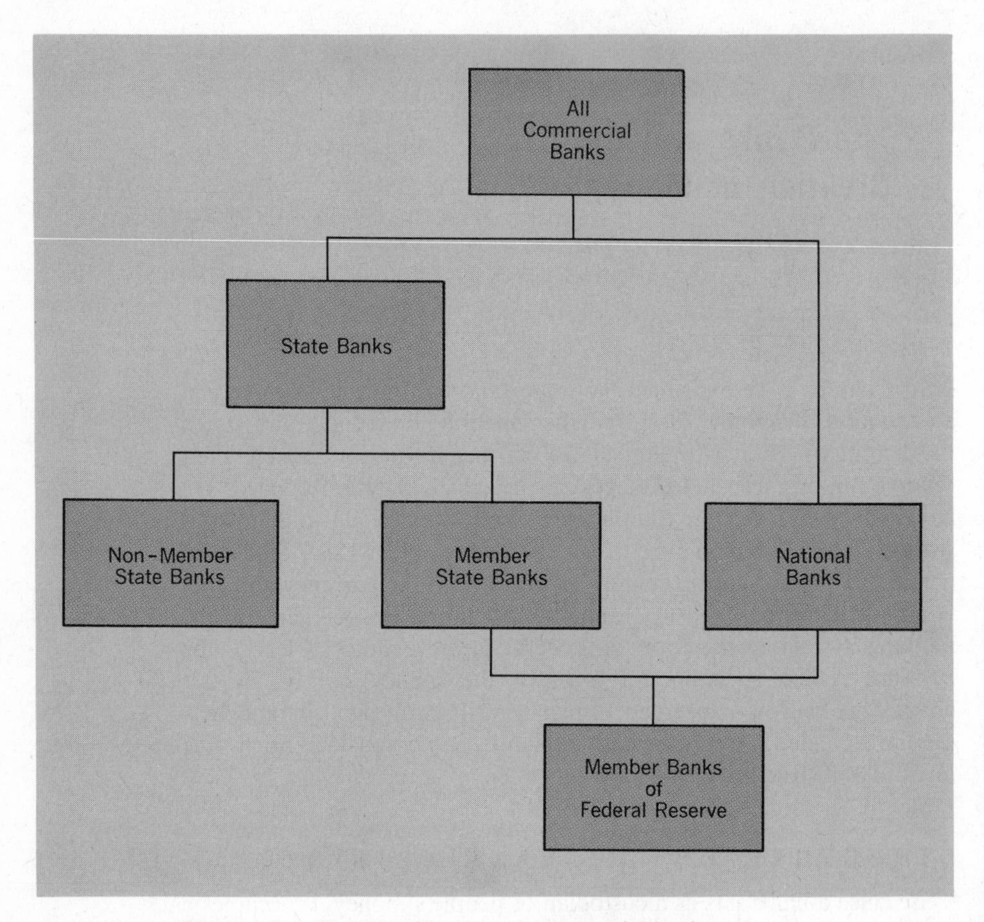


**Figure 10–1.** The classification of commercial banks.

We can summarize the relationships by means of the diagram shown in Figure 10–1.

## THE FEDERAL RESERVE SYSTEM

**Federal Reserve Banks.** For organizational purposes the United States is divided into 12 Federal Reserve Districts. Each of these contains a Federal Reserve Bank located in a major city. Thus we have the Federal Reserve Bank of New York, of Boston, and so on.[1] This system of 12 regional banks operates as a central bank, playing the same role in the United States as the Bank of England does in Great Britain. Clearly, though, the system is decentralized in much the same way as our political system, with its Federal, state, and local governments. The geographical outlines of the districts and the locations of the Federal Reserve Banks are shown on the map in Figure 10–2.[2]

Each Federal Reserve Bank is owned by the member banks of that particular district. In fact, each member bank is required to subscribe to stock in the Federal Reserve Bank of its district when it joins the system. In the sense that its capital is provided by the member banks, a Federal Reserve Bank may be said to be privately owned. Each bank is run by a nine-man board of directors, six being elected by the banks of the district and three being named by the Board of Governors of the Federal Reserve System. Of the three members appointed by the Board, one serves as president—that is, as chief executive officer. Each bank holds the reserves that the member banks of that district are required to maintain against their deposits. Because the Federal Reserve Banks do not accept deposits from private individuals, they are primarily *bankers' banks*. In addition, they are not run primarily in order to make money, but rather with a view to realizing certain public goals. In the course of their operations they do, however, regularly earn a profit. Periodically, the Federal Reserve turns over these profits to the government rather than allowing them to accumulate indefinitely.

**Board of Governors.** At the head of the system is the seven-member Board of Governors, appointed by the President of the United States and confirmed by the Senate for 14-year terms. Because a new member is appointed only every other year, a substantial period of time elapses before an incoming President can appoint a majority of the Board. Such length in the term of office gives the Board a degree of independence from immediate political considerations. Although it reports periodically to Congress on the pursuit of goals established through legislation, the Board is left essentially free to carry out the law according to its own interpretation.

[1] There also are 24 branch banks located in other major cities. Thus there is a Federal Reserve Bank in San Francisco with a branch in Los Angeles.

[2] This is taken from the *Federal Reserve Bulletin*.

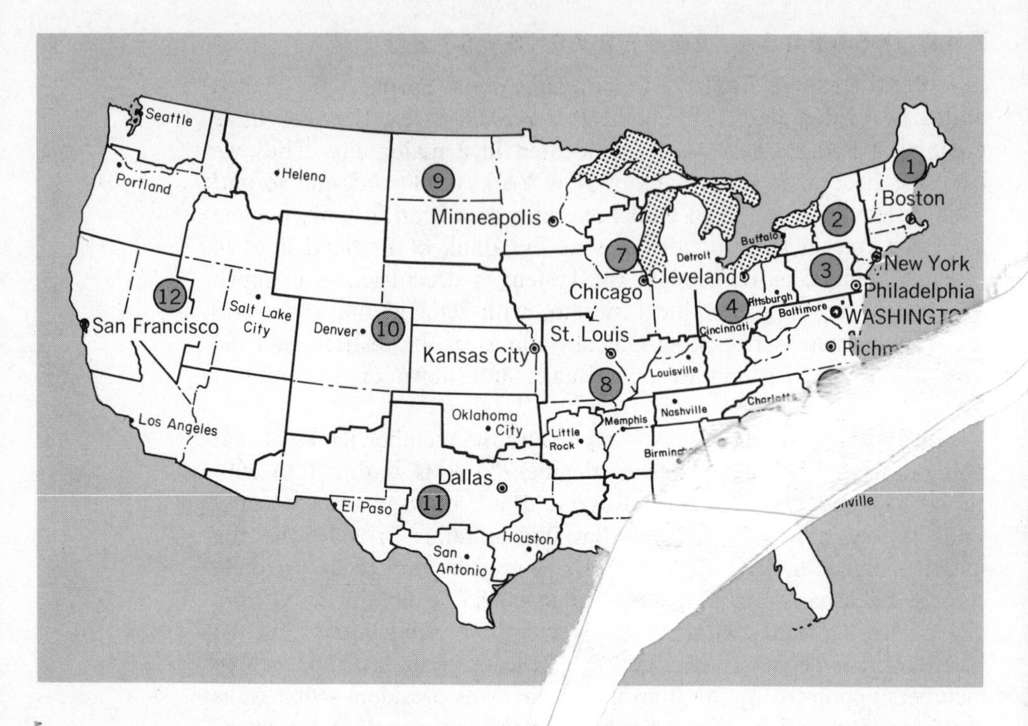


The Federal Reserve System

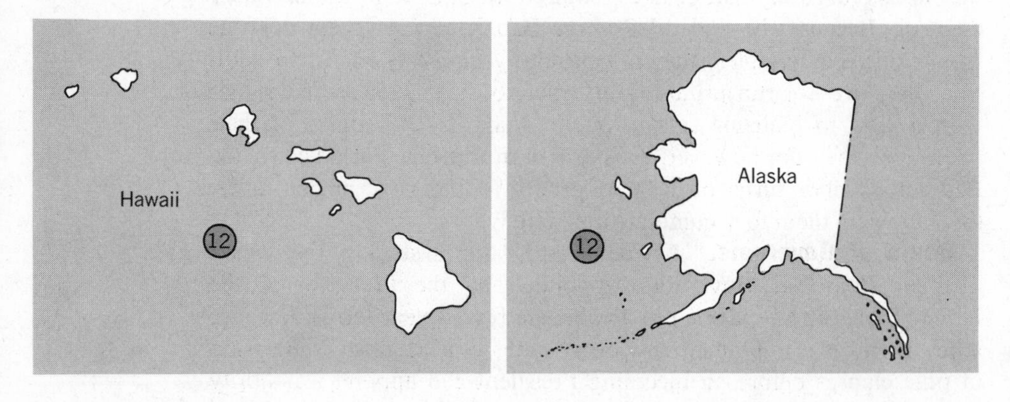


Legend

—— Boundaries of Federal Reserve Districts —— Boundaries of Federal Reserve Branch Territories

✪ Board of Governors of the Federal Reserve System

◉ Federal Reserve Bank Cities • Federal Reserve Branch Cities

**Figure 10–2.** Boundaries of Federal Reserve Districts and their branch territories.

With the assistance of the Federal Reserve Banks the Board acts to control the supply of money in the interests of economic stability. Thus the entire system, including the member banks, takes on a social character. In short, although the system, consisting of member banks and Federal Reserve Banks, is privately owned it is controlled in the public interest.

Assisting in the control of the money supply is the Federal Open Market Committee. Composed of the seven members of the Board and five presidents of the several Federal Reserve Banks, chosen in rotation, this 12-man committee governs the purchase and sale of government securities by the Federal Reserve Banks. Because "open-market operations" constitute the primary method for controlling the money supply, the Open Market Committee necessarily plays an important role in the operation of the system. Inasmuch as the Board constitutes a majority of the members, it will tend to control the policies of the Committee. Another body in the structure is the Federal Advisory Council, a 12-man committee, composed of bankers, which advises the Board of Governors on monetary policy. This group has no authority, its power coming solely from its influence on the Board.

## FUNCTIONS OF THE FEDERAL RESERVE SYSTEM

**Service Functions.** Member banks are required to hold a certain fraction of their deposits with the Federal Reserve Bank in their district. By means of these deposits the Federal Reserve Banks can acquire the assets they need to carry on their operations. Because banks hold only a small part of their cash in their own vaults in any event, it is quite logical to pool these reserves with a view to strengthening the entire system. In case of emergency member banks will be able to turn to the Federal Reserve Banks, which can respond in virtue of these pooled reserves. Later, we shall see that the quantity of reserves held in this way by member banks is a critical factor in determining the money supply.

A second function is to collect checks for the member banks. In fact, the entire system serves as a gigantic clearing house for all checks written on the member banks. Because most of the work of banks revolves around cashing checks, the job of collecting checks drawn on other banks is a very substantial one. In the absence of the Federal Reserve System banks would be forced to settle accounts through private clearing houses.

Finally, the Federal Reserve systematically sends out auditors who check on the condition of the various member banks. Each bank must meet certain minimum standards required of members. In view of the vital importance of the banks to the public it is absolutely essential that each bank be in a safe condition at all times.

**Fiscal Agent of the Treasury and Foreign Governments.** In carrying out its enormous financial operations, including the handling of a $100-billion yearly budget, the Federal government has to maintain a substantial bank balance. Rather than favor a certain group of private banks, it keeps its balance with the Federal Reserve Banks. Under certain conditions, especially when the Treasury is "refinancing" a large volume of government bonds, the Federal Reserve Banks will conduct operations designed to facilitate the task. In addition to acting for the Treasury the Federal Reserve acts in various capacities for foreign governments and central banks. This function arises because many countries maintain dollar balances and "earmarked gold" in the United States as a basis for their money.

**Control of Money Supply.** Finally, the Federal Reserve System is responsible for controlling the supply of money. Nowadays this is regarded as the principal function of the system, and we will consider it fully in the next chapter.

Our sketch of banking institutions is now sufficiently complete to pass on to the operations of individual banks. Here we will try to show how banks, both individually and collectively, operate to create deposit money.

## HOW BANKS CREATE DEPOSITS

**Banking As a Business.** Our banking system is founded on the individual, privately owned bank. Consequently, it is logical to begin the study of bank operations from this viewpoint. Private banks have two main functions: (1) to accept deposits—from individuals, firms, and governments, and (2) to make loans. In the discussion to follow we will concentrate on the second of these functions and show how it is tied in with the first. Thus we will concentrate on the means by which banks can make loans and the consequences of such actions.

**Accounting Concepts.** For purposes of discussion it is essential to make use of basic accounting concepts. Let us note these briefly. A bank, like any other firm, has certain sources of funds. In the case of a bank the two main sources are *deposits* of individuals, business firms, and other institutions and the *equity* of the owners represented by stock. The main uses of bank funds consist of cash reserves, loans to firms and individuals, and various financial instruments, such as government bonds and mortgages. Actually, these financial instruments represent loans by the holder to the issuer, so that all holdings of bonds, mortgages, and loan contracts represent loans by the bank.

Consequently, it would not be inaccurate to say that the uses of funds break down into cash reserves and loans.

**Deposit Creation by an Individual Bank.** To facilitate discussion we will make the drastic simplification mentioned above of breaking down all assets into "cash" and "loans," where the latter refers to all income earning assets of the bank. The sources of funds we have classified as deposits and net worth, or the capital supplied to the business by the owners (the stockholders). Because the latter element is small compared to deposits in almost all cases, we can neglect it for elementary purposes. This means that deposits will constitute the only source of funds in the cases to be discussed.

**Accepting Deposits.** To start the discussion, let us assume that a new bank opens its doors and accepts deposits. On the first day an individual shows up with $100 in currency (to make it simple) and opens an account. At this stage the bank's books look as follows, ignoring sums contributed by the bank's owners.

**TABLE 10-1**
**Acme Receives a Deposit of $100**

| Acme National Bank | | | |
|---|---|---|---|
| **Assets** | | **Liabilities** | |
| Cash reserve | $100 | Deposits | $100 |

Obviously, the cash reserve is the $100 in currency just deposited and now held by the bank. Also the $100 in deposits represents the obligation on the part of the bank to pay currency to the depositor on demand or honor checks drawn against the account by the depositor. So far the bank is only a passive participant in this little drama.

**Making Loans.** Now let us investigate how a bank in this situation can create deposits. Suppose a reputable businessman presents himself at the bank and applies for a loan. He convinces the proper official that he has in mind a sound use of the money, one that should earn a satisfactory return on the investment. An agreement is reached to loan the businessman $50. A contract is drawn up between the bank and the businessman, establishing the rights and obligations of the parties. In the first place, the borrower is to be entitled to secure access to $50. Therefore the bank will simply establish a checking account for this man in the amount of $50. He can draw checks against this account in the usual manner.

On the other hand, the contract will establish the obligation of the individual to repay the amount borrowed at some future date, as well as the interest on the principal, which is usually deducted in advance. Suppose the principal is due a year from today—also neglect interest. One part of the contract that takes effect right away is the responsibility of the bank to establish a deposit balance in favor of the borrower. Because this is an obligation of the bank, it falls on the liability side. At the same time the contract states that the borrower will repay the principal in a year, and this aspect of the loan is recorded under the asset side. Recording these two changes, we come to the following balance sheet.

**TABLE 10-2**
**Acme Lends $50, Creating a $50 Deposit**

| Acme National Bank | | | |
|---|---|---|---|
| **Assets** | | **Liabilities** | |
| Cash reserve | $100 | Deposits | $150 |
| Loans | 50 | | |
| Total | $150 | | $150 |

Inspecting this balance sheet, we see that deposits have gone up by $50. Also the item "Loans" appears on the assets side in the amount of $50. At this juncture something very important has happened. Because deposits form an element of the money supply, and because they have increased in amount by $50, the money supply has increased as a result of the loan. Tentatively, we may conclude that *an individual bank can create money by the act of making a loan.* Why tentatively? We have not yet said what the borrower does with his money on deposit with Acme.

**Use of a Loan.** We have just seen that an individual bank can create deposits in the act of making a loan. Is this new money, consisting of the deposit, a transitory phenomenon? Will the deposit somehow vanish when the borrower makes use of it? The answer is no. Let's see why.

Suppose the borrower elects to make use of his deposit balance the following day by purchasing some equipment. In order to pay for the equipment he makes out a check for $50, drawn against his account at the Acme National Bank. He presents this to the General Machine Company in return for certain equipment. This company takes the check and deposits it at its own bank, the Fourteenth National. Then the Fourteenth National credits General Machine Company with the $50 check and collects the $50 check on Acme National in cash. At Acme National cash is down by the $50 paid to the Fourteenth National; the borrower's account is down $50, because of the check drawn against that account. At this juncture things at Acme National look as follows.

**TABLE 10-3**
**Acme After Check Clears: Final Position**

| Acme National Bank | | | |
|---|---|---|---|
| **Assets** | | **Liabilities** | |
| Cash reserve | $50 | Deposits | $100 |
| Loans | 50 | | |
| Total | $100 | | $100 |

**Summary.** Note that deposits have returned to their initial level of $100. Assets are the same in amount, but have changed in composition. Now half of the assets are in cash, half in loans. From this result it might appear that deposits do not really increase. However, this is not the case, because the Fourteenth National's balance sheet shows the following changes where the + indicates an increase.

**TABLE 10-4**
**Fourteenth National Receives Deposit Originating at Acme**

| Fourteenth National Bank | | | |
|---|---|---|---|
| **Assets** | | **Liabilities** | |
| Cash reserve | +$50 | Deposits | +$50 |
| Total | +$50 | | +$50 |

As a result of General Machine's deposit, Fourteenth National shows a growth of $50 in deposits. The total of deposits in *both* banks together has therefore grown by $50. Thus our last two balance sheets combined indicate essentially the same result as the second, namely *making a loan creates a corresponding amount of deposits that shows up thereafter at some point in the banking system.*

## LIMITS ON DEPOSIT CREATION

All we have shown so far is that a bank can create deposits in the act of making loans. By creating a deposit the bank brings new money into being. This is a rather surprising feature of banking, and one not generally understood by either the general public or businessmen in particular. However, it is a very general proposition: banks can create money. All well and good, but *how much?* If banks have this immensely important power, what limits exist to its exercise? An understanding of this subject is facilitated by consideration first of an individual bank, then of the banking system as a whole.

**Preliminary: Fractional Reserve Banking.** Banking as we know it seems to have originated in the Middle Ages. In those days the principal form of money consisted of gold or other metallic coins. To a wealthy man this presented a problem of safekeeping. How could he best safeguard his stock of gold coins? In these circumstances it was quite natural to take these coins to a goldsmith for safekeeping. In return, the goldsmith would issue a receipt for the coins. The owner could then come in at his discretion and call for the return of all or part of his deposit. Meanwhile, the person's money was on deposit, as evidenced by the goldsmith's receipt. This is deposit banking.

Later the goldsmiths discovered that people who deposited these sums rarely called for all of their deposit at once. Moreover, if one person withdrew some gold, it was not long before another person deposited some. In brief, they found that it was not actually necessary to keep all this gold on hand at all times. Instead, they used part of this gold to acquire some income-earning assets. Perhaps a goldsmith made a loan to a business at interest. Then the goldsmith would be earning interest by putting part of the gold to work. If he loaned 10 per cent, and kept 90 per cent in gold, he would find that at no time would a group of his depositors come in and demand over 90 per cent of their gold. In fact, he would doubtless find that a considerably smaller percentage sufficed to meet any temporary withdrawals until such time as more deposits took place.

In this way the practice of holding only a fraction of the deposits in gold developed. Thus *fractional reserve banking* had its beginning. Such a system conferred benefits on both the depositor and the goldsmith banker. To begin with, the acceptance of gold deposits implied an obligation to keep records and to safeguard the store physically from theft. Such obligations justified the goldsmiths in charging depositors for the service. As they learned the system of fractional reserves, the charges could be diminished or eliminated, because the earnings on the loans would cover the costs and risks in large part.

Later the reserve held by banks came under legal regulation. Member banks of the Federal Reserve System (discussed below) keep their cash with the Federal Reserve Bank of their district, except for a small percentage held in the vault. The amount of cash reserve to be held there is set by the Federal Reserve within legal limits. For the moment we will assume that a bank must hold a 20-per-cent reserve against its deposits.

**Individual Bank Expansion.** From our earlier discussion we know that an individual bank can create deposit money by making loans. Now let us consider *how much* money a single bank can create under given conditions. To carry through our discussion we need several definitions. First, *cash reserve* means cash in the vault or held at a Federal Reserve Bank, and we assume all this may be counted in the 20-per-cent requirement. Second, *required reserve* is the quantity that must be held in cash reserve according to regulations; by assumption this amounts to 20 per cent of deposits. Third, the *excess reserve* is the amount by which the cash reserve exceeds the required reserve.

Now the ability of a bank to lend or create deposits depends strictly on its excess reserve. If a bank has a larger reserve against deposits than is required, it will be able to lend more and create more deposits.

On the other hand, a bank with a zero excess reserve, which has cash reserve just equal to the amount needed for a given amount of deposits, cannot lend any more.

Now let us get back to the Acme Bank and see how much it can lend in the situation to be described. Let the cash reserve, loans, and deposits be as shown in the following balance sheet.

**TABLE 10-5**
**Acme Has an Excess Reserve of $100**

| Acme Bank—Stage 1 | | | |
|---|---|---|---|
| **Assets** | | **Liabilities** | |
| Cash reserve | $150 | Deposits | $250 |
| Loans | 100 | | |
| Total | $250 | | $250 |

At this juncture the required reserve is $50 = 20% ($250), whereas the cash reserve is $150, giving an excess reserve of $100 = $150 − $50. Clearly, Acme has a larger cash reserve against deposits than it needs. This is evidenced by the $100 in its excess reserve.

How much can Acme lend? Let us consider the effect of lending the entire amount of its excess reserve, or $100. Assume a $100 loan is made to a businessman and the sum credited to the account of the borrower. After this occurs the account looks as follows.

**TABLE 10-6**
**Acme Expands Deposits by Making a Loan of $100**

| Acme Bank—Stage 2 | | | |
|---|---|---|---|
| **Assets** | | **Liabilities** | |
| Cash reserve | $150 | Deposits | $350 |
| Loans | 200 | | |
| Total | $350 | | $350 |

The balance sheet shown above is purely transitional, because the borrower has not yet made use of his newly created deposit. Note, however, that $100 in new money (deposits) has been created. Once created by a bank this sum continues in existence.

Suppose the borrower now draws a check against his account for $100 and sends it to a business firm in return for supplies. In turn, the latter firm deposits the $100 with our old friend the Fourteenth National, the check clears, and both cash and deposits go down $100 at Acme National. Cash reserves and deposits go up by $100 at the Fourteenth National. This leads to the following situation at Acme National Bank.

**TABLE 10-7**
**Acme Reaches Final Position**

| Acme National Bank—Stage 3 | | | |
|---|---|---|---|
| **Assets** | | **Liabilities** | |
| Cash reserve | $ 50 | Deposits | $250 |
| Loans | 200 | | |
| Total | $250 | | $250 |

At this juncture Acme's excess reserve is down to zero. Excess reserve = cash reserve − required reserve = $50 − 20% ($250) = $50 − $50 = 0. Clearly, Acme National has a zero excess reserve and is therefore all loaned up. So we made the right guess when we picked $100 or the amount of the excess reserve as the largest amount Acme could lend. Why is this true? When an individual bank makes a loan, say to a businessman, it can expect the borrower to buy goods with the money. This results in the loss of reserves and deposits by the lending bank; these reserves and deposits go to a bank in the area where the goods are bought. Because we can assume that the check drawn will be redeposited elsewhere, the cash and deposits corresponding to the loan are lost to Acme National.

**Summary.** We can summarize this discussion briefly: an individual bank can expand deposits by the amount of its excess reserve. An individual bank tends to lose an amount of reserve equal to new loans. This means that the lending of all its excess reserve will leave a bank completely loaned up.

**Expansion of Deposits by the Banking System.** Should we assume that the banking system has the same property as the individual bank? Not necessarily. What is true of the part is not necessarily true of the whole. Let us trace out our argument again with the aid of the example above.

Assume that all banks in the system are loaned up with the single exception of Acme National. Then Acme National can lend the amount of its excess reserve, or $100, as shown above. When it has done so, its excess reserve is exhausted, and it has done all it can by the creation of $100 in new deposits. Now consider the Fourteenth National, taking account only of changes as registered by + and − signs. Recall that the supplier of goods to the borrower at Acme National has deposited a $100 check at the Fourteenth National. This raises cash reserves and deposits by $100 at the Fourteenth National, as shown in the accompanying balance sheet.

**TABLE 10-8**
**Fourteenth Receives $100 Deposit Lost by Acme**

| Fourteenth National—Stage 1 | | | |
|---|---|---|---|
| **Assets** | | **Liabilities** | |
| Cash reserve | +$100 | Deposits | +$100 |

Now a quick calculation shows that excess reserves equal $100 − 20% ($100) = $80. Actually, the excess reserve amounts to $80, or ⅘ of the new deposit. Why? When a bank receives $100 in cash by a deposit, it must set aside 20%, leaving 100% − 20% = 80%, or ⅘ in excess reserve. Consequently, the receipt of a $1 deposit creates an excess reserve equal to the following:

$$\begin{aligned} &\$1 - \text{the reserve requirement} \\ &= \$1 - 0.2\ (\$1) \\ &= \$.80, \text{ or } 80\%\ (\$1). \end{aligned}$$

It is this 80% of the deposit taking the form of excess reserve that the Fourteenth National can now use as a basis for loans. Evidently, it can hold $20 as reserve and lend the rest, $80.

Now the Fourteenth National proceeds to lend $80. The balance sheets then shows an increase in loans of $80 and in deposits of $80. Then the balance sheet looks like this.

**TABLE 10-9**
**Fourteenth Expands Deposits by Making $80 Loan**

| Fourteenth National—Stage 2 | | | |
|---|---|---|---|
| **Assets** | | **Liabilities** | |
| Cash reserve | +$100 | Deposits | +$180 |
| Loans | +80 | | |
| Total | +$180 | Total | +$180 |

As the borrower uses his $80 in funds to buy goods, the recipient of the check will deposit it, causing cash and deposits to go down by $80. At this final stage the balance sheet looks as follows:

**TABLE 10-10**
**Fourteenth Reaches Final Position**

| Fourteenth National—Stage 3 | | | |
|---|---|---|---|
| **Assets** | | **Liabilities** | |
| Cash reserve | +$ 20 | Deposits | +$100 |
| Loans | + 80 | | |
| Total | +$100 | | +$100 |

Evidently, the Fourteenth National is now all loaned up. Suppose the $80 was deposited in what we will call the Third Bank. Then we can already tell what will happen; this bank can lend 80% of the new $80 deposit, or $64, while setting aside $16 in cash reserve. This process continues through an indefinite succession of banks. Suppose we add up the amounts of deposits and loans created in the several banks.

**TABLE 10-11**
**Expansion of Loans and Deposits by the Banking System**

| Bank | Excess Reserves = Loans and Deposits Created | Deposits Received by Bank | Additional Cash Reserves Held |
|---|---|---|---|
| Acme National Bank | $100.00* | | |
| Fourteenth National Bank | 80.00 | $100.00† | $20.00‡ |
| Third Bank | 64.00 | 80.00 | 16.00 |
| Fourth Bank | 51.20 | 64.00 | 12.80 |
| Fifth Bank | 40.96 | 51.20 | 10.24 |
| Sixth Bank | 32.77 | 40.96 | 8.19 |
| Seventh Bank | 26.22 | 32.77 | 6.55 |
| Eighth Bank | 20.98 | 26.22 | 5.24 |
| Ninth Bank | 16.78 | 20.98 | 4.20 |
| Tenth Bank | 13.42 | 16.78 | 3.36 |
| Sum for above banks | $446.33 | $432.91 | $86.58 |
| Sum for an indefinite number of banks** | $500.00 | $500.00 | $100.00 |

* See balance sheet for Acme National Bank—Stage 2.
† See balance sheet for Fourteenth National Bank—Stage 1.
‡ See balance sheet for Fourteenth National Bank—Stage 3.
** Some banks will be repeated as the list of banks is extended indefinitely.

As we see in Table 10–11 the loans and deposits created by the banks listed add up to \$446.33. At this point the process is not ended, because the last loan of \$13.42 will be spent by the borrower, then deposited by someone in the Eleventh Bank, which permits a continuation of the expansion. If carried on indefinitely, the sum of loans and deposits will add up to or approach \$500. Concurrently, the reserves will add up to \$100; this amounts to 20% of the \$500 of deposits that can be created.[3] The sum \$100 is the original amount of excess reserves. Clearly, the amount of deposits equals the excess reserves, \$100, times 5.

This can be expressed by a formula:

$$E = p \cdot D, \qquad \textbf{(1)}$$

where $E$ represents the amount of excess reserves held by the banks, $p$ is the reserve ratio, and $D$ is the *maximum* amount of additional deposits that can be created on the basis of these excess reserves. Thus, we are given $E = \$100$ and $p = 0.20 = 20\%$. Then we calculate $D$ on the basis of these excess reserves with this reserve ratio. If we try the value $D = \$500$, we see that

$$\$100 = 20\%\,(\$500) = \$100. \qquad \textbf{(2)}$$

Clearly, the total, \$500 in new deposits (and loans), is the largest total the banking system can create.

[3] We can get this sum by the following method. The $\$500 = \$100 + \$80 + \$64 + \ldots = \$100\ (1 + 0.8 + 0.64 + \ldots) = \$100\ (1 + 0.8 + [0.8]^2 + \ldots)$. Examining the series in parentheses, we find that each term is 0.8 times the preceding one. But the sum of a series of this kind is found by a formula $S = 1 + r + r^2 + r^3 + \cdots = 1/(1 - r)$, where $r$ is the common ratio of the successive terms. In this case $r = 0.8$, so that $S = 1 + 0.8 + (0.8)^2 + (0.8)^3 + \cdots = 1/(1 - 0.8) = 1/0.2 = 5$. We can substitute the value of $S$ in the parenthesis above to get:

$$\begin{aligned} &\$100 + \$80 + \$64 + \ldots \\ &= \$100\ (1 + 0.8 + [0.8]^2 + [0.8]^3 + \cdots) \\ &= \$100\ (1/[1 - 0.8]) = \$100(1/0.2) = \$100 \cdot 5. \end{aligned}$$

Here $r = 0.8 = 1 - 0.2$, where 0.2, $p$, is the reserve ratio. We may call $r = 1 - p$ the coefficient that passes along the dwindling reserves for further use. In general the sum for the expansion is going to be:

$$\begin{aligned} D &= E(1 + r + r^2 + r^3 + \cdots) \\ &= E\frac{1}{1 - r} \\ &= E\frac{1}{1 - (1 - p)} \\ &= E\frac{1}{p}, \end{aligned}$$

where $E$, $r$, and $p$ have the meanings assigned above.

Actually, we want to put $D$ in the position of the unknown. So we rewrite the equation in the form

$$D = E \cdot \frac{1}{p}. \tag{3}$$

In this form the equation enables us to compute $D$ with a knowledge of $E$ and $1/p$.

We can verbalize this relation by this statement: *maximum deposit expansion D, with given excess reserves E, equals excess reserves times the reciprocal of the reserve ratio, 1/p.*

In the case just discussed the excess reserves were \$100 and the reserve ratio $p$ was 20%, or 0.20. Then the formula states that maximum deposit expansion is $\$100 \times (1/0.20) = \$100 \times 5 = \$500$. Here the important thing is the number 5. This is the number of times that extra deposits can be multiplied in generating excess reserves. But this multiple depends on the reserve ratio; change the reserve ratio and you change the multiple. For example, suppose the reserve ratio were 25%. Then excess reserves could be multiplied only *4* times. Why?

**A Puzzling Point.** Why can a system of banks expand credit by 5 times excess reserves, whereas a single bank can expand only by the amount of its excess reserve? The answer lies in the differing relation to reserves. Where a single bank loses part of its reserve when it lends money, the banking system does not. It retains all its reserves, because what is lost by one bank is gained by another. (Here we are neglecting a leakage of cash into circulation and a possible loss of gold to foreign countries.) As a result of this stability of reserves, the several banks, working in unison, can expand loans and deposits by a multiple of excess reserves.

**Summary.** In this chapter we have outlined the basic institutional structure of the banking system that led to a discussion of how individual banks can create and expand deposits. In the next chapter this information will serve as a background to the discussion of monetary policy. We have noted that commercial banks are classified as state or national, according to the governmental level at which they are chartered. All national and some state banks belong to the Federal Reserve System. Although fewer than half the total number, they hold about 84 per cent of the deposits. The Federal Reserve System centers around the 12 Federal Reserve Banks, which hold reserves deposited with them by the member banks. At the head of the system is the Board of Governors, which, together with the Open Market Committee, helps to control the supply of money in the United States. In addition to performing certain service functions, the system acts as fiscal agent for the United States Treasury.



In the second part of the chapter we were concerned with an essential feature of individual banks—their ability to extend loans and thereby to create deposit money. It was shown that individual banks can expand deposits only by the amount of their excess reserves. On the other hand, the banking system is not subject to a loss of reserves, as is an individual bank. As a result it turned out that member banks can expand loans and deposits by a *multiple* of excess reserves. This expansion is given by the formula $D = E/r$, where $D$ is maximum deposit expansion. $E$ is the amount of excess reserves, and $r$ is the reserve ratio, stating reserves held by banks against their deposits as a ratio to deposits.

## QUESTIONS

1. Describe briefly the number, location, ownership, control, and purpose of the Federal Reserve Banks.
2. What is the Board of Governors? How are its members named, and what are the purposes of the Board?
3. What is the Federal Open Market Committee, and what are its functions?
4. Outline the several functions of the Federal Reserve Banks.
5. Using a balance sheet, explain the results that follow immediately on a loan made by an individual bank.
6. Explain why it is said that an individual bank can create money by making a loan.
7. What is fractional reserve banking, and how did it originate?
8. What is the maximum amount by which an individual member bank can expand its deposits?
9. What is the maximum amount by which the banking system can expand its deposits? How do you explain the difference between this and the previous answer?
10. What happens to excess reserves as deposits are expanded to the limit in an individual bank? In the banking system?
11. What is the relationship between the additional deposits created and the additional loans extended when a bank or the banking system expands deposits?

CHAPTER

11

# The Federal Reserve and Monetary Policy

In this chapter we will outline the objectives of monetary policy and the ways in which the Federal Reserve attains them. Because the basic aims can be stated rather briefly, most of the discussion will concern itself with ways and means. It is clear that the Federal Reserve System lacks sufficient power to achieve all the ends it is concerned with. Further, the ends themselves may prove to be inconsistent under certain circumstances. In view of these difficulties it is suggested that an appropriate fiscal policy might be necessary to solve certain problems. This is the topic of the next chapter.

**Objectives of Federal Reserve Policy.** The act establishing the Federal Reserve System was passed in 1913 and amended in 1935. Lacking in this legislation is a clear statement of objectives, leaving the area of policy somewhat confused. As the present Chairman of the Board of Governors sees it, the task of the system is to "lean against the prevailing economic winds." What this seems to mean is that the aim of Federal Reserve policy is to stabilize economic activity, checking recessions or depressions, on the one hand, and spasmodic expansions leading to inflation on the other. For a long time this statement appeared to be relatively adequate. However, for reasons to be stated below this guide will no longer suffice.

In the last 30 years it has become quite evident that both depressions and inflationary periods can be extremely lengthy and stubborn. For well over a decade between 1929 and 1941 the United States languished in a depressed state. At no time in this period did the economy approach full employment despite considerable effort by the Federal Reserve. Again, following World War II the economy has been marked by a "creeping inflation," in which prices have tended to rise at a rate of about 1.5 to 2 per cent a year.

A further economic tendency became evident in the period 1955–64, namely a rate of economic growth inadequate in relation to our own needs and by comparison with that of other countries. Of particular note is the presence of a moderate but steady volume of unemployment and unused productive potential. If the economy could be encouraged to develop more rapidly, these problems would be minimized. Thus an obvious policy objective is to achieve a higher rate of growth. Achievement of this goal would tend automatically to take care of depression and unemployment, but would not eliminate inflation. In recognition of this problem the Federal Reserve now takes as a guideline the achievement of "the highest sustainable rate of economic growth consistent with avoidance of inflation." Thus the encouragement of a *high rate of economic growth with a minimum of inflation* now takes its place alongside economic stabilization as one of the principal objectives of policy.

In this chapter we will concern ourselves primarily with economic stabilization. This is the more elementary and easily understood of the two goals, because the actions required under any given set of conditions are generally clear. Actually, then, we will deal here primarily with (1) plans to avert depression, on the one hand, and (2) plans to avoid inflation, on the other.

**How the Federal Reserve Helps to Avert Depressions.** Perhaps the most characteristic symptom of depression is a low level of investment spending. A number of causes may be advanced to explain the phenomenon: a failure of business confidence, which reduces the expectation of profit; a slowing down in the growth of consumer demand; the exhaustion of immediately profitable avenues of investment; the failure of businessmen to develop innovations requiring new investment spending. Whatever the causes, spending on output tends to lag, and it must be stimulated if the depression is to be overcome. Only when total spending, including the fickle element of investment, is sufficiently large to take off all output at full employment will the problem be solved. Now consider how the Federal Reserve may help to increase expenditure on output.

Through its various powers the Federal Reserve can expand the excess reserves of the member banks of the system. With given excess reserves, member banks are *able* to expand loans and deposits by a multiple of excess reserves. Now, in line with the argument in Chapter 10, the increased (excess) reserves of member banks will make it possible for banks to lower interest rates to existing customers or to make available credit to new customers. This will (it is hoped) stimulate additional investment and government spending, $I$ and $G$. Each such dollar of additional spending will generate further *NNP,* so that the total rise in *NNP* will amount to about 3 times the initial increase in $I$ and $G$.

In schematic form this may be summarized as follows.

Federal Reserve creates excess reserves.
Member banks are able to expand loans.
Member banks lower interest rates and increase availability of loans.
Investment and government spending, $I$ and $G$, increase.
*NNP* rises by an amount equal to about 3 times the increase in $I$ and $G$.

If this sequence of effects takes place, the easy-money policy in question will have a favorable effect on employment. Keep in mind, though, that the desired goal is *full* employment. Thus the Federal Reserve is faced with a distinctly quantitative question, namely, whether it is possible to push this easy-money policy to the point where full employment is achieved. If it is, good; if not, additional action must be taken, possibly by the Treasury working through spending and taxing policies.

So far we have talked about curing depressions. What about checking booms or inflationary periods? Here the opposite moves are made: the Federal Reserve takes steps designed to reduce reserves and excess reserves, setting in motion a sequence of events like the above but working in the opposite direction. Later, some differences in the way the process works in the case of a tight-money policy will be indicated.

## HOW FEDERAL RESERVE POLICY IS CARRIED INTO EFFECT

**Balance Sheet of the Federal Reserve Banks.** In order to learn how the Federal Reserve carries out its policies we need first a little information about the way the Federal Reserve Banks do business. To this end let us turn to the consolidated balance sheet of the 12 banks, as shown in Table 11–1.

Consider first the asset side. As the first item we have "Gold certificate reserve." According to law the Federal Reserve must maintain a gold reserve equal to at least 25 per cent of Federal Reserve notes (the reserve against deposits having been eliminated). In this balance sheet Federal Reserve notes amount to \$33.747 billion, 25 per cent of which equals \$8.437 billion. Because the gold certificate reserve is \$14.871 billion (the figure in Table 11–1 includes other cash), excess reserves of \$6.434 billion exist. The item "Gold certificate reserve" consists primarily of Federal Reserve claims (credits) against gold owned and held by the Treasury.

Consider how this item comes to appear on the books. Suppose a foreign government wishes to sell gold in the United States. By law all monetary gold must be sold to the United States Treasury. The Treasury pays for the gold with a check drawn against its account with, say, the Federal Reserve Bank of New York. This action depletes its account while adding to that of the foreign government. In order to replenish its deposits the Treasury notifies this Federal Reserve Bank that it is granting a claim against the new Treasury gold (by crediting its "gold certificate account" with the Treasury). Taking note of this action, the Bank adds to Treasury deposits a like amount. In the end gold certificate reserve is up, Treasury deposits are unchanged, and foreign deposits have increased.

"U.S. government securities" consist primarily of interest bearing "bills" and "notes" issued by the Treasury that mature within a year.

**TABLE 11-1**
**Combined Balance Sheet of the Twelve Federal Reserve Banks: January 27, 1965 (Billions of Dollars)**

| Assets | | Liabilities and Net Worth | |
|---|---|---|---|
| Gold certificate reserve (and other cash) | 15.050 | Federal Reserve notes | 33.747 |
| | | Deposits | |
| U.S. Government securities | 36.723 | Member bank reserves | 17.820 |
| | | U.S. Treasury | .907 |
| Discounts and advances, acceptances | .354 | Foreign and other | .327 |
| | | Other, including capital | 6.096 |
| Other (about 80% consists of items being collected) | 6.770 | | |
| | 58.897 | | 58.897 |

We will explain how these are acquired under the heading "Open Market Operations," below. Income from these securities, although very useful, does not constitute a significant factor in motivating purchases or sales. In fact, the primary objective is to influence member bank reserves, and a secondary purpose is to stabilize government security prices.

The next item consists primarily of "Discounts and advances" to member banks. The larger item of the two, advances, represent loans to member banks, with government securities used as collateral. The borrowing bank receives the loan in the form of an increase in its reserve account or Federal Reserve notes issued for the occasion by the Federal Reserve Bank.

The item labeled "Other" consists mostly of items in process of collection.

On the Liabilities and Net Worth side the largest item consists of

"Federal Reserve notes" issued by the 12 Federal Reserve Banks. In value terms these notes amount to over 80 per cent of all currency and coin issued in the United States. Being liabilities of the Federal Reserve Banks, they constitute claims against the assets (primarily government securities and gold). Only currency actually issued to the member banks, the government, and the public counts in this total.

The next item is "Deposits," "Member bank reserves" being quantitatively much the most important subhead. The latter part of deposits includes the reserves that member banks are legally required to hold with the Federal Reserve Banks. Although these reserves are liabilities to the Federal Reserve Banks, they are assets to the member banks. The treasury also maintains a deposit of roughly $0.9 billion to finance its transactions. In fact, the Treasury uses its Federal Reserve bank account in the same way that we use our own checking accounts. Again, this item is an asset to the Treasury, though it is a liability to the Federal Reserve Banks. Finally, foreign governments and central banks have small balances that arise mainly in connection with sales of gold. Most foreign money in the United States is held in two forms, "earmarked gold," held in United States government depositories but owned by these governments, and deposits in private banks. Of course, these items are distinct from the small deposits held with the Federal Reserve Banks.

## DISCRETIONARY MONETARY POLICIES

The system has at its disposal three major instruments of control, listed in order of importance: (1) open-market operations, (2) control of the rediscount rate, and (3) control of reserve requirements. In addition, there are two other minor weapons: (4) moral suasion, and (5) control over margin requirements. Let us consider these policies in the order named.

**Open Market Operations.** Open market operations consist of the purchase or sale of government securities on the open market rather than by direct dealings with the Treasury. This activity is directed by the Open Market Committee, consisting of the seven members of the Board of Governors and five of the twelve presidents of Federal Reserve Banks, chosen in rotation. Because actual Committee operations are conducted in the New York Federal Reserve Bank, the president of that bank is an ex officio member and chairman of the Committee. Once every three weeks, approximately, the Open Market Committee meets and decides on policy for the ensuing period. This policy is carried out by the *system manager,* who, from a "desk" in the Federal Reserve Bank of New York, conducts the actual buying and selling of government bonds on the open market. He is assisted in translating general verbal instructions of the Committee into concrete actions by the Chairman, who is physically nearby. In addition, he can and does communicate by telephone or otherwise with the other Committee members.

Open market operations consist in the purchase and sale of government securities on the "open market." In practice, this means buying or selling through the few (less than two dozen) dealers in these securities, most of whom are located in New York City. By long established convention the system manager follows the practice of dealing primarily in short-term securities—bills, notes, and certificates—that fall due within a year or two. Although the restriction to dealings in short-dated securities has been challenged in Congressional hearings, there is, as yet, no evidence of change in this policy.

The operations are designed primarily to influence the reserve position of member banks. Purchases on the open market tend to increase member bank reserves; sales, to decrease them. If reserves (and excess reserves) increase, a basis is created for the further expansion in member bank loans and deposits. In fact, as we know, $1 of excess reserves can result in additional loans and deposits amounting to about $5. Let us consider now the effect of a purchase by the Federal Reserve of $100 in government bills from a private individual.

In order to effect payment the Federal Reserve, through the system manager, draws a check against, say, the Federal Reserve Bank of New York. When the individual deposits this sum in his bank, the Acme National, deposits go up to the same extent. Because Acme is a member of the Federal Reserve, it sends in the check to the Federal Reserve Bank of New York, assuming Acme to belong to the New York district. When it is received, the Federal Reserve Bank credits this sum to the account of Acme National. In Table 11–1 this appears under the heading of "Deposits—Member bank reserves." Such a sum will appear on the books of the member bank as an increase in its cash reserve held at the Federal Reserve Bank.

Let us summarize the effects of this action on the member bank by a balance sheet showing only changes. Such an action creates $100 in actual reserves, whereas required reserves against the added deposits are 20 per cent of $100, or $20, leaving excess reserves of $80. By our previous argument the banking system can expand deposits by 5 times excess reserves, provided the reserve ratio is 20 per cent.

**TABLE 11–2**
**Effect of Federal Reserve Bill Purchase on Acme National**

| Assets | | Liabilities | |
|---|---|---|---|
| Cash reserve (held at Federal Reserve Bank) | +$100 | Deposits | +$100 |

Consequently, an expansion of 5 times $80 (equals $400) can now occur under our assumptions, as loans are extended to firms and individuals. Altogether the original deposit of $100 plus the expansion occuring later will amount to $500. Such borrowing will undoubtedly be facilitated by lower interest rates present with such excess reserves.

The purchase of government bonds from private parties thus tends initially to cause an equal increase in private deposits and reserves. It also causes an increase in excess reserves. Under favorable conditions deposits will increase by a total of 5 times the original amount of bonds purchased. At the level of the Federal Reserve Bank the effect is to increase the holdings of government securities and member bank deposits by equal amounts. This is given in the following balance sheet, showing these changes.

**TABLE 11-3**
**Effect of Federal Reserve Purchase of a Bill on the Condition of Federal Reserve Bank**

| Assets | | Liabilities | |
|---|---|---|---|
| Government securities | +$100 | Member bank reserve deposits | +$100 |

Clearly, by purchasing government securities the Federal Reserve increases reserves and excess reserves of member banks, thus creating a basis for further expansion of deposits and loans. Such actions favor the low interest rates and easy availability of credit needed in time of recession. If the reverse policy is needed in time of inflation, the Federal Reserve can sell securities. The detailed working out of the effects may be left to the reader.

Open market operations constitute an extremely flexible tool for easing or tightening credit and thus affecting interest rates and credit availability. Operations can be carried on in any volume from millions to billions, with results ranging from small to great. If it is difficult to be sure what action it is appropriate to take, the Federal Reserve may operate in the open market without fanfare or publicity in what appears then to be the correct manner. If a change in the economic situation occurs, it can alter its policy without the necessity of reversing itself in public. This ability to adjust to changing conditions quietly, rapidly, and in the desired degree is the greatest advantage of this device. As a result, open market operations are regarded as the principal method of controlling the supply of money.

**The Rediscount Rate and the Rate on Advances.** Let us consider briefly the meaning and origin of discounts and advances. When a member bank needs reserve cash, it may sell short-term paper (a process called "rediscounting") to the Federal Reserve Bank of its district. Alternatively, the bank may obtain a loan, backed by suitable government securities, thereby obtaining an "advance." In either case the Federal Reserve Bank charges the member bank a rate of interest, called the "rediscount rate" in the first case and the "rate on advances" in the second. The evidence indicates that there is a direct relation between the member banks' interest rates to their borrowers and the rediscount rate. Actually, member banks seem to try to keep their rates somewhat above the rediscount rate, raising and lowering them with the latter. Under the law each Federal Reserve Bank sets the rediscount rate and the rate on advances that apply to the member banks of that district. The rates thus set are subject to the review of the Board of Governors. To summarize, the Board of Governors can influence or determine these two rates and thereby the rates charged by member banks.

Now consider how the Federal Reserve uses these two rates to influence loans and deposits. For simplicity we will refer this discussion only to the rediscount rate, because the two are closely tied together. If the Federal Reserve wishes to ease money and credit, it can lower rediscount rates. Statistical evidence indicates that the interest rate on short-term loans at banks conforms closely to the rediscount rate. For the moment, take this to be a fact. Then a reduction in the rediscount rate will lead to a corresponding decline in member banks' interest rates on loans to their customers. Such a decline in the interest rate will lower the cost of borrowing. When businessmen compare the reduced cost of borrowing with the presumably unchanged returns, they may decide to undertake some capital expansion financed by bank loans. Such borrowing will be the fruit of lower member bank interest rates and will be accompanied by deposit expansion. As this takes place, the economy will receive a corresponding boost. Thus, lower rediscount rates tend to encourage expansion of deposits and economic activity.

Let us insert here a word of caution. Although lower rediscount rates usually lead to lower member bank rates and higher rediscount rates to higher bank rates, this says nothing about the volume of loans. A potential borrower from a member bank may or may not be brought to a point of decision by a lowering of the interest rate. If this borrower fails to discern a sufficiently attractive profit opportunity, even after the cut in the interest rate, he will not seek a loan. In short, businessmen cannot be made to borrow simply by pushing the button of lower interest rates.

Left untouched here are a number of points. Frst, why do member banks adjust their rate to that of the Federal Reserve? There is no pat answer to this question. However, one thing is clear. The rediscount rate signals the attitude of the Federal Reserve toward the credit situation. If the Federal Reserve lowers the rate, this is a signal that it wishes to expand credit. If it raises the rate, the reverse is true. Now the system can always wheel up its heavy artillery—open market operations and reserve requirements—to bolster its actions. Knowing this, the member banks doubtless take the hint without further ado.

Next, a reduction of the rediscount rate cannot be effective unless excess reserves are reasonably plentiful. Without such excess reserves the member banks will not wish to expand credit. Consequently, it is necessary for the Federal Reserve to buy bonds to create such reserves concurrently with a reduction in the rediscount rate. Only in this way can the lower interest rates be made effective through member bank lending.

Finally, a member bank probably wants its rate a bit above the rediscount rate, but not much above. It wants the rate above, because in case of emergency it would like to rediscount paper without loss at the Federal Reserve Bank. If the rediscount rate is 4 per cent and the member bank rate is 5 per cent, a member bank can rediscount a loan with a slight gain (1 per cent) on the transaction. On the other hand, competition prevents the bank from raising its rate very far above the rediscount rate. Let us note here that tradition prohibits large-scale rediscounting by member banks except in case of emergency.

**Reserve Requirements.** The Board of Governors has the power to fix member bank reserve requirements within defined limits. Not only can the reserve ratio vary within the limits established by law at the discretion of the Board, but they vary according to the place in which the bank is located. On this basis banks are now classified into two groups—Reserve City Banks and Country Banks. The legal limits for the reserve ratios and the actual values at a recent date are given in Table 11–4. It is the reserve ratios against demand deposits that are considered to be of vital importance.

Manipulation of reserve requirements is the most powerful but least used of the major weapons of the Federal Reserve. Because of its im-

**TABLE 11–4**
**Reserve Requirements of Member Banks: Actual Requirements on February 1, 1965, and the Legal limits (in Per Cent)**

| | Demand Deposits | | Time Deposits | |
|---|---|---|---|---|
| | Central Reserve City and Reserve City Banks | Country Banks | Central Reserve City and Reserve City Banks | Country Banks |
| February 1, 1965 | 16½ | 12 | 4 | 4 |
| Minimum | 10 | 7 | 3 | 3 |
| Maximum | 22 | 14 | 6 | 6 |

mediate and drastic effect on member banks, this tool is used rather infrequently. By reducing reserve requirements of member banks the Federal Reserve can create excess reserves at a stroke. An increase causes a corresponding reduction in excess reserves. Suppose that in dull times member banks are loaned up. Then the Federal Reserve lowers reserve requirements. Now actual reserves are the same. So are deposits. But required reserves are lower, and as a result excess reserves are brought into existence. With such excess reserves the member bank can lower interest cost in order to expand. The rest of the story is the same.

To illustrate, suppose the Acme National Bank is a Reserve City Bank, that the current reserve requirement is 20%, and that it is loaned up. Then its balance sheet would appear as in Table 11–5. At this juncture its actual reserves are $200, as compared with required reserves of $200 = 20% ($1,000), so that excess reserves of $200 − $200 = 0 now exist. Evidently, Acme is loaned up.

**TABLE 11–5**
**Acme National Is Loaned Up**

| Assets | | Liabilities | |
|---|---|---|---|
| Cash reserve | $ 200 | Deposits | $1,000 |
| Loans | 800 | | |
| Total | $1,000 | | $1,000 |

Now suppose that the Federal Reserve, sensing a major depression, decides to go all out in combating this situation, and cuts the reserve requirement to 11%. The balance sheet is unchanged, but excess reserves are created. Comparing the actual reserves of $200 with required reserves of $110 = 11% ($1,000), we find excess reserves to be $90 = $200 − $110. Clearly, Acme can now expand credit by $90 and the banking system by a multiple of this amount. This illustrates the ability of the Federal Reserve to vary excess reserves and thus create a basis for deposit expansion by changing reserve requirements.

**Minor Controls, Moral Suasion.** If the Federal Reserve officials decide that a given policy, such as easy money, is desirable, it may attempt to persuade the member banks to go along voluntarily. Probably, pronouncements by the Chairman of the Board of Governors are regarded as a sign of the direction in which monetary policy is turning. Such an approach is effective insofar as the system stands ready to back up its words on other fronts.

**Minor Controls, Margin Requirements.** The Board of Governors has the power to determine margin requirements on loans for purchasing or holding securities. A margin requirement amounts to a minimum required down payment stated as a percentage of the market value of the security. It is a common practice for speculators to buy stock on a margin. Under this scheme the individual instructs his broker to buy a share of stock in a certain company at the market price. The buyer may put up 60 per cent of the price in cash, and the broker lends him the remainder in order that he may purchase the share. Such a practice facilitates speculation in stocks. By increasing the margin that must be put up by the purchaser, the Board of Governors can discourage excessive speculation. Conversely, lowering requirements may stimulate a needed flow of funds into the securities markets and thus establish a somewhat easier availability of funds to business.

## GOLD AND MONETARY CONTROL

**Basic Facts.** As of February, 1965, the Federal Reserve Banks are required by law to maintain a 25 per cent reserve in gold against Federal Reserve notes and deposits (mostly member bank reserves). Legislation in process as of this time, proposing to drop the reserve requirement against deposits, seems certain to pass. It appears, then, that we will have in the near future a 25-per-cent reserve against Federal Reserve notes only. (This change was enacted into law in 1965.)

The gold reserve consists of two types of claims. The first consists of *gold certificates,* a form of currency or paper money that constitutes a claim against a corresponding value of gold bullion held by the Treasury. This type of money, once in general circulation, is now used only in the hallowed precincts of the Federal Reserve Banks. The second type is known as *gold certificate reserve* and constitutes a claim by the Federal Reserve Banks on Treasury gold. Essentially, it amounts to an entry, on the books of the Treasury, acknowledging the claim that the Federal Reserve Banks have on the gold. This is the principal way that the gold reserve is held.

Let us note the way in which gold and currency are related. The *dollar* is defined by law as a certain weight of gold—at present, $1/35$ of an ounce. This gives the Treasury buying price for gold as $35 an ounce. If the Treasury possesses a certain stock of gold, the gold content of the dollar, $1/35$ oz, determines a corresponding dollar value of that stock. Thus if the Treasury holds 1 million oz of gold, the dollar value of that gold stock is $35 million. Now suppose Congress reduced the gold content of the dollar from $1/35$ to $1/40$ oz. Then the dollar is said to have been *devalued,* because it contains less gold. Such a change raises the buying price of gold from $35 to $40 per ounce and increases the value of the existing stock of gold in proportion. Thus the dollar value of a gold stock of 1 million oz will be raised from $35 million to $40 million.

If Congress increases the gold content of the dollar, thus lowering the purchase price of gold, revaluation is said to occur. Changes in either direction are very infrequent, the last having taken place in 1934, when the Treasury buying price was raised from $21 an ounce to $35. A devaluation generally rises from a drastic and persistent loss of gold to foreign countries, an event preceding our last one.

**Gold Stock and Money Supply.** As of February 1, 1965, a 25-per-cent reserve in gold must be held against Federal Reserve notes and deposits of Federal Reserve Banks. However, our gold stock has been declining in the last few years. Between December 1, 1957, and March 1965 the stock fell from about $22.7 billion to slightly under $15 billion. The free gold reserve, the excess of our gold stock over the 25-per-cent requirement, has been declining, year by year, as we have used gold to settle accounts with foreign countries. Federal Reserve notes and deposits amounted to nearly $53 billion on January 30, 1965, requiring about $13.3 billion of gold compared to an actual reserve of about $14.9 billion. Thus the free gold reserve amounted to only about $1.6 billion. Feeling this margin to be too close for comfort, the Administration has introduced legislation to drop the requirement of gold reserves against deposits.

If the revised rule were currently in effect, the required gold reserve would be only about $8.4 billion, or 25 per cent of the $33.7 billion Federal Reserve notes outstanding (as of January 30, 1965). Then there would be about $6.5 billion free reserves, which equals $14.9 billion actual reserves less the $8.4 billion required reserves. This change would enlarge the free gold reserve to the point where no immediate problem would exist.

The existence of a law requiring a 25-per-cent gold reserve against Federal Reserve notes limits the amount of this form of money that can be issued. Suppose the gold reserve is about $15 billion, as in January 1965. Then about $60 billion of Federal Reserve notes could be issued, compared to the roughly $34 billion as of that date. Thus the gold reserve sets a definite limit to the amount of currency that can be issued. It seems very likely, however, that the United States might well cut loose from the 25-per-cent reserve rule against Federal Reserve notes, if the gold reserve began to drop to the minimum.

It appears that the main significance of the gold reserve is to settle debts that occur in the course of international trade. It is universally accepted for that purpose. If our gold reserve continues to shrink, as it has in the past few years, it will eventually force on us some measures to retain at least some gold for that purpose.

## ASSESSMENT OF MONETARY POLICY

**Review.** In a period of recession the Federal Reserve can ease credit conditions by buying government securities, lowering the rediscount rate, and lowering reserve requirements. Such steps should lower interest rates and make credit more readily available. In turn, this ought to stimulate additional investment and government spending, which would lead to a rise in *NNP*. Eventually, it is hoped, full employment would be attained. In a period of boom accompanied by inflation, the reverse steps should check the rise in prices.

**Criticisms of Monetary Policy in Recession.** A very basic criticism of easy money is this. Granted the Federal Reserve can create additional reserves for member banks and that they will make loans available at low rates, it does not follow that anyone will want to borrow. Investment is low in recession periods primarily because the level of expected returns is low. If existing plants are not being used to capacity, additional borrowing to build more plant is not likely to be attractive. Thus the interest rate is not necessarily a decisive factor in a recession. Neither is the ready availability of credit. In the case of government investment in capital projects a low interest rate is very helpful. However, in recession, tax receipts are low, and governments are not likely to be disposed to make large capital outlays, because such action creates a large public debt. Thus credit may be had for the asking at low rates with very few takers.

A second criticism hinges around the gold problem. If an easy money policy is pursued far enough to be effective, it will probably lead to some rise in the price level. If this goes far enough, it may lead to a loss of gold as foreigners buy less from us and we more from them, resulting thus in a deficit. To avoid this an easy-money policy may have to be abandoned before full employment is attained. Thus easy money would prove to be an inadequate policy under actual conditions.

**Criticisms of Monetary Policy in Boom or Inflation.** There is little doubt that the Federal Reserve can wipe out the excess reserves of member banks and otherwise raise interest rates and reduce the availability of credit. This policy may be pushed far enough to restrict significantly the funds available for investment and government spending for capital projects. To some extent this may be offset by the use of certain cash balances that are normally idle. Even so, it seems likely that this policy could reduce *I* and *G*. The result would be a dampening of the inflationary fires. The criticism is that the impact of credit restriction is very unequal on different classes of borrowers.

Consider now this claim. Large corporations are able to meet a great part of their need for investment funds by internal saving. In addition, they hold rather large working balances and can draw on these for investment in fixed capital. Finally, they are the first to be accommodated and the last to be cut off by banks. On the other hand, the small borrower is likely to rely heavily on banks for expansion purposes but be a less favored customer. Thus the impact of a tight-money policy is likely to fall quite heavily on the small businessman. In short, a prime objection to a tight-money policy lies in its effect on the small borrower. This is deemed unjust.

A second factor lies in the effect on the government. With a large public debt, tight money and a higher interest rate mean higher service charges on the national debt. Because our debt amounts to about $300 billion, a 1-per-cent increase in the interest rate would cost the government $3 billion annually. Thus the government has, at times, resisted increases in the interest rate because of the added expense.

**Defense of Monetary Policy.** Nowadays there is almost a consensus among economists that monetary policy is inadequate as a tool for economic stabilization. Other, probably more powerful weapons, such as government fiscal policy, need to be used as well .Once this point has been established, much of the edge of the criticisms is removed. There are certain additional virtues of monetary policy that can be summarized under the heading of *flexibility*. Monetary policies can be changed quietly, quickly, and over a wide range in quantitative terms. No political decision is required, because the management of the system is essentially independent. Such an ability to move quickly to check an incipient recession or inflation is most valuable.

**Summary.** Objectives of Federal Reserve action are (1) to stabilize the economy by halting inflation and checking recessions, and (2) to stimulate the growth of the economy if it is too slow. In this chapter only the first has been discussed.

The Federal Reserve attempts to stimulate the economy in recession periods by easing credit conditions. The expected pattern is as follows. (1) The Federal Reserve takes actions designed to create excess reserves. (2) Member banks are able to expand loans. (3) Member banks lower interest rates and increase availability of loans. (4) Investment and government spending, $I$ and $G$, increase. (5) *NNP* rises by an amount equal to about 3 times the increase in $I$ and $G$. Inflations are dealt with by roughly opposite policies.

The balance sheet of Federal Reserve Banks contains as assets (1) gold certificate reserve, (2) United States government securities, (3) discounts and advances, acceptances, and (4) other. The first consists of a claim against gold held by the Treasury. The second represents government securities, mostly of short maturities, purchased on the open market. The third is a collection of short-term items, mainly consisting of loans to member banks. The fourth consists of items in process of collection. The liabilities items are (1) Federal

Reserve notes, (2) deposits—member bank, United States Treasury, foreign, and other, and (3) other, including capital. The first arises because the Federal Reserve Banks issue these notes. The second consists almost entirely of member bank reserves held to fulfill legal requirements. The third is small and includes the capital stock of the Federal Reserve Banks.

Major weapons of the Federal Reserve against depression or recession consist in (1) buying short-term government securities in the open market to increase member bank reserves, (2) lowering the rediscount rate as a signal to the member banks that the authorities are seeking to ease credit, and (3) lowering reserve requirements to create excess reserves. And minor powers consist of (4) moral suasion, and (5) control over margin requirements on buying securities.

Gold presents a problem in the United States, because short-term foreign assets of $25 billion outweigh our monetary gold stock of $15 billion (including free reserves of $6.5 billion). A conversion of these assets to gold or excess imports could lead to a crisis in which free reserves are eliminated. Such a possibility necessitates something of a tight-money policy at all times. This constitutes a restriction on the use of easy money as an antidepression measure.

Criticisms of the effectiveness of monetary measures for curing depressions include, in addition to the above problem, the explanation of the possible unresponsiveness of investment to an easy-money policy. During inflation a tight-money policy is hindered by the fact that this policy impinges primarily on the small, vulnerable borrower. It is generally agreed that monetary measures alone will not suffice to stabilize the economy. A prime virtue of monetary policy consists in its flexibility.

## QUESTIONS

1. State the objectives of Federal Reserve policy in several alternative versions.
2. Outline the sequence of steps by which the Federal Reserve could hope to bring the economy out of a depression or recession.
3. What are the main items on the assets side and on the liabilities and net worth side of the 12 Federal Reserve banks (the consolidated statement)?
4. How important a part of the total volume of currency and coin are Federal Reserve notes?
5. Who may deposit funds with Federal Reserve banks? Explain.
6. What is the primary objective of open market operations?
7. Explain the immediate effects of a purchase of government bonds by the Federal Reserve from individuals. Explain how this happens. Do the same for a sale.
8. What are the expected effects of a decline in the rediscount rate? Of a rise?

9. Outline the reserve requirements, the legal limits, for member banks of the Federal Reserve system.
10. How does an increase in reserve requirements affect the money supply? A decrease?
11. What is *moral suasion* and what are *margin requirements?* How are these methods of control used?
12. In what way does the gold reserve limit the money supply (assuming current bills pass)?
13. Give the pros and cons for the use of monetary policy.

CHAPTER

# 12

## Fiscal Policy and the National Debt

In the previous chapter we discussed stabilization of the economy by the use of monetary remedies. As we indicated there, such measures are not sufficient to bring about this result under all conditions. The weakness of monetary controls is traceable to the fact that fluctuations in the level of investment constitute the principal cause of economic instability. Because investment depends more on expectations of future returns and the level of consumer demand than on the interest rate or credit availability, monetary stimuli may fail on certain occasions. Then resort must be had to other means to achieve and maintain full employment. This brings us to the role of fiscal policy in economic stabilization.

**Fiscal Policy.** Let us note that the term *fiscal* is derived from the word *fisc,* the name that Rome gave to the treasury. Thus the word *fiscal* refers literally to the Treasury. And fiscal policy refers literally to all practices adopted by the Treasury in the receipt and expenditure of funds. We are concerned here only with that part of Treasury actions that concerns such general economic objectives as (1) attainment of full employment, (2) avoidance of inflation, and (3) achievement of a sufficiently rapid rate of economic growth. In the ensuing discussion we will concern ourselves with fiscal policy as a means to economic stabilization, or the attainment of full employment without inflation.

As we will bring out in the course of the chapter, the handling of the national debt is a factor that cannot be ignored in discussions of fiscal policy. In fact, it impedes to a degree the use of Treasury powers to stabilize the economy. Also the nation's gold reserve poses an indirect problem for the Treasury, because certain actions leading to full employment may precipitate a gold crisis. We reserve this problem for discussion in a later chapter. To summarize, in this chapter we shall consider, under the heading of fiscal policy, Treasury effort in the interests of economic stabilization, taking into account the national debt.

The national debt is a problem that seems tremendously important to many people. In this chapter we attempt to show that its significance is less than is commonly believed. Certain popular misconceptions are discussed, and the real trouble spots are brought into focus.

**Background for Present Policy.** During the dreary nineteen thirties, when unemployment ranged between 10 and 25 per cent, the American people became fully aware of the problems and costs of such depressed periods. The war came along at this point and demonstrated dramatically how heavy government spending can bring a country out of a depression. In the latter part of the war, fears were expressed by many that cessation of government spending would be followed by economic collapse. At this time some serious thinking was done on ways and means to avoid a repetition of the depression of the thirties.

**The Employment Act of 1946.** The upshot of this ferment was that government was entrusted with the responsibility for maintaining approximately full employment. This draft of power was formalized in the Employment Act of 1946. This law is so important that we will quote the policy section, No. 1021, in full.[1]

> The Congress declares that it is the continuing policy and responsibility of the Federal Government to use all practicable means consistent with its needs and obligations and other essential considerations of national policy, with the assistance and cooperation of industry, agriculture, labor, and State and local governments, to coordinate and utilize all its plans, functions, and resources for the purpose of creating and maintaining, in a manner calculated to foster and promote free competitive enterprise and the general welfare, conditions under which there will be afforded *useful employment opportunities, including self-employment, for those able, willing, and seeking to work, and to promote maximum employment, production and purchasing power.*

Under the provisions of the act there was created a Council of Economic Advisers, composed of three members, to be appointed by the President and confirmed by the Senate. Each member was to be a trained economic analyst, capable of interpreting economic conditions and preparing programs and policies that would assure full employment. Every year the President is required to submit to Congress a document known as the *Economic Report of the President.* Essen-

[1] *United States Code Annotated* (St. Paul, Minn.: West Publishing Co. and Edward Thompson Co., 1948), p. 261. Italics added for emphasis.

tially, this is a report of the Council of Economic Advisers, designed to review the economic developments of the past year. In this report the adequacy of current policies is considered, and possible changes are suggested.

Finally, there is constituted under the act a Joint Committee on the Economic Report. This committee consists of 14 members, seven from the Senate, seven from the House, whose composition reflects the relative numbers in the majority and minority parties. This committee has a number of duties. It makes studies pertaining to the *Economic Report of the President*. It considers how the program of the Federal Government may be coordinated to fulfill the purposes of the act. Finally, on March 1 of each year it must file a report with the Senate and the House that contains its suggestions and advice concerning each of the main recommendations made by the President in the Economic Report. Clearly, the Employment Act imposes a responsibility on the President, Congress, the Council of Economic Advisers, and the Joint Committee that must be shared and coordinated by an interchange of ideas and concerted action.

**Fiscal and Monetary Policy.** In the previous chapter we explained that the Federal Reserve System has assumed the task of "leaning against the prevailing economic winds." Apparently, this is equivalent to the task of fiscal policy, as defined earlier. This raises some questions.

If the desired goals are to be met, fiscal and monetary measures must be coordinated. Clearly, this involves the cooperation of the Council of Economic Advisers, the Board of Governors of the Federal Reserve, the Secretary of the Treasury, as the official responsible for preparing the annual budget, and the President. In practice, it seems that the President usually confers with the Chairman of the Council, the Chairman of the Board of Governors, the Secretary of the Treasury, and possibly some other advisers or assistants. This helps to keep the Federal Reserve System aligned with the executive branch in economic policy. Because the Board of Governors is a quasi-independent agency, it is not required by law to comply with the wishes of the President. Under the law it is charged with certain general responsibilities, as indicated above, but it is allowed discretion in the pursuit of these goals. For this reason the President must try to persuade the Board to follow plans that will lead to a coordinated fiscal-monetary policy designed to provide full employment.

## STABILIZATION OF THE ECONOMY

**Overall Plan.** In order to maintain full-employment *NNP* without inflation (if that is possible), the flow of total spending $(C+I+G)$

must be maintained at a high level. Speaking rather roughly, we may attack this problem from two points of view. (1) We seek certain automatic or built-in stabilizers that will maintain the level of spending in spite of various adverse changes. (2) We seek discretionary powers to be exercised by the President or other appropriate authorities with a view also to the maintenance of spending. Ideally, of course, the automatic stabilizers would do the entire job with no need for the exercise of discretion by the authorities. However, our knowledge of the economy is insufficient to permit us to design an ideal and automatic plan for all future situations. Improvisation is necessary to meet unforeseen circumstances. Let us consider first the built-in stabilizers.

**Built-in Stabilizers, Taxes.** In Chapter 7 we explained how the imposition of taxes affects consumption. Briefly, the additional tax bite lowers the amount of *NNP* passed back to become *DPI* (Disposable Personal Income or take-home pay). Because the consumer always tends to spend over $9/10$ of any additional *DPI,* the *MPC* out of *NNP* is reduced. To illustrate the statement that *MPC* falls let us ignore all differences between *NNP* and *DPI* except taxes, and assume the tax bite to be 26%. Then 74% of *NNP* (100% − 26%) becomes *DPI,* and, say, 90% of this additional *DPI* is consumed. Then the fraction of $1 of *NNP* that will be consumed is equal to $0.9(0.74) = 0.666 = 2/3$, approximately. In brief, *MPC* is reduced from $9/10$ to $2/3$. Literally, this means that *consumption spending is stabilized by the imposition of taxes.*

Let us give an example to clarify the above statement. Suppose *NNP* falls off by $30 billion. Under our present tax system *MPC* is about $2/3$, and consumption will fall by $2/3(\$30) = \$20$ billion. If no tax bite existed, a fall of *NNP* by $30 billion under our assumption would imply a like decline of $30 billion in *DPI.* Then consumption would be reduced by $9/10(\$30) = \$27$ billion. Thus the decline in consumption spending is much less with the tax system we actually have than it would be without these taxes.

The stabilizing effect of this change is best expressed by means of the multiplier. In the absence of taxes with an *MPC* of 0.9 the multiplier would be $K = 1/(1 - 0.9) = 10$. Under actual conditions with a substantial tax bite, *MPC* is reduced to about $2/3$. In turn, this gives rise to a multiplier of about $K = 1/(1 - 2/3) = 3$. In short, the multiplier is reduced from 10 to 3. Here the important thing is not the precise numerical values, which are included for the sake of definiteness, but the general concept. Consider now the implications.

The principal cause of variations in *NNP* consists in autonomous changes in *I* (investment spending). These are caused by such factors as changes in profit expectations and innovations and alterations in the pattern of consumer demand. Independent changes in $I$ are translated through the multiplier into severalfold changes in *NNP*. The larger the multiplier $K$, the greater the effect on *NNP* of a given change in $I$; the smaller is $K$, of course, the smaller the change in *NNP*. If there were no tax bite and the multiplier were 10, a decline of, say, $1 billion in investment would lead to a fall of $10 billion in *NNP*. On the other hand with a tax bite of 26 per cent, as above, and a multiplier of 3, a decline of $1 billion in investment causes a decline of only $3 billion in *NNP*. Therefore the *tax bite lowers the multiplier and reduces fluctuations in NNP caused by changes in I.*

**Built-in Stabilizers, Further Details.** As we have just explained, taxes reduce *MPC* and thus the multiplier. Let us now spell out the various taxes that constitute the sums taken from *NNP* before *DPI* is found. Of course, there is the sizable element of personal taxes, including income taxes, having exactly the type of effects described above. Also corporation income and excess profits taxes take a slice out of *NNP* by absorbing about one half of corporate profits with similar results. On the other hand the effects of indirect business taxes and social security taxes cannot be stated with certainty.[2]

An even more positive effect is produced by transfer payments. In a recession, payments are made to the unemployed out of the unemployment compensation fund built up for this purpose. As *NNP* and employment decline, payments increase, thus maintaining *DPI* and consumption. A similar effect is provided by farm price supports, which go into operation as *NNP* falls and with it the level of farm prices. In effect, the price supports help to guarantee that the output produced can be sold at certain minimum prices. This assures that the given output will yield at least a given money income.

To summarize, the built-in stabilizers tend to cause *DPI* to fluctuate less than *NNP*. With reduced fluctuation of *DPI* consumption is also more stable. Because *NNP* must equal $C + I + G$, the stabilization of $C$ tends also to stabilize *NNP*. In terms of the multiplier, the built-in stabilizers reduce *MPC* (consumption is more stable) and the multiplier. This reduced multiplier lowers the fluctuations in *NNP* caused by independent changes in $I$.

By the very way we have explained this it is clear that these stabilizers allow fluctuation in *NNP*. The measures are designed to reduce the magnitude of changes in *NNP* resulting from changes in $I$. Unless further steps are taken, ups and downs in activity will occur. It is the function of discretionary measures to take care of the remaining problems.

[2] Indirect business taxes, for example, provide the same kind of deduction from *NNP* as the other taxes. They obviously tend, therefore, to check consumption and lower *MPC*. On the other hand, these taxes tend to raise prices, to increase consumption in terms of money, and thus raise *MPC*.

## DISCRETIONARY FISCAL POLICY—GOVERNMENT SPENDING

**Identifying Full-Employment Income.** The first step in establishing a proper fiscal policy is to determine full-employment income. Such an income level will correspond to and measure the largest obtainable quantity of output for the economy. Very properly, the Council of Economic Advisers has actually studied this problem, coming up with estimates of full-employment income for a number of recent years.[3] Assume that we have found such a value for the current year, estimated in terms of Net National Product. Then the actual figure of *NNP* is noted, as well as the gap between actual and full-employment *NNP*. An appropriate objective of fiscal policy is to push *NNP* up to the desired full-employment level. Consider now the way in which government spending may be manipulated to reach this objective.

## UNDEREMPLOYMENT TENDENCY

**Use of the Multiplier.** Suppose the full-employment *NNP* is found to be $500 billion, as compared with an actual *NNP* of $470 billion. How much is the government going to have to spend in order to raise *NNP* by the difference of $30 billion? At first glance we might guess $30 billion, but this would be wrong. As we showed in our study of the multiplier, the spending of $1 extra in the economy leads to additional income and spending elsewhere. Eventually, the spreading effect of the $1 of additional spending leads to a total rise in the level of income equal to about $3 in our economy. Therefore, we can count on a leverage in the ratio of about 3:1, which magnifies the effect of the initial spending. This being the case, additional spending of $10 billion will have its effects multiplied 3 times, giving rise to $30 billion, or $10 billion × 3, additional income.

**Gap Analysis.** Essentially the same approach is one stimulated by the use of a total-spending graph. Suppose we have an estimate of the current levels of spending at every income level. Graphically, this means that we have in hand a $C + I + G$ line that actually holds true for our economy. We then study the gap or margin between total spending, $C + I + G$, and total supply, *NNP,* at the full-employment income level.

In Figure 12–1 there is a deflationary gap of *GH* at full-employment *NNP*. At this point demand for goods is *FG,* whereas supply (*NNP*) is *FH,* leaving excess supply of *GH*. If government spending is increased by *GH,* this margin of surplus output available at full employment can be sold. Then the entire full-employment output could be

[3] See the discussion in the 1962 *Economic Report of the President* (Washington, D.C.: U.S. Government Printing Office, 1962), pp. 49–56.

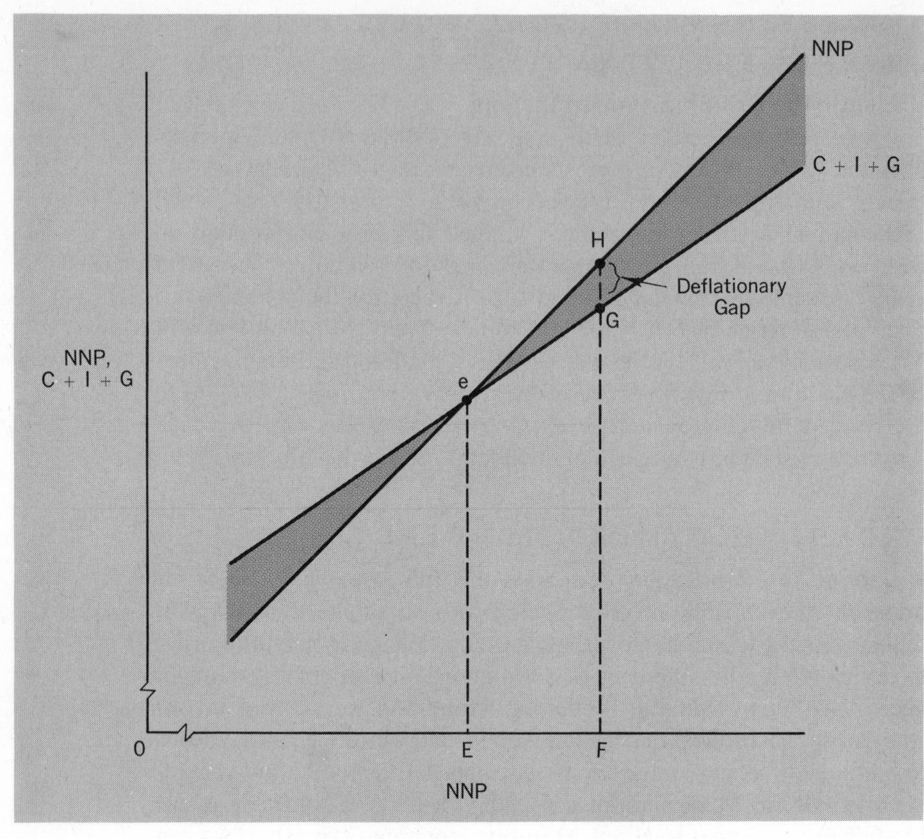


**Figure 12–1.** Deflationary gap at full-employment *NNP*.

sold, and full-employment *NNP* equal to *OF* could be maintained. Let us remark that the gap of *GH* to be filled by government spending is equal to the $10 billion figure reached by multiplier analysis. By either process of reasoning an amount of government spending is indicated that will generate full-employment *NNP*.

**Cost of the Action.** How much does it cost society to carry out the policy of sustaining full employment through government spending? Well, it all depends on how you want to estimate cost. First, there is the immediate outlay by government to "fill the gap," amounting in this case to $10 billion. From a very short-run, practical viewpoint this can be said to be the cost. Second, one might estimate the budget deficit that would result. Very superficially, it might appear that government would go in the hole an extra $10 billion. However, the additional income of $30 billion that marks the advance of *NNP* to the desired level will produce additional net revenue. For all levels of government this will amount to about 20 per cent of the extra $30 billion, or $6 billion in extra taxes. Therefore the deficit incurred will amount only to about $4 billion.

Finally, one might say, quite reasonably, that the entire $30 billion *NNP* represents pure gain. After all, this sum represents increased output available to society. Any increase in the output of society must confer a benefit on the public. This argument surely contains a great measure of truth, because it has proven to be almost impossible to refute.

Actually, the gain involved is extremely obvious and is realized as actual output. The loss, if any, consists in the problem of handling the additional public debt, say $4 billion. Once the government has gone into debt, it must pay the interest on this debt forever. This represents an encumbrance against the future taxes of the government, necessary to pay interest to the bondholders. Because the bondholders are themselves members of society, this payment does not represent a dead loss. What the taxpayers as a whole lose, the bondholders gain. However, the debt and interest payment tie up a part of government receipts and the *NNP*. Such a fixed charge reduces the flexibility of the economy. This is the real cost of the added government spending.

**Use of Extra Output.** In the situation just reviewed *NNP* is increased by about $30 billion. By our previous discussions this is evidence of a corresponding increase in supply. Who claims this additional output? First, there is the government, which claims an additional $10 billion in virtue of its spending program. As we pointed out, the multiplier operates, causing *NNP* to rise by about $30 billion. If the marginal propensity to consume is ⅔, the approximate figure in the United States, consumption will expand by ⅔ of $30 billion, or $20 billion. This serves to exhaust the remainder of the additional output. Note that none of the $30 billion is allocated to private investment. Under the circumstances, however, this is natural, because present plant capacity will meet the total demand for goods.

## PROPER FISCAL POLICY—TAX CUTS

**Objections to Government Spending Manipulation.** Let us set aside arguments that it is not worth pursuing fiscal policies leading to full employment. There appears to be a large consensus in favor of using these tools, among others, to achieve this goal. Nevertheless, there are two basic objections to the specific method of varying government spending. First, the approach requires excessive time to implement. If government spending is to take effect soon, projects involving the spending of large addtional sums must be initiated rapidly. It is never easy to start and carry through on short notice a government project involving large sums of money. Either a delay ensues, the usual occurrence, or an early start is made marked by spectacular misuse of public funds. This unfortunate dilemma appears to be rooted in the nature of the problem.

Second, the increase in government spending involves a rise in the part of output bought by the government. Thus ⅓—$10 billion out of $30 billion—of the extra output goes to the government, as compared with the average fraction of about 23 per cent in the United States. Although this output is serviceable to the public, consisting possibly in additional roads or school buildings, it is not subject to the decisions of private individuals. It is *collective spending*.

**Effects of a Tax Cut.** Suppose an across-the-board cut is made in individual income taxes. Such a step enlarges Disposable Personal Income out of a given *NNP*. In turn, this will tend to increase consumption out of a given *NNP*. On our typical graph this raises the consumption line relative to the *NNP* axis. Assume that investment and government spending remain the same. Then a rise in consumption will raise the $C + I + G$ or total spending line to the same extent that it raises the $C$ line. By a sufficiently large cut in taxes $C + I + G$ can be raised sufficiently to erase a deflationary gap—for example, the gap *GH* in Figure 12–1.

Let us note here that people will probably not spend on consumption all of the extra money they realize from reduced taxes. Very likely the fraction will be about 93 per cent of the taxes remitted. In order to realize the same impact as $1 of additional government spending the tax cut would have to be about $1.07, or at any rate, somewhat more than $1.

**Virtues of the Cut.** Perhaps the greatest virtue is that the effects are felt immediately by a large number of people. In turn, these people will proceed to spend money on consumption, thus setting in motion a rise in the level of income without delay. Also the additional spending will consist primarily of extra consumption and thus add to the private sector of the economy under individual control. One may, of course, question whether this is invariably a good idea, if the economy needs additional public services.

**How Deficits Are Financed.** Either increased government spending or tax cuts involve a budget deficit, or a decrease in the surplus. Suppose the measures taken involve a deficit. How does the government dig up the money with which to spend in excess of tax receipts? Obviously, it must borrow money, and the outward sign of this is found in the sale of new government bonds or bills. Initially, the new bonds and bills may be sold to the banks who create new deposit money when they write checks against themselves in payment. An alternative method that is equally effective is to sell bonds to individuals who are holding more bank balances than they require to finance their current transactions. This flow of money helps generate the rise in *NNP* to the new, higher level. However, as *NNP* rises to the new level, taxes rise and reduce the size of the deficit. If the additional spending is $10 billion and *NNP* rises $30 billion, with additional tax receipts of 20 per cent of $30 billion, or $6 billion, the deficit is $4 billion. Of course, this reduces the size of the problem.

There is another element to take account of, and that is additional savings out of income. As *NNP* rises, people with extra incomes will save more. Because private business is expanding at an unchanged rate, the *additional* savings will not be channeled off for investment purposes. Instead the extra saving could be used to finance the final government deficit. In fact, we can resort to one form of our equilibrium equation to show this situation. When the economy has reached equilibrium,

$$S + T = I + G.$$

This can be written:

$$G - T = S - I$$

or

Government deficit = Private surplus of investors.

Whatever the deficit of the government, when the economy reaches equilibrium, there will be an adequate surplus of private saving available to buy the bonds issued to meet the deficit.

In conclusion, the deficit may ultimately be financed out of *NNP*, with no recourse to the banks. Thus there is no "inflationary" creation of money. Finally, once the equilibrium has been reached, *NNP* will tend to continue at this level without further change. We now offer a capsule review of the opposite case where an inflationary tendency is present. This stresses gap analysis.

## INFLATIONARY TENDENCY

Suppose an inflationary gap develops at full-employment *NNP*. If allowed to develop unchecked, the situation will tend to produce an inflation. This is a dynamic situation, with rising prices, wages, income, and money supply. Such a situation can become extremely chaotic, and is harmful to orderly economic growth. Appropriate policies are essentially opposite to those used during underemployment.

**Inflation and Reduced Government Spending.** If the government should cut its spending by the exact amount of the inflationary gap, the problem would tend to disappear. For a graphic illustration, let us refer back to Figure 8–8. Recall that, originally, equilibrium existed with full employment at $H$. Then an upward shift of the aggregate demand line from $C+I+G$ to $C+I+G_1$ occurred. In turn, this gave rise to an inflationary gap equal to $HI$. It is the presence of this gap that sets off the inflationary spiral shown by the subsequent successive shifts in the $C+I+G$ curve. If government spending were to be cut by $HI$ ($JK$ or $LM$ at later points of time), the gap would be eliminated, and demand would exactly equal the supply. There would then be no continuing tendency for prices to run away. Let us summarize briefly the results of this action.

First, inflation is avoided in the absence of other events; this is a definite social gain. Second, in virtue of reduced spending government voluntarily accepts a reduced claim on the output, leaving a larger share to private claimants. In boom times private investment has probably increased due to favorable profit expectations. If the share of output going to investment is excessive, it will not be directly checked in this way. Third, a surplus or a reduced deficit will be realized. This raises a question of what is to be done with any surplus realized. Consider this point briefly.

Suppose a net surplus is created to the extent of the cut in spending (though a reduction in the deficit would have the same effect). Since

$$S+T=I+G,$$

in equilibrium, we get, by rearrangement of terms:

$$T-G=I-S$$

or

Government surplus = Private deficit of investors.

The extra sums that government does not need to finance government spending can be used to finance the excess of investment over saving.

How does the extra money get to businessmen? If the government realizes a surplus, it may use this to buy up existing government bonds from private owners. When the government takes in the bonds, it may tear them up or cancel them, the debt having been discharged. More important, the funds in question are turned over to the private sellers, who can then use these sums to assist new private investment. We will not follow the exact mechanics of this move; it is one of the functions of the capital market to effect such an interchange of resources.

**Reduced Consumption by Increased Taxation.** If the government raises personal income taxes, it can reduce Disposable Personal Income out of a given $NNP$. In turn, this will lead to reduced consumption out of a given $NNP$. If consumption declines while investment and government spending remain the same, the $C+I+G$ line will shift downward; the inflationary gap of $HI$ in Figure 8–8 will be eliminated.

In this case the burden of adjustment falls entirely on consumers, who are forced by taxation to give up part of their claim on output. Here the government's claim remains constant, whereas the investment share is allowed free rein. Thus, increased investment, which has caused or accentuated the gap, is allowed to assume its full value. Again, this must be listed as a possible defect of this scheme.

Again, as when government spending is cut, a surplus on government account tends to arise and is disposed of in the same manner.

## FISCAL POLICY AND THE NATIONAL DEBT

**Background.** We all know there is a huge national debt, which equaled $304.6 billion in February 1962. At this time the debt amounted to about $1,618 for every man, woman, and child in the United States. Impressive? Yes. But on this basis, not so large as the mortgage on the house, perhaps. In fact, it is the massive size of the debt in the aggregate and the knowledge that we are all responsible for it that may appall us. Consider now just how it got to be this large.

To a substantial degree the national debt can be accounted for by three events: (1) World War I, (2) the great depression, (3) World War II. From only about $1 billion before World War I the debt jumped to nearly $24 billion in 1920. This was cut down to a bit over $16 billion in 1929, through the prosperous decade of the 1920's. Then the great depression of the nineteen thirties supervened. As a result of the recovery effort the debt rose steadily, until in 1940 the debt reached about $43 billion. Even this increase in the debt was nothing compared to the rise during the immediate prewar and war years. By the year 1945 the debt was about $259 billion, representing nearly a sixfold increase. Between the end of World War II and the middle of 1963 the debt grew $47 billion or less than 20 per cent.

Actually, the burden of the debt or its importance is best judged by comparing it with some measure of national income, say Net National Product. We can also record the interest cost and compare it with *NNP*. Notice how the debt soared from 47 per cent of *NNP* in 1940 to 129 per cent in 1945, but since has sunk to about 60 per cent in 1962. Thus the enormous growth in the size of the economy implies that the debt is only a little larger now than in 1939, in relative terms. Thus it is a remarkable fact that the debt, if it is a burden, is little more of one now than in 1940. The fact that interest charges, as a fraction of *NNP,* have risen from 1.80 per cent to 1.86 per cent between 1945 and 1963 is accounted for by a substantial rise in interest rates. In 1945, interest rates were being held low in an effort to mini-

**TABLE 12–1***
**The Quantitative Importance of the Public Debt; The Debt and Interest Payments in Relation to *NNP*, 1910–1963**

| Year | *NNP* (billions of dollars) | National Debt (billions of dollars) | Interest Cost (billions of dollars) | Debt as Per Cent of *NNP* | Interest Cost as Per Cent of *NNP* |
|---|---|---|---|---|---|
| 1910 | 28.9 | 1.1 | 0.02 | 4.0 | 0.07 |
| 1920 | 83.0 | 24.3 | 1.02 | 29.3 | 1.23 |
| 1929 | 95.8 | 16.9 | 0.68 | 17.7 | 0.71 |
| 1940 | 92.5 | 43.0 | 1.04 | 46.5 | 1.13 |
| 1945 | 201.0 | 258.7 | 3.62 | 128.7 | 1.80 |
| 1950 | 265.5 | 257.4 | 5.50 | 96.9 | 2.07 |
| 1955 | 365.5 | 274.4 | 6.37 | 75.1 | 1.74 |
| 1960 | 459.6 | 286.3 | 9.18 | 62.3 | 2.00 |
| 1961 | 474.2 | 289.0 | 8.96 | 60.9 | 1.89 |
| 1962 | 507.5 | 298.2 | 9.12 | 58.8 | 1.80 |
| 1963 | 533.1 | 305.9 | 9.90 | 57.4 | 1.86 |

* Source: Information on public debt in U.S. Bureau of Census, **Statistical Abstract of the United States: 1964** (Eighy-fifth ed.; Washington, D.C.: U.S. Government Printing Office, 1964), p. 403.

mize the cost to the Treasury of borrowing large sums of money. In any event these interest charges now constitute less than 2 per cent of *NNP*.

## GENERAL PROBLEMS OF THE NATIONAL DEBT

**Business Debt and Public Debt.** Although there is a large public debt, there is an even larger private debt owed by business firms in the form of bonds, notes, loans, and the like. Yet we do not hear a dirge constantly sung about this private debt. Why? Is there something good or inherently natural about private debt, whereas public debt is wicked? Not exactly, but a crucial difference does exist, and thereby hangs a tale.

Almost invariably business firms, which hold the overwhelming bulk of private debt, use borrowed money to acquire capital goods. These capital goods consist of buildings, machinery, equipment, and the like, which enter into the productive process. When utilized, this capital improves the productive power of the firm and leads to an increase in output. Therefore the indebtedness of business is offset by capital endowed with the power to increase production and yield a net return. Of course, this net return can be used to pay the original lenders a return called interest.

Contrast this with the debt of the Federal government, almost all of which was incurred during wartime, especially World War II. In this war the government resorted to borrowing in order to meet a large fraction of the enormous outlay. The funds were used to pay all of the various military expenses—the pay of military personnel, military hardware in the form of ammunition, planes, and the rest. After the war ended practically none of this had any value. Consequently, the Federal government found itself with a large debt and no corresponding capital. Also there is no return available from capital with which to defray the interest that must be paid on the bonds. Actually, the public debt somewhat resembles a consumer loan incurred to buy a car. Corresponding to the debt, the consumer has the car, true. Still the car yields no return with which to pay the interest, let alone the principal.

**Consumer Debt and Public Debt.** Evidently, public debt is different from business debt but somewhat similar to consumer debt in that the latter too does not correspond to an *income earning asset.* Reasoning that public debt is like consumer debt, people sometimes reach the conclusion that an undue growth of public debt will lead to dire results. We know that if a person with a limited income goes further and further into debt, he will eventually run into trouble. Because the goods bought yield no return, he is forced to rely on his income to meet the rising tide of payments. Eventually, disaster! If the same rules held true for public debt, there would certainly be cause for worry. However, a crucial difference exists between public and private consumer debt.

Characteristically, a private debt signifies that one person owes another person a certain sum of money. Just as typically, the national debt signifies that the government owes the bondholders a sum of money. But the government can raise its money only from the taxpayers. Evidently, then, the taxpayers owe the bondholders the debt, and the interest also. Now for argument's sake, assume that everyone is a bondholder and a taxpayer as well. In this case we can say: the public owns the bonds that represent the debt, and the government in turn is responsible to the public for the debt. But the public stands behind the government as taxpayers. Therefore the public owes itself the debt! One can think of the typical citizen paying interest on the debt by reaching into one pocket, taking out a $100 bill, and giving it to a government tax collector. This gentleman then hands back the $100 as interest on the bonds. Our citizen is then neither richer nor poorer. In fact, he could tear up his bondholdings, and his situation would be little changed.

**Internal and External Debt.** In the course of two world wars the government rejected the idea of raising all the needed money by taxes and borrowed a large fraction from the public instead. Suppose that we had borrowed from abroad rather than at home. Of course, this option was not available to us, because no country or combination of countries would or could have done this. We would then be faced with a $300-billion debt owned abroad. Such a debt would constitute, in truth, a mortgage against the wealth of the country, held by foreigners. Each year part of our national income would have to flow abroad in order to pay interest on the debt. To that extent, we would be able to enjoy less of that income ourselves. Note the immense difference between this and a domestically owned debt, in which case the interest is retained within the country. We may conclude that *an external public debt constitutes a true claim on the wealth and income of a country. An internal debt does not.*

**Figure 12–2.** Defense and civilian output in war.

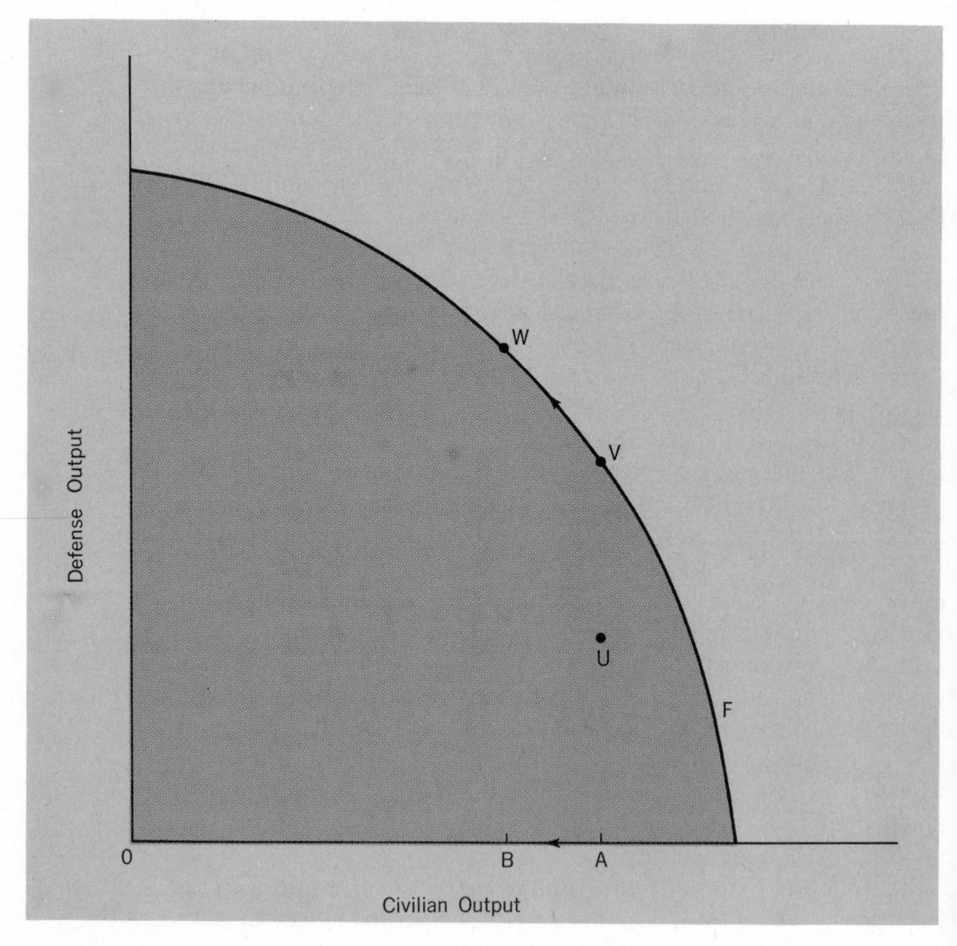

We are not concerned here to inquire whether borrowing abroad would have been beneficial. This is entirely possible. Our purpose here is merely to note the different effects flowing from internal and external ownership of the debt. Let us now consider a kind of assertion often encountered in discussions of public debt, namely: "By borrowing the money represented by the debt we have shifted the burden of the two wars and the great depression onto future generations."

**Shifting the Burden of the Debt.** The burden of a debt necessarily consists in the surrender of real income, a flow of goods and services, in order to accomplish desired objectives at a particular time. Consider the borrowing in the two wars. Did the public, by avoiding taxation during these wars, also avoid the surrender of a current flow of goods and services to the end that the wars be won? Were the sacrifices they made reduced by borrowing instead of taxing?

During wars the economy tends to operate at full employment and thus to produce the largest possible total output. According to the production frontier spoken of in Chapter 1, the economy moves onto the frontier as it makes use of all its available resources. If there has been a movement from inside the frontier at *U* onto the curve at *V*, in Figure 12–2, defense output increases by *UV*, with no sacrifice in civilian output. If the funds for buying the extra output have been raised by borrowing, there still has been no sacrifice of output on the part of the public. Suppose that the defense output needed to win the war in the desired time is found at *W*. Then a sacrifice of civilian output equal to *AB* is necessary, as the economy moves from *V* to *W* along the production frontier. This sacrifice must be made immediately by the public! It cannot be deferred until a later date. No matter how the money is raised, by means of which the government buys the output in place of civilians, civilians or the public must forego present enjoyment to achieve the objective. Therefore the burden cannot be shifted to future generations.

**The True Problem of a Debt: The Transfer Problem.** In our earlier discussion of an internal debt we assumed that the debt was evenly held by the public. Actually, it seems probable that more of the debt is held by those with above-average incomes than is held by those with below-average incomes. If this is true, taxes are going to be levied on the entire public to pay interest on the national debt, but the payments will be made primarily to the well-to-do. Ignoring the part of the taxes and interest payments that cancel for any individual, this means that poorer persons are being taxed to pay interest to the richer.

There is more to it than this, though. Of two equally well-off persons one may have sacrificed to buy bonds during the war, while the other spent all his income on consumer goods. After the war the bondholder who made an earlier sacrifice is going to receive some interest raised by taxing the other persons, who did not buy bonds. Consequently, the frugal among equally well-off individuals are going to benefit by interest payments raised by taxes on the spendthrifts. Thus one may claim that, to this extent, virtue is rewarded.

Leaving aside all questions of identifying the two groups, taxpayers and interest recipients, it seems likely that they will not coincide. As a result, net payments are made, through taxes, from nonbondholders to bondholders. Such payments constitute a redistribution of income and give rise to *the transfer problem*. Because these payments amount only to about 2 per cent of *NNP,* the problem is not currently critical. Obviously, if the debt grew to the point where interest charges absorbed 10 to 20 per cent, the problem would become acute. From a political viewpoint the issue would be like a loaded bomb. In time of depression the interest charges, being fixed, tend to become a larger fraction of *NNP*. The nonbondholders are squeezed progressively with the decline in *NNP*. To avoid this problem it is necessary to prevent recessions and keep *NNP* rising so that the ratio of interest charges to *NNP* will never become very large.

**The True Problem of a Debt: Reduced Output.** The transfer problem tends to generate a further undesirable result, a loss of output. To sharpen up the case, assume that individual *A* must be taxed at a 10-per-cent rate in order to pay corresponding interest to individual *B*. Regardless of circumstances, individual *B* is going to receive his interest, so that the receipt of this income affects his actions only in that he may slacken his activity slightly because he feels richer. On the other hand, *A*'s actions are influenced by the imposition of the tax. Without the tax (and ignoring other taxes) he will tend to work up to the point where the productivity of the last hour's work is just offset by the sacrifice or effort involved in doing that work.

Suppose that *A* can choose to work a longer or shorter time on a given day and that he is able to produce $10 worth of output in an hour. Assume also that if he works 8 hours, the last hour's effort measured in money "cost him" $10. Clearly, it is just worth it to work the eight hours. If a 10-per-cent tax is in force, however, the government is going to take $1 of this $10, leaving him $9. Now this return is not sufficient to induce him to work the eighth hour, and he will cut back on his working time to 7 hours or less. Clearly, this is going to reduce output. Thus the necessity of imposing taxes tends to reduce output. This may be the greatest burden of the debt.

**Effects of the Debt on Consumption.** Here there are conflicting points to be made. On the one hand the possession of bonds by the members of society will give them a greater sense of security, reduce the need for further saving, and thus increase consumption. If demand is deficient, this will increase production, as well. On the other hand the transfer problem works to shift income from nonbondholders to bondholders. The latter group is probably better off, with a lower marginal propensity to consume. If this is, in fact, the case, consumption will tend to be reduced. Thus the first, favorable effect tends to be canceled by the second.

**Retiring the Debt.** The Federal debt now exceeds $300 billion, and the question of whether to pay off the debt naturally arises. If the public debt was strictly analogous to consumer debt, we would probably seek to do so. Because the debt is internal, however, there is no drain of *NNP* abroad. In fact, the problems and losses involved in a continuance of the debt are not severe. From a technical viewpoint the Treasury suffers the inconvenience and worry associated with continual refunding of the debt. Each year a large fraction of the debt falls due, and must be paid off. At this point the Treasury seeks to persuade these or other lenders to acquire new government securities in the same amount. Generally, there is no difficulty, and the Federal Reserve offers its support during temporary situations in which large-scale refunding takes place.

What would happen if the Treasury did attempt to retire the debt? To be specific, suppose the Treasury attempted to work off the national debt by retiring $15 billion a year for 20 years. To do so, starting from, say, a balanced budget, it would be necessary to cut government spending or raise taxes by the amount mentioned. Suppose government spending were to be cut $15 billion, tax rates being left the same. By the multiplier principle *NNP* would tend to fall by 3 times this, or $\$15 \times 3 = \$45$ billion. Obviously, taxes would fall as *NNP* fell, and the surplus would be smaller than expected. By a further slight cut in government spending and decline in *NNP* a point could be found at which this surplus would be generated. In so doing, however, *NNP* has been driven down by over $45 billion, or about 10 per cent of 1961 *NNP* of about $470 billion. Thus a severe loss of output would be suffered in each of the 20 years.[4]

If a rise in taxes were attempted, *NNP* would again decline, and a similar result would ensue. In fact, it seems rather clear that no matter how you cut the cake, retiring the debt will involve worse consequences than living with the debt. By far the best policy seems to be to encourage the most rapid possible expansion in *NNP* to the end that the debt becomes easier to handle as time passes. Mean-

[4] If the Treasury were to expand both government spending and taxes sufficiently, a point could be found at which the surplus would be realized without a decline in *NNP*. However, this would involve a substantial increase in the government share of output, which would probably be politically unacceptable.

while it appears that we shall have to learn to live with this debt and service it without attempting to retire it.

**Treasury, Federal Reserve, and Interest Rates.** In 1961 the Treasury paid $7.3 billion in interest charges, amounting to nearly 9 per cent of the total Federal expenditure of $84 billion. Naturally, the Treasury would like to minimize this expense, because it contributes nothing to the services the government renders to the public. For this reason the Federal Reserve was encouraged to provide easy money during World War II and even afterward. With the Federal Reserve taking action to create ample reserves, banks were willing to lend at low interest rates. Eventually, the Federal Reserve felt the strong necessity of tightening money, and in 1951 an "accord" between the Treasury and the Federal Reserve was reached. Under the agreement the Federal Reserve agreed to help the Treasury maintain an orderly market for government securities. On the other hand, the Federal Reserve was left free to exercise its powers to loosen or tighten credit, according to the requirements for economic stabilization.

Since that time interest rates have moved substantially upward from their formerly low level. At present there is ample range within which the Federal Reserve could exert either upward or downward pressure on interest rates. Additional considerations are that current American economic growth is rather slow, and the gold situation is somewhat shaky. On the one hand, low interest rates would prompt greater investment and faster economic progress. On the other hand, low rates might prompt a conversion of short-term foreign assets into gold and a further deterioration of the gold situation. Thus there appears to be no simple solution.

Some writers have come up with a suggestion that the Federal Reserve change its holdings of United States government securities to include more long-term securities. Thus it could sell from its extensive holdings of bills and notes and add to its holdings of bonds. This, it is argued, would tend to raise short-term rates and lower long-term rates. Because investment is related more to long-run than short-run rates, this action would encourage expansion. Moreover, the higher short-term rates would encourage foreigners to retain their present holdings of short-term United States assets. It seems doubtful that the Federal Reserve, with holdings of about $30 billion, could have much influence on interest rates quoted on about $300 billion of United States government securities. It is, however, an ingenious suggestion and may be worth a try.

**Summary.** Fiscal policy as the subject of this chapter is taken to be concerned with the attainment of full employment without inflation. Following World War II Congress asserted in the Employment

Act of 1946 that it proposed to try to provide full employment. Under the Act the three-man Council of Economic Advisers was created to advise the President on economic matters and to help prepare the annual *Economic Report of the President*. Also the Joint Economic Committee of Congress was created as a kind of watchdog to evaluate the *Economic Report* and otherwise assist in the performance of the Act.

Maintaining full employment without inflation is implemented by two methods: (1) the creation of built-in stabilizers that tend automatically to sustain the flow of spending in the face of adverse effects, such as reduced investment; and (2) discretionary fiscal policy by means of which the government takes deliberate action designed to maintain spending at the full-employment level. The principal built-in stabilizer consists in a tax system that takes a substantial fraction of each additional dollar of *NNP*. This is shown to reduce *MPC* and thereby to stabilize consumption. Also it reduces the numerical value of the multiplier, which reduces fluctuations in *NNP* arising from autonomous changes in *I*.

The tools of discretionary fiscal policy consist of variations in government spending on output and tax changes. Government spending may be changed by an amount sufficient to "fill the gap" between full-employment spending and full-employment output. Another approach is through figuring the difference between present and full-employment *NNP* and using the multiplier to compute the extra government spending. (Divide this difference by the multiplier to get the extra required government spending.) Tax cuts on individual incomes are slightly less certain in their effects, but have about nine tenths of the effects of government spending. Deficits resulting from increased spending or reduced taxes are found to be rather small as compared with the increased *NNP*.

Analysis of the national debt shows it to be different from business debt in that no assets are held against that debt and no earnings realized with which to pay the interest. Also, national debt differs from consumer debt in that, although the consumer must pay interest and principal to an outsider, the government raises the taxes from roughly the same group to which it pays the interest. Our internally held debt presents no critical problems as compared with one held externally. In the latter situation the payments of interest and principal to outsiders constitute a deduction from the flow of output, leaving to this society a reduced total. It is shown that the burden of a war cannot be shifted to future generations, because winning the war requires the current sacrifice of civilian goods in order to acquire more war goods.

The true problems of the debt are found to consist in the transfer problem and the loss of output. The transfer problem arises because the owners of bonds do not coincide precisely with the taxpayers. Therefore net payments are made from nonbondholders to bondholders, which constitutes a government-approved transfer of income. This involves difficulty when the transfer becomes large. The debt involves a loss of output, because taxes levied to pay interest discourage productive effort.

Retirement of the national debt is found to be undesirable because cuts in government spending or increased taxes designed to yield a surplus drive down the level of *NNP*. The best approach is to encourage the growth of *NNP* relative to the debt so that it will become more easily handled.

The Treasury likes low interest rates in order to minimize its interest charges, but the Federal Reserve likes to vary rates in accordance with its desire to "lean against the prevailing economic winds." It has been suggested that the Federal Reserve reshuffle its holdings of United States securities to lower long-term and raise short-term interest rates to meet the objectives of faster growth and retention of foreign short-term assets.

## QUESTIONS

1. Give in your own words the basic objective of the Employment Act of 1946.
2. What mechanism was set up by Congress to carry out the objectives of the Act?
3. Outline an overall plan for the stabilization of the economy.
4. What is a built-in stabilizer? Explain in detail how the income tax serves as a built-in stabilizer, assuming that this tax is a constant percentage of income.
5. Do automatic stabilizers eliminate changes in *NNP?* Explain.
6. What is the first step in establishing a proper fiscal policy?
7. Approximately how much government spending (with no change in tax rates) would be required to raise *NNP* by 60 billion? Explain.
8. Assuming a tax rate of 20 per cent, what deficit would be caused by the action outlined under question 7?
9. Outline the effects of a proportional or a uniform percentage tax cut in all brackets.
10. How could such an action serve to bring about full employment?
11. Why are there always sufficient funds *in equilibrium* to finance a government deficit from private saving?

PART

# 4

# The Pricing of Consumer Goods and Services

In the introductory chapters of this text a simple model of competitive supply and demand was sufficient for understanding the fundamental forces operating in a capitalist society. But the actual determination of the prices for all the multitude of goods and services is clearly much more complex than this simple competitive model. Some prices are set by supply and demand in a competitive market, but others are established by the decisions of individual firms. If we want to know the price of wheat, we get the last market report, but for the price of a certain model of Chevrolet, we check the price list issued by General Motors (though we may attempt to secure a special trade-in allowance with the local dealer). We shall try to probe these complex problems of price determination in the next few chapers.

CHAPTER

13

# Structure and Operation of Product Markets

In Chapter 2 the analysis of the functioning of pure capitalism revealed the key role played by markets in the circular flow of income. What products will be made available to consumers, how they will be produced, and how much each person will be able to buy are matters largely determined in the markets for goods and services. These functions performed by markets are so vital to the effective operation of our society that we sometimes use the term *market economy* as a synonym for the capitalist system. It is time now to turn from the macroeconomic analysis of the preceding chapters to a study of the operations of markets for particular products and for factors of production. In this microeconomic analysis we shall first examine the markets for goods and services in Chapters 13 through 17; this study is usually referred to as *value theory*. Then in Chapters 18 through 22 we shall consider the functioning of factor markets in which services of the production factors of land, labor, and capital are bought and sold. The study of markets for factors of production is called *distribution theory,* because the pattern of prices paid to factors largely determines the way in which income is distributed.

## THE COMPETITIVE MARKET

**Benefits of the Competitive Market.** Almost two centuries ago Adam Smith in his famous book *The Wealth of Nations,* argued that the best way to run an economy was by reliance on the free operation of the "unseen hand" of competition. This philosophy of economic control through the operation of competitive markets became the basis upon which the economies of the United States and other Western countries were established. If the control of the capitalist system is to depend upon the proper functioning of markets, then it is vital that we understand both how they are supposed to operate under ideal conditions and how they actually do operate.

In the treatment of demand and supply in Chapter 2, it is pointed out that in a competitive market a price tends to be established that equates the quantity people wish to purchase with the quantity other persons are willing to sell. In this explanation of the way a perfect market is supposed to work under ideal conditions the price of the product moves to that value which provides an equilibrium between the forces of supply and demand. Demand is defined as *a schedule of the amounts of a good that the buyers will seek to purchase at a corresponding schedule of prices*. Supply is defined as *a schedule relating the quantities and prices on the side of the sellers*. These two schedules are illustrated in Table 2–4 and in the graph drawn in Figure 2–4 of Chapter 2. The analysis given there shows that only at one price of 6¢ for apples was the quantity demanded equal to the quantity offered for sale. At any other price there was either a surplus (more offered for sale than demanded), which drives the price down, or there was a shortage in the market, which drives the price up. We must understand that in this perfectly competitive market the price is not fixed by the seller (or the buyer) but results entirely from the pressures exerted by supply and demand in the market. Under perfect competition individual buyers and sellers do not fix prices; they only react to prices established by the market.

The analysis in Chapter 3 points out that any change in demand or supply (shift in the position of either curve) causes a change in the market price and in this way alters the quantity being exchanged. This change in quantity provided through the market as the result of a change in price is the mechanism by which the free-enterprise economy answers the desires of the people. The quantity of a good being produced under such a system does not increase as a result of an order by a government official; it increases, rather, when an increase in demand by the consumers causes a rise in price that increases profit possibilities for the producer.

In *The Wealth of Nations* Adam Smith argued that government control of production reduced public welfare. National wealth would be increased, he believed, by permitting businessmen to produce the things that would earn them a profit. Only the goods and services that people were willing to buy could be sold at a profit, and thus the search for business gain would compel producers to bring to market the items most desired by the public. In this way the selfish search for personal gain was made the motivation for work beneficial to all. This laissez-faire philosophy was the basis upon which the United States and other free nations built their economic systems.

To a remarkable degree the free pursuit of self-interest, in conjunction with other capitalistic institutions, has had the results Adam Smith predicted. We have enjoyed almost two centuries of unparalleled growth in production, culminating in a standard of living and a wealth of choices in consumption beyond the wildest dreams of the absent-minded old Scotch economist in 1776.

We have found, however, that this highly successful system of free enterprise is not perfect. Like other human institutions, it has its weak points. Clever men have found ways of making profit that do not always advance the public welfare. Competition does indeed exist and bring the benefits we have mentioned, but it does not operate perfectly. Only by understanding the weaknesses and problems faced by our competitive system can we hope to improve its functioning. In this need for comprehension of the economic problems facing our nation lies one of the most important reasons for the study of economics.

**Basis for a Competitive Market.** In Chapter 2 we listed the following necessary conditions for the existence of a competitive market: (1) The product is homogeneous in quality. (2) Buyers and sellers possess perfect information about the price and quality of the item being exchanged. (3) There are many buyers and sellers, so many that no buyer or seller can affect the market price by his actions. (4) Perfect mobility for the item exists within the market area.

Economists use two terms in referring to competitive markets that meet these four requirements, *perfect competition* and *pure competition.* The distinction between the two terms varies somewhat among economists, but in this book we shall use the expression *perfect competition* when we are dealing with markets that are completely free of any interference with the perfect operation of the competitive market. We shall use *pure competition* in any connection in which we wish to emphasize the freedom of the market from monopolistic control.

Only when perfect competition exists can we be certain that the market will operate effectively in determining the prices and quantities of goods and services being bought and sold. Unfortunately, most markets fail to meet one or more of these requirements. In such markets the absence of perfect competition may permit an individual to exercise control over price. When this occurs, the businessman begins manipulating the market rather than responding to it, the ideal results of the competitive system are lost, and the public welfare suffers. Let us examine now some of the reasons for the appearance of imperfections in our competitive economy.

## TRENDS IN COMPETITIVE CONDITIONS

**Effect of Modern Technology upon Competition.** In some fields, such as the automobile, airplane, and steel industries, modern methods of production require large size for efficient operation. We shall examine in the next chapter the reasons why large-scale production in such lines reduces the cost per unit. At this point, we want only to notice the impact of this increase in mass production methods on the competitive market. Earlier we stated that many sellers must be present in a market to prevent control of price by any one of them. But when the industry requires large output by each firm in order to keep costs down, then only a few producers will be needed to supply market demand. If the demand for the item is limited, it is possible that a single firm producing at the most efficient level can meet all needs.

The fact that modern technology gives rise to large-scale production poses a serious dilemma for followers of Adam Smith's notion of a self-regulating market system. On the one hand, if there exist the number of producers required in order to secure effective competition, each firm will be small and inefficient. On the other hand, the presence of the large firms, which alone can achieve low costs, implies a small number of producers and a market that is no longer truly competitive.

Modern technology has also created another barrier to the maintenance of perfect competition. Consumer goods have become far more complex and susceptible to differentiation than they once were. The differences between one buggy and another a century ago were relatively minor and obvious in character. But in the modern automobile, today's consumer is offered a bewildering array of choices as to power, size, accessories, and style. Other consumer goods have also tended to develop a great variety of special features in order to attract buyers. This increase in product differentiation makes it more possible for each buyer within the limits of his income to satisfy his individual needs or desires. Unfortunately, this development interferes with the operation of competitive markets. One of the conditions for the existence of perfect competition is that all firms in a given industry sell a homogeneous product. When each seller is offering a slightly different product, the price for that particular product can be fixed by the manufacturer. Because a Chevrolet differs in certain ways from a Ford, Plymouth, or Rambler, buyers' preferences will permit price variations. Modern technology has given us a great variety of low-cost consumer goods, but one loss we have felt is the weakening of competition as the force controlling our economy. We shall examine this problem further in Chapter 15.



The great variety of goods among which the buyer can choose

weakens the ability to satisfy another essential condition of perfect competition, namely, that buyers and sellers possess complete knowledge about the price and quality of each product. The very profusion of choices offered the buyer makes it impossible for him to learn all he needs to know about each product in order to make an intelligent choice. Increasingly, the consumer is influenced by advertising or other sales efforts, because rational choice based upon personal knowledge has become an impossibility. Differentials in price as well as in quality add to the complications facing the buyer. Modern technology has added to the rich variety of modern life, but the resulting complexity of consumer choice has weakened the assumption of rational response to price upon which the competitive market depended for its effective functioning.

Although weakening competition in some respects, modern technology has strengthened it in others, as in the improvement of transportation and communication methods. Our fourth basic requirement for a competitive market is that perfect mobility exist for the product being bought and sold. Fifty years ago a person living in a small town had to buy his groceries at the local store, but today, if local prices are high or the quality poor, he can use his car to go to a nearby town. Mobility within the market area has been greatly increased by improvements in modern transportation. Improved communications, exemplified in radio and television, have given people more information about conditions in other parts of the market and reduced the ability of the local seller to control prices or quality.

It is not easy to ascertain whether our present economy is more or less competitive on balance than it was in the nineteenth century. Modern technology has strengthened competition by increasing mobility within the market, but in many industries mass production methods and product differentiation have greatly increased the ability of some firms to exercise control over price. One thing appears to be certain: the many and varied products and processes of modern technology are here to stay. We cannot go back to markets as they existed in an earlier period. Neither can we be certain that methods of controlling those markets that were effective in an earlier period will continue to be so after they have been altered by a changing technology. We must look at problems as they exist today and seek to determine what changes in our laws or institutions will meet today's needs.

**Effect of Organizational Changes upon Competition.** The shift from the sole proprietorship or partnership to the corporation as the predominant form of business organization has had a great impact on competition. As technological change brought cost advantages to the large industrial producer, it became increasingly difficult for the single proprietor or partnership to raise the needed capital. Before the end of the nineteenth century, corporations, with their advantages in financing large-scale enterprise, were becoming increasingly important in such industries as petroleum, steel, copper, textiles, and meat packing. Even earlier, the corporate form had been used in banking, canal building, shipping, and railroads. After the turn of the century, giant corporations demonstrated their profit-making advantages in the production of automobiles, chemicals, aluminum, airplanes, and electric power.

Markets have been greatly affected by the increased use of the corporation as a method of organization. Business units of the size of American Telephone and Telegraph, General Motors, United States Steel, Du Pont, and General Electric would have been impossible under the simpler organizational forms of an earlier day. The very size of these giants enables them to exercise control in many of the markets in which they buy and sell. Their share of the goods and services being traded is so important that they tend to determine market price, even though the corporation may not deliberately attempt to exercise such control. The big business unit no longer merely reacts to decisions made in the market place; instead, the market reacts to the decisions made by the managers of the large corporations.

Again we are faced by a dilemma. Modern production methods require large aggregations of capital for efficient operation. Such large sums can be raised only by the use of the corporate form or through governmental investment. But the use of the corporation as a method of business organization reduces the effectiveness of competition as an agency of economic control. On the other hand, governmental finance and control of production carries with it various dangers and disadvantages. We must have production units making use of large amounts of capital, and for most industries we have decided that we prefer the loss of competition, brought by the corporation, to the dangers of centralized control, which would result from governmental ownership of the means of production under socialism.

Another result of the rise of the corporate form has been the separation of the function of management from that of ownership. Under sole proprietorship or partnership, the owner (or owners) almost always is the active manager of the business. But most of the thousands of holders of common stock in our large corporations take no significant part in the management of these businesses even though they are the legal owners. The complex problems of managing a large business make it impossible for these small stockholders to participate intelligently in the making of important decisions. They may participate formally by sending in their proxies each year, but the real management decisions are made by a small inside group of corporation officials, sometimes joined by a few large stockholders. The theory of profit as the motivating factor underlying our market economy must take account of this separation of ownership and management in the large corporation. We examine this problem further in Chapter 21.

The possibility of financial manipulation is also greatly increased by the existence of the corporate form. Shares of stock represent the physical assets of the company, but the intangible nature of the property right represented by the stock certificates greatly increases the opportunities for unearned profit through unwarranted issues of stock or speculative management of its price. Men like Commodore Vanderbilt, Jay Gould, John D. Rockefeller, and J. P. Morgan are sometimes referred to as the "robber barons" as a result of their financial manipulations in the last half of the nineteenth and the early part of the twentieth century. Much of the governmental regulation concerning the organization of corporations, the issue of stock, and the operations of stock exchanges was made necessary by the misuse of the corporate form by ruthless executives and investment bankers. The competitive market was not able to exercise effective control over these financial manipulations.

Mergers of existing businesses also became much simpler under the corporate form. Such devices as the trust certificate, the holding company, and the subsidiary firm were frequently used and abused. International Harvester, Standard Oil, U.S. Steel, and General Motors were formed in these ways. Many mergers brought with them real increases in productive efficiency, but others brought increased profits only by the monopolistic control over prices that resulted from the elimination of many of the previously competing firms.

**Measure of Concentration in American Industry.** Many attempts have been made to assess the reduction in the effectiveness of competition by measuring the degree of concentration in various important industries. All the studies show essentially the same thing, that in many important American industries only three or four large firms control a major part of the total output. Table 13–1 is taken from Walter Adams' *The Structure of American Industry* and is based on figures developed by the Federal Trade Commission in 1947. It clearly illustrates the degree of concentration in many lines of production. These particular industries were labeled "extremely concentrated," because in each case the three largest firms controlled more than 60 per cent of net capital assets.

In these "extremely concentrated industries" the danger of monopolistic control over the market is certainly increased by the smallness in the number of sellers who produce the major part of the output. We must remember, however, that many industries with significant monopolistic power are not included in the above list, because they operate only on a local or regional basis. Some industries (brick or concrete tile, for example) may be composed of as many as a hundred firms in the United States and still not be competitive if each firm is the only seller in a local market.

It may not be possible to determine statistically whether American business is becoming less competitive as a result of changes in our economy, but it is easy to prove by measures of concentration, movements of industrial prices, comparisons of profit levels, and various other methods that significant elements of monopoly control do exist in the market structure. The recognition of the danger of monopoly came early in American history. Part of the reason for the failure to recharter the Second Bank of the United States in 1836 was the charge by President Jackson that the Bank's monopolistic character was a

**TABLE 13-1***
**"Extremely" Concentrated Industries**

| Industry | Per Cent of Net Capital Assets Held by the Three Largest Companies |
|---|---|
| Aluminum | 100.0 |
| Tin cans and other tinware | 95.3 |
| Linoleum | 92.1 |
| Copper smelting and refining | 88.5 |
| Cigarettes | 77.0 |
| Distilled liquors | 72.4 |
| Plumbing equipment and supplies | 71.3 |
| Rubber tires and tubes | 70.3 |
| Office and store machines and devices | 69.5 |
| Motor vehicles | 68.7 |
| Biscuits, crackers, and pretzels | 67.7 |
| Agricultural machinery | 66.6 |
| Meat products | 64.0 |

* Source: **The Structure of American Industry** (ed. Walter Adams) (rev. ed.; New York: Macmillan Company, 1954).

danger to free institutions. Unfortunately, neither was the competition of state banks free of danger to our economy, and banking was increasingly subjected to government control. By the 1870's the American people were also alarmed by the monopolistic practices of the railroads, and began to insist that the government control their rates. Businessmen in other industries, such as meat packing, tobacco, petroleum, steel, and sugar, were quick to see and take advantage of the possibility of large profits from the elimination of control over firms by a competitive market. In order to protect the public against high prices and excessive profits the government was forced to take action against the emerging monopolies.



Such governmental control can take either of two forms: (1) the price and service can be regulated, or (2) the competitive market may be restored by destroying the monopolistic control exercised by the large business unit. The first method of control has been applied to public utilities, such as railroads, airlines, bus lines, telephone systems, gas distributors, and electric power companies. The second method, attempting to restore the competitive market, is the basis for our long series of antitrust laws. Because in value theory we are particularly concerned with the operation of markets, let us take a quick look at the more important laws that have been passed in the attempt to maintain competition as a method of effective economic control.

## LEGAL CONTROLS OVER MARKETS

**Sherman Act of 1890.** In the presidential election of 1888 the Democratic candidate, Grover Cleveland, charged the Republicans with favoring monopoly through the elimination of foreign competition brought about by high protective tariffs. Because the public was becoming more and more aroused by the monopolistic practices of "big business," the victorious Republicans decided to meet the issue by the simple device of making monopolies illegal. The Sherman Act, which was passed in 1890, contained the following two important provisions:

> Section 1. Every contract, combination, or conspiracy, in restraint of trade or commerce among the several states, or with foreign nations, is hereby declared illegal. . . .
>
> Section 2. Every person who shall monopolize, or attempt to monopolize, or combine or conspire with any other person or persons, to monopolize any part of the trade or commerce among the several states, or with foreign nations, shall be deemed guilty of a misdemeanor.

The Sherman Act is still the basic law upon which the American people depend to maintain competition. The constitutionality of this legislation is based upon the authority of Congress to regulate interstate and foreign commerce. Its provisions are general and must be interpreted by the courts. Sometimes the court decisions have reflected a broad interpretation, and big corporations have been heavily penalized or ordered dissolved. At other times the interpretations have been narrow, and business executives have felt free to pursue monopolistic practices. The vigor with which different administrations have enforced the law also has varied widely; McKinley, Harding, and Coolidge were generally lenient toward the big corporations, whereas, both the Roosevelts were strong opponents of the "trusts."

In the first few years after the passage of the Sherman Act the courts refused to apply it vigorously against the corporations. However, they did apply it to control the growing power of labor unions. The law that was supposed to control "big business" was used instead by the corporations to control the trade unions. At the request of business firms threatened by strikes, courts issued injunctions forbidding unions to take actions constituting interference with interstate commerce. When a strike took place contrary to an injunction, the court would order imprisonment of the leaders involved. The railway strike of 1894 was broken in this way.

A new champion of the competitive system, Theodore Roosevelt, became president in 1901, and a period of vigorous enforcement of the law against monopoly was inaugurated by this famous trust buster. Although some significant successes were achieved in the courts as a result of his efforts, particularly the decisions ordering the dissolution of Standard Oil and of American Tobacco in 1911, it was becoming obvious that many legal loopholes had been discovered by businessmen in their search for monopoly profits.

**The Clayton Act and the Federal Trade Commission Act.** In 1914, during Woodrow Wilson's administration, two acts were passed to close some of the legal loopholes used by monopolies and to provide for more effective enforcement of existing laws. The Clayton Act declared illegal a number of specific business practices, such as interlocking directorates, stock purchases that lessened competition, price discrimination, exclusive sales agreements, rebates, and tying contracts. This legislation also recognized the injustices resulting from court decisions that had applied the Sherman Act to labor unions and exempted them from many provisions of the antimonopoly laws.

The Federal Trade Commission Act was passed at the same session of Congress. It provided for the establishment of a commission of five members appointed by the President who were empowered to hold hearings whenever they had reason to believe that any business firm was acting in violation of the laws against monopoly. If violations of the laws were revealed, the Federal Trade Commission could then issue cease and desist orders.

Unfortunately, corporation executives, sometimes assisted by sympathetic courts, were able to find new methods of evasion as rapidly as the old loopholes were closed. World War I demanded the attention of government officials during the latter part of the Wilson administration and little effort was made to curb the large corporations during the Harding, Coolidge, and Hoover era of the 1920's. When the depression of the 1930's called the nation's attention once again to the dangers of unregulated "big business," new efforts were made to deal with the problem of monopoly.

**Business Regulation Under the New Deal.** Although Franklin D. Roosevelt was very critical of many business practices of the large corporations and believed that their actions helped bring on the great depression, he also recognized that the cooperation of business with government was necessary for recovery. One of the first attempts of the New Deal to find a basis for this cooperation of business and government was the National Industrial Recovery Act of 1933. Far from being an effort to restore competition this law was designed to secure cooperation of all parts of the economy in order to hasten recovery from the disastrous business collapse that had brought bankruptcies and unemployment. Codes were drawn up for each industry, giving rise to more than 800 separate instruments. The provisions of these codes protected business from the "unfair" competition of excessive price cutting, shoddy quality, and cost advantages secured by exploitation. The NIRA legislation provided that the firms covered by the codes could not thereby become subject to court action under the antitrust laws.

In order to make this relaxation of control over monopoly acceptable to labor the workers in these industries were given minimum wage guarantees, limitation on hours of work, permission to bargain collectively, and various other rights and benefits. Although the codes were supposed to provide for consumer representation, business and labor gained at the expense of buyers as controlled prices were raised. The government was not prepared to deal effectively with the many complex problems that developed from this attempt to substitute legally controlled cartels in each industry for the control exercised by competition, imperfect though it was. Accordingly, it came as a relief when in 1935 the Supreme Court declared the NIRA unconstitutional. Subsequently the government returned to its efforts to make competition effective by maintaining restrictions on monopolistic practices.

A number of other New Deal laws concerning business turned out to be much more permanent than the NIRA. The banking system was reorganized and strengthened. The Federal Deposit Insurance Corporation was formed to insure depositors against losses. The issuance and trading of corporate stocks and bonds were regulated and placed under the supervision of the Securities and Exchange Commission. Protection of labor, which had been one aspect of the NIRA codes, was continued under the Wagner Act of 1935, and the National Labor Relations Board was created to aid in enforcing the law. Excessive concentration of public utility operating companies by the use of multiple holding companies was made illegal. A vigorous effort was made to offset the monopolistic tendencies introduced by the NIRA through improved enforcement of the earlier antitrust laws.

Gradually in the last half of the 1930's the nation began to emerge from the depression, and confidence in market competition under the

TABLE 13–2
**Classification of Market Types**

| Type of Market | Number of Producers | Nature of Sales Effort | Control over Price | Examples |
|---|---|---|---|---|
| Pure monopoly | One seller of product with no good substitute | Advertising for general goodwill | Limited only by consumer resistance or government control | Telephone service, nylon and aluminum for many years |
| Oligopoly | Few sellers of standardized product | Goodwill advertising and use of special credit terms or service | Limited by fear of what other producers may do | Steel, copper, many chemicals |
| Monopolistic competition | Many sellers of similar but differentiated products | Heavy use of advertising and other selling methods, with stress on brand names, trade marks, style variations, quality differences, etc. | Limited by fear of shift by consumers to competing product | Cigarettes, tooth paste, soap, gasoline, refrigerators |
| Pure competition | Many sellers of standardized product | None | None | Some agricultural products |

new legal structure was restored. The one important exception to dependence upon the market system was in agriculture. The collapse of the farm economy, beginning in the early twenties, was so disastrous that the American people decided to attempt governmental regulation over supply in an effort to guarantee farmers a fair price. Despite the limited success of these efforts and the many problems encountered, this country is still attempting to substitute governmental decisions for the controls formerly exercised by the market over many farm products.

Although the past three decades have seen a great increase in the role of government in our economy, we still depend primarily on the regulation provided by supply and demand. Experiments with governmental control have been limited mainly to those markets where competition was ineffective, or where the answer of the market was not politically acceptable, as was true in the case of farming.

**Role of Value Theory.** Because the American people still depend on competition as the primary agent for economic control, it is vitally important that we understand how these markets function. We must examine the basis of monopoly so that we may identify the practices that limit competition. We should understand the strong points as well as the weaknesses of our competitive system, so that we can adapt it to the needs of our people in the decades of continuing change and growth that lie ahead. In the next few chapters we hope to contribute to that understanding by a detailed study of value theory.

In Chapter 14 we shall examine the problems of production costs as they are analyzed by the economist. Chapter 15 deals with the problems faced by the businessman as he attempts to determine the price he should establish for his products. In the analysis of price policies we shall use the normal classification of markets utilized by the economist, as shown in Table 13–2. It should be noted that some industries, such as automobile production, are examples both of oligopoly and of monopolistic competition.

Although most producers (except under the unusual conditions of pure competition) have some control over the prices charged for their output, this control is limited for most businessmen by the nature of the market in which they sell. Because control over the selling price is the most important aspect of the monopoly problem, almost all producers are in some limited degree monopolists. On the other hand almost no producers are pure monopolists. The normal business situation is one in which competing firms exist, but with such a limitation in numbers or differentiation of the product as to leave some control over price. Although our economy is not purely competitive, it is far from being purely monopolistic.

Chapter 16 examines the factors considered by the businessman when he makes the decision whether or not to build a new plant. These decisions, made in response to the profit motive, are basic in determining whether our economy will enjoy a period of growth or suffer stagnation. Construction of additional plants and of facilities involving the latest technology are essential parts of economic growth.

In Chapter 17 we look at these actions by individual producers and by consumers as they appear in the total market. Some attention is also given to problems of interdependent prices and governmental control of prices.

**Summary.** Adam Smith's advocacy of reliance upon supply and demand operating in competitive markets as the basic method of control for our economy still forms the philosophic basis for our capitalistic society. Unfortunately, the four requirements for the effective functioning of a competitive market (homogeneous products, perfect information, many buyers and sellers, and perfect mobility) do not always exist.

Modern technology with its large-scale production has reduced the number of sellers by the low costs secured in mass production. Product differentiation has made impossible perfect knowledge about price and quality of all the many complex consumer goods. On the other hand, improved transportation has strengthened competitive conditions by increasing market mobility.

Expanded use of the corporate form of business has reduced the effectiveness of the competitive market by increasing firm size and making financial manipulation easier. Complications have also arisen as a result of separation of ownership and management in the large corporations.

Various statistical measurements have shown significant concentration of control in many industries. Although earlier efforts were made to control the monopolistic power resulting from this concentration in such specific industries as banking and railroads, the Sherman Act of 1890 was the first general law to declare all monopolies illegal. The Clayton Act and the Federal Trade Commission Act of 1914 strengthened the legal control over monopolies. But in 1933 the NIRA temporarily permitted the formation of monopolies under regulation by codes in the effort to secure recovery from the depression. Various other laws passed by the New Deal during the depression improved the functioning of the competitive market in such areas as banking, sales of corporate securities, labor relations, and holding company arrangements. On the other hand, governmental control over the price of farm products developed as a result of depression conditions, and it forms one important exception to our general reliance upon the impersonal control by the market.

## QUESTIONS

1. What does control of an economy by a competitive market imply about the proper role of government?
2. What are the four conditions essental to the existence of a competitive market?
3. In what ways has the development of modern technology reduced the amount of competition in our market system?
4. Has modern technology done anything to increase market competition?
5. Why was the development of the modern corporation essential for efficient industrial operations in the twentieth century? In what way did this new organizational form tend to reduce competition?
6. Which industries in the United States appear to be owned by the smallest number of corporations?
7. Explain briefly the provisions of the following laws:
   a. Sherman Act of 1890.
   b. Clayton Act.
   c. Federal Trade Commission Act.
   d. National Industrial Recovery Act.
8. List and explain the characteristics of each of the four types of markets. What are typical examples of each?

CHAPTER

# 14

## Production Costs

Earlier, we stated that the prospect of profit is the motivating factor stimulating business to produce goods and render services. Because profit is the difference between revenue and costs, the firm will be searching constantly for ways to increase revenue and to decrease costs. In this chapter we shall study first how the economist classifies costs and then examine forces that cause changes in costs. *The economist treats as a cost any payment that must be made for productive resources in order to secure their use in a particular industry.* Taxes can be thought of in this connection as payments for services provided by the government.

Costs of production exist because the supplies of productive resources are scarce relative to the need for them. These resources normally have a number of alternative uses, and if they are not paid as much as they can earn in other fields a particular industry will find that the productive factors tend to shift to lines of production in which they are better paid. Economists refer to the price that will prevent the transference of factors to other uses as *opportunity cost.*

There is a close relationship between costs as defined by the economist and expenses as treated by the accountant, but significant differences do exist. Accountants must organize their records for the basic purposes of determining profit (or loss) earned by the owners and taxes due the government. Contractual relationships between the owners and persons with whom the firm is dealing must be the basis of the accounting records, and tax liability must be calculated according to definitions established by legislation. Accountants apply, therefore, a very detailed set of rules for the determination of each expense. For example, depreciation entries have as their primary purpose the provisions for the replacement of worn-out capital goods, but the exact amount that can be treated as depreciation expense is very carefully prescribed by accounting practice and by legal limitations.

On the other hand the economist is not reporting income to a particular business management, nor is he calculating tax liability. Instead he is trying to examine the operation of the basic forces that will accomplish this purpose. The economist must treat the wearing out of productive equipment as a cost, but he is not bound by legal technicalities in calculating depreciation. Although the accountant must answer questions that require a knowledge of the law, the economist is much more likely to be searching for answers to the question of *what the law should be.*

The owners of firms must be paid for their efforts and the use of their capital, and so the economist usually includes these payments as costs, whereas the accountant counts them as part of the profits. Certain other differences in treatment will emerge in the next few chapters. With this distinction between economic costs and accounting expenses in mind, let us now proceed to examine costs as they are classified and analyzed by the economist.

## SHORT RUN COSTS

**Fixed Costs and Variable Costs in the Short Run.** When the firm already has its plant built and machinery installed, it finds that costs fall naturally into two categories, fixed and variable costs. (1) *Fixed costs* are those payments that continue at a constant total amount whether production levels are high or low, indeed, even when production temporarily ceases. (2) *Variable costs* are those expenditures that increase or decrease in total amount as production levels rise or fall.

Among the many examples of fixed costs are depreciation of fixed assets, interest, rent, and salaries of executives or supervisors. Businessmen sometimes use the term *overhead costs* when speaking of such expenses. Whenever the economist deals with problems that assume that certain factors used by the firm, such as plant and equipment, are fixed in amount he calls the time period involved the *short run.* In contrast, he refers to the *long run* as a time period long enough to permit the firm to vary the quantity of any of the productive factors being used.

Among examples of variable costs are wages of production workers, expenditures for power, and raw material outlays. The term *out-of-pocket costs* is sometimes used in speaking of what the economist calls variable costs. Although variable costs will change in total amount as production levels alter, it is not necessarily true that they will change in exact proportion to variations in output. The economist applies the principle of diminishing returns when he considers changes in variable costs.

**Variable Costs and Diminishing Returns.** When any business firm builds its plant, it has in mind a level of operations that it expects to attain. The plant is built to operate efficiently at this anticipated output. Although output can depart from the level at which the plant is designed to operate, it is usually true that labor and materials will not be as efficiently used at these higher and lower levels as they would be at the output planned for the plant. This situation is really an example of the broader concept of diminishing marginal returns: *When the quantity of certain factors of production are held constant while the amount of at least one other factor changes, the output added by each additional unit of the variable factor will at first rise, but after a certain level of output is reached, the amount of production added by each additional unit of the variable will begin to decline.* The student should note that we are paying particular attention here to what happens at the margin. We are studying the effect upon output of adding one more (marginal) unit of a particular factor of production.

Table 14–1 provides an illustration of diminishing returns applied to an imaginary industrial plant. We assume that the plant that has been built is a given size, as indicated by the fact that it has just 20

**TABLE 14–1**
**Variations in Average and Marginal Output with Changes in Number of Workers**

| (1) Number of Machines | (2) Number of Workers | (3) Total Output per Day | (4) Average Output per Worker | (5) Output Added by 10 Workers | (6) Marginal Output for Individual Worker |
|---|---|---|---|---|---|
| 20 | 50 | 2,100 | 42.0 | | |
| 20 | 60 | 2,600 | 43.3 | 500 | 50 |
| 20 | 70 | 3,200 | 45.7 | 600 | 60 |
| 20 | 80 | 3,900 | 48.7 | 700 | 70 |
| 20 | 90 | 4,500 | 50.0 | 600 | 60 |
| 20 | 100 | 5,000 | 50.0 | 500 | 50 |
| 20 | 110 | 5,400 | 49.1 | 400 | 40 |
| 20 | 120 | 5.700 | 47.5 | 300 | 30 |
| 20 | 130 | 5,900 | 45.4 | 200 | 20 |
| 20 | 140 | 6,000 | 42.9 | 100 | 10 |
| 20 | 150 | 6,050 | 40.3 | 50 | 5 |

machines. Although the owner could have built a larger or a smaller plant, he decided that this size would probably be best able to produce the amount that he expects to be able to sell. Any variation in his sales would have to be met by operating the plant beyond or short of its most efficient output. The most efficient operating level in this plant would require the employment of approximately 120 men, because this point of operations yields the lowest total cost per unit of output, as revealed by column (7) in Table 14–3. Let us now examine how these costs are determined.

As we see in Table 14–1 the plant can be operated with as few men as 50, but total output, column (3), rises as more men are used. Column (5) shows the output added by each extra group of 10 men employed. We can calculate the added output by subtracting one total output from the next. We notice that at first output increases very rapidly, but after 80 men have been employed the added output begins to diminish. In column (6) (calculated by dividing the figure in column (5) by 10) we can see how much on the average each extra man has added to output. This amount is referred to as his marginal product.

The average output per worker in column (4) (calculated by dividing the number of workers into the total output) also rises at first and then declines, but it should be noted that the change is much more gradual than the marginal change per worker shown in column (6).

Perhaps it is easier to see the nature of the changes taking place as a result of diminishing returns if we show the movement in columns (4) and (6) on a graph, as in Figure 14–1. The relative position of these two curves should be carefully studied to understand the relationship between average output per worker and marginal output. When the plant is operating below its most efficient level (with 50 workers, for example) the average output curve shows a lower level than at the planned level of operation between 100 and 120 men. The highest average output per man is 50 units when either 90 or 100 workers are used. The average output curve begins to drop when the attempt is made to expand production beyond this most efficient use of labor. Average output per worker falls almost to 40 units when 150 men are employed.

The marginal output curve in Figure 14–1 shows that the increase in output secured by adding additional workers is relatively high when the firm is producing at low levels, but falls rapidly as normal operating levels are approached and then exceeded. It should also be noted that the marginal output curve passes through the average curve at the latter's highest point. This intersection of the two curves is the natural result of the mathematical relationship involved, because the

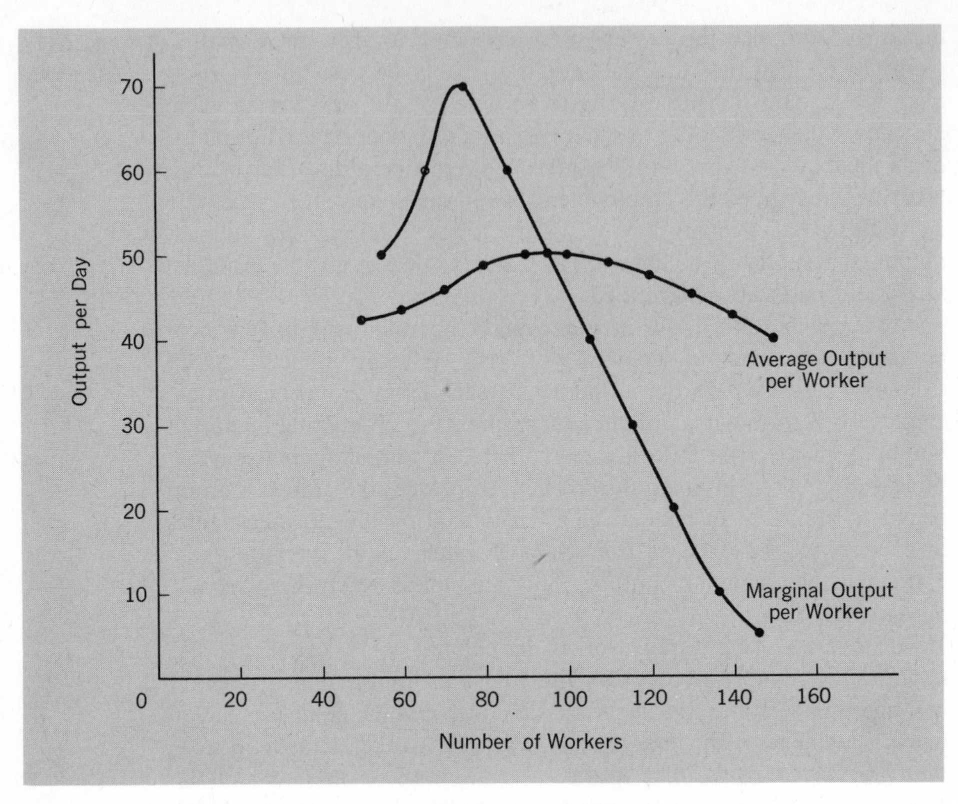


**Figure 14–1.** Effect of changing the number of workers upon average and marginal output per worker in a given plant.

average must always rise as long as the number added is above the average and fall when the added figure is below the average. If a baseball player with a .300 batting average has a .200 day his average will fall, but it will rise if he has a .400 day. In the same way average output will be rising whenever marginal output is above the average and falling when marginal output is below. As a result of this relationship, the marginal output curve must pass through the average curve at its highest point.

**Physical Output and Variable Costs.** Figures of days worked and output secured can be changed into dollar costs by applying a price to the labor used. In order to simplify our illustration we shall assume that the only variable cost in this plant is represented by the labor employed, and the only fixed cost is that associated with the use of the 20 machines. Let us assume that the workers in Table 14–1 each receive $25 per day. We can then calculate the cost figures shown in Table 14–2. Column (4) is gotten by multiplying the number of men employed by $25, and column (5) is the result of dividing the resulting total variable cost by the total output figure.

The most important point to notice in Table 14–2 is the close relationship between column (3), which shows average output per worker, and column (5), which shows the variable cost per unit of output. We have already noticed that the average output per worker rises when employment increases toward the more efficient levels of operation for the plant, and we can now observe that variable costs per unit of output are falling when average output is rising. The lowest variable cost of 50¢ per unit is achieved at the same level of operations that gives the highest average output per worker. As production increases beyond 100 workers, we notice in Table 14–2 that average output per worker falls, and variable cost per unit of output rises.

The nature of this movement of costs can best be seen by graphing the average variable-cost curve, as in Figure 14–2. In this graph we measure units of output on the horizontal axis. On the vertical axis we measure variable cost per unit of output. The average variable-cost curve (labeled *AVC*) has a saucer shape, with its lowest point between 4,500 and 5,000 units of output. If we now look back at Figure 14–1, we are struck by the fact that this variable-cost curve has the same shape as the average output per worker curve in the previous graph except that it is now turned over. Where the average-output curve had its highest point in Figure 14–1 at between 90 and 100 workers, with an output between 4,500 and 5,000 units, the average variable-cost curve in Figure 14–2 has its lowest point at the same level of operations. The economist must always remember that money costs are a reflection of the real costs of production, which are the services of scarce factors of production (labor, capital, and land).

**Fixed Costs and Total Costs.** Because total fixed costs remain constant regardless of the level of output, the fixed cost per unit of

**TABLE 14–2**
**Changes in Variable Cost per Unit Resulting from Variations in Output Levels**

| (1) Number of Workers | (2) Total Output per Day | (3) Average Output per Worker | (4) Total Wages or Variable Cost ($) | (5) Variable Cost per Unit of Output (¢) |
|---|---|---|---|---|
| 50 | 2,100 | 42.0 | 1,250 | 59.5 |
| 60 | 2,600 | 43.3 | 1,500 | 57.7 |
| 70 | 3,200 | 45.7 | 1,750 | 54.7 |
| 80 | 3,900 | 48.7 | 2,000 | 51.3 |
| 90 | 4,500 | 50.0 | 2,250 | 50.0 |
| 100 | 5,000 | 50.0 | 2,500 | 50.0 |
| 110 | 5,400 | 49.1 | 2,750 | 50.9 |
| 120 | 5,700 | 47.5 | 3,000 | 52.6 |
| 130 | 5,900 | 45.4 | 3,250 | 55.1 |
| 140 | 6,000 | 42.9 | 3,500 | 58.3 |
| 150 | 6,050 | 40.3 | 3,750 | 62.0 |

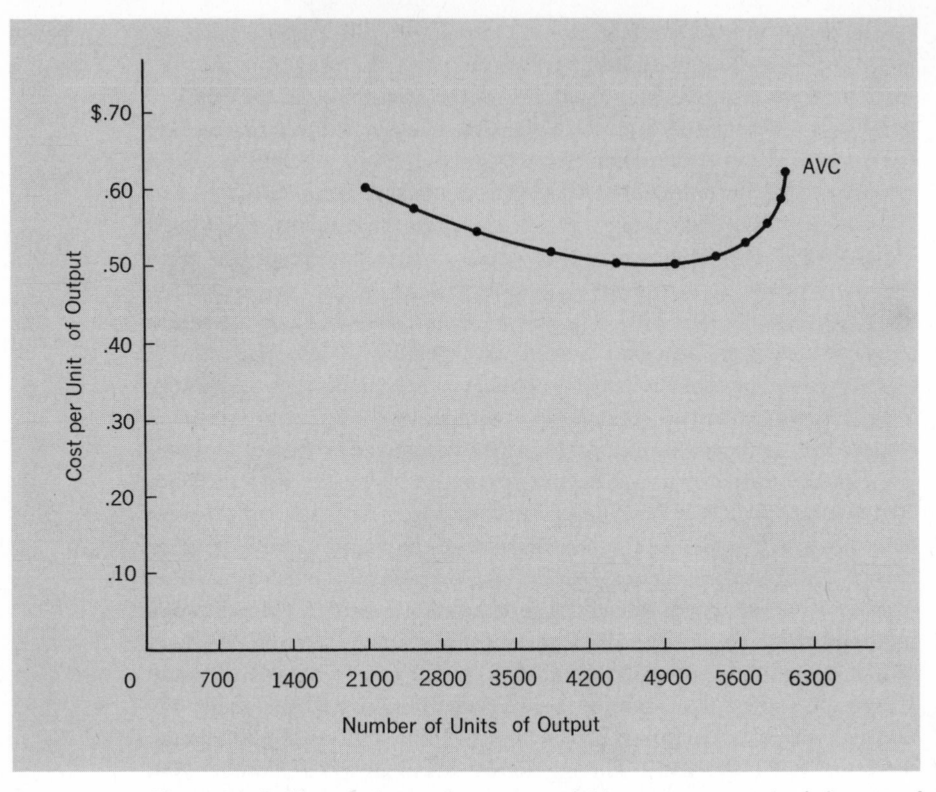


**Figure 14–2.** Normal shape of average variable-cost curve under influence of diminishing returns.

output will decline as production increases. In Table 14–3 we have calculated average fixed cost per unit in column (5) by dividing the total output shown in column (1) into the total fixed cost of column (4). In order to get the total fixed cost of $2,000 we have assumed that each of the 20 machines has associated depreciation and other costs of $100 per day. If we now show on a graph the figures for average fixed cost per unit from column (5) of Table 14–3, we get the *AFC* line shown in Figure 14–3. Because fixed costs per unit of output must decline as production increases, the *AFC* curve naturally drops downward to the right but tends to level out as output approaches the limit of plant capacity.

When considering profit margins management is naturally more interested in total cost per unit of output than in either average variable or fixed cost alone. In Table 14–3 we have calculated the total unit cost shown in column (7) by adding together the variable cost per unit in column (3) to the fixed cost per unit in column (5). The total cost per unit of output can also be calculated by dividing the

**TABLE 14–3**
**Changes in Various Costs as Affected by Variations in Output Levels**

| (1) Total Output per Day | (2) Total Wages or Variable Cost ($) | (3) Variable Cost per Unit of Output (¢) | (4) Total Machine or Fixed Cost ($) | (5) Fixed Cost per Unit of Output (¢) | (6) Total Cost, Fixed & Variable ($) | (7) Total Cost per Unit of Output ($) | (8) Marginal Cost per Unit of Output ($) |
|---|---|---|---|---|---|---|---|
| 2,100 | 1,250 | 59.5 | 2,000 | 95.2 | 3,250 | 1.547 | |
| 2,600 | 1,500 | 57.7 | 2,000 | 76.9 | 3,500 | 1.346 | 0.500 |
| 3,200 | 1,750 | 54.7 | 2,000 | 62.5 | 3,750 | 1.172 | 0.416 |
| 3,900 | 2,000 | 51.3 | 2,000 | 51.3 | 4,000 | 1.026 | 0.357 |
| 4,500 | 2,250 | 50.0 | 2,000 | 44.4 | 4,250 | 0.944 | 0.416 |
| 5,000 | 2,500 | 50.0 | 2,000 | 40.0 | 4,500 | 0.900 | 0.500 |
| 5,400 | 2,750 | 50.9 | 2,000 | 37.0 | 4,750 | 0.879 | 0.625 |
| 5,700 | 3,000 | 52.6 | 2,000 | 35.1 | 5,000 | 0.877 | 0.833 |
| 5,900 | 3,250 | 55.1 | 2,000 | 33.9 | 5,250 | 0.890 | 1.250 |
| 6,000 | 3,500 | 58.3 | 2,000 | 33.3 | 5,500 | 0.916 | 2.500 |
| 6,050 | 3,750 | 62.0 | 2,000 | 33.1 | 5,750 | 0.951 | 5.000 |

total output per day in column (1) into the total costs in column (6).

Because the total cost per unit of output is the sum of the variable cost and the fixed cost per unit, it is natural that it should fall when each of its parts is declining. It is not surprising, therefore, that when we plot *ATC* (average total cost per unit) in Figure 14–3, the curve should be falling until we reach the most efficient operating level of the plant, with output somewhat beyond 5,000 units per day. At about this point the average variable cost begins to rise, but the average fixed cost continues to fall, as we can see in Figure 14–3. If one component

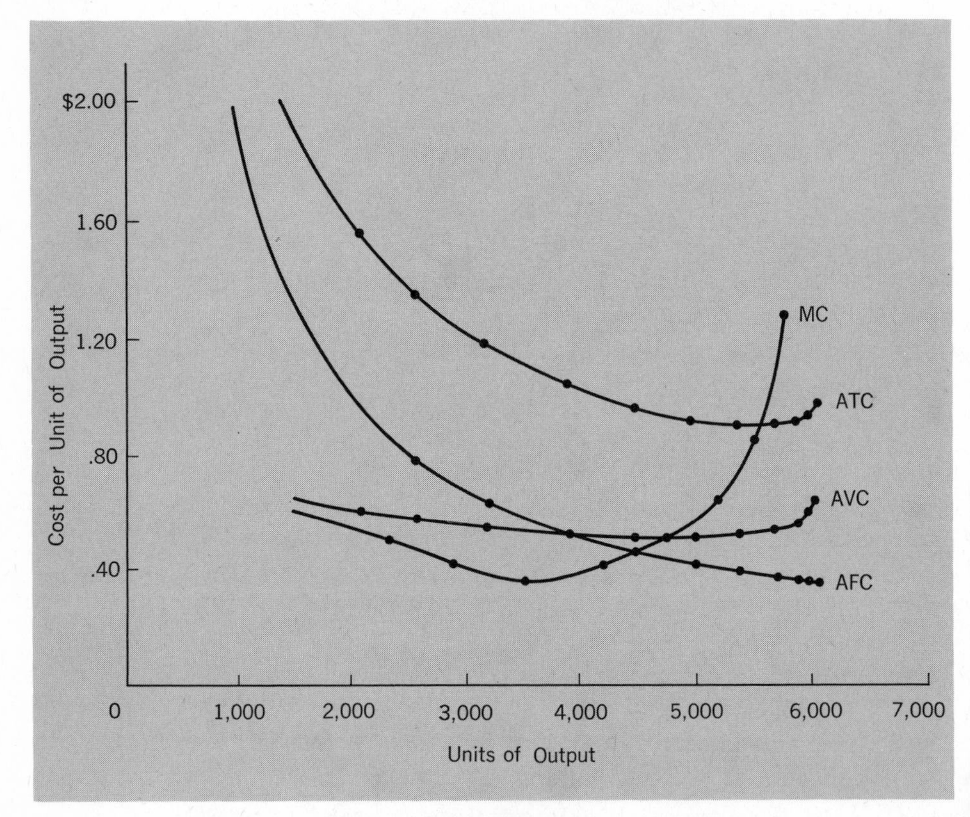


**Figure 14–3.** Total-, variable-, fixed-, and marginal-cost curves per unit of output in typical industrial plant.

of average total cost per unit is declining and one is rising, it is inevitable that the *ATC* curve will fall as long as *AFC* is falling more than *AVC* is rising. But *ATC* will begin to rise when the *AVC* rises more than *AFC* falls. We have already observed that the *AVC* curve rises more and more sharply as normal operating levels are exceeded, but that *AFC* tends to level out as maximum output is approached. An inspection of Figure 14–3 shows that the upward slope of the *AVC* curve begins to exceed the downward slope of the *AFC* curve at about 5,500 units of output, and a glance at the *ATC* curve verifies that its lowest point also comes at this level of output.

**Marginal Costs.** *Marginal cost is the amount added to total cost when total output is increased by one unit.* For example, if a tractor plant is producing 50 tractors a day at a total cost of $100,000 and 51 tractors could be produced at a total cost of $101,000, the marginal cost (the added cost of the last tractor) would be $1,000. The student must be careful to understand the difference between average total cost per unit and marginal cost. When this plant is producing 50 tractors the average total cost is $2,000 ($100,000 ÷ 50), but as we have just seen, the marginal cost is $1,000. Marginal cost is an important concept and will be used in many different problems of economic analysis.

The calculation of marginal cost is not always as simple as it is in the example we have just used. When we look at Table 14–3 we see that total output does not increase by just one unit at a time. The first change in output is from 2,100 to 2,600, or an increase of 500 units. In order to achieve this increase in output total costs rose from $3,250 to $3,500, a rise of $250. If we can achieve an increase of 500 units of output by the expenditure of an additional $250, on the average the marginal cost for each unit at this point is 50 cents ($250 ÷ 500), as shown in column (8). Each of the other figures in the marginal cost per unit of output column has been calculated by dividing the increase in total cost by the increase in output that results from the change.

In Figure 14–3 we find the *MC* (marginal cost per unit of output) plotted from the figures in column (8) of Table 14–3. It is particularly important to notice that the *MC* curve crosses both the *AVC* and the *ATC* curves at their lowest points. These intersections, as we have already noticed in this chapter, are the natural result of the mathematical relationship between average and marginal figures. In any graph showing both average and marginal curves, therefore, we can always be certain that the lowest variable or total cost per unit is found where the marginal-cost curve intersects the average variable- and total-cost curves.

**Graphs of Total Cost.** Economists sometimes wish to analyze a problem dealing with total costs rather than unit costs. The classification of fixed and variable costs treated as total amounts, then, is frequently presented as in Figure 14–4. On the horizontal axis we still measure quantity of output, but on the vertical axis we now measure total dollar costs rather than unit costs. Because by definition fixed costs remain constant regardless of output level, the fixed-cost curve

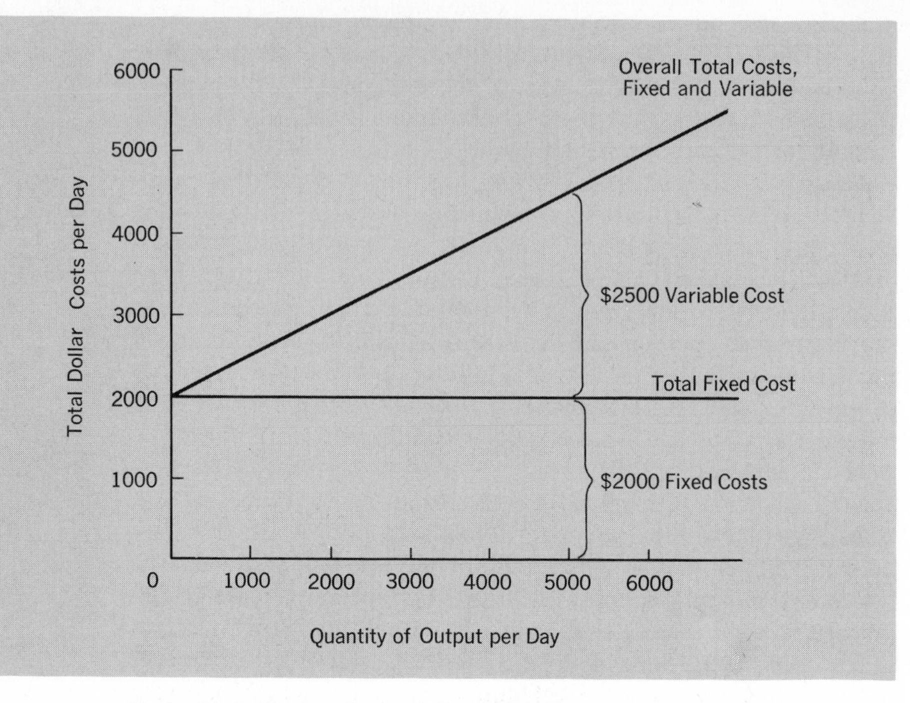


**Figure 14–4.** Changes in total, fixed, variable, and overall costs with changes in output under assumption of proportional variable costs in break-even chart.

is a horizontal straight line. If we use Table 14–3 for our illustration, the total fixed cost is $2,000.

In this presentation of total costs the principle of diminishing returns is frequently ignored, and the assumption is made that variable costs increase at a constant rate. When this simplifying assumption is made, variable costs are represented as the distance between the total fixed-cost line and the overall total-cost curve drawn as a straight line. If we now ask what the costs are at a given level of output, such as 5,000 units, the answer would be: fixed cost of $2,000 (vertical distance from the base to the total fixed-cost line), variable cost of $2,500 (distance from total fixed-cost line to overall total-cost line), and overall total costs of $4,500 (vertical distance from base to the overall total-cost line).

If we decide that accuracy requires us to include in our graph the effect of diminishing returns, we then find the overall total-cost line altered as in Figure 14–5, which is plotted from the figures in Table 14–3. Because variable costs per unit are high at low levels of production, we must show the overall total-cost curve rising more sharply in its early stages. As normal operating levels are reached the overall total-cost curve tends to level out somewhat, but as the capacity of the plant is approached variable costs per unit are again high, and the curve rises more sharply. We can see the amount of departure from the assumption of proportional variable costs by comparing the plotted *AVC* line in Figure 14–5 with the perfectly straight dotted line.

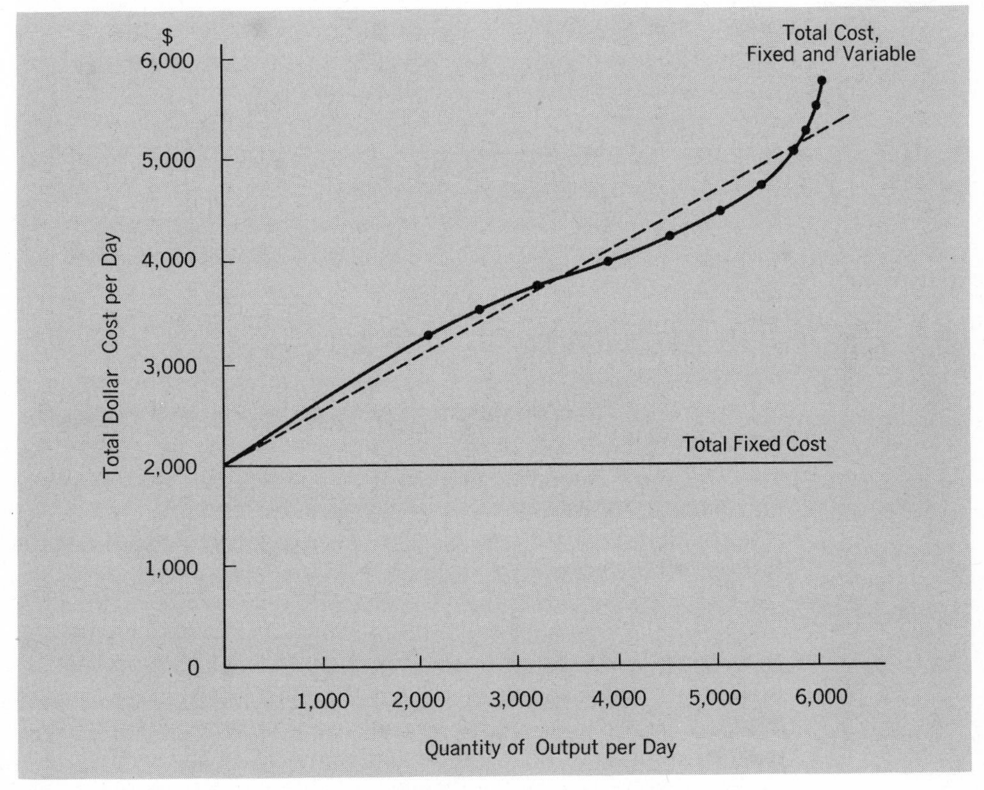


**Figure 14–5.** Changes in total and variable costs with changes in output under the assumption that variable costs are affected by the principle of diminishing returns.

**Variations in Nature of Variable Costs per Unit.** We must be careful not to assume that all industrial plants have a smooth saucer-shaped average variable-cost curve, such as we have shown in Figure 14–2. Many plants, particularly in the chemical and oil refining industries, are designed for constant operation at a given level of production per day. In such a plant the variable-cost curve would look much like Example A in Figure 14–6, with a low cost per unit at the intended level of operation and very high costs at any output that required even a small shift away from proper operating levels.

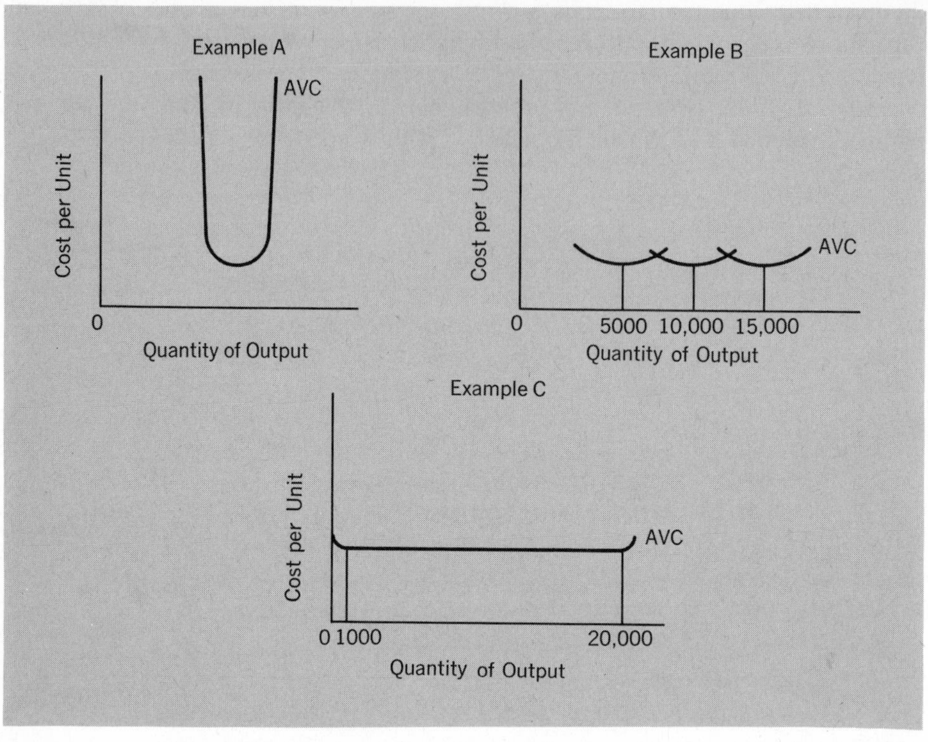


**Figure 14–6.** Examples of differently shaped variable-cost curves in various types of industrial plants.

On the other hand, some industrial plants can operate on one, two, or three shifts of eight hours per day, with each shift being almost as efficient as any other. In this case we would have an *AVC* curve formed from separate average variable cost per unit figures for each separate shift, as in Example B. If the most efficient operating level is around 5,000 units of output with one shift per day, approximately the same average variable cost per unit would result also from outputs of either 10,000 or 15,000, depending on how many shifts were being worked.

In Example C of Figure 14–6 we find still another type of variable cost that results from the assumption that the operating efficiency of the plant will not be reduced by closing down part of the plant. In our earlier illustration of costs in this chapter we assumed that the plant had 20 machines. If any one of these machines could operate independently at about 1,000 units of output per day, we could change output anywhere between 1,000 and 20,000 units and still have about the same variable cost per unit of output.



Although the *AVC* curve is likely to have a saucer shape as a result of the operation of the principle of diminishing returns, the student should always keep in mind that the costs in each type of plant will respond somewhat differently as production levels are changed. In economic theory we must use graphs that reflect usual changes in costs in an average plant, but when some particular plant or industry is being studied the analyst must remember that the shape of its cost curves may depart significantly from the idealized typical plant of the economist.



## LONG RUN COSTS

**Variations in Time Periods.** The costs with which we have so far been dealing in this chapter were in the time period referred to as "short run." Basic to the concept of the short run is the fact that decisions to change the quantity of output must be made within the limitation that certain factors of production are fixed in amount and cannot be varied. In our earlier examples of cost we assumed that a plant containing 20 machines had already been built.

In the long run we attempt to analyze what happens to costs as a result of changes in the level of output when we allow the firm all the time needed to vary the quantity or nature of any of the factors of production. In the long-run period we are asking what will happen to costs if a larger plant is constructed or a different method of production adopted, involving perhaps the use of machines to replace men.

**Production Costs in the Long Run.** American businessmen have become world famous for the lowered costs they have attained by mass production. It is sometimes thought that the larger the plant, the lower the unit costs. The economist usually refers to this lowering of unit costs by increasing the quantity of output as *increasing returns to scale* or *economies of large-scale production.*

We must be careful, however, not to assume that the larger plant is always more efficient. The large-scale producer will have lower costs only if by having the larger plant he is able to take advantage of one of the following savings. (1) *Use of more efficient machinery.* Many industrial operations can be performed efficiently by automatic machinery with great saving in labor costs over methods in which each unit is produced by hand. These machines, however, lower costs only when the heavy investment in expensive machinery can be spread over many units of ouput. This automatic machinery is usually economical only in sizes producing a large output. (2) *Increased specialization in the use of manpower.* In the typical assembly line of mass production each man performs a specific operation day in and day out. The first saving from this division of labor comes through the proficiency achieved by the man in performing this one task. A second saving comes in the short training period for each man before he takes a regular place on the assembly line. A third saving comes from the possibility of assigning each man to the task for which he is best fitted by strength, intelligence, or dexterity. (3) *Better use of by-products.* The large meat packer can make use of parts of the animal for fertilizer, glue, or pharmaceuticals that are a complete loss to the small-town butcher. Effective use of by-products is also important today in such major industries as oil refining, steel, cotton, and many others. (4) *Specialized management.* Large firms separate the tasks of management into production, marketing, credit control, personnel, finance, purchasing, accounting, and so on. A specialist can be placed in charge of each of these functions. Lower costs will result from this separation of functions if the departmental manager becomes more efficient by devoting all his attention to the limited tasks of his special assignment.

**Diseconomies of Large Scale.** We must not make the error of assuming that the larger the plant, the more efficient it will be. Once the firm is large enough to have the best machinery, effective division of labor, specialized management, and full use of by-products it cannot lower costs further by an increase in size. Instead, at this point the large firm begins to run into certain inefficiencies of large size. Managerial decisions cannot be wisely made unless full information is available, but the collecting of accounting and statistical information for the large firm becomes expensive. In the small firm management can secure most of this information by personal observation, but in the large firm it must come from detailed reports prepared in multiple copies. Red tape is the result of large size, whether in government or in a business corporation. Separation of management into specialized functions also leads to divided authority and buck-passing. In an effort to avoid these inefficiencies that result from large size, firms such as Du Pont, General Motors, and U.S. Steel divide their operations into semi-independent units, but this device is able to overcome only some of the difficulties.

**Long-Run-Cost Curves.** When we attempt to express economies and diseconomies of scale graphically, a diagram such as the one shown in Figure 14–7 is the result. If the firm builds a plant with lowest unit cost at 1,000 units of output per day, the result is an average total cost curve similar to *ATC*–1 in Figure 14–7. This plant is too small to take full advantage of the various economies of scale. If the firm builds a somewhat larger plant (*ATC*–2), it finds that at 2,000 units of output the unit cost is lower than in the smaller plant. It should be noted, however, that at 1,000 units of output the smaller plant has lower unit costs than the larger one.

The still lower unit costs shown in *ATC*–3 demonstrate that even greater economies of scale are possible with a plant designed to produce 3,000 units per day. But the fact that costs did not decline still further with the larger plant represented by *ATC*–4 indicates that a plant with an output of 3,000 units is large enough to exhaust all the economies of scale that are possible with types of machinery and methods of production available at the present time. The somewhat higher unit costs of *ATC*–5 at its lowest point show that diseconomies of scale have commenced and that efficiency has begun to decline.

The heavy line in Figure 14–7 is called the long-run average cost curve (*LRAC*). Because this heavy line shows what would happen to costs if plants of different sizes were built, it is also sometimes called the planning curve. If the plans of the firm call for sales of less than 1,000 units per day, cost considerations demand that a small plant, such as that shown by *ATC*–1, should be built. But if sales can be as high as 3,000 per day, the firm should construct a larger plant, such as that shown in *ATC*–3, which will give significant economies of scale. The planning curve thus shows the size of plant that will give the lowest costs per unit at various levels of output. In Figure 14–7 we have shown only five possible plant sizes, but normally an almost infinite number of possibilities for plant variation exist. If the cost curves for all these possible plant sizes were drawn, we would find that their tangencies to *LRAC* give us the almost perfectly smooth curve we have shown by the heavy line in Figure 14–7.

**Figure 14–7.** Derivation of the long-run average-cost curve from separate *ATC* curves resulting from construction of plants of various sizes.

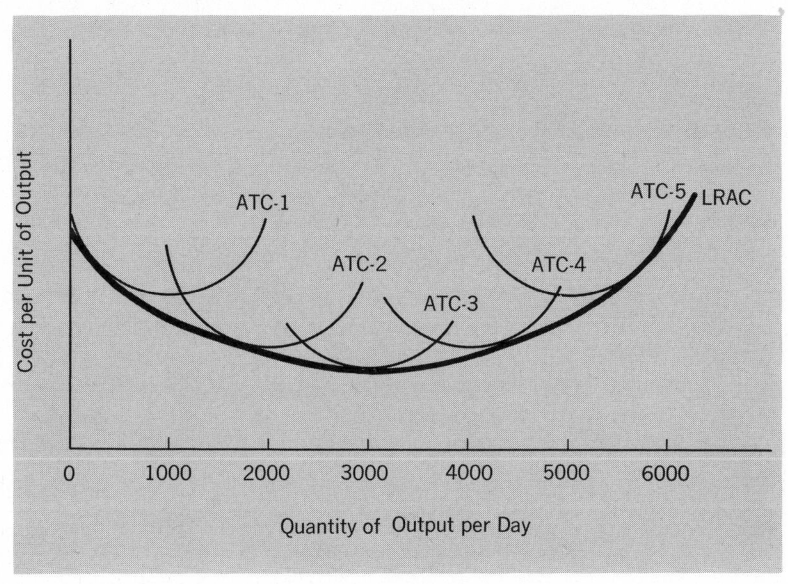

**Increasing- and Decreasing-Cost Industries.** Some factors that affect the costs of production are external to the firm. When consumer demand causes a significant expansion in the output of a particular product, the resulting increase in demand for the factors of production frequently forces up their prices. The increased demand for citrus fruit in recent years has forced up the price paid for suitable land for orange groves in Florida. When the firm pays a higher price for specialized land, skilled labor, or other essential elements of production, its cost curves move up, as in Figure 14–8. If the solid line *ATC* represents the short-run costs of this firm when a particular type of skilled labor is paid $3.00 per hour, then the dotted line *ATC′* would show the average total costs when this type of labor is being paid $4.00 per hour. When the costs of production for all the firms in an industry are forced up by the increased demand for the product because of the pressure upon the prices paid for limited quantities of scarce factors of production, we call it an increasing cost industry.

On the other hand expansion of production may sometimes cause changes external to the firm that lower costs of production. Expan-

**Figure 14–8.** Effect upon the short-run *ATC* curve of the individual firm resulting from increased prices of factors of production when output in the industry is expanded.

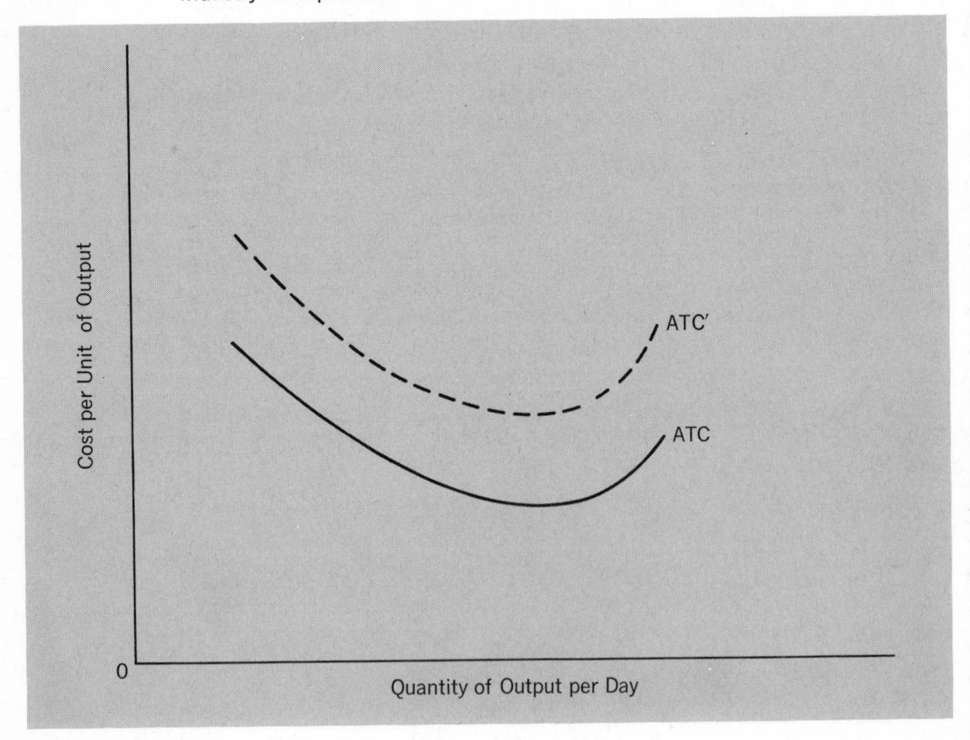

sion of demand for citrus fruit has been one factor that caused increased expenditures on highways and other transportation facilities in central Florida and resulted in a lowered transportation cost for the orange producers. An expanding industry also frequently finds that its expenditure for specialized machinery is declining as the producers of such equipment find economies of scale reducing their costs. Types of production which for reasons external to the firm find their costs declining as output increases are referred to as decreasing cost industries. It is much more common, however, to find industries responding to increasing cost than to decreasing cost pressures.

Sometimes the industry may be so unimportant that it can increase output without affecting the prices of the factors of production. For example, the output of radishes can be doubled without increasing the price paid for suitable land. The same statement cannot be made for important crops like wheat or corn. When an expansion of output will not significantly influence the costs of the individual producers, it is called a constant cost industry.

**Summary.** A production cost is any payment that must be made in order to secure the services of a productive resource in a particular industry. Fixed costs are those payments that remain constant in total amount in the short run regardless of changes in production volume. Variable costs are those payments that vary in total amount as volume of production changes.

Producers normally find that when the quantities of certain factors of production are held constant while others are varied in amount, the output added by additional units of the variable factor after a certain point will begin to decline. This general principle of production is called the law of diminishing marginal returns. The principle of diminishing marginal returns causes average variable costs per unit of output to exhibit a saucer shape when graphed. The average fixed-cost curve will decline throughout its length. The average total-cost curve will tend to exhibit a saucer shape as the result of changes in per unit costs in the variable-cost and in the fixed-cost curves. Marginal cost is the amount added to total cost when total output is increased by one unit. The marginal cost curve will intersect the average variable-cost and the average total-cost curves at their lowest points. The shape of the average variable-cost curve will vary in each plant, depending upon the nature of the production process.

Due to certain savings resulting from large-scale production, costs in the long run frequently decline as the plant expands output. Beyond the firm size that permits full use of economies of scale, certain diseconomies begin to influence costs. The long-run average-cost curve can be drawn by combining a series of short-run average total-cost curves for plants of various size. Certain factors external to the firm may cause the industry as a whole to have either increasing, decreasing, or constant costs in the long run.

## QUESTIONS

1. How does the economist define cost? How does this differ from the accountant's definition of expense or cost?
2. How long is the long run? The short run?
3. Distinguish between "fixed costs" and "variable costs."
4. State the principle of diminishing returns, and then draw a graph showing its effect upon average output and marginal output as more workers are added in order to expand production.
5. Why does the average variable-cost curve (*AVC*) normally have a saucer shape? In Table 14–2 why does the lowest variable cost per unit of output come with the same utilization of labor as the one that gives the highest average output per worker?
6. How is marginal cost in column (8) of Table 14–3 calculated?
7. Draw a graph showing the following short-run cost curves in their typical shapes:
   a. Average variable cost (*AVC*).
   b. Average fixed cost (*AFC*).
   c. Average total cost (*ATC*).
   d. Marginal cost (*MC*).
8. In question 7 why should the *MC* curve cross the *AVC* and the *ATC* curves at their lowest points?
9. Discuss the possible variations in the shape of *AVC* curves in different industries.
10. What is meant by *increasing returns to scale?* What are the basic causes that sometimes bring reduced costs with large-scale production?
11. Draw a graph showing the relationship of short-run *ATC* to long-run *ATC* in an industry with increasing returns to scale.
12. What is meant by *increasing cost industry?* Give illustrations of both increasing- and decreasing-cost industries.

CHAPTER

15

# Price Policy of the Firm

In the last chapter we examined cost conditions within the firm. Because profit equals revenue minus cost, the firm's profit will depend on revenue conditions, as well as cost. Now the revenue received by the firm equals the price of the product times the number of units sold. In what follows we will examine with particular care the factors influencing price under short-run assumptions. Under certain conditions the firm will have almost complete freedom to decide the price charged for the product, although the quantity that can be sold at the various possible prices will depend upon the decisions of the consumers. Under other circumstances producers find that they exert no control over the price of the product. Here price is determined in a free market by the bidding of numerous buyers and sellers. Between these two extremes lie a number of situations in which the firm has some influence over price. Any study of the determination of price by the firm is complicated by these variations in the product markets. These market conditions fall into four categories: (1) monopoly, (2) oligopoly, (3) monopolistic competition, and (4) pure competition.

## CLASSIFICATIONS OF THE MARKET

**Monopoly.** Monopoly exists when there is only one seller of a product for which there is no close substitute. Since no substitute is available and there is only one seller of the product, the monopolist can set the price where he will. The buyer must pay this price or go without the item entirely. Significant examples of such complete monopoly are not easy to find today. Until about 1940 the Aluminum Company of America enjoyed a monopoly in aluminum production, but World War II saw the entry of Kaiser and Reynolds as competitors. For many years Du Pont held a monopoly position in the production of nylon by virtue of patents. Although aluminum and nylon are among the best examples of industrial monopoly, it is well to remember that even these products have substitutes. Rayon and silk are satisfactory substitutes for nylon in some uses, though not, for example, in women's hose. For some uses magnesium, steel, or even plastics can be substituted for aluminum.

Perhaps the most significant examples of monopoly exist in public utilities, such as transportation, electric power, gas, and telephone service. If the consumer wishes to buy electric power, he finds only one company offering to sell. If he wishes to have a telephone he must deal with the Bell System in most communities. In such industries efficient service requires that only one producer be allowed to operate in a given area. Costs would rise and inconvenience to the public would result, if, for example, two telephone or two electric power companies were allowed to string lines along every street. Because public utilities are inherently natural monopolies, public policy sanctions them. At the same time, the prices of such firms are regulated by governmental agencies to protect the consumer.

Many examples of local monopolies exist. Small towns frequently have only one bank or one hotel and sometimes only one hardware or grocery store. Control over prices by local monopolists has been reduced in recent years, however, by the ability of consumers to use their cars to go to other towns to buy when they are overcharged.

**Oligopoly.** Oligopoly exists when there is more than one seller of a product for which there is no close substitute, but where the number of sellers is small enough for each to exert some control over price. Although the production of aluminum in the United States is no longer a monopoly, the Aluminum Company of America can still change the price it charges for its output (as can also Reynolds and Kaiser). But the freedom to change price is not as great in the case of an oligopoly as in a monopoly. Before World War II Alcoa could raise the price of aluminum, and the consumer had no recourse but to buy at that price or go without. Now, the buyer may decide to buy from one of the other producers unless they also have raised their prices.

Under oligopoly a firm can change its price, but it always faces the danger of losing customers, if its price exceeds that asked by the other producers. Oligopolistic producers would naturally like to arrange mutually satisfactory prices with their competitors, but this is illegal under the antitrust laws. The conviction in 1961 of General Electric and Westinghouse officials for price fixing illustrates the continuing efforts of antitrust authorities to protect consumers from collusion aimed at obtaining monopoly prices in such industries.

Firms that operate in an oligopolistic market face the possibility of severely competitive price changes by other firms. Businessmen have often responded to this pressure in ways that are difficult to control by law. For many years U.S. Steel initiated prices in the steel industry, and other producers followed suit; a basing point system was used to determine how transportation costs would be included in the price. "Price leadership" of this kind has been practiced as well in such industries as cigarettes, sugar, copper, and petroleum. Trade associations have also been used to stabilize prices at a level that the industry considers to be satisfactory.

**Monopolistic Competition.** When a number of firms are engaged in selling products that differ to some degree, but are reasonably good substitutes for each other, monopolistic competition is said to prevail. A trip to the supermarket would reveal that most consumer goods are sold under these conditions. A customer does not buy just toilet soap—he must choose among Lux, Camay, Cashmere Bouquet, Ivory, Dial, and various others. The same situation prevails in such products as breakfast cereals, canned milk, crackers, cooking oils, toilet paper, bread, cake mixes, and so on. Differentiation of product is one of the most significant aspects of our modern economy. The housewife in a supermarket has an almost bewildering choice of products, representing many shades of quality and price. Product differentiation has made it possible for consumers both to satisfy wants more precisely and to adjust to differences in buying power arising from variations in income levels or family size. At the same time this very profusion of products has greatly complicated the problem of choice itself. Intelligent buying of consumer goods thus involves problems never faced by the individual in an earlier period.

In some ways differentiation of product can be regarded simply as a special type of monopoly; there is, for example, only one producer of Dial soap or of Chevrolet automobiles. The significant difference between monopolistic competition and monopoly is that the monopolist has a product for which there is no close substitute. If the power company raises the price of electricity, the consumer is almost forced to pay it. But if the user of Dial soap finds the price has been increased, he may decide to shift to Lifebuoy or Ivory. On the other hand, if I believe that Chevrolet is a better car than Ford or Plymouth, General Motors may be able to raise the price of Chevrolets significantly before I would consider buying another make.

Effective product differentiation depends upon psychological as well as physical differences in the product. Although scientific tests may demonstrate that two brands of gasoline are essentially the same, the belief that one is superior may well lead the consumer to pay a higher price for it. Thus, the difference between monopoly and monopolistic competition is a matter of whether or not good substitutes exist, and only the reaction of consumers can determine how good the substitutes are.

Because producers of differentiated products approach the position of a monopolist most closely when consumers believe that other brands are not acceptable substitutes, businessmen make strenuous efforts to convince consumers that their product has desirable qualities found in no other. Advertising and other sales efforts are primarily attempts to influence the relative acceptability of differentiated products by the consumer. Although there is relatively little advertising by various producers of copper, steel, or cotton, the selling expenditures for soap, cigarettes, gasoline, and automobiles are tremendous.

Product differentiation is accomplished in a great variety of ways. Sometimes the quality of the product is altered (perhaps by putting a little menthol in the cigarette), but on the other hand it may be only the package that is changed (a cereal box that can be reclosed). An effort is made to get an appealing brand name. In the case of durable consumer goods, such as washing machines, the ability to provide good repair service is a vital differentiating factor. Pleasant surroundings may induce people to pay much more for a dinner than they would in a more poorly furnished restaurant. Finally, it is not enough to make a better product; the businessman must also convince the buyer that it represents a better buy, quality and price considered.

**Pure Competition.** When a great many firms produce an essentially identical product, the price will be determined by supply and demand under what is known as pure competition. This ideal situation is the one characterizing the perfectly functioning market described in Chapter 2. Although good examples of pure competition are hard to find, such industries as cotton textiles, children's apparel, dry cleaning, and lumber closely approach this situation. Major farm products are produced under conditions of pure competition, with the incidental complication of government price supports.

Economists a generation ago assumed that most prices were determined under conditions approaching pure competition. This assumption fell into disfavor after it was subjected to critical examination and was replaced by a theory that treated most markets as mixtures of competitive and monopolistic forces. This approach was developed by Edward Chamberlin in this country and Joan Robinson in Great Britain some 30 years ago. Today, economists generally assume that conditions of oligopoly or monopolistic competition are typical, and that monopoly and pure competition are special cases of importance primarily for theoretical purposes.



Despite its diminishing importance in market situations pure competition still serves as a standard by which to measure the effectiveness of competition in a particular market. Such a standard is also useful as a guide in studying the best allocation of resources and the proper distribution of income. But when we wish to study the actual functioning of most markets we must make the assumptions of partial monopoly, not of pure competition.

**Profit Maximization and Other Goals of the Firm.** Economists normally assume that profit is the primary goal sought by businessmen in the determination of prices and other policies. It is also assumed that, other things being equal, a larger profit is preferred to a smaller one. The assumption that firms attempt to maximize profits should be clearly understood, because it is sometimes said to be invalid.

The goal of maximum profits is not as completely selfish as it seems at first glance. Most businessmen sincerely believe that their firms are rendering important services to the public. They further believe that the only way they can survive and grow is through the realization of profits that directly provide funds for investment and indirectly attract them from other sources. But the individual firm does not attempt normally to secure the maximum profit on each separate transaction. Producers in industries marked by oligopoly or monopolistic competition are well aware that future profits will depend upon customer goodwill. In order to retain this favorable attitude the firm will frequently charge less for a particular item than it might be able to secure.

Some critics of the assumption of profit maximization have suggested that economic theory should be based upon the assumption of other goals. One that has been suggested is security for the firm and its management, either in terms of survival or maintenance of a given share of the market. Another possible goal is financial stability and soundness. Sometimes simple growth in volume of transactions is urged as a basic goal. Other aims attributed to the firm are the best possible service to the public at the given price or the maximization of employee welfare.

Although economists as a whole have not been willing to accept any of these alternative assumptions, they admit that the actions of businessmen are not motivated entirely by the desire for profit. The study of the causal factors underlying business decisions needs to be carried much further. Nevertheless, the earning of profit is felt by economists to be essential to practically all the goals suggested above, whether they deal with the survival of the firm or the welfare of the employees. As a result, economists tend to accept the assumption that the primary motivation of businessmen is the maximization of profit, but with numerous qualifications and exceptions.

## REVENUE AND PRICE

**Price Changes and Sales Volume.** In attempting to maximize profit the producer adopts a price policy only after careful consideration of its effect upon the number of units sold. As we have noted in the preceding chapter, a change in output will alter the unit cost of production. The effect of variations in output upon average fixed costs will be particularly important in many cases. But in addition to causing variations in unit costs changes in the volume of output will be a critical factor in determining the total revenue received.

Because prices charged and quantity sold will almost certainly move in opposite directions with any change in price policy, it is difficult to tell in advance what the effect may be upon total revenue. A decision to increase the selling price of a product may not bring an increase in total dollar sales, but rather a decrease. Total revenue is the result of multiplying the selling price by the number of units sold, and if the increase in price is more than offset by a decrease in output sold, total revenue will decline. On the other hand, a reduction in price will cause dollar sales volume to increase if it attracts enough additional customers. The businessman can only adopt an intelligent policy after he has an accurate estimate of the effect of a change in price upon the volume of sales.

**Elasticity of Demand.** The economist makes use of a concept entitled the *elasticity of demand,* which measures the response of quantity purchased to a price change. Elasticity is a number that states the percentage change in quantity purchased caused by a 1-per-cent change in price. The mathematical formula for elasticity is $E = \frac{\text{percentage change in quantity}}{\text{percentage change in price}}$. For example, if the price of a sack of oranges goes up from 50¢ to 55¢ and the quantity sold declines from 1,000 sacks to 800, we would say that quantity changed 20 per cent, and price rose 10 per cent (using original quantity and price as the base for our calculations). Applying our formula we find an elasticity of 20 per cent divided by 10 per cent, or 2. The fact that this coefficient of demand elasticity actually has a negative or minus sign is of no particular significance and normally is not even shown.[1]

In discussions of elasticity we apply the adjectives *elastic* and *inelastic* to demand. If the percentage change in quantity is greater than

[1] The figures would be changed somewhat if we used the quantity and price after change as the base. For a compromise calculation we may use a formula that averages quantity and price before and after change, as follows:

$$E = \frac{\dfrac{q - q'}{(q + q')/2}}{\dfrac{p - p'}{(p + p')/2}} = \frac{\dfrac{q - q'}{q + q'}}{\dfrac{p - p'}{p + p'}} = \frac{\dfrac{1000 - 800}{1000 + 800}}{\dfrac{50¢ - 55¢}{50¢ + 55¢}} = 2.33.$$

the percentage change in price, we say that the demand is elastic, and the application of our formula gives an answer greater than 1. Although any relationship that gives a number greater than 1 will be called elastic, there will still be great variations in the degree of elasticity included under this general term of elastic demand. Inelastic demand will, of course, be used in referring to relationships where the elasticity is less than 1. The dividing line between elastic and inelastic demand then is an elasticity of 1, which is referred to as *unitary elasticity*.



Variations in elasticity can be illustrated by changing the slope of segments of the demand curve. In Example A of Figure 15–1 the demand is elastic over the range shown, because a decline of only 10 cents, or 10 per cent, in price brings a 100-per-cent change in quantity. Such a relationship prevails with a straight-line demand curve on a segment close to the price axis. On the other hand the relatively steep curve in Example B is inelastic, the large percentage change in price from $1.00 to 50 cents being accompanied by a comparatively small percentage change in quantity.

The mathematically inclined student will recognize the care that must be exercised in using slope to indicate elasticity. A straight-line demand curve drawn from one axis of the graph to the other will be changing from elastic to inelastic, even though slope does not change, due to the fact that the base for calculating percentage change will vary along the curve. A straight-line curve may relate throughout its length a 10 cents change in price to a change of 10 units in quantity

**Figure 15–1.** Variation in elasticity associated with changes in slope of segments of demand curve.

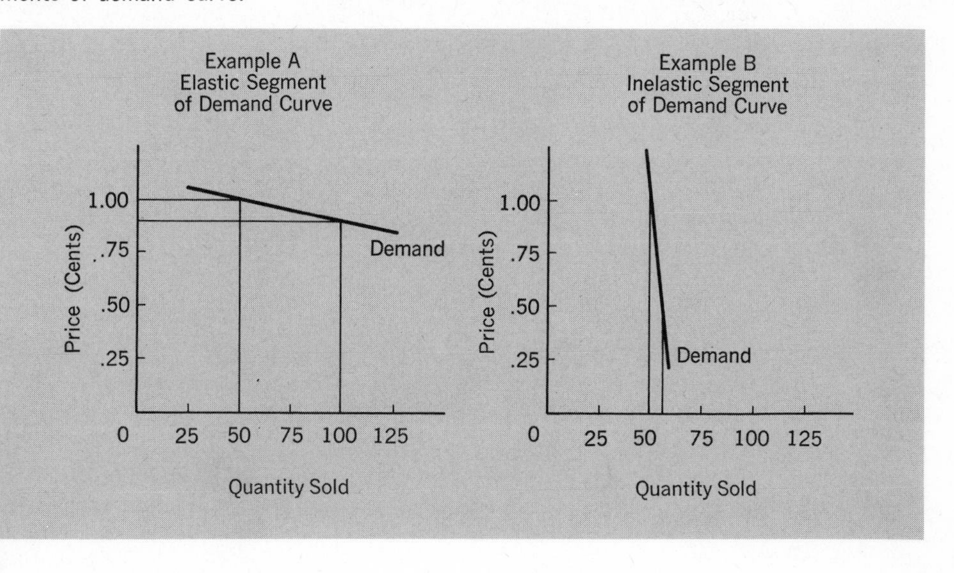

purchased, but the percentage change in price is not the same when price drops from $1.00 to 90 cents as when it drops from 20 cents to 10 cents. Figure 15–2 indicates the nature of this change in elasticity. The upper end of this demand curve is elastic because a drop of 10 per cent in price brings an increase in quantity of 100 per cent. On the other hand, the lower end of the curve is inelastic, because the same drop of 10 cents in price now represents a decrease of 50 per cent, whereas the increase in quantity of 10 units is now only slightly more than 10 per cent. If one end of a straight-line curve is elastic while the other end is inelastic, we should suspect what is actually true—that somewhere in the center of the curve elasticity will be unitary.

**Figure 15–2.** Variations in elasticity along a straight-line demand curve.

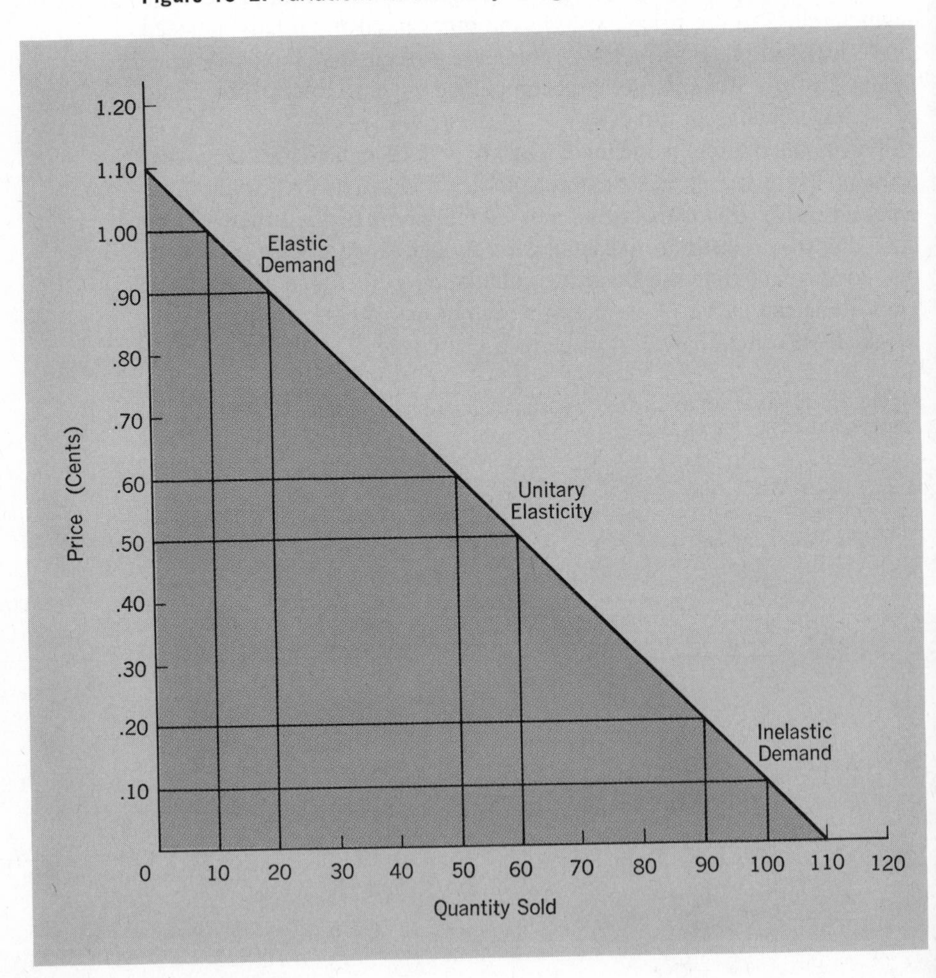

**Criteria for Determining Elasticity of Demand.** Economists and businessmen are constantly faced with the need to predict whether the demand for a particular product is elastic or inelastic. There are certain basic rules that we can apply in making this estimate. One of the more obvious factors is the *urgency of the want.* If the need for the product is so urgent as to be a necessity, it is likely that increases in the price will not cause much of a reduction in purchases, and the demand will tend to be inelastic. The consumer reduces the quantity of less urgently desired goods more readily when the price rises.

Another criterion that can be applied is the *existence of substitutes.* If numerous good substitutes are available, there will be a strong tendency to shift consumption to them when the price of the product rises, and demand will be elastic. When the consumer does not have the option of shifting to substitutes, the demand will tend to be more inelastic.

*Habitual or customary items* of consumption tend to have inelastic demands, because people are reluctant to vary consumption patterns when price changes. If the product takes only a small *proportion of personal income,* the buyer tends to have an inelastic demand for the good because he considers the price change to be relatively unimportant. On the other hand *postponable purchases,* such as automobiles or air conditioners, are influenced by price changes, and so tend to have an elastic demand. If the price of a new car is greatly reduced at the end of a model year, the buyer may decide to buy now at this low price rather than delay his purchase until the price has gone back up to its normal level.

Products that are *used jointly* with other goods to satisfy a consumer need are likely to have an inelastic demand, because a change in the price of this product will play an insignificant role in determining the final cost of satisfying the need. A fall in the price of nails will not cause many more frame houses to be built, and therefore will not greatly increase the quantity of nails purchased. Carpenters and steelworkers probably push harder for wage increases because they believe the demand curve for their labor to be inelastic as a consequence of its joint use in production.

**Relationship of Elasticity to Total Revenue.** If demand is elastic in a given range, a decrease in price will result in a proportionately greater increase in quantity sold, and total revenue must increase. This situation is illustrated in Figure 15–3, Example A. The relatively horizontal curve indicates that demand is elastic in a range close to the price axis, and by multiplying the separate prices by the quantity sold at each price, we find that the reduction in price from $1.00 to 90¢ has caused an increase in total revenue from $100 to $180.

Because the price is measured on one side of the rectangle *ABCO*

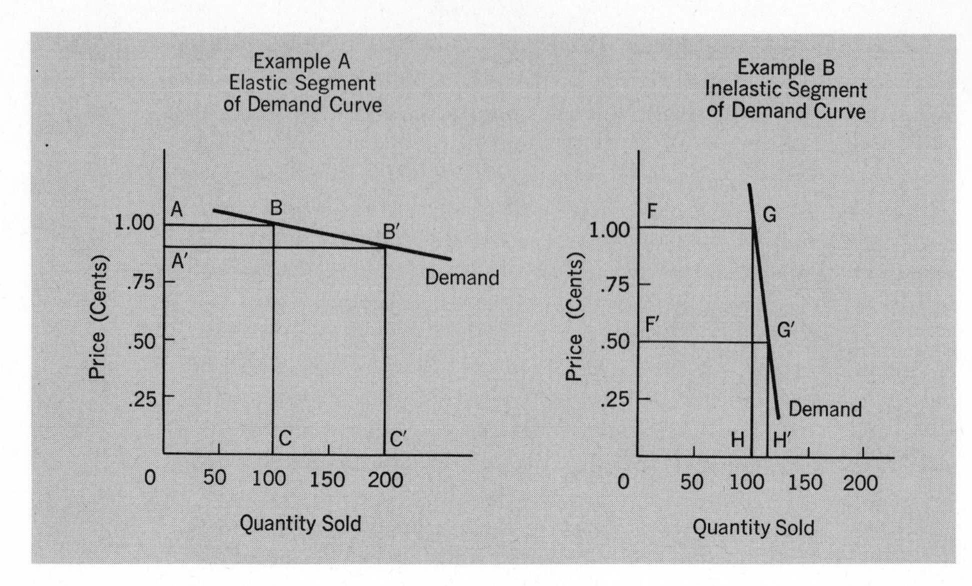


**Figure 15–3.** Effect upon total revenue of price changes with varying elasticity of demand.

and quantity on the other side, the area of the rectangle secured by multiplying the two sides measures the total revenue. The effect of the price change on total revenue is thus shown by a visual comparison of area *ABCO* at a price of $1.00 with the larger area of *A′B′C′O* found when the price is 90 cents. Reversing the direction of price change, we see that any increase in price when demand is elastic will result in a decrease in total revenue.

The reverse will be the case when demand is inelastic, because any reduction in price with such a demand will reduce total revenue, and any increase in price will increase total revenue. An examination of Figure 15–3, Example B, which illustrates a range of inelastic demand, reveals the direct effect upon total revenue caused by a price change; rectangle *FGHO* at the higher price has a larger area than rectangle *F′G′H′O* at the lower price.

The importance of elasticity in practical problems is illustrated in agriculture. Since nearly all farm products have an inelastic demand, farm income can be increased as a rule by raising price and reducing output. On the other hand, any firm with an elastic demand for its output will find total revenue increasing rather than declining with output. The businessman seeking to increase his total gross revenue should lower price (increase quantity) if demand is elastic, and raise price (reduce quantity) if demand is inelastic. In the determination of net revenue, of course, costs must also be taken into account.



**Marginal Revenue.** Marginal revenue is the name used by economists to designate the effect upon total revenue of an increase in output. It can be defined as *the amount added to total revenue by an increase of one unit in the number of units offered for sale*. When the individual producer finds that additional units of his product can be sold only by reducing the price of all units sold, it becomes important to know what the effect of this price change will be upon total revenue.

In Table 15–1 we find a simple example of the calculation of marginal revenue at a series of corresponding prices and quantities. The basic assumption underlying this table is that a series of reductions in price will bring a steady increase in the quantity sold, but when we look at the total revenue column we see that not all increases in quantity bring equally satisfactory results. The first two price reductions bring an increase in total revenue, but the third reduction to 15 cents leaves the total revenue the same, and the last price reduction actually results in a smaller total revenue. The column labeled "Marginal Revenue" shows the amount by which total revenue increases as quantity increases by one unit. Each such increase in quantity is caused by a corresponding price reduction. It should be noted that the zero figure for marginal revenue occurs at the point in the table where the elasticity of demand is equal to 1.

**TABLE 15–1**
**Calculation of Marginal Revenue**

| Price (¢) | Quantity | Total Revenue (¢) | Marginal Revenue (¢) |
|---|---|---|---|
| 30 | 1 | 30 | |
| | | | 20 |
| 25 | 2 | 50 | |
| | | | 10 |
| 20 | 3 | 60 | |
| | | | 0 |
| 15 | 4 | 60 | |
| | | | −10 |
| 10 | 5 | 50 | |

In Figure 15–4 the data for price and marginal revenue derived from Table 15–1 are plotted against corresponding quantities. The price–quantity relationship is the demand curve, whereas the relationship between marginal revenue and quantity is called the marginal-revenue curve. In referring to the demand curve for the product of a single firm rather than an entire market, economists frequently use the designation Average Revenue (*AR*). Two important points concerning marginal revenue stand out in the graph. (1) The *MR* curve lies below the *AR* curve at all points and ultimately falls below the base line as marginal revenue becomes negative. (2) The marginal revenue curve drops off more sharply than average revenue; a look at the table shows that each increase of one unit sold brings a 5¢ decline in selling price but a 10¢ reduction in marginal revenue.

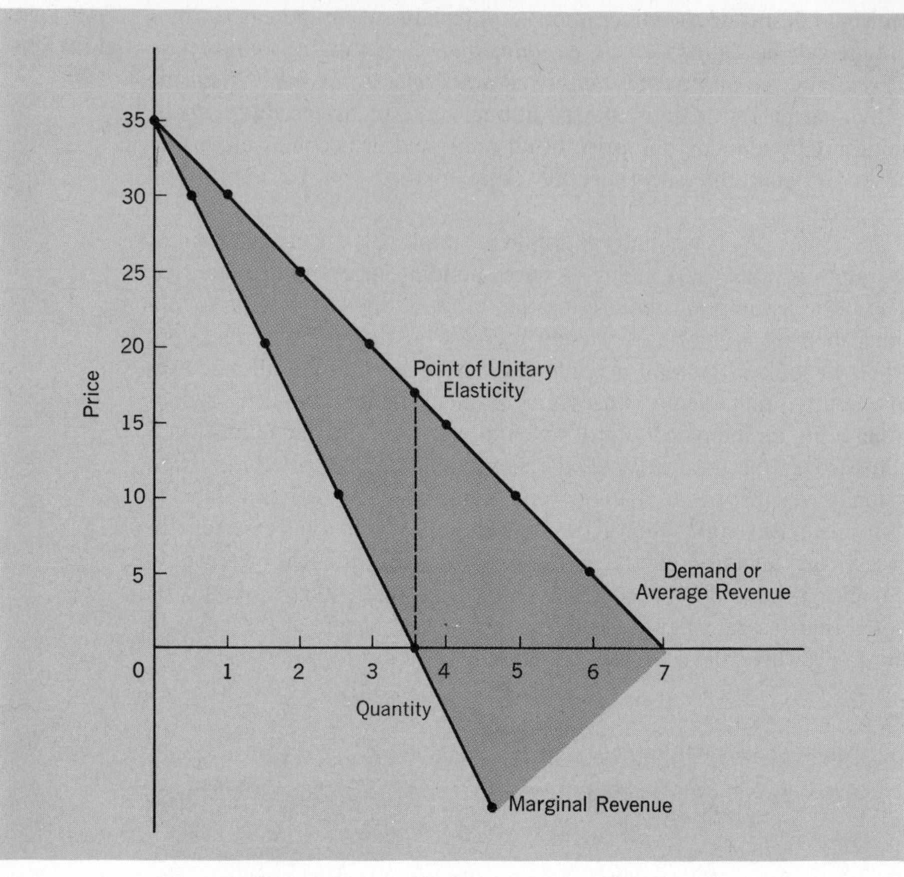


**Figure 15–4.** Relationship of the marginal revenue curve to the average revenue or demand curve.

In an earlier section of this chapter we noted that a straight-line demand curve reaching from the vertical to the horizontal axis would first exhibit an elastic section, then a point of unitary elasticity, and finally an inelastic segment. The *MR* curve lies above the quantity axis as long as the corresponding *AR* is elastic, cuts the axis at the point where *AR* has unitary elasticity, and falls below it when the *AR* is inelastic.

The reasons for this position of the *MR* curve should not be hard to understand. When *AR* is elastic a decline in price accompanied by a more-than-proportionate increase in quantity will bring an increase in total revenue. Thus marginal revenue must be a positive value. On the other hand, if *AR* is inelastic, an increase in quantity sold can only be secured by a more-than-proportionate price decrease, total revenue will fall, and marginal revenue will be negative, so that the corresponding point on the *MR* curve lies below the quantity axis. The point where the *MR* curve crosses the quantity axis corresponds precisely to the point of unitary elasticity on the *AR* curve; only at this point is the change in price exactly offset by a proportionate and inverse change in quantity so that total revenue remains the same and marginal revenue is zero.

## SHORT RUN PROFIT MAXIMIZATION

**Profit Maximization by the Monopolist.** The market demand for a monopolist's product corresponds exactly to that firm's individual demand curve, because no close substitutes are available for purchases by the consumer. The elasticity of the monopolist's average revenue curve depends at any point upon how essential customers consider the product to be in its various uses. If it is a good of habitual or customary use, or if it is used jointly with other items, the monopolist may be able to raise the price charged significantly without serious reduction in the volume of sales.

In Table 15–2 we have assumed that if the monopolist charges 98¢ he will be able to sell 5,700 units per day, but that any increase in price will reduce the units sold at the rate of 100 for each addition of 2 cents to the price. For example, if the price is increased 6 cents, from 98 cents to $1.04, the number of units sold will decline by 300, or from 5,700 to 5,400 per day. Conversely, any reduction in price of 2 cents is assumed to increase units sold by 100.

Given the series of prices shown in the selling price or *AR* column of Table 15–2, total revenue is derived by multiplying each total output by the price at which it can be sold. The marginal revenue column is then calculated by subtracting each successive total revenue from the preceding one and dividing by the number of units of increase in total output that brought the change. As we would expect from our preceding discussion, the figures in the *MR* column are smaller than those in the *AR* column and become negative beyond 5,400 units of output.

The cost figures in columns 2, 3, and 4 of Table 15–2 are taken directly from Table 14–3 of the preceding chapter. With these costs and revenue figures we can now show graphically in Figure 15–5 the process of profit maximization by a monopoly in the short run.

In the final column of Table 15–2 net profit or loss is listed. The largest profit figure occurs at an output of 4,500 units. By inspecting the marginal cost and marginal revenue columns we see that marginal revenue exceeds marginal cost up to, but not beyond, an output of 4,500 units. Beyond this point each change in output involves add-

**TABLE 15-2**
**Calculation of Profit or Loss by Monopolist at Various Possible Output Levels**

| Total Output | Total Cost ($) | Total Cost per Unit of Output (*ATC*) ($) | Marginal Cost (*MC*) ($) | Selling Price (*AR*) ($) | Total Revenue ($) | Marginal Revenue (*MR*) ($) | Net Profit or Loss ($) |
|---|---|---|---|---|---|---|---|
| 2,100 | 3,250 | 1.547 | | 1.70 | 3,570.0 | | 320.0 |
| 2,600 | 3,500 | 1.346 | 0.500 | 1.60 | 4,160.0 | 1.18 | 660.0 |
| 3,200 | 3,750 | 1.172 | 0.416 | 1.48 | 4,736.0 | 0.96 | 986.0 |
| 3,900 | 4,000 | 1.026 | 0.357 | 1.34 | 5,226.0 | 0.70 | 1,226.0 |
| 4,500 | 4,250 | 0.944 | 0.416 | 1.22 | 5,490.0 | 0.44 | 1,240.0 |
| 5,000 | 4,500 | 0.900 | 0.500 | 1.12 | 5,600.0 | 0.22 | 1,100.0 |
| 5,400 | 4,750 | 0.879 | 0.625 | 1.04 | 5,616.0 | 0.04 | 866.0 |
| 5,700 | 5,000 | 0.877 | 0.833 | 0.98 | 5,586.0 | −0.10 | 586.0 |
| 5,900 | 5,250 | 0.890 | 1.250 | 0.94 | 5,546.0 | −0.20 | 296.0 |
| 6,000 | 5,500 | 0.916 | 2.500 | 0.92 | 5,520.0 | −0.26 | 20.0 |
| 6,050 | 5,750 | 0.951 | 5.000 | 0.91 | 5,505.5 | −0.29 | −244.5 |

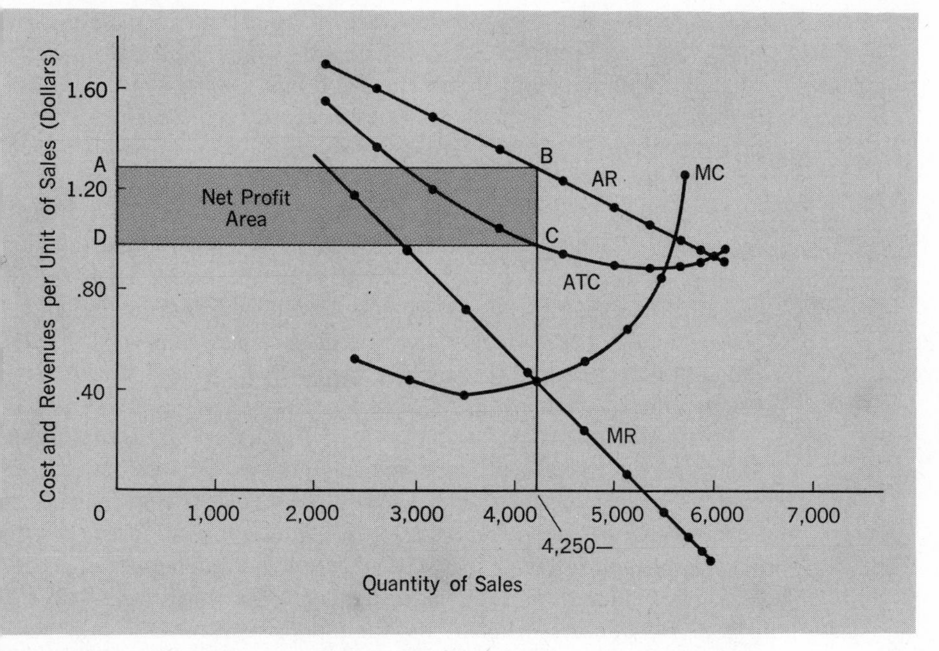


igure 15–5. Determination of maximum net profit by firm with monopolistic ontrol over selling price.

ng more to cost than to revenue. Such changes naturally reduce net rofit. We know that these changes add more to cost than to revenue, ecause the word *marginal* refers to the amount added to cost or to evenue when output expands by one unit. Stated in terms of the raph, then, *maximum profit will be achieved at the point at which the IC curve intersects the MR curve.*

An inspection of Figure 15–5 reveals that the maxmum profit posi-ion is actually achieved by selling 4,250 units at a price of about 1.26, although this output level is not listed in Table 15–2. At this oint the net profit is somewhat larger than the $1,240 realized when ,500 units are sold. This net profit is shown in the graph by the ectangular area *ABCD;* it is the product of the profit margin (*BC*) nd the number of units sold (*CD*). The distance *BC* represents the nargin of profit on each unit sold, because point *B* on the *AR* curve hows the price at which 4,250 units could be sold, whereas point *C* n the *ATC* curve shows the total cost per unit when output is at this evel. The difference between selling price and unit cost gives the rofit margin.

It is important for the student to notice that this point of maximum et profit is not achieved at the point of lowest cost, just beyond ,500 units of output. Although the monopolist could reduce his costs by expanding output to the lowest cost point where $MC$ intersects $ATC$, his net profit would be reduced by any increase in output beyond 4,250 units. Beyond this point of maximum profit the possible reduction of costs per unit would be more than offset by the necessary reduction in selling price, as shown by the relative position of the $MR$ and $MC$ curves.

This tendency of the monopolistic firm to restrict output in order to secure higher selling prices, even at the expense of operating the plant short of its most efficient output level, is one of the most serious disadvantages of monopoly. Consumers find that selling prices tend to be high and that these higher prices tend to restrict sales so that plants frequently experience higher unit costs than would be the case under competitive conditions.

**Profit Maximization in Oligopoly.** When there are a small number of producers of a product that has not been differentiated, each of them will have some control over price and therefore will have a negatively sloped average-revenue curve similar to that of a monopoly. The significant difference between oligopoly and monopoly is that the oligopolist must always be concerned with the prices being charged by other producers, whereas the monopolist is not.

Expressed in graphical terms, the $AR$ curve in oligopoly, although negatively sloped, tends to be more elastic than it would be if the industry were controlled by a monopolist. The explanation for this greater elasticity is that under oligopoly a price cut increases the number of units sold for a reason not present under monopoly. Thus, the monopolist is concerned only with how many more units the market will absorb if the price is lowered. In contrast, the oligopolist must consider also how many more customers he can attract from other firms by a change in price. If a lower price nets a large number of additional buyers the $AR$ curve of the firm tends to be quite flat, as in Figure 15–6, Example A. The flatness of the $AR$ curve reflects the willingness of buyers to switch their patronage to this firm by virtue of its cut in price.

A great deal will depend upon whether the other firms in the oligopoly also change their prices at the same time and in the same amount as the first firm does. If all firms change their prices proportionately and simultaneously no producer will lose customers to other sellers as a result of a price cut. Such a situation might exist if price leadership were firmly established in the industry or if the producers joined together to set prices. A firm in an oligopolistic industry may also believe that other producers would follow any price increase spontaneously, especially if firms in the industry are producing at capacity or if costs recently have risen sharply. Whenever the firm believes that a price increase would be followed by others in the industry, the *AR* curve becomes steeper, as illustrated in Figure 15–6, Example B. Even though there is no fear of loss of sales by shift of customers, the *AR* curve will have some elasticity, because buyers still have the option of deciding to change their consumption at the various prices.

Once the oligopolistic firm has determined its average-revenue schedule the marginal revenue can be calculated, as shown in Table 15–2. Although that case pertained to monopoly, the calculation of *MR* under oligopoly is the same. Finally, the point of maximum profit is determined graphically under oligopoly, as under monopoly, by the intersection of the marginal-cost and the marginal-revenue curves.

One interesting variation of this treatment of the elasticity of the *AR* curve of an oligopolistic firm, as it is affected by the anticipated reaction of other firms to any price change, is the kinked *AR* curve. The kink results when a firm believes that its competitors will follow

**Figure 15–6.** Effect upon the average revenue and marginal revenue curves of changing the assumption in an oligopolistic industry about the willingness of other firms to follow a price change.

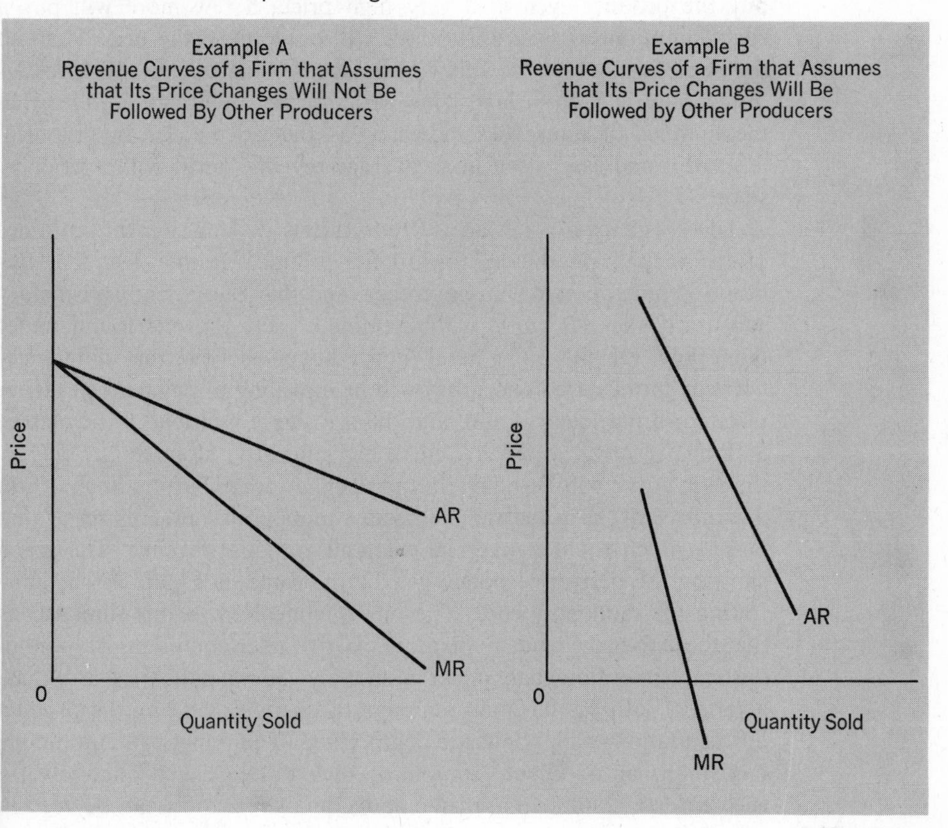

a price cut but will not follow a price increase. Some economists believe that the existence of such a kink provides some explanation for the observed price stability in many oligopolistic industries. A further discussion of this controversial analysis is found in the appendix at the end of this chapter.

**Profit Maximization in Monopolistic Competition.** Monopolistic competition is characterized by the presence of a number of competing firms, each of which sells a differentiated product. This characteristic tends to result in a negatively inclined average-revenue curve. Such an *AR* curve implies that the firm can raise price without losing all its customers. How, one may ask, is this possible in view of the numerous competitors faced by the firm? The answer lies in differentiation of product and the resulting attachment of the customer to a particular firm. To illustrate, those customers who believe that a particular brand of beer is better than any other will prefer paying a few cents more a can to changing brands. There may be some customers who will pay twice as much in order to continue the use of this particular beer. Such being the case, a few consumers will buy the product even at a very high price; a few more will pay a slight premium to secure it; others will buy only if the price is about the same as that of the other brands; and still others will buy this brand only if it costs less. This variation in preference implies that the number of units sold increases as the price falls. In graphical terms this expresses itself in an average-revenue curve with a negative slope.

The elasticity of such an *AR* curve thus depends on the attitudes of the various purchasers toward the product. If they feel that this brand is much better than any other, and that there is no satisfactory substitute, the *AR* curve will resemble closely the one found under monopoly. On the other hand, if the buyers believe that differences between brands are minor, they will be unwilling to pay a much higher price for a particular brand, and the *AR* curve will tend to be elastic. So long, however, as the *AR* curve has a negative slope to any degree, the *MR* curve will lie below it and decline more sharply. Such a firm maximizes profit in the same way as a monopolist; price is set at that output which equates marginal cost and marginal revenue. The graph showing the best price policy will be the same as Figure 15–5, illustrating the monopoly case. The one qualification to this similarity is that the *AR* curve tends to be more elastic under conditions of monopolistic competition than under monopoly. Some industries are characterized both by the small numbers of oligopoly and by the product differentiation of monopolistic competition. The American automobile industry is an excellent example of such differentiated oligopoly. In such cases a combination of the above analytical tools can be used in examining the problems of the industry.

**Role of Advertising and Other Selling Costs.** The purpose of most brand-name advertising is to convince the public that one brand is much better than any other. If a seller can make buyers believe in the superiority of his product, he will secure two very desirable results: (1) his customers will be willing to pay a higher price rather than shift to another brand, and (2) consumers who have previously purchased other brands will now buy his product. The effect of the first of these two results is to make the *AR* curve more inelastic, and the effect of the second is to shift the curve to the right.

Both of these changes in the *AR* curve create new possibilities for increasing profit. A change in demand that embodies both results is shown in Figure 15–7. In this graph the *AR, MR, ATC,* and *MC* lines show the initial situation, and the *AR′, MR′, ATC′* and *MC′*

**Figure 15–7.** Effect of a successful advertising campaign on revenue curves, cost curves, and profit areas.

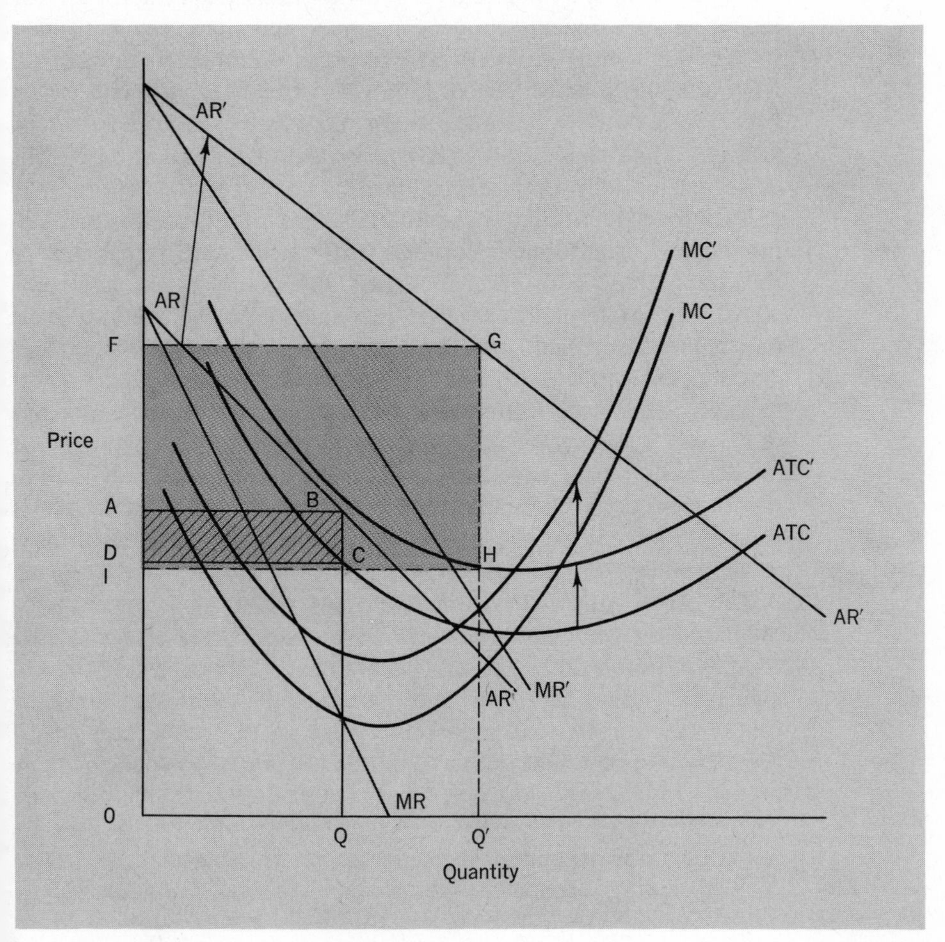

lines indicate the situation after the advertising campaign has gone into effect. As a result of the new sales effort the two cost curves have shifted upward, but as an offset to this increase in costs, the *AR* curve has shifted to the right and become somewhat more inelastic. The profit area *ABCD* represents the maximum profit attainable with the old cost and revenue curves and corresponds to the intersection of *MR* and *MC*. It is clear by inspection that the new profit area *FGHI* is much larger than the old, both because the volume of sales has been increased and because the margin of profit on each unit is greater. In this case the firm doing the advertising has decided to take advantage of the increased preference for its brand both in the form of a higher selling price and an increased sales volume. Thus price rises sharply from *OA* to *OF*, whereas quantity sold increases from *OQ* to *OQ′*.

Unfortunately for the firm, the final effect of a successful advertising campaign may not be as profitable as this graph indicates. The producers of competing brands naturally find that customers have shifted to the more heavily advertised brand. In turn, this causes their *AR* curves to shift to the left, and their profit declines as a result. Faced with this unpleasant development, the rival firms naturally attempt to lure back their old customers and to add more, if possible, by increasing advertising expenditures. These new sales efforts may redistribute sales in such a way that all firms' *AR* curves assume approximately their former positions. If this is the case profits will be smaller, because costs have increased as a result of the additional advertising. Many firms engaged in monopolistic competition have found that advertising costs cut seriously into their profits, but they dare not reduce these expenditures for fear that the loss of customers to their competitors will change their small profit position into one of net loss. Although the industry as a whole may be unhappy about the expenditures for advertising, any individual producer who tries to reduce this cost finds himself eliminated from the industry. It is this situation that has caused some critics to denounce much advertising as an economic waste.

The above analysis deals only with advertising aimed at changing the brand preference of customers. In addition, advertising may perform much more valuable services for the consuming public by enabling it to spend its money more intelligently. For example, many new products come to the market every year. Were it not for advertising the public would become informed of the advantages of these products much more slowly. A rapid increase in the demand for these new products may also reduce their cost and selling price, if they are produced under conditions of increasing returns to scale.



In a growing economy, with expanding productive capacity, we may find that the propensity to consume tends to lag behind the ability to produce. Under such conditions the special stimulation of demand that results from advertising may make an important contribution in pushing output closer to the full-employment position.

The social advantages of advertising, however, depend upon the correctness of the assumption that the information in advertising enables the public to spend its money more intelligently. This assumption is valid only if the information is relatively complete and honest. Obvious cases of dishonesty, of course, are dealt with in the courts. The real difficulties in attempting to make advertising serve the public welfare arise in those advertisements that are not obviously dishonest, but where the public is left with incomplete information or with misleading implications. For example, recent arguments about the responsiblity of the cigarette companies to inform their customers about the danger of lung cancer have been quite bitter. Advertising plays a major role in our society, but policies to assure that it serves the public interest are still in the formative stage.

**Profit Maximization Under Pure Competition.** Under pure competition the individual firm has no control over price. If a sufficient number of firms produce an identical item, none of them will be able to affect the price by changing its level of output. Moreover, customers will not be willing to pay more for one firm's output than for another's in the belief that it is superior. As such producers see the situation, the *AR* curve is horizontal. If chickens are selling at 25¢ per pound this morning, a farmer can sell 50 at this price. Even if he decides to dispose of his entire flock of 500, the price will remain unchanged. This lack of influence by the individual producer on the price is traceable partly to the fact that his chickens are essentially the same as others being offered for sale, and partly to the fact that a batch of 500 is an insignificant part of the total number sold daily. The price is decided by the action of supply and demand in the market as a whole.

In Figure 15–8 we find an illustration of the maximization of profit by the producer operating under pure competition. The cost curves are shown in the usual idealized form, because they will depend on the technical conditions of production rather than on the nature of the market. On the other hand the *AR* curve, being horizontal rather than negatively sloped, reflects the difference between pure competition and the market conditions discussed in the earlier sections of this chapter. The horizontal or perfectly elastic *AR* curve implies that the producer has no control over price, but can sell either part or all of his output at this same market price. Because additional units can be sold without the necessity of reducing the price on other units, the amount added to revenue by the sale of an extra unit is the same as the price at which the unit is sold. If the addition to revenue is the

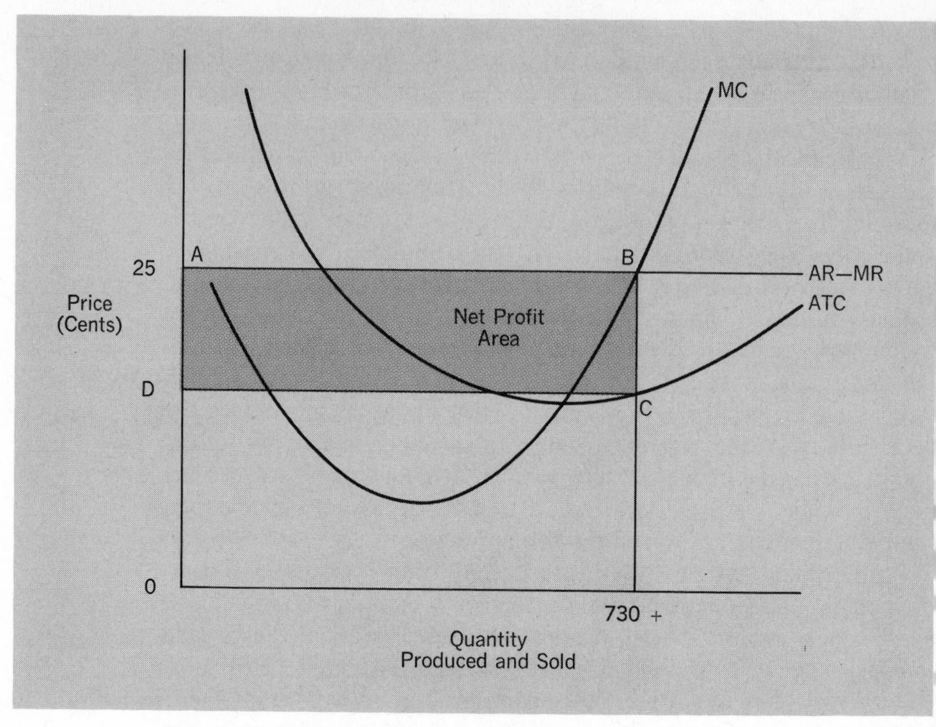


**Figure 15–8.** Firm under pure competition maximizing profit by carrying production beyond the least-cost point.

same as the selling price, it is clear that *AR* and *MR* are the same and the horizontal line at the market selling price represents both.

The producer as usual maximizes his profit by equating *MC* and *MR*. In Figure 15–8 maximum profit is attained at an output of approximately 730 units. The profit margin will be represented by the distance *BC* and the number of units by *CD*, so that the profit area is *ABCD*. If the market price rises there is a tendency for this producer to expand operations, because the intersection of the new *AR-MR* curve with the *MC* curve is above and to the right of the present intersection. On the other hand, a decline in the market price brings a tendency to reduce output with the decline of profit, because the new intersection is below and to the left of the intersection when the market price is 25¢.

If the price falls until the *AR-MR* curve drops below the *ATC* curve at all points, the distance between the *AR-MR* curve and the *ATC* curve will represent a margin of loss on each unit and the graph will show a net loss area, as in Figure 15–9. If the firm continues to produce while suffering a loss, it will try to minimize that loss by equating *MC* and *MR*. In other words, it will reduce its loss by expanding production so long as it is adding more to revenue than it is adding to cost. Conditions under which the firm suffering a loss will decide to continue operations will be examined in the next chapter. At that time the analysis of the long-run tendency for market price to approach equilibrium with *AR-MR* tangent to *ATC* at its lowest point will also be presented.

The student should be certain that he understands the different level of output that results when the producer operates under conditions of pure competition as compared with monopolistic operations. In Figure 15–8 the firm is making full use of its plant capacity by producing beyond the low-cost point shown by the intersection of *MC* and *ATC*. Production will not fall short of the low-cost point intentionally, unless the firm is suffering a loss. In contrast an examination of Figure 15–5 (also 15–7) shows that maximum profit has been

**Figure 15–9.** Firm under pure competition minimizing loss by carrying production to intersection of *MC* and *MR* short of the least-cost point.

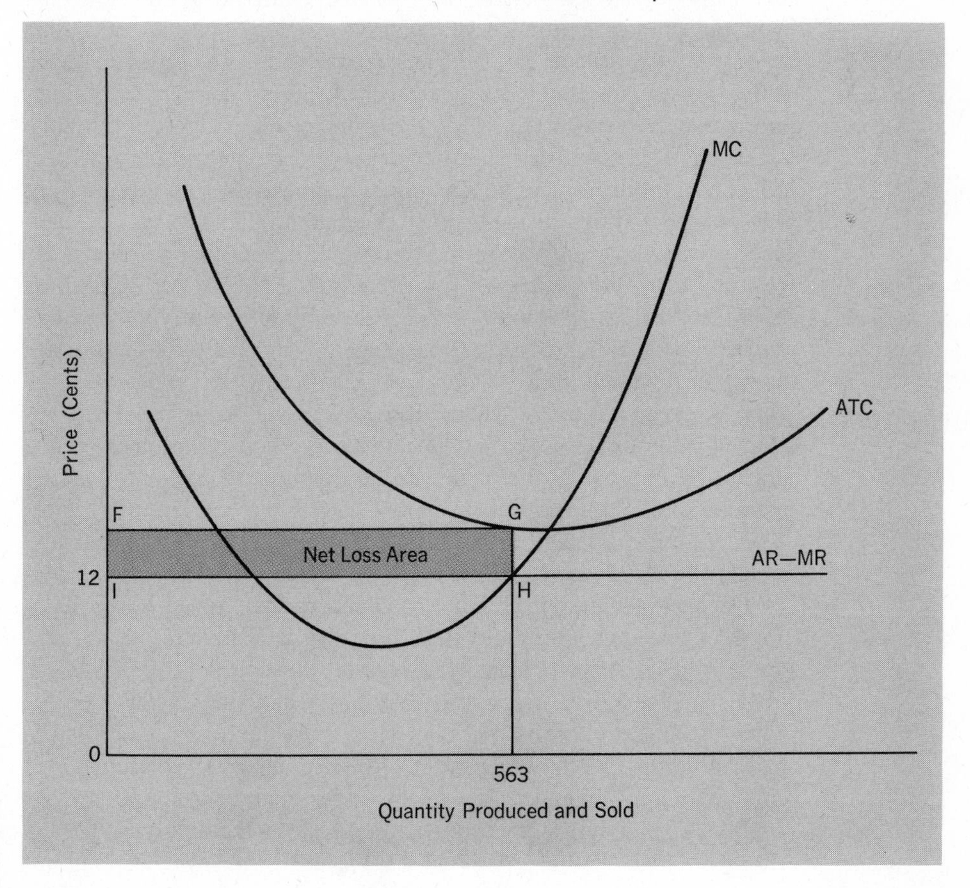

achieved by producing short of the low-cost point. Any firm under conditions of monopoly or partial monopoly, as revealed by a sloped *AR* curve, will tend to try to increase profit by charging a selling price that can only be secured normally by some restriction of output below the level that would be secured under competitive conditions.

An important reason why economists constantly emphasize the social desirability of competition is that it tends to encourage an expanded output and full utilization of valuable resources. The chief criticism of monopoly, either full or partial, is that it places the firm in a position where profit can be increased by restricting output. Economic welfare is normally increased by an expansion of the output of goods and services, not by a contraction.

**Summary.** The four categories of market conditions are monopoly, oligopoly, monopolistic competition, and pure competition. Monopoly exists when there is only one producer of a good or service for which there is no satisfactory substitute. Oligopoly exists when there are only a few sellers of a product with no good substitute. Monopolistic competition exists when a number of firms are selling differentiated products that are reasonably good substitutes for each other. An undifferentiated product sold by many firms characterizes pure competition with the price determined in the market as a whole.

The maximization of profit is assumed to be the primary goal of individual producers, although some qualifications and limitations must be recognized. Because price charged by the firm and the volume of sales change in opposite directions, a given price change by the firm may either increase or decrease total revenue, depending upon the elasticity of the *AR* curve. Elasticity of demand may be calculated by dividing percentage change in quantity by percentage change in price and may be expressed graphically by variations in the slope of segments of the curve. Demand will tend to be elastic for products that are not essential, have numerous substitutes, are durable and the purchase is postponable, are not habitual in consumption, are not used jointly, and take a significant part of the consumer's income. A decrease in price will bring an increase in total revenue if demand is elastic, but a decrease if it is inelastic.

Marginal revenue is the amount added to total revenue by an increase of one unit in quantity sold. The marginal-revenue curve on a graph will lie below a sloped average-revenue curve and will slope more sharply, falling below the base line when the elasticity of the average-revenue curve is less than unity. The monopolist will maximize his profit by restricting output to the point where marginal cost equals marginal revenue.



Under oligopoly the firm maximizes profit in the same way as the monopolist, but the elasticity of the *AR* curve will depend upon the estimate made about the action taken by other firms if a price change is initiated.



Differentiation of product under monopolistic competition also gives a negatively sloped *AR* curve and permits profit maximization by restricted output similar to what occurs under monopolistic conditions. Successful advertising of differentiated products results in a shift of the *AR* curve to the right and reduced elasticity. The shift in the revenue curves permits increased profit by expanded volume or higher selling price to offset the addition to total costs.

Under pure competition the *AR* and *MR* curves are horizontal and coincide. Maximum profit will still be achieved by equating marginal cost and marginal revenue, but now there is no advantage to the restriction of output, because price will not be increased.

## QUESTIONS

1. Why is the analysis of oligopoly or monopolistic competition more useful in studying real markets than is the analysis of monopoly or of pure competition?
2. What are the criticisms that are sometimes made of the economist's assumption that the primary goal of a business firm is the maximization of profit?
3. What is the formula for calculating elasticity of demand? What is the relationship of the slope of the curve to elasticity of segments of the demand curve?
4. List and explain the criteria for determining whether the demand for a particular product will be elastic or inelastic.
5. When the price falls for a product with inelastic demand, will total revenue increase or decrease? Why?
6. What is meant by marginal revenue? How is it calculated?
7. Why is the marginal-revenue curve (*MR*) separate from the average-revenue curve (*AR*) under monopolistic conditions but not under purely competitive assumptions?
8. Why is it advantageous for a monopolist to restrict output, but not for the firm operating under competitive conditions?
9. Why is the level of output that maximizes profit always the one that equates *MC* and *MR?* Draw the graph that illustrates this maximization of profit for the monopolist.
10. Explain why differentiation of products causes the *AR* curve for the firm under conditions of monopolistic competition to depart from the horizontal position that is characteristic of the firm under purely competitive conditions.
11. How can advertising increase net profit when it clearly adds to total operating costs? Explain how the cost curves and revenue curves of a business firm are changed by a successful advertising campaign.
12. Under what conditions does advertising perform a public service?

## Appendix

### KINKED AVERAGE-REVENUE CURVE IN OLIGOPOLY

Prices in certain oligopolistic industries, such as steel and copper, have been shown by statistical studies to be more stable than in industries operating under other market conditions. This stability may result simply from fear of change when firms are uncertain about the reactions of rivals to price adjustments. Some economists, however, seek to explain the absence of frequent price changes by assuming a kink in the *AR* curve.

Let us consider an oligopolistic industry selling a standardized product and composed of a small number of firms of approximately equal strength. Each firm doubts that the others will follow its lead if it decides to raise its price. If the rival firms do decide to hold their prices fixed, they stand to gain sales from the firms that have raised prices. Consumers will naturally tend to shift their purchases to the firms with lower prices. The result, then, of an independent price increase by an oligopolist is likely to be a sharp decline in the number of units sold by that firm. Thus, its individual demand or *AR* curve will tend to be quite flat at prices above the original level.

On the other hand, the firm may be reluctant to reduce prices to attract additional customers, because it believes (probably correctly) that its competitors would immediately match the price cut. A failure to meet the lower price by any firm in an oligopoly would cause it to lose business. Therefore, the prices of all firms tend to move downward together. With such recognition of interdependence in a sharply competitive market, any firm initiating a price cut cannot expect to sell more units by attracting buyers from its competitors. Accordingly, its *AR* curve is considered to be steep at prices below the original position.

In Figure 15–10 the *AR* curve of a typical firm in an oligopolistic industry is shown as it results from this consideration of how its competitors would react to any price changes. At any price above $1.00 (present price) the curve is relatively flat as a result of the fear that other firms will not follow a price increase. At prices below $1.00 the *AR* is steep because of the expectation that any price cuts will be matched by competing firms. As a result, the *AR* curve shows a sharp kink or change in elasticity at the present price.

We have noted in Figure 15–2 that a straight-line demand curve varies in elasticity throughout its length, and in Figure 15–4 it was shown that the position of the *MR* curve had a definite relationship to the elasticity of the demand or *AR* curve. So long as *AR* is elastic the corresponding *MR* curve will lie above the base line, but when *AR* is inelastic the *MR* curve lies below. With a perfectly straight *AR* curve, therefore, the *MR* curve steadily approaches the base line as demand elasticity declines and crosses it when the *AR* has an elasticity of one. But with a kinked *AR* curve we do not have a steady change in elasticity; instead we have a sudden change. Because the position of the *MR* curve is determined by the elasticity of the *AR* curve, a sudden change in the elasticity brings a sharp change in the

**Figure 15–10.** Maximization of profit by a firm in an oligopolistic industry under assumptions that cause a kink in the *AR* curve.

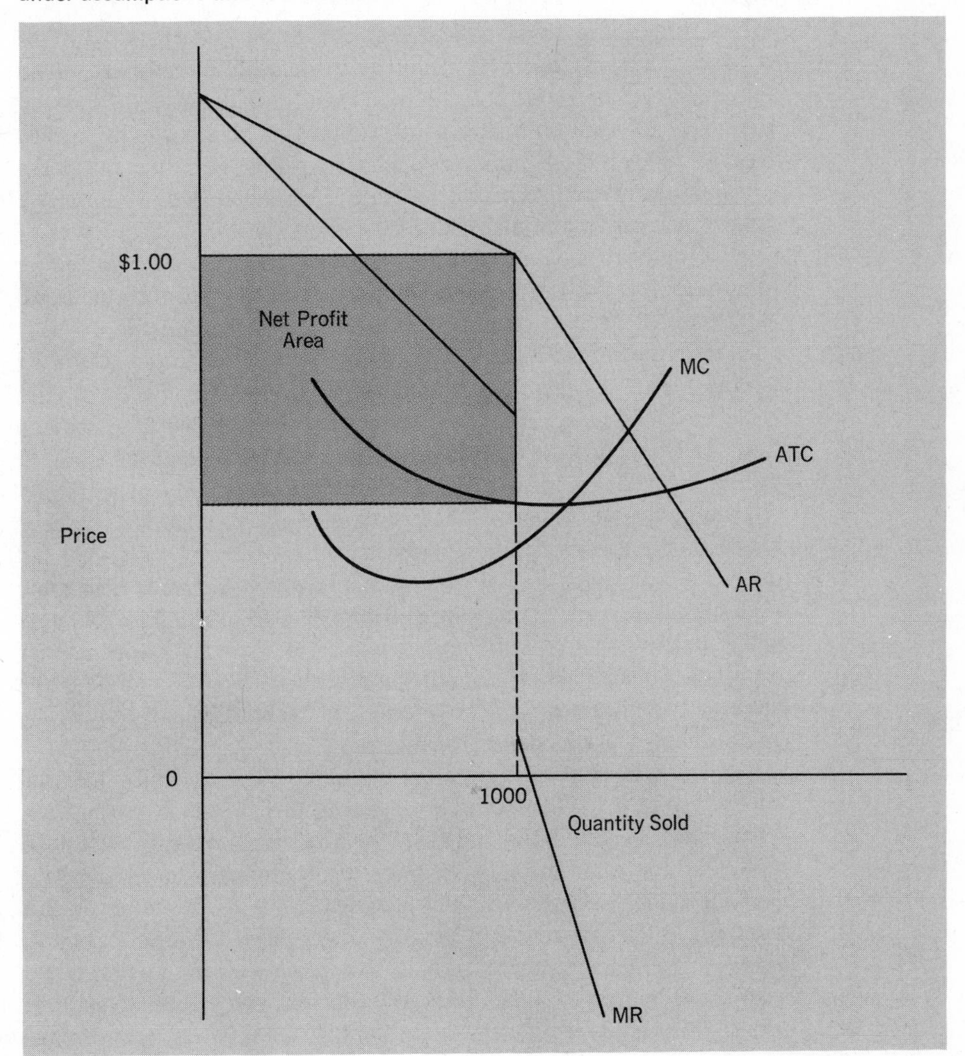

position of the *MR* curve. In Figure 15–10 we see that at the quantity of 1,000 units sold at the original price there is a gap or discontinuous section in the *MR* curve where it changes position sharply as a result of the change in elasticity of the *AR* curve at its kink.

In an extreme case we might assume that the kink is sharp enough that the *AR* curve at this point suddenly changes from being elastic to inelastic. In such a situation the *MR* curve would have to lie above the base line in the segment corresponding to the elastic part of the *AR* curve, but at the kink where it suddenly changes to inelastic, the *MR* curve would necessarily show a gap where it drops below the base line.

If we now place some typical cost curves on our graph with the *MC* curve crossing the *MR* curve at the discontinuous part, as in Figure 15–10, the point of maximum profit is clearly at the present price of $1.00, and with the quantity that can be sold at this price. What is perhaps more important, this price may continue to be the best price even though costs of production are changed. Suppose we assume that raw material or labor costs rise so that the position of the *ATC* and *MC* curves are shifted upward. So long as the *MC* curve still crosses the *MR* curve in the discontinuous part, this firm will find that, despite the reduction in net profit caused by the increase in costs, it cannot afford to raise the price. At any higher price profit would be less, as shown by the fact that marginal revenue on the lost sales would be above marginal cost. At any price below $1.00 the positions of the *MR* and *MC* curves show that the extra units sold add less to revenue than they add to costs and therefore reduce net profit.

**Disappearance of the Kink.** Although many economists believe that the existence of conditions indicated graphically by a kink has led to considerable price stability in various oligopolistic industries, some research has revealed other oligopolies where frequent price changes appear to show that no kink exists. In many of these industries further examination reveals that certain conditions exist that eliminate the uncertainty by each producer about what actions will be taken by rival firms if a price change is initiated.

For example, at certain times in the past U.S. Steel and American Tobacco were the accepted price leaders in their respective industries. When market conditions indicated that a price change would be profitable, the other firms waited for the traditional leader to make the change and then immediately matched it. No illegal collusion was required, but the price could be moved to a level yielding monopoly profit almost as certainly as though only one producer existed in the industry. Failure of some firms to follow a price leader, such as occurred in the steel industry in the spring of 1962, however, creates uncertainty about reactions to price changes and restores the kink.

Another situation that eliminates uncertainty about the reaction of rivals is the existence of considerable inflationary pressure. If production costs for all firms have recently increased because of inflationary conditions, the profit margins for all producers will have been reduced, and it is almost certain that all firms will be happy to follow the one who happens to announce an increase first.

A general increase in the demand for the product that shifts the *AR* curve of all the firms to the right will also reduce the uncertainty about price changes by competitors. If all the firms are producing close to capacity, each will be unable to benefit from attracting customers by quoting lower prices. The firm initiating the price increase can be almost certain that others will follow, because the higher price means a greater profit margin, and there is no opportunity to increase sales by maintaining the old lower price.

Various other conditions may lead to the elimination of uncertainty about the price policies of competing firms in an oligopoly. Whenever uncertainty disappears, the cause of the kink in the *AR* curve is eliminated. In such circumstances there is no fear of changing prices, and an important pressure for maintaining stability at the existing price level is gone. Nevertheless, it seems reasonable to believe that this fear does frequently exist in oligopolistic situations, and when it does we have a sound explanation for the price stability so often found in oligopolistic industries.

CHAPTER

16

# Changing Production Capacity of the Firm

In the preceding two chapters we considered the problems of cost and revenue faced by the firm as it deals with price and output adjustments in an existing plant. Under these conditions the maximization of profit involves a balancing of the effects of a change in the output level upon costs and upon revenue. Now we must turn to the question of when management should change its production capacity either by building a new plant or by abandoning an existing one. The aggregate of such individual decisions will determine the rate of growth in the production capacity of the private sector of the economy.

## DECISION TO BUILD A NEW PLANT

**Role of Expectations.** In the decision to build a new plant, as in any other business decision, the effects upon both costs and revenue must be considered. Because the construction of new capacity affects costs and revenues over a long period of time, prediction is an important part of the decision process. Uncertainty about the effect of such decisions is greatly increased by the movement from the short run into the long run. It is difficult enough for businessmen to estimate accurately the effect on costs and market prices of a 10-per-cent increase in output next month. But it is far more difficult to judge what selling prices will be three years from now when a new plant is completed or what production costs will be at that time. Changes in judgment by businessmen as to what the future will bring are extremely important in determining the rate of investment in plants and machinery. When management is optimistic about the possibility for future profits, investment will be high. Any adverse change in these expectations will cause a decline in investment, even though actual profits have not yet commenced to fall.

**Effect of Increased Consumer Demand.** Let us consider first a firm with some control over prices, such as in oligopoly, monopolistic competition, or monopoly. Such a firm will add to an existing plant when sales increase sufficiently to cause movement along the short-run average total-cost curve to a point where unit costs are unduly high. Such a firm will not add to production capacity unless it believes that the increase in sales will be sufficiently permanent for the additional plant to earn a regular profit, not just a temporary one. In Figure 16–1 we see a shift in the *AR* curve adequate to cause management to consider the building of a new plant. The original *AR* or demand curve gives a maximum profit position, indicated by the intersection of the *MR* and *MC* curves, well short of the low-cost point. Any small increase in demand gives rise to a welcome increase in profit, because unit costs fall and volume rises, but the firm would not necessarily feel any need for additional productive capacity.

As increased consumer demand shifts the *AR* curve out toward its position at *AR′* in Figure 16–1, the situation would begin to change. Each movement of the *AR* curve to the right would pull the *MR* curve with it. As the shift in the position of the intersection of the *MR* and *MC* curves moves output toward the low-cost point and then beyond it, as shown by the *MR′* curve in Figure 16–1, each increase in sales volume would involve a rise in unit costs. Cost per unit at *X′* may still be below the original level at *X*, but it has risen above the unit cost shown where *MC* crosses *ATC*. At some point in this steady increase of output management would decide that unit costs would be lower with a second plant, even though neither plant would have sales adequate to enable it to reach its low-cost point.

It is worth noting in examining Figure 16–1 that the firm is benefiting from the increased consumer demand, both by an expansion of sales volume from *Q* to *Q′* units, and by the charging of the higher price at *P′* instead of *P*. After the construction of a new plant the total output of the firm would be divided between new and old, with each plant producing an appropriate share of total output. Under these conditions the price yielding the maximum profit might move somewhat closer to the original figure. This change in the price yielding the greatest profit would be the result of benefits secured by operating each plant closer to its low-cost point and by the increased sales volume resulting from the price reduction. Management would determine the exact price by equating marginal cost and marginal revenue in each plant. Such adjustment of prices would be possible only in an

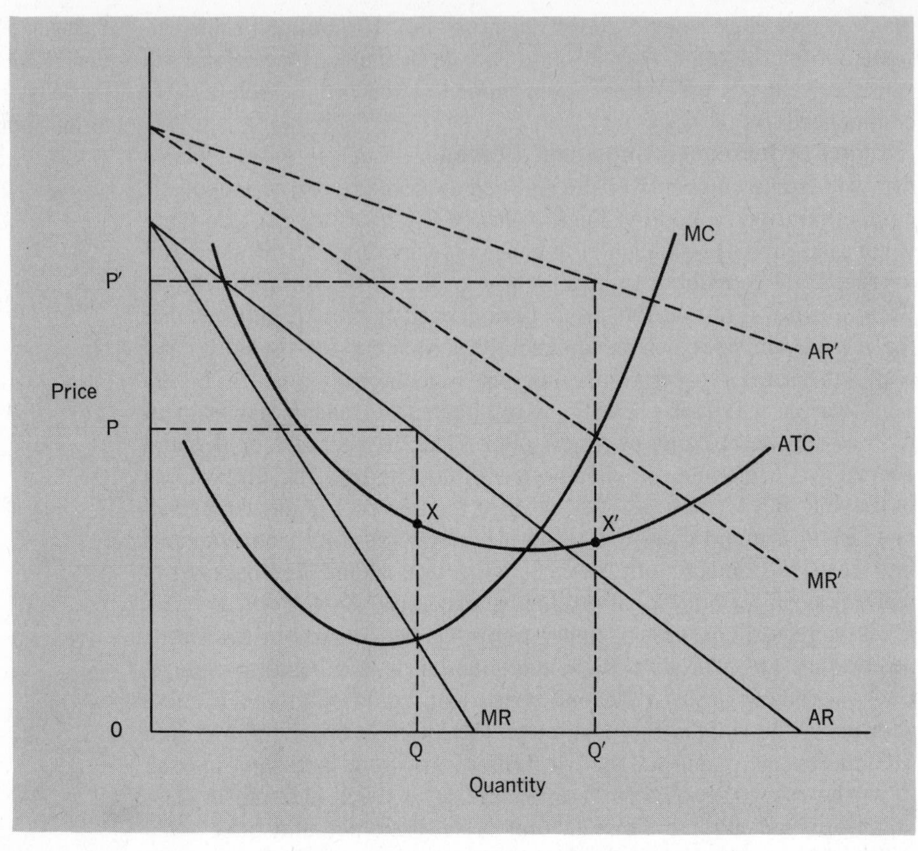


**Figure 16–1.** Effect upon unit costs of a firm with sloped *AR* curve when increased consumer demand forces an expansion of output.

industry where serious fears of a price war or other unpleasant repercussions did not exist. The marginal cost in each plant would depend upon a great many factors, such as size, location, and age.

**Effect of Technological Progress.** Another cause of investment in new plant capacity is technological progress. Research makes possible the development of new or improved products and cheaper ways of making existing products. The businessman who first makes successful use of these new methods has a significant advantage over his competitors. A new or improved product tends to cause a movement to the right in the *AR* curve as customers shift from the old to the new product and as entirely new buyers appear. The movement to the right of the average-revenue curve gives rise to a higher profit, both as a result of the increase in volume of sales and the higher price made possible by the improved quality of the product. The effect upon profit and output for the firm making the innovation resembles the result of an independent increase in consumer demand, as shown in Figure 16–1. But there is one significant difference in the two cases. All producers tend to benefit from an independent increase in consumer demand, but in the innovation situation only those firms that adopt the improved product at an early stage secure the benefits of a shift of customers from those with slower acting managements.

The effect of research that reduces production costs for an existing product is somewhat different. The advantage to the firm accepting this innovation comes largely from the increase in the profit margin that occurs when the cost curve is lowered, as pictured in Figure 16–2. The old profit area *ABCD* was secured with a profit margin of *BC*, and the new, larger profit area is based upon the higher profit margin *HI*. The decline in costs permits an increased profit margin despite a decline in selling price. The reduction in price is designed to take advantage of the possibility of expanded sales as a source of additional

**Figure 16–2.** Effect on profit of a drop in costs caused by a technological change in firm with control over price.

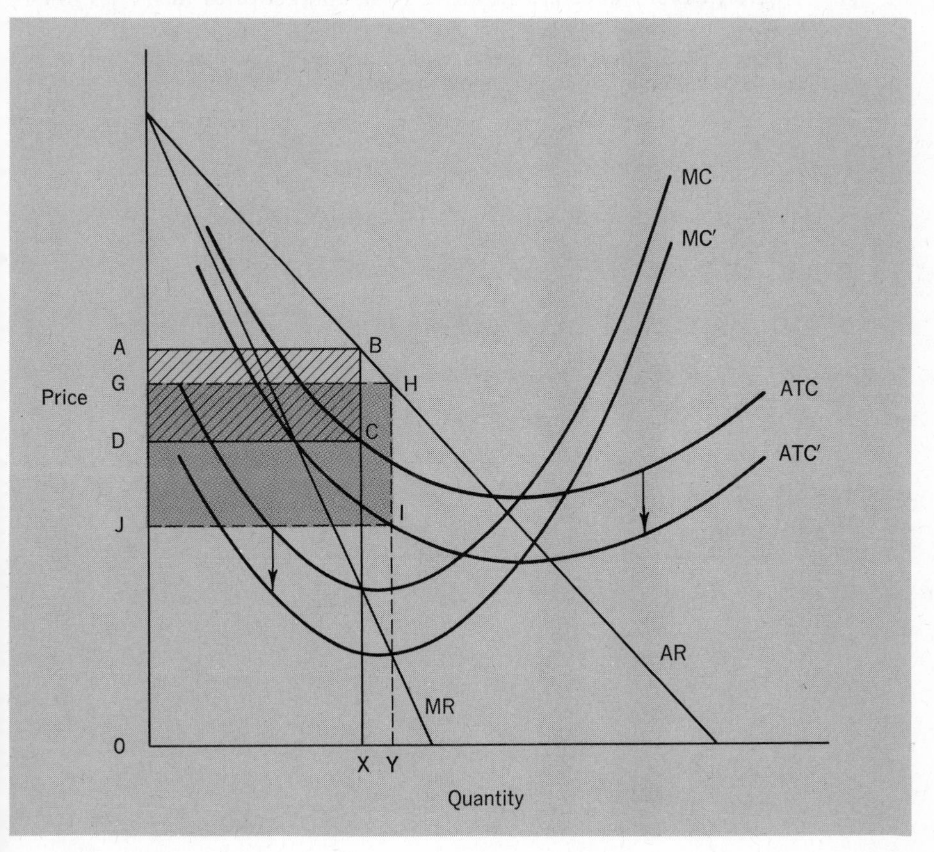

profit. The new profit area *GHIJ* has been increased both by the greater margin of profit per unit and by the increase in sales volume. As always, the exact operating level and selling price that will maximize profit is determined by the intersection of the *MC* and *MR* curves. The new intersection of the marginal curves after the decline in costs resulting from the technological improvement shows the point of maximum profit to be at an output of *OY* units and with a price of *OG*.

**Expansion by Firm Under Pure Competition.** When the firm has no control over the selling price, as under pure competition, it can only react to the profit possibilities created by the market. If demand and supply push the market price up to a level where the firm can earn a profit, and if the price is expected to remain at such a point, energetic managements will begin to plan expansion. Because the *AR–MR* curve of the firm under pure competition is horizontal, it must intersect the *MC* curve beyond the low-cost point if a profit is being earned. In Figure 16–3, at price *OP* the firm sells *OQ* units and barely covers all economic costs. If the market price then rises to *OP′*

**Figure 16–3.** Effect of an increase in market price upon levels of output and unit costs for a firm under pure competition.

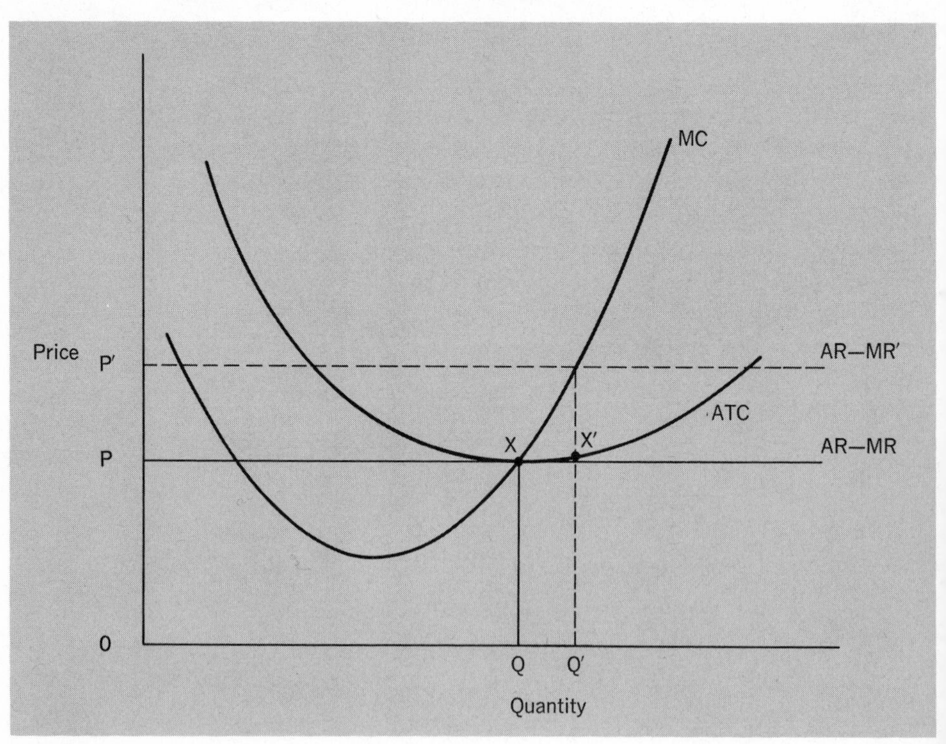

output will be expanded to $OQ'$ units. But this increase in output leads to a movement upward along the *ATC* curve from *X* to *X'*. This movement to a higher unit cost means that the firm has exceeded the most efficient operating level for this plant. Lower costs per unit under these conditions can be achieved only by an expansion of capacity. Thus, under pure competition the appearance of economic profit arising from an increased price is inevitably accompanied by a rise in average total costs in existing plants, which provides motivation for new construction.

The primary difference between Figure 16–3 and Figure 16–1 is that the negatively sloped *AR* curve found under monopoly or partial monopoly may permit the firm to earn a profit while it is still operating short of the low-cost point. Under such conditions a limited expansion of output will not bring a rise in average total costs. Thus, the firm with some control over prices will not necessarily expand capacity as a result of limited increases in consumer demand, even though a significant profit is being earned. On the other hand, under pure competition the earning of an economic profit will always provide the firm with an incentive to expand capacity, because it is operating in the rising segment of the *ATC* curve. This incentive becomes effective at a point where the combined output can be produced more cheaply in two plants than in one.

## DECISION TO ABANDON AN EXISTING PLANT

**Effect of Pessimistic Business Expectations.** The decision to abandon an existing plant, like the decision to expand, can be reached only after considering business conditions that are expected to exist sometime in the future. A plant is not abandoned or scrapped merely because it is currently operating at a loss, but only when management cannot see reasonable prospects for covering costs in the future.

Unfortunately, the decision to abandon an existing plant usually involves some loss. Although it may be possible to secure a partial return of investment funds by sale of the building and equipment, the amount is likely to be much less than the book value of the fixed assets. The loss suffered by abandonment, then, will be the difference between book value (cost less depreciation) and scrap value. Management normally will not abandon a plant and accept this loss unless it anticipates that the loss suffered by further operations will be even greater. Under these circumstances the businessman has given up hope of earning a profit and must be satisfied with minimizing his loss.

**Relationship of Fixed and Variable Costs to Plant Abandonment.** Once a plant has been built management must deal with problems involving fixed costs. Except for the small scrap value that can be realized by sale of the equipment and building, management must accept the costs relating to these fixed assets as an expense that cannot be avoided. Thus, plant value must be written off as a depreciation cost during the operational life of the equipment, or it must be written off all at once as a cost of abandonment. Management cannot avoid this sunk cost; it can only decide whether under unfavorable conditions the loss will be less by continuing to operate than by closing down.

As we have seen, the decision to close down the plant does not relieve management of the fixed or sunk costs. What costs, then, are eliminated by closing down the plant? Clearly, the only savings will consist in the variable costs avoided for such items as production labor, raw materials, and power. Sales revenues, of course, drop to zero with the cessation of operations. Because shutting down the plant eliminates variable costs but leaves the fixed costs as a net loss, *it is usually better to continue operations so long as sales revenues are at least adequate to cover variable costs at some level of operations.*

For example, let us suppose that a certain plant has fixed costs for depreciation and related items of $100 per day and variable costs of $400 at a particular level of operations. If sales revenues exceed $400 per day, losses will be minimized by continuing operations. At sales of $410 management will be able to cover variable costs and have $10 to apply on the fixed costs so that the loss will be only $90 per day. If the plant is closed down, on the other hand, the loss would be $100 (the entire fixed cost).

Sometimes management will decide to cease plant operations without taking the final step of scrapping the plant. This decision is likely to be made when present conditions will not permit variable costs to be covered, but it is anticipated that sales opportunities will improve before the plant ceases to be usable. It should be noted that there are special costs associated with closing and reopening a plant, such as the training of a new labor force and protection of machinery against deterioration. Under these conditions management must decide whether losses will be minimized by continuing operations or by adding the special costs of closing and reopening the plant to the losses from fixed costs.

**Decision To Close Down by Firm with Control over Price.** We must not assume that all firms operating under monopolistic or partially monopolistic conditions will be making a profit. Although such firms may sometimes secure a profit by adjusting the selling price (a possibility closed to firms under pure competition), changes in costs or consumer demand may still bring a loss. When such losses are suffered, the decision must be made as to whether the loss will be smaller by closing down or by continuing operations.



In Figure 16–4A we have assumed a decrease in consumer demand that has moved the *AR* curve to the left and down so that it no longer lies above the *ATC* curve at any point. The point of best operations still remains at the output indicated by the intersection of *MR* and *MC*. But when we extend the vertical line up to the *AR* and *ATC* curves, we find that cost per unit at *B* lies above the selling price for this quantity at *C*. The distance *BC* thus represents a margin of loss on each unit sold, and the rectangle *ABCD* represents the total loss suffered. Despite this loss, however, we can see that this firm should still continue operations as long as the plant is in usable condition, because the loss suffered from closing down would be greater than the loss from continuing operations. This fact is evident when we observe that the *AR* curve at this level of operations still lies above

**Figure 16–4A.** Firm with control over price continues to operate: although losing money, it is covering variable costs, and loss by closing would be larger.

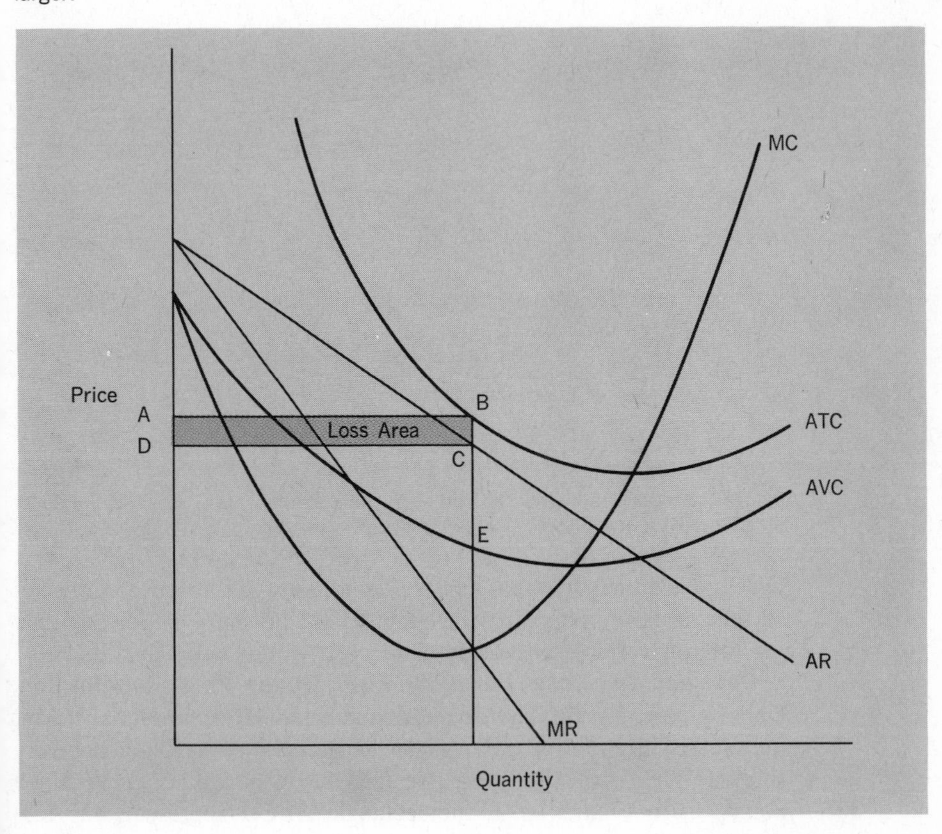

the *AVC* curve, so that variable costs are being covered and something additional is being earned to reduce the loss on the fixed costs.

On the other hand, when the *AR* curve is moved down still further and to the left to the position indicated by *AR′* in Figure 16–4B, we can see that the new loss would be so great that the firm now would find it desirable to close down the plant. Such a decision would be correct, because the *AR′* curve lies below the *AVC* curve at all points, so that operating revenue at no level of output covers variable costs.

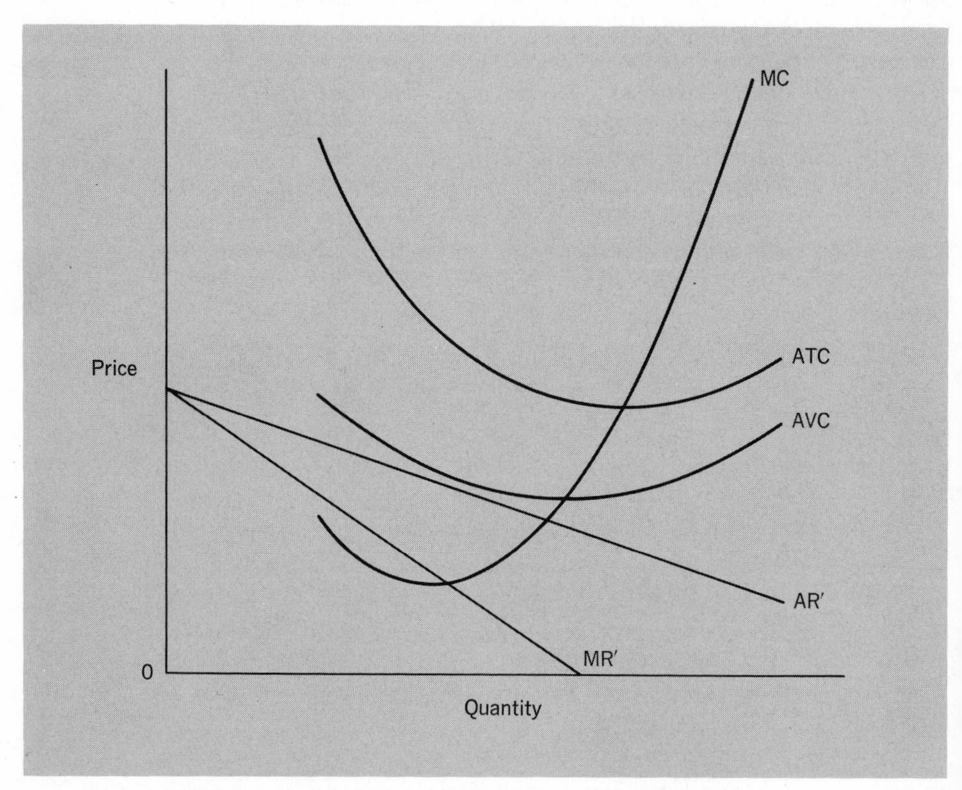


**Figure 16–4B.** Firm with control over price shuts down: it fails to cover variable costs, and loss by operating would be larger.

Unless it is anticipated that business conditions will improve very soon so that costs of reopening the plant might be more important than the loss on variable costs, the plant clearly should be shut down.

**Decision To Close Down by Firm Under Pure Competition.** Under pure competition with a horizontal *AR–MR* curve for the firm, the factors involved in the decision to shut down the plant are very similar. When the *AR–MR* curve falls below the *ATC* curve at all points, as in Figure 16–5, the rectangle *ABCD* represents the loss area. The distance $BC$ constitutes the margin of loss on each unit sold. But as long as the $AR–MR$ line lies above the $AVC$ curve, the firm will find that the loss involved in continuing operations will be less than the loss arising from the continued existence of fixed costs when the plant is closed down. Under these circumstances the firm will find it advantageous to continue operations.

When the selling price no longer covers variable costs per unit, as shown in Figure 16–5, where the $AR–MR'$ line lies below the $AVC$ curve, the firm will doubtless decide to close down, because losses from operations now would be even greater than those resulting from fixed costs. If we ignore the costs of closing and reopening the plant, the point of indifference in the decision to close down temporarily comes at the tangency of $AR$ to $AVC$. If the selling price of the product is expected to remain below $AVC$, the plant will be abandoned or scrapped.

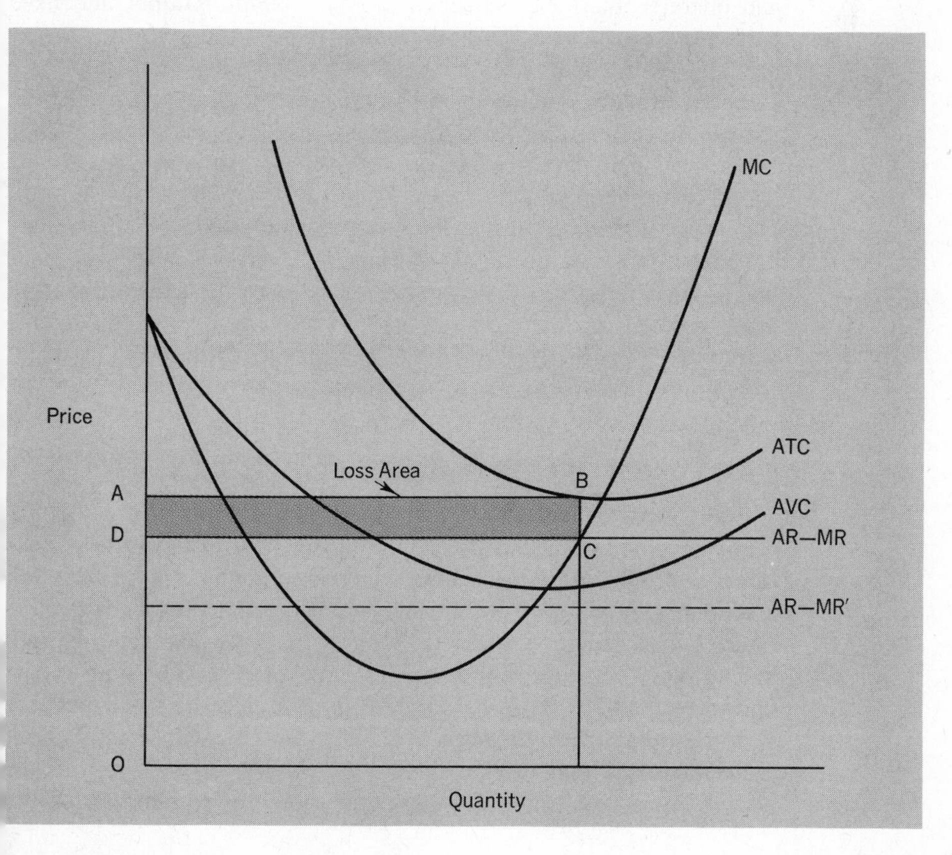


**Figure 16–5.** Loss by a firm operating under pure competition when the *AR-MR* curve drops below the *ATC* curve and abandonment when *AR-MR'* drops below the *AVC* curve.

**Comparison of Plant Shutdown Under Monopolistic and Under Competitive Conditions.** The only significant difference between Figure 16–5, showing the firm operating under competitive conditions, and Figure 16–4A, showing a monopolistic situation, is that when the *AR* curve is negatively sloped the shutdown point is at a lower per cent of output capacity than when the *AR* line is horizontal. Under pure competition a decline in market price brings the *AR* line to tangency with the *AVC* curve at its lowest point, but a sloped *AR* line can be tangent to *AVC* well short of its lowest point.

Elimination of excess capacity when demand decreases is, therefore, likely to come much more quickly under pure competition than it is under monopolistic conditions. For example, the complete monopolist, with several plants in operation, may have an option not open to the small competitive firm with only one plant. The monopolist may find that the restricted output essential to maintaining the desired selling price would reduce production in all of his plants well below efficient operating levels. But by appropriate allocation of output among plants the monopolist may be able to shut down some and operate others close to their low-cost points. Output and fixed costs are the same, but variable costs have been reduced, thus lowering total costs per unit. If the firm under oligopoly or monopolistic competition has a definite share of the market and several plants, the same option of shutting down some plants may also exist.

On the other hand, the firm under pure competition, even though it operates several plants, does not have this option. Restricted output by the individual firm will not prevent a decline in the selling price as a result of decreased consumer demand. Neither will combining sales help in reducing unit costs, because the competitive firm has a perfectly elastic demand and can sell any number of units it wishes at the market price. Thus it can operate at the low-cost point without the necessity of closing any plants.

## EQUILIBRIUM OF THE INDUSTRY

Equilibrium or balance is one of the basic concepts used by economists. It assumes that individuals in our society are subject to various forces that influence their actions, some pushing them in one direction and some in another. The individual is believed to respond to these forces by adjusting his actions as long as the force impinging on him in one direction is greater than the force or forces pushing in the opposite direction. Basic to this concept, however, is the belief that at some point these pressures on the individual will exactly offset each other, and that when a person has carried adjustments this far he will cease to change. For example, short-run equilibrium of the firm is based upon the idea that costs and revenues are the opposing forces acting upon business management and that changes in output will be made until additions to revenue exactly balance additions to cost. At this point the firm will maximize profit (or minimize loss), and there will be no reason for further changes in output until external pressures change costs or revenues.

In the same way that we think about a firm being in equilibrium or balance we can think of the output produced by an entire industry being in equilibrium. Such a balance will exist when the firms producing a particular item have no incentive either to open new plants or to close existing ones. An alternative way of stating the condition of equilibrium for the industry would be to say that decisions to open new plants were exactly balanced in terms of output capacity by decisions to close existing plants.

**Equilibrium of the Industry Under Monopoly.** The industry cannot be in equilibrium when the individual firms believe that they can either increase their profit by opening new plants or reduce their losses by closing existing ones. Suppose we start the study of equilibrium in an industry by analyzing the adjustments made by a complete monopolist who produces in several plants and controls the entire output of this industry. Let us simplify the analysis by further assuming that all plants including any new ones are exactly alike and have the same cost curves, with transportation costs to any part of the market being insignificant. Let us also assume that these plants have all achieved maximum economies of scale with presently known technological methods.

Under these conditions the monopolist would find his profit increased at the established selling price by building additional plants whenever consumer demand is expected to force operations in existing plants to undesirably high levels of unit costs. Because the margin of profit would be greatest for any individual plant when it is operating at the low cost point and additional plants can be built to operate at this same cost level, the number of plants required to maximize profit will be the number needed to satisfy customer demand at the previously determined selling price, with each plant operating at the low-cost point, as shown in Figure 16–6. In this graph the monopolist is shown with four plants, each producing 1,000 units per day at the low-cost point.

The price has been determined by equating *MR* and long-run marginal cost (*LRMC*). Because our assumptions permit all plants to have essentially the same costs, additional output from new plants will have the same low-cost point as previous ones, and our long-run average cost (*LRAC*) curve will be horizontal when we connect the series of low-cost points. Perfect adjustment of fixed factors is really assumed

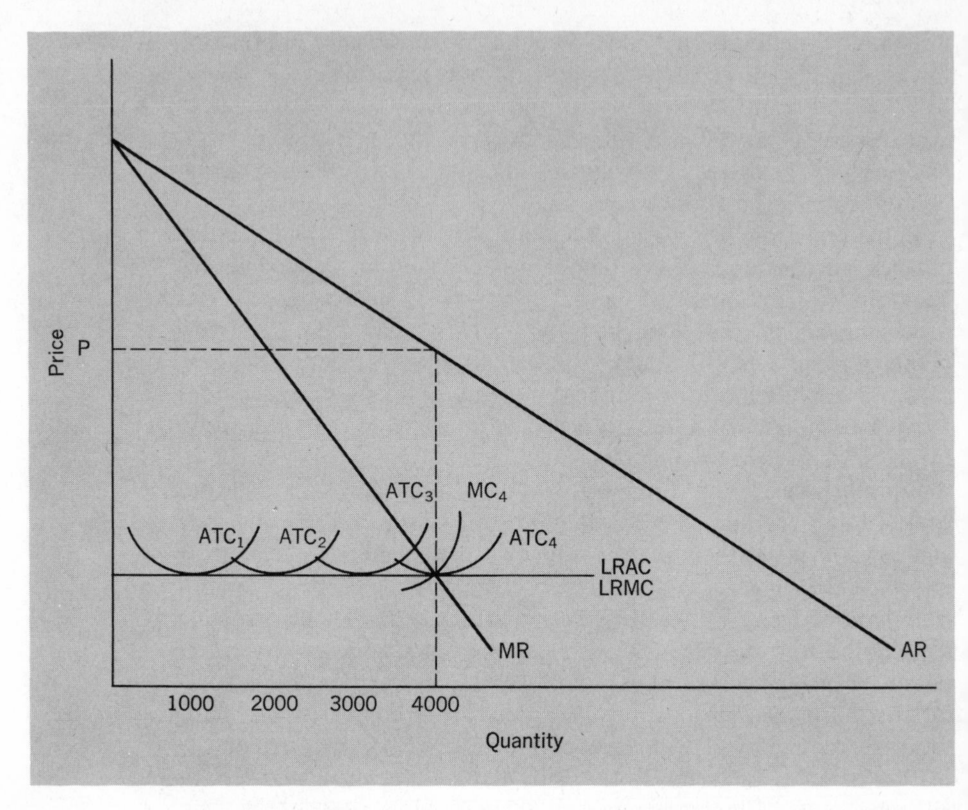


**Figure 16–6.** Equilibrium of a monopolized industry under constant cost conditions.

by this straight-line *LRAC*. This constant cost situation in Figure 16–6 will cause the *LRMC* to lie along the horizontal *LRAC*, and the intersection of *MR* with this *LRMC* will determine the total output capacity desired by the monopolist. The *AR* or consumer demand will then indicate the price the monopolist can charge for this volume of sales, shown as *P* in Figure 16–6.

Short-run profit earned by each plant is also being maximized as shown by the fact that the short-run marginal cost ($MC^4$ for plant No. 4) has been equated with the marginal revenue, as shown by the intersection of *MR* and $MC^4$. Marginal cost for each of the four plants would be the same if they were all operating at the same level of output. Therefore, the summation of the four *MC* curves would be equated with the total *MR* curve. This industry would now be in equilibrium, because any change in operating levels or in number of plants while consumer demand and technology remain constant would reduce total profit. Additional plants would be required only if a change in consumer demand shifted the *AR* and *MR* curves to the right or technological change permitted a lower position for the cost curves.

On the other hand, a movement of the *AR* and *MR* curves in Figure 16–6 to the left would mean that the equilibrium was disturbed as operations fell short of the low-cost point. For example, if the quantity that can be sold at the existing price drops from 4,000 to 3,000 units per day, the monopolist could either operate all four plants at outputs of 750 units or close down one plant and operate the remaining three at 1,000 units. Although charging the fixed costs of the closed-down plant to the income earned by the three plants remaining in operation would reduce the profits earned by them, the closing down of one plant would probably permit more efficient utilization of variable factors in the operating plants. A decision to close down one of the plants would be made, however, only if it would result in more efficient use of the variable factors and if the expenses of closing down and reopening did not exceed the savings made in utilization of the variable factors.

Plant shutdown under assumptions of varying costs in the various production units is a much simpler problem than with constant costs. The low-cost plants would almost certainly be making more efficient use of the variable factors, and production would be concentrated in them. The less efficient plants would be closed down first as a result of any decrease in consumer demand and would be abandoned unless future increases in demand were anticipated.

**Equilibrium of an Industry Under Oligopoly.** If each producer under oligopoly has an established share of the market, his reactions will be much the same as those of the monopolist when he considers expansion of plant capacity. One difference will be that fear of setting off a price war will make each member of the oligopoly reluctant to change selling prices when consumer demand increases. Only if there is a definite tradition of price leadership or some similar method of avoiding disastrous price competition will firms raise prices right away. Any movement of the *AR* curve to the right may, therefore, fail to result in a price change. Instead, it may lead to construction of new plant capacity at the point where the *MR* curve intersects the *LRMC* at the point representing a need for this additional output.

In an oligopolistic industry, closing down capacity no longer needed because of decreased consumer demand would follow the same pattern as that of the monopolist, provided each producer operates several plants. But if an oligopolist has a small share of the market and operates only one plant, the shift of the *AR* curve to the left will reduce profit and possibly even cause a net loss. This owner will not close his plant, however, unless the selling price of the industry fails to cover variable costs. Price wars can sometimes be caused by attempts of small producers facing plant closings to secure a larger share of the market by price concessions.

**Equilibrium of the Industry Under Monopolistic Competition.** With differentiation of the product, equilibrium of the industry is somewhat less determinate. Changes in consumer preference, whether autonomous or caused by selling effort, may result in expansion of plant capacity by the favored firms while other producers are forced to close down existing plants. Each producer in an industry characterized by monopolistic competition also has options for maximizing profit not open under oligopoly with undifferentiated product. Advertising expenditures and selling prices may be adjusted as the individual firm sees fit. Variations in product quality and reputation make price wars less feared than under oligopoly. The decision by the firm concerning changes in output capacity will still be made, however, on the basis of attempting over the long run to equate marginal cost and marginal revenue. The industry will be in equilibrium only when each firm is maximizing profit, or minimizing loss, and has no incentive either to expand or to contract. An alternative position of equilibrium might be said to exist when the expansion of capacity by some firms was exactly offset by the contraction of others.

The possibility of entry of new firms as the source of additional plant capacity does not exist under monopolistic conditions and is usually not significant in an oligopolistic industry. But under monopolistic competition it is usually possible for new producers to enter the market. Expansion of plant capacity by new firms will tend to occur so long as economic profit can reasonably be anticipated. As new producers enter the market they will take a share of the sales now being made by other firms. Such an expansion of capacity, therefore, will tend to move the *AR* and *MR* curves of existing firms to the left. This movement will continue so long as people outside the industry believe that economic profit can be earned by going into production. The point where such entrance ceases is shown in Figure 16–7 by the position of the *AR* curve tangent to the short-run *ATC* curve. If such a firm, which is earning no economic profit, is considered typical by other firms contemplating entrance into the industry, they will not be attracted by the opportunity. When this situation exists the industry will be in equilibrium, because outsiders will not be entering the industry. On the other hand, typical existing firms are not suffering net losses and will not be leaving the industry.

**Definition of Costs in Economic Equilibrium.** The use of the term *economic profit,* rather than simple *profit,* in the preceding analysis should be carefully noted by the student. The economist finds it desirable to define costs in calculating profit somewhat differently than the accountant or governmental tax expert. It has already been

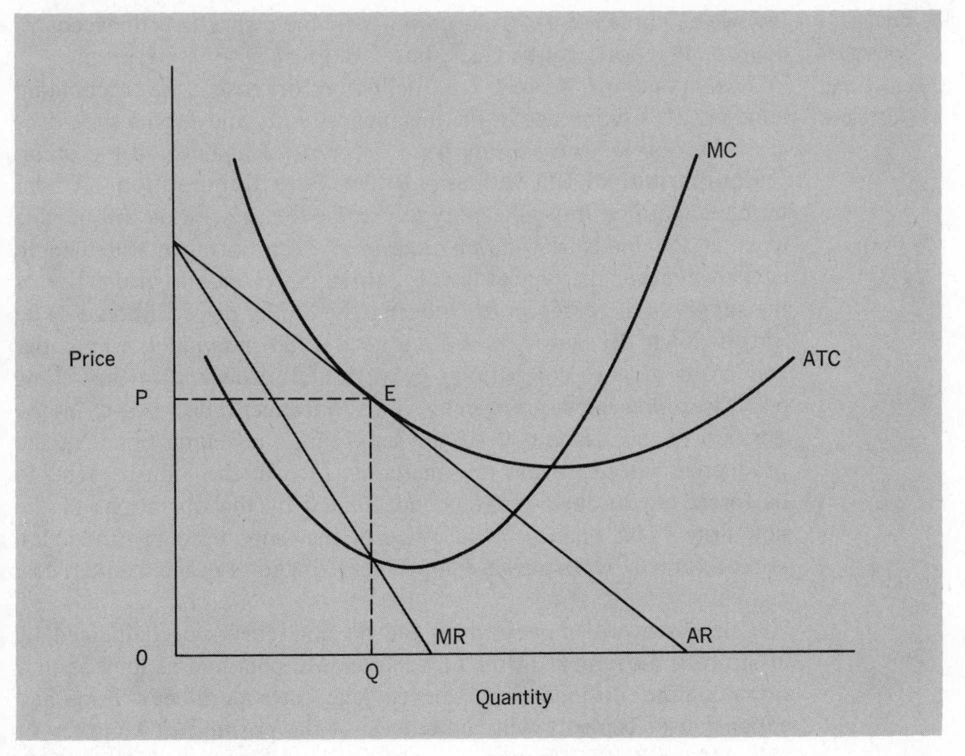


**Figure 16–7.** Equilibrium profit position of a typical firm in an industry under monopolistic competition.

pointed out in Chapter 14 that the economist includes as a cost any payment that must be made in order to secure the production of a particular good or service. In the long run, the owner of a business must secure a return for his labor and the use of his property equal to what he could secure by employing them in alternative opportunities, and the economist considers such payments to be a cost of production. On the other hand, normal accounting and tax procedures insist that payments made to the owner of a business be considered a share of the profit rather than a cost.

Let us apply these two separate definitions of cost to the situation represented by the typical firm in a differentiated product industry in equilibrium, as shown in Figure 16–7. The economist would say that this firm is earning zero economic profit because costs, including normal return to the owner, just equal sales revenue; but the accountant would say that the firm is earning an accounting profit or return to the owner about equal to that of firms in a similar situation in other industries. The difference results from the fact that the cost curves in Figure 16–7 were drawn according to the economist's definition and include as implicit costs those earnings by the owner that the accountant would report, not as costs, but as normal accounting profit.

The economist prefers one definition of costs; the accountant another. This difference in the meaning of costs and profits should be carefully observed in shifting from one type of analysis to the other.

**Equilibrium of the Industry Under Pure Competition.** Under pure competition it is customary to assume that new firms will be able to enter the industry without hindrance. Such entrance will tend to occur whenever the typical firm is earning an economic profit. But as the supply is increased in the industry the selling price will tend to be forced down. Because the *AR* curve for the individual firm under conditions of pure competition is horizontal, a decline in the selling price is represented graphically by a movement downward in the position of the *AR* curve. At the same time the selling prices of the productive resources and raw materials used in the industry tend to be forced up by the extra demand created by the operations of the new firms. This change in the price of the items used in production is represented by an upward movement of the *ATC* and other cost curves.

This downward movement of the revenue curves accompanied by an upward movement of the cost curves will continue as long as new firms continue to enter the industry. The entrance of new firms and expansion of capacity will continue until the position of tangency of *AR–MR* with *ATC* for the typical firm, as indicated in Figure 16–8, is attained. Until the movement of *AR–MR* and *ATC* results in tangency the existence of an economic profit, as shown by *AR–MR′*, provides an incentive for further movement of firms into the industry.

On the other hand, if a rise in costs or a decline in selling price causes the situation shown by the position of *AR–MR″* in Figure 16–8, it is obvious that this typical firm will be operating at an economic loss. Although this economic loss may not be large enough to prevent the appearance of some accounting profit, the income secured by the owner will be less than he can earn by using his resources in alternative occupations, and he will have strong inducement to leave the industry. Gradual closing down of plants, either when variable costs are not covered or fixed assets are worn-out, will tend to reduce bidding for the productive factors used in the industry and so reduce their prices. At the same time the reduced output of the product tends to increase its selling price. This rise in selling price of the product and fall in production costs continues until *AR–MR″* has shifted relative to the *ATC* curve to the point of tangency shown by *AR–MR*. At this point the typical firm will no longer be suffering an economic loss, owners will be securing normal returns, and exit of firms from the industry will cease.

Equilibrium of the industry under conditions of pure competition can exist, therefore, only when the typical firm is neither earning an economic profit nor suffering an economic loss. At this equilibrium position typical owners are securing normal returns for the use of productive resources supplied by them, but no more than normal, so that firms have no incentive to change productive capacity of the industry either by entering or by leaving. Productive capacity is in balance relative to the pressures being exerted on the firms, and the industry is in equilibrium.

Changing Production Capacity of the Firm

**Benefits of Competitive Equilibrium.** The student should note particularly that this position of equilibrium under conditions of competition gives a tangency of the *AR* curve with the *ATC* curve for the typical firm at the low-cost point. In other words, when equilibrium of the industry is reached under pure competition the typical firm will be able to cover all costs only at the low-cost point. It will, therefore, tend to be operating at its most efficient level of output. It should be noted also that at this equilibrium position the

**Figure 16–8.** Equilibrium in competitive industry with *AR-MR* curve tangent to *ATC* curve.

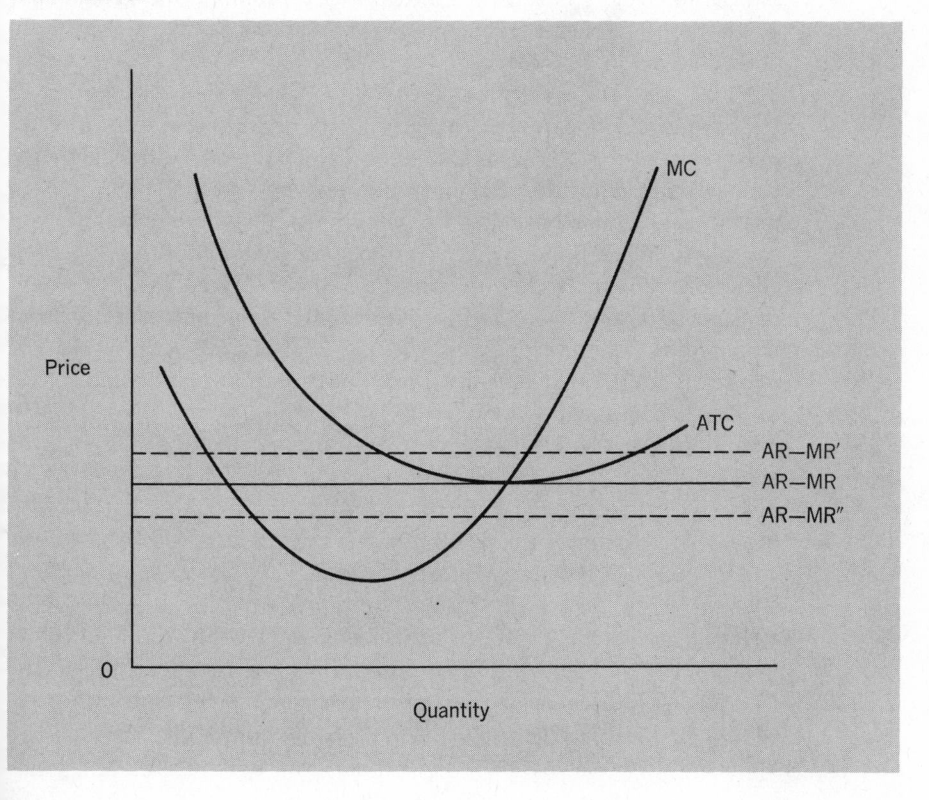

consuming public is paying the lowest possible price that will cover all costs of production. For the economist, then, the social advantages of having industries operating as closely as possible to conditions of pure competition are that firms tend to operate at their most efficient output levels and consumers get the product at the lowest possible price.

If the equilibrium of the industry under monopolistic competition, as shown in Figure 16–7 is studied, the disadvantages suffered by society become apparent. Although economic profit has disappeared, the point of tangency of the *AR* and *ATC* curves is short of the low-cost point. The individual firm is not operating at its most efficient output level, and the consumer is paying a higher price than would be required to cover all costs at the low-cost point.

**Function of Economic Profit in Growth.** As we have developed our analysis of the equilibrium of an industry above, it is clear that the existence of economic profit is not necessary to secure the continuance of production. Normal returns determined by alternative opportunities provide the incentive for carrying on production at existing levels. It must be remembered that this implicit cost of normal returns to owners is shown, however, as a profit by the accountant. The existence of some accounting profit is essential to the maintenance of production in an industry.

What, then, is the function performed by economic profit (or loss)? It is primarily to motivate changes in the productive capacity of an industry in response to changes in consumer demand or in technology. Our private enterprise economy depends upon economic profit to provide individual businessmen with the incentive to expand plant capacity in response to our needs. An essential aspect of the American economic system is that no central authority gives orders for expansion or contraction; rather, individual producers react to profit possibilities determined by impersonal changes taking place in the market. The fact that individual reactions to profit opportunities tend to cause these temporary profits to disappear under competitive conditions, as equilibrium is restored, means that the existence of economic profit serves a function only when the adjustment is taking place. The drive by the individual to earn this temporary profit also provides the assurance under competition that prices will be as low as costs permit and that plant capacity will be used at most efficient levels.

Under complete, or even partial, monopoly we have noted, however, that economic profit fails to perform these functions effectively. Monopolistic firms tend to avoid expansion of plant capacity in response to the existence of economic profit unless they are able to anticipate production that will force costs to undesirably high levels or will benefit from significant increasing returns to scale. If maximum profit can be earned by maintaining market price at a level that limits the volume of sales to levels short of the most efficient production points, then the existence of economic profit may provide no incentive for expansion of plant capacity. Nor under monopolistic conditions does the consumer have the assurance that the market price will be pushed down to a level barely covering all economic costs. In many industries the ability of producers with monopolistic power to prevent the entry of new firms enables them to avoid the downward pressure on market prices that would exist under competitive conditions.

The function of economic loss in an individual enterprise economy is to secure the elimination of unnecessary plant capacity. In the early days of this century it was quite as essential that the output of buggies and horse collars be reduced as it was that the production of automobiles and gasoline be expanded. As we have already noted, a shift of consumer demand tended to reduce the price of horse collars and left producing firms with an economic loss that eventually caused most plants to be closed. Although we can be sympathetic with the owners of firms no longer needed and with their workers, it is essential that a dynamic society have adequate incentives for the elimination of unnecessary production. Economic loss resulting from shifts in consumer demand or changes in methods of production performs this function.

**Change and Growth in a Dynamic Economy.** If an economy is to grow, the changes that take place in the positions of the *AR* and *ATC* curves must be such that they provide the individual firm with motive for expansion of plant capacity. Shifts of demand curves to the right or the cost curves downward must take place in order to provide the profit incentive and the relatively full utilization of capacity that will be essential in any industry that is to expand.

One important factor in determining the rate of growth in industrial output is change in population size. Since the end of World War II most nations in Western Europe and North America have had rapid increases in population. These increases that raise the number of consumers have shifted the demand curves of firms in many industries sharply to the right, increased profit margins, and caused existing plants to be operated beyond their low-cost points. During this same period increases in per capita income were resulting in higher standards of living, which also meant that firms selling consumer goods had their demand curves shifted to the right. Accumulated shortages in housing, automobiles, clothing, and many other items resulted from the depression of the 1930's and World War II. When these and other causes of increased consumer demand are examined, the satisfactory rate of growth that has been experienced by the private enterprise system in Western Europe, Canada, and the United States for most of the time since 1945 becomes understandable. It is only since about 1958 that some of these forces increasing consumer demand have commenced to weaken and that we have become concerned about the rate of growth in the United States.

Other changes that are important in determining the growth of our economy have to do with the cost curves. Technological progress that lowers the position of the cost curves for firms making the change also influences the profit margins and provides incentives for new plant construction. The research that brings technological progress depends upon proper financial support by government and industry and upon an adequate supply of qualified research personnel being trained in our educational system. Businessmen and consumers must continue to accept new processes and new products. We must also prevent the development of monopolistic controls that limit increases in output capacity because of the belief that profit will be maximized by maintaining high selling prices rather than by increasing the volume of sales.

**Governmental Policies and Growth.** If our economy is to continue to depend upon private initiative for the decisions that bring growth and development, government must encourage the necessary private actions. Because one powerful motivation for plant investment is the existence of opportunities for profit, our political leaders can take advantage of the continuous search for profit. Taxation obviously can be used to provide incentives for desirable action. During the Korean fighting, when the defense authorities believed that expansion of certain basic industries, such as steel, was essential, the government permitted the companies to charge off new plants over very short time periods. This enlarged charge for depreciation did not reduce actual profit, but it did reduce the reported profit upon which the amount of tax liability would be based. Because corporations generally paid a tax on profits of 52 per cent, this tax saving provided a strong motivation for plant expansion. It should be noted that the government did not try to motivate plant construction by increasing overall profits through a general tax reduction. Rather, it permitted the tax saving only in connection with a particular action. Such a tax cut would not necessarily be desirable under all conditions, but it does illustrate the point that taxes can be modified to encourage growth. It is obvious that other tax policies could seriously discourage industrial expansion.

Bitter struggles between labor unions and corporate management in recent years have increasingly forced the government to intervene for the protection of the general public. Laws dealing with these problems must attempt to secure justice for both parties without undue interruption in the production of essential goods and services. On the other hand, decisions reached in regard to such matters as wage levels, hours worked, and working conditions may also influence output, prices, and profits. Economic growth will be influenced by the results of bargaining over these matters.

Another area in which governmental policies will influence growth lies in the field of antitrust activities. We have already shown how profit under monopolistic conditions tends to be associated with restricted output. Antitrust laws have probably contributed to the encouragement of growth in many American industries by penalizing many of these restrictions.

We have noticed also that industries tend to build new plants when they can reasonably expect that sales will keep the added output capacity utilized. Governmental efforts to keep the economy stabilized at high levels of employment tend to assure a general level of sales and profits that encourage private business expansion.

Protective tariffs have frequently been used in the past to secure industrial expansion. This method of encouragement has serious disadvantages that can best be examined while studying problems of international trade in a later chapter. Special subsidies for locating plants in particular states or cities should also be used with extreme care.

**Summary.** Decisions to expand plant capacity depend more upon expected profits than upon realized profits. Increased consumer demand under conditions of monopoly, oligopoly, and monopolistic competition shift the *AR* and *MR* curves to the right and tend to cause plant expansion when efficient operating levels are exceeded in existing plants. Technological progress may either improve products or reduce costs and may motivate expansion for firms accepting the change.

Under pure competition changes in market price cause movement up or down in the horizontal *AR–MR* curve and motivate changes in plant capacity. The essential difference when compared with monopolistic conditions is that competitive profit exists only when output of the firm has passed the low-cost point, and therefore, additional capacity would be advantageous. If profit expectations are pessimistic and losses are suffered, the firm will close a plant only when revenues will not cover variable costs.

Under monopolistic conditions the point of least loss may be far short of the low-cost point, but under pure competition the point of least loss will be much closer to the low-cost point because of the horizontal slope of the *AR* curve. Elimination of excess capacity tends to happen more rapidly under pure competition than under complete or partial monopoly.

Equilibrium of the industry is achieved when plant capacity is neither being increased nor decreased. Under monopoly or oligopoly, where entry of new firms is restricted, significant profits may exist without causing expansion in the industry. When entry into the industry is relatively free the position of equilibrium requires the elimination of economic profit.

Economic profit differs from accounting profit in that the expenses or costs deducted include an implicit return to the owner for his labor and the use of his property. The primary function of profit or loss in our economy is to motivate changes in productive capacity in each industry. A dynamic economy has constant changes in such things as population size, products, methods of production, and personal income, which motivate growth through expansion of plant capacity. Governmental policies relative to taxes, labor–management relations, and economic stability will also influence the growth rate of an economy.

## QUESTIONS

1. Why is the role of expectations more important in the long run than in the short run?
2. Under what conditions will a firm decide to build an additional plant as a result of increased consumer demand for its product?
3. Explain the role of technological progress in decisions relative to new plant construction.
4. Why will the existence of economic profit always provide a firm operating under pure competition with an incentive to expand capacity? Why is this profit incentive not always effective under monopolistic conditions?
5. Under what conditions will a firm decide to abandon an existing plant even though it may not be worn-out?
6. Why will excess plants be closed down more quickly as output falls short of the low-cost point when the industry is competitive than when it is monopolistic?
7. What determines how much consumer demand must increase before a monopolist decides to build additional plant capacity? How much must it decrease before some existing plants are closed?
8. What is the difference between the definitions of costs by economists and by accountants that causes the economist to say that the equilibrium of an industry with freedom of entry is achieved when the typical firm is earning zero economic profits?
9. Why is the firm operating at a more efficient level when the industry is in equilibrium under competitive conditions than when it is in equilibrium under monopolistic conditions? What is the advantage to the consumer of the competitive equilibrium?
10. What is the true function of profit in a competitive economy? Why must loss sometimes exist?
11. How may government assist in securing economic growth through expansion of output capacity?

CHAPTER

17

# Demand, Supply, and Price for the Entire Industry

In the last three chapters we have focused attention on the decisions made by the firm in response to changing economic conditions. Let us now broaden our focus to an industry. We will consider the interplay of individual firms as they compete for a share of the market. Back in Chapter 2 we developed some basic ideas on demand and supply that have been adequate for our needs to this point but now require more detailed examination. In this analysis we will consider the psychological basis upon which demand rests and from this study develop some concepts that serve to explain certain aspects of consumer behavior.

## DEMAND FOR THE PRODUCT OF AN ENTIRE INDUSTRY

**Diminishing Marginal Utility As a Basis for the Law of Demand.** Even the early writers on economics recognized that an inverse relationship existed between the price charged for a commodity and the quantity purchased. But only within the last century has the analysis approached a finished form. The early economists also recognized that utility was essential if a product was to have value. But they were confused by the fact that value or price did not seem to be directly related to utility. A classic illustration was the *paradox of value* stated by Adam Smith: both bread and diamonds have utility, but diamonds (the product with the lesser utility) have the greater value.

This problem was solved when economists switched their attention from total utility to marginal utility. Although the total supply of bread usually has greater utility than that of diamonds, one more slice of bread normally has less utility than one more diamond. The utility of one more unit of any consumer good will depend upon the quantity already possessed by the person. To a starving person one more slice of bread will have great utility, but to a person who has just finished a big meal the utility of another slice of bread will be very small. This brings us to an important idea, the concept of diminishing marginal utility.

The *principle of diminishing marginal utility* is merely a generalized statement of the relationship between quantity consumed and the utility of additional units of a good or service. It says that as a person consumes increasing amounts of an item the marginal utility (utility added by the last unit) tends to decrease. The same idea can

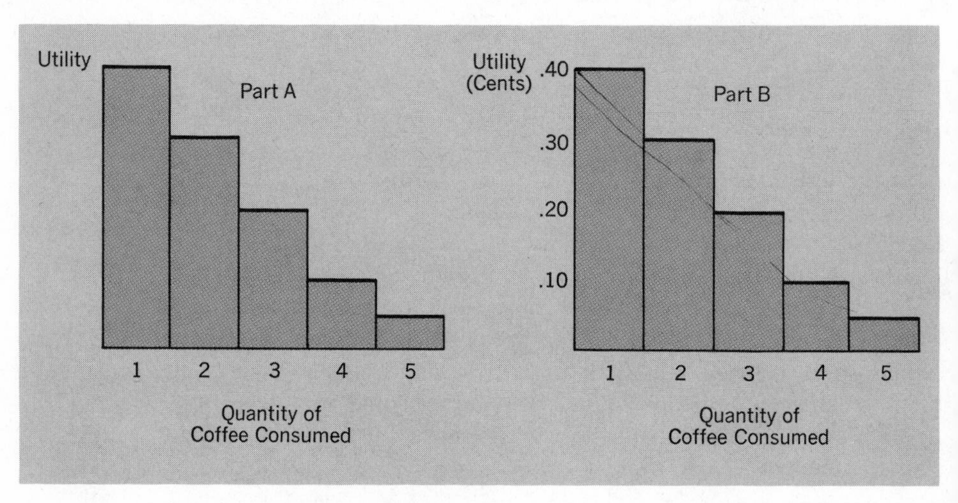


**Figure 17–1.** Diminishing marginal utility as additional cups of coffee are consumed related to quantity of money a person is willing to spend.

be expressed by saying that total utility will increase with the number of units consumed but that it will increase at a decreasing rate.

**Downward-Sloping Demand Curve.** With the aid of this principle we will seek to explain why people tend to buy increasing quantities of a product as the price drops. In Figure 17–1, Part A, we express the marginal utility of various cups of coffee in graphical form, measuring the utility attributed to cups of coffee on the vertical axis and the number of cups consumed in one morning on the horizontal axis. Notice that the successive bars decline in height. The shorter bar for the second unit reflects the fact that the second cup of coffee adds less satisfaction than the first. This decline in utility added continues as the third, fourth, and fifth cups are consumed.

One difficulty with this approach to the analysis of demand is that we have no means for a direct measurement of utility. Although the principle of diminishing utility expresses accurately what our common sense tells us occurs as we buy varying quantities of consumer goods, no exact measure of psychological satisfaction has been devised. For some purposes, however, it is useful to represent the satisfaction yielded by an additional unit of consumer goods, as we have in Figure 17–1, Part B. The diagram reveals that this person is so fond of coffee that he would purchase one cup of coffee each morning even if the price were 40 cents. But at that price he would find that the utility of a second cup was insufficient to warrant its purchase. At a price of 10 cents, however, he would be willing to buy four cups each morning, because the utility of the fourth cup is enough to warrant giving up a dime to secure it. From the psychological principle expressed above regarding diminishing marginal utility, therefore, we have derived the basic law of demand that was stated in Chapter 2.

The principle says that we can measure the marginal utility of coffee by the price the buyer is willing to pay for each unit. This gives us the price that the individual is just willing to pay for each successive cup of coffee. If we combine the price he is willing to pay for coffee with the number of cups, we arrive at the individual's demand schedule for cups of coffee. Moreover, this schedule embodies the law of demand; as the price of coffee is reduced, a person is willing to buy additional cups, because the lower price is in line with the reduced marginal utility. The analysis given above is essentially the one outlined by the English economist, Alfred Marshall. Once we have the demand schedule for each buyer in the market, we can add together the quantities purchased by each person at each price and secure the total demand schedule for the entire market.

Consider now some of the limitations of the argument. The amount of money a person is willing to give up for the marginal unit of an item can be used to measure its utility only under certain conditions. Thus, a dollar cannot be used to measure utility or satisfaction between two different people or for the same person at two different times. The amount of utility represented by a dollar will vary in response to changes in the number of dollars a person has. Also, variations in personal or family needs will alter the utility represented by one dollar. Despite these difficulties in the use of money as a measure of utility, the analysis provides much insight into the way consumer decisions are made.

For example, when a person says that a particular sport shirt is not worth $5 to him, he means that he would get greater satisfaction by spending that $5 for other goods. Money serves here as a measure of utility because it represents to this person the power to purchase a number of different products. The satisfaction that would have been secured by the purchase of five dollars' worth of these other goods is the measure of the utility that has been sacrificed if this part of his income is used to buy the sport shirt.

**Rational Expenditure for Consumer Goods.** The typical consumer has a limited income and, in view of his many wants, will try to spend it in a way that will provide the greatest possible satisfaction. A person would not consciously spend a dollar for any product if he believes that he would get greater satisfaction or utility by using that dollar to buy something else. We can formalize this statement by saying that *a consumer will acquire units of any item up to the point where the marginal utility of a dollar spent on it is the same as the marginal utility of a dollar spent on any other item.* Until the consumer has come as close as possible to this ideal allocation of income, he will tend to shift his expenditures from the uses of money that give lesser satisfaction to those that give greater. We can express this basic consumer equilibrium in a continued equation relating the marginal utilities of the several goods to their respective prices, as follows:

$$\frac{MU \text{ of good } A}{P \text{ of good } A} = \frac{MU \text{ of good } B}{P \text{ of good } B} = \frac{MU \text{ of good } C}{P \text{ of good } C}, \text{ etc.}$$

Let us illustrate the meaning of this equation. If good $A$ is a pair of shoes costing \$10 and $B$ is a sport shirt costing \$5, the purchaser will have his expenditures properly balanced only when the marginal utility of shoes for him is twice that of sport shirts. In the same way the individual must balance his present need for goods against his expectations of future needs. The amount of saving to meet future needs, therefore, conforms also to this rule.

Changes in the allocation of income from the purchase of one commodity to another will change the marginal utility of both items. If a consumer shifts part of his expenditure from neckties to socks, the reduction in the number of neckties raises their marginal utility, whereas the increase in the quantity of socks reduces their marginal utility. Such changes in marginal utilities enable a consumer to approach the equilibrium defined by the above equations. An increase in the price of one of these goods ordinarily sets in motion a decline in the quantity purchased of that item, which continues until the marginal utility has risen high enough to warrant paying the higher price.

Although the concept of marginal utility explains why a person will buy less of a product when the price is increased, it does not define the extent to which the quantity purchased will decrease with a rise in the price. Such quantitative measurements are expressed by means of the elasticity of demand, a concept we treated in Chapter 15.

**Changes in Demand.** Let us recall some features of demand theory dealt with in Chapter 2. Because the word *demand* designates an entire curve, a shift in the position of the demand curve represents a change in demand. But a movement from one point to another on the same curve does not constitute such a change. Thus a change in the quantity purchased as a result of a change in price is not a change in demand, because this change in quantity is already a part of the existing curve. Such a change in quantity represents a change in demand only when, at one or more of these prices, there is a change in the quantity purchased. In spite of the fact that price remains the same under such conditions, the quantity purchased changes. Clearly, some factor other than price is causing the change in the amount purchased. In other words, a change in demand exists only when the change in the quantity purchased results from some cause other than a change in price.

In Figure 17–2 both an increase and a decrease in demand are shown. With the original demand curve labeled *D* the quantity purchased is 1,000 units at a price of *P*. If the demand curve shifts to *D′* 1,500 units are bought at the same price of *P*. Because the

**Figure 17–2.** Effect of changes in demand upon quantities purchased at price *P*.

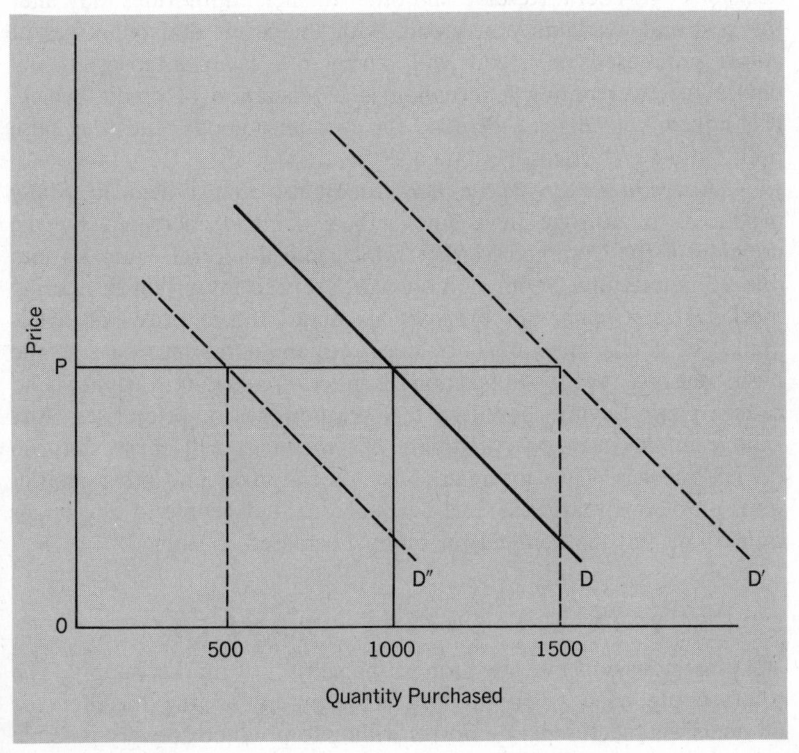

quantity taken at a price of $P$ has increased, this shift of demand from $D$ to $D'$ is entitled an increase in demand.

On the other hand, if the demand curve shifts from $D$ to $D''$ the quantity taken at a particular price decreases, indicating a decrease in demand. Evidently, a decrease in demand appears graphically as a shift of the demand curve downward and to the left, whereas an increase appears as a movement upward and to the right. The various demand curves in Figure 17–2 are parallel to each other, but many changes in demand will involve only portions of the curves and may involve changes in slope or in elasticity at the same time.

**Causes of Changes in Demand.** One of the most obvious causes of change in demand is the *variation in consumer tastes*. In some years consumers choose big cars with tail fins, whereas in other years they prefer compact cars with simple lines. Sometimes research reports or like information cause changes in demand, such as the one that occurred when reports on lung cancer affected the demand for cigarettes. Advertising and other selling efforts may also shift demand curves.

*Variations in consumer purchasing power* also cause changes in demand. During a period of prosperity rising incomes cause corresponding increases in demand for many consumer goods. Similarly, decisions by Federal Reserve and other financial authorities may alter the cost and availability of credit, with the result that quantities of goods purchased on credit will change. A favorite governmental device for overcoming a recession is a relaxation of credit, which, it is hoped, will increase demand for consumer goods, and thus raise both output and prices.

A *change in the size of the market* may also change demand. Many producers in Europe have found their demand increased by the creation of the Common Market, which joined several countries into one economic unit. Population changes are also important in altering market size. *Changes in expectations* about future prices or availability of goods may influence decisions about buying. One of the basic reasons for the imposition of price control in wartime is to reduce panic buying caused by fear of shortages or price rises. Any *change in the price or availability of substitutes* will cause shifts in demand curves. Thus the removal of special taxes and other restrictions on oleomargarine several years ago caused people to buy larger quantities, and the demand for butter decreased sharply.

## SUPPLY IN AN ENTIRE INDUSTRY

Let us now shift our attention to the subject of market supply. The total supply of a given product is found by adding together the amounts that each separate firm is willing to produce at every possible price. But the response of quantity supplied to a change in price is controlled principally by two factors: (1) the length of time allowed for the response, and (2) the degree of competition or monopoly existing in the market for the particular good. Let us begin by examining the short-run period, defined as a length of time sufficient to permit the firm to adjust output with existing facilities but not to build new plants.



**Short-Run Supply Under Pure Competition.** As we explained earlier, an individual firm under perfect competition will expand production to the point where its *MC* curve intersects the *AR–MR* line. Figure 15–9 affords a graphical illustration of the principle. If the *AR–MR* curve shifts upward as a result of an increase in the market price, the intersection will move upward and to the right. The new intersection corresponds to a larger volume of output for the firm. Thus, when the price rises from *P* to *P′* in Figure 17–3, output increases from *Q* to *Q′*. If, on the other hand, the price declines to

**Figure 17–3.** Quantities supplied by competitive firm at various prices determined at points on the marginal cost curve.

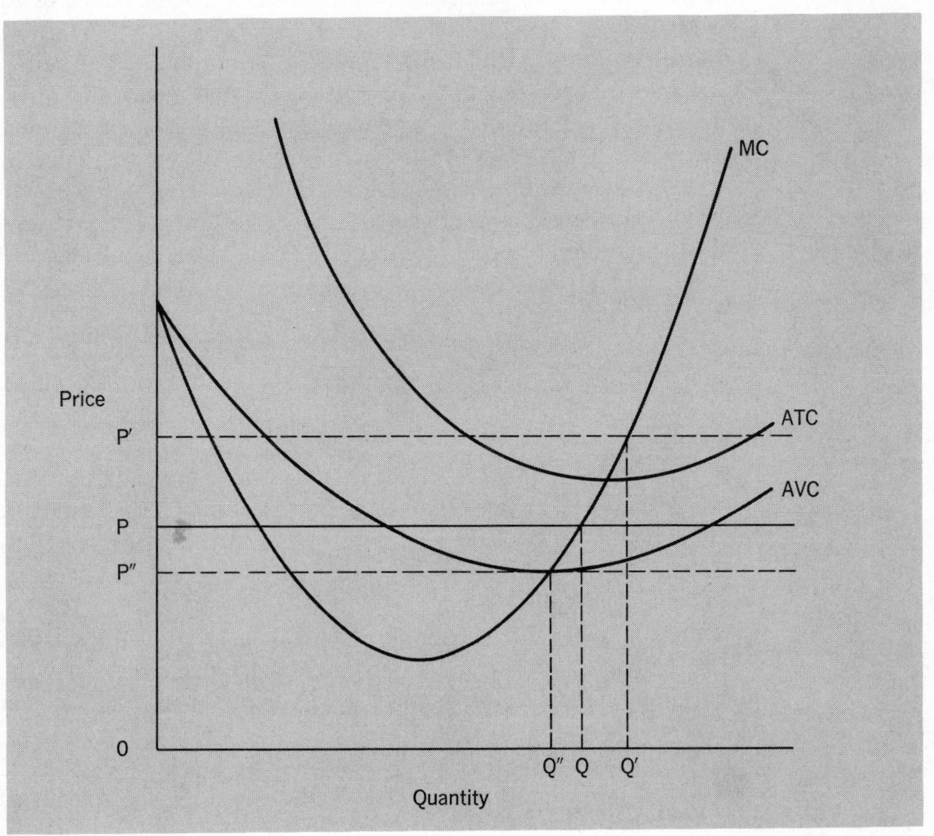

$P''$ the new intersection will be lower and to the left, giving a reduced output of only $Q''$ units. Still lower prices would cause the firm to fail to cover variable costs. This occurs when the price falls below $P''$. At this point, where the firm is barely covering variable costs, its losses equal the amount of the fixed costs, and it is in the same financial position as it would be if it shut down.

If we look again at Figure 17–3, we see that all the points showing the quantity this firm is willing to produce at each price lie along the *MC* curve. Because the quantities produced at various prices are simply points on the *MC* curve, this curve must represent the short-run supply curve for the competitive firm. However, only the part that lies above the price at which variable cost is being covered is included.

The supply for the entire industry is the result of adding together the outputs of individual firms at the various prices. If the cost curves of individual firms differ, the quantities they are willing to produce at the different prices will vary, but this will not prevent our getting an aggregate supply curve. The competitive supply curve of an industry is secured simply by adding together at each possible price the quantities that will be produced by the various firms, as indicated by their *MC* curves.

**Short-Run Supply Under Monopolistic Conditions.** The supply for an industry operating under complete or partial monopoly cannot be so simply determined. The downward-sloping average revenue curve, which results from control over price at which the product is sold, forces a separation of the *AR* and *MR* curves. The quantity to be produced, therefore, no longer equates selling price and marginal cost. Maximization of profit requires instead the equating of marginal revenue and marginal cost.

With the conditions shown in Figure 17–4 the firm achieves maximum profit by setting a price of *P* while producing *Q* units. But the point *X*, showing *Q* units at a price of *P*, does not fall on the *MC* curve, lying instead well above it on the *AR* curve. If an increase in consumer demand occurs, shown by a shift of the *AR* curve to *AR′*, the equilibrium shifts to point *X′* on the new *AR* curve, marked by an output of *Q′* units at a price of *P′*. Again, the equilibrium price lies above the intersection of *MC* and (the new) *MR′*. Although a monopolist considers his *MC* curve in reacting to changes in consumer demand, we cannot identify the *MC* curve with that firm's supply curve. Rather, we conclude that under monopolistic conditions, the quantity a firm will be willing to supply at a given price will be determined by the intersection of the *MC* curve and the *MR* curve appropriate to that market situation.

If the monopolistic industry is reluctant to change the price of the product, as is frequently the case under oligopoly, the firm tends

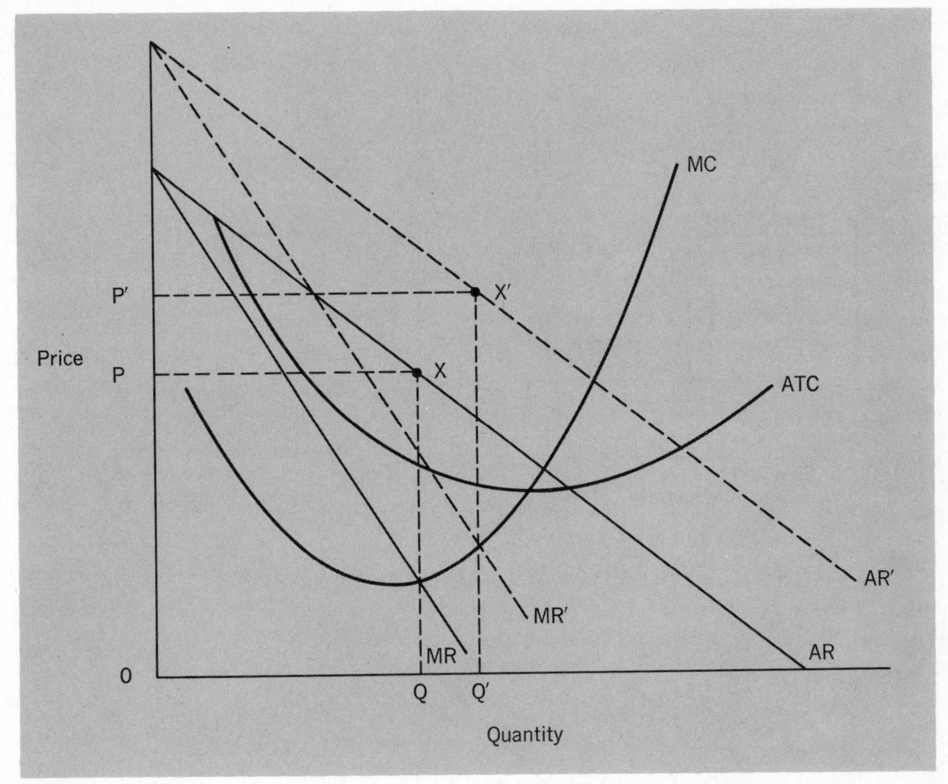


**Figure 17–4.** Effect on price and quantity produced of increase in demand under conditions of monopoly.

simply to produce the quantity that can be sold at the established price. For example, in the early months of 1961 the demand for steel declined considerably, but there was no drop in the price of steel. Rather, each firm reduced its production to the quantity that could be sold at the existing price. For a while output of the steel industry dropped almost to 50 per cent of what could have been produced. Under these assumptions of a rigid and generally accepted price in the short run the supply curves for each firm and in total for the industry are characterized by a horizontal supply line at the established price. Of course, if consumer demand continued to grow for a considerable period, it is probable that the established price would be raised. On the other hand, a prolonged weakening of consumer demand would probably result in an ultimate lowering of the selling price.

**Short-Run Market Price.** The market price of a particular product under conditions of perfect competition will be determined by the intersection of the demand-and-supply curve, as was pointed out

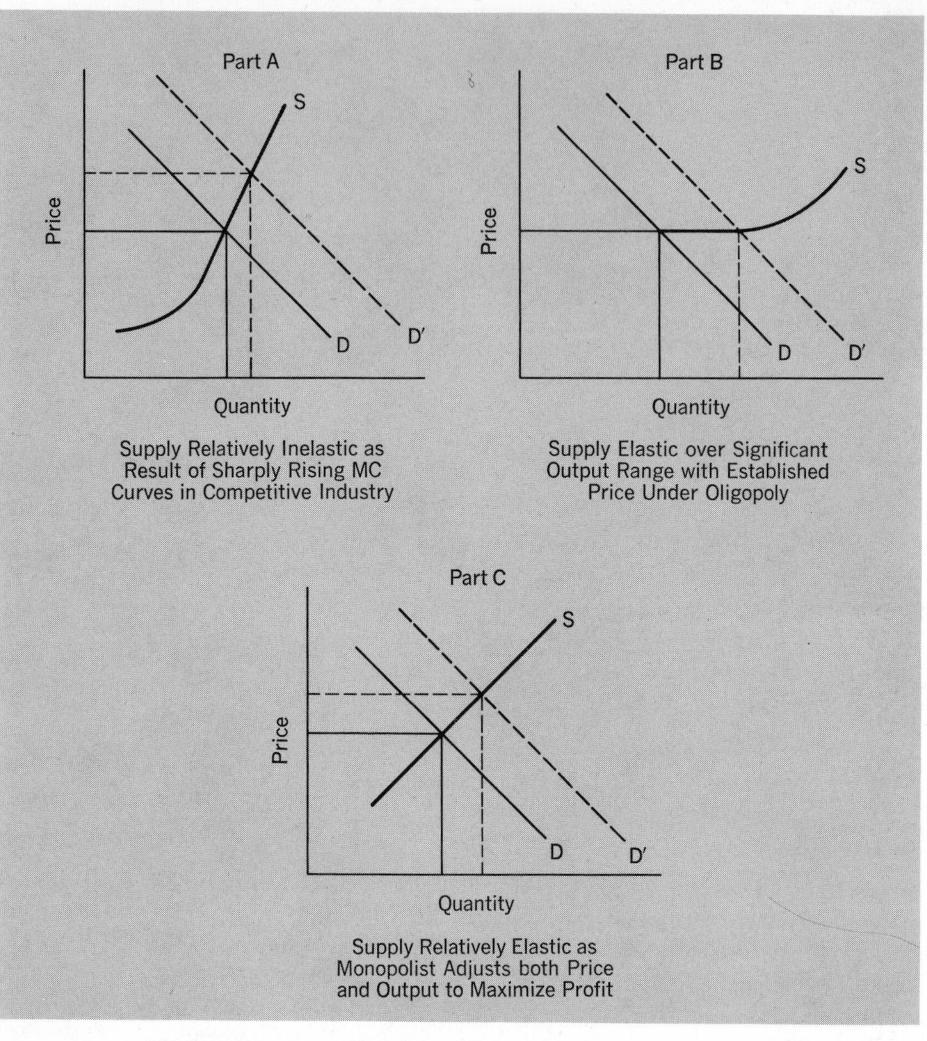


**Figure 17–5.** Price and output adjustments under various supply conditions with increase in demand in the short run.

in Chapter 2. We have been trying in the preceding three chapters to analyze the factors that enter into the decision of the individual producer as to how much he would supply under different market conditions, monopolistic as well as competitive. Let us now consider how the entire market would react to changes in consumer demand under different market situations. In the discussion that follows the concept *supply* applies in the strict sense only to the perfectly competitive case.



In each of the three graphs in Figure 17–5 we are assuming an increase in consumer demand, but the supply situation differs in each case. In Part A we are assuming that the firms in this market are operating under conditions of pure competition and have sharply rising *MC* curves. In this situation the total supply curve will therefore rise rather sharply and be relatively inelastic. The hook at the lower end of the supply curve shows that if the price falls below the level of variable costs, firms will tend to cease production and the quantity supplied will drop off sharply. The increase in demand shown in Part A of Figure 17–5 thus results in a very considerable rise in price and a relatively small increase in quantity sold as the intersection of the supply curve by the demand curve shifts to its new position.

In Part B of Figure 17–5 we are assuming that the industry is an oligopoly, with each of the small number of firms maintaining an established price because of fear that changing the selling price might set off a price war. The result of the demand increase from *D* to *D′* here is that the output increases very greatly. But there will be no increase in price unless a change is announced by a price leader or output increases far enough beyond the low-cost point of the individual firm so that profit margins are seriously threatened, as indicated by the upward slope of the supply curve at the right. Under these conditions we find a selling price that is not altered by limited shifts in the demand curve. Instead of changing price it is output level that varies as demand changes.

In Part C of Figure 17–5 we assume that the industry is controlled by a monopolist who is willing to adjust both price and output with changes in demand as required by the maximization of profit. When demand increases from *D* to *D′*, the monopolist finds that he can increase his profit by expanding volume and raising price at the same time. The relatively elastic "supply curve" [1] indicates that the changing intersection of the *MR* and *MC* curve has caused the monopolist to increase both output and selling price in response to the increased demand. If the demand (*AR*) curve is relatively elastic, the monopolist is likely to increase output considerably and raise the price very little. The reverse is true if the demand curve is inelastic. Another consideration in the changing of output and price to maximize profit is the existence of excess capacity. If the firm is operating at low levels of output, the decision is more likely to emphasize changes in output, but if operations are near capacity, output cannot easily be increased, and prices are more likely to be raised.

**Long-Run Market Price Under Competition.** The long-run supply curve of an industry under conditions of pure competition is

[1] We are referring here to the monopolist's reaction to a price increase, shown in the form of a curve. This "supply curve" will shift if the demand curve becomes flatter or steeper.

almost certain to be more elastic than the short-run supply. The existence of many producers indicates that entrance into the industry is not limited, so that any increase in price that results in economic profit causes the entry of new firms and an increase in quantity offered for sale. A market large enough to support many firms will already have permitted existing firms to exhaust the cost benefits of increasing returns to scale, as shown in our planning curve in Chapter 14. The new firms, therefore, will tend to have about the same cost per unit as the existing firms, unless the entrance of new producers into the industry results in bidding up the price of specialized labor or natural resources used in the production process.

In Figure 17–6 we show the long-run supply curve for this industry sloping slightly upward to the right, under the assumption that the prices of some productive factors have been forced up by the bidding of the new firms. The increase in consumer demand shown by the shift of the demand curve from $D$ to $D'$ results in only a small rise in

**Figure 17–6.** Long-run response of competitive market to increase in demand.

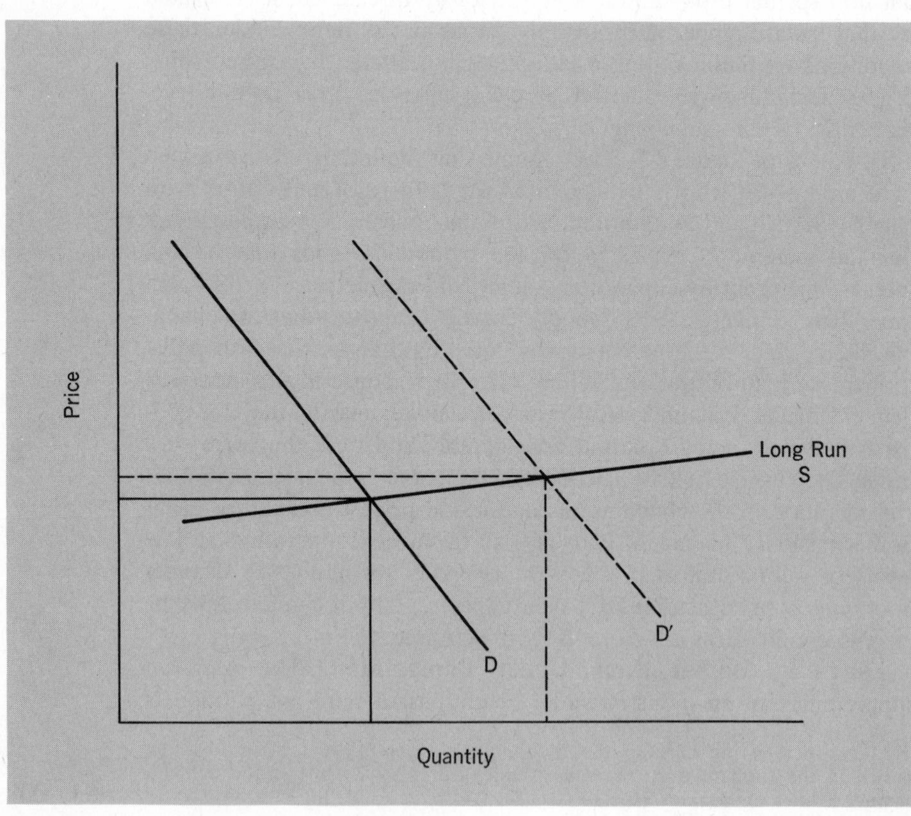

price; but the quantity sold increases greatly. Figure 17–6 shows what is probably a fairly typical long-run market situation for industries operating under pure competition. The desire of consumers for increased quantities of goods from such industries will be met in the long run by very limited price increases unless the productive factors needed are in very limited supply.

Although in the short run the increased consumer demand does increase the selling price, as shown in Figure 17–5, Part A, the resulting economic profit causes an expansion of capacity in the industry. The entry of the new firms causes a shift to the right of the short-run supply curve (not shown) and pushes the market price down to the long-run supply level.

**Long-Run Market Price Under Monopolistic Conditions.** In an industry characterized by monopoly or oligopoly we cannot depend upon the market price being forced down to the level of long-run average cost as we can under competition. In contrast with a purely competitive situation, entry of new firms into the industry in response to the existence of economic profit meets with resistance from existing firms. If the barrier consists of a series of patent rights or control over raw material, entry may be impossible. Because it does not have to meet competition from additional firms, the monopolist or price leader in an oligopoly will set the price in the long run that will maximize profit. Almost certainly such a price will be well above the long-run average cost to which it would be forced under competition.

Under conditions of monopolistic competition the entry of new firms is frequently possible. This expansion of capacity will certainly tend to reduce the general price level of the differentiated product and to eliminate economic profit. However, it is unlikely that the entry of new firms will push prices down to the level prevailing under pure competition. The downward-sloping average-revenue curve for the firm with a differentiated product causes the point of tangency of *AR* and *ATC* to fall short of the low-cost point, as we saw in Figure 16–7 of the preceding chapter. Even when economic profit has been eliminated, therefore, selling price will still be above the level that would exist under competitive conditions. This higher price is necessary to meet high unit costs arising from inefficient operation at a point short of capacity.

**Supply in the Immediate Market Period or Very Short Run.** In contrast to the relative elasticity of the supply curve in the long run, particularly under competitive conditions, the supply curve in the immediate market period or very short run will tend to be highly inelastic. This time period is defined as one that does not allow changes in output, so that the only possible supply is that drawn from existing stocks. If the product is one that cannot be stored, the supply curve will tend to be perfectly inelastic under competitive conditions, because the quantity on hand must be sold whether the price is high or low.

But when the product can be stored, the supply curve tends to become a bit less inelastic. A severe decline in price may cause producers to place part of current output into storage in the expectation that a later rise in price will make the withholding profitable. A rise in price, on the other hand, may bring additional quantities out of storage and add to the quantity offered for sale.

The monopolist, faced by a decline in demand, however, will not permit the price to fall to the same degree that it would under competition. Although he faces the same problem of sunk costs, he will not permit a decline in price that would reduce total revenue. From the viewpoint of the monopolist it is better to withhold units from the market and let them spoil than it is to permit a decline in price that decreases gross revenue. If demand for the monopolist's product, therefore, has an elasticity of less than unity, so that revenue is dropping, he will withhold units from the market in order to secure a higher price and so increase total revenue.

## INTERDEPENDENT PRICES

**Joint Supply.** Up to this point we have been treating each product as though it were produced separately from other goods. But the real problems are frequently complicated by the fact that many industrial operations result in the production of several different goods. Ham cannot be produced without also producing bacon and pork chops. When gasoline is refined, paraffin, fuel oil, asphalt, and many other items result as by-products. If the demand for gasoline increases and the rise in price causes an expansion of output; an unavoidable result is an increase in the supply of fuel oil. Unless the demand for fuel oil has changed, its price must drop. A technological change, such as the introduction of the cracking process, may permit some variation in the product mix, but normally it cannot completely eliminate the problem.

If one of the items in joint supply provides a small fraction of sales revenue and is, therefore, a by-product, it will tend to have a relatively inelastic supply. A rise in the price of asphalt will not be important enough to justify increased output of gasoline and fuel oil along with the asphalt. The main determinants of asphalt output are the prices of these major associated joint products.

**Joint Demand.** We have already noticed that goods demanded jointly tend to have inelastic demands, but there are also other effects of this relationship. If the supply of lumber decreases and the price of lumber rises so that fewer frame houses are built, the demand for carpenters' labor will be reduced. In the same way shortages of any complementary or jointly used products will tend to affect the markets for the related goods.

**Rival Supply and Rival Demand.** When one product can be substituted for another, we have rival supply. For certain purposes aluminum can be substituted for steel, and any change in the price of aluminum will alter the quantity of steel purchased at the existing price. Relationships between markets arising from possibilities of substitution are extremely common.

Another relationship of considerable importance is found in rival demand, which exists when the same product can be used for several purposes. Thus, new uses for aluminum, such as wrapping foil and house siding, now compete with old uses in cooking utensils and castings. Clearly, this tends to increase the demand for aluminum. But it also makes it more elastic; as the price falls, the product finds more uses.

As we analyze demand-and-supply forces in the market determination of prices, we must constantly be aware of the changes that are brought about by the complex relationships with other products either on the demand or on the supply side.

## PROBLEMS OF PRICE CONTROL

Under some conditions the public may not be satisfied with the answer that the market gives to the problem of prices. In such cases the government may be called on to secure the desired prices. If this is to be done, those in charge must understand the operation of the price mechanism. Thus, government price control does not mean that the basic forces of supply and demand are ignored; rather, it means that supply and demand are manipulated in such a way that the market gives the answer the government wishes. Our purpose here is not to determine whether such manipulation is desirable but to understand the methods by which it is accomplished.

**Wartime Price Control.** In time of war the demand curve is shifted sharply to the right by the rise in government buying and by the accompanying rise in personal income. If these changes are accompanied by a fear of shortages and of price rises leading to panic buying, there may be no real limit to the rise in price. Not only does the demand curve shift to the right, but its elasticity is reduced, because the government cannot permit cost increases to interfere with planned purchases for the war effort. Consumer demand curves also tend to become more inelastic as consumption of the more essential goods and services is limited by production controls and rationing. Such a change in the position and the elasticity of the demand curve for most products is represented in Figure 17–7, Part A, by the shift from *D* to *D′*.

If there are idle resources when the war begins, producers will put them to work to expand production. In consequence, the supply curve will shift to the right, shown by a shift of the supply curve from *S* to *S′* in Figure 17–7, Part A. The supply also will tend to become more inelastic when the economy reaches full employment and the production of nonessentials has been eliminated. At such times the individual firm cannot secure labor or raw materials for further expansion. Even small further increases in demand will push the price up sharply, but because the supply curve is highly inelastic at

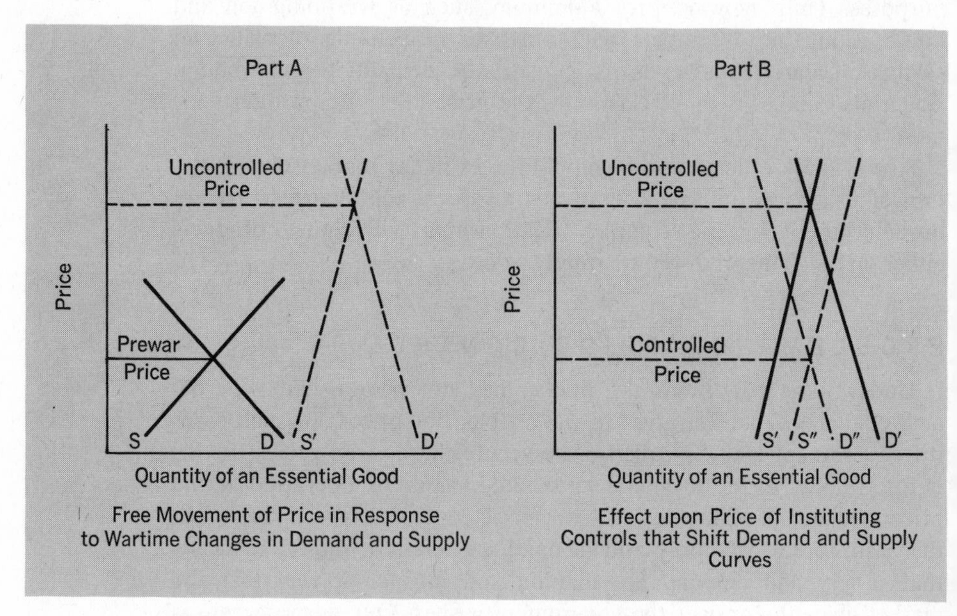


**Figure 17–7.** Inflationary pressures of war upon prices of essential goods and the effects of rationing and other price controls.

this stage, the price rise will not cause any significant increase in output. The real results of the price increase will be rising incomes for the lucky producers and hardship for those whose incomes are fixed or sticky. Another result will be the rapid rise of the public debt as the government is forced to pay higher prices for the goods it is buying.

Virtually all countries during World War II instituted price control programs to deal with the danger of runaway price rises. Part B of Figure 17–7 illustrates the effect of price control. By allocation of scarce resources and by special subsidies our government attempted to increase the supply of essential goods, as shown by the position of supply curve $S''$. At the same time rationing of scarce consumer goods and controlled demand for productive factors, such as steel, shifted the demand curve back to $D''$. The combined shift of the demand-and-supply curves was carried far enough to give an intersection at the price level desired by the control authorities. Because both curves were inelastic, relatively small shifts in either demand or supply resulted in relatively large changes in price.

Under properly administered controls the level of output should remain close to the possible maximum. This analysis requires that the government be able to enforce its price control regulations. If black markets develop and people begin to evade the rationing and allocation restrictions, prices in these illegal markets will move back up toward levels indicated by the uncontrolled intersection. Price control in time of war is much more complex and difficult than the simple illustration we have used, but this analysis is adequate to show the basic nature of the problem and its solution.

**Prices of Farm Products.** Farm prices pose exactly the opposite type of problem. Instead of trying to keep prices down the government seeks to force them up to a level acceptable to farmers. However, this result also is sought by means of a shift either in the demand or the supply curve.

The demand for many important farm products is rather inelastic. Small shifts in production resulting from weather variations or decisions about planning will, therefore, result in disproportionate changes in price. Farmers have long been aware that their income was frequently higher when crops were bad than when they were good. Adding to the problem of instability in farm prices, technological improvements in agriculture have caused a shift to the right of the supply curve in recent decades. Moreover, the supply curve has been shifting much more rapidly than the demand curve, despite rising population and per capita incomes. The result of this steady rise in farm output has been a constant downward pressure on farm prices relative to prices of other products.

Under the Hoover administration in 1929 the effort was made to raise farm prices by the purchase of surpluses that were then put into storage. In 1933 it became obvious that these stored surpluses could not be disposed of without depressing prices. At this time the New Deal of Franklin D. Roosevelt began a policy of limiting production by acreage restrictions and related policies.

Because the demand curve for most important farm products is inelastic, a relatively minor shift in the supply curve as in Figure 17–8 brings about a significant rise in prices. It thus appears that a plan designed to limit supply might well succeed in raising price to satisfactory levels. Unfortunately for the application of this plan,

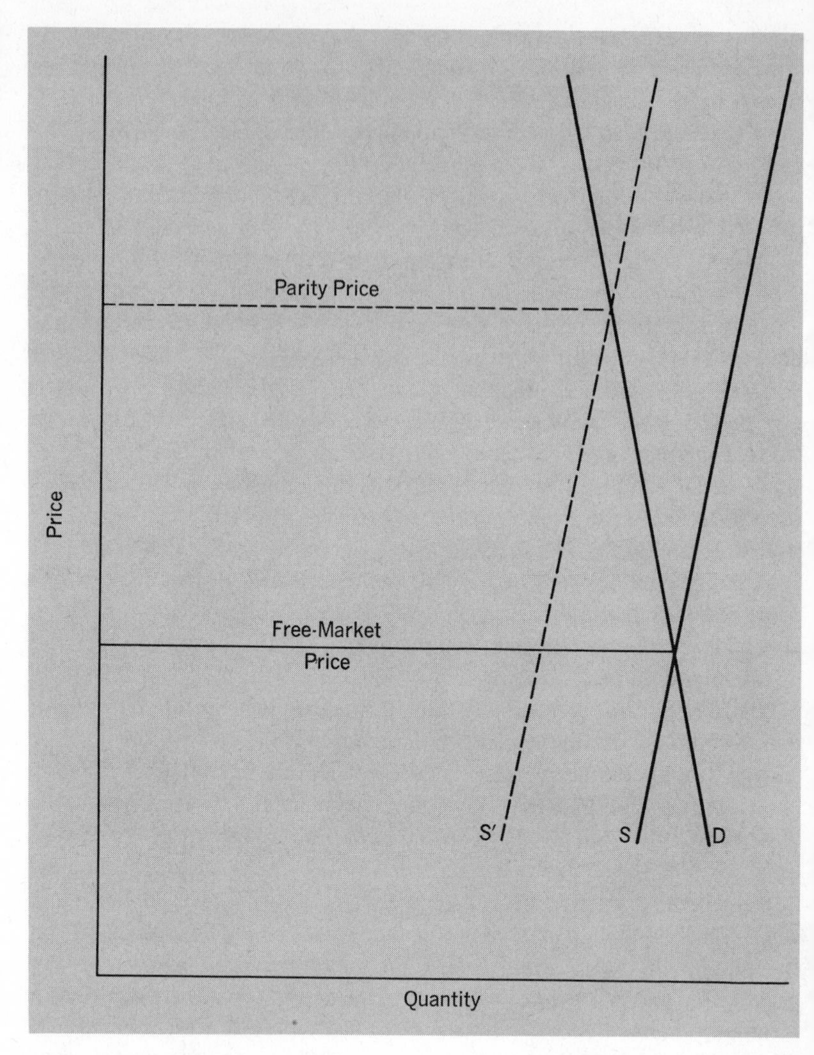


**Figure 17–8.** Effect upon farm prices of shift in supply curve caused by restriction of production.

the steady improvement in fertilizers, insecticides, and seeds continued to push the supply curve back to the right and to offset the limitation on planting. In order to maintain prices at the controlled or parity level it was necessary to reduce further and further the number of acres that could be planted. In addition, attempts were made to raise farm prices by shifting the demand curve to the right through a free school lunch program and special sales abroad. However, the main reliance has been on the shift of the supply curve, as in Figure 17–8, by restrictions upon production.

Whenever government decides to interfere with the price mechanism, the difficult problem arises of determining a fair price. In wartime, prewar prices are usually assumed to be normal and therefore fair. The method of determining a fair price for farm products, however, is more complicated. The basic solution has been to say that farm prices are fair (at parity) when they have the same relationship to things the farmer buys as they had at a time in the past when the relationship is thought to have been equitable. In other words, if things the farmer purchases have doubled in price since the base period, it is argued that farm prices also should be twice as high. In recent years some percentage of this statistically determined parity price has been supported as fair, but the question of what percentage of parity to accept has been bitterly debated. For a grasp of economic theory it is important to understand how prices can be manipulated, but the problem of what price is fair is more political than it is economic.

**Summary.** Consumer demand for a product is based upon the principle of diminishing marginal utility that relates utility of a unit to the quantity possessed. Taking as our measure of utility the amount of money a person is willing to pay rather than forego the use of each unit we can derive an individual demand curve that will slope downward to the right. The rational consumer will spend his income in such a way that the marginal utility of each good bears the same relationship to its price as for any other good which he is buying.

Changes in demand represent changes in the schedule and are treated graphically as shifts in the position of the demand curve. Demand changes may result from variations in consumer preferences, changes in purchasing power, alterations in market size, changed expectations, or variations in the prices of substitutes.

Short-run supply by the firm under competition follows the price and quantity relations indicated by the marginal cost curve when the price at least covers variable costs. Under monopolistic conditions the quantity supplied by the firm will be determined by the intersection of the *MC* and *MR* curves. Thus, the points showing price and quantity relationships will lie on the *AR* curves, and the *MC* curve is no longer the supply curve as it is under competitive conditions. Long-run supply for a product includes the effect of possible expansion of output facilities and, therefore, tends to be more elastic than the short-run supply. Expansion of productive facilities may not take place so easily under monopolistic conditions as under competition, and the long-run supply curve may be less elastic. In the immediate market period the supply curve tends to be highly inelastic, but this tendency may be modified by the possibility of storage or control of sales by a monopolist.

Prices may be interdependent under conditions of joint supply, joint demand, rival supply, and rival demand. Demand and supply curves may be manipulated to restrain price increases in time of war or to support farm prices in time of peace.

## QUESTIONS

1. How does the principle of diminishing marginal utility explain the apparent paradox that consumer goods with limited usefulness frequently sell for more than really essential goods?
2. Explain how money can be used to measure utility.
3. How does the individual decide whether he should buy additional units of one good rather than another?
4. What is meant by a change in demand? How is it shown graphically?
5. Why is a change in the quantity purchased as a result of a change in price not called a change in demand?
6. Give at least one significant illustration of each of the causes of a change in demand.
7. Why does the individual firm's short-run supply curve lie along its *MC* curve above the intersection with *AVC* when operating under competitive conditions? Why cannot the same statement be made of the firm operating under monopolistic conditions?
8. Why is the short-run supply curve under competitive conditions frequently more inelastic than it is under conditions of oligopoly?
9. Explain why the long-run price for a product under competitive conditions must equal long-run average cost. Why cannot the same statement be made about long-run prices under monopolistic conditions?
10. Why is supply in the immediate market period highly inelastic? If the product can be stored, how does this affect elasticity?
11. What are the four ways in which the price of one product may be related to product prices in other markets?
12. Explain the shifts that price control authorities must make in the position of the demand or the supply curves in order to prevent an undersirable increase in the price of a commodity. What are some of the devices used to accomplish such a shift in time of war? How can a similar analysis be used to explain the operations of the farm price support program?

PART

5

# *Income Distribution and the Prices of the Factors of Production*

Who shall get how much of what has been produced by the joint efforts of many people is one of the most difficult problems in economics. The basic answer given by capitalism is that each individual's income shall be determined primarily by the price at which he can sell the productive factors he controls. In the next five chapters we will examine the way the markets function as the factors of production are bought and sold.

CHAPTER 18

# Relationship of Income to Production

**Personal Income Results from Participation in Production.** In the American and other capitalistic economies, incomes individuals receive have generally been closely related to the role they played in producing goods and services to be shared. Because the work done by different people varied greatly, a very unequal distribution of personal income has resulted. The defense for this inequality has been that men work harder when the result is a higher income. Although we don't quite accept old Captain John Smith's decision that only those who work should eat, we certainly do allocate a greater share of output to those who make a greater contribution to production. Keep in mind, though, that contributions to production are made in many ways other than by physical labor. Only communist writers or closely related thinkers profess to believe that labor alone makes a contribution to production.

**Sources of Income.** Table 18–1 shows the national income for selected years broken down by types of income. The two categories "Adjusted Corporate Profit Before Taxes" and "Business and Professional Income" each more than quadrupled in the 35-year period between 1929 and 1964. They changed in about the same proportion as "National Income." On the other hand, "Farm Proprietors' Income" slightly more than doubled only, and this change was scarcely enough to offset the price increase during the period, leaving this group with a reduced fraction of total income. "Rental Income" and "Net Interest," as sources of income, also lagged behind the general growth of the economy, but not nearly to the same degree as farm income.

One category that has been absorbing a growing fraction of "National Income" in the past three decades is "Compensation of Employees." In 1929 employees received only 58.2 per cent of the "National Income," but in 1964 they received 70.9 per cent. A number of explanations can be offered for this increase, but the higher wage levels resulting from the operation of minimum wage laws and the increased strength of unions in collective bargaining should certainly be mentioned. Another factor has been the movement of population from farms to urban areas, thus lowering the number of people in the farm proprietors' group and increasing the numbers in the employee classifications. The change from the small retail store to the supermarket and large department store has reduced the number of independent businessmen and increased the percentage of

**TABLE 18-1***
**National Income by Type of Income (Billions of Dollars)**

| Year | Total National Income ($) | Compensation of Employees ($) | Business and Professional Income ($) | Farm Proprietors' Income ($) | Rental Income ($) | Adjusted Corporate Profits Before Taxes ($) | Net Interest ($) |
|---|---|---|---|---|---|---|---|
| 1929 | 87.8 | 51.1 | 8.8 | 6.0 | 5.4 | 10.1 | 6.4 |
| 1940 | 81.6 | 52.1 | 8.4 | 4.6 | 2.9 | 9.1 | 4.5 |
| 1945 | 181.2 | 123.2 | 19.0 | 11.8 | 5.6 | 18.4 | 3.2 |
| 1950 | 241.9 | 154.2 | 23.5 | 14.0 | 9.0 | 35.7 | 5.5 |
| 1955 | 330.2 | 223.9 | 30.4 | 11.8 | 10.7 | 43.1 | 10.4 |
| 1960 | 414.5 | 293.6 | 34.2 | 12.0 | 12.1 | 44.5 | 18.1 |
| 1964 | 509.8 | 361.7 | 39.3 | 12.7 | 12.4 | 57.0 | 26.8 |

* Source: **Economic Report of the President, January 1965.**

our labor force that is listed as employees. It is well to remember that not all of this increase in payments to employees went to low- or medium-income workers; corporate executives are also employees included in this category even though their incomes place them in the top brackets of the personal income tax. Nevertheless, this rise in the share of national income going to employees does appear to indicate that our working people are receiving an increasing percentage of a rising national income.

In later chapters we will classify sources of income according to types of productive contribution instead of following the "National Income" classifications. For purposes of analysis this will be a more useful approach.

## PATTERN OF INCOME DISTRIBUTION

**Inequality in the Distribution of Income.** Considerable inequality in the distribution of income results from the reliance by the American economy upon contributions made to production to determine the amount of income each family receives. Table 18–2 shows the extent of this inequality in 1958.

Critics of the American economy make a considerable point of the fact that the richest one tenth of our family or spending units, as indicated in Table 18–2, received an average income of $14,000 and 27 per cent of the total money income of the country, whereas the poorest one tenth received an average income of $690 and only 1 per cent of the total income. In other words, the wealthiest group received well over 20 times the income received by the poorest income group. However, the picture is not nearly so dark as these figures make it appear. The wealthier families have incomes that place them in the higher (personal income) tax brackets, and if these figures were adjusted to show incomes after taxes (rather than before) the degree of inequality would be considerably reduced. It is also well to remember that the families included in the lower-income groups include many for whom 1958 was a bad year because of temporary unemployment, illness, or crop failure. The income figure for such families would be much higher if we took the average for a five-year period.

**TABLE 18–2***
**Distribution of Money Income Before Taxes by Each Tenth of the Nation's Spending Units in 1958**

| Spending Units (Families or Single Persons) Grouped by Size of Income | Average Income of Group ($) | Percentage Share of Total Income Received by Group (%) | Cumulative Share Received by Each Group and Those of Lower Income (%) |
|---|---|---|---|
| Poorest Tenth | 690 | 1 | 1 |
| Second Tenth | 1,580 | 3 | 4 |
| Third Tenth | 2,360 | 5 | 9 |
| Fourth Tenth | 3,180 | 6 | 15 |
| Fifth Tenth | 3,990 | 8 | 23 |
| Sixth Tenth | 4,810 | 9 | 32 |
| Seventh Tenth | 5,680 | 11 | 43 |
| Eighth Tenth | 6,800 | 13 | 56 |
| Ninth Tenth | 8,390 | 16 | 72 |
| Richest Tenth | 14,000 | 27 | 100 |

* Source: **Federal Reserve Bulletin,** July 1959. Percentage shares are rounded to closest per cent and do not add to 100.

These low-income families also include older and retired people who have some independent income but are living with their children. Some farm families have only limited money income to report, but nevertheless have a reasonably satisfactory standard of living, because they produce for themselves a significant amount of food and other family needs. Despite these qualifications we can see from the table that a very significant inequality of family incomes exists when the richer half of our family groups receive 77 per cent of the money income, whereas the poorer half receives only 23 per cent or less than one third the income of the wealthier half.

**The Lorenz Curve—A Measure of Inequality.** A useful device for showing the amount of inequality in the distribution of income is the Lorenz curve. If we measure the per cent of family units on the horizontal axis and the per cent of income received on the vertical axis, we find that a perfectly straight line from the zero point to the far corner of the graph represents a perfectly equal distribution of income. This line would show any 10 per cent of the families receiving 10 per cent of the income, 20 per cent of the families 20 per cent of the income, and so on. In actual fact the lowest 10 per cent of the families received only 1 per cent of the income, so that our first point on the curve of actual income distribution is far below the line of equal distribution. The space between the two curves in Figure 18–1 shows the extent to which actual distribution of income in 1958 departed from perfect equality.

Any *decrease* in the inequality of income distribution would be shown by a movement of the lower curve upward toward the complete equality represented by the straight line. An *increase* in the inequality would be shown by a curve lying below the one showing actual income distribution in 1958. Statistics that would enable us to compare the present distribution of income with that existing before the New Deal of the 1930's are neither very complete nor very reliable. One widely used economics text [1] of the decade immediately after World War I estimated that the top 5 per cent of the income receivers got 26 per cent of the total income in 1918, whereas the top 14 per cent received 40 per cent. Using these two points as a basis we might assume an income distribution pattern somewhat similar to that shown by the dotted line in Figure 18–1. Although some economists doubt that there has been even the limited decrease in inequality of incomes shown by these figures, there is no statistical evidence to support the prediction of Karl Marx many years ago that under capitalism the rich would constantly grow richer and the poor poorer.

**Reasons for Inequality of Incomes.** The family income distri-

[1] F. W. Taussig, *Principles of Economics* (3rd ed. rev.; New York: Macmillan Company, 1929), II, pp. 259–260.

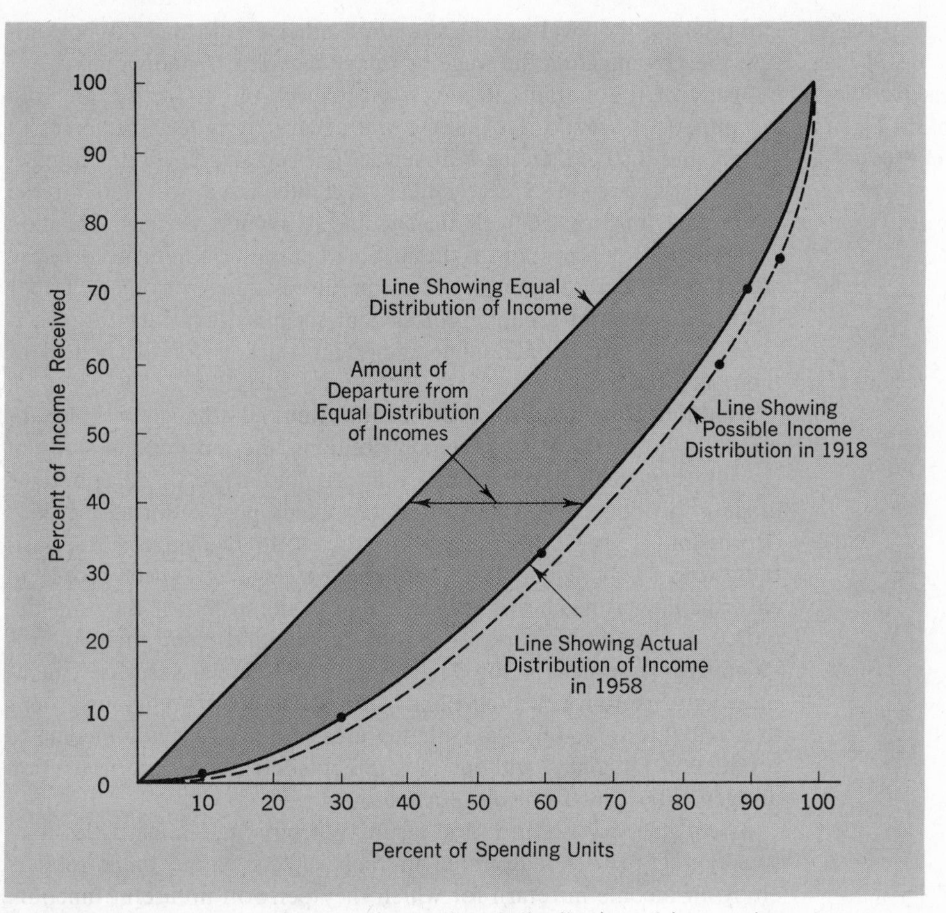


**Figure 18–1.** Lorenz curve, showing inequality of distribution of income by spending units in 1958.

bution must be uneven, because our system relates incomes to productive contributions that are necessarily unequal. Americans believe that all men are born equal in their legal rights, but not in strength of muscle, mental ability, willingness to work, or amount of property incomes. In the next few chapters we shall study how the market assesses the value of the contributions made to production and how the prices paid for these contributions are determined.

Another cause of inequality in the distribution of income is found in the operation of our social institutions. In many occupations women receive lower pay than men, although they perform the same work. Racial discrimination in employment frequently crowds minority groups into low-paying occupations. The institution of free inheritance has a twofold effect on income distribution. First, it affects the distribution of property and thereby of property income. Second, it causes variations in the level of education and other employment opportunities, thereby affecting the wage or salary received by individuals.

Many of the markets in which the factors of production are sold are imperfect and do not quickly and accurately reflect the forces of supply and demand. In these imperfect markets aggregations of political or economic power can influence greatly the price paid for the factor that, in turn, controls the income its owner receives. Taxation that takes away a portion of the income can also be influenced to the advantage of certain groups and to the disadvantage of others. Labor unions, managerial groups, professional societies, and farm organizations all attempt to manipulate imperfect markets for the benefit of their members.

**Incomes Not Resulting from Production.** Although we trace incomes primarily to productive contributions, the most casual study of the subject reveals some incomes that are not earned by contributions made to production. Severe suffering by many people during the deep depression of the 1930's forced our society to recognize a responsibility toward those unable to help themselves. We expect people to earn their own incomes if they are able to do so, but if they are too old or too young to work, or if they cannot find a job, help is provided by government action or private charity. Social Security, Unemployment Insurance, United Funds, and assistance by religious groups thus mitigate some objectionable features of a system tying income to production. Incomes without any direct contribution to production are generally called *transfer payments.*

There are certain incomes resulting from human activities that society regards as undesirable in their effects. Some bank robbers enjoy an income in return for which they perform no useful function. Bootleggers, smugglers, and gamblers can probably be classified in the same group, because these activities are also illegal, although some people can be found who will argue that productive functions have been performed. Fraud may also yield an income and is likewise illegal. However, it is difficult to draw the line between exaggeration and outright fraud. Thus the distinction between misleading advertising for patent medicines or cigarettes and the claims made by sellers of stock in risky or nonexistent corporations is a fine one. Our laws are constantly being revised in an effort to prevent the acquisition of income by people who are unwilling to contribute to production by socially acceptable methods. Unfortunately, the problem is more complex than is usually recognized. Gambling has usually been frowned upon, or at least closely regulated, but when it is unavoidably associated with a desirable activity, such as providing a ready market for investment securities or farm commodities, then we approve the action and the incomes that result.

**Classification of Productive Services and Income.** For purposes of analysis economists usually divide the contributions to production into four groups based on the nature of the function performed. The first productive function is *labor* performed by people. The work may be either physical or mental, and the payment for it is called *wages*. As we have already noted, a large part of the incomes earned by many persons comes from wages, and it will be most important to understand the principles that control the amount of wages paid for various types of labor.

The second productive function is that yielded by *capital goods* (the tools, machines, buildings, and other man-made items needed in production). In a modern economy the efficiency of production depends greatly upon the equipment with which men work. It is highly important, therefore, that we understand the operation of the incentive that leads to the supplying of capital goods. In a private enterprise economy the funds for the purchase of capital goods come largely from private investors, and the income these investment funds earn is called *interest*.

The third basic contribution to production is made by natural resources. We shall use the term *land* when referring to this factor of production, even though it includes such items as oyster beds, and oil fields under the Gulf of Mexico. The most important economic characteristic of land is that it is fixed in amount, because it is a gift of nature and cannot be changed by man's action. Under our system of private property these natural resources are usually owned by individuals, and the payment made for their use is referred to as *rent*.

The fourth contribution to production is performed by those people who organize, manage, plan, and bear the uncertainties of production. The function in question is variously referred to as *entrepreneurship* or *management*, and the payment is called *profit*. Because this last function is closely associated with ownership, it is difficult to separate profits from the interest income resulting from investment or the wages earned by the owner's labor. The chief distinction will be that entrepreneurship involves carrying responsibilities and uncertainties beyond those of the ordinary worker or investor.

The above description of productive services and the corresponding returns indicates that economists assign these terms meanings somewhat at variance with ordinary usage. In the development of economic thought it was natural that terms in general business usage should be employed, but it was quickly discovered that these terms must be strictly defined for purposes of logical discussion. In the study of income, therefore, economists adopted special definitions for words in common use that would permit them to relate the income received to the function performed. To the economist profits have come to mean income received primarily for the bearing of uncertainty in management decisions. In contrast the accountant takes profits to mean the income of the owner, including the reward for the use of funds or natural resources and (in the case of a sole proprietorship or partnership) payment for labor performed by the owner. The economist limits the meaning of rent to payments made for the use of natural resources alone, but the general usage of the term *rent* includes payments made for man-made things, such as cars or houses.

## MARKET FACTORS IN INCOME DISTRIBUTION

**Determination of Income by Supply Of and Demand For Productive Factors.** Earned income is merely the price paid for the services of the factors of production. These prices, like others in our private enterprise economy, are determined in the market through the operation of supply and demand. The supplies of labor, capital funds, natural resources, and entrepreneurship are subject to varying influences and must be individually examined in the following chapters. The corresponding demand, on the other hand, can be studied collectively as the result of the contribution made to production by the several factors. We can be certain that a rational businessman will be willing to pay no more for a factor than the increase in the value of the output that results from its services. We can be certain that the business that pays a greater sum for the factors it uses in its operations than the total it receives for its output is headed for failure. Thus the payment to each individual factor will be carefully compared to the contribution to production made by that factor. The technical term designating the contribution made by a factor is *marginal productivity*. We must next examine the production principle that underlies this theory and its relationship to the revenue of the firm.

**Principle of Diminishing Returns.** Like many other basic ideas in economics the principle of diminishing returns was clearly stated and recognized as a result of the need to solve a concrete problem. Early in the nineteenth century Napoleon controlled most of the European continent and threatened to cut off England's grain supplies. Urban population growth resulting from the burgeoning industrial revolution had already reduced the island's ability to feed itself. Some people were saying that the problem could easily be solved by putting more people to work on the land. Everyone was willing to admit that production of grain could be increased by using a larger number of farm workers on the limited amount of land. However, this raised a further question: would doubling the number of laborers double the output of grain? The answer to this question clearly was in the negative. Because the amount of land on the island was fixed and practically all of it already in productive use, additional labor would necessarily be less efficiently used and result in less output per man.

It was not long before economists began to realize that this concept of diminishing returns applied generally to situations in production where certain factors of production were held constant in amount and other factors were applied in varying quantities. Thus the principle of diminishing marginal returns took the form we gave it in Chapter 14. The economist now uses this principle to explain choices between the various possible methods of production as well as the shape of the cost curves for the individual producer.

**The Production Function.** The principle of diminishing returns describes the variation in output when production is carried on with different amounts of fixed and variable factors of production. It suggests a varying efficiency with different combinations of factors and leads to a study of what is the "best" way to produce. From the businessman's point of view this is the production method that secures the lowest cost per unit of output. In order to discover the lowest-cost method it is necessary to have the *production function* that shows us the various combinations of the input factors that will result in a given quantity of output. Then, if the businessman knows the prices for the input units, he can begin to compare the costs per unit of output that would result from the various possible combinations shown by the production function and select the one giving the lowest cost.

In Table 18–3 a simple illustration of the production function is given that shows how output of a plant will vary in response to changes in either the quantity of labor or the quantity of capital used. Across the top of the table we show plants with varying amounts of capital equipment. Along the left side of the table we show the num-

**TABLE 18–3**
**Possible Daily Outputs of Plants with Varying Amounts of Capital Equipment and Men Employed**

| Number of Men Employed | Plant Size Measured by Invested Capital | | | | | |
|---|---|---|---|---|---|---|
| | $50,000 | $60,000 | $70,000 | $80,000 | $90,000 | $100,000 |
| 10 | 37 | 41 | 45 | 50 | 54 | 57 |
| 11 | 41 | 45 | 50 | 55 | 59 | 63 |
| 12 | 46 | 50 | 54 | 59 | 64 | 68 |
| 13 | 49 | 53 | 57 | 62 | 67 | 72 |
| 14 | 50 | 54 | 58 | 64 | 70 | 75 |
| 15 | 51 | 55 | 59 | 65 | 72 | 78 |

ber of men working each day. The figures in the body of the table show the number of units of output with different combinations of men and capital. For example, if we use 11 men in a plant costing \$80,000, the output will be 55 units per day.

Such a table can be used, together with information on wages and capital cost, to derive estimates of production cost per unit. Presumably, the firm will wish to produce a given output at lowest unit cost. In an actual industrial plant the problem would be greatly complicated by the fact that many more than two factors of production must be used in such operations, but the basic idea of minimizing cost by the study of the physical results secured by the use of various combinations of factors would still apply.

**Use of Production Functions.** The production-function approach to costs assumes that it is possible within limits to substitute one of the productive factors for another. But the principle of diminishing returns tells us that as we increase any one of these factors while holding the others constant, the added output secured by additional units of the variable factor will diminish after a certain point. The basic question is when the substitution of one factor for the other should stop. In general, we can say that the businessman will achieve least cost per unit by continuing to add a factor as long as the output secured is greater than could be secured by spending the same amount on another factor. Least cost will have been secured when the added or marginal products are proportional to their respective factor prices, as shown in the following equation:

$$\frac{\text{marginal product of factor } A}{\text{price of factor } A} = \frac{\text{marginal product of factor } B}{\text{price of factor } B}.$$

This equation can be expanded to include all the factors that could be varied in a given production situation.

Of course, the equation really means that in the situation illustrated by the production function in Table 18–3 the businessman would be foolish to add more labor if he could secure a greater amount of added output by spending an equal sum devoted to increasing his use of capital. For example, let us suppose that the added cost for depreciation, interest, and related expenses is \$25 per day when the plant investment is increased from \$70,000 to \$80,000, and the wages per man are also \$25 per day. Assume that 11 men and the \$70,000 plant are being used to produce 50 units of output. If the firm plans to expand output beyond 50 units, it is more economical to do so by expanding plant than by adding labor. Thus the hiring of a twelfth man yields an extra four units, with an added cost of \$25. On the other hand, an added cost of \$25 resulting from the use of the \$80,000 plant with the same 11 men will increase output five units. If we fit these figures into the above equation we would see that it was out of balance as follows:

$$\frac{4 \text{ (marginal product of labor)}}{\$25 \text{ (cost of labor)}} < \frac{5 \text{ (marginal product of capital)}}{\$25 \text{ (cost of capital)}},$$

where the symbol < means "is less than." But we would have balance at the point where we consider expanding output from 55 units to 59, because this result could be secured by using the twelfth man in the $80,000 plant or continuing to use 11 men in the $90,000 plant. In this situation our equation would read:

$$\frac{4 \text{ (marginal product of labor)}}{\$25 \text{ (cost of labor)}} = \frac{4 \text{ (marginal product of capital)}}{\$25 \text{ (cost of capital)}}.$$

This equation indicates that the firm is proportioning its use of factors to minimize cost. Our next step will be to hold one of the factors constant and then decide how much of the other factor in the production table should be used.

**Measuring One Factor's Contribution to Production.** Suppose now that we assume that the $80,000 plant shown in Table 18–3 has been built and we are trying to decide how many workers should be used in it. Figure 18–2, Part A, shows how many units of output would be added by varying the number of men employed from 10 to 15. The descending marginal product (*MP*) curve in Part A shows graphically the operation of the principle of diminishing returns in this plant. But the businessman must calculate his costs, revenue, and profit in money, so it is necessary to change this curve of physical marginal product into a curve showing the money value of the marginal product. This result is accomplished simply by multiplying the amount of physical marginal product at each point on the *MP* curve by the selling price of the product as shown in Part B. If a day's labor by the twelfth man added increases the output by four units, point *P* in Part A shows the addition to physical output, but if the selling price per unit is $15, point *P* in Part B shows this same addition to output as $60, or the value in money of the four physical units. After we have multiplied the marginal product by the selling price we refer to the curve as the sales value of the marginal product (*SVMP*).

**Measuring the Contribution to Revenue.** If the businessman has some control over the price at which he sells his product, we must also introduce the marginal-revenue concept, because he will try to maximize profit by balancing the addition to revenue resulting from any change in output and price with the addition to cost. Table 18–4 shows the calculation of *SVMP* and of marginal-revenue product (*MRP*). In this table we find the diminishing returns that result from adding more units of labor in the column headed "Marginal Product." The

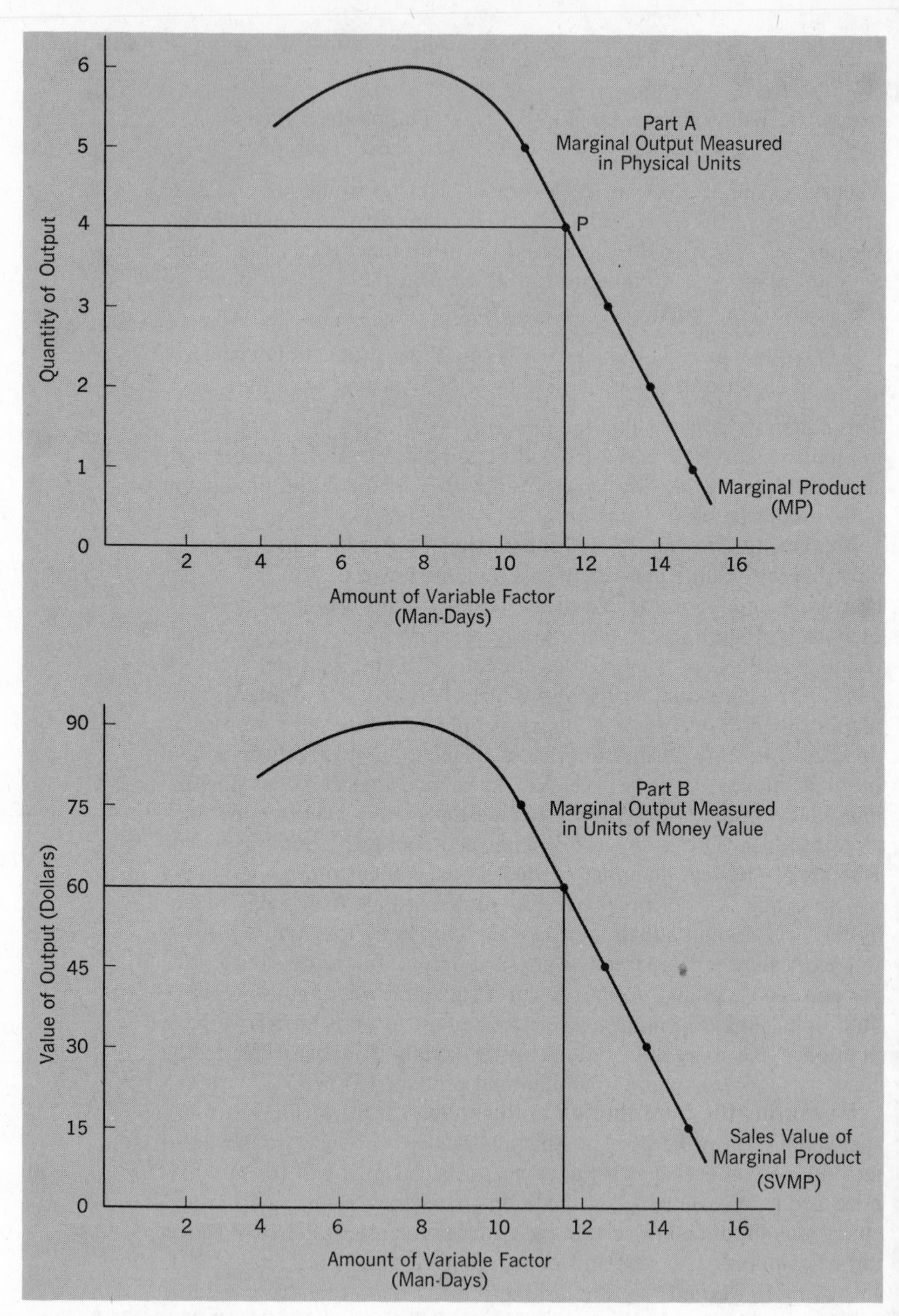


**Figure 18–2.** Effect of diminishing returns upon amount of output added as changes are made in quantity of variable factor used.

"Selling Price" column is based on the assumption that the firm must reduce its price 25 cents in order to sell each additional unit of output. *SVMP* is calculated by multiplying the marginal product at each level of input of the productive factor by the new lower price at which the new total product must be sold. *MRP* is simply the difference between two total revenues that results from the addition of another unit of labor.

**TABLE 18-4**
**Revenue Secured by Sale of Marginal Product Under Monopolistic Conditions**

| Total Output | Man-Days | Marginal Product | Selling Price ($) | *SVMP* ($) | Total Revenue ($) | *MRP* ($) |
|---|---|---|---|---|---|---|
| 50 | 10 | | $20.00 | | $1,000.00 | |
| | | 5 | | $93.75 | | $31.25 |
| 55 | 11 | | 18.75 | | 1,031.25 | |
| | | 4 | | 71.00 | | 16.00 |
| 59 | 12 | | 17.75 | | 1,047.25 | |
| | | 3 | | 51.00 | | 6.75 |
| 62 | 13 | | 17.00 | | 1,054.00 | |
| | | 2 | | 33.00 | | 2.00 |
| 64 | 14 | | 16.50 | | 1,056.00 | |
| | | 1 | | 16.25 | | 0.25 |
| 65 | 15 | | 16.25 | | 1,056.25 | |

Now if we place *SVMP* and the *MRP* curves on the same graph, the points showing marginal revenue product will be below those showing sales value of marginal product at each level of input of the variable factor. It is also significant that *MRP* will be more inelastic than *SVMP*. An example of such a graph is shown in Figure 19–3 of the next chapter.

**Demand for a Factor of Production.** We now have the basis for determining the demand for a factor of production, that is, the quantity that will be employed at a series of prices. If we ask how many men will be employed if the wage is $15 per day, it is clear that the employer will hire another man only if he increases revenue more than he increases cost. The *MRP* column in Table 18–4 shows that the twelfth man with his *MRP* of $16 has exceeded this amount. The same cannot be said of the thirteenth, fourteenth, or fifteenth man. It is true that the fifteenth man has added to production a quantity that can be sold for more than the wage, as shown by *SVMP*, but this sale will force down the price of all units sold and will reduce the marginal revenue to 25 cents, as shown by the *MRP*, or well below the wage to be paid. As a result this man will not be employed.

If only 12 men are employed at a wage of $15, how much will wages have to drop in order to cause the employer to take on another man? By looking at Table 18–4 again we see that the answer is that wages must fall to $6.75 per day (*MRP* of the thirteenth man), because at any wage level above this the thirteenth man will add more to cost than he does to revenue. Moving in the other direction we see that wages will have to go above $16 per day before the employer will cease to use the twelfth man and above $31.25 per day before it will cause him to discharge the eleventh man. Thus the *MRP* column shows the quantity of the factor that will be used at the various prices for the factor and is the demand schedule. This means that both in the table and on the graph, *MRP becomes the demand curve for the factor.*

Under special conditions (pure competition) when additional units of output can be sold without reducing price, the marginal revenue will be simply the amount for which the marginal product is sold. Therefore, *SVMP* and *MRP* will be the same under conditions in which the producer has no control over price and all units are sold at the same price.

The demand for a factor of production alone does not control the price that will be paid for the factor and, as a result, the income its owner will receive. It is only when the demand for the factor resulting from its contribution to production is combined with the supply schedule for the same factor that we can determine its price. In our illustrations in this chapter we have generally treated labor as the factor being varied, but in the following chapters we shall take the factors of labor, capital, and land in turn and examine the special characteristics of their demand and supply curves. From this treatment we hope to secure an understanding of the forces that control wages, interest, and rent.

**Summary.** In our economy income levels result generally from the contribution made to production and are therefore uneven. Incomes result from the contribution of providing labor (wages), furnishing capital (interest), making land or natural resources available (rent) or supplying the entrepreneurial or management function (profits). The amount of income earned by each of these four factors of production will be determined by the price paid for them as determined by the response of the market to the pressures of supply and demand.

The principle of diminishing returns and the production function show what happens to output when factors of production are combined in various ways. Combining physical output results with selling price for the product enables us to calculate the changes in revenue (*SVMP*) that will result from variations in the quantity of the factors of production. Under monopolistic conditions additional output can be sold only by a reduction in the selling price, and the addition to revenue (*MRP*) will be less than the sales value of the marginal product (*SVMP*). The schedule showing revenue change (*MRP*) then becomes the demand for the factor of production, because it shows the quantity that will be employed at each factor price.



## QUESTIONS

1. How does "Compensation of Employees" compare in amount with other types of income in the "National Income" statistics? How has this share changed since 1929?
2. How much inequality is there in the United States in the distribution of income?
3. What are the reasons for inequality in the distribution of income?
4. Why does capitalism permit some incomes to exist that do not result from contributions to production?
5. List the four categories of productive services and name the income resulting from each.
6. Explain how the production function makes use of the principle of diminishing returns.
7. What is the equation that can be applied to the production function to show the "best" method of production? Explain how this equation is used.
8. What does *SVMP* mean? How is it calculated?
9. How is *MRP* calculated? If the curve *MRP* for a monopolistic firm is put on a graph, where does it lie relative to *SVMP?*
10. Why is *MRP* the demand for the factor of production?
11. Under what conditions will the *MRP* curve be the same as *SVMP?*

CHAPTER

19

# Wages—Income Share of Labor

**General Wage Level in a National Market.** In a perfectly competitive, capitalistic system wages will be determined primarily by the forces of the market—by supply and demand. In order to understand why wages are high or low, then, we must study the nature of the market and the way in which it functions. The labor market is very complex and frequently subject to influence by unions or management. Unfortunately, it is also much more difficult to be objective when we study the labor market than when we study a commodity market. The sale of labor is a more personal matter than the sale of peanuts, partly because the person cannot be separated from the delivery of labor and partly because wages are such a large part of so many people's incomes. Despite these difficulties a real understanding of the determination of wage rates requires that emotion and bias be kept to a minimum.

In the last chapter the discussion showed that the demand curve for labor was the same thing as the marginal revenue product curve. This marginal revenue product is the marginal product multiplied by the marginal revenue. The height of the demand curve, then, will depend partly on the magnitude of the marginal product and the factors that determine it. The productivity of workers depends on their health, strength, intelligence, education, and willingness to work, but it also depends upon the nature of the tools they use, the richness of the natural resources available, and the efficiency of the management. Many other forces could be listed, but it is sufficient if we understand that labor productivity is influenced by a great variety of factors.



On the other hand, the supply of labor will depend upon the size of the population, the number of persons in the population who wish to work, and the amount of time they wish to put into the job. All of these points will need to be studied with some care, but we have already gone far enough to explain why wages in different countries vary so greatly. Figure 19–1 shows the determination of wage levels in the United States and in India. We notice two differences between these labor markets: (1) the demand curve is higher in the United States because of the greater productivity, and (2) the labor supply (relative to other factors of production) is much greater in India, because of past population growth.

These graphs bring out clearly the problem facing a country that wants to raise the wage level. Either it must raise the position of the demand curve (by increasing labor productivity), or it must limit the growth of the labor supply (so that the worker is not handicapped by having very little capital and land with which to work). In recent years American foreign aid has assisted many of the less developed countries by introducing technological changes and supplying capital goods, both of which contribute toward raising the productivity of labor. Unfortunately, in some of these countries the growth in population has prevented the anticipated rise in wages and per capita incomes.

**Total Supply of Labor.** One of the most famous treatments of labor supply was *An Essay on the Principle of Population* by T. R. Malthus in 1798. Although the ideas presented in the *Essay* have been widely criticized, any study of population and the supply of labor must take into account his analysis. Malthus's basic conclusion was that the tendency of population to increase more rapidly than food production would cause wages to fall to a subsistence level. He believed the whole world was faced with the same cruel pressures of limited

**Figure 19–1.** Comparison of real wage level in United States and India resulting from differences in productivity and in the supply of labor.

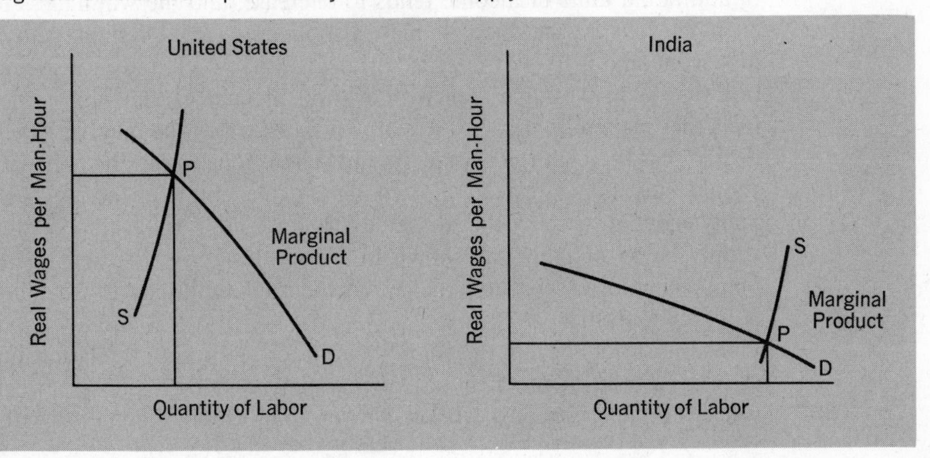

production and growing numbers that now appear in many underdeveloped countries.

Malthus thought that population unless checked was certain to grow rapidly because of the urgency of the sexual drive. On the other hand, the output of food for this increasing population, he believed, would be limited by the fact that the number of acres upon which food might be raised could not be expanded. The limitation of the food supply would result in malnutrition, disease, and other calamities that would tend to limit the growth in population. As we consider the fact that living standards have risen steadily in Western Europe and the United States during the past century and a half, we recognize that Malthus was in error. He failed to anticipate the impact of technological change on food output and the downward trend in family size. A continuation of the rise in the birth rate that has occurred since World War II, however, might yet bring to the Western world some of the serious consequences Malthus predicted.

Although population size is basic in determining the supply of labor, the fraction of persons willing to work must be considered also. If social custom permits women to work outside the home, the labor supply in the market will be larger than if they stay at home. The labor supply will be increased also if children leave school at an early age and if older people retire late in life. Finally, the labor supply, measured in hours of labor, varies directly with the work week. Thus a shift from a 30- to a 40-hour work week will increase hours of labor offered. The number of days of vacation per year will also affect the labor supply.

The effect of changes in the wage level upon the quantity of labor supplied is hard to predict. One's first thought is that people would work more hours if they were paid higher wages, but a little reflection casts doubt on this hypothesis. As wages and income rise, the utility of additional units of income tends to decrease, and the willingness to exchange leisure for income may also be reduced. A man with a higher income is likely to desire a shorter work week and more vacation time than the same man with a lower income. If the wage earner feels that his family income is relatively satisfactory, he may very well decide that the children should stay in school longer and that his wife should stay home instead of seeking outside employment. A good many economists think that these factors result in a backward-bending supply curve of labor, as shown in Figure 19–2. At the very least, many economists seem to believe that the total supply curve for labor is highly inelastic.

We must not confuse this supply curve for labor with a relationship showing the short-run effect of overtime pay offers on a laborer's work week. The decision of a worker with a comfortable income to work

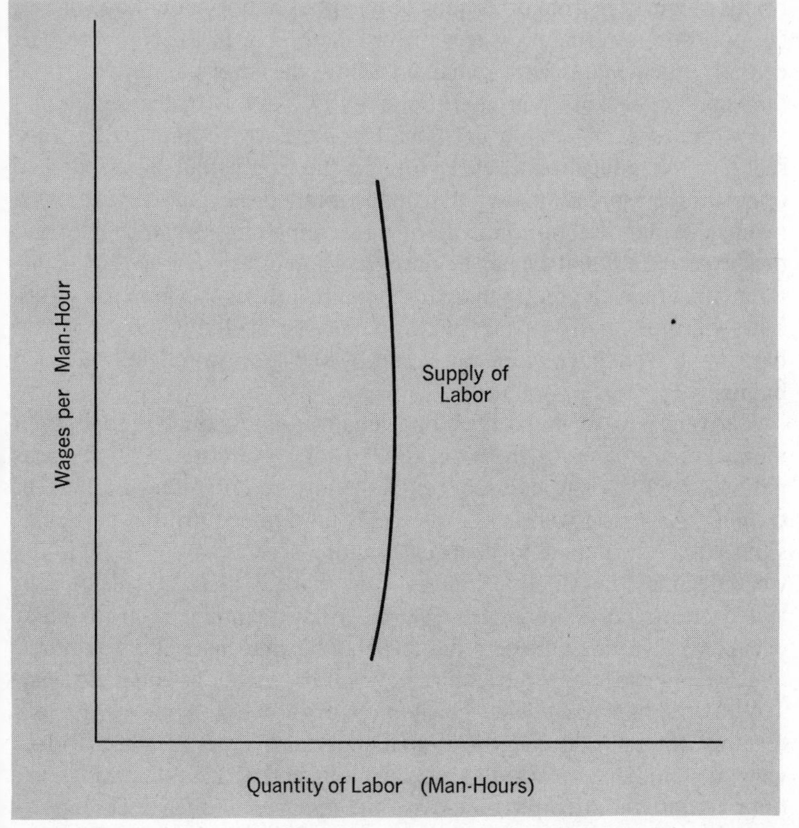


**Figure 19–2.** Inelastic or backward-bending supply curve for labor at various wage rates.

only a 40-hour week does not preclude his working 45 hours, if he is paid time and a half for overtime.

**Wages in a Particular Industry or Area.** Although demand and supply explain the general level of wages in a nation or region, we must look at the separate segments of the labor market if we are to discover the reasons for differences in wages in the various occupations or areas. A supply of skilled plumbers will not satisfy a contractor's need for electricians, and a demand for lathe operators cannot be met by a supply of truck drivers. We must look at the supply-and-demand forces for each particular kind of labor.

## SHORT RUN WAGE DETERMINATION

**Supply of Labor in a Particular Industry.** In any single occupation in a given locality the supply curve will be elastic if a high wage brings in workers from other jobs or localities and if a low wage causes the opposite movement. Wages of unskilled labor in the southern part of the United States long remained below the level of other parts of the country, because marginal productivity was low in the region and the workers were unable or unwilling to move to the higher-wage sections. As educational levels rose in the South and knowledge of opportunities spread, many unskilled workers did begin to move. As a result, the marginal productivity of those remaining began to rise, and the wage differential began to narrow. In Western Europe such differentials are even greater than in the United States, because the possibility of moving from one place to another is limited by political barriers, by language differences, and by variation in religion or living habits.

Hard as it is to make locational changes, individuals find it even more difficult to move from one skilled job to another. Skilled occupations, such as carpentry or brick laying, require long periods of training. A person who has invested his time in acquiring a particular skill will be reluctant to change to another occupation, even if the wage declines. On the other hand, if the wage is high, he will be protected from the depressing effect of workers coming in from other occupations. Until outsiders have spent the time and effort required to secure the specialized training they will be unable to enter the field.

Workers in a particular occupation or profession may also join together to limit the supply of that particular type of labor with a view to stabilizing or raising wages. Unions and professional organizations frequently attempt to increase the incomes of their members by decreasing labor supply.

**Short-Run Demand for Labor in a Particular Industry.** As we discovered in the preceding chapter, an employer will hire additional workers, or other factors of production, only so long as they add more to revenue than to cost. Thus the *MRP* curve of a firm was identified as its demand curve for labor. This demand curve will tend to be made inelastic by two conditions: (1) production arrangements that require a relatively fixed number of workers so that the addition of more labor does not add significantly to output, and (2) a market where additional units of output can be sold only at considerably reduced prices.

In some plants it is quite possible to add more workers without running into sharply diminishing returns. This situation tends to occur under several conditions: for example, where additional shifts can be used, where the plant can be operated on either a four- or five-day basis, or where a portion of the plant can be closed down without affecting the efficiency of the part that remains in operation. On the other hand, in many industrial plants the combination of men and machinery is highly inflexible, and marginal productivity resulting from the addition of more units of labor decreases very rapidly. The elasticity of the short-run demand curve for labor, therefore, will vary greatly between different plants as a result of technological factors that control the shape of the marginal-product curve. The persistent tendency of modern industry to increase the use of automatic machinery appears to be causing a growing rigidity in the combination of men and equipment. The result appears in the form of a very inelastic short-run demand curve for labor in the typical industrial plant.

If the producer has a degree of monopoly, gained by a differentiated product or limitations on the number of sellers, he will thereby acquire some control over price. In the last chapter it was shown that control by the businessman over the price charged causes the *MRP* curve to lie below the *SVMP* curve and to decline more sharply. Because the *MRP* curve constitutes the demand for the factor of production, it follows that control over the price of the product makes the demand for labor more inelastic. As shown in Figure 19–3, the demand for labor (*MRP*) has become quite inelastic because (1) the

**Figure 19–3.** Inelastic demand for labor by firm with control over price of its output and producing with automatic machinery.

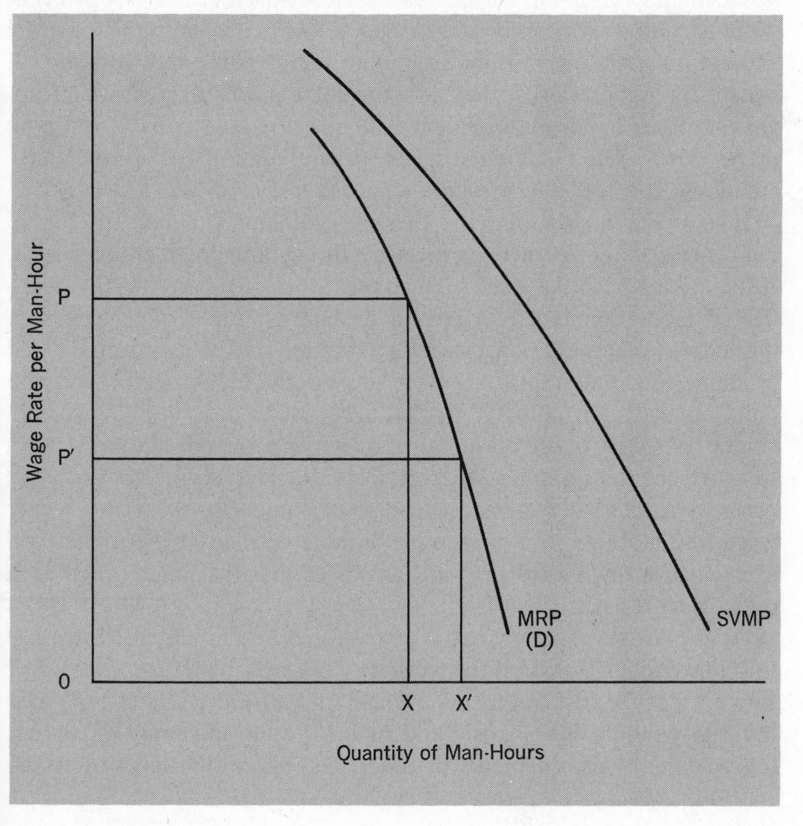

industrial plant involved has considerable automatic machinery, limiting variation in the use of labor and causing the *SVMP* curve to decline sharply as more labor units are added, and (2) the firm is avoiding an unprofitable drop in the price of its product, as shown by the separation of the *MRP* curve from *SVMP*. As a result, even a significant decline in the wage rate from *P* to *P′* in Figure 19–3 causes only a very slight short-run change from *X* to *X′* in the quantity of man-hours used.

**Effect of Unions and Collective Bargaining on Wages in the Short Run.** In a great many industries, then, we find that the labor market is characterized by highly inelastic short-run demand curves because of monopolistic elements in the market for the product and technological rigidity of the production process. If in addition the labor used in the industry has a considerable degree of skill, so that entry from other types of work is not easy, we also have a highly inelastic short-run supply curve. The steel industry, for example, appears to embody these characteristics. In an industry of this kind the supply-and-demand curves for labor would appear to resemble those of Figure 19–4. As a result of this inelasticity of the supply and demand for labor the curves lie close together for a significant distance, and wages can be established at any point between $P^1$ and $P^2$ without creating a significant disequilibrium. Because the workers will benefit by higher wages, they will use their power to push them up. On the other hand, management will try to reduce costs by pushing wages down. The resulting struggle presents one of the most bitterly emotional spectacles in present-day society.

It is worth noting that the demand-and-supply curves in Figure 19–4 are not represented as inelastic throughout their entire length. If the unions push the wage high enough, they will find that the quantity of labor demanded begins to decline as the weaker firms are pushed out of production (variable costs are not being covered) and as management attempts to replace some of the high-priced labor with more automatic machinery. At the higher wages the supply curve becomes somewhat more elastic also, as workers outside the area begin to move in and as other workers increase their efforts to learn the necessary skills. The spreading apart of these curves at the higher wage levels above $P^2$ represents a surplus of unused labor that will exert such a downward pressure on wages that the union will find it difficult to resist.

At the lower wage levels the reverse will be the case. If the wage falls low enough, many of the workers will leave the industry for other jobs even at the cost of the loss of their special skills. The lower wages indicate possible lower costs and higher profits that may encourage the opening of closed plants or other possible output expansion and

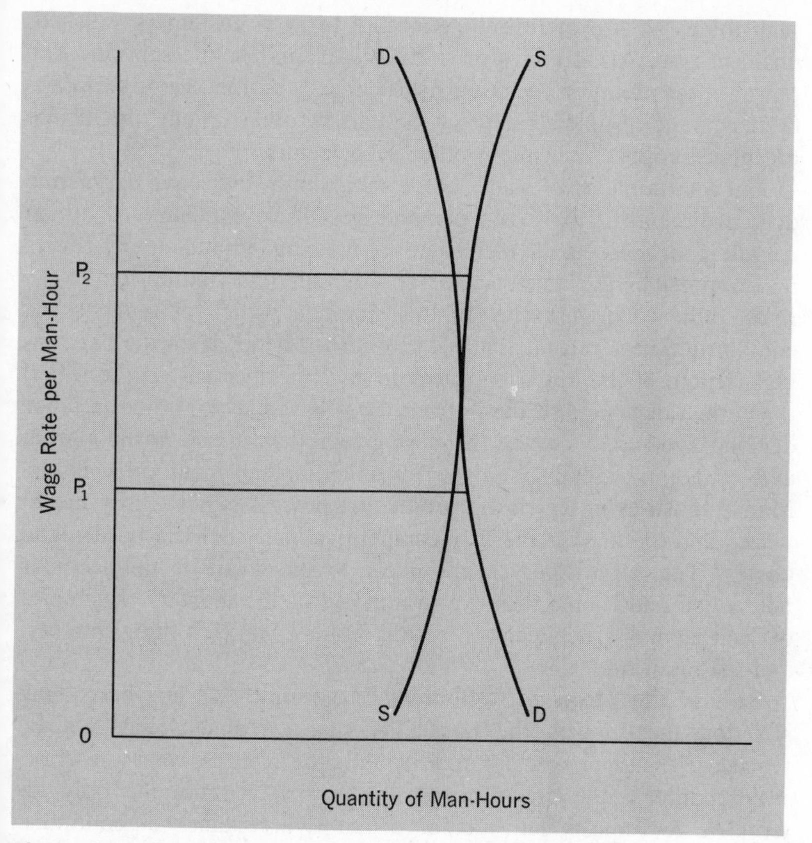


**Figure 19–4.** Range of possible wage rates that can result under collective bargaining with inelastic demand and supply curves for labor.

cause the quantity of labor demanded to increase. The spreading apart of the demand-and-supply curves below $P^1$ indicates that at such low levels the shortage of labor would tend to push wages up to a point where balance would be approached.

Although management might be willing to accept some shortage of labor at the lower wage levels and refrain from bidding up the wage rate, a more serious shortage would be hard to resist. In the same way the union could keep its members in line if the higher wages resulted in some unemployment, but not if the labor surplus became large. In between these two extremes collective bargaining can establish a wage rate that results in a stable equilibrium in the sense that there are no significant forces working to disturb the balance. Under these circumstances the actual wage rate depends on the bargaining ability and the capacity of each side to hold out. Such a struggle involves many factors, with the strength of management depending upon such things as size of inventory, ability to keep customers satisfied, financial reserves, attitudes of stockholders, and public support. The power of the union on the other hand depends on the size of the strike fund, attitude of union members, support by other unions, the degree of public support, and many other such factors.

The determination of wages in the short run by collective bargaining does not replace supply and demand as a basic explanation. But in certain labor markets the inelasticity of the demand-and-supply curves makes possible the existence of several different equilibrium wage rates, rather than just one. In this situation, which of the possible equilibrium wage rates actually is established depends on the bargaining strength of the union on one side and management on the other.

On the other hand, if the industry does have elastic short-run labor demand-and-supply curves, the wage level is determined by the market and cannot be greatly changed by either management or a union. Many industries in which the production process is not rigidly mechanized and the market is freely competitive have such elastic demand curves. The supply curves are likely to be elastic if the labor is not skilled and is free to move in and out of the industry. Examples of such labor markets exist in cotton textiles, work clothing, lumber, and the retail trades.

**Role of the Strike in Collective Bargaining.** In any bargaining situation there exists the possibility that agreement may not be reached. When management and the union disagree on wages or working conditions, the union may call a strike, because the only alternative to some effective labor action is acceptance of continued employment on terms set by the management. The strike, of course, works hardship on both sides and puts pressure on both for a settlement. If a strike is called and proves effective, the employer's plant is closed, and revenue from sales is lost while many costs continue. Union members, on the other hand, suffer a loss of wages, and their families may experience serious hardship unless they have adequate savings or receive strike benefits from union funds. Such a struggle may last many days or weeks and bring serious losses to both sides. Even if a wage increase is finally granted, it may take a long time for the increase to match the lost wages of the workers. If management wins and wages are kept low, the saving in cost may be more than offset by the revenue lost during the strike. Collective bargaining over wage rates is not likely to fail and result in a strike, therefore, unless one side or the other incorrectly estimates the possibility of success or unless tempers have risen to the point where irrational action is taken.

Unfortunately, a serious strike brings hardship upon persons other than the bargaining parties. The general public may be able for a short period to avoid serious inconvenience. The products that are held in inventory or are produced in plants not closed will satisfy the most essential needs. But if the strike is industry-wide and if it lasts very long, consumers will begin to suffer from the resulting shortages. If the strike occurs in transportation or communications industries, the hardships may be immediate and severe. Whenever the public begins to suffer from the private struggle of the contending groups, there is certain to be strong pressure for the intervention of a third party, usually the government.

The most difficult aspect of the intervention by government officials (or other peacemakers) is that they are obliged to determine the conditions upon which the strike is to be settled. Simply ordering the end of the strike would almost certainly mean that the workers accepted the wages and working conditions currently being offered by management. Intervention, therefore, really means that government has accepted the responsibility for fixing wage levels and controlling other working conditions. No wonder that government officials in a democratic society try desperately to avoid taking over the control of such an important market as the one in which wages are determined. But frequently the only alternative to severe hardship to the public is a significant increase in government power. The result has been a steady increase in the amount of intervention by government in quarrels between labor and management.

**Effect upon Wages of Monopsony.** Just as unions attempt to push wages up when they have the power, business management will try to push them down. One situation in which this is possible exists when there is only one buyer of a particular kind of labor in a certain market area. Under these conditions the employer will be faced with a rising supply curve of labor. He will find some workers with poor alternative opportunities who are willing to work at a low wage; but in order to secure a larger number of workers a somewhat higher wage must be paid.

The result is an upward-sloping curve of average expenditure for wages as shown by *AE* in Figure 19–5. At a wage of $1.00 per hour 10 workers will be available, but in order to attract more employees a higher wage must be paid. Because a smaller number of workers would offer their services at a rate less than $1.00 per hour, and a larger number at a higher wage, management must decide what wage it ought to set. If management wishes to maximize profit, it must add workers as long as the addition to revenue is greater than the addition to cost. Under this rule the best point of operation is shown at *X*, where *ME* (marginal expenditure for labor) crosses the *SVMP–MRP* curve. At this point 10 workers would be employed at a wage rate of $1.00 per hour.

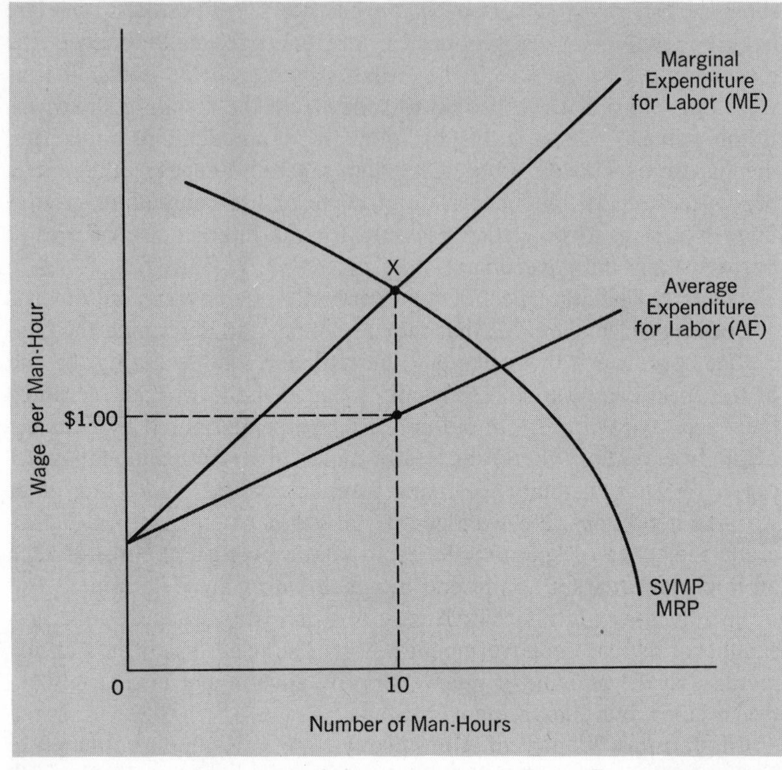


**Figure 19–5.** Tendency of monopsony in labor market to depress wages and limit quantity of labor used.

No distinct *MRP* curve is shown in Figure 19–5 in order to simplify the graph. However, this picture is relevant only if the firm has no control over the price of the product it sells. If such control exists, then the best point of operation is where *ME* intersects *MRP*.

It is important to understand why the *ME* line lies above *AE* in Figure 19–5; that is, why the addition to cost occasioned by another worker is greater than the wage he is paid. An examination of Table 19–1 reveals the relationship between wages paid and additions to cost when more workers are available only at higher wages. It is clear that at each level of employment the *ME* figure in the last column is well above the *AE* amount in the second column and that *ME* is rising 10¢ with each additional labor unit employed, whereas *AE* is rising more slowly at 5¢ per unit. Expressed graphically, the *ME* curve must lie above the *AE* curve, as in Figure 19–5, and be rising more rapidly. The effect of this relationship is that *ME* will rise quickly to equal *MRP*, causing the management to stop adding workers well before *MRP* equals *AE*, the wage. This reduced employment occurs because the addition of more workers will force the wage rate up for all employees, and thus the situation quickly reaches the point where more is added to cost than to revenue. As in any situation where one side of the market is able to control the price—in this case the wage—there is an advantage in restricting the quantity and thus securing a more favorable price. This tendency to restrict quantity is the basic problem posed by the presence of monopoly and monopsony in our society.

**TABLE 19-1**
**Relationship of Wages Paid to Additions to Cost**

| Number of Men | Hourly Wages *AE* ($) | Total Wages Paid ($) | Additional Cost *ME* ($) |
|---|---|---|---|
| 8 | 0.90 | 7.20 | |
| 9 | 0.95 | 8.55 | 1.35 |
| 10 | 1.00 | 10.00 | 1.45 |
| 11 | 1.05 | 11.55 | 1.55 |
| 12 | 1.10 | 13.20 | 1.65 |

## WAGES IN LONG RUN

**Long-Run Wage Adjustments in a Particular Industry or Area.** Although management or unions may be able to influence the wage in the short run, it is well to recognize that in the long run the demand-and-supply curves become more elastic. As the time period becomes longer, therefore, the influence of market forces upon wage rates increases in strength, and bargaining dwindles in importance. Figure 19–6 illustrates market conditions in the long run, with relatively more elastic supply-and-demand curves. The clear-cut intersection here affords a distinct contrast to the situation pictured in Figure 19–4. At any wage above *P* a sizable excess supply of labor would exist; and at any wage below *P* an excess demand would be present. These forces would tend to push the wage toward the equilibrium indicated by the intersection of the supply-and-demand curves.

Consider the reasons why these curves are more elastic in the long run than in the short run, starting with demand. In the long run management faces the need periodically to replace wornout plants or to expand capacity. Because the capital–labor mix can be reconsidered, a new flexibility arises in the amount of labor to be hired. If wages have been high, management is almost certain to construct a new plant with more automatic machinery in order to reduce the use of the high cost factor. If, on the other hand, wages have been low, management will tend to limit its use of high-priced machinery. The long-run decision with respect to the quantity of labor used will be

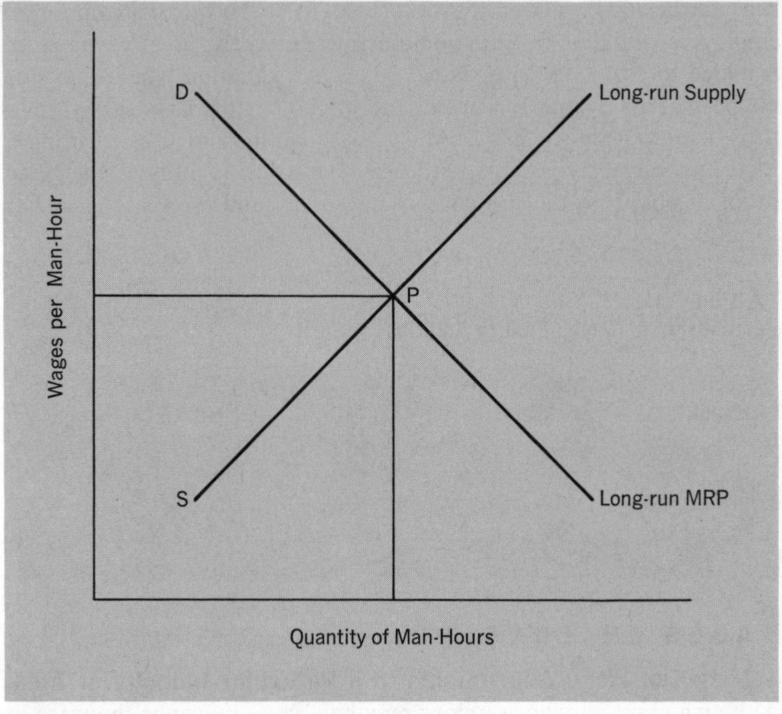


**Figure 19–6.** Long-run equilibrium level of wages in market with relatively elastic demand and supply curves for labor.

based on a comparison of costs involving alternative methods of production. All this implies that a more sensitive adjustment of the use of labor is made to wage changes in the long than in the short run. The demand for labor is more elastic.

In addition, the long-run supply curve in a particular industry will tend to be much more elastic than the short-run curve. Although men with special skills, seniority, and pension rights will be reluctant to leave their jobs when wages are reduced, many of them will gradually find more attractive opportunities. Even more important will be the reluctance of young people to take positions in an industry with unattractive wage scales. The reverse will be the case at higher wage levels, and the industry will find many people who are anxious to take advantage of these more attractive incomes. Labor mobility may be limited in the short run, but adjustments do take place in the long run.

**Wages in Particular Jobs Within a Given Plant.** In any particular plant a good many different wage rates will be paid to workers with varying degrees of skill and experience. The contribution that each worker makes to production helps to determine the wage that the employer is willing to pay for his services. The *MRP* is still the basis of the demand for workers of a particular type, as well as for labor in general. The supply curve for each kind of labor will vary also according to the number of employees able and willing to qualify. When these individual demand-and-supply curves, with all of their possible variations, are taken into account, the wage for a particular kind of work is determined.

It must not be supposed, however, that exact measurement of the marginal revenue product for a particular worker is possible. Management must make the best estimate it can of the importance of particular types of workers to the production process. As a result of management's imperfect knowledge of productivity, relative wage levels become the focus of many labor disputes. Many labor contracts tend to be extremely complex documents because of the need to define carefully the nature of the work to be done within each job classification and the wage to be paid for it. Such problems are dealt with in considerable detail in the study of labor economics or personnel management.

**Summary.** The general level of wages in different countries will vary with the productivity of labor and inversely with the quantity of labor relative to the other productive factors. The general supply curve for labor depends upon the size of the population and the willingness to work, and is generally thought to be inelastic or even backward-bending. The elasticity of the supply of labor for a particular industry depends upon whether higher wages will attract workers from other areas or other jobs.

The elasticity of the demand for labor in a particular industry will depend upon how rapidly marginal output declines as workers are added and whether the price of the output must be reduced to dispose of additional output. In many industries the short-run demand and supply curves for labor are highly inelastic, and in such cases the lack of a clear intersection of the curves permits wages to be forced up or down in the process of collective bargaining. Losses caused by strikes are used by unions to secure a higher wage settlement and by management to force settlement by the workers at a lower wage level. Monopsonistic control of the labor market by management will cause a smaller amount of labor to be employed and a lower wage to be paid than would be the case under competition. The long-run supply and demand curves for labor in a particular industry or area tend to be more elastic than in the short run, and either union or management is less able to manipulate the wage rate.

## QUESTIONS

1. What part of Malthus's ideas on population do we not accept today?
2. Discuss the possible validity of the arguments used to support the belief that the general labor supply curve is backward-bending.

3. What factors determine whether the labor supply in a particular locality or industry will be elastic or inelastic?
4. What are the two basic conditions that tend to make the short-run demand for labor inelastic in a particular industry?
5. Explain the relationship between inelasticity of the supply and demand curves in a particular industry and the operation of collective bargaining.
6. What is the role of the strike in collective bargaining?
7. Explain why the existence of monopsony in a labor market causes the wage rate paid to be less than the *SVMP* for the quantity of labor employed.
8. Why are long-run supply and demand curves for labor in a particular industry frequently more elastic than the short-run curves?

CHAPTER 20

# Interest—Income Share of Capital

Man's labor is much more productive when it is used with proper tools and equipment. Because production is increased by the use of capital goods and because those who provide the funds for their purchase forego alternative uses of these amounts, it is not surprising that a payment should be made for their use. Interest is the payment made for providing the funds that are needed to acquire productive capital goods.

**Special Problems in the Use of Capital.** The need to provide capital goods before starting production introduces many complexities into our economic system. Unless someone is willing to put up the funds required for buildings, equipment, tools, and raw material inventories, they will not be provided. When the economist deals with wages, however, he does not need to worry about a supply of funds, because the man is not bought, only his labor. Because the payment of wages and the sale of goods take place almost concurrently, the economist can treat wages as being paid out of the revenue from sales. But capital goods must usually be fully paid for in advance of their use, even though their services will be realized over a period of 10 or 20 years and sometimes even longer. The willingness to provide the funds and to give up for several years having them readily available for any other use is the service that must be paid for by interest.

This distinction between money capital and capital goods is one that has caused much confusion in the past. In the Middle Ages it was thought that money was barren or unproductive and that to charge interest for its use was sinful. It was not until we moved into the more modern period that clearer thinkers began to point out that, although money might be barren, capital goods purchased with the same money were highly productive. Consequently, a payment of interest for the use of money to be invested in productive goods became a morally acceptable practice.

Orthodox communist theory argues that labor alone among the factors is productive. In practice, however, Soviet planners have found it essential to levy an accounting charge against plants for the use of capital funds. This charge constitutes one of the plant's costs and must be met unless it is decided to let the product be sold at a loss. The use of interest charges permits the planners to compare the efficiency of a plant containing large quantities of automatic machinery with one using more labor but provided with limited equipment. By using an interest charge the planners force plants to limit their borrowing in the light of costs and the price at which the product is to be sold.

Another problem results from the fact that capital equipment wears out and must be replaced. Accountants give recognition to this problem by including a charge to cover the wearing out or depreciation of the capital goods. The accounting entry also permits the business to accumulate resources (not necessarily in the form of cash) adequate to recover the cost of the equipment and presumably sufficient to replace it. For example, if certain machinery is expected to last 10 years, the business will charge off 10 per cent of the cost each year. Thus the cost of using capital goods is a combination of the depreciation charge and the interest paid for the use of funds invested in the equipment.

It should be understood that we are using the term *interest* to designate the payment made for the use of capital funds, whether provided by the owners in the form of capital stock or by creditors in the form of bonds or shorter-term liabilities. The accountant and the lawyer must concern themselves with detailed problems of ownership, type of liability, and tax reporting, but the economist is concerned with the social cost of providing capital funds and capital goods for production and not the legal characteristics of the claims to those assets.

## DEMAND FOR INVESTMENT FUNDS

**Productivity of Capital Goods and the Demand for Capital Funds.** In arriving at a decision as to the needed amount of capital goods, businessmen balance the anticipated added revenue to be secured from an additional unit of capital goods against the added cost. The increase in revenue resulting from the increased use of capital goods is measured by the *MRP* curve. On the horizontal axis shown in Figure 20–1 we measure the quantity of capital funds invested in capital goods in one particular plant. Although it is units of machinery or other productive equipment that are being added, the only common denominator for all the different kinds of capital goods used is the money invested in them. Of course, the most essential machines will be provided first, but additional units of equipment will be purchased as long as they add more to revenue than to cost. In measuring cost Figure 20–1 shows that depreciation must be covered first, but that an additional investment will be made only if the anticipated *MRP* will also cover the interest charge on the funds. Measurement of *MRP* here becomes even less certain than it does in wage theory, because the anticipated revenue from capital investment will be yielded several years ahead, whereas the revenue from labor is much more immediate.



**Figure 20–1.** Factors which will enter into determination by firm as to the quantity of capital funds it will use.

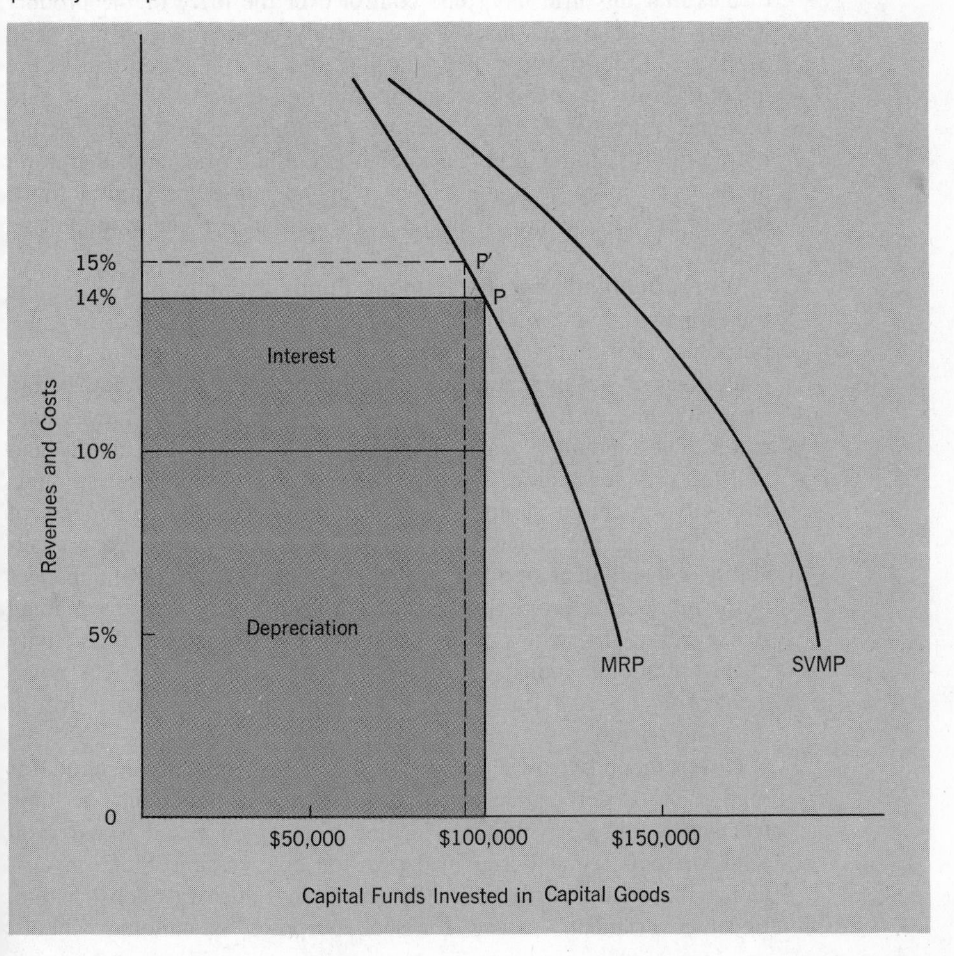

If a machine costs $1,000 and lasts 10 years, it will be purchased only if the businessman believes that it will increase revenue $140 per year measured on the vertical axis; that is, $100 for depreciation at 10 per cent and $40 for interest at 4 per cent of the $1,000 investment. If the interest rate rises to 5 per cent the cost rises to $150, and the investment will not be made unless the addition to annual revenue increases to the same figure. In other words point *P* on the *MRP* curve shows that $100,000 of capital funds will be required by this plant if the interest rate is 4 per cent, but point *P′* indicates that only $95,000 will be used if the interest rate increases to 5 per cent. *Because both P and P′, as well as other points showing quantity of capital used at various other rates of interest, lie along the MRP curve, we may conclude that this line shows the demand for capital as it relates to the rate of interest.*

The separation of the *SVMP* and *MRP* curves in Figure 20–1 indicates that this firm has some control over the price of the product it sells. If the selling market were purely competitive, *SVMP* and *MRP* would lie together. The fact that they are separated causes the quantity of capital demanded in this situation to be less than it would be under pure competition, because the producer here is restricting output in order to maintain an established selling price and, therefore, needs less capital equipment. The demand curve for capital funds has also been made more inelastic by the existence of the monopolistic element.

**Other Demands for Investment Funds.** Funds that might be used for investment in capital goods may also be demanded for other purposes. Consumers frequently wish to purchase automobiles, air conditioners, washing machines, and other consumer goods before they have the cash to pay for them. In order to do so they secure credit. The amount of such consumer credit outstanding at the end of 1962 was $63 billion. This use of funds diverts significant amounts from investment in capital goods and introduces some elements of instability into the demand for durable consumer goods. Easy availability of installment credit seems to have contributed to recent changes in the number of automobiles sold from year to year, thereby tending to exaggerate the swings of the business cycle. Changes in the activity of the automobile industry were clearly reflected in the upward movement of the economy in 1955 and 1964 and in the downward drift at the end of 1960.

Government borrowing also constitutes a significant demand for funds. The Federal government borrows heavily from time to time to cover defense expenditures in time of emergency and to carry on relief or recovery activities in depression or recession. State governments frequently borrow in order to finance highway construction. Local governments borrow for such purposes as building schools, paving streets, and installing sewers. The combined demand of the different levels of government constitutes a significant portion of the total demand for funds in our economy.

**Demand for Investment Funds Relatively Inelastic.** Economists vary considerably in their estimates regarding the elasticity of the demand for capital funds. Some writers have stated that a lowering of the interest rate would greatly increase the volume of investment, but in recent years other economists have begun to question this assertion. Three main reasons are advanced for believing that the demand for investment funds is relatively inelastic: (1) the increased control over prices in many industries results in a more inelastic *MRP* curve, as shown in Figure 20–1, (2) heavy investment in machinery results in greater concern by management for the depreciation element of cost than for the interest cost (if the depreciation is 10 per cent and the interest 4 per cent, even a 50-per-cent change in interest rates will give a relatively small change, from 14 per cent to 16 per cent in the annual cost of using equipment), (3) efficient methods in mass production industries require a relatively rigid amount of machinery of quite definite types (if the plant is to be built, it requires an investment of a given amount to be efficient regardless of normal changes in the interest rate).

The above points give significant support for the belief in an inelastic demand for capital funds, but they do not prove that investment is completely unresponsive to changes in the rate of interest. Many industries have production processes in which a choice can be made about the mix of capital and labor. In such industries a decline in the interest rate relative to the wage level will lead to an increase in the use of capital. In industries where firms lack control over prices, investment will also be more responsive to changes in the interest level, particularly if the demand for the product is elastic.

The durability of capital is also a factor bearing on the elasticity of the demand for it. It should be obvious that some types of investment do not carry a charge for depreciation, and the interest cost then becomes significant. If a capital good depreciates over a long period of years, the interest charge becomes a more significant part of the cost of using the equipment. If a hydroelectric dam is estimated to serve 100 years the annual depreciation will be only 1 per cent and a change in the 4-per-cent interest rate assumed previously becomes relatively more important than when depreciation is 10 per cent, as in our previous illustration. This would tend to indicate that the demand for more durable capital equipment will be somewhat responsive to interest changes. On the whole, however, it seems likely that the demand for industrial capital funds in most uses tends to be rather unresponsive to such changes.

Consumer demand for funds also seems to be relatively unresponsive to changes in the rate of interest. It is doubtful whether most installment buyers of refrigerators, washing machines, and air conditioners know what rate of interest they are paying. If they believe that they can manage the monthly payment (of which an indeterminate amount is interest), they proceed to buy. Changes in the interest rate probably do not change the size of the monthly payment enough to influence the decision to buy goods of moderate price. In case of expensive items, such as automobiles, interest charges amount to a larger fraction of the cost, so that interest variations are more significant. The buying of homes probably responds more to changes in the interest rate than any other credit purchase by the family. Because the amount involved is rather large and the capital repayment is stretched over a good many years, the monthly payment on the purchase of a house contains a very heavy proportion of interest, and changes in the rate charged will significantly affect the size of the monthly payment. Despite these exceptions it is probably accurate to say that most families do not alter their decisions to purchase durable goods on credit to any significant degree because of changes in the rate of interest.

The Federal government normally borrows heavily only in time of war or deep depression. In such emergencies factors other than the interest rate will control the decision to borrow. On the other hand, when the state government borrows for highway construction and the local government for building schools, interest cost on the bonds will be an important charge on future budgets, and certainly may influence the quantity of funds demanded. In general, therefore, we may conclude that Federal government demand for funds tends to be highly inelastic, but that the demand by state and local governments is somewhat more elastic.

The total demand for investment funds on the part of businessmen, consumers, and government, therefore, would appear to be rather inelastic despite the fact that certain uses for funds may respond somewhat to changes in the interest rate. As we shall see later in the chapter this relative inelasticity of demand means that relatively small changes in the supply will tend to bring about marked changes in the interest rate. Changes in demand, as a result of altered expectations in the various phases of the business cycle, also play an important role in the theory of interest.

## SUPPLY OF INVESTMENT FUNDS

**Sources of Supply for Investment Funds.** Funds can be made available for investment purposes only if income is saved and thus withheld from consumption or new money is created and loaned to those demanding investment funds. The supply of investment funds thus requires two separate decisions: (1) to refrain from consumption, and (2) to give up the advantage of holding these savings in liquid form. The most obvious source of investment funds is personal savings; 50 years ago economists believed that abstinence from consumption by the individual provided the basic supply of funds for the purchase of capital goods. More complete statistics today reveal that personal saving is a significant source of funds, but less important than originally believed. Savings by corporations in the form of undistributed profits and depreciation reserves provide an important portion of the investment funds required by our larger business units.

**TABLE 20–1***
**Personal Income, Consumption and Saving, Selected Years, 1929–64 (Billions of Dollars)**

| Year | Disposable Personal Income ($) | Consumption Expenditures ($) | Personal Saving ($) | Saving as Per Cent of Disposable Income |
|---|---|---|---|---|
| 1929 | 83.1 | 79.0 | 4.2 | 5.1 |
| 1932 | 48.7 | 49.3 | −0.6 | −1.2 |
| 1939 | 70.4 | 67.6 | 2.9 | 4.1 |
| 1944 | 146.8 | 109.8 | 36.9 | 25.1 |
| 1947 | 170.1 | 165.4 | 4.7 | 2.8 |
| 1950 | 207.7 | 195.0 | 12.6 | 6.1 |
| 1952 | 238.7 | 219.8 | 18.9 | 7.9 |
| 1955 | 274.4 | 256.9 | 17.5 | 6.4 |
| 1957 | 308.8 | 285.2 | 23.6 | 7.6 |
| 1960 | 349.9 | 328.2 | 21.7 | 6.2 |
| 1962 | 384.6 | 356.8 | 27.8 | 7.2 |
| 1964 | 431.8 | 399.2 | 32.6 | 7.5 |

* Source: **Economic Report of the President,** January 1965.

The creation of deposits by our commercial banking system, as explained in Chapter 10, also provides a significant supply of funds at certain times. Government, by taxation, may also bring about a reduction of consumption, and if the funds raised by taxation are not totally expended for routine governmental expenses, the remainder becomes available for investment purposes. Thus we have four possible sources of investment funds: (1) personal savings, (2) corporate savings, (3) creation of bank credit and (4) governmental budgets.

**Factors Affecting the Volume of Personal Saving.** Individuals have the choice of spending their income for consumption goods or of saving it. Table 20–1 shows how this choice has been exercised.

Although personal saving as a per cent of disposable personal income has remained relatively stable since 1950, the table shows clearly that depression in the decade of the 1930's and war in the 1940's greatly affected the rate of saving. The figures for 1932 show that when the depression reduced personal incomes, consumption was forced down also, but saving disappeared entirely. The negative saving indicates that many people were liquidating capital assets or borrowing to maintain acceptable living standards. A more normal situation was restored by 1939, but World War II forced down the percentage of income consumed through a shortage of available consumer goods, and in consequence the percentage of personal income saved in 1944 reached its highest point in recent history. After the war people rushed to purchase the things they had been unable to get during the war, and personal saving in percentage terms dropped to a postwar low. By 1950 more normal conditions had returned. Since that time consumption has accounted for between 92 and 94 per cent of disposable personal income, whereas saving has fluctuated around the 7-per-cent level.

Table 20–1 seems to indicate that personal saving is determined by decisions relative to the level of consumption. As depression or war changes living standards, the fraction of personal income saved fluctuates widely. On the other hand, when stable economic conditions are restored, Americans increase their consumption expenditures proportionately as personal income rises, and the percentage of saving seems to change only within narrow limits.

The relative stability of the percentage of personal income saved during the decade beginning with 1950 appears to indicate that the rising interest rate during the Eisenhower administration did not significantly influence the share of personal income going into savings. The average rate on Corporate Bonds Aaa (Moody's) in 1952 (according to the *Economic Report of the President*) was 2.96 per cent, and in 1960 it was up to 4.41 per cent. Yet this rise in the interest rate of approximately one half did not seem to motivate any significant change in the fraction of disposable personal income going into savings. People do not seem to save primarily in order to earn interest, but rather to have funds for emergencies, to pay for educating children, to take a vacation, to retire, or to provide for similar personal needs. A great deal of personal saving is also made almost automatically through purchase of insurance and retirement annuities.

**Corporate Saving.** Some decisions to save are made by business firms and the funds taken out of their net income before dividends are declared. In 1964 corporate profits after taxes amounted to $31.6 billion, whereas dividends were only $19.8 billion. The corporations had obviously retained $11.8 billion to be used for expansion of the firms. This plowing back of profits has never been less than

$6.4 billion per year since the end of World War II and has gone as high as $13.6 billion. Corporate executives believe that dividends paid out should be kept relatively stable, and the result has been that corporate savings in the form of undistributed profits have moved up and down somewhat with changes in the level of profits caused by shifts in the business cycle.

The amount of corporate saving seems to be inelastic with respect to changes in the rate of interest. The decision to plow back a portion of the firm's profits is governed largely by the level of the profits being earned and by the need for new capital. Because management wants the business to grow and concurrently wishes to maintain control, it seeks to expand by internal saving rather than by issuance of new securities. This motivation, rather than the desire to secure an added interest return for the shareholders, seems to explain corporate saving.

The process of accumulating depreciation reserves also plays a significant role in the supply of investment funds. Although depreciation charges are basically a way of providing for replacement of wornout assets, it is important to understand that the funds thus recovered can either be used to replace the wornout equipment or *to pay for an entirely different kind of production asset.* Funds derived from the depreciation process do not constitute a net addition to the capital goods of society, but they do provide funds for particular uses when they are shifted in this way out of less productive forms of investment and into more profitable uses. Depreciation reserves may also provide actual additions to investment funds when the rate of depreciation allowed by the tax authorities will cause the value of the asset to be written off before the end of its useful life. For example, if the depreciation is charged at 10 per cent on an estimated life of 10 years, but in actual fact the asset will continue to produce for 20 years, it is obvious that the charge for depreciation expense has been excessive. The overstating of expenses for depreciation results in understating profits, and after dividends are declared the actual profits left in the firm are even larger than are revealed in the accounting statements. The policy followed by most accountants in making conservative estimates of asset life is undoubtedly desirable for protecting the financial position of the firm, but it also results in significant amounts of saving in our economy.

**Governmental Budgets As a Source of Capital Funds.** The functions of the government in spending for such current needs as police or fire protection, defense, provision of water supply, and other similar activities, are so frequently in the forefront of our attention that the role of government in providing capital goods from tax funds is commonly overlooked. The American economy normally relies upon private enterprise to provide the capital equipment necessary for efficient production. But capital goods incident to government-operated enterprises, such as public docks, municipal water systems, post offices, school buildings, and highways, must be brought into being. Each of these governmentally supplied assets has the basic purpose of any capital equipment, namely, to assist in the production of goods and services.

Sometimes government will turn over to private enterprise the task of providing the capital goods but will cover part or all of the cost from tax funds. Subsidies paid to finance a portion of the cost of building privately owned vessels in our merchant marine is one example of this. Most of the railroads in this country were built in part from funds provided by various governmental units. Many rural telephone and electric power systems have been heavily subsidized by the Federal government.

When a governmental unit provides capital goods purchased with tax funds, a special form of social saving has taken place. The taxes reduce disposable personal income and, consequently, the level of consumption. Although the economic sacrifice required by saving has been felt by the individual, the decision to save was taken by governmental authorities. Although this form of saving is of limited importance in the United States, it is almost certain to be much more important in many of the less developed countries. Here voluntary personal saving is certain to be small in amount, because the low-income levels mean that almost all family earnings are needed for food and other essential items. In these poverty-stricken societies saving is very painful, and only limited amounts of capital funds will be voluntarily provided in this way. Yet the possibility of economic growth depends upon their having an adequate supply of funds for essential capital investment. Because these underdeveloped economies cannot depend upon funds saved willingly by their own people, the government must force saving for capital investment by the levying of taxes for this purpose or must secure the funds from outside the country. Unless Americans recognize the inability of the private sector to provide sufficient funds in other economies they will not understand why government plays a different role in the underdeveloped countries than it does here.

It should be kept in mind that the government may (by deficit financing) be a user of savings, as we noted previously in this chapter. But we must also recognize that the government sometimes becomes a supplier of investment funds through its taxing power. In many poor countries this role of supplier of capital funds will be much more important than it is in a wealthy and highly developed economy.

**Bank Credit As a Source of Investment Funds.** Commercial banks and other financial institutions perform an important economic function in providing a channel for the movement of saving into investment. However, a study of the operations of these institutions lies outside the present text, concerned as it is with such basic concepts as the primary sources of supply of funds. In Chapter 10 it was explained that commercial banks actually *create deposits* in the process of making loans. Because the ability of the banks to make loans and to create deposits is limited by their reserve position, it is possible for the Federal Reserve authorities to change significantly the amount of funds available for investment (and other uses). As we discovered in the earlier treatment of the banking system, the Federal Reserve can control excess reserves and loans by three methods: changing reserve requirements, engaging in open market operations, and varying the rediscount rate. This ability of our banking system to react quickly to the need for funds is a highly important factor in securing economic stability and meeting special emergencies.

Table 20–2 shows the changes in demand deposits in recent years.

**TABLE 20–2***
**Recent Changes in Demand Deposits**

| December of Year | Demand Deposits (Billions of Dollars) |
|---|---|
| 1950 | 90.8 |
| 1951 | 99.2 |
| 1952 | 103.0 |
| 1953 | 103.9 |
| 1954 | 107.7 |
| 1955 | 110.2 |
| 1956 | 111.5 |
| 1957 | 110.4 |
| 1958 | 115.5 |
| 1959 | 116.1 |
| 1960 | 115.2 |
| 1961 | 119.2 |
| 1962 | 120.3 |
| 1963 | 124.1 |
| 1964 | 128.7 |

* Source: **Economic Report of the President**, January 1965.

The increase in demand deposits between 1950 and 1964 indicates that almost $40 billion were created and made available to borrowers. The timing of the most important of these increases indicates that the banking system was reacting to special conditions of war or of recession. The increase in 1951–52 was clearly in response to national needs connected with the Korean War. The jumps in 1954, 1958, and 1961 probably resulted from a desire on the part of the Federal

Reserve to encourage business expansion by making loans more easily available. The banking system was simply being permitted to perform its function of providing a supply of money appropriate to the needs of the economy. The supply of funds thus created naturally influenced the rate of interest, but there is little indication that changes in the interest rate motivated the decisions by the banks to provide more or less funds. The quantity of demand deposits created apparently responded to changes in the reserve positions that were controlled by the Federal Reserve System in response to need for price stability or higher levels of employment. Variations in interest rates in different uses for funds may be significant in allocating bank credit to various borrowers, but the total supply of capital funds from this source is probably interest inelastic.

## SPECIAL FACTORS AFFECTING INTEREST RATE

**Liquidity Preference.** The entire supply of money must be held by someone. Whether the individual holding these funds decides to make them available for investment or possibly to hold them in liquid form will be important in determining the availability of investment funds. Keynes very properly pointed out in his *General Theory* that the supply of funds for investment depended not only upon the volume of saving carried out by society but also upon a second decision regarding the form in which these savings would be held. There are significant reasons for desiring to have funds easily available or in liquid form, reasons that Keynes classified into four groups: (1) the income motive, or the need to hold cash in the interval between the time when income is received and the time when it is spent; (2) the business motive, or the need to be able to make payments in the interval between the payment of business costs and the receipt of income from sales; (3) the precautionary motive, or the need to be able to meet unforeseen needs or opportunities; and (4) the speculative motive, or the desire to have a hedge against changes in the value of securities. In a later addition to his liquidity preference analysis Keynes added the finance motive. All of these motives result in what Keynes called "liquidity preference," or the desire to hold assets in liquid form (cash) unless overcome by the payment of interest.

Although we are assigning liquidity preference a somewhat less important place in interest theory than Keynes did in the depression period of the 1930's, we recognize that it plays an important role in determining what part of savings will be made available for investment purposes. If the public experiences an increase in the desire to hold cash, part of the flow of savings will be diverted to this purpose.

Because less saving is available for lending, the supply of investment funds will be reduced. Graphically, this change is represented by a movement of the supply curve upward and to the left.

**Influence of Banks upon the Interest Rate.** In recent years it has been noted that an easy-money policy could move the interest rate down, whereas a tight-money policy would move it up. During the New Deal the interest rate was forced down by an easy-money policy, and during the Eisenhower administration it was pushed up by a tight-money policy. In our discussion of the supply of and demand for investment funds we found strong reasons for believing that these curves were relatively inelastic. Examining Figure 20–2 we can see

**Figure 20–2.** Ability of the banking system to raise or lower the interest rate by small changes in the supply of credit.

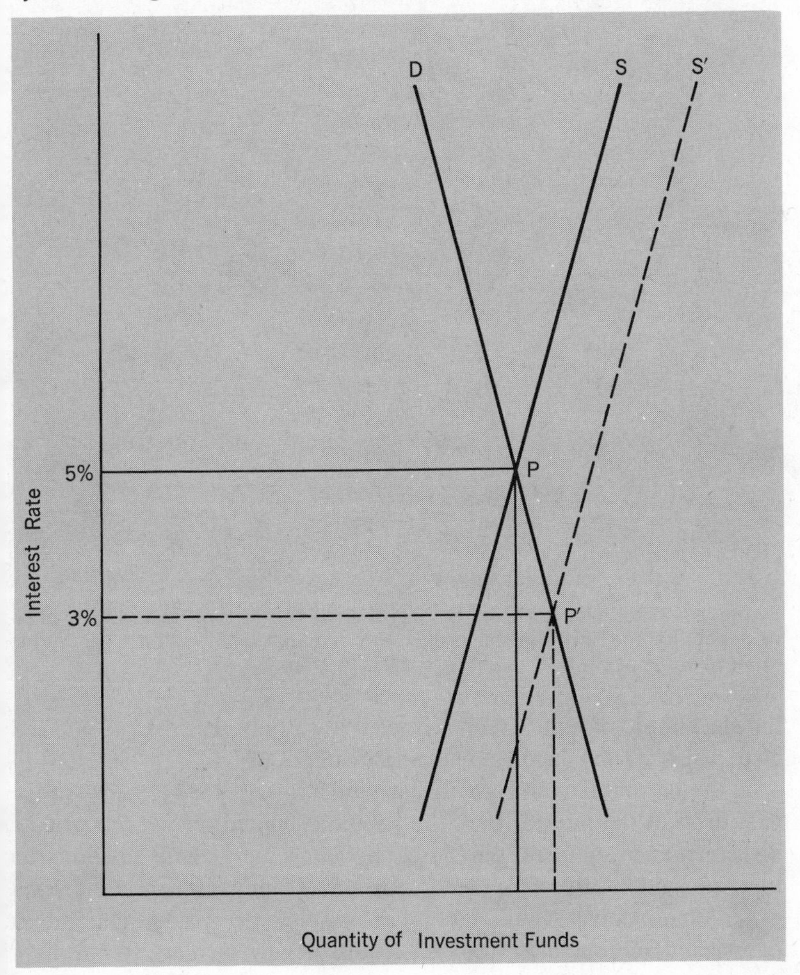

that when the demand and supply curves are relatively inelastic the interest rate can be forced down from $P$ (5%) to $P'$ (3%) by a relatively small shift to the right of the supply curve. Because one source of supply is the creation of new loans and deposits by the banking system, the Federal Reserve authorities by easing credit can increase supply and force down the interest rate. By reversing the process and decreasing the supply of loan credit the interest rate can be pushed up. We must remember, however, that the decision regard-

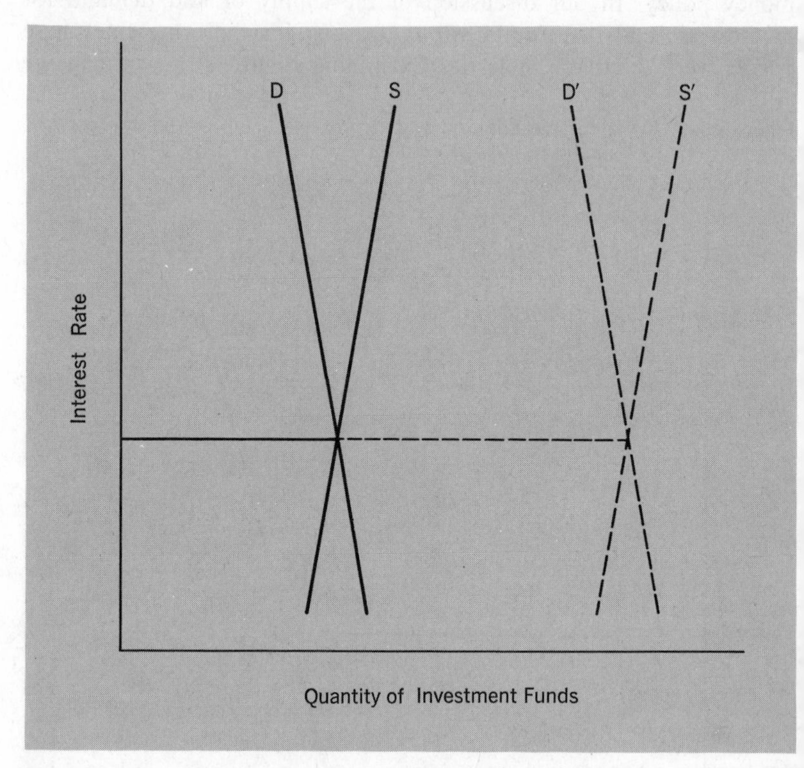


**Figure 20–3.** Relative stability of the interest rate during changes in business activity and shifts in the supply and demand for investment funds due to movements of the curves in the same direction.

ing the supply of bank credit will affect not only the interest rate but also the price level, income, and employment.

Although the demand for investment funds is not very responsive to a drop in the interest rate, the resulting limited changes in private investment, installment purchases by consumers, and construction by state and local governments can significantly influence the level of national income. By the multiplier principle every additional dollar of investment generates from $2 to $3 of new income. In the light of this fact we can attribute more significance to interest rate changes than seems likely at first. On the other hand, the relative inelasticity of the demand for investment funds makes monetary management of the interest rate a less satisfactory means of securing economic stability and growth than it would be if the demand were more elastic. Most economists have concluded that variations in the levels of government spending and taxation supplemented by appropriate monetary policies are necessary to assure satisfactory economic performance.

**Influence of Changes in Income upon the Interest Rate.** In our examination of personal and corporate saving we noted that the amount increased greatly with increases in the levels of personal and corporate income. Since we have indicated that the demand for capital funds is inelastic, it might be thought that large increases in savings as income begins to rise incident to a movement out of a recession would cause the interest rate to fall. What actually happens, however, is that as increased income causes increased saving and a shift of the supply curve to the right, it will be accompanied, or even preceded, by a shift of demand in the same direction. This is illustrated in Figure 20–3. The demand for capital equipment must be based upon the *anticipated* productivity or revenue-yielding capacity of the investment, and changes in the level of business activity will result in large changes in the anticipated profit possibilities from additional investment. The fact that the ups and downs of the business cycle cause both the supply and demand curves for investment funds to shift in the same direction, and at approximately the same time, makes it possible for changes in business activity to take place without great changes in the interest rate. Limited variations in the rate, of course, do occur as adjustments are made to changed market conditions.

Perhaps it would be easier to understand why the supply and demand curves for investment funds shift together, if we assume that the change takes place because of a decision of businessmen to increase their investment outlay. As our earlier study of the multiplier showed, a rise in the level of investment causes an even greater rise in the level of national income. But this rise in income results in an increase in the quantity of saving, the amount of the increase depending upon the fraction of additional income that society wishes to save.

Keynes in his *General Theory* argued that equilibrium in the desire to save and the desire to invest was brought about more by changes in the level of income than by changes in the interest rate. By looking again at Figure 20–3 we can see the logic in Keynes's argument. The intersection of the new supply and demand curves shows that it was not a change in the interest rate that brought the new equilibrium, but rather that changes in income caused both curves to shift to new positions where the equilibrium occurred at about the same rate of interest.

**Variations in Interest Rates.** When we look at the interest yield on bonds in the financial pages of the newspaper we find that there is not one rate of interest but a collection of rates. This interest cost, however, is a payment for risk of loss as well as for the use of the funds. Therefore, the interest yield on any particular bond or note will be much lower if the borrower is a government or private business having a good record on repayments. If there is doubt that the debt will be honored, the lender will insist on a high rate of return for the extra risk assumed. Also an additional charge is usually added for small loans to cover the extra costs for record keeping and efforts in collection. The length of time covered by the note or bond also introduces variations in risk and the liquidity sacrificed, and for these reasons affects the interest charged.

**Summary.** Interest is the payment made for the use of funds which when invested in capital goods contribute to the efficiency of production. The basic demand for investment funds is derived from their marginal productivity (*MRP*) when invested in capital goods. Additional funds will be demanded by business as long as the anticipated increase in revenue from the use of the capital goods exceeds the cost (depreciation and interest charge) of using those goods. Additional demand for funds comes from borrowing for the purchase of durable items by consumers and governmental deficit financing.

The supply of funds for investment comes from personal savings, corporate savings, governmental budgets, and bank credit expansion. All of these sources appear to respond more to changes in income than to changes in the interest rate.

Because the demand for funds is relatively inelastic, it is possible for the banking system to push interest rates up or down by changes in the quantity of bank credit being created. Movements in the business cycle cause both the demand and supply curves for investment funds to shift in the same direction and at about the same time. Changes in the level of income with variations in business activity, therefore, are more important in bringing equilibrium between saving and investment than are changes in the interest rate.

## QUESTIONS

1. What are the special problems in the use of capital that must be dealt with in interest theory?
2. Why are both depreciation and interest included as costs of using capital when we establish the demand curve for capital funds?
3. In addition to the demands by business for funds, what are the other significant sources of demand?
4. What are the reasons for believing that the demand for investment funds by business is relatively inelastic?

5. Do you believe that a change in the interest rate used in calculating the monthly payment on automobile purchases would significantly alter the number of cars sold? Would your answer be the same for refrigerators? For houses?
6. Will changes in the interest rate alter the quantity of funds borrowed by the Federal government? By state and local governments?
7. What are the four sources of funds that can be used for investment purposes?
8. What per-cent of disposable personal income have Americans saved in recent years? What happened to this normal saving level in World War II? In the depression of the 1930's?
9. Do changes in the interest rate appear to have any significant influence upon decisions by corporate executives about the level of dividends or corporate saving? If not, what factors do influence these decisions?
10. How can governments "save" for investment purposes? Why is such governmental saving more important in the poorer countries?
11. Why do we list bank credit as a source of investment funds? Can commercial banks lend more than people have saved and put on deposit?
12. What are the reasons that Keynes gave for the preference to hold funds in liquid form?
13. How can the banking authorities force down the interest rate? Would this action be possible if the demand curve were more elastic?
14. Is the equilibrium between the desire to save and the desire to invest established by changes in the interest rate or by changes in the level of national income? Explain.

CHAPTER

# 21

# Rent and Profits

## RENT

Although labor and capital are the two most important factors as measured by income shares flowing from production, natural resources also provide essential productive services. Farm land, plant and dam sites, oil pools, iron ore reserves, and other gifts of nature are essential to a modern economy. Such natural resources are unlike capital goods in that returns are not required to call them into being, yet each bears a price that reflects the scarcity relative to the need for it. The payment made for the use of natural resources is called *rent*. The term *land* is frequently used when referring to any type of natural resources. The payment of rent performs the function of limiting the quantity of land demanded and of determining who shall use scarce natural resources.

**Demand for Land.** As with any other factor of production, additional units of land will be demanded as long as they add more to revenue than to cost. Perhaps the easiest way to see how marginal productivity determines the addition to revenue is by examining its operation on a typical family farm. In such a situation the supply of labor is that provided by the family and can be considered fixed in amount. Equipment, buildings, and other capital goods can also be taken as given for the time being, but the farmer may have the option of buying or leasing a few more acres of land from a neighbor. He must decide whether the addition to output secured by spreading a fixed amount of labor and capital over more acres will justify the new rent payment.

An examination of Figure 21–1 will show that the standard method of analysis can be applied to the demand for land by this farmer. We measure the payment made for rent on the vertical axis and the quantity of land on the horizontal axis. Because the farmer ordinarily accepts the market price or the government support price, the *SVMP* and *MRP* curves coincide. Despite this constant price for the product these curves slope downward to the right, because the output added by the additional land will decrease as the farmer applies his fixed supply of family labor more thinly over the larger area. Because we are assuming here that land properly cultivated never wears out, we do not need to take depreciation into account in our cost calculations.

Under these conditions the *SVMP* and *MRP* curve constitutes the farmer's demand for land. If the rent per acre is $25 he will only make use of 160 acres, as shown by point *P* in Figure 21–1. But if the rent should decline to $20, the farmer would find it to his advantage to expand the area cultivated to 200 acres, as shown by point *P′*. Because these and other points show the relationship of rent paid per acre to the number of acres the farmer uses, the *SVMP–MRP* curve is also the individual demand curve for land. The total

**Figure 21–1.** Demand for farm land determined by marginal productivity for an individual farmer.

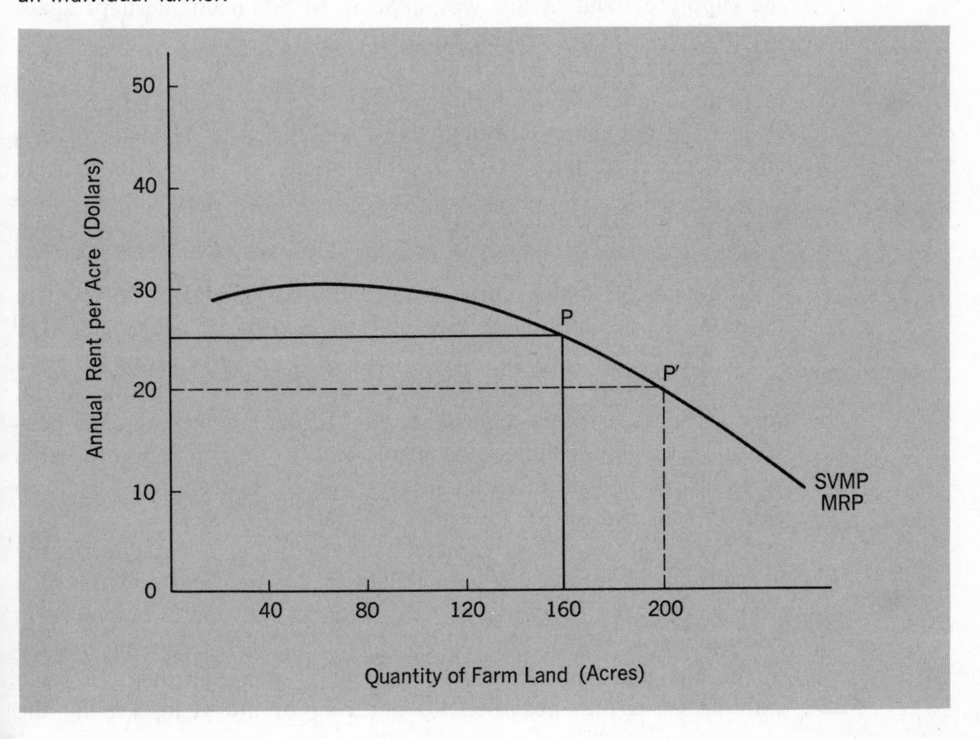

demand for land, then, will simply be the addition of such individual demands for land at each of the various possible prices. We are assuming here that all the land is of the same quality, but we shall analyze the problems of different grades of land later in the chapter.

**Supply of Land.** As we have already observed, the essential difference between land and capital depends upon supply characteristics. Although the quantity of land, being given by nature, is fixed, capital goods, being man-made, can be changed in amount. Because the total quantity of land cannot be changed by man in response to changes in the price paid for its use, we normally depict the supply curve for land as almost completely inelastic. As exceptions let us note that land surface may be increased by such devices as the dikes used to push back the sea in the Netherlands, or the fill at the edge of Lake Michigan in the vicinity of Chicago. But the qualification is obviously rather limited in its application. Also the supply of good farm land can sometimes be increased by proper drainage, fertilization, or irrigation of previously poor land. Another qualification is that land can be destroyed as a valuable resource either by bad farming practices or by depletion of the oil, coal, iron ore, and other similar gifts of nature. At one time it was possible to increase the area of available land by extending the frontier to the west, but addition to the supply of land in this way appears to be ended. Perhaps space exploration will open up new prospects.

**General Level of Rent.** In Figure 21–2 we have combined the inelastic supply curve for farm land with the market-demand curve derived from our marginal-productivity analysis. The demand curve is labeled *D* rather than *MRP* to simplify the graph and to indicate clearly that it is a market demand curve. With the supply curve labeled *S* and the demand curve labeled *D* rent is determined at the intersection marked *P*.

Although the supply curve is normally considered to be fixed in position, the demand curve may shift as a result of a change either in the physical productivity of the land or in the price of the product. In certain heavily populated and less developed areas of the world, such as Southeast Asia, high rents paid to the landowning class constitute an extremely difficult problem. The rise in population over the years has pushed up the price of food, which, in turn, has forced up *SVMP,* as shown in the movement of demand from *D* to *D′* in Figure 21–2. As the rise in demand pushed up the rent payment, the distribution of income between the owner of the land and the men who actually did the work of cultivation shifted more and more in favor of the landlord. The owner of the land then frequently moved to the city and lived in idle luxury on his rental income. In some extreme cases rent absorbed 90 per cent of the yield, leaving the

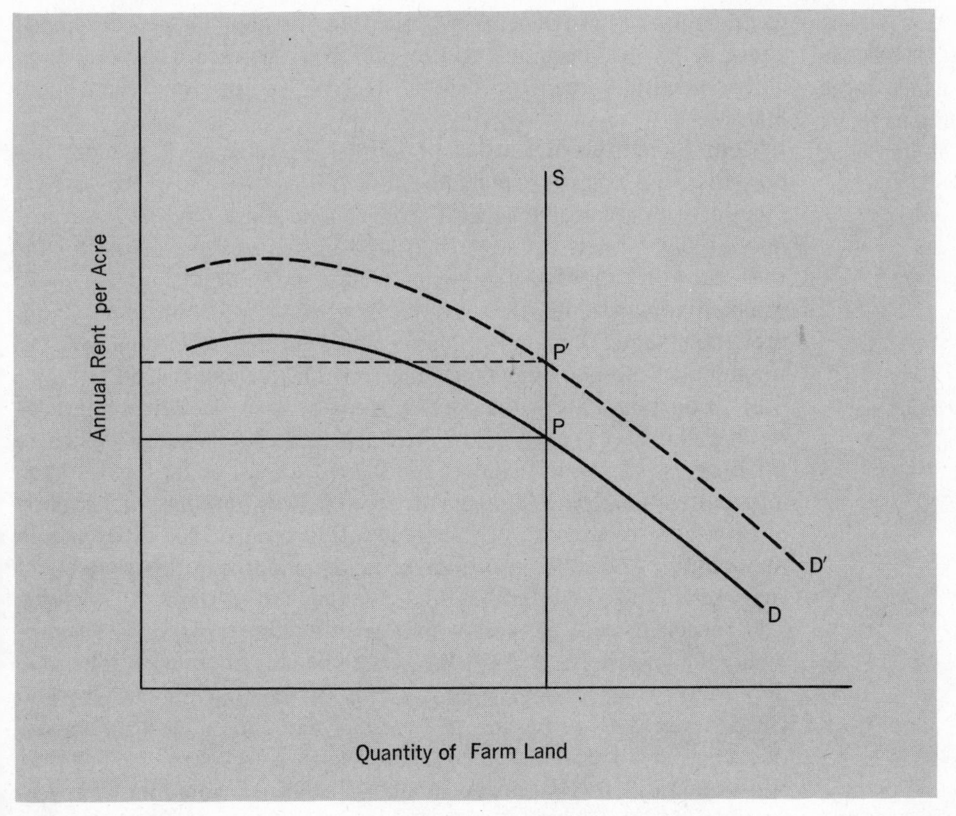


**Figure 21–2.** Effect upon rent of increase in demand for land caused by higher product prices resulting from increased population.

peasant only 10 per cent of the product. Communist propaganda has sometimes made the most of this inequity, and reform of land ownership has been necessary to give the people confidence in the justice of income distribution.

In a more general way we can say that whenever population begins to press against a scarce supply of land the result will be a rise in the level of rent. In the Western world this rise in rent has been limited during the past century and a half by the steady stream of technological improvements in agriculture that have enabled us to produce more and more output per acre. The pressure of increasing population upon a limited amount of land has in this way been kept from becoming a serious problem. Although the rise in population tended to force up the price of grains and other food stuffs and to increase rent, as is shown in Figure 21–2, by pushing up the demand curve, the improved methods of production tended to reduce food prices and to reduce rent by pushing down the demand curve. Unfortunately, technological improvement in agriculture in many lesser developed countries has not been able to keep ahead in the race with population as has generally been the case in Western Europe and the United States.

**Rent for Different Grades of Land.** Frequently, it is more important to be able to explain the rent on a particular piece of land than it is to explain the general level of rent. Corn land in Iowa produces more bushels per acre than land in dry sections of the Southwest. Store locations in the center of the shopping district are more productive of revenue than in places where few people pass. More productive land commands a higher rent than the less productive, but some land is so poor that it justifies no rent payment at all.

Ricardo pointed out the way to measure rent on different grades of land almost a century and a half ago in this statement: "When in the progress of society, land of the second degree of fertility is taken into cultivation, rent immediately commences on that of the first quality, and the amount of that rent will depend on the difference in the quality of these two portions of land." Following this suggestion, suppose we take four grades of land, the best (Grade A) yielding 100 bushels of corn per acre with a given amount of labor and equipment, the next best (Grade B) yielding 80 bushels with the same application of labor and capital, Grade C yielding 60 bushels, and Grade D yielding 40 bushels. If the labor and capital used on an acre of each grade of land had to be paid 60 bushels of corn (or its equivalent in money) for wages and interest, no farmer would be willing to pay rent for the use of Grade C land. On the other hand, farmers would be willing to pay the difference in yield as rent for the privilege of using the better grades A and B; note that this difference is also the excess of yield over cost. The alternative to cultivating better land would be to use Grade C land with its lower yield on which no rent is paid and yield is equal to cost. Not only will farmers be *willing* to pay a rent for the better grades of land; the scarcity of the better land will set in motion competitive bidding that will *necessitate* the payment of rent. The payment for Grade A land will be forced up to 40 bushels and for Grade B land to 20 bushels, or the difference in the yields between these grades of land and the yield on Grade C land that is marginal or "no rent" land. Labor and capital would be receiving the same 60 bushels per unit regardless of the grade of land used and variations in the rent paid. Keep in mind that the 60 bushels is a cost and that the rent is an excess of the yield over the cost.

Unfortunately, the calculation of rent is complicated by the fact that as the growth of population forces up the price of corn (relative to the price of labor) and makes farmers willing to cultivate land other than Grade A, it will also cause them to employ more labor and capital on the better land. In Figure 21–3 we assume that suc-

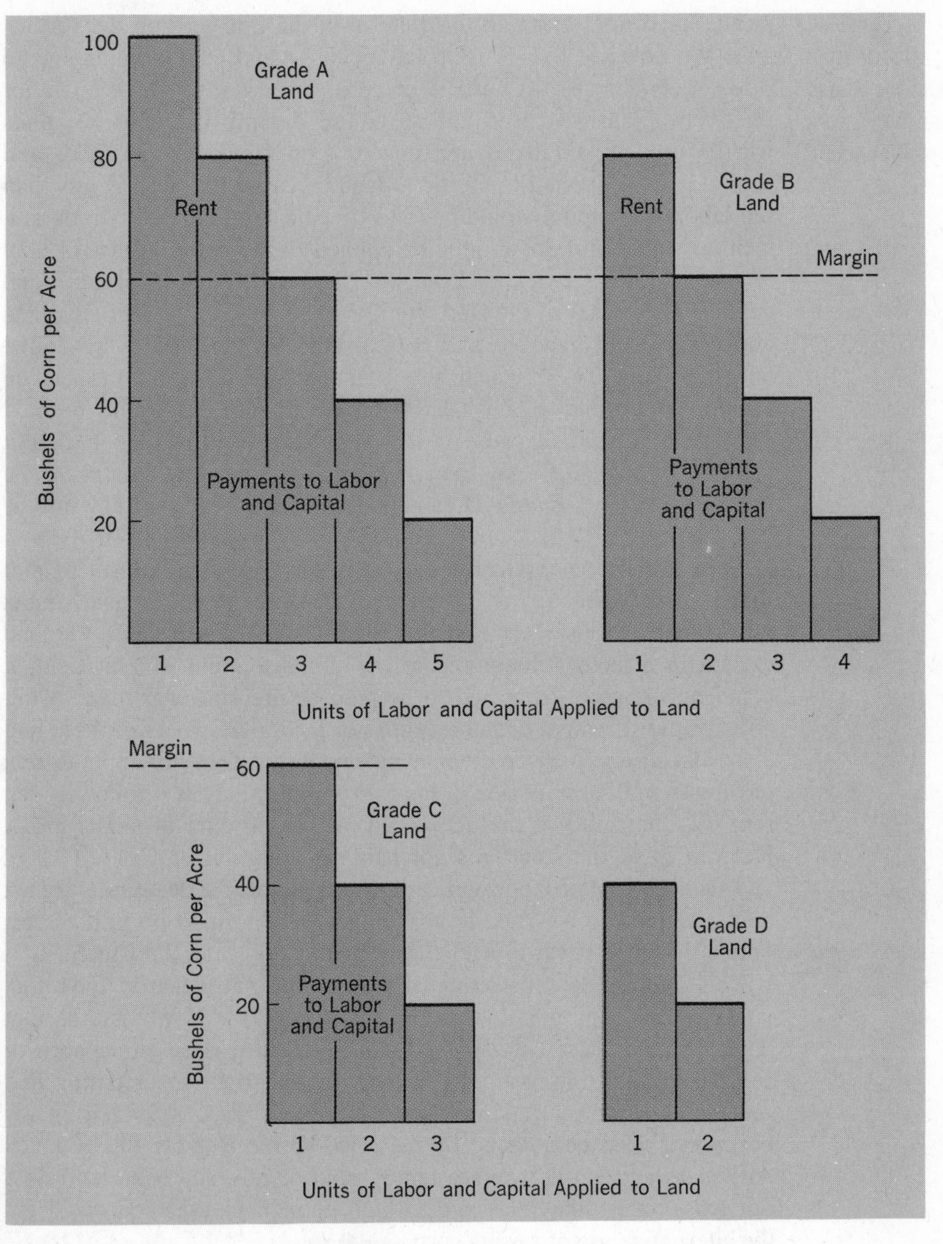


**Figure 21–3.** Determination of rent paid on various grades of farm land with units of labor and capital used on each grade until margin is reached.

cessive units of labor and capital are applied to Grade A land, subject to the principle of diminishing returns. The diagram shows the number of units of labor and capital employed on each grade of land on the horizontal axis and the yield in bushels of corn on the vertical axis. We now see that if each unit of labor and capital commands a price equivalent to 60 bushels of corn, three units will be used for relatively intensive cultivation on Grade A land, but only two units will be used on Grade B and one unit on Grade C. No labor and capital will be applied to Grade D land, because the yield is less than the labor and capital would have to be paid in a competitive market. Neither would additional units be applied to the better grades of land after the additional yield drops below the payment made for labor and capital. The owner of the land would be able to keep as rent any yield above that paid to labor and capital (the surplus above the dotted line in Figure 21–3, which shows the margin), or 60 bushels on Grade A land and 20 bushels on Grade B. No rent would be paid for Grade C land, because it is barely worth cultivating in that it yields only enough to pay the going rate for labor and capital on the one unit applied. Grade D land is submarginal and would not be cultivated.

**Rent and Price.** Ricardo argued in his famous treatment of rent that "Corn [wheat to us] is not high because a rent is paid, but a rent is paid because corn is high." He reasoned that because the land existed in a fixed amount regardless of the amount of rent paid, it could not be a cost that had to be paid before land was made available for use. If wages or interest are not paid, the owners of these factors will cease to provide them, a statement that does not apply to rent payments and the provision of land. From this analysis it followed that rent was the result of the price paid for the product of land (corn). Keep in mind that rent was not paid on marginal or Grade C land and that the cost of labor and capital was equal to price. On marginal land, assumed to be of basic importance, rent formed no part of cost (price). Hence Ricardo said that rent did not enter into price.

This analysis is satisfactory if we assume (as Ricardo did) that land has only one possible use, but it is not valid if we assume that land has alternative uses. If land can be used to raise either corn or soy beans, then the soy bean farmer is quite right in assuming that rent he pays for the land he uses is a part of the cost of raising soy beans and must be covered by the price he receives for this product. Although land exists whether rent is paid or not, soy bean land does not exist unless the rent paid is high enough to take it away from the alternative use of raising corn.

**Henry George and the "Single Tax."** Because rent is a payment made for the use of natural resources that are not man-made but simply appropriated for his use, this source of income has always been hard to justify from an ethical viewpoint. Our forefathers in the Revolution had struggled against a government run by a nobility whose income was derived from land inherited in large estates, and our abolition of entailed estates at that time reflected our determination not to allow rent to become the basis for a privileged class.

Henry George in his book *Progress and Poverty,* published in 1879, launched a famous attack upon rent as a source of private income. His proposal, simply stated, was that the government should place a tax upon land sufficiently high to capture the entire amount of rent. He believed that the income from this tax would be adequate to cover all governmental expenditures and, therefore, could serve as government's "single tax." Although the tax revenue might have been adequate for the United States in 1879, it certainly would not be sufficient as a sole support for government today. But Henry George's argument is not destroyed by the growth of governmental expenditures. His case was based upon the alleged injustice of collecting income for which no work had been done and upon the belief that the collection of rent interfered with the best utilization of the land from a social viewpoint. It was argued that land frequently was withheld from use until the growth in population had increased its rental income and, therefore, its sales price. It is certainly true that in Henry George's time the rapid growth of cities like Chicago permitted the accumulation of large fortunes by speculators who gained control of urban land and simply waited for population growth to increase its value. It is also true that the hope for capital gains from the holding of land has sometimes prevented it from being used in ways that would currently be the most useful to society.

**Modern Land Taxes.** The most serious barrier to applying the single tax today is that it would confiscate the entire income earned by owners of land, and by eliminating this income it would destroy the market value of their property. Because our legal system has permitted people to invest in land, it seems unjust to confiscate this type of property while leaving other property rights intact. For this reason advocates of the single tax idea usually argue that only future increases in land rents should be taxed away. This tax on rent increases would not confiscate present property values, but it would prevent the securing of additional income as a result of population growth pressing upon limited natural resources. Although this proposal has certain attractions, the administrative problems involved in the determination of the amount of land rent would be rather difficult, and politicians have not been enthusiastic about the proposal.

On the other hand, the single tax theory has been important in providing opposition to efforts for the lowering of taxes on land. Imposing a new tax on land rent would be the same as confiscating a part of the property, but by the same reasoning a reduction in taxes on land would increase the value of the land to its owner and give him an unearned capital gain. Such a free gift, granted at the expense of the rest of society, would be quite unjustified. As a result, land taxes have been continued as a source of local government revenue despite the many difficult problems of securing fair assessments upon which to base land taxes.

**Rent and Inelastic Supply.** We have treated land as being different from other factors of production because it is a gift of nature with a supply not susceptible to change by man's efforts. Some economists do not accept this distinction, arguing that other factors of production have this same inelasticity of supply under certain conditions. For example, they argue that there are only so many people born with the physical qualities necessary to be good baseball pitchers and that their income in large part should be classified as rent. If we turn to capital goods, these same economists assert that once a plant is built or a railroad line is laid the short-run supply is inelastic and the owner is forced to accept whatever return the market affords. Such economists usually define rent as the income received by any productive factor above what it could earn in its next best use. Although there are some valid arguments for this type of definition, most writers still prefer to treat rent as being the payment made for the use of natural resources.

## PROFITS

If our economic system were perfectly competitive and there were no problems of adjusting to the changes that come in a dynamic society, all the units of labor, capital, and land would be receiving incomes based upon and measured by their marginal productivities. The sum of the payments to these factors of production would then exhaust the total output of the economy, and there would be no fourth source of income. But, as we have already found, our economic system is not perfectly competitive, and we do have to allow for unpredictable developments that occur in a dynamic society. Under these conditions we find that the payments made by the owner of the business for wages, interest, and rent sometimes do not absorb all the revenue secured by the sale of the product and that a residual is left, commonly called profit. On the other hand, the payments to labor and the owners of land and capital sometimes are greater than the revenue received, and the enterprise suffers a loss. Imperfections in our competitive system, therefore, force us to include a fourth source of possible income in our scheme of distribution. Profit (either positive or negative) becomes the residual income that results when payments to the three previously analyzed factors do not exactly equal the revenue received by the firm.

In general the economist thinks of profit much as the accountant or businessman does, but as we have already explained, there is a difference in what they consider cost to be. The accountant must include in cost only those items that the law and accepted accounting practice approve. To illustrate, if the owner of the corner drug store works in his own store, his earnings will be included in the accounting profits, not in the wage expense account, by the accountant. But the economist wishes to connect the income received to the function performed, and it is obvious that part of the owner's income is a reward for labor performed. We refer to this income as *implicit* wages. *Explicit* wages, in contrast, are those actually paid to workers by the business as a result of contractual arrangements and are shown in the expense accounts of the firm. The economist treats both implicit and explicit wages as costs, because if either is not paid, the person performing the work will sooner or later switch to a job in which he will be paid. In the same way the economist treats as cost implicit interest on capital and implicit rent on land supplied by the owner. Economic profit thus tends to be less than accounting profit, because we deduct implicit costs from revenue in addition to the explicit costs already subtracted by the accountant.

The economist identifies the equilibrium or normal position of the competitive firm as a situation in which economic profit is zero. However, a business firm in such a situation earns an accounting profit in this position, because implicit wages, interest, and rent are being earned by the owner. Thus the equilibrium position of zero profit as defined by the economist is the same as a normal accounting profit. In other words, the businessman considers his accounting profit as normal if it is about the same as he could secure by using his labor, capital, and land in any other industry. But if these implicit returns are treated as cost, as the economist does, the profit figure is reduced to zero.

**Uncertainty and Profit.** If the normal or equilibrium position for the competitive firm is one of zero profit, why consider profit as an item of income? The answer is that the business firm in a dynamic economy is seldom at this equilibrium position, with the result that costs are less than revenue and an economic profit results; or else costs (including the implicit items) are greater than revenue and there is a loss or negative economic profit. Because these profits (either positive or negative) enter into the actual income of the owner of the business, it is necessary for the economist to take them into account when he studies the distribution of income.

Economic profits (or losses) under competitive conditions are thus the result of changes in the dynamic society. If the businessman is lucky and the change favors him, a profit results. If, on the other hand, he is unlucky and the change goes against him, he suffers a loss. This is not to say that the businessman depends entirely upon luck and cannot increase his income by hard intelligent work, but the reward for this virtue is found in increased implicit wages, not in increased economic profit.

Professor Frank H. Knight made a basic contribution to economic theory by relating economic profit to the uncertainties of a dynamic society. He classified dynamic changes into two categories, risk and uncertainty. He argued that the businessman can protect himself against some changes, and these he called risks. For example, the business owner cannot predict with certainty whether he will have a fire next year, but he can carry insurance against this possibility, and so will regard the premium as a cost. Hedging against price changes is another method of protection against unfavorable changes. Although for the individual businessman these risks carry the possibility of loss, he can insure himelf by joining with others in averaging out these losses through dependence upon the law of averages.

*True economic profit,* Knight said, *must result from uncertainty,* the changes that cannot be accurately predicted, even on an average basis, by the businessman. What are some examples of such uncertainties? Style changes, advances in production methods, increased advertising by competitors, new international tensions, political change affecting foreign markets, labor troubles, and general business recession are but a few of the many uncertainties that will influence the profit of the businessman. He cannot predict such changes accurately nor can he provide protection against them. If he is lucky, these unforeseen changes will bring him a profit; if he is unlucky, a loss. For many people these uncertainties make business management an unpleasant occupation they would not undertake unless they received pay well beyond implicit wages and interest. On the other hand, many men obviously enjoy the excitement that uncertainty brings to business, just as they enjoy betting on a horse race. In our economy we assume that there are enough men who enjoy these uncertainties so that no payment beyond the implicit return for wages and interest is necessary in order to attract an adequate supply of people to carry on necessary business activity.

The normal equilibrium position of the firm under conditions of perfect competition is, therefore, assumed to be one characterized by zero economic profit where no specific payment needs to be made for the bearing of uncertainty. Economists frequently use the term *entrepreneur* in referring to the person who bears these uncertainties as owner of the business and who makes the basic decisions as the firm adjusts to the conditions created by these changes.

**Innovation.** Some economists, notably Joseph Schumpeter, have argued that innovation is the most important source of profit. If an entrepreneur is fortunate in seeing the possibilities inherent in some new product or new method of production, he may secure considerable profit before his competitors can capture part of the market or reduce the price by copying him. The search for profits resulting from innovation is certainly one of the moving forces for change and progress in our dynamic society. If these innovations come in waves, as Schumpeter believed, they may also help to account for fluctuations in business activity. Although we do not give innovation the central place in our theory, we must certainly recognize that it is a special and important type of uncertainty. The profit or loss of the entrepreneur will be greatly influenced by the guesses he makes about new products or methods, and his income will be reduced if his competitor makes the successful change first.

**Profit Without Social Justication.** In our society profit may result from monopoly or monopsony as well as from uncertainty or successful innovation. Manipulation of either the market in which the firm sells or in which it buys is subjected to legal controls in our economy, but the problem is much too complicated for complete control by the courts. When monopoly results from patent rights, economies of scale, or goodwill resulting from past efficient operations, the courts find it difficult to apply the antitrust laws. In the case of natural monopolies, such as public utilities, the only solution appears to be to limit the amount of accounting profit the firm will be allowed to earn. Despite the best efforts of our lawmakers and the courts, the economic realist is forced to recognize that a significant amount of economic profit is earned as a result of the market conditions that we studied under oligopoly and monopolistic competition, not to speak of pure monopoly.

Another type of profit that should be kept to a minimum in our society is the kind that results from fraud or deception. The entrepreneur ought to find his income increased by serving the public, not by leading them to believe that they will receive benefits which in fact they will not realize. We do not permit the old-fashioned medicine man to promise impossible cures today, but the Federal Trade Commission must be on constant alert against misleading advertising. The Securities and Exchange Commission was created partly because of the need to protect investors against false information put out in order to sell securities. Our economy tries to prevent the realization of profits by fraud, as well as by monopoly, but it is never completely successful.

**Functions of Profit and Loss.** The most important functions of profit (positive or negative) are to provide businessmen with the indication of what products the public wants and to provide entrepreneurs with the incentive to meet these needs. For example, if the public decides that it wants smaller automobiles, the firm that responds first to this market demand will find its profits increasing. When American Motors demonstrated the operation of this principle at the end of the 1950's, even the oligopolistic position of General Motors, Ford, and Chrysler did not protect them from the pressure exerted through profit changes. So long as there is a reasonable amount of competition, the possibility of profits will provide a powerful motivation for entrepreneurs to meet the market demand as it expresses the desires of consumers.

One of the most unfortunate aspects of monopoly profit is that it is achieved by limiting the volume of goods supplied to the public and thereby keeping prices high. The true function of profits, which is to encourage an increase in output, is thus perverted. In fact, increased monopolistic income frequently results from limiting service to the public rather than by increasing it.

Another function performed by profit is to exert pressure upon producers to use the most efficient methods of production currently known. As innovators demonstrate the cost advantages of new production methods, the profits they earn will attract imitators. The firms that are slow to adopt these new methods or products will inevitably find themselves suffering losses which, if continued, will eliminate them from the field. The efficiency of production by businessmen is largely the result of pressure exerted by profit as a reward for acceptance of desirable change, or the losses that will result from failure to keep up to date in a changing world.

**Profit in the Modern Corporation.** Profit is associated in our theory with the performance of two separate roles: bearing economic uncertainties inherent in a dynamic economy and making basic decisions of adjustment or innovation. In an older, simpler society the owner of a firm bore the risk of loss and also made the important decisions, but in the modern large corporation this is no longer the case. The common stockholder is the main bearer of uncertainty with its associated possibility of loss, but the thousands of scattered stockholders cannot be well enough informed to make the real decisions of business management. Although holders of common stock are legally entitled to any profits the corporation may earn, there is a strong tendency among our major corporations to stabilize dividends at a rate that can scarcely be distinguished from interest paid to bondholders. The role of the stockholder as decision maker is reduced to the almost meaningless ritual of filling out a proxy that authorizes management to vote his shares as they wish at the annual meeting. As the stockholders are eliminated from certain important entrepreneurial functions, a professional management class arises to perform the function of decision making and innovation. This basic change in the business structure raises two difficult questions: (1) How much of the profit is the stockholder entitled to receive in dividends, and how much shall management be allowed to withdraw in the form of corporate salaries or special bonuses? (2) What are the limitations upon management in the chances they take with the stockholders' funds as they make decisions? We are still searching for final answers to these questions.

**Relation of Profit to Growth.** Among the many basic requirements for securing a satisfactory rate of growth are some items closely related to the going rate of profits: (1) a level of investment adequate to provide the capital goods needed by an expanding population, (2) a replacement of productive equipment rapid enough to make effective use of new methods of production, and (3) continued search for new ideas or innovations. Unless the entrepreneur believes that a real possibility of profit exists he will not be willing to take the chances involved in making new investments or experimenting with new methods or products. In determining tax policies or governmental regulations of business for our economy, we must keep firmly in mind the role that profits play in motivating the entrepreneur. The need for maintaining reasonable prospects for business profit does not mean that taxes cannot be levied upon such income nor that necessary controls should not be imposed, but it does mean that policy makers must keep the role of profit in mind as such policies are made.

It is important also to remember that profits are one source of funds needed to pay for investments, as well as to provide an incentive for making them. As we noted in Chapter 20 undistributed corporate profits amounted to almost $12 billion in 1964. Although there are other sources of investment funds than undistributed corporate profits, this source is currently playing a significant role. Either personal saving or governmental investment would need to be increased if undistributed corporate profits were to be reduced by governmental tax or control policies.

**Summary.** Rent is the income earned by providing the services of scarce natural resources (land), and its amount is determined in the market. Demand for land is a function of marginal productivity and can be measured in much the same way as for labor or capital. The supply of land is highly inelastic, which makes rent tend to increase rapidly under pressure of population growth. The basic limitation upon the increase of rent in capitalist economies has been our rapid technological progress. Rent can also be measured as a differential return earned by better grades of land.

Rent plays a special role in tax theory and in the analysis of prices. Our thinking along these lines is still influenced by the ideas of Henry George and Ricardo, although we do not fully accept their analyses.

Economic profits are the residual part of revenue of the firm after costs (including implicit wages, rent, and interest of the owner) have been paid. The principal source of profits is the uncertainty inherent in a dynamic society, which may result in either a positive o a negative return to the owner. Innovations are a particularly impor tant type of uncertainty and source of profits. Profits may also resul from monopoly or fraud, but our society attempts to limit profit from these sources. The rise of the modern corporation has divide the entrepreneurial function between stockholder and management

The basic functions of profits are (1) to act as a guide to entre preneurs in satisfying consumer needs, and (2) to provide the incen tive for efficient adaptation to new ideas and the changes of a dynami society.

A desirable rate of growth depends upon the existence of a possi bility for profit that provides the incentive for an adequate rate o investment. Business profits may also be an important source of th needed investment funds.

## QUESTIONS

1. What is the elasticity of the general supply curve for natural re sources? Why?
2. Explain how we can secure a demand curve for land from the prin ciple of diminishing returns. If we draw a graph to illustrate thi demand, what will be measured on each axis?
3. Why does an increase in population tend to raise the proportion o income paid for the use of land?
4. Will improved methods of farming raise the rent paid for farm land by increasing physical productivity or lower rent by reducing th prices paid for farm produce?
5. Explain why competition will force the payment as rent of any sur plus production on the better grades of land above the competitiv payment made for the services of labor and capital.
6. Does the payment of rent cause the price of farm produce to b higher than it would be without the payment of rent? Or does th higher price for farm produce cause the rent payment to be highe than it would be with lower farm prices?
7. What is meant by the "single tax"? What would be the difficulties i applying this proposal today?
8. Explain the difference between the accountant's definition of profi and that of the economist.
9. What is the relationship of uncertainty to profit?
10. If business activity is motivated by the search for profit, should w ever disapprove of profit earned by whatever means?
11. What are the functions of profit in our economic system? Does los ever perform a function?
12. What basic problem in profit theory is raised by the separation o decision making and uncertainty bearing in the management of th modern corporation?
13. What is the relationship of profit to the problem of economic growth

CHAPTER

22

# Income Distribution and Growth

**Conditions Essential to Growth.** Economic growth is a complex phenomenon and takes place only when many different conditions have been satisfied. Some of these essential conditions are closely related to the distribution of income. The most important tie is that the prospect of increased income is one of the great incentives in securing human actions. Among the important human actions necessary for economic growth are (1) willingness to work hard, physically and mentally, (2) ready acceptance of change, and (3) willingness to provide an adequate supply of funds for capital investment. As we have seen in our study of the theory of income distribution, the performance of these essential acts is closely related to the income that it is hoped will result from them.

## PERSONAL ATTITUDES

**Willingness To Work.** Men are much more willing to labor if they believe that their efforts will be rewarded. When we related the demand for labor and the wage level to marginal productivity, we provided the theoretical tie between effort made and reward received. Because either hard or intelligent work increases the productivity of the worker, it tends to raise the wage the employer is willing to pay. Unfortunately, we found that there are numerous imperfections in the labor market that tend to prevent as close a tie as we should wish between the quality and quantity of work performed and the amount of wages received. If any economy is to attain the rate of growth of which it is capable, it must have a wage structure that gives proper reward for the performance of tasks.

We do not assume that men work for monetary rewards alone, but we do believe that money income is one of the important motivations of human conduct. Men also work for prestige, for satisfaction of a well-done job, for the pleasure of aiding others, for love of country, and for fear of punishment. In some countries the "man of distinction" is the one who lives without hard work, and in these areas it is difficult indeed to motivate performance of essential work. For this reason a growing economy needs to reward the worker with social approval, as well as wages, if his best effort is to be forthcoming.

The worker also needs to feel a sense of pride in the job he is doing. One problem of modern industrial society lies in the fact that specialization often leaves the individual with the feeling that he is just a cog in a big wheel. If he assigns a low value to his work, he will have little incentive to try to do the job well. One partial solution is to inform the worker of the role he is playing in the enterprise as a whole, so that he can take personal satisfaction in the accomplishments of the firm. Under some circumstances, such as war, this sense of personal achievement is secured by the understanding that national survival requires the maximum effort of each individual. Totalitarian economies make national survival and social progress a prime motivating force, not only in wartime, but also in time of peace. Where these motivations are found inadequate, authoritarian governments frequently rely upon the application of force. But the people of a free society believe that the most efficient work is done by the free choice of the individual.

**Acceptance of Change.** Increases in productivity that are essential to growth cannot be secured unless the individuals in a society are willing to accept new ways of doing things. In a dynamic economy scientists are constantly engaged in a search for new products and for new processes of production. Business management is constantly searching for methods that will increase efficiency in production, marketing, and accounting.

Economic change resulting from this constant effort by the firm to increase profits by developing new products and increasing efficiency of operation involves hardships for some people. Automation may reduce costs for the firm, but leads to a loss of employment for certain workers and possibly the necessity of retraining for other jobs. These unpleasant results naturally cause some individuals to oppose such changes. If society loses sight of the broader gains from innovation, it may find that individual opposition to change precludes the economy from making technological progress. One characteristic mark of a static society is an adherence to traditional methods of production and the ways of life associated with them. In such a stagnant economy the individual is protected against loss of job or value of skill by the absence of change, but he has lost thereby a more significant thing, the hope of a rising standard of living for himself and his children through increased productivity.

Therefore, the distribution of income should reward people who are willing to initiate, or accept, change. Profits should continue to exist for the successful innovator, and the wage structure should not be allowed to become inflexible for the protection of employees whose jobs can be eliminated by change. We can sympathize with the firm whose profits have been reduced by the new methods or with the employee whose job has been lost, but we must not allow this feeling to prevent the change from taking place. Public policy should aim at easing the hardships caused by change, but it should not prevent change. Therefore, distribution of income must include as one of its basic aspects the incentive for change, if an economy is to achieve a satisfactory rate of growth.

## FINANCIAL FACTORS

**Investment Funds for Growth.** A growing economy requires a constant flow of funds for investment in order to assure a supply of capital goods adequate for production of consumer goods and replacement of technically obsolete equipment. The distribution of income has a dual role to play in providing these investment funds: it must put sufficient income into the hands of those people who will save, and it must provide an incentive to these people to save the necessary funds and then to make them available for investment.

At one time it was believed that considerable inequality in the distribution of income was necessary if saving was to take place. The argument was that poor people were so close to bare subsistence that, rather than save their money, they would spend any increase in income upon badly needed consumer goods. Saving, it was believed, would result only if the extra income were placed in the hands of the wealthy classes who had already satisfied their basic consumer needs. As a matter of fact, however, statistical evidence indicates that saving is taking place in significant amounts among the middle- and even lower-income groups. The broadening in sources of personal saving seems to have developed as a result of a general rise in income levels. This development has raised the living standards of the middle-income family to a par with that of the wealthy consumer a century ago and still permitted some saving. The growth of a variety of savings institutions, such as life insurance companies, savings and loan associations, and mutual funds, has also encouraged saving among groups to whom this practice was unknown a century ago.

In the chapter dealing with the theory of interest we noted that a large part of our present supply of investment funds derives from sources other than personal savings. Undistributed profits provide a major part of the sums required for expansion by our major corporations. In many of the lesser-developed nations the government, through its power to tax, has satisfied a large part of the necessary investment funds. Although there are several sources of funds for providing capital, it is essential that the distribution of income permit an adequate volume of saving.

Along with saving must go the act of investment in order to complete the process of capital accumulation. As Keynes pointed out, people like to hold assets in liquid form. The rate of return on capital must be sufficient to induce consumers to surrender cash for less liquid assets and to motivate the movement of savings into investment in capital goods.

**Balance Between Consumption and Saving.** It is essential that the proper balance between consumption and saving be maintained in the utilization of disposable personal income. If too large a portion of income is used for consumption, the volume of savings is reduced and adequate funds for investment cannot be realized from this source. On the other hand too great an allocation of income into savings causes a reduction of consumption purchases which, in turn, leads to underutilization of productive capacity. If the machines already in existence are not being fully used, it is difficult to get businessmen to make investments in more capital goods. A high level of personal saving is a virtue only if it results in the creation of a greater supply of capital equipment that will increase the production of the nation. If the rate of saving rises to the point where it results in idle men and machines because consumption has been depressed, then the high propensity to save lowers the real income (*NNP*) of society. Saving and consumption must be balanced so that funds for investment are provided and yet adequate consumption makes additional investment profitable.

**Inflation and Growth.** History is full of examples of the close relationship between a high rate of growth and inflation. Rapid growth almost inevitably involves a high rate of investment, which puts a strain upon the limited productive capacity of the economy. The same machines, land, and men cannot be used to produce both consumer goods and capital equipment. The resources for the production of investment goods can come from only four sources: (1) putting idle factors of production to use, (2) bringing newly created capital equipment into production, (3) shifting resources away from producing consumer goods, or (4) importing capital goods from abroad. If the production of investment goods can be limited to an amount that can be supplied from previously idle factors, from newly built plants or from other countries there will be little danger of inflation. The additional investment under these conditions only serves to push the economy toward the full-employment position.

On the other hand, if the extra investment expenditure is added at a time when the economy is already at full employment, an inflationary gap is created. At this juncture the total expenditure on output exceeds the volume of output available at current price and cost levels. Of course, this puts an upward pressure on prices and costs. This inflationary gap can be eliminated only by reducing another type of expenditure to compensate for the increase in investment. Although it may be possible to reduce government spending or exports, the most obvious item to reduce is consumption. If the public is willing to increase its saving in conjunction with the increase in investment, the resulting decline in consumption will free factors of production for the output of investment goods. Ultimately it will be desirable for consumption to increase in order to provide a market for the output of the new plants, but in the period when the extra investment is taking place a fully employed economy must free resources for this purpose by reducing other demands upon productive capacity.

This need to reduce consumption in order to free capacity for production of capital goods is a source of difficulty for many lesser developed countries. Investment in such nations is an essential for growth, but living standards there are usually so low that it is difficult to reduce consumption enough to free factors for the production of capital goods. The difficulty in providing the needed flow of saving is primarily one of low productive capacity, not of finances. The inflationary pressure results from the excessive demands on limited capacity to produce regardless of the financial policies that may be followed. Monetary policy will be useful only to the degree that it assists in reducing the excessive demands upon the resources of the economy.

On the other hand, it will be possible to finance essential investment more easily once the actual growth process is under way. The expansion of output can then be diverted into investment uses without the need to depress consumption. The developing economy then moves into the pleasant cycle where increased saving essential for investment is secured out of larger output, and some small part of the rising *GNP* can even be allocated to a limited rise in the standard of living. The real hope of avoiding inflation by the developing country lies in this possibility of financing the major part of its investment needs out of increased production. We will develop these points in more detail in later chapters.

**Effects of Inflation.** When inflation results from the added investment needed in a growing economy, problems are created that make the continuance of stable growth difficult. Rapidly rising prices distort the pattern of income distribution and give rewards to clever or lucky people who have not made significant contributions to production. Speculators take advantage of shortages and hoard needed goods in order to profit from rising prices. On the other hand, workers or investors whose wage or interest returns rise at a slower rate than consumer goods prices suffer undeserved losses.

Public resentment may become aroused against an economic system that permits serious injustice in the distribution of income. Because lesser developed countries have large numbers of people very close to the subsistence level, such dissatisfaction can grow to revolutionary proportions. Accordingly, political instability faces the government of a poor nation that is unable to secure an acceptable income distribution. Rigorous controls on the flow of income may be a partial answer, but the resulting loss of individual freedom makes such a policy one to be followed only in extreme situations. Clearly, growth for an underdeveloped country presents difficult problems of both an economic and political nature.

Deflation may have an even more serious effect than inflation upon an economy, but is less likely to characterize a society consciously oriented toward growth. Deflation results from a shortage of expenditure for consumption, investment, and government services; but spending for all of these purposes is almost certain to increase in a growing economy. Thus, inflation becomes the more common danger to a growing economy, whereas deflation is more characteristic of a stagnant one.

**Role of Interest Rates in Growth.** In the chapter on interest theory we noted the strong tendency for private investment to have an inelastic demand for funds. Because saving in a less-developed economy is small relative to investment needs, interest rates tend to rise beyond socially acceptable limits in a free market. Not only is the supply curve in a position close to the interest axis as a result of limited saving, but the curve also tends to be highly inelastic because of the urgency of consumer needs, the absence of a tradition of saving, and the lack of effective institutions for channeling these savings into investment.

As we see in Figure 22–1, illustrating this situation, any increase in investment demand, as shown by the shift to the right of the demand curve, will result in a sharp rise in the interest rate. Unfortunately, this rise in the interest rate does not bring a significant increase in the volume of saving because of the inelasticity of the supply curve. Neither does this higher interest rate choke off much of the demand for funds, because this curve is also inelastic. The operation of a free

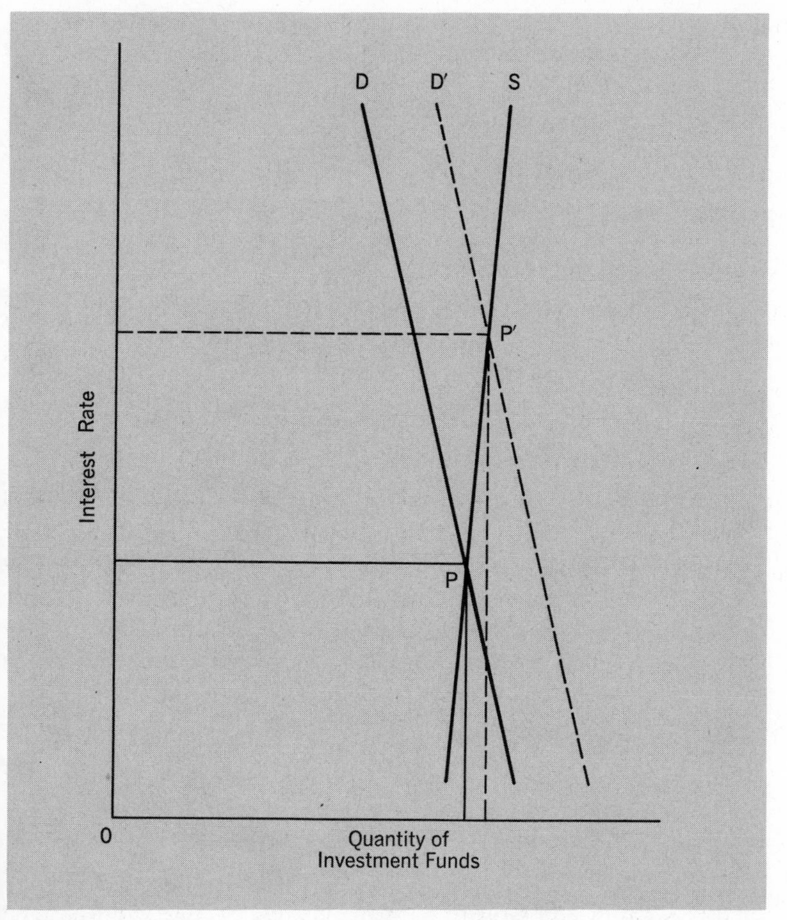


**Figure 22–1.** Tendency of interest rate to rise sharply with increased investment demand in underdeveloped country due to inelasticity of supply and demand curves.

market for investment funds under these conditions will result primarily in redistribution of income in favor of the few wealthy families who have funds to lend. Any such redistribution of income favorable to the wealthy portions of the population is almost certain to increase the political instability that often is already a serious problem in a developing economy.

The inevitable result of this undesirable rise in the interest rate is that the government of the growing economy places controls upon the use of investment funds to assure their use in the most essential ways. The demand curve is thus shifted back to the left, and the rationing of scarce funds is accomplished by control over investment rather than by a rising interest rate. On the supply side, the government will undertake to compel saving by rationing of consumer goods, restricting unnecessary imports, and securing investment funds by taxation. Again, controls replace the interest rate as a means of securing an adequate supply of capital funds. After growth is well under way and normal capitalistic conditions and living standards are established it will be possible for the interest rate to play a somewhat more important role, because rises in income will increase the volume of saving. But in the early stages of development governmental control over the flow of investment funds appears to be almost inevitable.

One exception to this limited role of interest rates in the early stages of growth exists when it is possible for the underdeveloped economy to obtain capital from abroad. If investors in highly developed countries are willing to invest in the less advanced economy, higher interest rates will be a valuable incentive in securing this movement of capital. American investment in Canada, Western Europe, and certain Latin-American countries illustrates the role played by interest rate differentials in such situations. But recent years have provided too many illustrations of loss of foreign investment by Americans to believe that the role of interest rates as an incentive for long-run investment can be very great in many parts of Asia and Africa, or even some parts of Latin America. Our losses in Cuba and Indonesia will be very much in the minds of American lenders as they consider the possibility of investment in the politically unstable countries. Interest rates will be an incentive for international capital flow only when the lender can be reasonably sure that principal and interest will be paid.

## SPECIAL GROWTH PROBLEMS

**Land Reform and Growth.** In the chapter dealing with rent and profits we have already noted the danger to political stability that results when the pressure from population increase forces rents to unusually high levels. Poverty-stricken peasants will inevitably resent the payment of a large part of agricultural production to absentee landlords, who make no apparent contribution to production. Communist propaganda has made very successful use of this resentment.

A purely short-run solution to this problem can be found in a land reform program that transfers ownership of agricultural land to the families who till it. This type of program may raise the living standards of the peasant group and provide incentive for a better utilization of the land. At the very least it should relieve the political pressure that results from the belief that the distribution of income lacks justice. On the other hand, land reform may reduce the size of the farm to uneconomic levels. With lower total production the per capita income of the peasant may even fall.

The longer-run solution for food scarcity and high rents must be found in increased productivity, both agricultural and industrial, in the less-developed country. Better health, improved education, modernized techniques, and increased supplies of capital goods will ultimately increase per capita output. Income of the individual farmer can be increased by transferring part of the population into industrial jobs and increasing the size of the average farm and its output. The increased agricultural output will prevent further rises in food prices with their resultant increases in rent. These beneficial results of increased productivity will be secured, however, only if the rise in population resulting from a high birth rate and a low death rate does not force a distribution of the increased output over so many people that the living standard is kept from rising.

**Skilled People and Growth.** Modern industrial societies require large numbers of skilled people both for management and for technical work in production. Developing countries almost inevitably face severe shortages of skilled personnel in all categories. Many causes contribute to these shortages. A poor country has difficulty in financing an adequate educational system. Many people may not even learn to read and write, so that they are unable to educate themselves outside of school. The poor quality of teaching handicaps many who are able to attend school. Education at the university level suffers from limited financial support as well as from the poor basic training of the students. Highly specialized and professional education is very expensive, and the quality of such training is likely to be particularly low.

In many backward societies education has been a social status symbol possessed only by the governing class and associated with established professions, such as law or medicine. When the possibility of increased education opens up for larger groups of the population, therefore, the people tend to crowd into these prestige professions rather than into agricultural science, engineering, accounting, business management, or chemistry. Yet these occupations are perhaps more essential to growth than the older professions.

If growth is not to be retarded by inadequate supplies of workers with the necessary technical and professional skills, the income structure must reward these people adequately. In the short run the backward economy may be able to meet the need by bringing in trained personnel from other countries, but in the longer period a nation must draw people for essential occupations from its own population or suffer from excessive foreign control.

**Productivity and Growth.** The problem of securing economic growth is essentially that of increasing productivity. The ability of an economy to produce results from a very complex set of social, political, and economic conditions. In any backward society production is hampered by many causes, but a distribution of income that fails to reward the necessary human actions can be one of the most serious limitations. In many stagnant societies income is determined by social tradition that must be broken before a market-regulated income system can offer proper rewards as incentives to the supplying of necessary productive functions.

If an economy is to depend upon the free choice of individuals rather than the controls of the government, individual income must be tied to the performance of productive functions. Income is not unjust because it provides a low standard of living; rather, it is unjust when it fails to reward properly, and therefore to motivate, the performance of socially desirable functions. If an economy is to grow by increasing its productivity, labor must be performed, investments must be made, uncertainties must be faced, and difficult responsibilities must be accepted. If individuals are not willing to perform these functions under the motivation of securing added income, then an authoritarian government using controls to force performance offers the only alternative route to growth. A system of income distribution that properly rewards performance of productive functions is an essential part of an economy based upon human freedom.

**Summary.** Economic growth depends in great measure upon willingness to work, acceptance of change, and the provision of adequate capital. Income distribution must reward these actions if they are to be efficiently performed.

Essential supplies of investment funds result from providing adequate incomes to people who will save and then rewarding investments made out of the savings. A possible alternative is for the government to perform the saving and investment function through its power to tax. Growth also requires a balance between consumption and saving. Consumption must be reduced enough to provide saving for essential investment, but it must be high enough to provide a market for the output of the new investment goods.

Economic growth requires investment, but if added investment expenditures are imposed upon a fully employed society an inflationary gap results. Inflation disrupts income distribution and interferes with production. A market-determined interest rate is of limited usefulness in an undeveloped economy either to motivate savings or to ration limited investment funds. One exception may be that high interest rates attract funds from outside the country.

Less-developed countries with large populations find that political instability results from high rents. Land reform may be necessary in the early growth stages before increased productivity eases the population pressure. Distribution of income must provide the incentive for providing personnel for jobs requiring special skills or technical training. If the system of income distribution does not provide for the performance of essential productive functions in a free society, economic growth can be obtained only by governmental controls that force the performance of these functions.

## QUESTIONS

1. What are the basic human attitudes essential for economic growth?
2. Explain the relationship between wage payments and the motivation of essential work. Why is this relationship not as perfect as we should like?
3. How does capitalism attempt to secure acceptance of change?
4. How important is inequality in personal incomes in securing essential saving for capital investment?
5. What are the undesirable effects of too little saving? Of too much saving?
6. Why do so many underdeveloped countries find it hard to avoid inflation as they attempt to secure economic growth?
7. What is the proper role of the interest rate in securing economic growth in developing countries?
8. Why is land reform so often essential in an underdeveloped nation?
9. What is the relationship of the income structure to the problem of securing adequate numbers of skilled workers and managers?
10. Why can capitalism depend primarily upon free choice in getting essential work done whereas communism depends more upon the use of force?

PART

# 6

# *International Trade*

Following an explanation of the theory of trade, balance of payments, exchange rates, and reinterpretation of national income—adding foreign elements to the domestic determinants of income (*NNP*), this section deals with the reciprocal relationships between income (*NNP*) and the balance of payments. This study is followed by an analysis of measures to restore equilibrium in the balance of payments. The problem of the United States balance of payments is discussed, and approaches to the problem are considered.

CHAPTER

# 23

# The Basic Theory of Trade

## INTRODUCTORY REMARKS

In this section of the text we will direct our attention to international economic relations and problems. As we do so, let us recognize that international economics is not a separate study in itself. Rather, it is that branch of our discipline in which the relationships between the foreign and the domestic sectors of the economy become the objects of study. The above statement seems necessary at the outset of this section for two main reasons. First, students often fail to relate happenings in the international sector of a nation's economy to the behavior of income, prices, and wages at home. Second, United States foreign policy is a more important determinant of national goals today than it has ever been in the past.

The principles studied in this chapter are closely related to ideas developed earlier in the text. Thus we devote much attention to the allocation of factors among different uses, their costs, and their returns. These topics relate to principles discussed in Chapters 3 and 18. In Chapter 24 the determination of a relevant set of prices (foreign exchange rates) is shown to depend upon the forces of demand and supply discussed previously in Chapters 2 and 17. In a similar fashion, we will employ tools of income determination developed in Chapters 6 and 7 to describe the effects of foreign trade on the level of income. The latter will be our task in Chapter 25.

## THE BACKGROUND OF TRADE

It should now be evident that both micro- and macro-economics play a role in the study of international economics. In this respect, the prices (costs) of a nation's firms engaged in exporting and importing influence the average level of prices within the country. Furthermore, prices of numerous firms scattered throughout the world affect the average level of prices among the various nations. Macroeconomics, the study of the whole, will absorb our attention as we proceed to analyze the familiar elements of consumption, saving, and investment, along with some not-so-familiar factors of imports, exports, and lending, which together help to express why it is that relative income levels vary among nations.

The second point that was made in the first paragraph of this introductory statement indicates that United States foreign policy is playing a relatively more important role today than it did in prior periods. It is not difficult to explain why in our historic past we have treated international economics as a kind of special study supplementing our national economics. We have been a wealthy nation in terms of resource endowments. Consequently, we have not had to rely on trade to the same extent as foreign nations. Furthemore, our foreign trade amounted to only a small part of our total ability to produce goods and services. Today scarcely 3 to 4 per cent of our production is shipped abroad; and a similar percentage of goods and services consumed in our country comes from abroad.

This situation presents a paradox: although total trade contributes only moderately to our national income (output), it makes a substantial contribution to the income (output) of other nations. As we shall see in a subsequent chapter, many nations depend upon our imports—their exports—to yield a large portion of their national income. For example, Venezuela's exports account for nearly 40 per cent of the total national income of that country. Similar high percentage figures are found in several Western European countries. In the same manner, imports from the United States are important to the economic growth of many countries, because they provide capital and other goods that are needed to increase production.

It has become evident since World War II that the United States was destined to take a more active part in world affairs. At the conclusion of the war the United States was the world's leading industrial nation. Consequently, we began to recognize more clearly our obligations in the world.

In the aftermath of World War II, the world became divided into two camps: the communist bloc and the free nations. This development promoted the creation in the West of mutual defense arrangements that provide a necessary counterweight to Russian military power. A spirit of cooperation in the free world has thus become vital in the postwar period of the cold war.



All of our attention in this postwar period has not been devoted to the problems of the divided world. It has become apparent that our factor endowments are not inexhaustible. Foodstuffs, minerals, and metals are increasingly in short supply or destined to become quite scarce. As a result, the growth of our economy is more directly dependent on foreign sources of supply than ever before. On the other hand, our productive capacity in some lines exceeds the ability of the nation's economy to absorb these commodities. Absorption of this output requires an expansion of the market for such products.

The next five chapters will bring together some of the fundamental principles, tools, and analyses in the area of international economics. The last group of chapters in the text is reserved for the purpose of integrating the leading principles of economic growth developed throughout the book.

## SPECIALIZATION AS THE BASIS FOR TRADE

It has long been asserted that a region or nation stands to gain from specializing in the production of certain goods and services and exchanging the resulting surpluses with other regions or nations. In discussing production costs in Chapter 14 we analyzed the advantages of specialized large-scale production. At that time we pointed out the advantages of specialized use of labor and the employment of automatic machinery. Knowing that specialization yields certain gains where it is applied, we will stress its application in our study of international economics.

There are many differences between countries that influence the exchange of goods and services. Three important differences are noted at this juncture. They are (1) variations in the relative abundance of the several factors of production, (2) differences in the level or pattern of demand, and (3) the existence of differing political and socioeconomic organizations. Let us proceed to develop these three points in more detail.

**Supply Characteristics.** The relative abundance of factors of production controls the terms under which resources will be supplied. When these supplies are related to the demands for them, their prices emerge and with these prices the allocation of resources in producing various types of goods and services. Because all productive factors are scarce, technically speaking, and some of the factors are immobile, or nearly so, their prices are determined indirectly through the market forces of supply and demand for the goods that are produced from them.

One can easily apply the principle of unequal relative abundance of productive factors on a regional basis. Alabama produces cotton;

California and Florida, oranges; Illinois and Iowa, corn; and Kansas, wheat. In like manner, the remaining sections of our country may be cited for their specific products. The explanation of such regional specialization is that the peculiar climatic conditions, the location of mineral and metal deposits, the characteristics of the soil, the quantity and quality of labor, and the application of capital combine to yield low cost of production for some products and not for others.

Does this principle continue to hold true when applied to nations? The answer is an emphatic yes. Political boundaries do not, or should not, impair the operation of this principle. If, for example, we know something about relative factor supplies throughout the world, we should also know something about the various kinds of goods that can best be produced and exchanged by the several countries. Between World War I and World War II the approximate distribution of productive factors followed rather well the pattern indicated in Table 23–1.

**TABLE 23–1**
**Relative Supplies of Productive Factors in Selected Areas**

| Relative Factor Supply | Tropics | United States | Great Plains | United Kingdom |
|---|---|---|---|---|
| Ample | Labor | Capital | Land | Capital |
| Moderate | Land | Land | Capital | Labor |
| Scarce | Capital | Labor | Labor | Land |

In an absolute sense all factors are scarce in supply. Relatively speaking, some factors are more or less abundant (or scarce) than others. The relative distribution of factors is indicated by the terms *ample, moderate,* and *scarce,* shown in the first column. Reading across the rows we get a general view of the relative factor supplies in the various areas.

One would expect that each of the several areas would produce goods which allow for the generous use of the ample supply factor. *Any factor in abundant supply relative to the remaining factors is cheaper to employ, and hence, contributes to a larger output when used to its fullest extent than would be possible with the relatively scarce, high-cost factors.* This basic rule informs us that the tropical areas tend to employ as much labor as possible on moderate amounts of land and with limited capital. Consequently, production is primarily oriented toward tropical agricultural products and handicraft goods. In contrast, the United States devotes a large part of its production to a variety of industrial goods utilizing much capital and relatively small amounts of labor. In the Great Plains area, where land is relatively abundant, much grain, meat, and wool are produced. The relative scarcity of land and a moderate quantity of labor in the United Kingdom explains why much of its production is directed into light and heavy industrial products. One would not expect this area to produce large amounts of crops or meat.

There is a tendency over a given period of time for the distribution of factors to become altered. The United States is a good example of the change that takes place in the relative supply of factor endowments. In the 1860's land was the factor in ample supply relative to labor and capital, but more recently capital has become the abundant factor. The closing of our frontier, improvements in technology, the improved quality of labor, foreign investment, our tariff policy, the rise in income, and the changed pattern of demand all contributed to the alteration in the relative supplies of productive factors. At the same time, other regions of the world were experiencing changes in their relative factor supplies, and for the same reasons as the United States. In the case of England, the repeal of the Corn Laws in the 1840's had much to do with the accumulation of capital and the development of industry. The scarcity of land caused the prices of agricultural goods to rise above those at which she could obtain similar commodities from abroad.

In recent years a few of the countries in the tropical region have witnessed a change in the relative abundance of factors. Heavy foreign capital inflows into Mexico and Brazil, and the gradual increase in the production of industrial goods may, in the foreseeable future, cause capital to become moderate, or even ample, in supply relative to labor and land. Perhaps the same holds true with respect to the future of Canada, which is presently classified among the group of nations making up the Great Plains area.

Past and present experience indicates that in the future we can reasonably expect continuous changes to occur that will influence the relative distribution of factors among nations. The success of future economic growth will require, then, that the changing pattern of productive factors be understood and that nations employ these factors in the most efficient combination possible.

**The Role of Demand.** The demand for a factor—like supply—helps to determine its price (cost). Let us assume that each nation specializes in the production of goods that require large amounts of the factor in ample supply. When trade starts up, the present systems of internal prices within the trading nations become altered. To demonstrate the price movements, suppose one of two trading countries has an ample supply of land relative to labor and capital. The lower priced factor will experience an increase in demand as a result of increased exports of the low-cost goods produced on the cheap land. The price of this factor (or the goods produced from its employment) will therefore begin to rise. In converse fashion, the scarce and high-cost factors —labor and capital—will be affected by a decline in demand and price, and the country may import these factors (or the goods made from them). As far as this first country is concerned, we may conclude by stating that the price of the factor in relatively abundant supply increases, and the prices of the factors in relatively moderate and scarce supply decrease.

Our analysis may now be applied to a second country where either labor or capital is the original factor in ample supply and the remaining two are relatively scarce in supply. For similar reasons, our conclusion with respect to the price of the factors is the same as that for the first country—that is, the price of the factor in relatively abundant supply rises, whereas the prices of the factors in relatively scarce supply fall. A brief summary statement applicable to this line of reasoning is that changes in demand cause the internal prices of factors and their products to become altered. In fact, Professor Bertil Ohlin, a noted Swedish economist, contended that the trend is toward more equal factor and commodity prices in the countries involved.[1]

Factor pricing also depends on the relative elasticities of demand and supply and the relative levels of income among trading nations. If the foreign demand for goods produced with liberal use of land is inelastic in the first country mentioned in the above paragraphs, the rise in the price of this factor would be accompanied with a less-than-proportional decline in the quantity demanded of land-made goods. The price of land in this country will tend, therefore, to become quite high. If greater supply efficiencies are not possible, the foreign country may soon find it profitable to employ some of its own land rather than pay such a high price for similar imported goods from the first country. Changes in supply further affect the ultimate prices of the factors and, hence, the prices of goods made from them.

Countries with relatively high levels of income (and large amounts of capital as a result) often tend to import large amounts of raw materials and semifinished goods. In contrast, countries where the pace of economic development is slow, and the relative levels of income are low, tend to import large quantities of capital or capital-made goods. An exchange of mutual advantage appears possible among the nations with varying income levels based upon the distribution of resources.

Our discussion of factor supply and product demand indicates that many complications are involved in the study of international economics. A tentative conclusion emerges at this point: international trade is beneficial as long as factor supplies are unequally distributed and some degree of specialization is practiced. We will return shortly

[1] *Interregional and International Trade* (Cambridge, Mass.: Harvard University Press, 1935), pp. 35–37.

to substantiate this statement by developing the classical concept of trade. Before we do so let us consider the influence on trade exerted by the ways in which society is organized.

**Differing Political, Social, and Economic Organizations.** Given the relative supplies of productive factors and the influence of demand for them and their products, various market prices are established in which exchange takes place. Yet there are other differences of great importance among different economies. These include differences in taste and levels of education as well as the major political, social, and economic institutions of the society in question. In some way each of these items exerts effects on demands and supplies and thereby on the prices and quantities of things produced. For example, the demand for a particular good is influenced by the pattern of consumer tastes and the distribution of income. The latter element is partly the result of government tax policy. We also know that the relative abundance of factors in each country tends to be different. This leads to different supplies of the item in each country. Accordingly, the price of an item tends to vary both within and among nations. We have already noted the tendency of individuals to purchase additional quantities of more expensive goods when their incomes rise relatively to those of other countries. Refrigerators, machines, and various other products are produced in the United States, Europe, Russia, Latin America, and elsewhere under different technical conditions, within a different political and social setting, and at different prices.

John Stuart Mill, a distinguished economist writing in the mid-nineteenth century, developed a provocative issue set forth in terms of the "laws of production" and "laws of distribution." Because the issue relates to our discussion, it is worthy of repetition. He explained that the basic laws of production—law of population, law of increasing returns to industry, law of decreasing returns to agriculture, and so on—were laws concerning physical truths, and therefore unchangeable. The laws of distribution were social laws and, therefore, pertain to such things as property rights, taxes, tariffs, farm price supports, pensions, and unemployment benefits. These laws are subject to change, the responsibility for which lies in the hands of society. No doubt Mill had in mind, among other things, the idea that political, social, and economic organizations adopted by people influence the performance of an economic system.

We have generally assumed thus far that the unequal distribution of productive factors gives rise to differing prices (costs) for their various uses. Though factors tend to be employed according to differences in prices as trade begins, they may be restricted in their uses by economic nationalism, fear, ignorance, or monopoly ownership.

Nonetheless, we will see later in this chapter that gains from trade may come about from the movement of goods that substitute for the flow of productive factors. As citizens of the world come to recognize and to want improvements in their material welfare, political, social, and economic differences will become more clearly recognizable and understood. Perhaps many of these differences will tend to disappear with a freer flow of ideas.

Our ultimate purpose is to set up a framework of analysis that is both consistent with that previously developed in the text and useful in studying problems of international trade. Later, we will introduce further notions into our analytical scheme. The classical concept of trade will serve as our point of departure in the ensuing discussion.

## THE CLASSICAL CONCEPT OF TRADE

**Some Assumptions.** As a starting point let us state the basic assumptions of the classical theory insofar as it relates to international trade. Classical writings contained four general assumptions pertaining to the functioning of an economy: (1) pure competition exists in all markets; (2) full employment prevails in the economy; (3) labor cost determines value; and (4) production takes place under conditions of constant cost. In previous parts of this book we modified these general assumptions to conform to the present-day functioning of an economy. In this section of the book we shall make use of these basic classical assumptions, but shall modify them at times to provide a more realistic treatment. In their study of international trade, the classical writers added three more assumptions. First, labor and all other productive factors were mobile within a country but immobile between nations. Second, there were no cost obstructions to the transfer of goods between countries. In other words, commercial and financial restrictions affecting the movement of goods were ruled out. Finally, the balance of payments included only trade items—that is, tangible goods being exchanged. The classical economists were content with analyzing the physical movement of goods. For the present it will suffice simply to identify these three assumptions of classical theory relating to international trade. They will be put to use at appropriate points in subsequent chapters.

**Theory of Comparative Advantage.** Consider the following hypothetical situation. Suppose that Mr. X, who is considered to be the best lawyer in town, is also the best typist. Should the lawyer do his own typing or hire a secretary? The answer is quite obvious. He should devote his talents exclusively to his law practice and employ a secretary. Although Mr. X has an absolute advantage in both employments, the application of his time to the law will afford him a higher monetary return. In short, he enjoys a comparative advantage in the practice of law. Furthermore, when he decides to concentrate on law, Mr. X will necessarily hire a secretary. Although a secretary will suffer an absolute disadvantage in both occupations, she necessarily enjoys a comparative advantage in typing by reason of her competence in this field contrasted with her lack of legal training. By specializing in this way the lawyer and his secretary would pool their talents to maximum advantage.

**A Simple Case of Comparative Advantage.** Let us apply this same line of reasoning to our study of international trade. We will use a simple case of the two-country, two-commodity model. Essentially the same results would be obtained should we employ more than two countries or two commodities. Our task is to determine whether or not there is a basis for trade between two countries and to establish the possible gains.

Consider a further hypothetical example, this time involving countries. Suppose the United States and England are engaged in producing wheat and shirts. For simplicity in discussion let us combine all productive factors under the single heading of *labor,* the number of units of which we assume to be fixed. Now five man-days of labor will yield outputs of each of the two goods in the two countries, as shown in Table 23–2.

An inspection of these figures reveals that the United States possesses an absolute advantage in the production of both wheat and shirts. Yet, from our earlier example of the lawyer and his secretary, we understand that absolute advantage does not determine the choice of occupation. In the present example the United States can produce both goods at lower labor costs. However, the United States possesses an even greater advantage in wheat than in shirts. Specifically, she can outproduce England in wheat in the ratio 20:8 (2.5:1), but only 10:8 (1.25:1) in shirts.

**TABLE 23–2**
**A Simple Case of Comparative Advantage**

| | Output from Five Days' Labor: | |
|---|---|---|
| **Country** | **Wheat** | **Shirts** |
| United States | 20 | 10 |
| England | 8 | 8 |

Economists tell us that a nation has a *comparative advantage* in that product in which its *absolute advantage is greater* or its *absolute disadvantage is less.* Hence, even though the United States has an absolute advantage in both products, its absolute advantage is relatively greater in wheat than shirts. Therefore, it may be said that the comparative advantage of the United States lies in wheat. On the other hand, England suffers an absolute disadvantage in producing both products, but its absolute disadvantage is comparatively less in shirts than in wheat. As a result, England is said to have a comparative advantage, but an absolute disadvantage, in shirts. Clearly, the people of both countries can benefit from trade through an exchange of some American wheat for some English shirts. This is the case, we shall find, because of the relative productivity (cost) within each country.

**Comparative Cost.** The foregoing discussion suggests that specialization as between individuals or countries leads to increased production. The classical economist, David Ricardo, went further in developing and applying the principle of comparative cost.[2] *The principle holds that the cost of a unit of one commodity is the reduction in the output of a second commodity that its production necessitates.* This is an opportunity-cost concept, which expresses the relative gains or losses realized from alternative uses of factors. Let us illustrate.

A given piece of land may be used to produce either corn or cotton. Hence, we may say that the (total) cost of the corn crop is the amount of cotton that might otherwise have been produced. Comparative costs can be computed from the output data given in Table 23–2. The opportunity cost in the United States of one bushel of wheat is one half shirt (that is, it costs as much labor effort to produce one bushel of wheat as it does two shirts), whereas in England the opportunity cost of one bushel of wheat is one shirt (that is, it costs England as much labor effort to produce one bushel of wheat as it does one shirt). Thus the opportunity cost of wheat is lower in the United States than it is in England (one bushel of wheat costs one half shirt in the United States, but costs one shirt in England). On the other hand, the opportunity cost of shirts is lower in England than it is in the United States (one shirt costs one bushel of wheat in England, but costs two bushels of wheat in the United States). It is cheaper, therefore, for the United States to produce wheat and England shirts; and the two countries gain by the interchange of their respective surpluses.

An application of the principles of comparative advantage and cost to our illustration reveals what common sense does not, namely, that the two countries can benefit from specialization and trade.

[2] Ricardo's major contribution to the theory of trade was an idea that was later formalized into the principle of comparative costs. See Chapter 7 of his *Principles of Political Economy and Taxation* (3d ed.; London: John Murray, 1821).

Before congratulating ourselves on this fortunate outcome, we may revert back to the basic assumptions underlying classical thought. Of special significance to our case of comparative advantage are the assumptions of constant costs and absence of transportation cost as well as other impediments to trade. The assumption of constant cost ignores the fact that goods might be produced under increasing cost conditions. Furthermore, the assumptions preclude such hindrances as tariffs, quotas, and exchange restrictions. Freedom of trade is essential if both countries are to maximize their gains from trade.

Let us try to summarize our basic trade theory to this point. International trade occurs because of international differences in cost. Because factors are unevenly distributed and lack complete mobility as between nations, differences in cost arise. Countries tend to benefit most from trade when they specialize in the production of those goods and services in which they enjoy a comparative advantage and least comparative cost.

**The Physical Terms of Trade.** Though the people of both countries in our illustration can benefit through an exchange of United States wheat for English shirts, we need to consider the terms upon which such an exchange is possible. Referring to our illustration, we find that the United States gains by trading wheat for shirts if she can secure one shirt for anything less than the cost of two bushels of wheat. Of course, a gain is possible, because in England the comparative cost of one shirt is one bushel of wheat. Similarly, England gains by trading if one bushel of wheat can be obtained by anything under the domestic cost of one shirt. This is possible because in the United States one bushel of wheat is worth only one half shirt.

The United States will offer no more than two bushels of wheat for one shirt, because one shirt can be produced at home at the cost of two bushels of wheat. Likewise, England will offer no more than one shirt for one bushel of wheat, because one bushel of wheat can be produced at home at the cost of one shirt. Now the range within which trade will occur lies somewhere between the ratio of two bushels of wheat for one shirt and the ratio of one bushel of wheat for one shirt. Thus, trade will be beneficial to each country on *any* terms of trade between these limits, because it is possible for each to acquire some goods from abroad at a lower real cost than if the goods were produced at home.

Up to this point we have set only the outside limits to trade. Whether the *actual terms of trade*—the amount of exports required to obtain a given amount of imports—will settle near the ratio of 2:1 or the ratio of 1:1 depends upon the location and elasticities of the demands of the two countries for one another's goods. Suppose the terms of trade settle at 1.5:1 (one and one half bushels of wheat in exchange for one shirt). Given the actual terms of trade we can reason through the nature of the gains for each country.

Suppose that at this trade ratio of 1½ bushels of wheat for 1 shirt we arrange to exchange 9 bushels of wheat for 6 shirts. Let us further assume that the United States, in order to get the wheat for this trade, shifts one half of the labor it has been using for shirt production into wheat production. With our assumption of constant labor costs in each industry wheat output would rise from 20 to 30 bushels and shirt output would fall from 10 to 5, as shown in column (2) of Table 23–3. At the same time let us assume that England shifts all its labor into shirt production. In other words, each country moves labor into the industry in which it has a comparative advantage. How much labor (and other factors of production) would actually be shifted into the industries having a comparative advantage would depend primarily upon elasticity of demand for each product. The final adjustment would be controlled by changes in the relative money prices for each product. Because introduction of money into the analysis makes it more complicated, we have placed this part of the theory in the appendix at the end of the chapter. At this time we shall simply assume that the operation of the price mechanism has brought a shift of only one half of the labor in the United States that has been

**TABLE 23-3**
**Comparative Advantage and the Physical Gains from Trade**

| Country | (1) Product of Five Days' Labor Before Specialization | (2) Output of Same Amount of Labor After Specialization | (3) Amount of Goods Traded | (4) Goods Available After Trade |
|---|---|---|---|---|
| United States | 20 bushels | 30 bushels | −9 bushels | 21 bushels |
| | 10 shirts | 5 shirts | +6 shirts | 11 shirts |
| England | 8 bushels | 0 bushels | +9 bushels | 9 bushels |
| | 8 shirts | 16 shirts | −6 shirts | 10 shirts |

producing shirts, but that all of England's labor in wheat has been shifted into the production of shirts. The advantage of this labor shift can easily be seen by comparing total outputs for each product in column (2), after specialization, with outputs in column (1), before the change. Total output of wheat in column (2) is 30 bushels, whereas in column (1) it is only 28. The change in shirt production is even more gratifying, because it rises from 18 to 21 units.

We can now demonstrate that trade at any ratio between 2:1 and 1:1 will benefit each country. Using the halfway point in the possible ratios of 1.5:1 and trading 9 bushels of wheat for 6 shirts, we can see the gain for each country by comparing total goods available in column (4) with those of column (1) in Table 23–3. The United States has 21 bushels of wheat (after trade) instead of 20 and 11 shirts instead of 10. England's wheat available for consumption has risen from 8 to 9 bushels and shirts from 8 to 10. The figures in this illustration have been kept small for ease in demonstrating the basic principle, but in actual international trade the figures would be in the millions of dollars. These increases in the amount of goods available for consumption as a result of specialization in production permit significant increases in the standards of living in both countries. It is this assurance of mutual advantage that has caused economists to urge the general removal of barriers to international trade.

**Trade and Growth.** The main thesis of this chapter is that trade can contribute to a more efficient use of current resources. In this sense our analysis is basically of short-run duration. To express the analysis in terms of the production frontier, as explained in Chapter 1, we can state that unrestricted trade (regional and international) yields an altered combination of goods measured along the frontier curve at full-capacity output.

In long-run analysis we assume the possibility of a larger output, because a larger quantity of resources can be had or improved productive techniques can be introduced, or both. Under these conditions expanded trade can give a vital assist to a growing economy. As countries continue to trade on the basis of comparative advantage a larger volume of trade will help secure for each country a growing volume of efficiently produced output.

**Summary.** Our analysis of trade makes use of the basic concepts of the classical writers and employs the same simplifying assumptions they made. From this analysis we derive the fundamental theories of comparative advantage and of comparative cost.

The principle of comparative advantage states that a nation has a comparative advantage in that product in which its absolute advantage is greater or its absolute disadvantage is less. In our illustration the United States has an absolute advantage in both products, but its absolute advantage is relatively greater in wheat. Though England has an absolute disadvantage in both goods, its absolute disadvantage is comparatively less in shirts.

The principle of comparative cost is an opportunity-cost concept that holds that the cost of a unit of one commodity is the reduction in the output of a second commodity that its production necessitates. On the basis of this principle we found that the opportunity cost of producing wheat in the United States is less than that of shirts. The reverse holds true for England.

The physical terms of trade establish the limits within which trade will occur. These limits are determined by the cost ratios in each country. The actual terms of trade—the amount of exports required to obtain a given amount of imports—depend upon demand conditions in the two countries. Hence, the actual terms of trade result from the interaction of supply (cost)-and-demand forces.

Because money is used to establish values in the real world, the final form of our illustration requires a translation of physical values into monetary values—costs, prices, and profits. The introduction of money significantly complicates the analysis, and is, therefore, treated in the appendix to this chapter.

Comparative cost does not require a complete specialization of labor (and other resources). Gains accrue to a country by specializing in the production of goods in which its advantage is great: it imports other goods in which its advantage is less. This more efficient use of resources makes a significant contribution to the growth possibilities for an economy.

## QUESTIONS

1. Why is international trade more important to the United States today than it was at the beginning of the century?
2. Explain the relationship between the relative abundance of the various factors of production and the nature of the goods that can most efficiently be produced in each region or country.
3. How does the demand for each of the factors of production change as a result of an expansion of exports? What happens to the demand for factors used in producing goods competing with an expanded supply of imported items?
4. Explain the influence of the legal structure of a country upon income levels of different groups and how the resulting differences may affect the demand for goods moving in international trade.
5. What is meant by "comparative advantage"? Why will opportunity costs in the production of each good be reduced by having each country concentrate on the product in which it has a comparative advantage?
6. Work out a table similar to Table 23–3 for the following set of figures.

| | Product of Five Days' Labor Before Specialization (Bottles) | |
|---|---|---|
| United States | Coca-Cola | 400 |
| | Rum | 100 |
| Jamaica | Coca-Cola | 160 |
| | Rum | 80 |

7. Explain how the principle of comparative advantage demonstrates that each country can benefit from specialized production and international trade.

# Appendix

## USE OF MONEY IN THE ILLUSTRATION OF COMPARATIVE ADVANTAGE

In the real world goods are not normally exchanged directly for goods. Instead, money enters into the process of exchange to facilitate the flow of goods. If our analysis is to be convincing, we must express costs,[3] prices, and profits in money terms. Our immediate task is to establish money wages and to translate the comparative differences in cost into money terms in the two countries. The output data in Tables 23–2 and 23–3 show that the United States has an absolute advantage in producing both wheat and shirts and a comparative advantage in wheat. Hence, the United States will specialize in wheat and England in shirts. These data are reproduced in column (1) of Table 23–4. The remaining columns in the latter table will be useful in the following discussion.

We simplify our transition to monetary terms by expressing all figures in dollars. Although the British would express costs in pounds, we can assume a conversion at the existing exchange rate of dollars for pounds. The ratio of money wages between the two countries must lie somewhere between an upper and lower limit determined by ratios of productivity. Let us assume a daily wage rate in England of eight dollars (column (2)). Now the daily wage rate in the United States cannot exceed $20, or two and one half times that of Europe, because the upper limit is fixed by the greater labor productivity in the United States in wheat—that is, 20:8. Similarly, the daily wage rate in the United States cannot fall below $10, or one and one quarter times that of England, because the lower limit is set by the relatively greater productivity in the United States in shirts—that is, 10:8. A $12 wage rate in the United States satisfies these requirements. Clearly, actual wage rates in each nation would be determined by demand-and-supply forces in the labor market.

Given the output relations (column (1)) and the wage rates (column (2)) in the two countries, we next establish the money costs (also selling prices under long-run competitive conditions). The price per bushel of wheat in the United States is $3 (five days' labor at $12 per day gives total cost of $60, divided by 20 bushels of output). Other prices in column (3) are determined in the same way. For example, the price per shirt in England is $5 (five days' labor at $8 per day gives total cost of $40, divided by output of 8 shirts).

[3] Though costs are expressed in terms of money wages of labor, we hold to our earlier assumption that labor includes all productive factors.

**TABLE 23–4**
**Costs, Prices, and the Value of Trade**

| Country | (1) Product of 5 Days' Labor | (2) Wage Levels ($ per Day) | (3) Prices Before Trade | (4) Prices After Trade | (5) Value of Trade | (6) Relative Values Before Trade | (7) Product After Specialization | (8) Product After Trade |
|---|---|---|---|---|---|---|---|---|
| United States | 20 bushels | 12 | 3 | 4 | 9 bu @ $4 = $36 | 2 wheat = 1 shirt | 30 bu | 21 bu (30 − 9) |
| | 10 shirts | | 6 | 6 | | | 5 shirts | 11 shirts (5 + 6) |
| England | 8 bushels | 8 | 5 | 4 | 6 shirts @ $6 = $36 | 1 wheat = 1 shirt | 0 bu | 9 bu (0 + 9) |
| | 8 shirts | | 5 | 6 | | | 16 shirts | 10 shirts (16 − 6) |

**Money Terms of Trade.** Unfortunately, we do not know from the cost data alone exactly where, within these limits, the ratio of wages will settle when trade begins, and consequently the ratio at which United States wheat will exchange for England's shirts. As explained earlier, this ratio depends upon the conditions of consumer demand. Assume that the opening of trade does not affect wages and that, accordingly, wages settle at the amounts shown in column (2)—that is, $12 in the United States and $8 in England. Then prices of the products that satisfy the conditions of exchange of 1½ bushels of wheat for 1 shirt are $4 per bushel of wheat and $6 per shirt (column (4)). We illustrate this fact below.

**Value of Trade.** Having established the relative prices for the traded goods, we seek an equilibrium position for the two countries. If, at a price of $4 per bushel, the United States exports 9 bushels of wheat, making a total value of exports equal to $36, and if, at a price of $6 per shirt, England exports 6 shirts, giving them exports of $36 and imports of $36, this exchange would then result in an equilibrium position. A long-run equilibrium could not exist if the trade did not balance import and export values. The balance of these values is shown in column (5). Notice that prices are not equal, but that the ratio of prices determined by relative costs is such that the total value of exports is equal to that of imports.

It is important to note that with the opening of trade prices tend toward equality, except for transport costs, which are omitted here. A glance at columns (3) and (4) suggests this result. Neglecting a detailed explanation, we may say that it is the forces of supply and demand that create this effect. When trade begins, each country tends to concentrate on producing that product in which it has a cost advantage. Output rises as a result of this specialization, and the supply of each product in each country is increased. The interaction of supply and demand tends to cause the price of the exported good to rise in each country and that of the imported item to fall. It is this change in prices and profits that provides the motivation for shifting labor (and other productive factors) into the production of the good in which comparative advantage exists.

**Some Important Points in Conclusion.** This illustration of comparative advantage enables us to clarify a number of significant points. One of the most important facts demonstrated is that trade can take place to the advantage of both countries even though one is a high-wage country and the other has low wages. Wage rates are determined primarily by the productivity of labor, and if labor is sufficiently productive a country can have low costs per unit of output while paying a high wage rate. For example, in Table 23–4 we see

that the United States can produce wheat at a lower dollar cost pe
bushel even though it pays a 50-per-cent higher wage rate.

Another point of significance is that we can depend upon th
market to give us the correct allocation of resources in trade betwee
nations as well as in trade within a nation. The rise in profits tha
goes with the increase in the price of wheat in the United States—
for example, from $3 to $4—provides the motivation for the in
creased use of labor in that industry. With relative freedom of trad
it is not necessary for the government to control production or t
tell businessmen what goods to import or to export. The free function
ing of a competitive market will perform this function.

However, caution must be exercised in adopting this theory t
practical policy decisions. For example, the proper allocation o
resources as treated above requires the existence of effective competi
tion. The presence of monopoly can be as disastrous to public welfar
in international markets as it is in domestic markets. One of th
dangers of trade with the communist countries is that we are dealin
with a governmental monopoly, not a free competitive market.

Another important point to notice is that international trade tend
to increase consumer living standards. But if our national aim become
military strength rather than a high living standard, the operation o
a freely competitive market may not help us to achieve our goals.

CHAPTER

24

# International Trade: Balance of Payments Equilibrium

The theory of trade presented in the last chapter should have convinced us that regions and nations benefit from trade. In this chapter we will examine financial and other aspects of the movement of goods and services between countries. It is easy to visualize a rise in income taking place when an American exporter ships goods abroad. The foreign buyer either pays in money, promises to pay later (gives IOUs), or makes available some kind of asset acceptable to the American exporter. The transaction results in a receipt of money or claims to money that increases the income (purchasing power) of the seller. Conversely, an American importer pays out income or gives the foreign seller claims to income.

Exports and imports comprise only a part of the total financial transactions between nations. In order to understand the significance of these transactions we need to examine a country's international balance of payments. By doing so, we shall see how income affects the balance of payments and how it, in turn, affects the level of income.

International prices also influence the movement of goods and services. We shall find that an exchange rate is a price expression, the rate being determined by the forces of demand and supply. A country's exchange rate may be free to fluctuate or it may be quite inflexible. Later in the chapter we shall explain how fluctuating exchange rates and changes in internal prices correct a disequilibrium in the balance of payments.

To sum up our points, the objectives of this chapter are (1) to introduce monetary aspects of trade, (2) to analyze the international balance of payments, (3) to examine the role of exchange rates and adjustments to equilibrium, and (4) to indicate the nature of long-run adjustments and growth. Let us develop these ideas in more detail.

## FINANCING A TRANSACTION: FOREIGN EXCHANGE

One may hear a statement to the effect that goods bought at home keep money in the country, but goods imported from abroad cause money to leave the country. This is not the case. On the contrary, a more accurate statement is this: "Exports finance imports." When a resident of the United States buys goods from abroad the foreign seller wants to be paid in his own currency just like an American exporter wants payment in dollars. Let us follow a typical transaction to demonstrate how payments and receipts take place.

Suppose an American firm buys $3,000 worth of English bicycles. The rate of exchange—the price of dollars in terms of pounds—is, say, $3 equals £1. The $3,000 is exchanged for a £1,000 check at the firm's bank (or any bank that deals in foreign money). The firm then sends the £1,000 check to the English bicycle firm. We might inquire where the American bank gets the pounds sterling. It acquires them from an English bank or a branch of an American bank located in England in exchange for dollar deposits. These dollar deposits provide a source of foreign exchange (dollars) for English importers who purchase goods in the United States.

A reverse transaction occurs when an American firm exports $3,000 worth of tools to an English company. The United States firm receives a $3,000 check in payment after the English company converts £1,000 to dollars. This is a simple, and balancing, type of transaction. In practice there are several alternative techniques available to finance international transactions; and there may be hundreds of individual transactions taking place each day. The important point to keep in mind is that a nation's importers create a demand for foreign exchange, whereas its exporters create a supply of foreign exchange. Or in terms of the two trading countries, American exporters create a foreign demand for dollars, and American importers create a foreign supply of dollars.

The above transactions involve a movement of goods. Actually, many other types of transactions take place between nations, and they are financed in essentially the same way. Presently we shall analyze the transactions of one country, namely, the United States, with the rest of the world; this analysis goes under the name, the balance of payments. In this connection we should understand that individuals and firms carry on most of the trade between nations. Nonetheless, we shall find governments engaged in exporting goods, making loans and grants, and providing other forms of payments.

## THE BALANCE OF PAYMENTS

We said that exports finance imports. We also indicated that there are many types of transactions that do not involve the movement of goods. Now we can state with more accuracy that a nation can import (requiring payments) more goods than it exports (requiring receipts), if other transactions provide the country with sufficient receipts to make up the deficiency. (Opposite transactions occur when exports are greater than imports; that is, payments take place to finance the export surplus.)

The international balance of payments is, strangely enough, a kind of income statement that *records all transactions between individuals, firms, and governmental units of one nation and individuals, firms, and governmental units of all other nations*—in short, the world. Transactions include goods, services, and various kinds of capital movements. Because of the double-entry nature of the accounting employed, total receipts and payments always balance. This balance occurs because every transaction that gives rise to a payment requires an offsetting transaction that gives rise to a receipt. However, each export transaction is not necessarily offset by a corresponding import of goods. Instead, the payment may be in the form of a service, some type of capital movement, or gold flow. In essence, a balance of payments balances in the sense that total receipts and payments must be equal. Let us analyze the accounts in Table 24–1 and see what the various transactions reveal.

**The Current Account.** As the name implies, the current account contains a record of yearly transactions of goods, services, and money that produce current receipts and payments. This account is divided into two parts: private and governmental. Government is included because it had transactions in goods and services during 1964.

Exports by individuals and firms totaled $25.2 billion. Because export transactions give rise to foreign payments, they are recorded as receipts (+'s) in the United States current account. Similarly, imports of foreign goods create obligations on the part of Americans to persons and governments abroad. As a result, they are recorded in our current account as payments (−'s). In fact, any item in the balance of payments is a receipt item if it is, like exports, supplying us with foreign currencies or other assets. Conversely, payment items, like imports, cause us to use up our foreign currencies or other assets.

The balancing column in Table 24–1 shows the difference between receipt and payment items. In this connection, the balance of trade, $6.6 billion, reveals an export surplus. The old mercantilists used to thrill at such a result! We know, however, that many other transactions take place besides the movement of goods.

**TABLE 24-1***
**The United States International Balance of Payments, 1964 †**
**(Billions of Dollars)**

| | Receipts +($) | Payments −($) | Balance (+ or −) ($) |
|---|---|---|---|
| **Current Account** | | | |
| Private | | | |
| Merchandise (exports and imports, adjusted) | 25.2 | 18.6 | +6.6 |
| **Balance of Trade** | | | +6.6 |
| Transportation | 2.2 | 2.4 | −0.2 |
| Travel | 1.0 | 2.1 | −1.1 |
| Miscellaneous services | 1.7 | 0.4 | +1.3 |
| Investment income | 4.6 | 0.9 | +3.7 |
| Unilateral transfers (net): | | | |
| Private remittances abroad | | 0.5 | −0.5 |
| Totals | 34.7 | 24.9 | |
| Net balance on private account | | | +9.8 |
| Governmental | | | |
| Unilateral transfers: | | | |
| Military expenditures abroad | | 2.8 | −2.8 |
| Other grants and payments | | 1.9 | −1.9 |
| Military sales abroad | 0.8 | | +0.8 |
| Other government transactions | 0.5 | 2.3 | −1.8 |
| Totals | 36.0 | 31.9 | |
| Net balance on government account | | | −5.7 |
| Net balance on current account | | | +4.1 |
| **Capital Account** | | | |
| Private long-term investment (net) | | 4.3 | −4.3 |
| Government long-term investment (net) | | 2.6 | −2.6 |
| Totals | | 6.9 | |
| Net balance on Capital Account | | | −6.9 |
| Basic deficit | | | −2.8 |
| **Settlement Transactions** | | | |
| Private short-term capital movement | 2.2 | 2.1 | +0.1 |
| Government short-term capital movement | 3.5 | | +3.5 |
| Gold | 0.1 | | +0.1 |
| Errors and omissions | | 0.9 | −0.9 |
| | $41.8 | $41.8 | $0.0 |
| Offset to basic deficit | | | +2.8 |

* Source: United States Department of Commerce, **Survey of Current Business** (March 1965), pp. 12–14.
† Preliminary estimates.

The remaining items of private trade involve current services and money transfers. For example, the $4.6 billion of investment income recorded as a receipt refers to current income (interest, dividends, and so on) received by American investors in foreign securities. The $900 million in the payments column means that Americans, mainly firms, paid out this amount in the form of interest and dividends to foreign holders of American securities. On balance, current investment income received by us was $3.7 billion greater than investors abroad received from us.

Unilateral transfer items deserve special mention. Technically speaking, they pertain to one-way movement of funds or goods for which no repayment is expected. For instance, private remittances abroad amounted to $500 million and appear as a payment item in the United States current account. Because it is recorded as a payment (−), Americans, mostly persons, sent dollars abroad to relatives, friends, and others. Even though these transactions require no return payments, we may conceive of such payments in the form of satisfaction enjoyed by foreign recipients.

A part of total governmental transactions are in the form of unilateral transfers. They are important to us as well as other countries, because grants under our international aid programs help promote economic growth abroad. Moreover, military expenditures strengthen the defense systems of our allies and, thereby, enhance our own security.

Total private receipts on export type of transactions were some $9.8 billion greater than comparable payments on import type of transactions. This figure is reduced, however, by the payments balance on governmental transactions, which amounted to $5.7 billion. The result is a net balance on current account of $4.1 billion. This surplus in our current transactions means that other nations must have received more goods and services from us than they sent to us. In other words, their current accounts would reveal a deficit of $4.1 billion, or a payments (−) balance of this magnitude.

But how was it possible for other countries to purchase so much from us? How did they finance their deficit? We must examine the capital account to find the answer to these questions.

**The Capital Account.** The capital account shows the (net) movement of long-term capital that took place during the year. The figures indicate that long-term loans and investments of individuals and firms were much larger than those of governmental units. What is not so clear is the direction of flow of long-term capital. To clarify our thinking in this matter, we can say that whenever payments exceed receipts the United States is making dollars available abroad. Capital flows out of our country. An alternative is to think of payments as imports. But what is imported when we invest abroad? Well, we import assets—securities, property rights, and so on. Should more long-term capital flow into our country than we invest abroad, the net inflow would be recorded in our capital account as a receipt (+). Or we would export assets, on balance, like securities or property rights.

The net balance on capital account was −$6.9 billion. Not only was this capital outflow sufficient to offset our current account surplus of +$4.1 billion, we made more than enough dollars available abroad than foreign nations needed to settle their current account deficit with the United States. Because the current and capital accounts did not balance, they induced movements of short-term capital and gold.

**Settlement Transactions.** As indicated above, an imbalance is apparent in the two major accounts of the United States balance of payments. This imbalance amounted to a −$2.8 billion ( = [−$6.9 billion] − [+$4.1 billion]). The −$2.8 billion is the basic deficit. It shows that the current account failed to match the net outflow of long-term capital by this amount. Because short-term capital and gold are balancing items that flow in response to an imbalance between the two major accounts, we combine them into what we call settlement transactions. In recording these items, short-term capital is handled in the same way as long-term capital. Private and government short-term capital items show that we received, on balance, some $3.6 billion from abroad.

Although short-term capital flowed into the United States, we exported $100 million in gold. This is the case because gold is treated like any other commodity for recording purposes. Furthermore, by exporting gold we obtained claims to dollar assets abroad. And because foreign nations held an excess of dollar assets, exports of gold were required to offset these holdings. The sum of the short-term capital receipts (+$3.6 billion) and the gold outflow (+$0.1 billion) equals +$3.7 billion.

Let us summarize our findings for 1964: from the American point of view the trade and grants surplus was inadequate to cover the flow of long-term loans and investments abroad, the difference amounting to −$2.8 billion. Because the receipt of short-term loans and investments and the gold outflow amounted to +$3.7 billion, a discrepancy of some +$0.9 billion occurred. This difference was resolved in the errors and omissions item. To conclude, there was an imbalance in the accounts even though the United States balance of payments was in balance.

## EQUILIBRIUM AND DISEQUILIBRIUM

It is clear that a balance of payments always balances; nonetheless, nations are not necessarily in equilibrium in establishing a balance. As a general rule nations do encounter imbalances—that is, deficits and surpluses. In a moment we will see why. But first let us define equilibrium in the balance of payments. *A nation's balance of payments is in equilibrium when its normal demand for foreign exchange is equal to its normal supply of foreign exchange.* It signifies a stable condition, one which is maintainable for a period of time. Disequilibrium is just the opposite: a nonmaintainable condition with changes expected to take place. In contrast, an *imbalance* pertains to a temporary condition. The United States balance of payments in 1964 revealed an imbalance in the accounts. Should the imbalance not be corrected over a series of years, we would refer to it as a disequilibrium. A nation must correct this situation and try to restore equilibrium.

**Normal and Settlement Items.** We determine whether or not an imbalance exists in a balance of payments by computing total receipts and payments on goods and services, grants, and long-term loans and investments—or more simply stated, from Table 24–1, the current and capital accounts. These are the normal items involving transactions of an autonomous nature. Goods are bought and sold, and loans and investments take place for the purpose of making a profit. Grants and other forms of aid are given to restore war-devastated countries and to promote economic development. Accordingly, nations can achieve an equilibrium even though they import more goods and services than they sell abroad. How? They cover their excess purchases by receiving grants and long-term investments. Hence, a normal supply of foreign exchange is made available to match their normal demand for foreign exchange. Conversely, countries with export surpluses can achieve equilibrium by making grants and long-term investments abroad.

Our analysis leads us to the following conclusion: if a nation's current surplus is exactly offset by capital account outflows, the receipts implied by the former are offset by the payments required by the latter, and the balance of payments is in equilibrium. It follows that a nation would also achieve equilibrium if the payments implied by its current account deficit are exactly offset by the receipts resulting from capital account inflows.

An imbalance giving rise to short-term capital and gold flows is not a serious problem for a country to face. Surpluses and gold inflows of some years offset deficits and gold outflows of other years. A persistent imbalance—that is, a disequilibrium—is, however, a serious problem for a nation. Continuous surpluses on normal items mean that a nation is accumulating unwanted stocks of gold and foreign bank deposits; and a nation experiencing a persistent deficit continually loses gold and foreign bank deposits.

Now we understand why a disequilibrium in the balance of payments leads to change. Nations experiencing persistent surpluses are exporting more goods and services than they purchase abroad. Therefore, they must finance the import deficits of foreign countries. The do so by making grants and long-term investments in deficit countrie and receiving gold from them. The deficit nations cannot earn suffi cient foreign exchange to finance current transactions in goods an services and must obtain grants and long-term capital from expor surplus countries. Furthermore, their gold reserves become exhausted At this point they are forced to reduce imports. Further repercussion set in on both sides which lead to changes in national income an foreign exchange rates.

Before examining exchange rate levels and adjustments in th following section, let us first introduce a few examples of balance o payments problems in the postwar period. Immediately after Worl War II most nations of Europe suffered from a balance of payment disequilibrium. Specifically, they encountered persistent deficits i their trade with the United States. The trade surplus of the Unite States was evidenced by our grants, loans and investments, and short term credits to those nations and gold inflows from them. The situa tion existing in this period is often designated by the term *dolla shortage*. After recovering from the war Europe made substantia progress, part of which is attributable to United States assistanc Later, we abandoned the Marshall Plan and are now considering othe adjustments. The term *dollar surplus* is sometimes employed to de pict the recent outflow of gold from the United States.

Many of the less developed nations are plagued by a persisten disequilibrium caused by deficits in their trade with the more in dustrialized countries. The intense desire to become more full developed produces deficits. Domestic output often falls short c yielding sufficient exports to pay for imported goods and service In addition, grants and investments are insufficient, and gold reserve become depleted.

## EXCHANGE RATE DETERMINATION

We understand that an imbalance in the balance of payments ma produce a disequilibrium. The latter is a condition that sets in motio adjustments leading to a new equilibrium. There are two mai avenues of adjustment: (1) income changes, and (2) exchange ra variations. With respect to the first of these, a change in the incom of a nation relative to the rest of the world has the effect of produ ing changes in the nation's balance of payments. Consider a rise i our exports as a result of increased foreign demand. This implies a imbalance, because exports rise relative to imports. The increase exports generate a rise in output and income. Some part of the highe income will be spent on imports. Thus the rise of income produc changes in the balance of payments, tending to right the previous imbalance. These few short statements indicate the nature of income adjustments. Because we intend to develop income concepts in the following chapter, let's pass on to exchange rate adjustments.

**The Rate of Exchange.** Before examining exchange rate adjustments, it is essential that we understand what an exchange rate is and how it is determined. As mentioned earlier in this chapter, *an exchange rate is simply the price of one currency in terms of another*. Thus, the exchange rate for pounds sterling is $2.80. This is the dollar price of pounds. Likewise, the dollar price of a French franc is about 20 cents, the Indian rupee approximately 21 cents, the Venezuelan bolivar nearly 30 cents, and so on for other foreign currencies. In foreign countries the price of the dollar is expressed in domestic currencies. For example, in England the pound price of dollars is £0.357; in France the franc price of dollars is fr. 5. To find the comparable foreign price of dollars for any currency, one merely finds the reciprocal of its dollar price. For English pound sterling the reciprocal is 1/$2.80, or £0.357, and so on.

The reciprocal relationship between currencies reveals an important point. Whenever the price of one currency changes it causes a reverse change in the price of other currencies. Suppose the dollar price of pounds rises from $2.80 to $3.00. In England the pound price of dollars falls from £0.357 to £0.333. The increase (appreciation) in the dollar price of pounds means that dollars have depreciated in terms of pounds, because an American gives up more dollars to acquire pounds. To an Englishman, however, the pound has appreciated in terms of dollars. He needs only £0.333 to obtain a dollar's worth of American goods, whereas previously he surrendered £0.357.

We are now familiar with an exchange rate, but how is it determined? Some of the elements that influence the market price were given in Chapter 23. Our analysis of the international balance of payments in this chapter also helps us to understand the forces lying behind the determination of an exchange rate. In brief, an exchange rate is a price determined by the market forces of demand and supply. In Figure 24–1 the demand curve for foreign exchange (£'s) slopes downward and to the right, whereas the supply curve for foreign exchange (£'s) slopes upward and to the right. The slopes of these schedules are similar to those encountered in determining the price of goods back in Chapter 2, except that here we are dealing with international prices.

As the dollar price of English goods falls, Americans want to import more goods from England; hence, they need more pounds. So the quantity of pounds demanded increases. This price-quantity re-

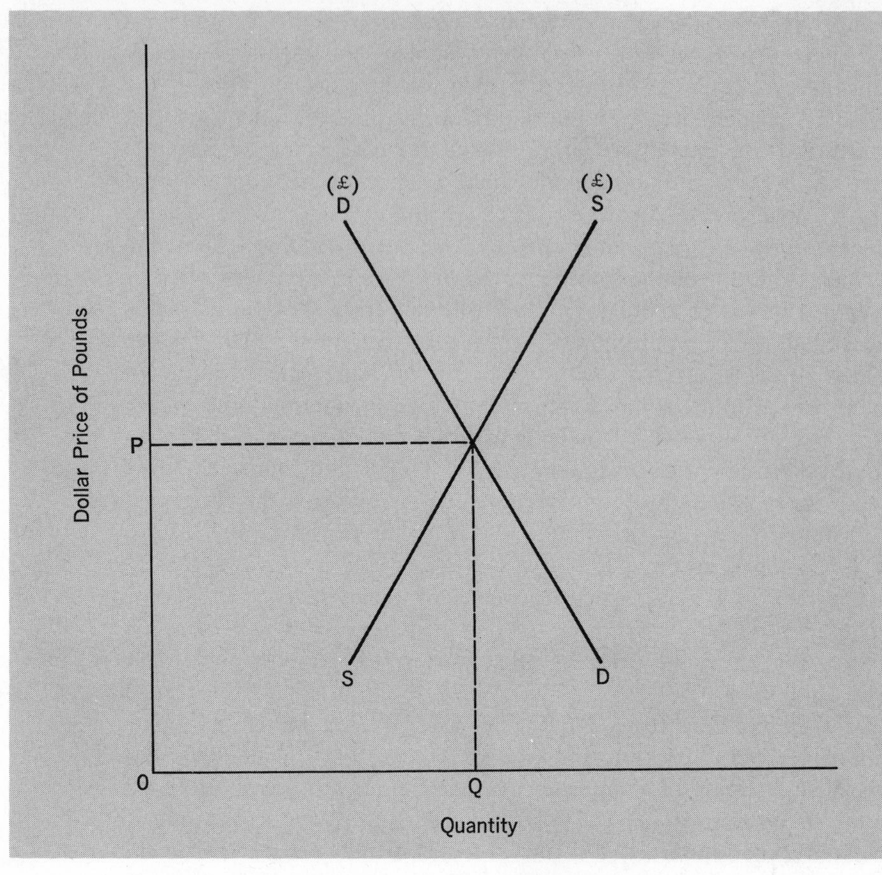


**Figure 24–1.** Demand and supply determine exchange rates.

lationship conforms to the law of demand. The upward-sloping supply schedule indicates that at higher values of pounds (lower prices of American goods to English buyers) English importers want to purchase larger quantities of American goods. Consequently, the quantity of pounds supplied in the United States increases at higher dollar prices.[1] At the intersection of the two schedules, trade between America and England is in balance. This equality between demand and supply expresses the equilibrium rate of exchange—*OP* in Figure 24–1.

Our analysis of the balance of payments yields similar results. Payment items, like imports, constitute the American demand for foreign exchange. Conversely, receipt items, like exports, make up the

[1] If the reader wants to pursue the income effects implied in this statement and other technical points, he might refer to a current international economics textbook.

supply of foreign exchange in the United States. As long as a surplus (deficit) in the current account is offset by an equal capital outflow (inflow), the rate of exchange remains stable.

On the other hand if normal United States payments exceed receipts, the demand for foreign exchange rises to intersect the supply curve at a higher point. (Pencil in the new demand schedule in Figure 24–1.) The new equilibrium rate of exchange for pounds involves a higher dollar price. What happens to the dollar price of foreign exchange (pounds) when normal receipts exceed payments? It should be clear by this time that whenever *normal* payments and receipts (demand and supply) become altered, the rate of exchange tends to vary. Notice that we said "tends" to change. A country may be able to forestall the change if it is able to acquire short-term loans or has available a large supply of gold. Furthermore, some countries hold the rate of exchange of their currencies stable. In doing so they force normal receipts and payments into balance. Thus, adjustments in the balance of payments are effected by fluctuating rates, introduced in the above paragraph, and rigid rates. Let us examine them and the adjustment processes.

## FLUCTUATING EXCHANGE RATES

Excluding governmental interference, a nation's exchange rate is free to rise and fall according to the dictates of demand and supply. In order to sharpen our insight into these two forces, let us briefly outline the determinants of the demand-and-supply schedules for foreign exchange. Consider first the basic determinants of the demand schedule. First of these is the level of national income or product. Earlier in this chapter we explained that a country tends to import more at a higher level of national income. Furthermore, the larger output (that is, national income) requires more raw materials and semifinished goods from abroad. An increase in demand for these goods and services shifts the demand curve for foreign exchange upward. The dollar rate on foreign exchange therefore rises. Of course, a decline in the level of income or output has the opposite effect—the demand curve for foreign exchange shifts downward and to the left—and the dollar rate on foreign exchange falls.

The second determinant of demand for exchange consists in preferences for foreign goods. In the automotive field the recent trend toward economy, the rise of the two-car family, and the search for new styles has led to an influx of foreign cars. Clearly, the increased demand for foreign autos raises the demand curve for foreign exchange, accompanied by a rising dollar price for foreign exchange. On the other hand, American manufacturers, by producing compact cars, are trying to decrease our demand for foreign autos. To the extent that they succeed in improving the relative desirability of the American variety, the demand curve for foreign exchange and the dollar prices of foreign currencies will decline. The same reasoning applies to other goods and services.

Relative prices and elasticities of demand for foreign versus American goods also affect the demand for exchange. The higher our prices are, relative to those abroad, the greater will be our imports relative to exports. Therefore, high prices at home and low prices abroad usually mean a high price for foreign exchange. With respect to elasticities of demand, the steeper (more inelastic) is our demand schedule for foreign goods and services, and hence foreign exchange, the more foreign currencies will change in price when the supply varies.

Our desire for foreign securities, grants and other aid administered by the United States, and our accumulation of short-term assets and gold imports also affect the demand for exchange. The above three points pertain primarily to our demand for foreign goods and services. Nevertheless, we know from the balance of payments items that capital movements exert an important influence on the demand for foreign exchange. As we increase our foreign loans and investments (and import securities thereby), so do we increase our demand for foreign exchange. Hence, the dollar price of foreign currencies increases. Of course, American loans and investments abroad depend upon foreign interest rates adjusted for risk compared with yields on the domestic variety. If we American investors feel that the prospective earnings are inadequate in the light of the risks, then our demand for foreign exchange falls, and so does the dollar price of foreign exchange.

Government grants and aid payments affect our demand for foreign exchange in a similar way. A large portion of governmental foreign aid has taken the form of dollar grants. Dollar balances are created in our country and drawn off by other nations. Normally, these funds are used to buy goods in the United States. A part of the increased output occasioned by the receipt of dollar balances will end up as imports in the United States. And an increase in imports is associated with an increase in the demand for foreign exchange.

Settlement balances also make up a part of our demand for foreign exchange. When United States residents, firms, and governments buy short-term assets (bank bills, commercial paper, and so on) from abroad, they need foreign exchange to pay for these assets. What amounts to the same thing, Americans are obligated to make payments to foreigners. Likewise, claims for payment arise on behalf of foreign nations, when we import gold. Hence, in these situations our demand for foreign exchange increases, and the dollar price of foreign exchange rises.

The determinants of the supply of foreign exchange are the reverse of those influencing the demand for foreign exchange. Transactions that produce receipts in the United States balance of payments help create a supply of foreign exchange. Accordingly, the dollar price of foreign exchange falls as the quantity of foreign exchange (supplied) increases.

Because the supply determinants are the same factors applied to the demand of other countries for a given country's currency, we can list them in the order presented above: (1) the levels of income or product in foreign countries; (2) foreign tastes and preferences for United States goods and services; (3) relative prices and elasticities of supply of American versus foreign goods; and (4) foreign desire for American securities, grants and other aid administered by foreign countries, foreign holdings of short-term assets, and United States gold exports.

Because an exchange rate is a price, determined like all purely competitive prices by the forces of demand and supply, it is obvious that any element that influences these forces will also affect prices and amounts of goods and services entering the foreign market.

**Adjustments to Equilibrium.** We found that the intersection of the demand-and-supply curves determines the dollar price of foreign currency. As long as the exchange rate is free to fluctuate it will rise and fall in response to changes in the determinants of demand and supply mentioned in the above paragraphs. The altered exchange rate is indicative of a disequilibrium in the balance of payments, because normal receipts and payments are no longer equated. Nevertheless, a disequilibrium sets in motion forces that restore equilibrium in the balance of payments. Let's see how a fluctuating exchange rate tends to restore equilibrium in the balance of payments.

Suppose the dollar-pound rate is $2.80 = £1. Now let us assume the United States level of income rises or our tastes change so that we import more goods from England. If the exchange rate on pounds is $2.80 and an increase in demand for pounds takes place, this implies that imports have risen relative to exports. This situation causes a shortage of exchange on pounds, which forces up the exchange rate on pounds. At $2.80 there is a gap between the supply of and demand for pounds. This is eliminated by letting the exchange rate on pounds increase.

Figure 24–2 shows the adjustments that lead to equilibrium. An increase in demand for pounds causes an upward shift of the demand schedule from *DD* to *D′D′*. Evidently, imports rise relative to exports, causing a shortage of exchange on pounds to occur. This shortage forces up the exchange rate on pounds to, say, $3.00. Now at $2.80 there is an excess of demand for pounds amounting to the horizontal distance *AB*. The gap is eliminated as the exchange rate of pounds

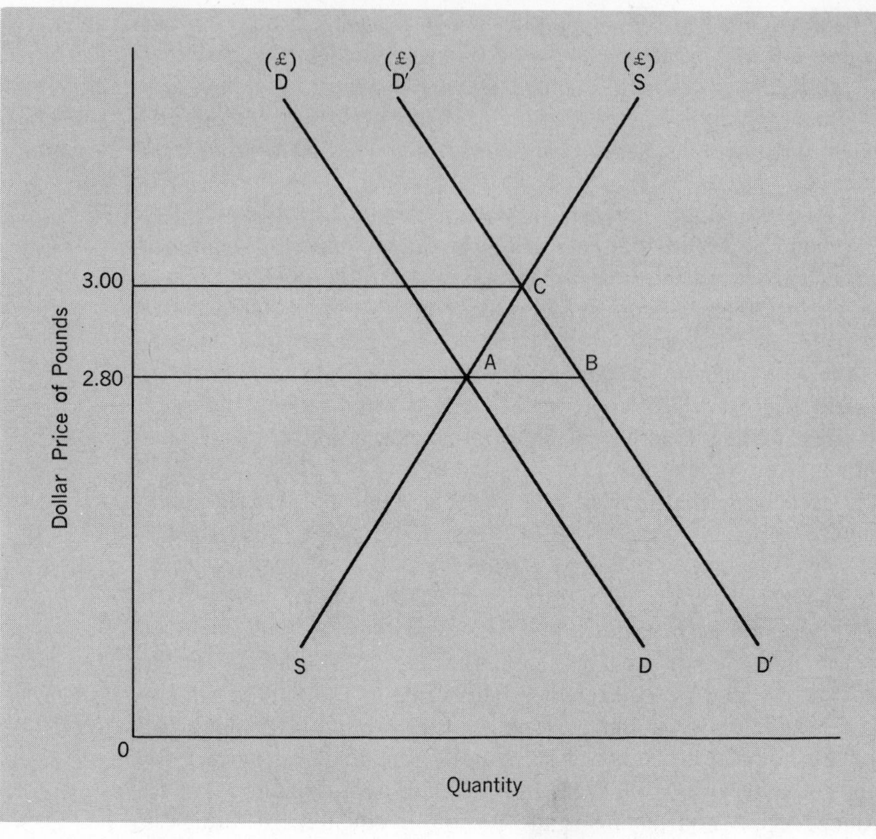


**Figure 24–2.** Fluctuating exchange rates restore equilibrium.

rises to point *C*. This is the case, because the rise in the rate from $2.80 to $3.00 implies that Americans reduce their purchases from England. Hence, our imports from England tend to decline. This condition is expressed graphically by a movement on the *D′D′* curve from point *B* toward point *C*. At the same time Englishmen find that our goods are cheaper, because they now secure $3.00 worth of American goods per pound, rather than only $2.80 worth. Thus, our exports to England tend to rise. This situation is indicated by a movement on the *SS* curve from point *A* toward point *C*. Consequently, at point *C* the fluctuating rate restores equilibrium in the United States balance of payments.

There are certain disadvantages associated with freely fluctuating exchange rates. First, frequent rate changes disturb normal trading relations. For instance, an American importer, who relies on an exchange rate of $2.80 = £1, buys 1,000 units of English goods only to find on delivery date that a new $3.00 = £1 rate is in effect. Instead of paying $2,800 for the goods he must pay $3,000. The difference in prices may destroy the importer's profit margin. Hence, he may decide to confine his business to the domestic market. Quoting the transaction in dollars does not solve the problem. It merely shifts the risk to the English exporter.

Second, the more inelastic are a nation's demand-and-supply schedules for foreign exchange, the greater is the rate fluctuation as the schedules shift. Furthermore, speculation may cause the exchange rate to fluctuate widely. For example, importers may buy (import) more goods and services in anticipation of a higher rate. The additional demand for foreign exchange causes the rate to rise to a higher level. As the process continues, the rising rate leads to further depreciation of the currency.

Third, a nation's terms of trade tend to become unfavorable when the value of its currency declines (depreciates). A higher dollar price for pounds, exemplified by the rise to $3.00 = £1 in our illustration, means that the United States must export more goods and services to buy the same quantity of imports from England.

Fourth, a depreciated exchange rate may cause inflation within the country. If a higher dollar rate causes exports to rise and imports to decline, domestic production and income would rise. The resulting increase in *NNP* (income) would cause total spending $(C+I+G)$ to rise. Prices would tend to rise sharply, if little excess capacity existed.

Because of the numerous disadvantages associated with freely fluctuating exchange rates, some countries resort to a type of control that prevents extreme rate changes. In the 1930's England set up an equalization account and the United States a stabilization fund. The idea was, and is, to establish a pool of domestic and foreign currencies and gold. Purchases or sales of various currencies are made from the fund whenever a country's exchange rate fluctuates widely. In other words, the exchange rate is allowed to fluctuate within limits in response to market forces. Should the rate tend to rise above or fall below the established limits, the fund sells or buys foreign exchange. Such funds or accounts are normally operated by governments or governmental agencies. Exchange rates influenced by their operation are usually referred to as flexible exchange rates rather than freely fluctuating rates.

Several other means have been employed to secure exchange rate stability. An outstanding example is the gold standard, which operated for many years prior to World War I and again in the 1920's. Exchange controls were practiced in the 1930's and revived in the post World War II period. In recent years countries have cooperated in various ways to maintain exchange-rate stability.

## RIGID EXCHANGE RATES

Exchange control is an important means used today by individual countries to maintain a stable exchange rate. Referring back to the American example, an excess of imports led to a higher dollar price of pounds ($3.00). If exchange control were in operation, the dollar rate would be held stable at $2.80. How is this possible? The government controls the rate by requiring exporters and others who receive foreign exchange to surrender their foreign earnings. Furthermore, importers and others who need foreign exchange purchase it from the government. Consequently, a shortage of foreign exchange, like the distance *AB* in Figure 24–2, requires the government to ration foreign currencies among importers. The government is then in a position to regulate imports to match the quantity of foreign exchange earned by exporters.

**Adjustments to Equilibrium.** The rationing process produces an equilibrium in the balance of payments. It does so because the government restricts imports to a level equal to exports at the fixed rate. In addition, the government can discriminate among importers and, thereby, limit imports to essential goods. For this reason the rationing process has particular appeal to the governments of the less developed countries that are trying to hasten economic growth.

We noted that the adjustment process with fluctuating rates involves the movement of rates; that is, the fluctuating rates serve as the link between nations through which adjustment to equilibrium is possible. It is, therefore, an external adjustment. Exchange control does not allow this kind of adjustment to take place. Instead, the adjustment is basically of an internal nature influenced by domestic price and income adjustments.

Assuming rigid exchange rates, United States imports are curtailed to match the smaller volume of exports at the fixed rate. The excess of imports implies that domestic goods cannot readily be produced or produced at a comparable cost at home. As imports are limited, the diversion of expenditure from foreign to home goods produces upward pressure on the domestic price level. This trend encourages imports and discourages exports, sharpening the original problem. Monetary and fiscal policies play an important role in the adjustment process. They must be directed toward lowering cost, especially wages, while at the same time preventing increases in prices of outputs. Such results tend to increase exports relative to imports.

In the above example, should the United States encounter an export surplus instead of an import deficit, then exports would be reduced to equal the lower volume of imports at the fixed rate of exchange. Assuming full-employment *NNP* at the outset, a decline in exports tends to reduce production, employment, and *NNP* (income). With a fall in income total spending $(C+I+G)$ declines. Thus equilibrium occurs at a lower level of *NNP*. It is apparent that monetary and fiscal policies need to be flexible to cope with changing conditions.

Because government exercises control over the exchange rate, it can periodically adjust the foreign exchange rate. For example, if the United States tends to import more than it exports or is plagued by unemployment, governmental authorities might depreciate the dollar by changing the exchange rate from $2.80 to $3.00. Exports, income, and employment tend to rise while imports decline. Of course, the opposite result occurs in, say, England: the pound appreciates in terms of dollars, imports rise and exports fall, income declines and unemployment increases. The attempt on the part of the United States to correct this condition may lead England to depreciate the pound in the hope of reversing its present condition. This form of retaliation leads to a lower volume of trade between the two countries because both want to sell more and buy less. Past experience with depreciation among countries bears out this conclusion.

## BALANCE OF PAYMENTS AND GROWTH

Up to this point we have been mainly concerned with short-run analysis. We observed, for example, how an increase in demand for imports (and foreign exchange) produced by a rise in income led to a rise in the dollar price of foreign exchange, restoring equilibrium in the balance of payments. In the next chapter we will continue our short-run analysis explaining, among other things, how changes in exports can cause changes in the level of *NNP*.

Though we defer a detailed discussion of growth to later chapters, we can indicate here the nature of the growth problem as it relates to the balance of payments. Assuming a given combination of relative factor supplies, the state of technological development, and the pattern of demand preferences, a country exports certain goods and imports others. In equilibrium, the volume of exports and imports of goods and services tends to balance within this framework of supply-and-demand conditions.

Let us suppose that a full-employment level of output has been maintained, output rising by a given amount each year. In short, we establish conditions for a growing economy at the outset.

Now a country may experience long-run changes that will upset the previously assumed relationships. These involve gradual changes in international demand, long-run shifts in the supplies of resources and goods and services, and even slow changes in institutional organizations—political, social, and economic. These types of changes tend to produce what is called *structural* disequilibrium and create a *persistent* disequilibrium in the balance of payments.

If conditions assumed in the theory of trade in Chapter 23 were applicable—that is, if resources were perfectly mobile and prices of resources and goods responded to free market forces—then adjustments would automatically set in to restore equilibrium in the balance of payments. However, in the real world we cannot expect perfect adaptability of resource use to changed conditions of a structural type. As a result of imperfections, a persistent disequilibrium in the balance of payments may develop. This gives rise to a level of output that continually falls short of what we would enjoy under more favorable conditions.

Returning to the real world, we use the term *potential output* to measure the performance of the economy. This is the output (aggregate supply) that could be *achieved* and *maintained* at full employment, the highest level of employment attainable under normal conditions. Because we assumed full employment within our framework, the economy has achieved its potential at the outset. Now if annual *GNP* (actual output or aggregate demand) matches potential output over a lengthy period, the economy would achieve maximum growth at a predetermined rate. Let's suppose that the economy functions in this manner.

Consider changes of a structural type to occur which, as we earlier stated, upset the previously assumed relationships. Neglecting the details, adjustments follow that restore the assumed supply-and-demand relationships. These adjustments also provoke changes in the balance of payments during the interim period, transforming a persistent disequilibrium into equilibrium. Clearly, we have simplified complex phenomena, employing several if's and other conditions. However, we have said enough to set us thinking about the growth problem, realizing that other nations influence a country's ability to grow.

Our analysis of the balance of payments and the adjustment process in this chapter gives us sufficient background for understanding the way foreign trade affects domestic economic activity. We shall examine the role of exports and imports in determining an equilibrium *NNP* in Chapter 25.

**Summary.** Exporters create a supply of foreign exchange, whereas importers create a demand for foreign exchange. In this sense we may say that exports finance imports.

A balance of payments records all transactions between one country and the rest of the world during a given period, usually one year. Because any one transaction gives rise to an offsetting transaction somewhere in the balance of payments, total receipts and payments must balance.

Apart from the recording of transactions, a balance of payments is in equilibrium if exports and imports of goods and services are equal, provided there are no unilateral transactions and long-term capital movements. Most countries engage in transactions of the latter type; therefore, we alter our statement to include them. A balance of payments is in equilibrium when the difference between current account receipts and payments, including unilateral transfers, is just offset by the appropriate (net) movement of capital. An imbalance exists if long-term (net) capital movements fail to offset the difference between current receipts and payments. This induces short-term capital and gold flows.

If an imbalance continues over a lengthy period, a disequilibrium occurs. The latter implies a structural problem, one that the country must try to solve.

An exchange rate is the price of one currency in terms of another. It is determined by a country's demand for and supply of foreign exchange. The determinants of demand for foreign exchange include the level of income, tastes or preferences for foreign goods, relative prices, and elasticities of demand for foreign versus American goods, and the desire for foreign securities. Supply determinants are the same factors applied to the demand of other countries for a given country's currency.

An imbalance in the balance of payments can be corrected in either of two ways. When a country's rate of exchange is free to fluctuate, the movement of the rate produces adjustments to restore equilibrium (see Figure 24–2). A rigid exchange rate produces internal adjustments via income, employment, and prices, whereas control of exports and imports forces an equilibrium in the balance of payments.

We indicated the nature of the growth problem as it relates to the balance of payments, reserving for later chapters a more detailed discussion of these relationships. We noted here that changes in the balance of payments, transforming a persistent disequilibrium into equilibrium, play an important role in the growth process.

## QUESTIONS

1. The balance of payments is a kind of income statement. Explain.
2. The balance of payments may be divided into three separate parts: current account, capital account, and settlement transactions. Make a list of items for each part, and explain why the items belong there. Can you identify each item as to a receipts or payments type of transaction?
3. What is meant by an equilibrium in the balance of payments? Was the United States balance of payments for 1964 in equilibrium? Why or why not?
4. Distinguish between an imbalance and disequilibrium. A balance of payments always balances; yet an imbalance may be present. Explain.

5. What is an exchange rate, and how is it determined? The French franc exchanges at a rate of fr. 5 to the dollar. What is the dollar rate on the franc?
6. Assume the dollar–pound rate is \$3.00 = £1. Now United States demand for English goods increases, and the rate on the pound rises to \$3.25. Trace through the steps, explaining how the fluctuating rate restores equilibrium in the United States balance of payments. (Refer to Figure 24–2 and the surrounding discussion.)
7. What is meant by rigid exchange rates? What form of control is needed to maintain a stable exchange rate?

CHAPTER

# 25

## Foreign Trade and Income Determination

Nearly all the countries of the world find themselves involved in trade with other countries. Goods are bought and sold, services are rendered, and money is lent or borrowed. In the present chapter we will focus attention on the ways in which such transactions affect the level of Net National Product. Of particular importance in this connection are the concepts of exports, the part of *NNP* not consumed at home, and imports, the part of consumption not produced at home. By directing attention to the role of exports and imports in the determination of *NNP* we will gain understanding of the way foreign trade affects domestic economic activity.

**TABLE 25–1***
**Exports as a Percentage of National Income, Selected Countries, 1963**

| Country | Per Cent | Country | Per Cent |
|---|---|---|---|
| Belgium | 44 | Germany, Federal Republic | 20 |
| Canada | 21 | Japan | 12 |
| Chile | 16 | United Kingdom | 17 |
| Denmark | 30 | United States | 5 |
| France | 13 | Venezuela | 41 |

* Source: United Nations, **Monthly Bulletin of Statistics,** March 1965.

Before analyzing the requirements for equilibrium *NNP,* let's clarify our understanding of the importance of trade. We can do this by comparing exports to national income, as shown in Table 25–1. Of course, the information provides us with an incomplete view of trade generally. Nevertheless, we can offer a few tentative statements. The low percentage figure for the United States is explained by the fact that the domestic sector is exceedingly large relative to the foreign sector. Yet the United States is the largest trading nation in the world. Hence, the low percentage figure is misleading as a surface fact. A few of the countries (Germany and Japan) are among the most rapidly growing countries of the world. Chile and Venezuela are typical examples of the less developed countries. In any event, the percentage figures indicate the varying influence of exports on income.

## BACKGROUND OF EQUILIBRIUM *NNP*

Back in Chapter 5 we discussed the accounting equality between national product and national income. The reader may recall that upper-loop expenditure on output was matched by lower-loop cost of output. The equation can be written:

$$\text{Expenditure on Output} = \text{Cost of Output} = \begin{array}{l}\text{the Income Generated}\\ \text{by the Production of}\\ \text{the Output.}\end{array} \quad \textbf{(1)}$$

Expenditure and cost approaches to national income were given in Table 5–6. By substituting symbols for the data and expressing the result in the form of equation (1), we get:

$$C + I + G = NNP = C + S + T\,, \quad \textbf{(2)}$$

the symbols having their usual meanings. Equation (2) was introduced in Chapter 6. This was the first of the two chapters dealing with income determination.

It was stated that $I$ consists of net private investment plus net foreign investment, the latter being the difference between exports and imports. Because our main purpose was to explain an equilibrium level of *NNP* for the domestic economy, we did not consider net foreign investment as a separate element. Hence, $I$ was interpreted primarily as private domestic investment. Now we intend to single out exports and imports, showing how these factors enter into the general framework explaining the determination of *NNP*. First, let's briefly review the domestic elements and introduce foreign factors.

## TOTAL SPENDING AND OUTPUT

**Consumption and *NNP*.** Consider a hypothetical consumption–*NNP* table, as shown in Table 25–2. This table is based upon data in Table 6–3. Notice the column entitled $S + T + M$, where $S$ and $T$

have their usual meanings and $M$ stands for imports. Earlier, it was stated that saving includes individual and corporate saving and that taxes refer to the excess of indirect taxes, corporation income taxes, personal taxes, and social security taxes over transfers, including interest on government bonds. As this point we add imports along with saving and taxes, because some part of income ($NNP$) is spent on imports. Specifically, we apply here a 3.33-per-cent figure. This amount of expenditure on imports out of income fits closely the pattern of the United States (see Figure 25–3).

**TABLE 25-2**
**Relation of Consumption and *NNP* (Billions of Dollars)**

| *NNP* | C | $NNP - C = S + T + M$ |
|---|---|---|
| 0 | 15 | −15 |
| 60 | 53 | 7 |
| 120 | 91 | 29 |
| 180 | 129 | 51 |
| 240 | 167 | 73 |
| 300 | 205 | 95 |
| 360 | 243 | 117 |
| 420 | 281 | 139 |
| 480 | 319 | 161 |

In the upper part of Figure 25–1 we have plotted consumption on the vertical axis against $NNP$ on the horizontal axis, using the figures in Table 25–2. Consumption is now used to mean domestic expenditure on domestically produced goods that yield direct satisfaction.[1] It is necessary at this juncture to note two points: (1) $NNP$ consists of four parts—consumption, saving, taxes (less transfers), and imports, and (2) it is convenient to divide the allocation of $NNP$ into two parts: consumption spending and the drains from the income flow not spent on domestically produced consumer items, namely saving, taxes (less transfers), and imports. Because $NNP$ = consumption plus saving plus taxes (less transfers) plus imports, we may write an allocation equation for $NNP$: $NNP = C + S + T + M$, where $M$ represents imports. In general, the drains—$S + T + M$—are grouped together.

[1] In our earlier analysis consumption referred to domestic expenditure on goods that yield direct satisfaction. It is actually quite difficult to get sufficiently good statistics to measure the part of this that comes from foreign sources. This fact accounts for our including all consumption in one total. Here we assume that imports both of consumer and capital goods can be identified, and we combine them in a total import figure $M$. Therefore the $C$ now identifies only expenditure on domestically produced goods of this type.

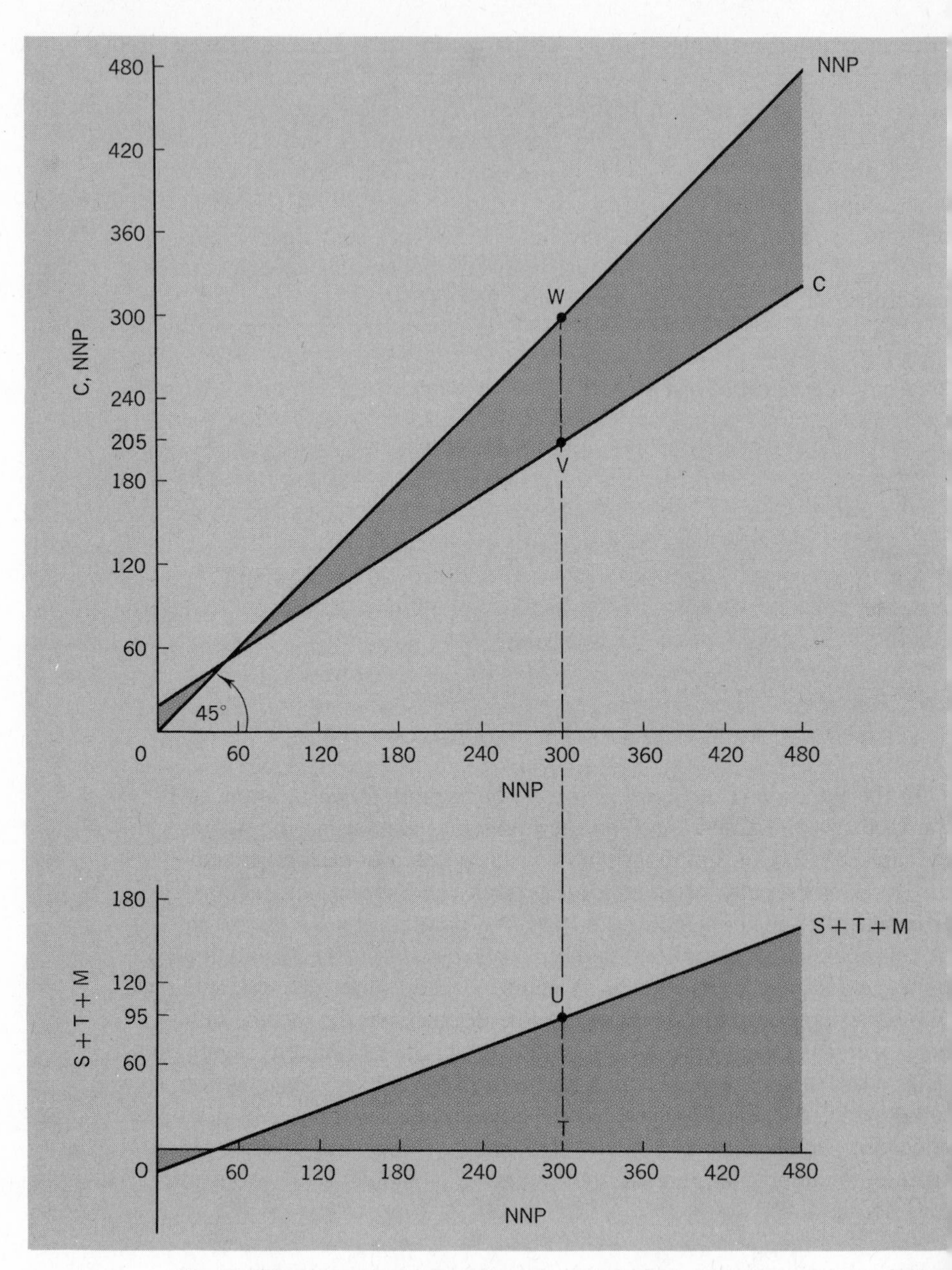


**Figure 25–1.** Consumption and saving plus taxes plus imports in relation to *NNP* (billions of dollars).

We see that consumption exceeds *NNP* at very low levels of *NNP*, so that $S + T$ is negative and $M$ is zero. As *NNP* increases, a point is soon reached at which *NNP* exceeds consumption and a margin is left for saving, taxes, and imports. We demonstrate this situation in

ʻigure 25–1 by selecting an *NNP* of \$300 billion. The vertical dis-ance to the 45-degree line measures *NNP* (= \$300 billion), for easons stated previously. At \$300 billion income consumption is ;205 billion. Then the vertical distance from the consumption line o the *NNP* line, $VW =$ \$95 billion, is saving, taxes, and imports. In virtue of the allocation equation:

$$NNP - C = S + T + M, \quad \textbf{(3)}$$

or that part of *NNP* not allocated to consumption is devoted to saving, axes, and imports. In the diagram this distance is the vertical distance *VW* between the *NNP* and *C* lines at *W* and *V*, respectively. The saving, taxes, and imports element is shaded to mark it off from con-sumption.

In the lower part of the diagram we have plotted $S + T + M$ against *NNP*. The shaded areas in the two diagrams exactly correspond. The only difference is that the base for saving, taxes, and imports is now the *NNP* axis instead of the *C* line, as in the upper diagram. Note that $TU = VW =$ \$95 billion $= S + T + M$ at an *NNP* of \$300 bil-lion. For certain purposes the $S + T + M$ line alone is useful. We shall refer to this line in later chapters dealing with economic growth.

**The Import Function.** Before examining other components of total spending, let's digress here to note a few important aspects of imports. A careful reading of the preceding paragraphs suggests a close relationship between imports and *NNP*. If this proposition has some validity, we should be able to develop a schedule or curve relating imports to the level of *NNP*.

Consider the period 1950–64, a period during which economic con-ditions were fairly stable. Plotting imports against *GNP* (deflated for price change) we get a set of 15 points in Figure 25–2, each repre-senting the import-*GNP* combination for a given year.[2] We then draw a line freehand through the middle of the points. We see that such a line represents fairly well the general tendency of the points. There-fore, we may assume that this or some very similar line represents a relationship between deflated imports and deflated *GNP*.

Such evidence as we have just given supports our belief in the existence of an import function; import variations seem to be ex-plained, in large part, by income changes in the 1950–64 period. How-ever, there are a number of other factors that ought to exert some in-fluence on imports. Because these factors have been mentioned in previous chapters, we will merely point them out in passing. First,

[2] Note that the base used in Figures 25–2, 25–3, and 25–4 is *GNP* instead of *NNP*. We use the former so that the data may be referred to in later discussion concerning economic growth. In any event, we do not destroy mean-ingful relationships here by using *GNP*.

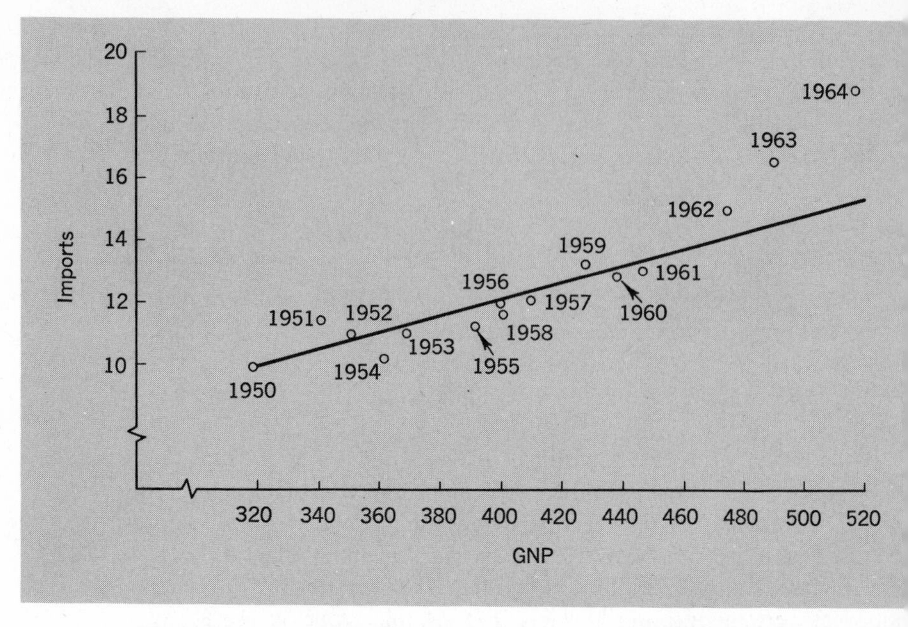


**Figure 25–2.** Import line, 1950–64 (billions of 1954 dollars).

*the distribution of income.* Suppose the government plugs a numbe of tax loopholes for the rich and cuts income tax rates in the lowe brackets. This action would take income from the "rich" and give it t the "poor" without changing the income level. Because the "poor consume larger fractions of their incomes than do the "rich," this ough to raise consumption in general. Some of the extra purchases woul probably include a variety of imported goods. The reverse action b government ought to stimulate the importation of raw materials an certain types of capital goods. Of course, the latter depends upon th present level of income, the extent of the tax alterations, and business men's expectations concerning future economic activity. Second, *taste and social attitudes.* Earlier, it was mentioned that the social attitud in the United States seems to favor a high level of consumption. I further appears that tastes have become altered so that a large part o one's material possessions includes an assortment of imported item —autos, watches, clothing, and so forth. However, it is doubtful tha these factors can undergo rapid change.

Third, *a rising population.* Clearly, an increase in the number o buyers implies a rising demand for goods and services. A part of thi increased demand is satisfied by the importation of additional con sumer and capital goods. Fourth, *inflation at home.* An uninterrupte inflation at home has the dual effect of increasing spending and increas ing purchases from abroad. Though imports may rise in any event hey are most likely to increase if prices rise faster at home than broad.

The relation between imports and *NNP* will undergo change if one r more of the underlying factors changes significantly. Consider the ata in Figure 25–3, where we plot again deflated imports against eflated *GNP*. Next we mark off a 3-per-cent-of-*GNP* (45-degree) ine and plot a set of points for the years 1929–64. Note the points or the years 1929–40. By dividing imports by *GNP* and striking an verage for the period, imports amounted to 2.8 per cent of *GNP*. If ve drop out the year 1929 and add the war and early postwar years, he average would fall below 2.5 per cent. It appears that the points

**igure 25–3.** Imports and *GNP*, 1929–64 (billions of 1954 dollars).

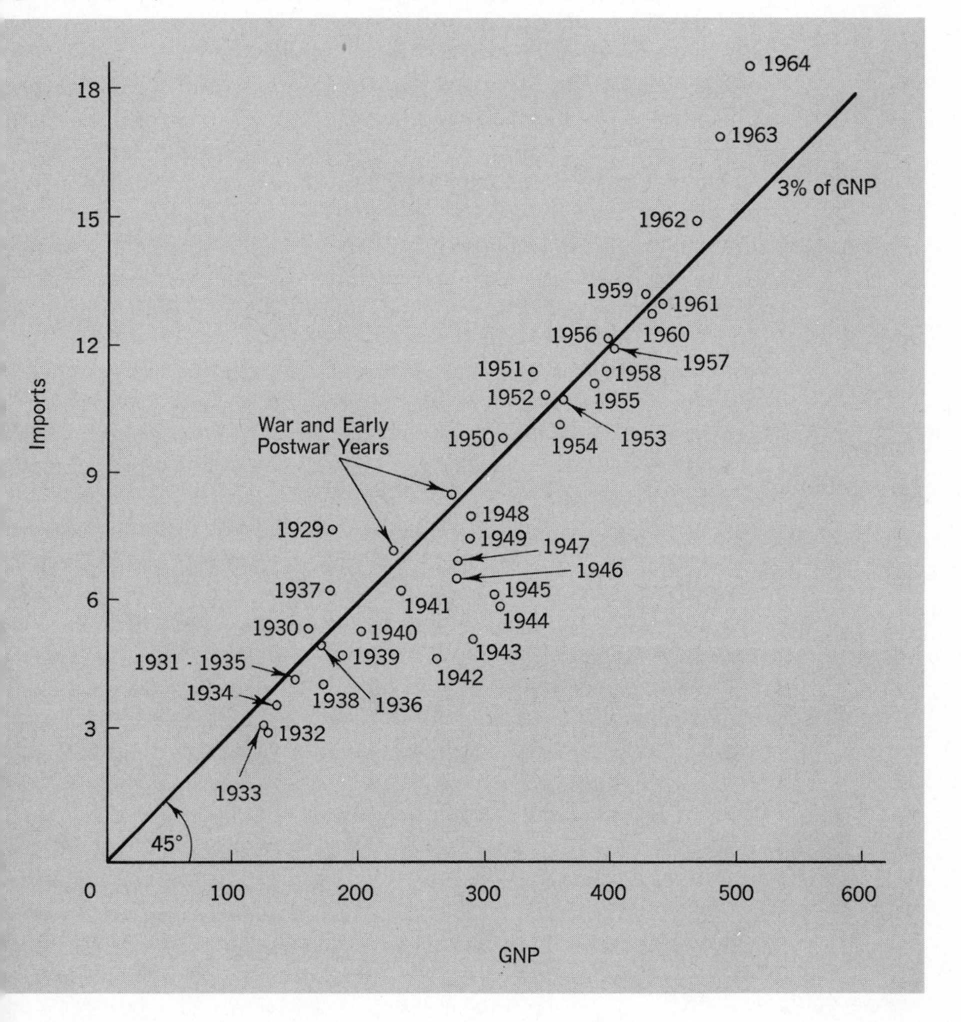

for the later period, 1950–64, cluster more closely around the 3-per-cent-of-*GNP* line. Using the same method applied to 1950–64 period we find that imports averaged approximately 3 per cent of *GNP* Clearly, the data reveal an upward shift in the import function ir recent years. This suggests that as a nation becomes richer it requires increased imports.

**Investment, Government Spending, and Exports.** Recalling ou earlier discussion concerning investment, we found that investment demand is unresponsive to variations in the level of *NNP* (see Figure 6–5). Therefore, we concluded that investment was not a function of *NNP* but was mainly affected by factors other than income. In a similar fashion, we discounted a direct relationship between governmen spending and the level of *NNP,* government spending being primarily determined by political and social factors. Because our exports represent that part of current output not consumed at home, they reflec foreign demand for a part of our *NNP*. As a result we add foreigr demand (for our exports) to domestic demand in arriving at aggregate demand.

Our first impression concerning exports might be that exports are not directly related to *NNP* and that we may treat exports as an autonomous factor along with investment and government spending Let us see if we can verify our preliminary thoughts in this matter Figure 25–4 shows exports of goods and services plotted against *GNI*

**Figure 25–4.** Relation between exports and *GNP*, 1950–64 (billions of 195 dollars).

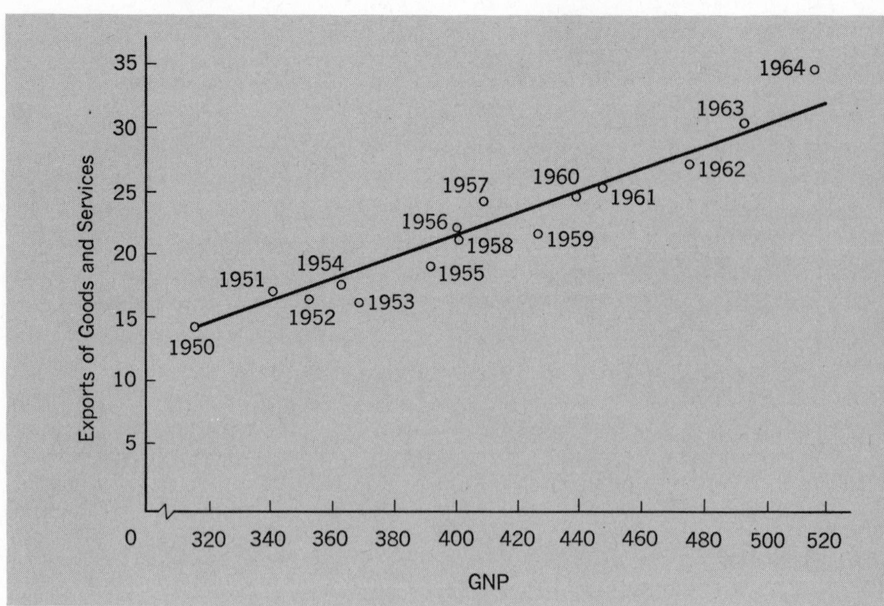

for a series of years (1950–64). We get a set of 15 points, each representing an export-income combination for a given year. We then draw a line freehand through the middle of the points. We see that the export line slopes upward, indicating a positive relationship between exports and *GNP*. (Compare the export line with the investment line in Figure 6–6.) Clearly, the data do not fully support our first impression concerning exports. Let us briefly consider the relationship between exports and income.

The forces leading to economic growth in this country generate a rising level of *GNP* and with it an increasing level of income and demand for foreign goods (imports). Although this increase represents a small fraction of our *GNP*, it is significant relative to the *GNPs* of foreign countries. (Our *GNP* is approximately equal to that of the rest of the free world.) [3] As foreign countries produce to meet this demand, their *GNPs* and incomes increase, causing them to import more from us, thus increasing our exports. Such an increase in our exports further stimulates the rise in our *GNP*, which initiated the changes, because it leads to additional production for export. Therefore the rise in our *GNP* tends to be correlated with increasing exports.

## DETERMINING EQUILIBRIUM *NNP*

We are now in a position to determine an equilibrium *NNP*. Let us begin with a review of aggregate demand and aggregate supply, adding foreign determinants (exports and imports) to domestic determinants of *NNP* (income). Demand consists of four elements: consumption of domestically produced items ($C$), domestic investment ($I$), government spending on domestically produced items ($G$), and exports ($E$). Adding these four we arrive at the total demand for domestic output, which may be expressed by the equation:

$$\text{Aggregate demand} = \text{upper-loop } NNP = C + I + G + E\,. \quad \textbf{(4)}$$

In earlier analysis we assumed that $I$ and $G$ were independent of *NNP*. Although we have just explained that exports are correlated to some extent with *NNP*, let's assume here for the sake of simplicity that exports are independent of *NNP*. This leaves us with $C$ as the one component of demand that varies with *NNP*. To represent all these assumptions graphically we superimpose on the $C$ line of Figure 25–5 an $I$ of \$40 billion, a $G$ of \$85 billlon, and an $E$ of \$14 billion. Thus, the $C + I + G$ line gives the variable amount of consumption spending plus a constant investment and government spending of

[3] In 1962 the fraction was estimated as 49 per cent of the total. Calculations were based on estimates of Gross Domestic Product for 62 countries. See United Nations, *Yearbook of National Statistics*, 1963, pp. 321–324.

$125 billion. In turn, a constant amount of exports (foreign spending on our output), $14 billion, is superimposed onto these three elements, giving the $C+I+G+E$ line. This gives aggregate demand for domestically produced output or total spending (*NNP*), at a corresponding level of income (cost of output, lower-loop *NNP*).

As previously defined, aggregate supply is the sum of money that exactly motivates the production of the current level of output. In short, this is the cost of output, *NNP,* or simply income. Keep in mind that part of the output whose cost must be covered is that produced for export. Thus the cost of output includes that of goods destined for the use of foreigners.

Since we are measuring (lower-loop) *NNP* along the horizontal axis, we need to find a way to compare it with total spending. As before, we use a 45-degree line, labeled $NNP =$ supply, to effect the comparison.

**Figure 25–5.** Determination of *NNP* by demand, $C + I + G + E$, and supply (lower loop) *NNP* (billions of dollars).

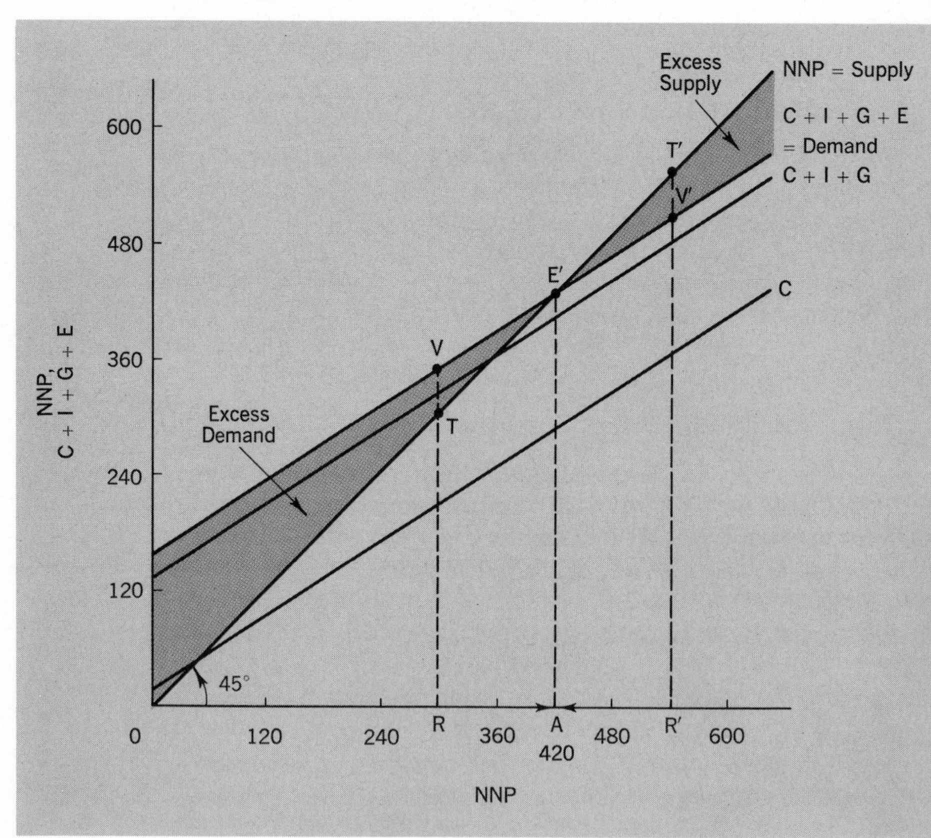

The point of equilibrium or balance is one at which supply equals emand. In Figure 25–5 a point of equality is found at $E'$, where $'NP$ = supply line intersects the $C+I+G+E$ = demand line. At ıe $E'$ point the demand $= C+I+G+E$ amounts to $AE'$, or \$420 illion. At the same time $NNP$ = supply amounts to $OA = AE'$, or 420 billion. This demand represents a sum of money that just suffices ) cover the incomes (costs) necessary to provide that level of output. .quilibrium then exists, because the output is just taken from the ıarket in a transaction precisely satisfactory to both sides, buyers nd sellers.

We can illustrate this process also by Table 25–3, which is merely 'able 25–2 with some new columns. Note the columns $M$ and $E$. At quilibrium $NNP$ (= \$420 billion) exports and imports are equal (at 14 billion). This means that the current account of the balance of ayments is in equilibrium at this level of output. (In national income ccounting this situation expresses zero net foreign investment or $; - M = 0$.) We should not get the idea that an equilibrium $NNP$ :quires an equilibrium in the balance of payments. It does not.

Recalling that an equilibrium $NNP$ requires an equality between emand $(C+I+G+E)$ and supply $(NNP = C+S+T+M)$, xports could exceed or fall short of a given level of imports, provided ıe imbalance is offset by the other demand components. Perhaps we an clarify the point by referring to Table 25–3. Notice the two col-mns entitled "Drains from Income Stream" $(S+T+M)$, and "In-:ctions into Income Stream" $(I+G+E)$. We need not consider onsumption $C$, because at equilibrium $NNP$ consumption is an ele-ıent common to $NNP$ $(= C+S+T+M)$ and $C+I+G+E$. 'o conclude, suppose the value of exports is \$16 billion instead of 14 billion at equilibrium $NNP$ (= \$420). Clearly, equilibrium $NNP$ 'ould prevail if $I+G$ were \$123 billion, because total injections into ıe income stream, $I+G+E$, would equal total drains from the in-ome stream, $S+T+M$ (= \$139 billion).

**Disequilibrium.** Suppose demand, $C+I+G+E$, exceeds sup-ly, $NNP$. This implies that the public is willing to spend a greater mount $(C+I+G+E)$ on current output than is necessary to pro-uce this output $(NNP)$. To single out the foreign elements only, if ex-orts $E$ exceed imports $M$, this means that foreigners are willing to buy ıore of our current output than we are of theirs. This margin implies n excess of demand in terms of the foreign elements. In any event, it ; profitable for businessmen to increase output with a view to meeting he excess demand. In turn, this leads to an increased $NNP$ as new actors are hired and production increases.

If demand falls short of supply, excess demand is negative and xcess supply is present. Again, the foreign elements may influence this

**TABLE 25-3**
**Income Determination (Billions of Dollars)**

| | Excess Demand $(C+I+G+E)-NNP$ | Supply—Cost of Output $NNP$ | Consumption $C$ | Drains from Income Stream $(S+T)$ | $+M$ | $=$ Total | Injections into Income Stream $(I+G)$ | $+E$ | $=$ Total* | Demand (Exp. on Output) $C+I+G+E$ | Behavior of NNP |
|---|---|---|---|---|---|---|---|---|---|---|---|
| | 161 | 0 | 15 | −15 | 0 | −15 | 125 | 14 | 139 | 154 | Grows |
| | 138 | 60 | 53 | 5 | 2 | 7 | 125 | 14 | 139 | 192 | Grows |
| | 115 | 120 | 91 | 25 | 4 | 29 | 125 | 14 | 139 | 230 | Grows |
| | 92 | 180 | 129 | 45 | 6 | 51 | 125 | 14 | 139 | 268 | Grows |
| | 69 | 240 | 167 | 65 | 8 | 73 | 125 | 14 | 139 | 306 | Grows |
| | 46 | 300 | 205 | 85 | 10 | 95 | 125 | 14 | 139 | 344 | Grows |
| | 23 | 360 | 243 | 105 | 12 | 117 | 125 | 14 | 139 | 382 | Grows |
| | 0 | 420 | 281 | 125 | 14 | 139 | 125 | 14 | 139 | 420 | Equilibrium |
| Excess supply | −23 | 480 | 319 | 145 | 16 | 161 | 125 | 14 | 139 | 458 | Shrinks |
| Excess supply | −46 | 540 | 357 | 165 | 18 | 183 | 125 | 14 | 139 | 496 | Shrinks |
| Excess supply | −69 | 600 | 395 | 185 | 20 | 205 | 125 | 14 | 139 | 534 | Shrinks |

* $I = \$40$, $G = \$85$, $E = \$14$; each is constant for the period under consideration.

temporary condition. If imports $M$ exceed exports $E$, this means that we are willing to buy—on balance—more current foreign output. Such action implies an excess of supply in terms of foreign elements only. With stocks piling up because they are unable to sell the current level of output, businessmen will cut back output, lay off factors, and reduce $NNP$. As a consequence, excess supply leads to reduced $NNP$.

We can interpret this more precisely in Figure 25–5. At a level of $NNP$ equal to $OA = AE'$, or $420 billion, demand $(C+I+G+E)$ $=$ supply $(NNP)$. If this level of $NNP$ exists, the market is cleared and no change in $NNP$ will occur.

Consider $NNP$ at the lower level $OR$. At this point supply $(NNP)$ is $OR = RT$, and demand $(C+I+G+E)$ is $RV$. Hence, there is *excess demand* of $TV$. As explained earlier, an excess demand prompts businessmen to expand $NNP$ to meet demand. As this happens $NNP$ increases from $OR$ toward $OA$, as indicated on the $NNP$ axis by an arrow.

Suppose $NNP$ happens to be at a level above the equilibrium value, falling at $OR'$. Then supply $(NNP)$ is $OR' = R'T'$, and demand $(C+I+G+E)$ is $R'V'$. Because $R'T'$ exceeds $R'V'$, supply $(NNP)$ exceeds demand $(C+I+G+E)$ in the amount of $V'T'$. In short, an *excess supply* of $V'T'$ exists. The apparent overproduction prompts businessmen to cut back production, lay off workers, and generally take actions that lead to a decline in $NNP$ (supply) from $OR'$ toward $OA$. This is indicated by an arrow on the base line from $R'$ extending toward $A$.

To conclude: if $NNP$ falls to left of the value $OA$, excess demand is present. Then $NNP$ rises. If $NNP$ falls to the right of $OA$, excess supply exists and $NNP$ falls. Hence, $NNP$ always tends to gravitate toward and remain at a level at which $NNP$ equals $C+I+G+E$.

## AN ALTERNATIVE INTERPRETATION OF EQUILIBRIUM

We can approach equilibrium in a slightly different manner. Notice that in equilibrium:

$$NNP = C+I+G+E\,. \tag{5}$$

Subtracting $C$ from both sides we find that $NNP - C = I+G+E$. But we already know that lower-loop $NNP$ is allocated into four parts: consumption, saving, taxes, and imports, so that $NNP = C+S+T+\text{M}$. Substituting this into the equation we get:

$$S+T+M = I+G+E\,. \tag{6}$$

Verbally, this says that equilibrium is marked by the equality of saving, taxes, and imports, on the one hand, and investment, government spending, and exports on the other. The basic reasoning is exactly the same.

We can verify the correspondence between equations (5) and (6) from Table 25–3. However, it is even easier to see the correspondence on a graph as in Figure 25–6. In this diagram $S+T+M$ is shown as the vertical distance between $C$ and $NNP$. At the same time $I+G+E$ is shown as the vertical distance between $C$ and $C+I+G+E$. In the lower diagram $I+G+E$ and $S+T+M$ are plotted separately instead of as distances between $C$ and $C+I+G+E$, $C$ and $NNP$. In each case the height of $I+G+E$ just equals the height of $S+T+M$ at an income of $OA$. Equilibrium of supply and demand implies that $S+T+M=I+G+E$, and representing this as the equilibrium simply stresses another aspect of the situation.

We need not stress here the monetary aspect of excess demand and excess supply. (For a review of this important topic, see Chapter 6.) Clearly, excess demand is associated with the creation of new money or the use of idle balances. Income in excess of spending (excess supply) is directed to paying off bank loans and increasing the idle part of bank balances.

## INCREASING THE LEVEL OF *NNP*

Up to this point we have merely added foreign determinants to domestic determinants to explain the notion that the level of *NNP* tends toward a definite equilibrium value. Now we would like to explain changes in the level of *NNP* with the aid of this framework, giving special attention again to the foreign elements. First, let us briefly review some important ideas relating to the present discussion.

In earlier analysis we found that economic activity is marked by continual ups and downs. This led us to seek causes for income variations. Seemingly, the main cause of these variations was the variability of investment. Hence, changes in the level of investment cause corresponding changes in total spending and in equilibrium *NNP*. Consumption and government spending also change from time to time. These changes will cause variations in the level of *NNP*, just as will changes in investment, but less frequently.

Now changes in the level of exports will also cause corresponding changes in total spending and in equilibrium *NNP*. Of course, changes in exports are the result of decisions made by persons, firms, and governments of other countries. In effect, any element that influences other countries' demand for imports will have some effect on the amount of goods we export. Anticipated changes in tariff duties, profit expectations, exchange rate changes, and changes in income abroad

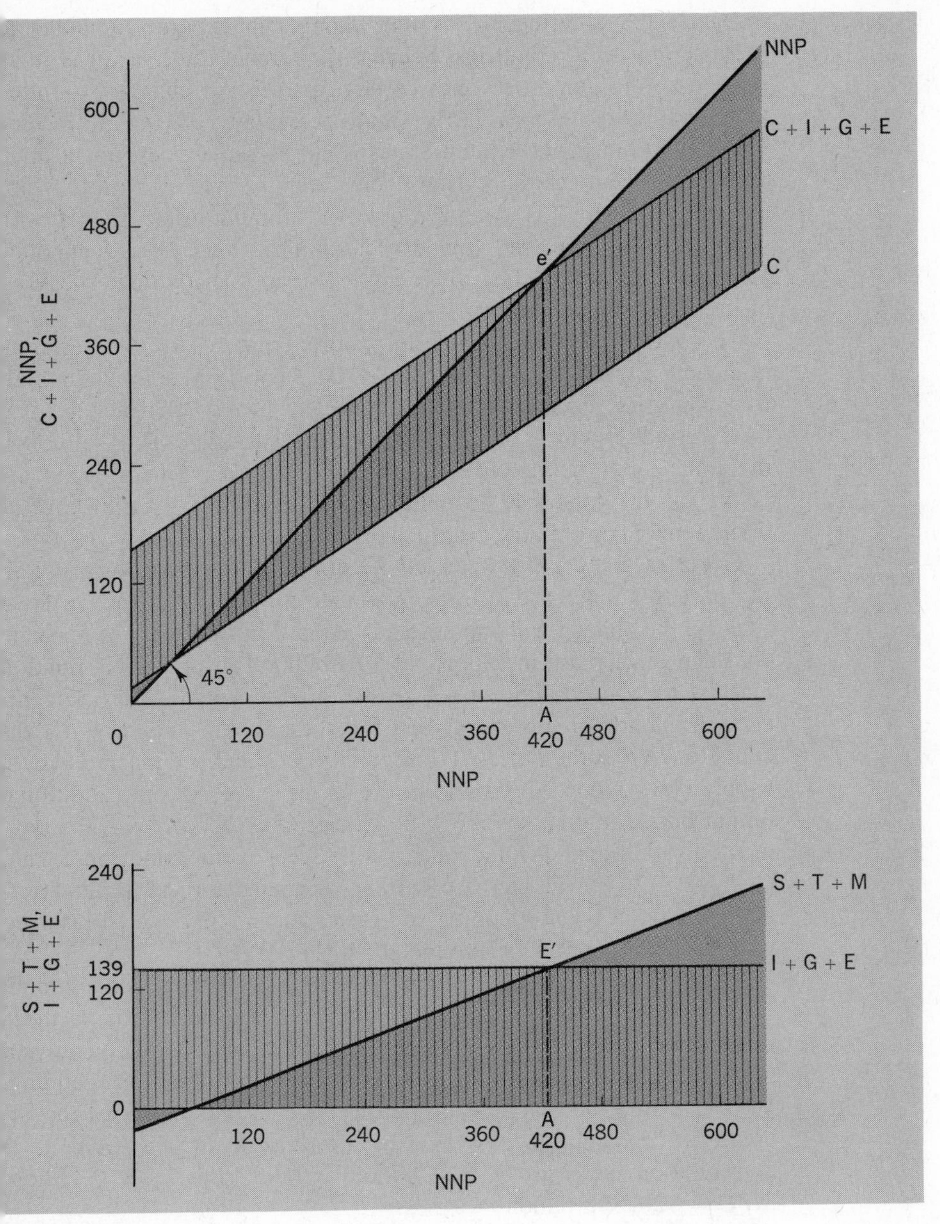


Figure 25–6. Determination of *NNP* by equality of $I + G + E$ and $S + T + M$.

are a few of the elements that influence our exports. To demonstrate: an increase in foreign income (*NNP*) induces a rise in imports that causes an increase in our exports. The latter sets off a chain of events leading to a higher level of income (*NNP*) in the United States.

Before we explain the details of this kind of expansion we should recognize the differing effects that changes in exports are likely to produce in various countries. Because the foreign trade sector is small relative to the domestic sector, a large percentage change in United States exports causes a fairly small percentage change in income (*NNP*). Although the United States is not as heavily dependent upon the international economy as are some countries, foreign trade is important to it. In this country, however, foreign trade shares with domestic investment the role of determining the level of economic activity. If exports decline, there still exists the strictly domestic level of investment to rely upon.

To contrast, a small change in exports creates a sizable variation in income (*NNP*) in many of the less developed and some industrialized countries, because they are generally heavily dependent upon foreign trade in virtue of their extreme specialization. Thus, although investment may be viewed as the basic factor that generates income (*NNP*) in the American economy, a similar role is played by exports in the economies of many other countries.

**Effect of Export Changes on Income.** Suppose exports rise in response to an increase in foreign demand for our goods and services. Clearly, the change will promote an increase in *NNP*. To be specific, consider an increase in exports of \$10 billion[4] in an initial situation marked by the equilibrium of $C+I+G+E$ and *NNP*. The increased exports create excess demand, because $C+I+G+E$ was equal to *NNP* at the outset. To meet extra demand producers increase supply (lower-loop *NNP*) and in the act generate not only additional output but additional income with which to buy goods. With the payment of additional income buyers will seek to consume more, and $C+I+G+E$ will increase further. Seemingly, there is an interaction between rising spending and rising income that can be resolved only if a point of equality is found at a higher *NNP*.

We need to know how much spending will rise with additional income (*NNP*). Recall that *I, G,* and *E* are considered to be independent of income, whereas *C* depends on income. Consequently, a rise in income (*NNP*) produces an increase in consumption spending. We recall that the marginal propensity to consume expresses the increase in consumption generated by a \$1 rise in income (*NNP*). If consumption increases by \$20 billion as *NNP* rises by \$30 billion, $MPC = \$20/\$30 \text{ billion} = 2/3$.

Now $C+I+G+E$ is \$10 billion above *NNP,* and both are increasing as a result of excess demand. Suppose *NNP* increases by precisely \$30 billion. Then *C* will increase by exactly 2/3 of this, because *MPC* is 2/3. Hence, this will lead to an increase in *C* of 2/3 (\$30

[4] Realistically, this figure is excessive in the light of United States experience. We use it for the purpose of facilitating the diagramatic presentation.

billion) = \$20 billion. Combining the increase in consumption of \$20 billion with the initial increase in exports of \$10 billion, and no change in investment and government spending, we find $C+I+G+E$ to have risen by \$30 billion. Clearly, this amount exactly suffices to buy the additional output of \$30 billion generated by the like increase in *NNP*. If *E* remains \$10 billion above the old level, *NNP* will continue to be in equilibrium at a level \$30 billion higher than before.

Evidently, a rise of \$10 billion in exports leads to a rise of \$30 billion in *NNP*. Accordingly, we can say that the ratio \$30/\$10 billion = 3 represents the rise in *NNP* per unit rise in *E*. As anticipated, we come up against an old friend—a knowledge of which is basic for understanding the expansionary process. This is the multiplier. It tells us the number of dollars income (*NNP*) will rise when *E* rises by one dollar. (See Chapter 7 for a detailed explanation of the *MPC* and multiplier.) In the present example the ratio is 3; for every dollar rise in *E*, *NNP* rises by \$3.

Let us illustrate the action of the multiplier (*K*). In Figure 25–7 equilibrium is shown at point *e′*, where $C+I+G+E$ equals *NNP*, or in the lower figure, at *E′* where $S+T+M=I+G+E$. Consequently, an income *Oa* in the upper or *OA* in the lower diagram represents the initial equilibrium income. Now *E* (exports) increases to $E_1$, causing the $C+I+G+E$ line to shift to position $C+I+G+E_1$ in the upper diagram and $I+G+E$ to shift to position $I+G+E_1$ in the lower diagram. In the upper diagram $C+I+G+E_1$ reaches equilibrium with *NNP* at point *h′*, giving a new income of *Ob* (an increase of *ab*). In the lower diagram $I+G+E_1$ intersects $S+T+M$ at point *H′*, giving an income *OB* (an increase of *AB*).

The same principle is at work in Table 25–4. An original equilibrium is found at *NNP* of \$420 billion, but the rise in $I+G+E_1$ $(C+I+G+E_1)$ upsets the equilibrium. Thus, $C+I+G+E_1$ is now \$430 billion as compared to the *NNP* of \$420 billion, implying an excess demand of \$10 billion. Clearly, this amount of excess demand is the result of an increase in exports of \$10 billion ($\Delta E =$ \$10 billion). As *NNP* expands by \$30 billion, $C+I+G+E_1$ increases by \$20 billion, which, together with the initial excess demand of \$10 billion, causes $C+I+G+E_1$ to equal *NNP* at \$450 billion.

## THE BALANCE OF PAYMENTS EFFECT

**Increased Exports.** Note that imports and exports are unequal at the equilibrium *NNP* (= \$450 billion), exports exceeding imports. (Refer to the figures shown in parentheses under headings *M* and $E_1$

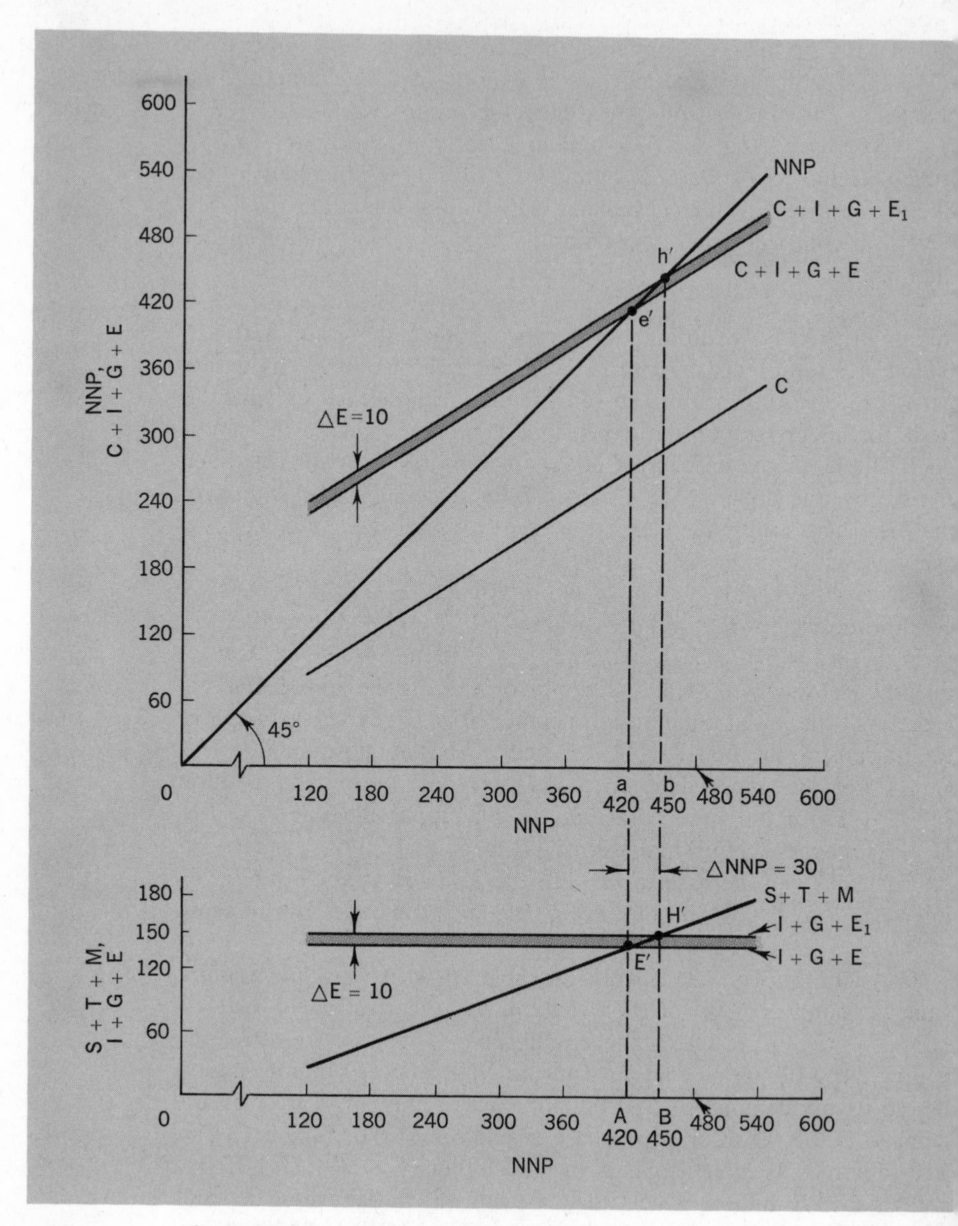


**Figure 25–7.** Expansion of *NNP* as a result of increasing exports operating through the multiplier.

in Table 25–4. Specifically, $E_1 = (25)$ and $M = (15)$ at $NNP$ $(= 450)$.) Evidently, an equilibrium *NNP* does not always give a corresponding equilibrium in the balance of payments. Let us see why.

TABLE 25-4
**A Numerical Illustration of the Multiplier (Billions of Dollars)**

| | **NNP** | **C** | **S + T + M** | **I + G + E*** | **C + I + G + E** | **I + G + $E_1$** | **C + I + G + $E_1$** |
|---|---|---|---|---|---|---|---|
| | 60 | 40 | 18 (2) | 140 | 180 | 150 (25) | 190 |
| | 120 | 80 | 36 (4) | 140 | 220 | 150 (25) | 230 |
| | 180 | 120 | 54 (6) | 140 | 260 | 150 (25) | 270 |
| | 240 | 160 | 72 (8) | 140 | 300 | 150 (25) | 310 |
| | 300 | 200 | 90 (10) | 140 | 340 | 150 (25) | 350 |
| | 360 | 240 | 108 (12) | 140 | 380 | 150 (25) | 390 |
| Original equilibrium | 420 | 280 | 126 (14) | 140 | 420 | 150 (25) | 430 |
| New equilibrium | 450 | 300 | 135 (15) | 140 | 440 | 150 (25) | 450 |

* $I + G = \$125$, $E = \$15$; each is constant for the period under consideration.

Consider an alternative explanation of the expansionary process just concluded. We shall concentrate on the external elements (*E* and *M*). First, it is clear that a rise in exports (an injection element) sets off an expansion leading to a rise in income (*NNP*). In our illustration, $\Delta E$ (= \$10 billion) at *NNP* of \$420 billion produces an excess demand of that amount. The expansion leads to a rise in income (*NNP*) amounting to \$30 billion (from \$420 to \$450 billion). As income rises by \$30 billion, consumption increases by \$20 billion (from \$280 to \$300 billion). Thus we can say that a higher equilibrium *NNP* is established, because $\Delta E$ (= \$10 billion) plus $\Delta C$ (= \$20 billion) = $\Delta NNP$ (= \$30 billion). But it is clear that not all of the rise in income is absorbed by additional consumption. The remainder is channeled into additional saving, taxes, and imports. We recall that these latter elements are referred to as leakages from the income stream. Therefore, we understand that a rise in income (*NNP*) leads to additional consumption and additional saving, taxes, and imports.

Now ignoring saving and taxes we can make the following observation: A rise in exports leads to increased income; and a rise in income results in increased imports. However, imports may not rise by the exact amount of exports. Essentially, imports depend upon the *marginal propensity to import* (*MPM*), a term used to denote the increase of imports generated by a \$1 rise in income (*NNP*). This expression can be written $MPM = \Delta M/\Delta NNP$. Now if the marginal propensity to save ($\Delta S/\Delta NNP$) plus the marginal propensity to tax ($\Delta T/\Delta NNP$) is greater than zero, the rise of imports will be less than the rise of exports. In essence, the balance of payments disequilibrium is only partially corrected through the income effects of the increased exports for the reasons just cited. However, certain elements may produce changes that might lead to an equilibrium in the balance of payments. These and other ideas are discussed in the appendix to this chapter.

According to our example, a rise in exports can lead to an inequality in the items, because the resulting rise in imports falls short of the initial increase in exports. Thus the current account of the balance of payments ends up in a state of imbalance (an export surplus) even though a higher equilibrium *NNP* is achieved. If this experience is repeated over a series of years, the level of exports would tend to exceed the level of imports.[5] This reasoning is supported by the experience of the United States. (See, for example, the

[5] The underlying reasons for this situation are found in the relative supply-and-demand conditions existing between nations. The latter were explained in detail in Chapter 23.

United States balance of payments for 1964, in Chapter 24.) From the balance of payments viewpoint, a nation with an export surplus must be willing to finance the excess exports by means of grants, long-term loans and investments, short-term loans, and gold.

**Summary.** In this chapter we emphasized exports and imports, adding them to the domestic determinants of income (*NNP*).

National income (*NNP*) is reinterpreted. National income expressed as Net National Product tends to reach an equilibrium marked by the equality of upper-loop *NNP,* total spending on output, and lower-loop *NNP,* output at cost. The main component underlying demand is consumption spending; this is shown to be functionally related to *NNP.* The relation of consumption to other elements is also considered. Like consumption, the sum of saving plus taxes plus imports is also functionally related to *NNP;* this follows, because the four together are equal to *NNP.*

Export spending is considered an autonomous element for analytical purposes. We justify our handling of exports in this manner, because they are influenced mainly by foreign demand for our goods and services. However, we understand that a change in income at home, induced increases in imports in foreign countries, and other changed conditions at home and in other countries may lead to induced changes in exports. Investment spending and government spending are treated as autonomous or independent variables, like exports, for reasons stated previously.

Equilibrium is described graphically in two ways. The equality of a $C + I + G + E$ line with a 45-degree *NNP* line designates the level of *NNP* at which upper- and lower-loop *NNP* are equal; total spending equals cost of output. We identify $C + I + G + E$ with aggregate demand for domestic output and the 45-degree line showing *NNP* with aggregate supply or total domestic output. If $C + I + G + E$ exceeds *NNP,* aggregate demand exceeds aggregate supply; total spending exceeds necessary factor payments. Under these conditions *NNP* must increase. If $C + I + G + E$ falls short of *NNP, NNP* must decrease for the opposite reasons. Hence, the equality of $C + I + G + E$ and *NNP* marks an equilibrium of aggregate demand and aggregate supply. Any departure of *NNP* from the equilibrium quantity at which this holds true leads to a return to this value. The equality of $C + I + G + E$ and *NNP* is found to be equivalent to the equality of $I + G + E$ and $S + T + M$.

A rise in exports tends to disturb previous relationships marked by an equality of $C + I + G + E$ and *NNP* at a given level of output. In our illustration (Table 25–4) the original equilibrium *NNP* is \$420 billion. An increase in $I + G + E_1$, initiated by a rise in exports, upsets the previous equilibrium. Thus, total spending ($C + I + G + E_1$) is now \$430 billion as compared to the *NNP* of \$420 billion. This implies an excess demand of \$10 billion. As *NNP* expands by \$30 billion, $C + I + G + E_1$ increases by \$20 billion, together with the initial excess demand of \$10 billion, and causes $C + I + G + E_1$ to equal *NNP* at \$450 billion. Consequently, the equality of $C + I + G + E$ and *NNP* is reestablished at a higher output. These results are also described graphically.

We observed that the changed conditions leading to a higher equilibrium *NNP* did not produce an equilibrium in the balance of payments: an export surplus still existed. Thus, our illustration suggests that imports may not rise by the exact rise in exports. We noted this possibility by making use of the marginal propensities to import, to save, and to tax, recognizing that if the marginal propensity to save plus the marginal propensity to tax is greater than zero, the rise of imports will be less than the rise of exports.

## QUESTIONS

1. We find that by comparing United States exports to national income the percentage figure is relatively low. Why is this figure misleading as a surface fact?
2. The meaning of consumption is changed from previous analysis. Explain. What are imports?
3. What is meant by the import function? Observe the points relating imports to *GNP* (Figure 25–3) for the periods 1929–49 and 1950–64. Can you detect a shift in the import function? Comment. What does this shift imply with respect to rising *GNP?*
4. Why are exports added to other elements ($C + I + G$) in determining aggregate demand?
5. Refer to Figure 25–5. Comment as to why the consumption ($C$) line is upward-sloping. The $C + I + G$ and $C + I + G + E$ lines lie above, and are parallel to, the $C$ line. Explain. What is the significance of the 45-degree *NNP* line? Excess demand or excess supply denotes a disequilibrium. Why ?
6. Assume an equilibrium in the balance of payments at an equilibrium *NNP* of \$500 billion. Now exports increase by \$5 billion and remain at the higher level. $I$ and $G$ are constant. The *MPC* is ⅔. What is the new, higher equilibrium *NNP?* By how much would consumption increase? Resolve the difference between the rise in income (*NNP*) and the rise in consumption.
7. Refer to Table 25–4 and the surrounding discussion. Draw a graph that accurately demonstrates the expansion of *NNP* as a result of increasing exports operating through the multiplier. (Compare your graph with Figure 25–7.)
8. Discuss the following statement: an equilibrium *NNP* does not always give a corresponding equilibrium in the balance of payments.

## Appendix

# BALANCE OF PAYMENTS EFFECT OF CHANGES IN EXPORTS AND OTHER DISTURBANCES

In our discussion we have explained that a balance of payments disturbance does not correct itself completely through income effects. In our illustration of Table 25–4 an export surplus exists even though *NNP* achieves an equilibrium. Now we can show how certain elements might produce changes that lead to an equilibrium in the balance of payments. To do this we need to relax previous assumptions and note changes that occur in other countries. Let us trace the reasoning as it applies to increased exports.

First, consider *induced investment*. As we have argued previously, an increase in exports causes a rise in *NNP* and consumption. Such increased demand for output may stimulate an increase in investment (or government spending). Such a further increase in total spending will set off a further rise in income (*NNP*). Let us also suppose that the rise in income is just sufficient to cause imports to equal the initial increase in exports, so that in equilibrium ($NNP = C + I + G + E$) the export surplus is eliminated. Our first reaction is that induced investment may be a factor that brings equilibrium. However, things may not work out so neatly. It is possible, for example, that the added investment may raise *NNP* and imports so much that the export surplus is changed into an import deficit. In this instance, the induced investment becomes a source of balance of payments disequilibrium.

Now let's note the *foreign effect*. Again we assume an increase in exports at the outset. The rise in, say, country *A*'s exports is equivalent to an increase in other countries' imports. However, the increased imports from *A* probably reduce the income (*NNP*) in the latter countries, notably where increased imports are carried out at the expense of consumption of those countries' products. In turn, the reduced income induces a decrease in imports. Thus, the induced decrease in other countries' imports has the effect of reducing *A*'s exports, and to the extent that this action is effective, country *A*'s current account surplus is reduced. This foreign effect produces uncertain results, because imports will not decline by the full amount of the decreased income, and out of the total amount of decreased imports only a part will effect *A*'s exports. As a result, it is unlikely that *A*'s export surplus will be eliminated completely.

**Increased Investment.** Consider a different situation involving an autonomous increase in investment. We begin with an equilibrium condition—that is, an equilibrium in the balance of payments at an equilibrium *NNP*. Now an autonomous increase in investment occurs. Because investment is an injection element—just like exports—the result will be a multiple expansion of income. Although the effects on income are the same as in the case of increased exports, the effects on the balance of payments will be different. This is so because the increased income does not directly effect exports, but it will cause imports to increase. In short, increased investment leads to an import deficit.

We wonder if there are forces at work that may reduce the import deficit created by increased investment. Clearly, there are. However, whether they are sufficiently strong to eliminate completely the import deficit is another matter. Let us examine the probable effects. We start with an increase in investment. The increased income generated by the increased investment leads to a rise in imports (exports being unaffected). An increase in country *A*'s imports is equivalent to a rise in other countries' exports and, thereby, income. As income rises in those countries, their demand for *A*'s exports will increase. Thus, an increase in *A*'s imports will lead to an increase in *A*'s exports. These results are indirect and uncertain, because not all of the increased income in other countries will be spent on imports, and out of the total amount spent only a part will be spent on *A*'s exports. It is therefore unlikely that the induced increase in *A*'s exports will be sufficient to match the increased imports.

Next, we examine possible repercussions on the balance of payments initiated by an increase in imports and a decrease in exports. Because we want to show the results of autonomous increases, we will discuss these elements separately.

**Increased Imports.** Let us begin with an increase in imports caused by a change in preferences for imported goods, a reduction in tariffs, and so on, and not because of a change in income. We also assume that the increased expenditure on imports is associated with a corresponding decline in spending on domestic output ($C+I+G+E$), so that the increased spending on imports leads to a decline in income (*NNP*) and a deficit in the balance of payments. The fall in income will ultimately be a multiple of the increased imports. Suppose, for example, that $\Delta M = \$10$ billion and the multiplier $(K) = 3$. Then, we can expect income to decline ultimately by \$30 billion (= \$10 billion times 3).

Let us be more specific concerning the income effect. Increased imports will probably take place, if *NNP* is constant, by displacing some production and demand for domestic goods. Therefore consumption, investment, or government spending (by definition for domestically produced goods) will be reduced. If so, total spending on domestically produced output, $C + I + G + E$, will drop at a given level of (lower-loop) *NNP* or supply. At this point supply exceeds demand, and production or lower-loop *NNP* must be cut, and a decline takes place. Clearly, if imports increase with no decline in spending, *NNP* will remain steady.

Assume that the increased imports accompanied reduced investment, both changes amounting to $10 billion. With a multiplier of 3 and an *MPC* of ⅔, the resulting fall in *NNP* will amount to 3 times $10 billion or $30 billion, and the decline in consumption to ⅔ of this or $20 billion. The combined decline in *C* and *I* is $20 + $10 = $30 billion, with no change in *E* and *G*. Because *NNP* or supply is reduced by a similar amount, aggregate supply and aggregate demand will be equal.

The same results can be explained by the drains-injections approach. Assume that *M* increases, displacing the production of domestic capital goods and causing *I* to fall by an equal amount, namely $10 billion. As a result of the fall in *I*, *NNP* falls by $30 billion and *C* by $20 billion = ⅔ ($30 billion). Hence, $C + S + T = NNP - C$ falls by ($30 − $20) billion = $10 billion. This is precisely equal to the initial fall of $10 billion in $I + G + E$, resulting from the fall in *I*. Because drains and injections have each fallen by $10 billion, equilibrium is restored.

The important point to note above is that the sum of the leakages will decline by $10 billion when income (*NNP*) declines by $30 billion. The import deficit would be eliminated completely only if $S + T$ did not decline as *NNP* fell by $30 billion, a highly unlikely situation, necessitating a secondary fall in imports of the full $10 billion, or if induced $I + G + E$ would rise sufficiently to offset any decline in $S + T$, making it necessary for *M* to fall $10 billion. In these unlikely cases the final value of *M* would be the same as the original one.

Of course, we can expect certain foreign repercussions. The autonomous increase in imports is equivalent to an autonomous increase in exports and, hence, income in foreign countries. Thus there will be induced increases in the imports of other countries and induced increases in the exports of the first country. However, the amount of change is likely to be insufficient, in itself, to balance the increase in its imports. Now let us summarize the possible effects of decreased exports.

**Decreased Exports.** Because we have already discussed the effects of increased exports we need not dwell on the possible effects of decreased exports. Consider for a moment a decline in exports marked by a decrease in foreign demand—and not by a prior decline in foreign income. In short, an autonomous decrease in exports occurs at the outset. This phenomenon leads to a decline in income via the multiplier process. The latter induces a decline in imports (and other leakage elements). Though a deficit occurs in the balance of payments, it is offset, in part, by the induced decline in imports.

Other adjustments take place through the foreign effect. Assuming that a rise in foreign income occurs because of the autonomous decline in imports (indicated above by a decrease in foreign demand), we can expect induced increases in imports in those countries. This implies a partial offsetting of the original autonomous decline in foreign imports. Thus, the decline in exports of the first country is mitigated to some extent.

CHAPTER 26

# Trade and Economic Stability

The brief analysis of the income and balance of payments effects given in Chapter 25 suggests a reciprocal relationship between income (*NNP*) and the balance of payments of each country, and between income (*NNP*) and the balance of payments of each country and those of all other countries. In the next two chapters we plan to investigate these relationships with a view to examining some problems of and policies for maintaining economic stability. The present chapter is devoted to a general discussion of problems and policies available to a country that is trying to achieve a high level of output. Special emphasis is to be given to policies designed to cope with the external (balance of payments) problem. In the following chapter we will deal with the United States balance of payments problem. We will reexamine policies already suggested and consider others with a view to estimating how they might alleviate this problem and what effects they are likely to have on economic activity.

## INTRODUCTORY REMARKS

Our earlier study of the theory of trade pointed up, among other things, the fact that trade contributes to a more efficient allocation of resources and a higher (real) income. In the last chapter we found that trade enters into the determination of income (*NNP*). Thus, we were able to explain the ways in which trade affects, and is affected by, changes in income (*NNP*). Recalling these twin aspects of trade, we can now draw up an important statement concerning the relationship between external trade (as revealed by the balance of payments) and domestic economic activity: a high level of economic activity is normally associated with a constantly expanding volume of trade, directed into lines of comparative advantage. Our statement suggests that a certain balance in the relationship between these dual aspects of economic activity is necessary if the economy is to perform at peak levels. To summarize, a country must try to harmonize the requirements for domestic stability at full employment with those for external stability at a high volume of trade.

Herein lies a problem. Measures employed to achieve domestic stability at a high level of employment may conflict, at times, with the requirements for external stability at a high volume of trade. In turn, measures used to achieve external stability at a high volume of trade may conflict, at times, with the requirements for domestic stability at a high level of employment. Consider a few examples to demonstrate the point.

Suppose events set in that point to a decline in income (*NNP*) and employment. Monetary and fiscal measures are therefore applied for the purpose of increasing spending, output, and employment of the sagging economy. Assuming an equality between imports and exports at the outset, the rise in income, resulting from the successful use of proper policies, brings forth an increase in imports. However, exports will fail to rise as output increases, if foreign demand for these goods remains unchanged. Thus, the altered conditions have temporarily disturbed the previous external balance. If the situation continues, we can expect certain measures to be employed to correct this imbalance. These measures may give rise to further adjustments in the domestic economy, and in foreign countries, leading to uncertain results with respect to the level of income (*NNP*) and the volume of trade.

Consider another possibility. Suppose the economy is fully employed in producing current output. Now a decline in price or an improvement in quality of foreign goods causes domestic consumers to increase their purchases of foreign goods. Hence, imports rise relative to exports. Assuming that the additional imports displace some domestic production, certain measures are suggested. If injured domestic producers can convince the authorities that increased imports have caused a decline in production, measures are likely to be imposed to restrict imports. In view of this action, foreigners may decide to adopt similar measures, leading to a decline in exports of the home country. In turn, monetary and fiscal measures may be applied in response to changed conditions within the domestic economy.

These few observations indicate that measures used in response to changed conditions bring about adjustments in both the domestic and external sectors of the economy, and in foreign countries, which result in uncertain effects regarding the country's level of income (*NNP*), employment, and volume of trade.

Because we want to emphasize the effects of trade, the following discussion will center on the balance of payments. We will therefore discuss some measures—or combination of measures—which would tend to correct an imbalance in the country's external trade. Also, we want to see how these measures might affect the performance of the domestic economy. Since adjustments often produce changed conditions in foreign countries, we will note these changes in passing. Let us begin by considering the general problem of economic stability.

## NATIONAL VERSUS INTERNATIONAL STABILITY: THE GENERAL PROBLEM

It is natural for a country to give first priority to national goals, especially high and stable levels of employment and output and stable prices. This implies that international stability may be sacrificed, at times, in order to maintain a certain level of internal stability. By this we mean that international trade may be altered by appropriate measures for the purpose of achieving domestic stability. Viewed from the standpoint of the balance of payments this means that international trade may exert a destabilizing effect. However, under certain conditions trade may produce a stabilizing effect. Perhaps a few, simple examples will clarify our points.

Taking the latter situation first, suppose a country is plagued by inflation. Foreign goods become cheaper relative to some domestically produced items. Thus imports increase relative to exports. The additional imports tend to exert a stabilizing effect on the domestic economy, because part of the excessive spending for domestic goods is diverted to foreign goods. This tends to hold down the rise in the domestic price level.

On the other hand consider a country whose income (*NNP*) is rising more rapidly than in foreign countries. As a result of this situation imports rise relative to exports. The induced increase of imports could lead to a multiple contraction of income (*NNP*) and reduced employment if it is not offset by an increase of *C, I,* or *G*. In this case, the changed trading conditions would provoke a destabilizing effect on the domestic economy.

Perhaps the above examples are sufficient to indicate the possibilities of trade complementing or conflicting with domestic stability. In any event, we can expect a country to institute actions designed to restore equilibrium relationships between income (*NNP*) and the balance of payments. Some such policies—for example, monetary measures designed to limit inflation—have in the first instance an internal impact; others—for example, depreciation of the exchange rate—primarily influence foreign trade. Clearly, an appropriate choice of policies is a condition essential to economic stability.

## BALANCE OF PAYMENTS DISEQUILIBRIUM: SPECIFIC PROBLEMS AND CORRECTIVE MEASURES

We understand that imbalances between the major accounts of a country's balance of payments lead to disequilibrium, a condition which, in the long run, must be corrected. There are several measures available which, if applied individually or in combination, may restore equilibrium. The measures chosen depend upon the severity and expected duration of the present imbalances; the manner in which they might affect the functioning of the domestic economy; and the probable repercussions that they are likely to have in foreign countries.

Disequilibrium results from a multitude of interrelated forces that are difficult to isolate. For this reason it is convenient to distinguish between measures pertinent to the two major types of disequilibrium: short run and long run. For a brief discussion of the nature of long run or structural disequilibrium the reader may review the section "Balance of Payments and Growth" in Chapter 24. In view of limitations of space we plan to focus our discussion here primarily on measures relevant to short-run disequilibrium and its sources. The sources of short-run imbalance can be classified under three headings: income, monetary, and commercial.

Two other points appear useful at the outset. The first is merely a restatement of what constitutes disequilibrium in the balance of payments. A deficit disequilibrium most commonly occurs when a country spends more on imported goods and services (payments) than it earns from exports of goods and services plus what it receives via net long-term capital and gift inflows (receipts). Expressed in terms of the balance of payments accounts this means that the current account deficit is not matched by an inflow of long-term capital (capital account).[1] As a result, the country is forced to borrow from abroad (short-term capital inflows) or export gold. Obviously, a nation's credit rating tends to worsen under these conditions, and its gold reserve is reduced. A surplus disequilibrium is, for practical purposes, the opposite of a deficit disequilibrium defined above.

Second, we assume a deficit disequilibrium in the following analysis.

[1] We assume that unilateral transfers are recorded as current account transactions.

## DISEQUILIBRIUM AND INCOME ADJUSTMENTS

Because we had an opportunity to express relationships between income (*NNP*) and the balance of payments in the latter part of Chapter 25 and in the appendix, we will draw upon some ideas already developed. In the discussion that follows we assume that the exchange rate is relatively stable. This leaves us free to concentrate on income adjustments.

**Changing the Level of Economic Activity.** Suppose an import deficit arises out of an autonomous increase in imports accompanied by a corresponding decrease in aggregate demand. In other words, if *NNP* is constant, an increase in imports displaces some production and demand for domestic goods. Therefore, $C$, $I$, or $G$ is reduced. Thus total spending on domestically produced output, $C + I + G + E$, declines at a given level of *NNP*. Now domestic supply (*NNP*) exceeds demand $(C + I + G + E)$ and a decline in *NNP* commences. In the course of the decline in income (*NNP*), $S + T + M$ falls to a new, lower level. The original import deficit would not normally be eliminated at the lower level of income, because the marginal propensity to save plus the marginal propensity to tax is greater than zero—that is, $S + T$ declines with $M$ as income falls. In short, an equilibrium *NNP* is established at a lower level of economic activity, and an import deficit of some amount still exists.

This situation requires further action. We noticed that the income effect brought about adjustments leading to a lower level of domestic economic activity. Demand must increase, especially if the economy is already operating below full-employment *NNP*. It is evident, then, that internal measures (monetary and fiscal) should be employed to encourage aggregate demand to rise closer to full-employment *NNP*.

Next, we noted that income adjustments do not completely restore equilibrium in the current account. A trade deficit still exists. Although the "foreign effect" would alter the above conditions (see the appendix to Chapter 25), the final outcome is uncertain. Let us therefore look at certain measures and see how they may effect adjustment to disequilibrium.

## MEASURES FOR ALLEVIATING MONETARY DISEQUILIBRIUM

Monetary adjustments to disequilibrium refer to changes in the general level of prices and money costs in one country as compared to others. There are two sorts of price adjustments that may be effected. The first, a rather remote possibility, is to alter the domestic price level so as to bring it into a new relationship to foreign price levels. A second method consists in altering the exchange rate, an adjustment that changes the price relationships between this and other countries. Recalling the discussion of exchange rates in Chapter 24, we understand that a change in the exchange rate yields higher prices in one country and correspondingly lower prices in a second country. We will make use of these and other measures in the discussion that follows, assuming as before a trade deficit. Although price and income changes are closely related, we want to stress the pricing aspect at this juncture.

**Lowering Domestic Prices.** Assume that the levels of income and prices are such in various countries that at a given rate of exchange a country, say the United States, experiences a sharp rise in imports relative to exports. Assuming that relative demand elasticities are favorable, the said country may be able to correct this condition and restore external balance by lowering the domestic price level. Clearly, this course would impose strict demands on the economy, including a reduction in costs through technological and managerial improvements, the acceptance of lower wage rates, and other efforts designed to reduce domestic prices relative to foreign prices.

Assume that the domestic price level is reduced and that this development evokes an increase in exports and a decrease in imports. Then external balance may be restored between imports and exports, both of which have increased. However, such corrective measures may set in motion or accelerate an internal tendency to underemployment or falling income. With excess productive capacity and rigid wage rates in some industries (as under oligopoly), a fall in general prices is likely to result in a further decline in income (*NNP*) and employment. This may be a higher price than the public is willing to pay for external balance.

Because world prices have showed an upward trend in recent years, a country may be able to achieve the desired goal without the side effects noted. If it takes action to hold the rise in its price level below that of other countries, it might increase exports without adverse effects on income and employment. For example, during the 1950's Western Germany was able to hold back its price level sufficiently to secure lower prices relative to other countries. In her case the rise in exports served as a stimulus to an already expanding economy.

**Exchange Depreciation.** Assume that imports have increased relative to exports. Instead of lowering domestic prices, a country depreciates its currency in order to restore external balance. Such an action reduces the value of a country's currency relative to foreign currencies, resulting in higher domestic prices for foreign goods and services. At the same time the country's products will now be cheaper to foreign buyers. Suppose that the present dollar-pound rate of

$2.80 = £1 is altered to $3.00 = £1. (Refer back to Figure 24–2.) This amounts to a depreciation of the dollar and an appreciation of pound sterling. What will be the effect of the altered exchange rate? Well, an English product worth £100, which previously cost $280 to American buyers, will now cost $300. In turn, Americans will buy less of this product, and imports will decline. At the same time, dollar goods are cheaper in England. Thus, an American product worth $300 to English buyers, which formerly cost £107.14 in England, would now cost only £100. Englishmen would tend to buy more of it, and United States exports would increase. Thus, increased exports and reduced imports result from a depreciation of the exchange rate, tending to bring about the desired equality between exports and imports.

Note that we said that depreciation tends to bring about external balance. Whether it does or not depends, in part, upon the response in physical items traded to a change in the exchange rate. Because each imported item costs more (in dollars) than before, and fewer are purchased, and because each exported item costs less (in pounds) than before, and more are sold, our trade balance would improve only if the changes in physical terms are sufficient to outweigh the adverse effect of the cheapening of our currency. In short, the result depends upon the elasticities of demand in the two countries—that is, the elasticity of United States demand for English exports and the elasticity of English demand for United States exports. Textbooks on international trade tell us that a country's trade balance will improve if the sum of these two elasticities is greater than one—that is, elastic. Because we assumed an import deficit at the outset (imports rising relative to exports), restoration of external balance would require this condition to be met. The greater the elasticity (the excess of the sum over one), the smaller the depreciation required.

Besides these technical aspects of financial adjustment, the decline in imports resulting from exchange depreciation may prevent the importation of capital or consumer goods necessary to maintain a given level of output or to achieve a minimum plane of living. Clearly, these effects are most pronounced in less developed countries, where both capital and consumption goods are in short supply. If the deprivation is severe, public opposition to this cure might develop.

**Depreciation and Exchange Control.** The effects of depreciation depend on the manner in which exchange rates are determined. Suppose that the depreciating country in the example above employs exchange control.[2] As we explained in Chapter 24, a system of ex-

[2] Exchange control is associated with a fixed rate of exchange made effective by direct government control of exchange operations. Normally, depreciation would be employed only at infrequent intervals.

change control implies that the government or governmental agency regulates the purchase and sale of all foreign exchange. Moreover, the controlling agency can regulate the amount and types of goods imported. Thus, it is in a position to select from the reduced quantity of imports those goods that are most needed to permit economic growth and to meet basic consumer needs.

On the other hand, it is not entirely clear how much depreciation is needed to reduce imports to just the right level. The rate may be set too high or too low. If depreciation is excessive—that is, if the value of the country's currency is cut too much relative to other countries—then the decline in imports may be greater than that required to restore external balance. Conversely, if depreciation is insufficient, import reductions may fall short of that desired level. Of course, exports are also affected by depreciation. The final adjustments depend, as stated above, upon the nature of the elasticities of demand in this and other countries.

Two problems are clearly discernible in connection with depreciation and exchange control: (1) imports are controlled by some public agency, thus taking such decisions out of the private sphere, and (2) there exists the possibility of excessive or deficient depreciation, either of which would fail to produce an equality between exports and imports. Thus, the remedy outlined may fail to meet the exact needs of the situation.

**Depreciation and Foreign Retaliation.** An attempt by one country to rid itself of an import deficit by depreciation might provoke similar action abroad. This is most likely to occur if other countries are currently marked by excess capacity and large-scale unemployment. In fact, retaliation may be nearly spontaneous, because depreciation is designed partly to reduce a country's imports—that is, to reduce the exports of other countries. Of course, the speed and extent of retaliation will depend upon the state of employment in the several countries, the loss of total exports by those countries arising from the reduction in imports by the depreciating country, the possibility of developing markets elsewhere, the relative importance of imports received from the depreciating country, the availability of substitute goods, and so forth.

Clearly, depreciation by one country does not preclude its use by others. Indeed, just this sort of retaliation occurred in the late 1920's and during the 1930's. If, for example, the United States dollar is reduced in price relative to the English pound, and this is later followed by action to reduce the price of the pound relative to the dollar, the situation can return to what it was in the beginning, with the total value of trade unchanged.

**Disinflation and Depreciation.** The next monetary device incorporates a combination of the first two measures. We assume that the domestic economy is plagued by inflation. Instead of trying to reduce the level of prices, a deflationary act that might involve unemployment, the authorities may apply monetary and fiscal policies just sufficient to halt the inflation without causing the general level of prices to decline—that is, to cause disinflation. Once inflation is halted, exchange depreciation may be employed to bring costs and prices into line with those in other countries. Presumably, imports and exports would then gravitate to proper levels.

Disinflation plays an important part in the adjustment process, because through its use the level of employment can be maintained, and at a time when inflation threatens, the benefits from depreciation on the trade balance can be secured without further inflation.

Although these measures require a certain precision in the application of monetary and fiscal policies and assume predictable results from depreciation, they would contribute greatly toward achieving domestic and external stability.

**Loans and Grants.** An import deficit not offset by an inflow of long-term capital and unilateral transfers gives a clear indication of a deficit disequilibrium in the balance of payments. However, if the balance of payments problem is regarded as temporary, the country may be able to obtain additional loans or grants to carry it along until the problem is corrected. Thus, although loans and grants are not corrective measures in the sense previously understood, they have the effect of extending the adjustment period so that the receiving country may adopt measures that will ultimately improve the performance of the economy. Seemingly, such was the case with the Western European countries during the years immediately following World War II. In the years 1948–51 inclusive, Marshall Plan grants were extended to Western European countries experiencing trade deficits. By 1951 the countries had recovered to a point where deficits were disappearing generally, and the Marshall Plan was terminated.

**Gold Flows.** We recall that a deficit disequilibrium, evidenced by an excess of normal payments over normal receipts, must be settled by an outflow of gold or an inflow of short-term capital or both. Though short-term capital inflows are an important source of temporary funds, we plan to use our limited space for a discussion of gold flows.

We should point out that gold flows are not measures, in themselves, that correct a disequilibrium in the balance of payments. Indeed, they indicate the presence of a disequilibrium. Thus, gold flows require the initiation of measures designed to eliminate a persistent movement of gold into or out of a country. Not only does such a gold flow indicate a balance of payments problem, it also affects the money supply and complicates the normal results expected from the application of monetary policy. We will demonstrate these and other points shortly. Since, at this juncture, we intend to present a reasonably complete picture of the effects of gold movements, we will trace changes in bank reserves and the money supply resulting when a country, say the United States, buys gold. Then we will observe changes associated with the sale of gold (gold outflow). Finally, we want to recognize other problems that are directly related to gold movements.

**Gold Reserves and the Money Supply.** We are presently concerned with changes in the monetary gold stock and the money supply caused by gold movements. Suppose, for example, that the Treasury *buys* a new shipment of gold amounting to $1 million from a foreign government. The immediate effects run as follows: (1) The Treasury pays for the gold with a check on its account at the Federal Reserve. (2) This reduces the Treasury deposit account at the Federal Reserve and adds to the account of the foreign government. Noting only changes, the transactions would appear as the entries designated by (a) in the Federal Reserve Banks balance sheet shown in Table 26–1. (3) The Treasury then makes use of its extra gold by crediting the gold certificate fund of the Federal Reserve Banks. The Banks' gold certificate reserve is, thereby, increased. (4) In turn, the Banks credit a corresponding amount to the Treasury, which now has the same balance with the Federal Reserve as before the gold shipment. The latter two transactions are recorded as (b) entries. So far the gold purchase has not affected member banks or the public at all. Consider now the further steps in the process.

The balance of the foreign government with the Federal Reserve has increased by the value of the gold shipment. Since foreign governments maintain only small balances at the Federal Reserve, further steps are indicated. (5) The foreign government will probably draw a check against its account either for deposit in, say, a member bank (or banks) or for purchase of securities or goods. (6) In any of these cases the deposits of a member bank increase.[3] When the check clears at the Federal Reserve, member bank reserve deposits increase at the expense of deposits of foreign countries. Therefore member bank reserves and deposits of member banks each increase by the amount of the original Treasury purchase of gold. These transactions are shown as (c) entries in the member bank's balance sheet shown in Table 26–2 under the name of Acme National Bank and the Federal Reserve Banks balance sheet in Table 26–1.

Assuming a deposit of $1 million and the reserve ratio of 20 per cent, only $200,000 in reserve would be required by the Acme bank.

[3] If the foreign government buys securities, it pays the purchaser with a check on its account. When the seller deposits this check, member bank deposits increase by the same amount. Of course, this assumes that the seller of securities does business with a member bank.

eaving a balance of $800,000 in excess reserves. Thus a further otential exists for creating deposits. Then, *the total of deposits, ncluding that shown in Table 26–2, could increase by about five imes the original gold purchase of $1 million—that is, by $5 million.* This follows from the deposit expansion ratio 5:1 on given reserves, vhen the reserve ratio is 20 per cent. The leverage effect is much reater, potentially, in the case of an outflow, especially a prolonged utflow. We will consider this point below.

**ABLE 26-1**
**alance Sheet of Federal Reserve Banks (Thousands of Dollars)**

| Assets | | Liabilities | |
|---|---|---|---|
| Gold certificate reserves | +1,000 (b) | Deposits | |
| | | Member bank reserves | +1,000 (c) |
| | | U.S. Treasury | −1,000 (a) |
| | | | +1,000 (b) |
| | | Foreign | +1,000 (a) |
| | | | −1,000 (c) |

**Gold Movements and the Money Supply.** What are the implica-ions of gold movements into and out of the United States? As we ave just explained, a shipment of gold bought by the Treasury could ead to a 5:1 expansion of deposit money. Also, an *outflow* of gold ould lead to a *contraction* of deposits, a $1 million outflow resulting n a $5 million contraction. Such inflows and outflows are the result f our foreign trade situation (an outflow being marked by an excess f payments over receipts on normal—that is, current and capital—ccount items) and are not planned or desired by the Treasury or ederal Reserve. In fact, *gold movements constitute a major inde-endent and uncontrolled source of variation in bank reserves and the noney supply.*

Consequently, a limited gold movement is a nuisance in that it nfluences economic activity and alters the effectiveness of monetary olicy. Let us summarize the proposition. Clearly, the United States as a gold reserve that is now more than adequate to back outstand-

**ABLE 26-2**
**cme National Bank—Stage 1 (Thousands of Dollars)**

| Assets | | Liabilities | |
|---|---|---|---|
| Cash reserves | +1,000 (c) | Deposits | +1,000 (c) |

ing Federal Reserve notes.[4] However, a gold outflow, say, reduces reserves and sets in motion a multiple contraction of deposit money. It will tend to encourage a contraction in demand and economic activity. The tighter credit conditions will involve higher interest rates, reduced availability of credit, a decline in investment, and a contraction of *NNP*. At some point the Federal Reserve is likely to be forced to intervene with a view to easing credit and heading off the consequences of these developments. More or less opposite results tend to occur in case of an inflow, resulting in inflationary pressure, particularly if the economy is presently operating at a high level of capacity and employment. In short, gold flows tend to require the Federal Reserve to take some sort of countervailing action.

Although we are discussing short-run sources of disequilibrium, it appears pertinent at this point to conclude our account of gold by noting some of the longer-run effects of persistent gold flows. If a gold flow in a given direction persists over a long period, serious problems tend to arise. Let us illustrate. Between 1933 and 1957 the gold reserves of the United States rose from less than $5 billion to nearly $23 billion. Such an enormous gold inflow created a great quantity of reserves and deposits. In turn, this made possible a very large expansion in loans and deposits. Thus, gold contributed to the postwar inflationary pattern. Since 1957 there has been an outflow of gold that has reduced the gold reserve to about $14.9 billion (as of January 1965). If this trend continues more or less indefinitely, it may well cause serious problems.

**A Prolonged Gold Outflow.** Suppose gold continues to flow out of the country. Eventually, the gold reserve would fall to that minimum at which it was just equal to 25 per cent of Federal Reserve notes.[5] In theory, a further $1 loss in gold would force a 4:1 contraction in Federal Reserve notes.[6] In turn, this would force a 5:1 contraction in

[4] Refer to Table 11–1 and compare gold certificate reserves with Federal Reserve notes. These reserves more than fulfill the statutory minimum of 25 per cent gold to be held against Federal Reserve notes.

[5] A 25 per cent requirement against member bank reserve deposits was suspended by Congress recently owing largely to the shrinkage in the gold reserve. This avoided the possibility of a multiple decline in deposits of a type similar to that discussed in the text.

[6] Let us check this line of reasoning. When the Federal Reserve Banks reached this point, they would be forced to sell bonds (bills) to the public. If the public paid in currency withdrawn from member banks (say, Federal Reserve notes), other cash of member banks would decline. Therefore, the effect on the Federal Reserve Banks is to reduce an asset, bills, by $1 and Federal Reserve notes by $1. But this action is not sufficient. At least $4 worth of securities must be sold before Federal Reserve notes would be reduced to the proper level. For 25 per cent ($4) = $1, and thus, a $4 decline in this liability would eliminate the necessity for $1 in gold reserves. Evidently, such an action would take care of the deficiency of $1 in gold reserves, provided the bills were all paid for with Federal Reserve notes.

member bank deposits. Altogether this amounts to a 20:1 decline in member bank deposits. At the limit, therefore, a $1 million loss of gold would force a $20 million loss in member bank deposits. In reality, this effect is so drastic that Congress would intervene long before this point was reached. (In fact, certain adjustments have recently been made in the law for similar reasons. See footnote 5, this chapter.)

To make it clear why this is a significant problem consider the following additional fact. Foreigners hold, as of January 1965, about $25 billion of bank deposits and such short-term assets as Treasury bills maturing within a year or two. This amount exceeds our total monetary gold stock of about $15 billion (including free reserves of $6.5 billion). If foreigners should decide to use these deposits and short-term balances to acquire gold, they could easily buy up all our free reserves. In turn, this would precipitate a monetary crisis in which the monetary rules would have to be changed to avoid a 20:1 contraction in deposits.

At last we come to a significant question bearing upon current monetary policy. What effects do large foreign balances combined with our limited free reserves have on monetary policy? Briefly the answer is that the Federal Reserve is no longer entirely free to pursue an easy-money policy. In fact, such a policy could lead to further loss of gold in several ways. First, easy money is associated with low interest rates, and such rates might be unattractive to foreigners holding government bills. As a result, they might cash in some short-term assets, buy gold, and with the gold buy short-term assets in other countries at a higher rate of interest. To preclude this the Federal Reserve would have to keep money reasonably tight and the interest rate high enough to retain the investment of foreigners in these assets. However, this is probably a secondary consideration, because these differences in interest rates may not be very important to foreigners in deciding whether or not to hold their short-term assets in the United States.

Second, an easy monetary policy is normally conducive to an expansion of economic activity. Along with this comes a rise in the level of prices even before full employment has been reached. As prices rise in the United States compared to foreign countries, our consumers will buy more goods and services abroad and foreigners will purchase less here. In addition, the larger incomes of consumers arising out of the easy-money policy will prompt additional purchases abroad. As a result of these trends (imports rise relative to exports) the United States will owe a balance to foreigners. They may insist on a settlement in gold that would deplete our already slim reserve. To head this off the Federal Reserve may feel obliged to resort to tighter money. Then the economy could be stopped short of full employment.

In summary, gold flows responding to a disequilibrium in the balance of payments constitute an independent and uncontrolled source of variation in bank reserves and the money supply. A deficit disequilibrium that evokes an outflow of gold tends to reduce bank reserves and sets off a multiple contraction of deposit money. In turn, tighter credit conditions involve higher interest rates, reduced availability of credit, a decline in investment, and a contraction of *NNP*. To ease the situation the Federal Reserve is likely to initiate action that would lower interest rates with a view toward increasing investment and expanding *NNP*. However, lower interest rates may induce foreigners to convert assets into gold for investment abroad. This action appears to intensify the problem.

A prolonged gold outflow could lead to an enormous contraction in member bank deposits. With limited gold reserves and large foreign balances interest rates cannot be held as low and credit cannot be extended as readily as the employment situation at home would suggest in depressed periods. This implies that the Federal Reserve cannot use its full power to combat recessions or to stimulate the economy that has experienced a sluggish growth pattern. An economy performing in this manner is not likely to resolve the balance of payments problem that gave rise to the initial gold outflow.

Because gold flows arise, in part, from the presence of imbalances between foreign receipts and payments and in part from domestic instability, these conditions suggest the need for other adjustments. We have already discussed some alternative measures that would tend to reduce the deficit and, thereby, the outflow of gold. (In the next chapter we plan to introduce other measures.) In addition, a country can exercise control over the physical movement of goods. Let us see how this kind of action affects the balance of payments and domestic stability.

## COMMERCIAL MEASURES: DIRECT CONTROLS

A country can resort to direct controls over the movement of physical goods by imposing tariffs on trade. For example, an import deficit implying an excess of imports over exports could be resolved by raising tariffs on imports sufficiently to restore equality between the items. However, if countries are unequally endowed with resources leading to differing comparative advantages, trade will be mutually beneficial. Clearly, barriers to trade are harmful under these conditions.

It is evident from what has been said that countries do not purposely establish a trade policy with a view merely to imposing restrictions on the flow of goods. Such action would simply hurt consumers. Why, then, do countries devise schemes that restrict the free flow of trade? Well, primarily because of the self-interest of various industries that are subject to foreign competition. These industries are represented by powerful lobbyists who are able to sway political opinion in their favor. In addition, consumers, who normally suffer from the imposition of trade controls, are not sufficiently well organized to bring effective pressure to bear on politicians. In short, they tend to be passive, leaving a free field to various pressure groups.

**Some Basic Facts of Trade Controls.** There are several kinds of trade restrictions that a country may utilize. For example, import quotas may be established on either a country or commodity basis. In the former case, a predetermined quantity of imports is allocated among several countries for a stated period—say, one year. When the respective quotas have been met, imports cease. The same reasoning applies to commodities, if the quota system is patterned along these lines. The reader is probably familiar with the United States import quotas on petroleum, zinc, lead, cotton, sugar, and dairy products. Quotas are highly effective because they can completely halt the inflow of foreign goods once the quota is filled.

The following discussion will be confined to tariffs on imports mainly because of their historical significance and general application. A tariff amounts to a tax on imports. The importer must pay either an ad valorem tax, comprising a given percentage of the value of the imported good, or a specific duty, amounting to so many dollars and cents per physical unit of the imported item. Some countries may even combine these two devices. Tariffs are of two general types. They may be imposed principally to obtain revenue (a revenue tariff) or to restrict trade (protective tariff). The distinction is blurred and of historical interest only, because any tariff will yield some income and, at the same time, reduce imports. As the term implies, a revenue tariff serves as a source of government revenue. Normally, the rate is fairly low. Obviously, the intent of the protective tariff is to reduce imports. Historians tell us that United States tariff policy was primarily directed toward securing revenue up to the 1860's; thereafter tariff policy leaned toward protection.

**Effects of Tariffs on Imports.** Tariffs produce varying effects. We have already indicated possible revenue and protective effects. In addition, tariffs normally cause an alteration in the distribution of income. Let us see how these and other effects can influence the operation of the economy. We begin by noting the price of a certain product determined by domestic forces of demand and supply before

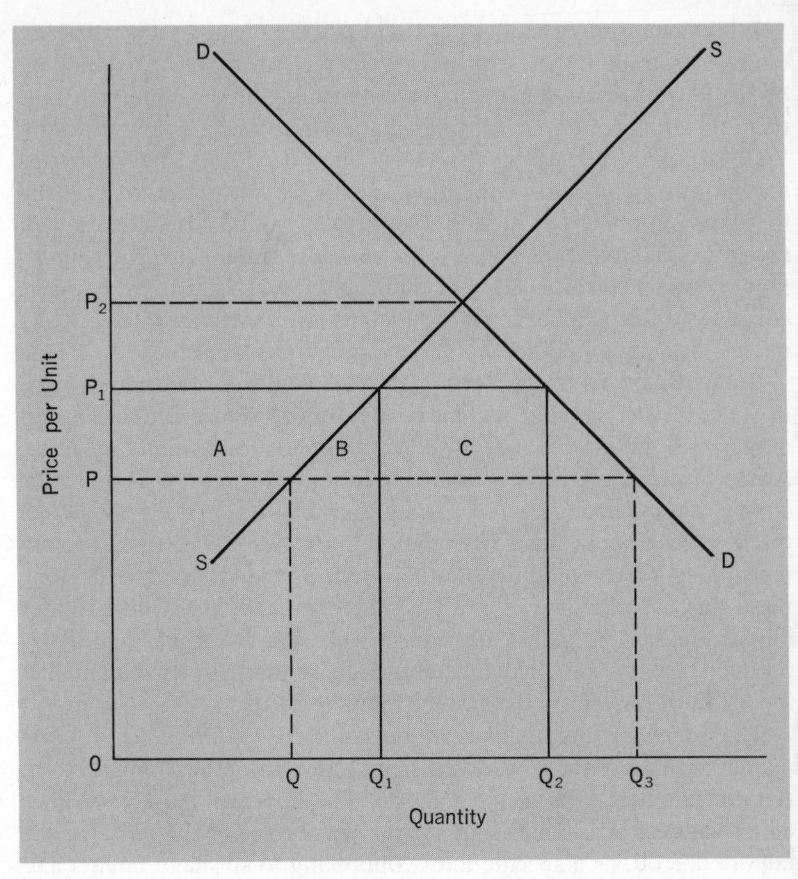


**Figure 26–1.** Effect of a tariff on imports.

trade commences. Such a price is indicated at $OP_2$ in Figure 26–1. Now let trade begin. Assuming that the world price for the commodity is lower initially than the domestic price, falling, say, at $OP$, then $OQ_3$ of the product is demanded and $OQ$ is supplied at home. The remainder, $QQ_3$, is imported.

Now for any one of a number of reasons to be explained shortly, a tariff is levied on the product. With the imposition of a specific duty amounting to $PP_1$ per unit, importers are obliged to pay the world price plus the tariff. Hence, importers will sell the product for $OP_1$. Reading across the line to the demand curve at this new, higher price we find that consumption of the product will decline from $OQ_3$ to $OQ_2$. On the supply side, domestic production will rise from $OQ$ to $OQ_1$, as price increases from $P$ to $P_1$. Consequently, domestic production rises, domestic consumption falls, and imports are reduced to $Q_1Q_2$.

**The Revenue Effect.** Government revenue increases by the amount of the customs receipts made possible by the tariff. The amount of the revenue is shown by the rectangular area labeled $C$ in Figure 26–1. This is equal to the tax per unit times the number of units imported, or $PP_1$ tax per unit times $Q_1Q_2$ units. Note, however, that the economy is less well off than before, because buyers of the imported goods will have to pay the amount of the tax and their consumption of the item has been reduced. In fact, we could defend with reasonable assurance a case for tax discrimination, because a tax for revenue purposes is borne mainly by the buyers of the product.

**The Protective and Redistributive Effects.** The protective effect is evident by the increased production at home in conjunction with the higher price. Domestic output increases by $QQ_1$ as the price rises from $P$ to $P_1$. Evidently some firms are being rewarded for inefficient production. This is the case since production costs (read off the supply curve) exceed price $P$ as output is increased by $QQ_1$. The triangular area $B$, lying to the right of the supply curve, measures the excess. The marginal producer, at $Q_1$, has production costs of $P_1$. He is just barely making a go of it with tariff protection.

It is evident from the above statements that income is being transferred from consumers to firms of the protected industry. All the firms except the marginal producer are receiving more profit than they need to maintain production. This increased profit to the industry is shown by the area labeled $A$, lying to the left of the supply curve.

The higher the tariff—that is, the closer the price moves toward $P_2$ in Figure 26–1—the greater is the burden shared by society. Of course, groups other than consumers feel the adverse effects of the tariff. Calling to mind earlier discussions, we remember that a reduction of a country's imports normally brings about a reduction in its exports. This clearly follows when other countries retaliate with corresponding tariff increases. However, similar results tend to occur even in the absence of retaliation. In fact, the proceeds received by foreigners from a reduced volume of exports fail to meet the cost of their imports. Of course, the tariff-imposing country may provide the means of payment by loans or grants. Nevertheless, we can expect that other countries will sooner or later demand the right to earn their own way.

Let's summarize our points on the general effects of tariffs: (1) The industry that receives tariff protection is benefited in that all firms are able to produce with reduced fear of competition from more efficient foreign producers. (2) Other industries are harmed, particularly the export industries. Although these goods are produced at relatively low costs, exporters are faced with declining sales. (3) Total domestic output is reduced because resources are diverted from products that enjoy a comparative advantage to those that do not. (4) Consumers pay a higher price for the imported product and obtain less of it.

If, on balance, tariffs tend to produce unfavorable effects, we may inquire why they are used. Our answer, couched in general terms, is that powerful self-interest groups often support tariff protection. Clearly, certain groups tend to gain from a tariff. For example, the protected industry cited above can charge higher prices, obtain greater profits, and employ more workers.

Specifically, there are a host of arguments in defense of the tariff. We would be remiss if we failed to examine some of them. The first argument is concerned with industry objectives; subsequent arguments, with national objectives.

**The Scientific Tariff.** This argument states that import duties should be high enough to equalize the cost of production at home and abroad. Suppose a product that costs 70 cents to produce in the United States can be imported for 40 cents. Accordingly, a 30-cent tariff is required to equalize costs and, thereby, maintain *fair* competition between American and foreign producers.

If the so-called scientific tariff is *scientific* in those cases in which it is applied, it presupposes a certain standard for determining costs. Consider this point and its possible effects. What is the standard for determining the costs of producers? Should costs be set on the basis of the lowest-cost producers presently engaged in supplying output? The highest-cost producers? Or, the highest cost of potential producers? Conceivably, the tariff could be applied at any point along the supply curve of Figure 26–1 between $P$ and $P_2$. At $P_2$ the principle of comparative advantage is ruled out completely. *Fair* competition is then resolved into *no* foreign competition. Obviously, the gains from trade would be zero.

Seemingly, the argument underscores two basic ideas, neither of which is valid. The first suggests that "what is good for a particular industry within a country is necessarily beneficial for the economy." This is an illogical form of reasoning, the results of which we have already cited. The second expresses the view that where foreign producers can undersell any American producer in any product whatsoever, the former's advantage should be nullified by our tariff. This approach can hardly be called scientific.

**Maintaining Full Employment.** It is sometimes argued that a tariff on imports can serve to push a stagnant economy to a higher level of employment. Suppose, for example, that United States imports are reduced in this manner and exports remain fairly constant. As explained earlier, this action tends to increase domestic demand, output, and employment. Although these effects temporarily benefit the United States, they work hardships in other countries, because a reduction of American imports puts people out of work abroad.



If a high-tariff policy is maintained for a lengthy period, we can expect other countries to retaliate with higher tariffs of their own. In turn, United States exports would decline, resulting in a lower volume of foreign trade. At this point the employment situation would probably have returned to much the same condition as before the original tariff change. With the reduction in trade, however, comes a failure to realize the fruits of comparative advantage. Real income will be reduced. This shortsighted policy ultimately reduces output without improving employment.

**High Wages and Income.** Tariff proponents explain that the only way to keep wage rates high is to restrict the inflow of goods and services produced by cheap foreign labor. Presumably, high wage rates in, say, the United States would be forced down because foreigners could undersell us in some lines. Tariffs are therefore needed to preserve high wage rates and a lofty plane of living. However, we recall that a high wage level is the result of high productivity. The United States wage level and plane of living are high because the productivity of American workers is high; restrictions against foreign competition are not required in such a situation. To illustrate: wages in the United States can be four times as high as in Italy, but the labor cost per unit of output will be no higher if each worker produces four times as much.

Basically, wage differences between the two countries mirror the differences in productivity per man-hour. Wages in the United States are high, then, because of greater skills, highly productive machines, and modern techniques. The point is this: wage differences are not to be feared. Indeed, they are necessary if countries of differing productivities are to compete on even terms. Clearly, the United States can undersell foreign countries in those lines where it has a comparative advantage; and wherever the United States has a comparative disadvantage foreign countries can undersell us. Thus, tariffs merely interfere with the ensuing gains.

**National Defense.** It can be argued that certain industries need tariff protection in order to remain intact during peacetime so that a ready supply of goods will be forthcoming should war break out. However, nearly every industry can demonstrate to some degree that it could and would contribute to a war effort. In other words, the argument can be carried too far. It is not difficult, for example, to show that the watch industry needs protection based upon this argument even though other industries are capable of producing excellent timing devices. But what about protection for the latter? As we can readily see, the need for protection on these grounds may be extended to the whole economy.

We may also question whether or not whole industries need protection during peacetime. An armed force of 12 to 16 million men and women may be required to fight a war, but only a small fraction of that number is on active duty in time of peace. Perhaps it is not advisable to grant protection to the entire watch industry cited above.

Clearly, all goods that we might want for war purposes need not be produced in the United States. Much strategic material can be stockpiled and some can be secured from foreign countries. Although tariffs applied on such goods would encourage domestic production, it would also reduce the future supply of these items. Even the fabulous resources of the United States can be reduced significantly, and some individual items may become seriously depleted unless suitable precautions are taken. For example, the maintenance of quotas on the importation of oil that drain domestic supplies tends to damage us in the long run. The unnecessary demands on our resources engendered by such quotas ultimately weaken the economy and reduce our military potential. In general, a country that cooperates with other nations tends to strengthen the national economy and to increase the military potential. Interdependence is, therefore, a mark of strength rather than weakness.

**Infant Industry.** Early economists, such as Friedrich List in Germany, Alexander Hamilton, and even some staunch free traders enunciated the benefits of protecting infant industries. The logic goes as follows: A nation with small but growing industries should be protected against competition from the more efficient industries of the highly industrialized countries. When the "infant" has gained experience sufficient to attain efficient operations, the tariff wall should be dismantled. Fundamentally, the argument applies to the less developed countries seeking a greater degree of industrialization. Today the countries of Africa, Asia, and Latin America make use of this argument, hoping by such a policy to expand their industrial base.

Although plausible in theory, the infant-industry argument encounters difficulties in application that shed doubts on the doctrine. According to this theory, tariff protection is to be granted an industry for some fairly definite period; permanent protection is not envisaged by the doctrine. Yet, such temporary tariffs for young industries never seem to be dropped. Protection granted the United States iron industry has been maintained on iron and steel products even as the steel industry matured. Apparently, experience under tariff protection becomes a customary way of doing things. Firms become accustomed to artificially high prices and large profits afforded by tariff protection. Therefore they resist a reduction in tariffs even though it was previously understood that they must face up to foreign competition at a later date.

It is taken for granted that protection is granted only those industries that offer prospects of becoming efficient—that is, that will at some time clearly possess a comparative advantage. Often there is no exact way of predicting in advance the prospects for new industries. In this connection, let us note that greater efforts aimed at defining areas of production where comparative advantage may be secured would tend to reduce the number of firms and industries seeking protection. In any event, this situation suggests the desirability of a flexible tariff policy with a view to relaxing tariff duties on those items where comparative advantage cannot be obtained by industries at the end of a reasonable trial period.

In retrospect, one finds it difficult to justify the above arguments on economic grounds. Some are based on false premises, and others are only partly valid.

We have discussed in this chapter only a limited number of policies aimed at promoting foreign trade and economic stability. Perhaps we have said enough to indicate that although there are numerous measures available to a country to achieve equilibrium in the balance of payments and to help restore balanced relations between income (*NNP*) and the balance of payments, the one best choice is not a matter of indifference. Apparently, the choice should fall on that measure or combination of measures that would tend to yield the best results in terms of a high level of domestic output and employment and a large volume of trade.

**Summary.** The discussion centered on the balance of payments, because we wanted to emphasize the effects of trade. Recognizing that it is natural for a country to give first priority to national goals, we examined each measure in terms of how it might affect the performance of the domestic economy. In each instance a deficit disequilibrium in the balance of payments was assumed to exist at the outset.

By examining income changes initiated by an autonomous increase in imports it is clear that—under the conditions given—an equilibrium *NNP* would be established at a lower level of economic activity and a trade deficit of some amount would still exist. Internal measures (monetary and fiscal) would be directed to reversing this trend in income, particularly if the economy is already operating below full-employment *NNP*. Although the "foreign effect" would alter the above conditions, the final outcome is uncertain.

Several measures were considered in the discussion of measures for alleviating monetary disequilibrium. At a given rate of exchange a lowering of domestic prices in response to a sharp rise in imports relative to exports imposes strict demands on the economy. Even if successful in evoking a rise in exports relative to imports and restoring equilibrium in the balance of payments, the decline in domestic prices could adversely affect a currently depressed economy.

Reducing the value of a country's currency would tend to cause imports to fall relative to exports. However, the results of this action are not entirely clear. The success of depreciation depends on several factors: the response in physical items traded, the types of goods given up where imports are reduced, and so forth.

Disinflation and depreciation involve the use of mixed measures where inflation is present. Clearly, this combination of measures requires a certain precision, the limits of error being extremely narrow.

Although loans and grants are not conceived as measures in the sense used here, additional grants or loans to offset the increased imports would have the effect of extending the adjustment period. In the meantime the affected country could develop measures needed to correct the problem.

Gold movements constitute a major independent and uncontrolled source of variation in bank reserves and the money supply. A prolonged gold outflow in response to a payments balance would lead to an enormous contraction in member bank deposits. Consequently, monetary policy cannot be applied with full impact where the domestic economy is performing at a low level of output.

We discussed the general effects of tariffs. In addition, we sought out some of the various arguments for tariffs, discussing them in terms of industry and national objectives. These arguments are difficult to justify on economic grounds.

## QUESTIONS

1. What is meant by a deficit disequilibrium? Review the explanation of *Changing the Level of Economic Activity*. Note the income (or cyclical) effect of an autonomous increase in imports (import deficit). Comment on the application of measures to be employed to encourage aggregate demand to rise closer to full-employment *NNP*.
2. Would lowering the domestic price level probably be an effective way of eliminating a balance of payments deficit? What objections are there to its use?
3. A country might depreciate its currency to achieve equilibrium in the balance of payments previously disturbed by an increase in imports. Explain.
4. Consider an economy plagued by inflation. How might disinflation and depreciation contribute toward achieving domestic and external stability?
5. In what way does the receipt of loans and grants benefit a country experiencing a temporary deficit in the balance of payments?

**6.** Suppose the Treasury buys a new shipment of gold from a foreign government amounting to $1 million. Trace changes in bank reserves and the money supply effected by this transaction. (Refer to Tables 26–1 and 26–2.) If the reserve ratio is 20 per cent, by how much would total deposits increase as a result of the original gold purchase of $1 million? Can you explain the possibility of a multiple contraction in member bank deposits (20:1) in the case of a prolonged gold outflow?

**7.** Discuss the following statement: An outflow of gold tends to require countervailing action by the Federal Reserve.

**8.** Examine the revenue, protective, and redistributive effects of a tariff on imports. (Refer to Figure 26–1.) Discuss the pros and cons of the arguments in defense of the tariff.

CHAPTER

# 27

# Restoring Equilibrium in the United States Balance of Payments

Up to this point we have been searching for ways, consistent with both domestic stability and a large volume of trade, by means of which a country may correct a disequilibrium in its balance of payments. In this regard, we found in the last chapter that any one measure may yield indeterminate results. However, certain measures tend to produce more or less definite effects. For example, if direct controls over trade are applied generally, they nearly always result in a less than maximum level of income (*NNP*) and a reduced volume of trade. In any event, we know that the selection of measures is not a matter of indifference when it comes to practical application. The choice is further complicated by political and social considerations that enter into the determination of measures to be employed.

For the reasons cited, we should understand at the outset of this discussion that a consensus of agreement has not been reached as to which measures will yield the best results in terms of an equilibrium in the balance of payments and a high level of domestic output. Thus, the following discussion concerning the United States is not intended to produce any one best answer. However, we will discuss the problem of restoring equilibrium in the light of recent experience and offer approaches to the problem similar to those outlined in Chapter 26.

## THE NATURE OF THE PROBLEM

Because the pattern of the American balance of payments has not changed materially in recent years, we will use the experience of

1964 as the basis for a review of the subject. Table 27–1 is set up for this purpose. It is a condensed version of the United States International Balance of Payments, presented in Chapter 24. The significance of this summary is indicated by the figures in the column headed "Balance." Note the individual balances on the current and capital accounts. Clearly, the current account failed to develop a net credit balance as large as the net outflow of long-term capital. The deficiency amounted to $2.8 billion, shown by the combined net balance on current and capital accounts. The difference was settled by the combined short-term capital and gold flows (including errors and omissions), shown by the net balance on settlement type transactions.

It is interesting to note that the disequilibrium, or more correctly the indication of disequilibrium, for this one year, differs from that of many countries. In this regard, we observe that the current account reveals a receipts balance of some $4.1 billion, rather than a payments balance typical of some countries. However, because net long-term capital outflows (capital account) exceeded the surplus earned on current transactions—after making the proper deduction for unilateral transfers—(current account), the difference resulted in a net payments balance on these two major accounts. This led to an inflow of short-term capital and a loss of gold.

**TABLE 27–1**
**A Summary of the United States Balance of Payments, 1964 (Billions of Dollars)**

| Item | Receipts (+) | Payments (−) | Balance |
|---|---|---|---|
| Current Account | | | |
| Private transactions | 34.7 | 24.9 | +9.8 |
| Government transactions | 1.3 | 7.0 | −5.7 |
| Net balance, current account | | | +4.1 |
| Capital Account | | | |
| Net balance, capital account | | 6.9 | −6.9 |
| Net balance, current and capital accounts | | | −2.8 |
| Settlement Transactions | | | |
| Short-term capital movements | 5.7 | 2.1 | +3.6 |
| Gold | 0.1 | | +0.1 |
| Errors and omissions | | 0.9 | −0.9 |
| Net balance, settlement transactions | | | +2.8 |

Clearly, the deficit cannot continue unabated. The above summary of the accounts suggests the need for corrective measures to bring about the desired adjustment to equilibrium. Apparently, efforts should be directed to increasing exports, decreasing imports, widening the gap between rising exports and rising imports, reducing long-term capital outflows, and/or unilateral transfers or some combination tending to result in an equality between total receipts and total payments of the two major accounts.

Viewing the apparent disequilibrium from a monetary standpoint, we cannot expect foreigners to hold short-term claims of unlimited amounts for lengthy periods. As stated earlier, they are likely to convert their short-term assets into gold and with the gold build up their balances abroad. Hence, a large withdrawal could lead to exchange depreciation or even exchange controls unless some other measures would produce successful results. In view of this situation—and the fact that an expansion of money will be needed to facilitate future growth of output—Congress passed legislation that resulted in a larger free gold reserve to help meet this contingency. Of course, if annual losses continue for an indefinite period, the gold reserve would fall to that minimum at which it was just equal to 25 per cent of Federal Reserve notes. Any further loss would probably force the United States to cut loose from the 25-per-cent reserve rule against Federal Reserve notes.

Perhaps the most significant point to be raised in connection with the disequilibrium is the fact that the foreign trade sector of the economy has become an important factor in determining domestic economic policy. Thus, freedom of action in the area of economic policy making is limited by the deficit in the balance of payments. We saw that the Federal Reserve is no longer entirely free to pursue an easy-money policy when gold continues to flow out of the country. In short, gold outflows tend to reduce bank deposits. This action restricts the money supply and exerts upward pressure on interest rates. The latter discourages business investment and leads to a decline in income (*NNP*) and employment. Thus a chain of events is set off, moving the economy to a lower level of economic activity.

## RESTORING EQUILIBRIUM: SOME ALTERNATIVE APPROACHES

What can be done to head off the adverse consequences of a deficit disequilibrium? Well, several proposals have been offered as possible remedies. In the last chapter we examined policies that might bring about an equilibrium in the balance of payments. Here we plan to analyze certain measures in detail to see how they might reduce trade deficits and contribute to economic stability.[1]

[1] For the sake of conserving space we will not make reference to short-run versus long-run (structural) causes and remedies associated with a deficit disequilibrium. However, the choice of measures would be influenced by identifying short- and long-run sources of disequilibrium.

Before proceeding further we want to set out the criteria to be used as guidelines in appraising the possible effects of the policies to be considered. We can do this merely by adding to the propositions established in the last chapter the requirement of a liberal trade policy. Our goal is, then, to eliminate the United States balance of payments deficit by measures that are consistent with domestic stability and a liberal trade policy.[2] Now let us examine the various measures.

**Hold the Line.** This approach suggests that we maintain a wait-and-see attitude in contrast to the imposition of stringent measures that might result in long-run instability and a reduced volume of trade. This reasoning is based on the assumption that market forces will eliminate the deficit before a serious crisis develops. Thus, the accumulation of international reserves [3] in a given period, secured by an excess of receipts over payments, can be drawn down in a subsequent period when payments exceed receipts. Accordingly, the vast accumulation of international reserves by the United States during the period 1940–58 have been drawn upon since the latter date.

Now the loss of reserves is attributable to economic conditions at home and abroad. Among the factors that account for our deficit and, thus, loss of reserves, the following two are especially important. They are (1) the rapid increase in productivity of Western Europe and Japan, and (2) domestic inflation in the United States, tending to cause our exports to be sluggish. Although these point up serious problems with respect to the American balance of payments situation, proponents of this approach inform us that certain changes have already set in that will reverse this trend. The restoration and growth of the Western European and Japanese economies have resulted in an increase in demand for United States goods. Also, the rise in prices of our closest competitors abroad has been greater than ours in recent years. These changing trends may cause our exports to rise at a faster rate. In turn, the rise in exports may become sufficient to reverse the flow of international reserves, resulting in a more favorable situation for the United States. According to this line of thought, our best bet is to wait things out.

Although the above is a plausible argument, it appears to stand on somewhat shaky grounds. First, any changes that have occurred probably did not come about automatically; that is, they were accompanied by certain actions at home and in foreign countries that resulted in these changed conditions. Because it is difficult to predict what form these actions will take in the future, we have little assurance of the outcome. Hence, a more positive course is suggested.

[2] We include the phrase *a liberal trade policy* because it appears to express the United States' attitude toward trade. This attitude was reaffirmed by Congress in the passage of the Trade Expansion Act of 1962.

[3] These are held mainly in the form of gold and foreign exchange.

Second, and more to the point, there is little indication that our export surplus will grow very much in the absence of a determined effort by American firms to introduce a more advanced technology and to expand foreign markets. For these and other reasons more positive measures are indicated.

**Depreciation of the Dollar.** We could depreciate the dollar relative to other currencies. Recalling earlier discussion, we know that this action reduces the value of a country's currency relative to foreign currencies. Thus, depreciation of the dollar would tend to lower the price level *relative* to other national price levels. Because American goods become cheaper to foreigners and foreign goods become dearer to Americans, our exports would tend to increase and imports would tend to decrease, alleviating or possibly eliminating the deficit in our balance of payments. Let us check recent experience of the United States in this regard.

**TABLE 27-2***
**Price Movements, Selected Countries, 1963 Versus 1958 (1958 = 100)**

| Index | United States | Belgium | France | Western Germany | Italy | Japan | United Kingdom |
|---|---|---|---|---|---|---|---|
| Consumer prices | 106 | 106 | 105 | 112 | 117 | 127 | 112 |
| Wholesale prices for finished goods | 101 | na† | 119 | 107 | 107‡ | 101‡ | 108 |
| Export prices, unit value | 103 | 96 | 115 | 101 | 95 | 96 | 105 |

* Source: United Nations, **Monthly Bulletin of Statistics,** March 1965.
† Not available.
‡ Producers' goods.

An examination of index numbers of money prices shows that the price level of the United States has risen less than many foreign countries. In Table 27–2 the consumer price index rose less in the United States between 1958 and 1963 than in any other country in the list except France and Belgium; the latter country exhibited the same price rise as the United States. The trend in the wholesale price index shows similar results, prices in the United States and Japan having risen less than other countries in the list. Apparently, the United States did not fare so well in the unit value of export prices. Export prices of all countries in the list rose less than the United States, with the exception of only two countries, France and the United Kingdom. Of course, each of these indicators is defective for various reasons. For example, the consumer price index fails to include prices of producers goods; the wholesale price index is restricted to finished goods; and although the export price is fairly comprehensive, it and the other indexes reflect average price trends. Barring these limitations, the figures appear to support the thesis that, although we had some inflation in the United States, it was probably even more pronounced in foreign countries. However, the rise in export prices indicates that our export industries became less competitive. Let us pursue this point further.

If we turn to sectoral prices, we find that prices of certain goods have risen relative to those of some foreign countries. This has been the case with respect to steel and our various machinery industries. The data in Table 27–3 point up this trend in sectoral prices. Labor costs rose in the basic metal industries of the United States by 20 per cent between 1953 and 1960. Although labor costs also rose in Germany and Japan, the rise was much less than in the United States. In the remaining countries—Belgium, France, and Italy—labor costs actually declined during the period. Similar results could be shown with respect to the industrial raw materials industries.

During the period 1953–60, the greater-than-average rise of labor costs in the American metals industries resulted from wage increases greater than the average rise of wages in manufacturing, whereas gains in productivity were less than for manufacturing as a whole. Relative to the other countries our increase in labor costs was primarily the result of a much slower increase in productivity.

**TABLE 27–3***
**Index of Productivity, Earnings, and Labor Costs in Basic Metal Industries, Selected Countries, 1960 Versus 1953 (1953 = 100)**

| Item | United States | Belgium | France | Germany | Italy | Japan |
|---|---|---|---|---|---|---|
| Output per man-hour | 115 | 146 | 163 | 146 | 212 | 153 |
| Hourly earnings | 137 | 131 | 135 | 161 | 136 | 159 |
| Labor costs | 120 | 90 | 83 | 110 | 64 | 104 |

* Source: Bela Balassa, "Recent Developments in the Competitiveness of American Industry and Prospects for the Future," Joint Economic Committee, **Factors Affecting the United States Balance of Payments,** 87th Congress, 2nd Session (Washington, D.C.: U.S. Government Printing Office, 1962), p. 38.

Prices of basic metals affect export prices, because the items in question provide raw materials for machinery and transport industries. The products of these industries make up about one half of world exports of manufactures. Thus, our trade balance could improve if some firms and industries made greater efforts to increase productivity while holding costs in line with these gains.

In agriculture our productivity is extremely high compared to that of other countries. Yet world trade in agriculture is marked by nationalistic controls designed to protect vested interests of farmers in each country. Consequently, despite a very favorable competitive position in these goods—which account for one quarter of our total exports—the United States cannot achieve large export surpluses. In the absence of these controls our exports would probably increase greatly.

United States imports have been rising, though erratically, in recent years. Increased purchases from abroad are explained by various factors: lower costs of certain foreign goods, including some that we normally export—barbed wire, transistor radios, toys, and so on—increased domestic income, and a change in taste in favor of foreign goods. As stated earlier, it seems that as a nation becomes wealthier it tends to import more goods, and people seek a greater variety of items.

Is currency depreciation a suitable remedy to this problem? Normally, the immediate effect would be a decline in our imports and a rise in our exports. Subject to qualifications set out in the last chapter, the effects would probably be favorable in the short run. However, if export prices rise because of such factors as the failure of firms to employ the latest equipment available, depreciation may yield unfavorable effects in the long run. Because export prices of some American goods have been rising relative to those of other countries, depreciation may not be beneficial. Moreover, it is possible that foreign countries may follow the lead of the United States in this policy. If several countries depreciate by the same proportionate amount, the canceling effect would leave them in the same position as before, with the original rates of exchange in force. Because the volume of trade is not likely to change much in this situation, the United States deficit would continue to exist. Only where foreign countries accept our depreciation as desirable will the policy work.

Instead of depreciating the dollar in relation to other currencies we might *devalue the dollar in relation to gold.* Suppose the dollar price of gold is doubled or, what is the same thing, the value of the dollar in terms of gold is cut in half. The dollar is therefore devalued. Under the assumed conditions only one half of the present gold reserve would be needed to satisfy the gold reserve requirement; that is, the requirement that Federal Reserve Banks hold a 25-per-cent reserve in gold against Federal Reserve notes. Thus, devaluation increases free gold reserves, which gives freedom of maneuver to the Federal Reserve Banks—that is, it increases potential liquidity.

Why do we hesitate to devalue the dollar? Well, one reason is that devaluation would jeopardize the dollar as a key currency. A large part of the international reserves of many countries are held in dollars. Devaluation would force large losses upon these countries that are relying on the stability of the dollar. In addition, the political and psychological effects of the weakness thus demonstrated would tend to threaten the leadership of the United States. Perhaps the most devastating result of devaluation would be an undermining of the world trade and payments system. This system functions best when it is tied to stable currency units.

If the above observations are correct, depreciation and devaluation are not likely to be used, particularly where other measures may provide relief. Depreciation may not be desirable, because the price level has not been rising faster than national price levels in many foreign countries. Also, other countries might respond to a depreciation of the dollar by depreciating their currencies. This action could result in a reduced volume of trade and a decline in incomes (*NNP*s). Devaluation could weaken the position of the dollar as a key currency and threaten the economic leadership of the United States. For these and other reasons unilateral depreciation of the dollar in relation to other currencies and devaluation of the dollar in relation to gold are usually considered as measures of last resort, used only if other measures fail to produce desirable results.

**General Devaluation.** If unilateral devaluation by the United States is rejected and a shortage of gold reserves exists generally, major countries could raise the price of gold by overt agreement. Were they to double the price from, say, $35 to $70 per ounce, the value of the world's gold reserves would automatically double. The purpose of this action would be to increase the world's international liquidity. At the end of the third quarter of 1964 total world reserves amounted to approximately $84.3 billion—gold: $40.5; foreign exchange: $25.6; and gross *IMF* positions (holdings of the several countries with the International Monetary Fund): $18.2.[4] Thus, doubling the price of gold would raise total world reserves to about $124.8 billion—that is, $84.3 billion (total world reserves) plus $40.5 billion (increase in world gold reserves effected by doubling the price of gold). Hence, total world reserves would rise by nearly 50 per cent. Countries with deficits accompanied by outflows of gold (United States) would then have a larger cushion of international reserves. A doubling of the United States gold reserves (from $15 to $30 billion) would greatly reduce the fear of potential gold outflows in the immediate future and relieve the threat of an enormous multiple contraction of the money supply associated with a prolonged outflow of gold.

Perhaps the most serious aspect of general devaluation is the fact

[4] United Nations, *International Financial Statistics,* February 1965, pp. 16–19.

that it would not eliminate, in itself, recurring deficits in the balance of payments. In turn, the existence of a deficit might reduce the effectiveness of monetary policy. Consider these points. Now general devaluation would increase the gold reserve of the United States; however, it would not necessarily produce adjustments in our trade accounts to restore equilibrium. Certain measures (or actions) are usually employed to bring about desired changes in the international accounts. In the absence of these measures the trade deficit would continue to exist. Until the deficit was eliminated authorities might hesitate to use an easy-money policy to bring about expansion of economic activity in time of recession, because the anticipated rise in income would lead to a rise in imports without affecting exports immediately. The resulting deficit would tend to grow larger, necessitating increased gold outflows. In short, increased liquidity will not permit the correction of a trade deficit and a policy to counter recession at the same time.

One other drawback is worthy of mention. General devaluation tends to yield unequal blessings, benefiting most those countries with large gold holdings (United States and Russia) and gold mining countries—for example, South Africa. Countries that normally have small amounts of gold are not likely to be enthusiastic at the prospect of general devaluation.

**Appreciation of Foreign Currencies.** We might hope that foreign countries would ease the burden of adjustment by appreciating their currencies in terms of the dollar rather than the United States' depreciating its currency. Perhaps there is some justification in this proposal. First, our deficit disequilibrium means a surplus disequilibrium in certain foreign countries conducting trade with us. These are the countries that would presumably appreciate their currencies. The presence of a surplus disequilibrium indicates an *undervaluation* of these currencies against the dollar.[5] Appreciation would therefore realign the values of currencies at home and abroad.

Undervaluation occurs if, over a series of years, we find that there was a significant inflow of gold and dollars into these countries. Thus, a higher price for a foreign currency in terms of the dollar would help to bring about an equilibrium in such a country's balance of payments. Exactly the opposite set of conditions obtain in the United States. Accordingly, the term *overvaluation* applies to the United States. We found that over a series of years there was a large outflow of gold and dollars associated with deficits. Therefore, it would take a lower price of dollars in terms of foreign currencies to restore equilibrium in our balance of payments.

[5] *Undervaluation* is a money expression applied to currencies of foreign countries that have surpluses in their trade with the United States.

Second, some part of the surpluses occurred because of large American expenditures abroad in the form of loans and grants for economic development. Also military aid relieved foreign countries of some of the burden of national defense and, thereby, freed some of their resources for expanding private output. The upshot of this is that the United States was able to develop an export surplus large enough to make transfers in the form of real items (goods). However, this required import deficits of foreign countries by the same amount. As a group, foreign countries did not develop deficits to this extent. As these countries found surpluses accompanying economic recovery, they used some of their receipts to buy gold and to build up short-term claims (purchased securities and increased bank balances) in the United States.

It is argued, therefore, that the surplus countries should reciprocate for American aid by appreciating their currencies. This action would cause their imports to rise relative to exports. Presumably, United States exports to these countries would rise relative to imports, reducing the deficit in our balance of payments.

Assuming that foreign countries want to maintain domestic stability at a high level of output and to expand trade, they may not find it desirable to appreciate their currencies at this time. To explain: in countries where few idle resources exist appreciation is likely to be self-defeating. Such a move would increase imports relative to exports, reduce demand for domestically produced goods, and reduce employment. These results tend to run counter to a policy aimed at maximum production and full employment.

On the other hand countries where idle resources are present can be expected to make an effort to expand output to higher levels. This is more consistent with a rise in exports relative to imports rather than the reverse movement of trade, which normally brings appreciation.

There are other reasons to explain why countries may not want to appreciate their currencies. Some countries would probably be reluctant to increase the value of their currencies relative to the dollar —that is, to lower exchange rates in terms of the dollar—because the new rate may later prove to be too low (or too high), necessitating further rate changes. In addition, measures other than appreciation are available, and some would not require changes in exchange rates.

**Higher Tariff Duties.** It would be a relatively simple matter for the government to raise tariff duties on imports sufficiently to reduce, or eliminate completely, the deficit in our balance of payments. However, recalling to mind the general effects of tariffs in Chapter 26, the decision to raise tariffs is complicated by factors tending to produce unfavorable results at home.

Although the precise effects of a given increase in tariff duties depend on many factors, including the present level of the tariff, increased rates may be met by foreign retaliation.

At this juncture we can add the fact that the imposition of tariffs tends to disrupt cost–price relationships by altering the price of imports previously set by market demand and supply conditions. Thus, tariffs tend to interfere with private trade transactions.

In terms of the criteria set forth in the earlier part of this chapter it is not difficult to understand that tariffs tend to cause a misallocation of resources, domestic instability, and a reduced volume of trade. For these reasons, and in view of the effort the United States has put into the multilateral reduction of tariffs since the war, it is unlikely that the United States would resort to higher tariffs as a primary measure to eliminate the balance of payments deficit.

Although any one of the measures cited would tend to correct a deficit in the balance of payments, the United States has avoided their use in recent years. We have indicated some of the reasons why these measures might prove to be ineffective. Now let us examine measures that have been used lately for the purpose of relieving the balance of payments problem in the immediate future.

## RESTORING EQUILIBRIUM: RECENT MEASURES TO REDUCE THE UNITED STATES DEFICIT

As might be expected, numerous measures have been put into effect in the last few years for the purpose of reducing the payments deficit. We will merely point out some of these measures, discussing them in terms of the basic elements in the balance of payments.[6] Recalling the nature of the United States balance of payments problem, improvement in the deficit involves either a reduction in the (net) outflow of long-term capital or an increase in the current account surplus.

**Exports of Goods and Services.** Although receipts earned from transactions in goods and services were larger than payments incurred for similar transactions, the (net) receipts balance on private account ($9.8 billion) was too small in 1964 to effect an equilibrium in our balance of payments. Certain measures have been (and are being) devised to remedy this situation. In an effort to assist private businesses in enlarging sales abroad a National Export Expansion Program was established by the Federal Government (1960). Specifically, the government has stepped up export promotion by improving com-

[6] For a more detailed explanation of the points made here refer to the *Economic Report of the President,* annual issues, January 1961–65.

mercial services abroad, establishing trade centers in foreign countries, planning trade fairs, improving the trade mission program, and working with businessmen on export opportunities through field offices of the Department of Commerce and Small Business Administration.

In this same connection, the Export-Import Bank began a new program of export credit insurance and guarantees (1962). The former makes available export credit insurance to American businesses covering both political and credit risks on short- and medium-term credit sales. The latter consists of guarantees issued to financial institutions that finance exporters' medium-term credit sales. The program enables exporters to apply for assistance through local banks.

Opportunities for negotiating lower foreign tariff duties have been strengthened by the passage of the Trade Expansion Act (1962). The government intends to use the authority granted to secure more liberal access to foreign markets for our agricultural and industrial products.

The United States Travel Service of the Department of Commerce (created in 1961) launched the "See America Now" program in 1963 to encourage foreigners to travel more in this country. This program is expected to increase purchases of some of our current output of goods and services and expand our foreign exchange holdings as larger numbers of foreigners visit the United States.

Some of the following measures will also tend to encourage the expansion of our exports.

**Government Loans and Grants.** The existence of the balance of payments deficit has necessitated certain actions to reduce the dollar outflow of foreign aid programs. (Note that government grants and long-term loans totaled $4.5 billion in 1964.) Aid agencies have been instructed to tie military and development aid directly to the purchase of United States goods and services wherever possible. In 1963 the Agency for International Development was able to get foreign countries to spend over 80 per cent of their new grants on American-made goods. In addition, efforts are being made to return to the United States much defense procurement. In this regard, some of our allies (for example, Germany and Italy) have agreed to offset all or a part of our military expenditures in their countries by increased purchases of American defense materiel.

Measures directed to conserving dollar expenditures abroad include, in addition, increased spending by other industrial countries to institute or strengthen their aid programs to less developed countries. Arrangements were made recently among several industrial countries to help underwrite the development programs of India and Pakistan. Also, some countries, notably Western Germany, France, and the

Netherlands, have made advance repayments of long-term debts owed the United States government. In this same regard, we have secured advance payments for future delivery of military items from some of the allied countries. These actions help strengthen the liquidity position of the United States.

**Private Long-Term Investment.** Transactions of this type revealed a net outflow of private capital amounting to $4.3 billion in 1964. Clearly, a reduction in this item would serve to reduce the deficit. This could be achieved either by a reduction of American investment abroad or by an increase of foreign investment in the United States. Let us note first how United States foreign investment might be discouraged by certain modifications of tax rules. We will then consider possible ways of increasing foreign investment in the United States.

Income earned abroad by foreign corporations where American shareholders own 50 per cent or more of the outstanding stock is now taxable at United States income tax rates in the current year even though actual distribution of the earnings is deferred until later. Not only does this discourage some foreign investment, it permits a certain equality in tax treatment between American firms operating abroad and competing firms in the United States.

Other legislation has been put into effect that reduces the "tax haven" privilege connected with foreign investment. It includes the tax on profits derived abroad by foreign subsidiaries of American corporations and distributed as dividends at full domestic corporation income tax less a tax credit for income tax payments made abroad; removal of tax advantages granted to investment companies created in foreign countries; restrictions on the exemption from United States taxes on earned income of American citizens establishing their residence abroad; and so forth. However, these provisions do not apply to American investment in less developed areas. This policy is in keeping with our intention to provide investment funds for the economic development of these countries.

The President asked the Congress (in February 1965) to extend the Interest Equilization Tax (IET) through 1967, and to broaden its coverage to nonbank credit of one-year to three-year maturity. This tax tends to restrict United States investment in foreign securities. In effect, IET amounts to an excise tax on American purchasers of new or outstanding foreign stocks and bonds equivalent to 1 per cent increase in interest cost. In addition to other measures, the President called on the Federal Reserve System, in cooperation with the Treasury, to work with all banks to limit lending to foreigners that is not directly for the purpose of financing exports of United States goods and services.

Although our points relate to the possible discouragement of some American investment abroad, we should mention the fact that the Revenue Act of 1962 contained certain "tax credit" privileges to encourage private domestic investment. Now let us turn our attention to some of the ways in which we have been trying to attract foreign capital.

The United States government is urging friendly countries, particularly those in Western Europe, to facilitate investment abroad by their residents so that more of their capital can be made available in the United States and less developed countries. In this connection, the United States Treasury has expanded its foreign exchange operations by issuing medium-term, nonmarketable securities whose face value is stated in terms of foreign currencies—for example, in pounds or francs. By selling these bonds abroad the Treasury acquires supplies of foreign currencies for its various needs.

The above measures should have two effects: (1) a reduction in net capital outflows, and (2) a strengthening of the domestic economy by attracting a large supply of investment funds.

**Private Short-Term Investment and Gold.** These items comprise the settlement items in the balance of payments. They reveal the magnitude of the deficit and indicate the change in the international liquidity position of the dollar. The relation of settlement items to the payments deficit for 1964 is shown in Table 27–4. Here we regard borrowing less lending and gold as constituting an offset to the deficit—that is, they come into being to an extent called for by the deficit. Because economists suspect that errors and omissions consist mainly of "flight capital" that does not get recorded, we list these transactions as the short-term lending item. However, this group of items gives rise to changes in our short-term assets and liabilities with foreign countries. Thus, by arranging the items to show changes in assets and liabilities, we can view the change in the United States' liquidity position. The net effect of short-term capital movements and gold flow was to cause a reduction in monetary assets and an increase in short-term liabilities, and by the same magnitude ($2.8 billion).

We noted earlier that the Export-Import Bank offers export credit insurance and guarantees on short- and medium-term credit sales. Not only do these services increase exports; they also provide assurance of short-term funds to businessmen, and thereby act as a stimulant to continued production for export. On the other hand much short-term capital moves in response to other criteria—for example, interest rate differentials, possible changes in exchange rates, and certain regulations. Monetary and Treasury officials have been devising policies in cooperation with foreign central banks to reduce the impact of shifts of this kind of capital between financial centers For example, high interest rates in Europe were lowered in late 1960 and early 1961. At about the same time the Federal Reserve System and the Federal Deposit Corporation raised permissible interest rates on commercial bank time deposits.

In 1962 the Federal Reserve System began to operate in foreign exchange markets on the System's own account. In carrying out its operation the System enters into "swap" arrangements, where equivalent currency claims on, and liabilities to, other central banks can be

**TABLE 27-4**
**United States Balance of Payments Deficit and Change in the Liquidity Position of the Dollar, 1964 (Billions of Dollars)**

| Item | Amount | Item | Amount | Total |
|---|---|---|---|---|
| **Basic Deficit:** | | | | |
| Deficit (sum of current and capital account net balances) | | | | −2.8 |
| Offset to deficit | | | | |
| Short-term borrowing (net) | | | 3.6 | |
| Short-term lending (errors and omissions) | | | −0.9 | |
| Gold outflow | | | 0.1 | |
| Total | | | | 2.8 |
| Decrease in Monetary Reserve Assets * | | Increase in Liquid Liabilities * | | |
| Gold | 0.13 | Short-term official and banking liabilities and foreign holdings of marketable U.S. government bonds and notes | 2.22 | |
| Convertible currencies | −0.22 | U.S. nonmarketable, convertible bonds and notes | 0.38 | |
| IMF position | 0.29 | | | |
| | 0.20 | | 2.60 | |
| Change in United States liquidity position | | | | 2.8 |

* Figures taken from **Survey of Current Business,** March 1965, p. 12.

created by mutual consent. Thus erratic outflows of short-term capital may be compensated in part by making foreign exchange available to the System. These actions help stabilize the value of the dollar.

With respect to gold, regulations prohibiting the holding of gold in the United States were extended to holdings of gold abroad by individuals and businesses subject to the jurisdiction of the United States. This action reduces private accumulations of gold and augments official holdings.

In an effort to moderate the temporary drain of gold the International Monetary Fund (IMF) has sold gold to the United States. The sale of gold was beneficial to the IMF in that it enlarged the income earning assets of this institution. The IMF has also made available to the United States a stand-by drawing, or line of credit, arrangement. Consider how this arrangement would tend to reduce the gold outflow.

The IMF has certain financial arrangements with member countries.[7] To summarize: members create a pool of funds with the IMF in the form of quotas consisting of their own currencies, foreign exchange, and gold. The percentage for each is set forth in the regulations. The several countries may borrow from the IMF other foreign currencies or gold that they need in order to make current payments. However, the prescribed percentages of total holdings in the IMF must be maintained. In recent years many countries that have repayments to make to the IMF have not been able to use additional dollars, because the dollar part of their total holdings has already been met. Therefore, these countries have had to seek either to buy gold from the United States or to sell dollars for other currencies in foreign markets that are acceptable to the IMF. Now the stand-by drawing arrangement permits the United States to draw other currencies that it can sell, for dollars, to countries needing them. This tends to lessen the purchase of gold from the United States and to strengthen the dollar in foreign markets.

Although we have not exhausted the various measures presently in use to reduce the deficit in the United States balance of payments, we have demonstrated that much is being done to bring about this result. Clearly, some of the measures, particularly those relating to short-term capital and gold movements, are employed chiefly to maintain the international liquidity of the dollar (that is, to stabilize monetary reserves), whereas others are used mainly to reduce the deficit.

It is clear that if certain measures discussed in the first part of this chapter were employed, they would be unpalatable to our allies or to certain groups in the economy. All of them would influence to some extent the operation of the domestic economy and, in turn, would be affected by its operation. We await more clearly defined results of recent measures to reduce the deficit described in the latter part of this chapter.

**Summary.** The presence of the disequilibrium in our balance of payments makes the foreign trade sector of the economy an important determinant of domestic economic policy. Several attitudes toward the problem were considered. The first considered the deficit as a

[7] There were 102 member countries at the end of 1964.

temporary difficulty not requiring actions that would threaten the achievement of full employment at home. However, it is not clear as to how long it might take market forces to produce adjustments needed to restore equilibrium. Because changes of this kind usually involve policy decisions both at home and abroad, and because it is difficult to predict what form these decisions might take in the immediate future, there is no sure way to predict how such changes would affect domestic stability, the volume of trade, and a liberal trade policy.

Depreciation may not be desirable at this time, because the price level of the United States has been rising more slowly than is the case in many foreign countries. Though prices in industries basic to export goods have been rising at a relatively rapid rate, the rise could be offset by improved efficiency in the various lines of production.

Devaluation could jeopardize the dollar as a key currency by forcing large losses on other countries that hold dollars as a reserve currency. In addition to the political and psychological effects that would tend to threaten the leadership of the United States, devaluation could result in an undermining of the world trade and payments system.

General devaluation by major countries has the effect of increasing the world's international liquidity. However, the existence of a larger gold reserve would not necessarily produce adjustments in our trade accounts to restore equilibrium. In the absence of certain actions usually employed to bring about these changes, the deficit would remain and gold outflows would continue.

Foreign countries could appreciate their currencies in terms of the dollar. The upshot of this action would be to cause their imports to rise relative to exports and thus assist in the reduction of the United States deficit. However, appreciation by these countries might yield results that are inconsistent with a policy directed to maximum production and full employment.

Although an increase in tariff duties sufficient to reduce our deficit can be effected, the action would produce many side effects. In general, tariffs tend to lead to certain unfavorable results at home. Other countries might retaliate by raising tariff duties. Also, tariffs disrupt cost–price relationships and, therefore, interfere with private transactions.

A concerted effort has been made in recent years to improve our balance of payments position. Several new programs were established for the purpose of increasing receipts on current account. Measures are directed to conserving dollar expenditures abroad in connection with government grants and loans. In turn, efforts are being made to attract foreign investment in the United States. Certain actions are being directed to improve the liquidity position of the United States.

## QUESTIONS



1. Table 27–1 reveals a deficit in the United States balance of payments (1964). Relate this fact to the statement that the foreign trade sector of the economy has become an important factor in determining domestic economic policy.
2. Evaluate the "hold-the-line" approach to eliminating the deficit.
3. Why might currency depreciation yield unfavorable effects in the long run?
4. What is meant by devaluation of the dollar? Why is devaluation so strongly resisted?
5. Would general devaluation eliminate, in itself, recurring deficits in the United States balance of payments? Why or why not?
6. Suppose that certain foreign countries decide to appreciate their currencies relative to the dollar in view of the United States deficit. Trace the trade effects (changes in exports and imports) in the United States and in foreign countries as a result of this action. Assuming that foreign countries want to maintain domestic stability at a high level of output and to expand trade, they may not find it desirable to appreciate their currencies at this time. Discuss.
7. Consider the following statement: It is unlikely that the United States would resort to higher tariffs as a primary measure to eliminate the balance of payments deficit. Defend this statement in terms of the criteria set forth in the earlier part of this chapter.
8. Outline recent measures employed to reduce the United States deficit.

PART

# 7

# *Economic Growth*

In this section the concepts of economic change are outlined. An explanation of the levels that employment, income (*GNP*), and other variables assume over a period of time is followed by a discussion of the problem of allocating larger output. Finally, consideration is given to factors that would bring about a higher rate of growth.

CHAPTER

# 28

# The Growing Economy

In the next two chapters we intend to investigate the nature of a growing economy with a view to determining the causes of economic growth and to examining some problems related to growth. The present chapter is devoted to causes, the one following to certain problems.

## A GENERAL STATEMENT ON GROWTH

Economic growth may be expressed as the expansion of real *GNP* or real *GNP* per capita. We recall that *real GNP* measures the amounts of goods and services currently produced by the economy. This figure is equal to *GNP* in current dollars deflated for changes in prices according to the method shown in Table 5–4. In analyzing economic growth, economists find it convenient to distinguish three different aspects of output: *capacity* output, *potential* output, and *actual* output. Much of the discussion to follow hinges around the notion that government policy should be directed toward pushing actual output to a level reasonably close to potential output.

**Capacity, Potential, and Actual Output.** Let us now consider the meanings of these terms. In ordinary business terminology *capacity output* is the output produced when plant and equipment is being used at the maximum possible rate. However, this is not necessarily the preferred rate of operation, the one at which the greatest possible economies of production are being realized. According to recent data the preferred operating rate averages at 92 per cent of capacity in manufacturing.[1] Let us refer to the output level achieved at the 92 per-cent rate as capacity output and the output level achieved at 100-per-cent rate as full-capacity output. This small variation o accepted usage should not be difficult to keep in mind.

Changes in the rate of operation are accomplished in some case by putting additional laborers to work on unused machines an equipment. In other cases the number of shifts may be increased fron one to two or three. In some industries, such as iron and steel, a increase in production may involve starting up an entire plant an running it continuously. No matter how the variation takes place th distinction between actual output, capacity output, and full-capacit output still exists. In the present discussion capacity output is th basic concept.

Next, we will consider *potential output,* which may be defined a the output that could be achieved at full employment, the highes level of employment attainable under normal, peacetime conditions Although estimates differ as to the highest employment level attain able, most economists would probably accept full employment as th condition existing when 95 to 97 per cent of the civilian labor forc is employed, or when unemployment ranges from a high of 5 per cen to a low of 3 per cent. In recent years the United States economy ha attained a 3-per-cent unemployment rate only during the Korean Wa period of 1952–53. In essence, potential output is a measure of wha the economy could produce under normal operating conditions, an over a lengthy period of time, without either excessive strain o undue slack. For the sake of precision let us say that potential outpu is the measure of what the economy could produce at a 4-per-cen unemployment rate. Actual output is, of course, the yearly outpu (*GNP*) of the economy.

What is the relation between potential and capacity output? Recen evidence suggests that capacity output is the larger of the two. I 1964 the per cent of the work force employed was 94.8 per cent, wit 5.2 per cent unemployed. Employment could have expanded by 1. per cent before actual output reached potential output. Comparably the operating rate in manufacturing was 88 per cent, compared to preferred rate of 92 per cent. This implies that there was a 4-per-cen deficiency in the rate of operation. The fact that the deficiency o 4 per cent in the operating rate exceeded the excess unemploymen of 1.2 per cent, suggests that if this 1.2 per cent of unemploye workers were absorbed, industry would still be operating below th preferred rate. In short, it appears that capacity output exceede

[1] *Economic Report of the President,* 1965 (Washington, D.C.: U.S. Govern ment Printing Office, 1965), Table 10, p. 90.

otential output in 1964. It is quite clear that full-capacity output is till larger.

## MEASURING POTENTIAL OUTPUT

One of the significant matters to be considered in any study of an xpanding economy is the growth that takes place at full employment. n measuring such full-employment growth we make use of the notion f potential *GNP*. Thus for any given year there is a maximum output hat is consistent with full employment of the nation's available labor upply. This maximum output is determined by the supply of labor nd the productivity of labor and is termed potential output. By way f contrast, the output currently produced (actual output) is both neasured and determined by total spending, or $C + I + G$. Hence, otential and actual *GNP* are not necessarily equal in any given year. f actual *GNP* exceeds potential *GNP* at full employment, expenditure n output exceeds the output available at current price levels. In this ituation an inflationary pressure exists. Conversely, if potential *GNP* xceeds actual *GNP*, a recession or depression threatens for the opposite reasons.

**The Nature of Potential *GNP*.** Potential *GNP* is equal to the upply of labor multiplied by the productivity of labor. We take as he measure of labor supply the total man-hours per year that can e provided at a 96-per-cent employment rate. The productivity of abor is interpreted as the potential *GNP* per man-hour. In order to ompute potential *GNP* we start at a time when the unemployment ate was about 4 per cent. At such a time potential *GNP* can be taken s the same as actual *GNP*.

In the lower panel of Figure 28–1 the varying unemployment rate n the period 1953–64 is shown. In the middle of 1955 the unemployment rate was almost exactly 4 per cent, and therefore actual and otential *GNP* can be taken as identical as of that time. The technique f estimating potential *GNP* is to decide on a plausible rate of growth f potential *GNP* from mid-1955 on, and to project the mid-1955 alue forward at this rate. In the upper part of the figure this procedure is put into effect. From mid-1955 through 1962 a 3.5-per-cent ate is used, and a 3.75-per-cent rate thereafter. How were these ates derived?

The Council of Economic Advisers estimated the rate of growth f the two components of potential *GNP*, potential man-hours, and utput per man-hour, and combined them to get an overall percentage.[2] Between 1954 and 1960 potential *GNP* per man-hour rose at

[2] See the 1962 *Economic Report of the President*, pp. 112–117.

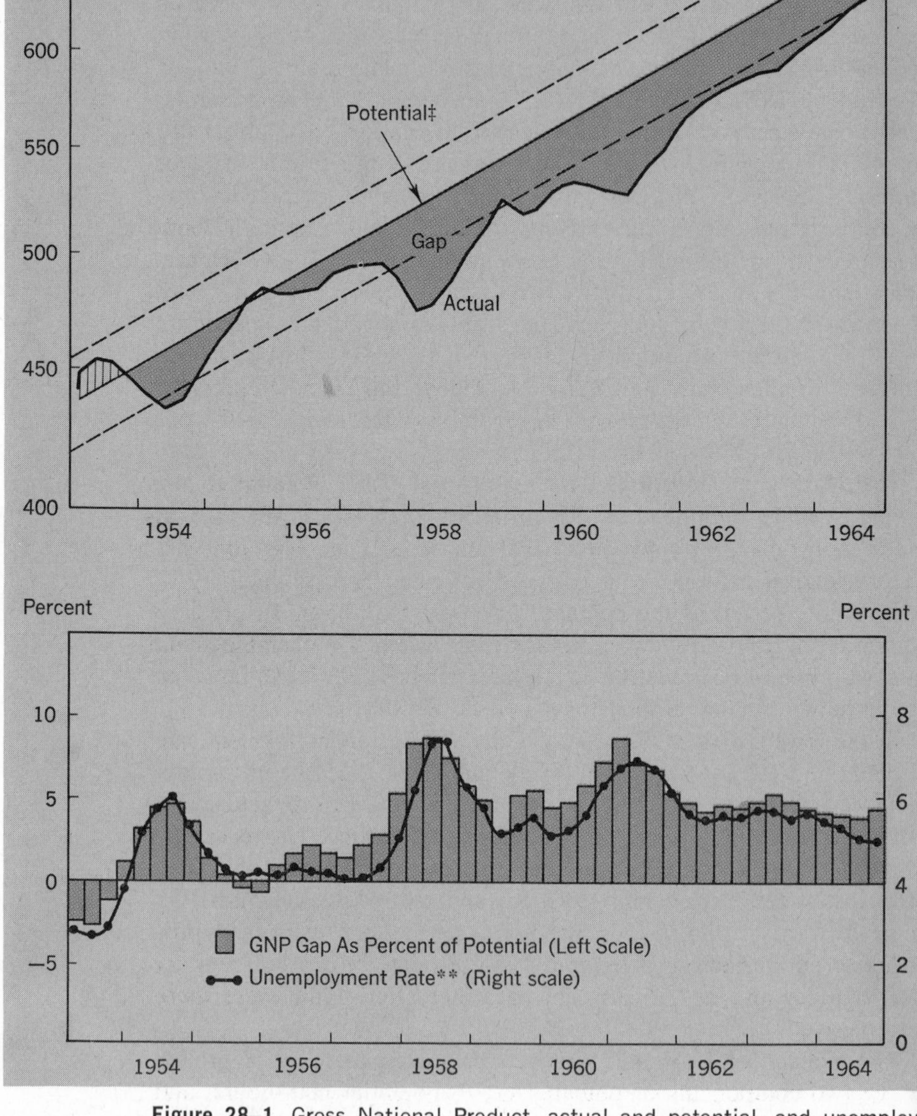


**Figure 28–1.** Gross National Product, actual and potential, and unemployment rate.*

* Sources: Department of Commerce, Department of Labor, and Council of Economic Advisers.

† Seasonally adjusted annual rates.

‡ 3½% trend line through middle of 1955 to 1962 IV; 3¾% trend line thereafter.

** Unemployment as per cent of civilian labor force; seasonally adjusted.

the rate of about 2.6 per cent per year, and potential man-hours rose at about a 0.9-per-cent rate. The rate of growth of *GNP* is found (approximately) by adding 2.6 per cent and 0.9 per cent to give 3.5 per cent. In short, taking account of upward trends both in productivity and labor supply, potential *GNP* seems to have risen at about a 3.5-per-cent rate from mid-1955 to the end of 1962. Since that time it appears that the growth rate has been slightly higher, namely, 3.75 per cent.

In the upper panel of Figure 28–1 the Council of Economic Advisers' calculations are shown in graphical form. Since 1955 it seems that actual *GNP* has fallen below potential *GNP*. The difference between the two is called the gap. For 1964 the actual *GNP* was estimated tentatively at $622 billion (preliminary figures). Potential *GNP* was estimated at $649, leaving a gap of $27 billion, amounting to about 4 per cent of potential *GNP*. This deficiency was caused by an unemployment rate of 5.2 per cent, which is 1.2 per cent more than the 4-per-cent norm.

The graph, Figure 28–1, is a ratio or semilogarithmic chart. The fact that potential output is a straight line, broken in 1962 to reflect slightly faster growth, indicates that constant percentage rates of growth for the periods 1955–62 and 1963–64. Between 1958 and 1964 actual output has been following a path roughly parallel to potential output. This implies that output is expanding at a rate sufficient to absorb additions to the labor supply accruing since 1958. However, output and employment opportunities have not risen sufficiently rapidly to absorb any substantial number of the unemployed already present in 1958. Only if actual output expands faster than potential output will the gap be eliminated.

**Remarks on Potential *GNP*.** In this approach to the estimate of potential *GNP* we relate *GNP* to the labor force and its productivity. Actually, the productive potential of a nation depends on a complex of things, including, in addition to the size and quality of the labor force, the availability of natural resources, the stock of capital, and the state of technology. Why the simplified approach sketched above? First, it is nearly impossible to devise precise measurements of the supplies of natural resources or the state of technology. The problems of measuring capital inputs are nearly as difficult. In contrast, labor yields more easily to measurement than do the other factors of production. Accordingly, it is convenient to use labor as the factor around which to build the analysis. The other determinants of *GNP,* such as the availability of natural resources, can be regarded as determinants of the productivity of labor. Like the two hands of a clock, the labor force and its productivity are the outward indicators of the unseen machinery of the economic system in all its complexity.

Next, the Council of Economic Advisers sets as a reasonable goal the achievement of a 4-per-cent unemployment rate. There appears to be a consensus among American economists that such a rate is both reasonable and attainable. The persistent failure to attain it in the period from 1955 to date suggests the need for measures to achieve that objective. At the same time it is recognized that a 4-per-cent unemployment rate is too precise a goal. As mentioned before, a level of activity in the economy involving between 3-per-cent and 5-per-cent unemployment is considered to be tolerable. We might draw two lines, one above and one below the line representing potential *GNP* in Figure 28–1, representing the estimated *GNP* at the 3-per-cent and 5-per-cent unemployment rates. According to the Council of Economic Advisers a reduction of 1 per cent in the rate of unemployment leads to about a 3-per-cent rise in potential output.[3] In line with this idea we have inserted two dashed lines in the Council's diagram to suggest these limits. As long as actual output or *GNP* falls within these limits the result may be regarded as tolerable. If *GNP* begins to touch or pass the upper, 3-per-cent unemployment limit, inflation begins to pose a distinct threat. If *GNP* begins to touch the lower, 5-per-cent unemployment limit, loss of output and employment becomes a problem.

**Importance of Potential *GNP*.** The potential *GNP* is a measure of the aggregate output that could be achieved at full employment. Using another type of terminology, this aggregate output is the potential supply available at full employment. We must contrast this figure with actual demand, which is regarded as total expenditure on output, or $C + I + G$. Because actual demand generates corresponding actual output, the actual *GNP* at any time can be assumed to represent actual demand, or $C + I + G$. Furthermore, when actual *GNP* is below potential *GNP*, $C + I + G$ is deficient at full employment; there is a deflationary gap. If actual *GNP* exceeds potential *GNP*, $C + I + G$ is excessive at full employment; there is an inflationary gap.

Considering Figure 28–1, we see that potential output exceeds actual output for most of the period shown and for the entire period since 1956. According to our interpretation, then, demand or $C + I + G$ has fallen short of full-employment output, or potential *GNP*, over this period. For portions of 1953 and 1955 actual output exceeded potential, and $C + I + G$ was larger than full-employment output, or potential *GNP*. As we have already stated, the 1956–64 period was marked by some unemployment and lost output; the portion of 1953 marked by the excess of actual output represented, perhaps, a brief inflationary threat.

**Graphical Interpretation.** There are two approaches to interpretation: a static and a dynamic. The first is a sort of snapshot of



[3] *Economic Report of the President*, 1963, p. 26.

the situation at a moment of time. The second involves the comparison of a series of situations through time. Let us begin with the first in order to get the feel of the situation.

In Figure 28–2 equilibrium is found at *E*, where $C+I+G=GNP$, giving rise to actual *GNP* equal to *OA*. By the methods previously outlined potential *GNP* is computed. This value is laid out along the horizontal axis, terminating in point *P*. In short, potential *GNP* is determined and introduced into the diagram as *OP*. Clearly, there is a gap of *AP* between actual and potential *GNP*. Let us call this the output gap. This corresponds to the shaded vertical distance between actual and potential *GNP* in Figure 28–1 at any one time, say in the period 1956–64.

Notice that if actual *GNP* were expanded to equal potential *GNP*, there would be a deflationary gap between *GNP* and $C+I+G$. This implies that demand is insufficiently strong to sustain potential

**Figure 28–2.** Output gap and deflationary gap.

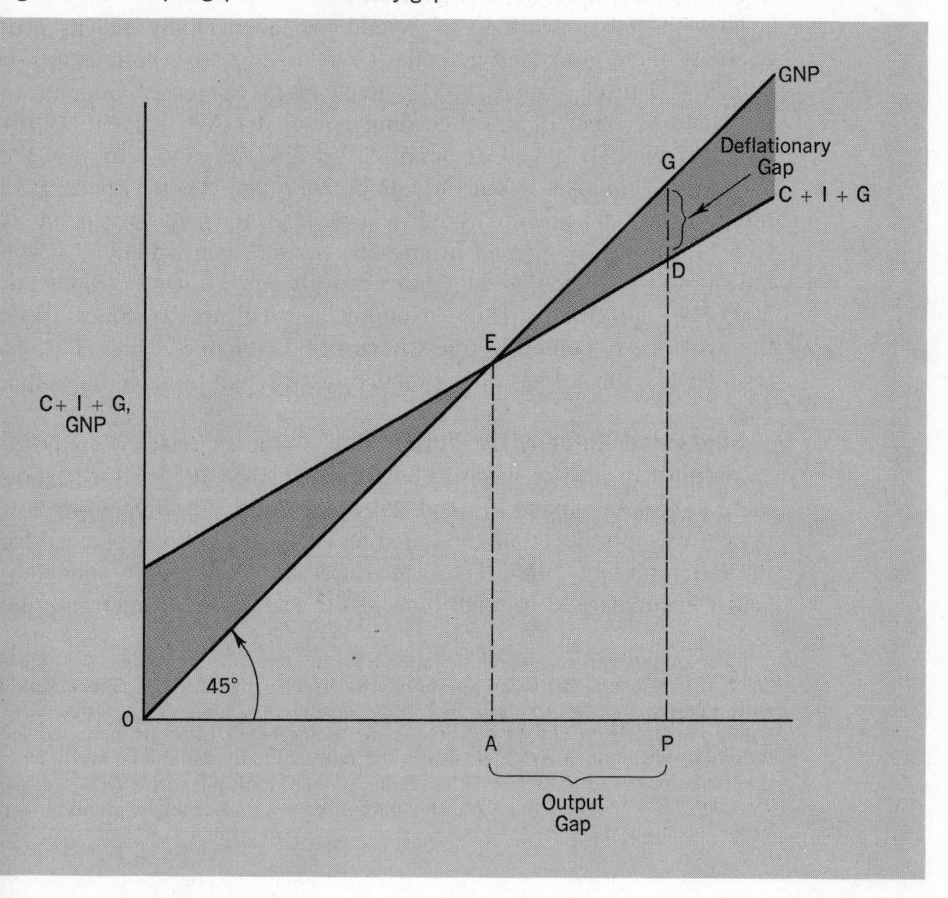

*GNP*. Consequently, *GNP* would have to decline toward a level *OA*, if it happened to be at a level *OP* at the outset.

The output gap is larger than the deflationary gap. The deflationary gap is the difference between $C + I + G$ (when *GNP* equals potential *GNP*) and potential *GNP*. The output gap *AP* is the gap between equilibrium $C + I + G$ (= equilibrium $GNP = OA = AE$) and potential *GNP*. Now equilibrium $C + I + G$, or $C + I + G$ at equilibrium *GNP*, is less than $C + I + G$ at potential *GNP*; that is, *AE* is less than *PD*. As *GNP* expands from the equilibrium value to the potential value, $C + I + G$ increases. Hence the margin between $C + I + G$ and potential *GNP* is narrowed. In short, the deflationary gap is smaller than the output gap. No confusion should exist on this point.[4]

Now let us consider the dynamic aspect of the problem. In Figure 28–3 we assume that no output gap exists, that actual output equals potential output. Thus the equilibrium at *a* generates an actual *GNP* of *OA*, or 300, equal to potential *GNP*.

Now the forces working to expand the labor supply and its productivity serve to expand potential *GNP* in successive periods to *OB* equals 400 to *OC* equals 533⅓. Each of the increases amounts to the same per cent of the preceding potential *GNP*, namely, ⅓, or 33.3 per cent. If actual demand, $C + I + G$, expands, so that the $C + I + G$ line rises to cut through points *b* and *c* at the appropriate times, actual and potential *GNP* will be kept equal to each other. If $C + I + G$ *fails to expand* in any one period, then actual *GNP* will fall short of the potential that is successively equal to *OA, OB, OC*, or 300, 400, and 533⅓. Thus an output gap will appear. Since 1955, the evidence presented by the Council of Economic Advisers seems to indicate, demand has not expanded fast enough to avoid an output gap.

**Suggested Remedy for Output Gap.** One suggested remedy for an output gap such as seems to have existed since 1955 is for government to seek to expand demand. Pursuant to the objective an income tax cut was introduced in 1964, and an excise tax cut was planned for the latter part of 1965. These measures are designed to spur consumer spending and to contribute to the expansion of aggregate de-

[4] The output gap equals the deflationary gap times the multiplier. In Figure 28–2, if $C + I + G$ increased autonomously by *DG*, the $C + I + G$ line would shift upward parallel to itself and pass through point *G*. As a result *GNP* would expand from *OA* to *OP*. The ratio of increased *GNP* to increased autonomous spending is $AP/DG$; this is the multiplier, by definition. Multiplying the deflationary gap *DG* by the value of the multiplier $AP/DG$, we get $DG(AP/DG) = AP$. Thus *AP*, the output gap, equals the deflationary gap times the multiplier.

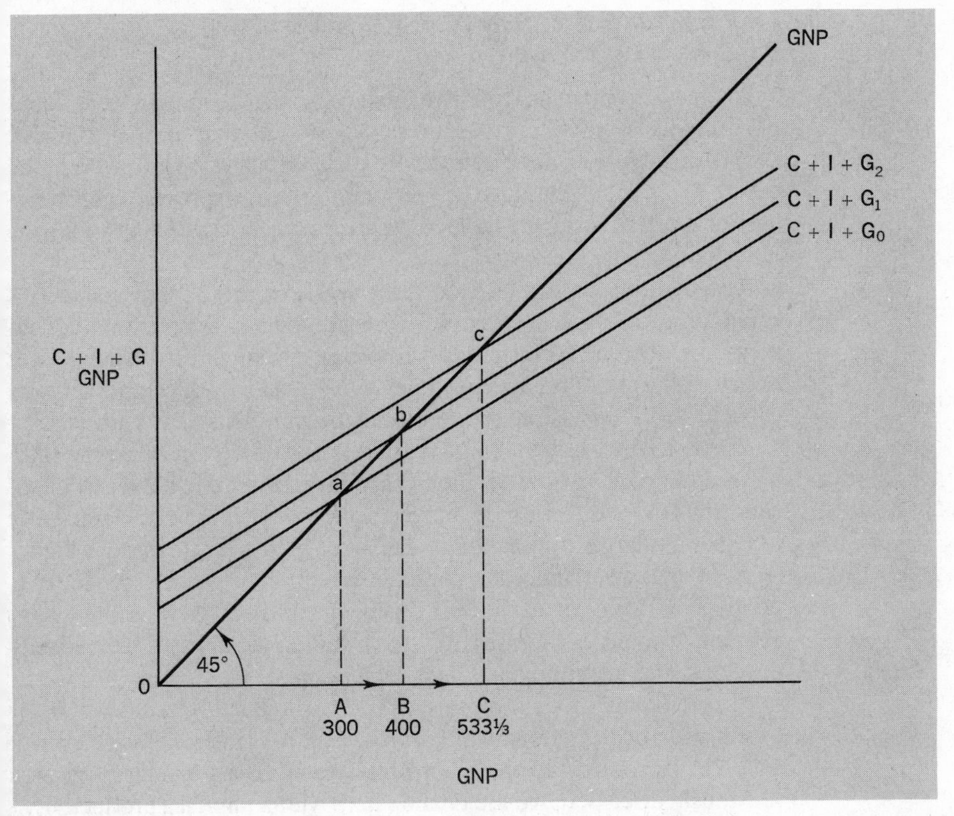


**Figure 28–3.** Expanding potential *GNP* matched by means of rising government spending.

mand. It is too early to judge how effective these measures will prove to be.

**Final Evaluation of Potential Output.** The value of this concept is that it permits the introduction of a fairly steady autonomous trend in *GNP* to be compared with actual output. Accordingly, the notion serves as a goal for the economy—a level toward which actual output should be pushed. Appropriate fiscal and monetary policies can be selected to help reach this end.

The chief drawback is that it fails to assign any reason why demand, $C + I + G$, should increase from period to period to meet potential *GNP*. Therefore it fails in some degree to explain the nature of a dynamic economy, why demand and supply increase concurrently. Perhaps a theory could be developed, but it is not explicitly present in this discussion. It is because of this deficiency that we turn to a second approach to growth.

## INVESTMENT AND GROWTH: CAPACITY *GNP*

In the foregoing analysis we made use of the notion that labor productivity is the key to growth. We found that if the available supply of labor and the productivity of labor grow, so must potential *GNP*. The second measure of economic growth expresses the expansion of *GNP* occasioned by increased investment. Let us consider the latter notion.

Any addition to capital stock last year generates extra productive capacity in the current year. Suppose production and income are increased to the new capacity level. Since consumption demand rises by a smaller amount than income (*GNP*), a gap develops between capacity *GNP* and expenditure on this output. This year's investment must rise to fill the gap. This means that last year's investment brings forth additional capital facilities that give rise to a higher level of capacity *GNP*. In terms of income, investment must rise sufficiently to equal the larger volume of saving associated with this year's higher level of income. Hence, a continuous capacity growth of *GNP* is possible as long as each year's investment rises by the necessary amount. Should businesses fail to invest sufficiently, idle capacity develops, and unemployment and depression result.

The remaining pages of this chapter will be devoted to a fuller explanation of the way in which investment promotes capacity growth of *GNP*. In contrast to the labor-productivity measurement of growth previously discussed, we are dealing here with a capital (productivity) growth measurement.

**The Dual Functions of Investment.** Referring back to the explanation of equilibrium *NNP*, we recall that investment is a component of total spending on output. Equilibrium is achieved at the output marked by the equality of total spending and *NNP*. Or, what is the same thing, equilibrium *NNP* is established at a level of output at which planned saving and planned investment are equal. Now investment is a vital factor generating increased income in that it stimulates consumption through the multiplier process. Consequently, one major function of investment is its ability to generate income. We refer to this function as the *income creating* aspect of investment. The second basic function of investment pertains to its ability to stimulate productive capacity. We call this the *capacity creating* aspect of investment.

The earlier *NNP* equilibrium analysis is fundamentally a short-run analysis. We recall that we were then dealing with a relatively fixed supply of resources. Under these assumptions full-employment *NNP* expresses a definite output produced with given resources. Of course, it is important to understand the fundamentals of short-run analysis. But once we inject growth into our discussion—that is, growth in labor supply, capital stock, or natural resources and their productivities—short-run analysis no longer applies.

Suppose growth sets in: this means that capacity *GNP* increases so that it becomes associated with a larger employment of resources.[5] (*Capacity* as used here means the possibility of a larger—potential—*GNP* because of additional resources forthcoming over a number of years.) In long-run analysis *GNP* must therefore rise to permit employment of the additional resources. Herein lies the crux of the growth problem. With additional resources forthcoming—including a rise in capital facilities—this year's real *GNP* must exceed last year's, and future *GNP*s must exceed this year's, or unemployment and depression will result. Let us summarize our points thus far. (1) A rise in investment generates both income and additional productive capacity. (2) Additional productive capacity must be absorbed by rising output. But the yearly rise in output to a capacity *GNP* level depends upon businessmen's willingness to invest more each year. (3) Unlike the earlier short-run analysis, associating a given level of *NNP* with a given employment of resources, long-run (growth) analysis associates capacity *GNP* with an ever larger employment of resources.

## CAPACITY GROWTH

Having presented the dual functions of investment and reviewed the short-run nature of equilibrium *NNP* analysis, we are ready to analyze long-run growth based upon the productivity of capital investment. The following analysis ignores the influence of government, because our purpose is to express important principles without resorting to added complexities posed by government intervention. Furthermore, growth in our capitalistic system depends mainly upon private investment. In fact, government decisions to invest are not a vital part of normal growth in output. This is not to say that government is neutral with respect to investment decisions. The Employment Act (1946) implies that it is a proper function of government to do what it can to encourage growth in *GNP*. Usually it does so by influencing aggregate demand (spending) and, thereby, creating a

[5] In our previous analysis we used net investment in association with *NNP*. Technically, it is net investment that increases the stock of capital. However, our analysis will run in terms of *GNP* to be consistent with the concept of full-employment *GNP* discussed earlier in this chapter. In any event little harm is done by assuming that total investment increases the nation's stock of capital.

climate conducive to further private investment. We will discuss various aspects of government's responsibility for growth in the next chapter.

**Long-Run Consumption and Saving Functions.** In shifting from a short-run equilibrium analysis to long-run growth equilibrium it is necessary to make the consumption and saving functions conform to people's long-run tendencies to consume and save out of income. We recall the upward-sloping consumption curve of our earlier short-run analysis. Since we assume a constant marginal propensity to consume, changes in the amount of consumption depend mainly on changes in the amount of income. At low levels of income families dissave, and at high levels of income positive saving occurs. In other words, families fail to consume in proportion to income. When income rises, they tend to save more out of the higher income: and when income falls, they tend to save less rather than accept a lower plane of living.

In long-run analysis the consumption pattern becomes altered. Historically, individuals tend to improve their level of living by increasing consumption almost in proportion to a rise in real income. (Refer to Figure 6–3 for the long-run trend.) Why do they act in this manner? For various reasons. In the first instance, consumers have sufficient time to adjust spending in accordance with changes in real income. Their decisions are also influenced by other consumers. Seemingly, the nature of people is such that low-income families strive to move up to the standard set by higher-income earners. Those who set the pace also try to improve their position with reference to other groups. In addition, consumers are tempted to spend more with the growth of output accompanied by the continued appearance of such new products as transistor radios, autos with gas turbine engines, and the like.

These examples indicate that the long-run level of consumption tends to vary in direct proportion to real income. Hence, unlike the short-run analysis, where consumption is positive at zero income, so that the consumption line intersects the vertical scale above the origin, the long-run consumption line begins at the origin and rises in direct proportion to the rise in real income. Thus, it is a straight line passing through the origin. Because consumption is a fraction of *GNP,* the consumption line lies below the *GNP,* or 45-degree line. Therefore, the ratio between consumption and *GNP,* $C/GNP$, or the average propensity to consume, is less than 1. Since the average propensity to consume is assumed to be constant or independent of changes in *GNP,* the marginal propensity to consume ($\Delta C/\Delta GNP$) is also constant and equal to the average propensity to consume. A numerical example will illustrate the point. Suppose $C = 5$ and $GNP = 10$, which implies an average propensity to consume of $5/10 = 1/2$. Then output rises so that $GNP = 20$ and $C = 10$; that is, $C = 1/2\ GNP$. Clearly, the marginal propensity to consume out of

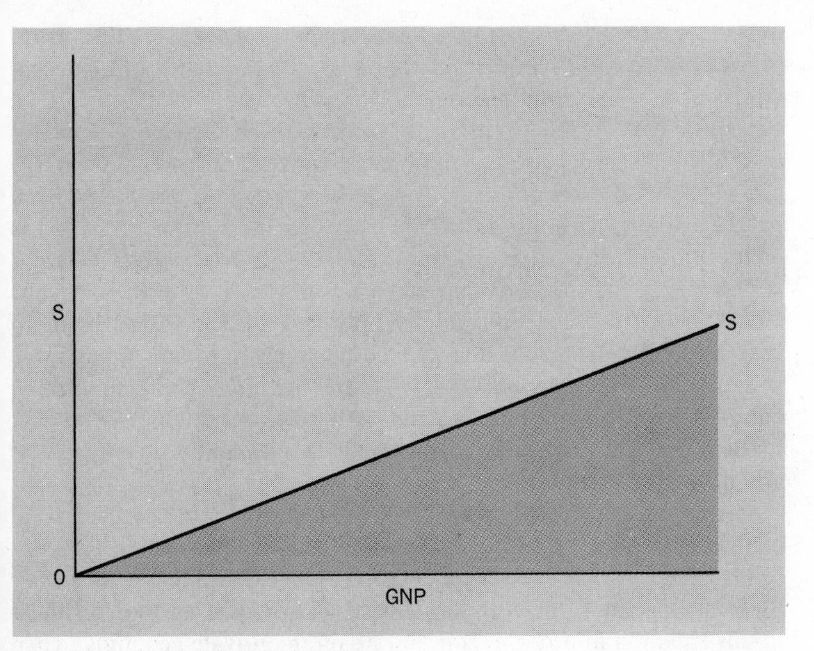


**Figure 28–4.** Long-run saving line.

*GNP* is ½, since $\Delta C = 5$, $\Delta GNP = 10$ and $\Delta C/\Delta GNP = 5/10 = 1/2$.

Referring once again to the earlier short-run equilibrium analysis, we found that what is not spent for consumption out of income is necessarily saved. Thus $NNP - C = S$, assuming taxes to be zero. At higher levels of income people spend proportionately more. In a growing economy the relationship between consumption, saving, and *GNP* reveals similar properties; that is, $C + S = GNP$. But because the level of consumption varies in direct proportion to *GNP*, the saving function must also take on this characteristic. Hence, the saving curve is drawn so that it begins at the origin and rises in direct proportion to the rise in *GNP*. What we said with respect to the long-run consumption function applies equally well to the long-run saving function, because that part of *GNP* not spent on consumption is saved. Figure 28–4 shows a long-run saving line. Note that it is a straight line rising from the point of origin, revealing that saving varies in direct proportion to *GNP*. The saving line lies below the 45-degree or *GNP* line (not shown), because saving is a fraction of real income.

**Investment and Growth.**[6] In the analysis to follow we formally

[6] The theory of growth presented here follows precisely that of D. Hamberg in *Principles of a Growing Economy* (New York: W. W. Norton & Company, 1961), Ch. 13. Hamberg's treatment is, in turn, a variation of the theory of E. D. Domar, "Expansion and Employment," *American Economic Review* (March 1947), pp. 34–55. A still earlier treatment is that of R. F. Harrod, "An Essay in Dynamic Theory," *Economic Journal* (March 1939), pp. 14–33.

introduce into the discussion a new variable, capacity *GNP*. We abbreviate this *CGNP*. Earlier in the chapter we defined this concept and contrasted it with potential *GNP*. The new concept creates a slight problem. In the discussion of determination of *NNP* in Chapter 6 we distinguished between supply and demand, or lower-loop *NNP*, and $C+I+G$, upper-loop *NNP*. Briefly, equilibrium was defined by the equality $C+I+G=NNP$, or demand = supply. In terms of the present discussion we would say $C+I+G=GNP$. Here $I$ is defined as gross, rather than net investment. If we now introduce *CGNP* as a third concept and try, like a juggler throwing balls, to keep these three concepts in a moving relationship to one another, we will probably become confused. We are therefore going to assume equilibrium of supply and demand as a basic condition. We take it for granted that the reader understands this equality, and how it is attained, from earlier discussion.

Let us refresh our memories on a related point. In the discussion of the equilibrium of supply and demand we concluded that the condition $C+I+G=NNP$ is equivalent to the condition $I+G=S+T$. We are going to assume that $G$ and $T$ are equal and cancel them in this equation in order to concentrate on the private economy. Then the equilibrium requires that $I=S$. If this condition holds true (in the revised version), $C+I+G=GNP$. Making use of our assumption that equilibrium prevails, then, we are going to interpret *GNP* as demand $(C+I+G)$ whenever $I=S$.

This is a variation from the practice of interpreting *GNP* (or *NNP*) simply as supply. In the discussion to follow it is convenient to think of *CGNP* as the supply to be disposed of and *GNP* as the demand. This is a simplification, because *CGNP* is only the maximum supply, but this will be the approach used.

There are two requirements of equilibrium in the analysis to follow. First, all goods produced must be sold or total supply must be equal to total demand. Under our assumptions this requires that $I=S$. As long as this is true $GNP=C+I+G$, and therefore, *GNP can be interpreted as demand*. Second, it is assumed that $GNP=CGNP$. Since, by the first condition, *GNP* can be interpreted as demand, this condition says that demand = capacity output. Accordingly, the economy is assumed to operate at capacity output in each period.

In Figure 28–5 *GNP* is laid out on the horizontal axis, and $I$ and $S$ are laid out on the vertical.[7] As we have stated earlier, we have $I=S$,

[7] This diagram is actually somewhat incomplete. It seems advisable to start from a combination of graphic, numerical, and verbal discussion, rather than to draw a more complicated or difficult diagram. The approach used here can be completed in two ways. One is outlined in the appendix to this chapter. The second appears as Figure 29–5 in the next chapter.

so that $GNP = C + I + G$. We will therefore interpret $GNP$ as demand for output. Now $CGNP$ is also represented on the horizontal axis. This creates no problem, since $CGNP$ is measured in dollars, as is $GNP$. However, $CGNP$ is shown here as a series of isolated points because of the way the analysis proceeds.

We will proceed to discuss the process of change in a sequence of time periods referred to successively as zero, one, two, and so on. In period zero we show saving and investment in equilibrium at $E_0$. This gives a $GNP$ of $OL$. The $CGNP$ is assumed to be equal to $OL$. Accordingly, $GNP = CGNP = OL$, or demand = capacity output. Thus equilibrium prevails in period zero.

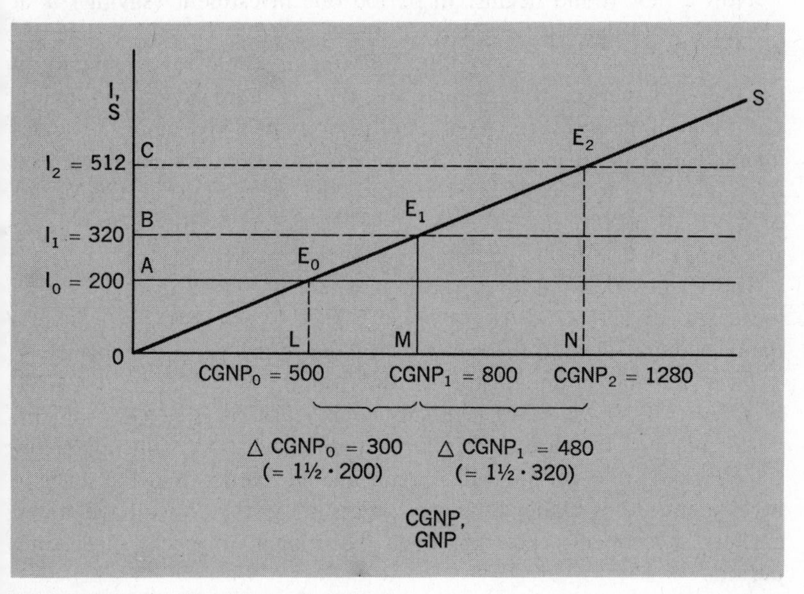


**Figure 28–5.** Growth of capacity output.

As a result of saving and investment of $OA$ in period zero, capacity output increases. However, it takes time for the investment to be completed. Accordingly, we assume that the increased productive capacity does not become available until period one. This shows up as an increase in $CGNP$ from $OL$ to $OM$. The ratio of increased $CGNP$ to investment is called the *productivity ratio of investment*. It is defined as $p' = \Delta CGNP/I$ and can be read from Figure 28–5 as equal to $p' = \Delta CGNP_0/I_0 = 300/200 = 1.5$.

At this juncture $CGNP$ has expanded to a new high of $OM$, labeled $CGNP_1$. As a result *capacity saving* or saving from $CGNP$ has expanded to $ME_1$. If the second condition of equilibrium is to be met, if the level of $GNP$ is to be raised to equal $CGNP$, $I$ must rise from

$OA$ (200) to $OB$ (320). Failing this, capacity output will not all be sold. Here we may contrast the two sides of investment: the capacity creating aspect and the income (demand) creating aspect. Saving and investment of $OA$ generates an increase in $CGNP$ equal to $LM = 300$. If this is to be met with increased $GNP$ (demand), investment must rise by $AB = 120$ from $OA$ to $OB$. There is an inherent dynamism in the situation. Investment (saving) generates increased capacity, which requires an *increase* in investment.

In this case the marginal propensity to save, $MPS$, is $\frac{2}{5}$, whereas $MPC$ is $\frac{3}{5}$, and the multiplier is $2\frac{1}{2}$. Increased investment of 120 raises $GNP$ by $120 \times 2\frac{1}{2} = 300$, the needed amount.

Now a new round begins. In period one investment (saving) is at a higher level than in period zero, namely, $OB = I_1 = 320$. The existence of *any* level of saving and investment would raise capacity in the following period. But, beyond this, there is more saving and investment than in period zero. As a result period one's investment provides an increased jump in $CGNP$. By period two capacity has increased from $CGNP_1$ to $CGNP_2$. Moreover, the increment in $CGNP$ or $\Delta CGNP_1 = MN = 480$ exceeds $\Delta CGNP_0 = LM = 300$. The successive jumps in $CGNP$ are getting larger as time passes.

In this situation the increased investment of period one, $I_1 = 320$, increases capacity $GNP$ by $I_1 \cdot p' = 320 \times 1\frac{1}{2} = 480$. Since investment increased, so did the numerical value of the jump in capacity.

Now we may complete the second round. With increased $CGNP$ of $ON = CGNP_2 = 1280$, capacity saving has risen to $OC$, and investment must increase to this level. Otherwise, $GNP$ will fall below $CGNP$, and some output will remain unsold. Notice that the level of investment $OC$ is higher than any preceding level. As we have stated earlier, investment (saving) must be higher in each succeeding period.

Let us notice one more idea. We have explained that $\Delta CGNP_1$ (480) exceeds $\Delta CGNP_0$ (300); the jump in capacity grows. By the same token the jump in capacity saving (= investment) must grow. This is true because saving is proportional to $GNP$ (= $CGNP$). If the jumps in $CGNP$ grow, so do the jumps in capacity saving (investment). Therefore $\Delta I_1$ is greater than $\Delta I_0$; or $\Delta S_1$ is greater than $\Delta S_0$, since $I$ and $S$ are equal according to our first assumption of equilibrium. (Read these values from the graph and verify these statements.)

Clearly, this process may continue indefinitely, provided that investment rises in the manner necessary to keep $GNP$ equal to $CGNP$. Now let us summarize the conclusions that emerge from this analysis. First, both $GNP$ and $I$ ($S$) rise in each successive period. Second, both $GNP$ and $I$ ($S$) rise at an ever faster absolute rate. The jumps in $GNP$ and $I$, $\Delta GNP$, and $\Delta I$ increase in magnitude from period to period. The second condition sounds somewhat alarming, as though the situation may lead to runaway growth. In order to define the growth rate we need to investigate the successive jumps in capacity $\Delta CGNP$ and relate them to the preceding investment $I$. This would enable us to make more definite statements about growth.

Let us summarize the final conclusion that can be derived from this analysis. We first recall the concept of the productivity ratio of investment, symbolized by $p'$. This is defined by the equation $p' = \Delta CGNP/I$, or the ratio of increased capacity $GNP$ to the (previous) investment that gave rise to it. In the figure above $p' = \Delta CGNP/I = LM/OA = 300/200 = 1\frac{1}{2}$. Let us refer to the average and marginal propensity to save as $s$. This is seen in the figure above as $s = S/GNP = OA/OL = \Delta S/\Delta GNP = AB/LM$; the two ratios may be seen to have the common value $200/500 = 120/300 = 0.4$. Now the conclusion may be stated. A system marked by (1) a long-run saving line of the type assumed; (2) a constant productivity ratio of investment $p'$; (3) equality of saving and investment; (4) equality of $GNP$ $(= C + I + G)$ and $CGNP$ will grow at a constant percentage rate equal to:

$$p's\,,$$

which is the productivity ratio of investment ($p'$) times the propensity to save ($s$). We prove this condition in the appendix. In the graph analyzed above, $p' = 1\frac{1}{2}$, and $s = 0.4$, so that:

$$p's = 1\tfrac{1}{2} \cdot 0.4 = 0.6\,. \tag{1}$$

This says that $GNP$ grows by $0.6 = 60$ per cent annually. Considering the sequence of values of $GNP$—500, 800, and 1280—we see that the conclusion is verified.

Let us apply this very roughly to the United States economy. We are aware first that the condition of equilibrium in our economy is

$$S + T = I + G\,. \tag{2}$$

The present analysis ignores the $T$ and $G$, or government taxes and government spending. If $T$ and $G$ were approximately equal, they could be canceled on either side of the equation, leaving $S = I$. Now in peacetime $T$ and $G$ are proportionately rather close. In the five-year period 1960–64 the difference between $G$ and $T$ amounted to less than 1 per cent in four of those years and then exceeded 1 per cent by only a slight margin. Consequently, it will not introduce a large error to assume $G$ and $T$ equal and to cancel them.

Next, the saving rate or ratio of gross saving to gross income lies between 10 and 15 per cent. Let us take it to be $\frac{1}{8}$. Now we do not have very good information on the productivity ratio. As a rough guess it lies between ½ and ⅓. Let us use the second figure. Computing the growth rate on this basis we get

$$p's = \frac{1}{3} \cdot \frac{1}{8} = \frac{1}{24} = 0.04+ = 4+\% \ . \qquad (3)$$

In short, the growth rate would amount to a little over 4 per cent. Actually, the growth rate over a 50-year period has been a shade less than this, or about 3.5 per cent. This is not to be thought of as a verification of the theory. Rather it is an effort to give some concrete meaning to the idea of a constant growth rate under the conditions stated.

**Evaluation.** The theory presented is extremely valuable in one important respect. Our original discussion of *NNP* determination stressed the idea of a fixed equilibrium value toward which *NNP* should move. This approach is quite static, a characteristic that follows from the exclusive emphasis on the income creating (determining) aspect of investment. When the capacity creating aspect is introduced, the fact that *NNP* (or *GNP*) must change is brought out into the open. Then we are compelled to consider the way in which *GNP* will change through time.

A second valuable idea introduced is that of capacity *GNP*. This forçes us to concentrate on the conditions under which $GNP = CGNP$. Thus we are led to consider whether our economy can be expected to produce at a capacity level or not. If we find that it does not, in practice, we may begin to consider the implications of trying to reach such a goal.

A third idea introduced, though not proved, above (see appendix to this chapter) is the idea that an economy may grow at a constant percentage rate. The determinants of the growth rate are defined by a simple equation involving the product of two factors, $p'$ and $s$. This is a simple and thought-provoking possibility. It suggests that such a constant rate of growth may be set up as a tentative norm or goal for the economy. In turn, this will provide a suitable focus of public discussion on policy for economic growth.

There are numerous shortcomings of the theory. We mention only one. In order to preserve equilibrium so that $GNP = CGNP$ investment must grow at the rate $p's$. The necessity for ever-increasing investment was explained in the text with suitable references to the diagram. The meaning of the theory seems to be that continued growth at a constant rate $p's$ is possible provided that $I$ grows at this same rate. It appears that the theory defines a necessary growth path for investment. Well and good. There is, however, no reason to suppose that $I$ will actually tend to grow at this rate. The theory sheds no light on this. We are therefore left with an unsettled matter to deal with, namely, the actual behavior of $I$ through time.

It appears that the theory may well be primarily useful in providing a norm for economic policy. Efforts may properly be directed toward urging $I$ to grow at a rate defined by $p's$ in order to assure continued economic growth at a steady rate. In short, the theory is perhaps as much a guide to what *should be* as to what *is*.

## FULL-EMPLOYMENT AND CAPACITY GROWTH: A SYNTHESIS

In the first part of the chapter we found that full-employment growth of *GNP* requires actual *GNP* to increase sufficiently to equal yearly potential *GNP*. The full-employment growth rate necessary to satisfy this condition is one equal to the annual percentage rate at which the available supply of labor increases plus the annual percentage rate at which the productivity of labor increases. We later learned that capacity growth in *GNP* requires annual increases in investment large enough to expand output and to absorb the growing productive capacity. Both investment and *GNP* must rise to maintain capacity growth. The capacity growth rate required to satisfy this condition is one equal to the productivity ratio of investment times the long-run saving rate.

This brief summary of the two growth concepts indicates a basic similarity between them. Ideally, they could yield identical growth rates. Imagine an annual percentage increase in the available labor supply plus an annual percentage increase in the productivity of labor matched by an annual increase in the productivity of investment times the long-run saving rate. Then long-run growth would continue to maintain a fully employed labor supply with full utilization of productive capacity.

Suppose, on the other hand, the economy produces a less-than-full-employment growth in *GNP*. In terms of production, widespread unemployment means a sustained growth in *GNP* at some lower level of output. Or expressed as a growth rate, a steady growth of *GNP* is maintainable only at a lower rate of growth. The point is that a nation can encounter a steady growth of *GNP* that falls short of utilizing a growing labor supply. (Refer to Figure 28–1, which shows actual *GNP* falling below potential *GNP*, but at a positive rate of growth.) This outcome is possible, because a change in the labor supply creates, by itself, only one result: a change in productive capacity. If a growing labor supply is not fully utilized, then excess capacity develops, resulting in a slower growth of *GNP*.

Suppose that, instead of a less-than-full-employment growth in *GNP*, the economy produces a less-than-*capacity* growth in *GNP*. Then the required investment falls short of the level necessary to bring about the desired growth of *GNP*. Again, excess capacity develops. But by recalling the dual functions of investment, we know that investment decisions by businessmen affect both income and output via the multiplier and productive capacity. In connection with the latter, decisions to invest are directly related to expected profits. When businessmen anticipate a decline in profit possibilities, they are likely to reduce investment. Even in the light of favorable profits the level of investment may not rise above that of previous years—and we recognize that a steady rate of growth in *GNP* requires a constant annual rise of investment to absorb into production the excess productive capacity. On the income side, additions to capital stock in the form of buildings and equipment originate in saving out of income. If businessmen do not increase investment spending sufficiently to match the larger volume of saving, the level of income can no longer maintain a given rate of growth.

At a positive growth rate, such as 4 per cent, the alternative to steady growth of *GNP* is depression. In contrast, a positive rate of growth in the labor supply does not necessarily cause a depression. From what has been said in connection with full-employment growth, a steady growth of *GNP* is possible even though the level of production is not large enough to utilize the growing labor supply. These differing results are possible because a change in investment affects productive capacity and income, whereas a change in the labor supply affects only productive capacity.

**Growth in Less Developed Nations.** One final observation bears on the experience of the less developed countries. As a rule, capital facilities do not expand sufficiently to employ the growing labor supply. Workers who are unable to find employment in industry tend to gravitate back to the farms; disguised unemployment is often the result of their migration to less productive jobs. In short, the full-employment growth rate of *GNP* is higher than the capacity growth rate. It is evident, then, that the problem of growth lies mainly in the area of investment; and the latter is the key to the possible solution of the problem. Because investment constitutes such a small part of annual *GNP,* capital facilities expand too slowly to provide employment for a growing labor supply. The problem could be alleviated by channeling more resources into capital goods production. But we find that many less developed nations are unable to reduce consumer goods production except at the expense of near-starvation diets. The volume of saving and investment are such that it is nearly impossible to raise the capacity growth rate to the full-employment level. The more highly developed nations and at least a few of the less developed countries can increase the fraction of saving and investment out of *GNP* enough to raise the capacity growth rate to a full-employment level. The latter statement recalls an alternative method of speeding up the rate of capital formation in poorer countries.

The receipt of capital goods from industrialized nations increases productive capacity in the same way as a rise of internal investment. In fact, imports of consumer goods can also stimulate investment via shifting domestic resources to capital goods production. Hence, the receipt of capital equipment—or possibly consumer goods—expands the productive base and generates saving and investment within developing nations. This self-generating process is the basis for the "take off" to a sustained growth in yearly *GNP*. As a larger fraction of *GNP* goes to increased saving and investment, the capacity growth rate rises toward the full-employment level. Assuming all conditions for growth are satisfied, the need for external capital would progressively diminish.

**Summary.** Economic growth is the expansion of real *GNP* or real *GNP* per capita. Two methods of measuring growth were introduced and explained: full-employment growth and capacity growth.

Potential output is the output that could be maintained at full employment. The growth rate of potential *GNP* is approximated by adding the estimated percentage increase in the supply of labor to the estimated percentage increase in the productivity of the labor supply. Actual output is the yearly output (*GNP*) of the economy. Actual *GNP* would equal potential *GNP* in a given year if the percentage increase in the labor supply and the percentage increase in the productivity of the labor supply were equal to the estimated increases the economy is capable of achieving. In recent years the actual *GNP* has fallen short of potential *GNP*. Unless demand or $C + I + G$ expands steadily, the expanding potential output will not be realized in the form of actual output.

By projecting full-employment *GNP* (potential supply) and actual *GNP* (aggregate demand) over the next few years, government policy makers are better prepared to suggest a course of action to reduce the anticipated gap.

Investment is the crucial factor explaining capacity growth. Beginning with a capacity equilibrium *GNP,* where planned saving and planned investment are equal, this year's investment (or addition to capital stock) creates extra productive capacity in the following year. The amount of extra productive capacity depends upon the productivity of capital. The growth of productive capacity generates a larger potential volume of saving. To justify the growth of output in the latter year a larger volume of investment is necessary. The increased investment spending, stimulated by the multiplier, causes demand to rise sufficiently to take care of the added output resulting from the increased capacity.

Capacity *GNP* and potential *GNP* will yield identical growth rates if the annual increase in the productivity of investment times the long-run saving rate equals the annual percentage increase in the available supply of labor plus the annual percentage increase in the productivity of labor.

Because the potential growth rate of *GNP* in less developed countries tends to be higher than the capacity growth rate, the problem of growth lies mainly with investment. The solution seems to be one of channeling more resources into capital goods production and the receipt of capital goods from abroad.

## QUESTIONS

1. Define carefully the following terms and note the differences. *Potential output, full-capacity output, capacity output, actual output, output gap.*
2. According to information furnished by the Council of Economic Advisers, what is the behavior of actual output compared to potential output since 1953? How do you account for this?
3. What is the main value of potential *GNP* as a concept?
4. What is an important remedy for an output gap, and how does it operate?
5. What are the dual functions of investment? How does this property of investment tend to bring about a moving or dynamic economy?
6. Describe the long-run saving function. How does it differ from the short-run function?
7. Describe the basic conditions of equilibrium assumed in the discussion of growth of capacity *GNP*.
8. Why must capacity *GNP* and investment (capacity saving) be larger in each successive year?
9. Give and explain briefly the formula for the equilibrium rate of growth of capacity *GNP*.
10. What is the formula for the overall equilibrium growth of the economy? What happens if this condition is not fulfilled?

# Appendix

## FINDING SUCCESSIVE POTENTIAL OUTPUTS

In Figure 28–3 the potential outputs at successive points of time were laid out on the horizontal axis. No method of figuring these points was stated. There is an easy graphic method, however, that we can insert here.

First, we draw in the $C + I + G$ line in Figure 28–6 to help define our initial equilibrium. Then we draw in a 45-degree line; the hori-

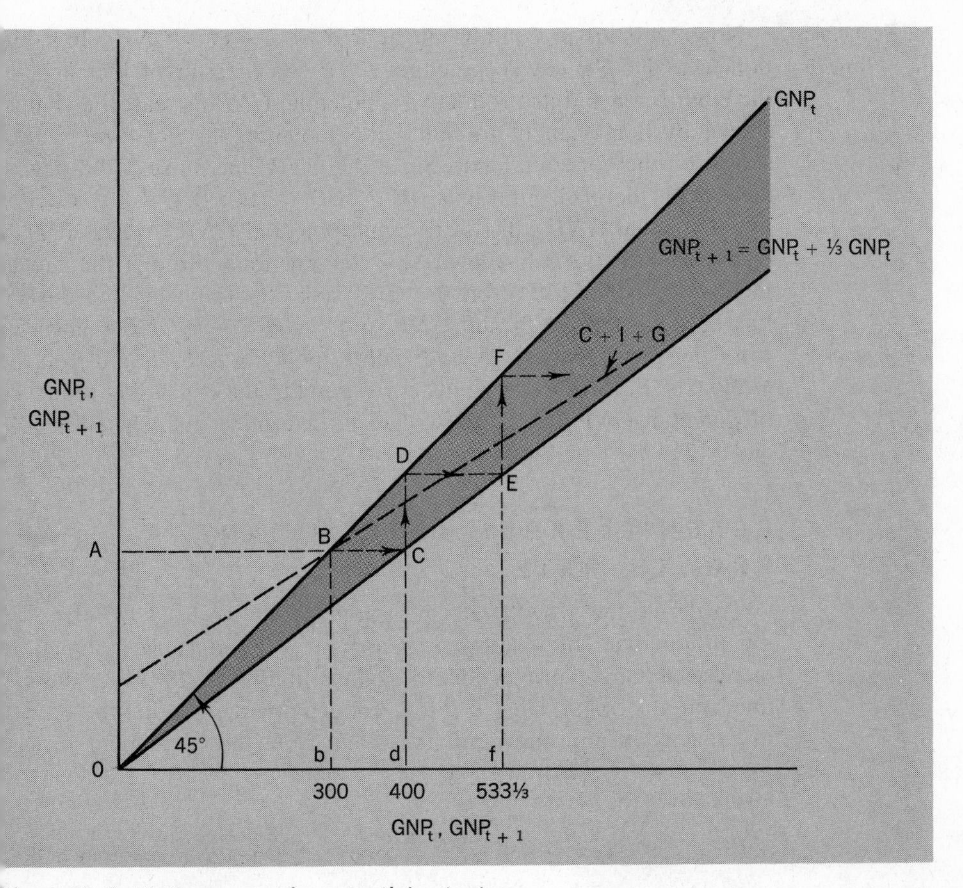


**Figure 28–6.** Finding successive potential outputs.

zontal and vertical coordinates of points on this line have the same value, which we may take to be $GNP_t$, or $GNP$ in period $t$.

Next, we tilt the *GNP* line downward. Let us do this in such a way that if we draw a horizontal line from *A* on the vertical axis, intersecting the 45-degree line in *B* and terminating in a point *C*, $BC/AB = 1/3$, or $33\frac{1}{3}$ per cent. This implies that each horizontal coordinate of the new line is $1/3$ greater than the corresponding one on the *GNP* or 45-degree line. We label this new line $GNP_{t+1} = GNP_t + 1/3\ GNP_t$. The *X* coordinate of every point on the new line is $1/3$ greater than on the 45-degree or $GNP_t$ line.

Now we assume two things. First, in the original equilibrium at *B*, potential output is equal to actual output. Second, the annual growth determined for *GNP* is $1/3$. This fact is then registered in shifting (tilting) the $GNP_t$ line, so that every *X* coordinate is $1/3$ greater than before.

Now, we start in equilibrium at $B$; $C+I+G=GNP_t$. In addition, actual $GNP$ equals potential $GNP$. As a result of increases in the labor force and its productivity, potential $GNP$ increases, a change shown by a movement to the right amounting to $BC = bd = 100$, shown on the horizontal axis. Since the $GNP_t$ line makes a 45-degree angle with the horizontal axis, $BC = CD = 100$. If $C+I+G$ rises by $CD$, actual $GNP$ will rise to equal potential $GNP$. Again, at $D$, a ⅓ increase in $GNP$ is shown (by construction) through the movement $DE = df = 133\frac{1}{3}$ on the $GNP$ axis. By following the dashed line between the $GNP_t$ and $GNP_{t+1}$ $(= GNP_t + \frac{1}{3}GNP_t)$ lines we can determine points $B$, $D$, and $F$ corresponding to $b$, $d$, and $f$ on the $GNP$ axis. In turn, these points correspond to the expanding sequence of potential $GNP$ values we wished to determine, namely 300, 400, and 533⅓.

## GRAPHIC PROOF OF CONSTANT GROWTH RATE

To derive the growth rate in graphic terms we need to introduce the productivity of investment. Capacity to produce is assumed to increase in direct proportion to saving. In Figure 28–7 we draw a line from the origin, labeled $P$ for Productivity, designating the growth in capacity in any one period resulting from the investment in that

**Figure 28–7.** The growth of capacity.

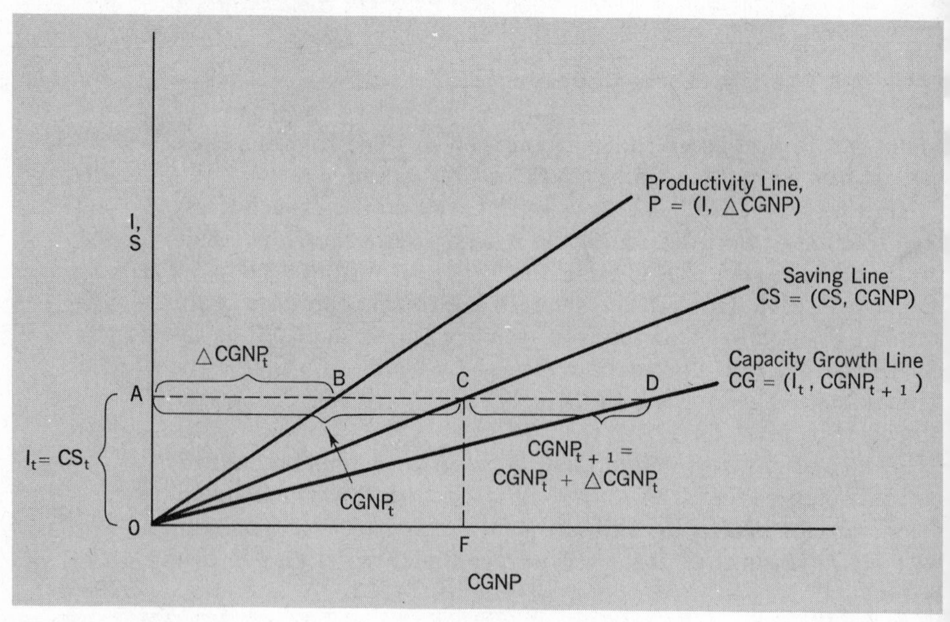

period. The capacity added is not completed until the following period. The slope of the productivity line with respect to the vertical axis is the productivity ratio of investment. Thus

$$p' = \frac{\Delta CGNP}{I} = \frac{AB}{OA}. \quad \textbf{(4)}$$

Next we draw in the usual long-run saving line. In drawing up this line we assume that $GNP = CGNP$ at all times. We refer to saving at $CGNP$ as capacity saving, or $CS$. The average and marginal propensity to save is interpreted in the graph as the slope of the saving line with respect to the horizontal axis, or as

$$s = \frac{CS}{CGNP} = \frac{FC}{OF}. \quad \textbf{(5)}$$

Now we must introduce the two conditions of equilibrium. Combined, these say that investment equals capacity saving ($CS$), or saving out of capacity $GNP$. In this discussion we assume throughout that

$$I_t = CS_t\,. \quad \textbf{(6)}$$

For this reason we label the horizontal axis $CGNP$ to indicate the assumption that capacity $GNP$ is being attained at all times. This is essential to the analysis.

We are now able to develop a line showing next period's $CGNP$ from a knowledge of this period's investment. We call this the Capacity Growth line. It is developed by the following reasoning. (1) By our assumption of equilibrium $I = CS$. Accordingly, $GNP$ is pushed to $CGNP$, because $CS$ can be absorbed by $I$ and the corresponding level of $GNP = CGNP$ can be sustained. In the given period, then, if $I_t = OA$, then $I_t = OA = CS$. We can then read $CGNP_t$ by moving horizontally from $A$ to $C$, where $AC = OF = CGNP_t$. This is read from the Saving Line. (2) We read the increment in capacity $GNP$ created by this level of investment from the productivity line. This is $\Delta CGNP_t = AB$. (3) We may now add the increment of productive capacity to the existing capacity. This gives $CGNP_t + \Delta CGNP_t = CGNP_{t+1} = AC + AB = AD$. We lay off $\Delta CGNP_t = AB$ beyond $C$, terminating in $D$, so that $AB = CD$. (4) We may now relate the volume of investment in one period, $I_t = OA$, to the capacity $GNP$ of the next, $CGNP_{t+1}$. The locus of points like $D$ is called the Capacity Growth line $CG$, and it relates $I_t$ to $CGNP_{t+1}$.

Operating under our equilibrium assumptions we are now ready to show the growth process graphically. We may drop the productivity line, because it is incorporated as the relationship between the common vertical coordinate of the Saving and Capacity Growth lines and the difference between their horizontal coordinates—for example, as the relationship of $OA$ to $OD - OC = CD = AB$.

In Figure 28–8, then, we draw in the Saving and Capacity Growth lines. We assume the equilibrium condition to prevail at the outset. Let us start in period zero with $I_0 = CS_0 = OA$. From capacity saving of $OA$ in period zero we know both current $CGNP_0$ and next period's $CGNP_1$. The first change, then, is an increase in $CGNP$ from $AB$ in period zero to $AC$ in period one. With a $CGNP_1$ of $AC$ in period one capacity saving rises to point $D$, or amount $OM$. To absorb this level of saving, investment must rise to $OM$. This raises $GNP$ to $MD = AC$, so that $GNP_1 = CGNP_1$, and demand clears capacity supply from the market.

Investment of $OM$ in period one leads to an increase in $CGNP$ from $MD$ to $ME$ in period two. Capacity saving rises to point $F$ or $ON$, and so on.

Clearly, the successive increases in capacity $GNP$, capacity saving, investment, and $GNP$ follow the stair-step pattern $BCDEFG$. We can also demonstrate the theorem on the growth rate. First we note that the productivity ratio can be written

$$p' = \frac{\Delta CGNP}{I} \tag{7}$$

$$= \frac{BC}{OA} = \frac{DE}{OM}.$$

The last equality is by construction. Since $p'$ is a constant, the spread between the saving line and the capacity growth line has been drawn up in such a way as to reflect this.

$$s = \frac{CS}{CGNP} \tag{8}$$

$$= \frac{OA}{AB} = \frac{OM}{MD},$$

by similar triangles.

The growth rate for capacity output can be represented by

$$g = \frac{\Delta CGNP}{CGNP} \tag{9}$$

$$= \frac{BC}{AB} = \frac{DE}{MD}.$$

To prove the last equality notice that the parallel lines $I_0$, $I_1$, and $I_2$ intersect the three lines from the origin, represented by the vertical axis, the saving line, and the capacity growth line. The lines from the origin intercept proportional segments on the parallel lines so that

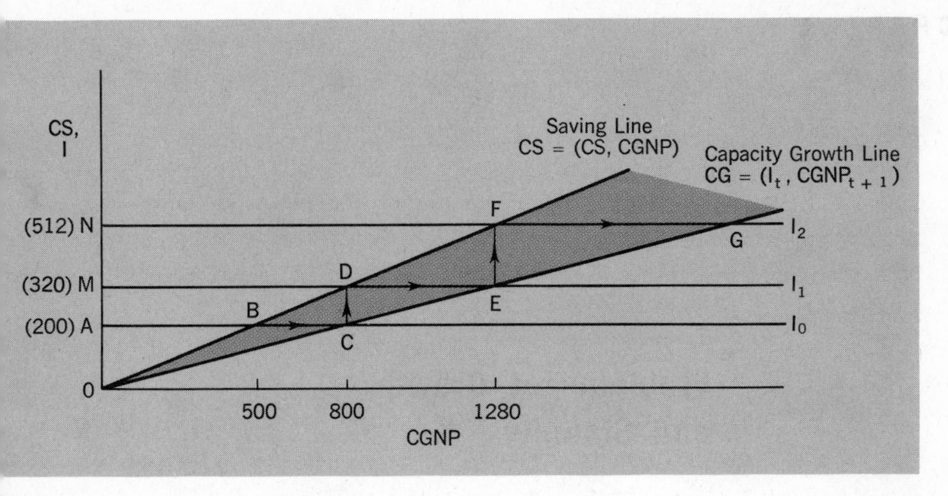


**Figure 28–8.** The growth process.

$BC/AB = DE/MD$. Alternatively, this may be proved by a repeated argument on similar triangles.

We now verify that $g = p's$ by a simple argument.

$$g = \frac{BC}{AB} = \frac{BC}{OA} \cdot \frac{OA}{AB} \tag{10}$$

$$= \frac{DE}{MD} = \frac{DE}{OM} \cdot \frac{OM}{MD} = p's\,.$$

Finally, noticing that triangles $BCD$, $OAB$, $DEF$, and $OMD$ are similar, we can find the growth rate for investment (capacity saving) to be

$$\frac{\Delta I}{I} = \frac{AM}{OA} = \frac{CD}{OA} = \frac{BC}{AB} \tag{11}$$

$$= \frac{MN}{OM} = \frac{EF}{OM} = \frac{DE}{MD} = g\,.$$

Clearly, investment grows at the same constant percentage rate $g$ as does *CGNP*.

The proof of this proposition by algebra is, perhaps, simpler. See the appendix to Chapter 13 in D. Hamberg, the source cited above. See also pages 611–12 below.

# CHAPTER 29

## Problems of Growth and Stability

Though it is not very difficult to acquire a basic understanding of the growth process, the study of policies that serve to promote full-employment *GNP* and stable purchasing power is another matter. The topic involves issues that arouse vigorous debate: nearly everyone adds his two cents' worth! Yet the complex problems involved call for the use of concepts found in all preceding chapters of the text. And do not think that a mastery of the tools of economics is sufficient. It is also necessary to make value judgments pertaining to the various methods of employing resources, the desirability of product mixes, and the distribution of output that may result. This is one of the reasons why there are so many persons willing to put in their two cents' worth!

Consider a few of the questions arising in this area: What is a desirable rate of growth for a mixed economy? What sorts of costs does growth involve? How can government surpluses (or deficits) or imports help to sustain a given growth rate? In this chapter we shall try to provide some tools of analysis that will be useful for dealing with such questions.

### PREREQUISITES FOR A CONSTANT RATE OF GROWTH

It is clear from the analysis in Chapter 28 that the rate of economic growth depends upon the relative availability of economic resources. In the labor force, capital facilities, and other economic resources are expanding at highly uneven rates, a constant rate of growth will not be consistent with the full utilization of resources. Consider a change in the annual rate of increase in the labor supply from 2 to 3 per cent. The rise permits a higher potential full-employment *GNP*. However, if the rate of growth remains constant, actual *GNP* will fall short of maximum output, and some unemployment will appear. On the other hand, if resources are increasing at a uniform rate, a fluctuating rate of output growth would not be consistent with the full utilization of resources at a maximum output. A drop in the growth rate in the presence of increased resources will create idle capacity and cause output to be held below the potential of the economy.

The above statements bring to mind two significant points: that the rate of growth is related to the availability of resources and that the rate of growth may fluctuate. Recall the unstable demand for durable goods and the variability of investment! But more about this point later in the chapter.

The requirements for a constant rate of growth can be explained with the aid of our tools of income analysis. Assuming an adequate supply of resources, capital must expand at a constant rate. For this to occur, saving must be sufficient to provide the necessary supply of capital. If the right fraction of current income is consumed, saving will rise by the amount necessary to maintain a constant rate of growth. Here we have it in a nutshell—saving, investment, real income, and consumption. But suppose too much of current income is consumed. Saving will then rise too slowly to support a steady rate of growth. (Recall capacity *GNP* analysis in Chapter 28, with its emphasis on saving, investment, real income, and consumption.) Not only is it essential that the level of saving be adequate: it is further necessary that the level of investment be high enough to absorb all the saving. In other words, aggregate saving and aggregate investment spending must be equal.

To sum up, a constant rate of output growth requires a fairly constant rate of increase in economic resources. The rate of output growth can be maintained only if the right proportion of current income is consumed and saved. In addition, aggregate saving must equal aggregate investment spending. Finally, if too little or too much is saved, or if aggregate saving and aggregate investment expenditures are not equal, the rate of growth will fluctuate, and some resources will be idle part of the time.

## THE PROBLEM OF ALLOCATING INCREASED OUTPUT

Suppose an economy is able to maintain a given growth rate. What is the value or worth of the extra output? If the United States growth rate of approximately 3.5 per cent per year is maintained, *GNP* in

1970 will amount to about $710 billion. At a 4.5-per-cent growth rate *GNP* would be approximately $790 billion in 1970.[1] The total value of the higher rate of growth is $80 billion. What the additional output is worth depends upon the kinds of goods produced in relation to the wants of the people. New baby shoes are important to a rapidly growing population. Steel plows, medical supplies, and new schools are critically needed in the less developed countries. Hula hoops or even additional economics textbooks may not be as high on the list of needs. Nonetheless, it is easy to imagine all kinds of uses for the additional $80 billion.

If society chooses those outputs that satisfy the most important needs, the first $710 billion will satisfy the most intense desires. The extra $80 billion will satisfy only the lesser needs on the lower end of the scale of wants. On the other hand, if no systematic scheme of choices is evident, the additional $80 billion may be as important dollar-for-dollar as the first $710 billion. If society elects to satisfy lesser needs ahead of more urgent ones, the extra $80 billion will be more important than the first $710 billion.

Thus the blessings of a more rapid growth of *GNP* depend in an important way on the way in which expected output is allocated among various needs. Should society allocate output to satisfy its most urgent needs, extra output will be only as important as the satisfaction of its less urgent needs. In earlier discussions the bearing of resource allocation on growth was emphasized. We now reverse the coin to show how the outputs resulting from the use of resources must be proportioned to achieve the right kind of growth.

There are several important problems pertaining to the allocation of a larger output. Only two will be brought out in the present discussion. The first relates to the distribution of output in the private sector; the second, to the allocation between private and public (government) uses.

**Private Shares in Larger Output.** Even though a larger output implies more goods and services for all, individuals may not share equally in the distribution of the larger *GNP*. Suppose that approximately 78 per cent of the *GNP* will be devoted to private needs. This is the present percentage share going to the private sector. If the *GNP* in 1970 is $790 billion, about $616.2 billion will be used for private purposes.

Let us assume that economic growth is a desirable goal. A redistribution of income may be needed to assure a rate of capital formation appropriate for the desired growth in output. If saving is too low in relation to income to provide the needed capital, persons in the higher-



[1] Figures are based on a *GNP* of $503 billion in 1960.

ncome groups who undertake a large part of the saving could be avored by tax cuts that would leave them a larger share of total in- ome and greater disposable incomes. With these larger disposable ncomes they would save more, thus helping to meet the need for extra aving. On the other hand, a high ratio of saving to income may re- ard economic growth. Under these circumstances, government could eek to raise the lower incomes by its actions. The effect of such in- ome changes, whether effected by taxes, transfer payments, or what- ver means, raises the share of total income they receive and reduces he fraction of income saved.

A rising *GNP* does not guarantee that everyone will share in the ise of per capita output. Furthermore, growth in output is not synony- nous with full employment. Unfortunately, adequate job openings are resently lacking for a certain segment of the population. By expand- ng educational and other opportunities for those who have turned 65 nd others who lack general educational requirements or specialized raining, the nation is more likely to attain a higher rate of growth. For example, specialized training increases the productivity of labor, nd as we found in the last chapter, a higher rate of productivity in- reases actual *GNP*. Both private firms and government participate n the expansion of employment opportunities. Many firms offer on- he-job training for new and old employees. They also sponsor adult nd other forms of educational training. The Federal government sub- idizes veterans' education, provides vocational retraining, and makes National Defense Scholarship grants. These and many other actions ielp to assure that all groups in society will share in a rising level of output.

**Government Shares in Larger Output.** In a mixed economy pub- ic expenditures are restricted to a figure well under half of total xpenditure. An arbitrary limitation on public spending may preclude he satisfaction of certain public needs. At the same time private needs of a kind that most people concede to be of less importance are being met. Thus the upward trend in government spending for basic esearch reflects a widely held conviction that prior expenditures in his area were quite insufficient. Perhaps the flight of the Russian Sputnik in 1957 and the gradual awakening of the public to our lag- ging growth rate prodded Congress to agree to larger public expendi- ures for research.

Consider the possibility that all levels of government will spend no nore than 22 per cent of the *GNP* for public needs. Out of a possible GNP of $790 billion in 1970, we will use $173.8 billion for public purposes. This allocation of output may leave unsatisfied certain public needs more important than a part of the $616.2 billion of private expenditures. Presumably the value or worth of the rising output is influenced by additional government spending made possible by the higher *GNP*. If society comes to believe that government spending is primarily responsible for increased output, we can expect a large increase in government spending. A proper limit to the expansion of the government share of output is set by the necessary private sacrifices. When these outweigh the benefits of additional public spending, a suitable limit has been reached.

There are two basic ways of raising public expenditures to a higher level: the first relies upon increased efficiency in tax collection and therefore a higher yield from present tax rates. The alternative is to increase tax rates. Greater efficiency results from closing tax loopholes, improved administration, greater economy in tax collections, and a host of other measures. With given tax rates and efficiency in collection only a rise in the rate of economic growth will afford additional taxes for increased spending.

Higher tax rates permit larger public expenditures, but certain tax changes, particularly those affecting investment incentives, might lessen the growth rate. Clearly, a sharp rise in tax rates of upper-income groups and corporations could retard investment. Chapter 28's analysis of capacity *GNP* showed that investment spending must rise continually in order to absorb the extra productive capacity required to sustain a given rate of growth.

If public expenditures are to be increased, higher tax rates may be necessary. Reducing exemptions or deductions on the personal income tax has the effect of broadening the tax base. The setting of higher beginning rates on individual incomes is another possibility. A further possibility consists of increases in sales or excise taxes. Such changes impose a burden on the consumer, but the decision to allocate a larger part of output to government implies a willingness to sacrifice some private consumption.

The rate of growth is influenced by the pattern of government expenditures. A large part of extra government spending is likely to be allocated to education, research, construction of dams, and other activities that lead to a higher growth rate. Yet government spending on these items involves foregoing private consumption of a corresponding amount. Obviously, a society must weigh the relative merits of allocating additional output to households and firms in the private sector, on the one hand, or to government, on the other. This is not a simple task.

## STEPPING UP THE GROWTH RATE

In the last chapter it was implied that a nation should take action to bring the level of actual output up to—or at least closer to—

potential output. The nation should also try in the future to keep the economy operating close to capacity—that is, close to the fullest possible utilization of resources consistent with price stability. We tried to demonstrate how an increase in the quantity and quality of labor and the growth of investment in capital facilities contribute to rising output, assuming in each instance the existence of a sufficient quantity of the remaining resources to work with this labor and capital.

If the long-run growth rate is to be estimated with more precision, it will be necessary to investigate the influence on the growth rate of the various elements that influence the supply and efficiency of productive factors. Assume, for example, a 2-per-cent annual increase in the available labor supply and a 2.5-per-cent annual increase in the productivity of labor. Though these figures are fairly realistic, a liberalization of the immigration laws to allow more foreign persons to settle here would probably cause both the supply and productivity of labor to rise in the future. Thus the long-run growth rate would rise by some specific magnitude—perhaps 1%.

In the following section we will content ourselves with a study of only a few of the many elements that influence the rate of growth. Subsequent discussion will therefore center around four main points: (1) increasing the supplies of factors, (2) public saving and growth, (3) increasing the efficiency of output, and (4) imports and growth. (The latter point is discussed in the appendix to this chapter.) We will confine the analysis of supply factors to labor and capital. In the interests of brevity, important social problems that may arise will be ignored.

## INCREASING THE SUPPLIES OF FACTORS

**A Growing Labor Supply.** In the last few years we have witnessed a rapid increase in the United States labor force. The annual increase between 1946–60 amounted to about 850,000 persons. According to the *Economic Report of the President,* 1961 (page 56), the unusually large number of younger persons reaching working age in the 1960s may raise the annual increase to 1.4 million persons. If the estimate turns out to be correct for the remainder of the decade, we can expect a yearly increase in the labor supply of about 2 per cent.[2] If, in addition, the productivity of labor rises by 2.5 per cent annually, a growth rate of 4.5 per cent would result.

Though the supply of labor is increasing, it is likely that many young people will find it increasingly difficult to fit into jobs demand-

[2] The current estimate is 1.8 per cent. See the *Economic Report of the President,* 1962, p. 116.

ing highly technical skills. If the education of the annual additions to the labor force is inadequate or inappropriate to changing needs of industry, unemployment will develop. Because rising output will be possible with the use of workers of greater skill, such growth does not assure employment of the improperly trained workers. Indeed, Professor Hansen tells us that employment in industries producing material goods (manufacturing, agriculture, and so on) has already reached its peak. Apparently, the growth in the labor force must be absorbed mainly by the service industries, public and private.[3]

Suppose that the changing structure of industry permits the full employment of a growing labor supply. In itself this adjustment may tend to inhibit growth for the following reasons. We recognize that full-employment *GNP* requires a steady increase both in the quantitative and qualitative aspects of labor. But economists generally agree that the productivity of labor in service industries is less than that in the material goods industries. Hence, even though the economy may be able to absorb increases in the labor force, the shift of labor from high to low productivity industries will tend to hold down the growth rate.

At least one other point deserves comment at this juncture. Suppose that the growth process is interrupted by a recession. An important question arises immediately: How will society share the burden of such a recession? If past experience is a guide, the answer seems to be that the major burden of a recession is transferred to the unemployed, the group least able to withstand it. Let us check recent experience in the United States to verify the suggested result. A brief analysis of the *GNP* and its components should do the trick.

Consider first aggregate consumption, defined here as the total purchases by consumers of all civilian goods, including nonmilitary goods and services of government. This total has risen in every year since the end of World War II. Of course, the rise was less during the three recession years (1949, 1953, 1958), when it averaged $6.7 billion. On the average, however, the increase in the flow of goods and services purchased by individuals was $10.3 billion in the period 1948–59, inclusive. Despite this remarkable feat, both the *GNP* and employment oscillated during the period. Evidently, we must look for the causes of these changes elsewhere.

If we subtract aggregate consumption, as defined above, from the *GNP,* we are left with (1) gross private investment, (2) net foreign investment (net export surplus), and (3) military expenditures. These three factors account for most of the fluctuations in *GNP,* because aggregate consumption (private and public) has risen fairly steadily.

[3] Alvin H. Hansen, *Economic Issues of the 1960s* (New York: McGraw-Hill Book Company, 1960), pp. 71–72.

For reasons explained elsewhere in the text, private investment has faltered at various times in recent years. Specifically, net investment in real terms fell by $11.7 billion in 1949 and $13.7 billion in 1958.[4] Unemployment naturally resulted from the reduction in capital outlays. As a consequence, the burden of the two recession periods rested heavily on the unemployed, because aggregate consumption, as defined above, continued to rise. (Incidentally, can you explain how a policy of rigid wage rates could intensify this problem?)

**Maintaining Standard Hours of Work.** People could produce and consume more goods and services if they worked harder and longer. During World War II we amply demonstrated our ability to enlarge output under emergency conditions. An expansion of the labor force and the lengthening of the work week brought a large increase in the output of military and civilian goods despite the mobilization of some 11 to 12 million men in the United States armed forces. Clearly, an increase in the number of man-hours of work per person has the effect of raising the growth rate of labor, provided the number of workers and the length of the work week do not decline. Thus, extra output increases, up to a point, as the number of hours worked per year is lengthened. In economic jargon, the economy gains most when the disadvantage of extra work just equals the value of the additional output.

But standards of work are not necessarily determined on the basis of economic efficiency. In fact, we do not know the exact relationship between standard hours of work and output. We do know that the amount of work a man performs in an hour is related to the number of hours he works. Shortening a particularly long work week will increase output. At some range of hours below this shortened work week, total output will decline, but output per man-hour will increase. To follow the sequence a step further, output per man-hour falls if hours are reduced further after some optimum work week is reached. The problem is that we do not possess the exact quantitative information that alone would permit us to use these relationships.

If economic efficiency is not the sole determinant of standard hours, what does fix the standard? It is established mainly by group efforts, exerted principally by unions and management, federal and state legislation, and custom. There is therefore some reason to doubt that this existing system for determining hours of work actually yields the greatest economic gain.

Granting certain imperfections inherent in establishing standard hours of work, the accepted standard exerts a great deal of influence on the ability of the economy to produce a continually increasing out-

[4] *Ibid.*, p. 145.

put of goods and services. The standard is especially significant, because we are presently considering a stepped-up growth rate. A higher rate of growth implies a higher rate of increase of output than previously—that is, a rising output concomitant with a higher growth rate. It is therefore important that the standard hours of work not be shortened beyond some point, because the lessened output involved in such action will retard long-run growth.

Of course, it is likely that standard hours of work may be reduced temporarily as a consequence of a decline in demand. This spreading-of-the-work to maintain short-run employment might be tolerated for a time. However, it is better for the economy in the long run to have plenty of jobs available to help produce a growing volume of goods than it is to reduce standard hours of work to increase employment.

**Lost Labor: A Possible Source of Expanded Supply.** Literally millions of hours of work are lost annually from illness, on-and-off the job accidents, labor disputes, criminals serving prison terms, seasonal fluctuations in industry, and excessive employment in agriculture and other occupations. We need only consult the daily newspaper or turn on the radio to be made aware of the magnitude of such losses. Without suggesting specific remedies for the various kinds of lost labor or attempting to measure the costs of such remedies, it is sufficient for our purposes merely to indicate the need for a reduction of these losses. Both individuals and society must somehow be brought to a fuller recognition of their responsibilities before net additions to the labor force can be expected from this kind of lost labor.

There are other types of lost labor that could help maintain the growth of output; we have in mind groups of workers who offer their services on a part-time basis. They include the senior citizens (those over 65), part-time workers among the school-age group, and married women in the middle-age brackets. If these persons are going to be absorbed into the labor force—and there is no guarantee that our mixed economy will absorb them—ways and means will have to be found to compensate for the additional cost and inefficiency involved in part-time employment. About all that can be said is that a failure to provide these potential workers with jobs will create some loss of labor input that would otherwise contribute to production.

**Immigration and Long-Run Growth.** A higher rate of immigration could add substantially to the economy's long-run output. Although he will experience some temporary loss in productivity because of changed environmental conditions, language difficulties, and unfamiliarity of work methods, the immigrant will soon adapt himself. Past experience of the United States bears out this proposition. Of course, future growth requires that a higher rate of immigration be associated with a rising per capita income and not merely with an improvement in long-run output.

Because many immigrants are likely to be drawn from the higher productivity groups who already possess skills or are generally better informed, and are therefore more capable of meeting standards for admission to other countries, it is assumed that the nations losing such persons will have to train others of the population to be as productive as those who leave. Otherwise, output per person will reach its peak at a lower population level. Yet the emigration of a limited number of persons might act as a stimulant to the economy that expects to lose workers. Comprehensive plans may be formulated to educate and train a larger number of the population than previously. Hence, productivity per person might rise enough—or more than enough—to offset the anticipated loss of productivity caused by emigration.

We do not pretend to have exhausted all the various aspects involving labor and the role it plays in maintaining a higher growth rate. Very likely, enough has been said to set us thinking about this problem.

**An Expanding Stock of Capital.** Suppose it were possible to expand the stock of capital at a faster rate. This would make possible the achievement of a more rapid rate of growth of output. Let us refer back to the model of economic growth introduced in the last chapter. Recall that the theory asserts the common rate of growth of capital and output to be

$$p's\,,$$

where $p'$ is the productivity ratio of investment (the number of dollars that capacity *GNP* rises as a result of one dollar of investment in the preceding period) and $s$ is the propensity (marginal and average) to save. If either of these two coefficients should increase, a more rapid growth of investment and *GNP* becomes possible.

Let us briefly state the sense of the two cases. Suppose the productivity ratio of investment increases. We start with a given saving and investment in period zero. With a stepped-up value of $p'$ capacity of *GNP* will increase by a larger amount and a larger percentage in the following period than it otherwise would. In order to absorb the larger volume of output from increased capacity, investment would have to increase. Through the multiplier the rise in investment would increase *GNP* (demand) sufficiently to absorb the enlarged *CGNP*. With the larger $GNP = CGNP$ comes enlarged *CS* (capacity saving), which is, of course, equal to the aforementioned larger flow of investment. With the larger investment comes, subsequently, an increased *CGNP*. The analysis follows the usual lines, with the enlarged productivity amplifying the growth directly or indirectly at every stage.

Before resorting to numerical illustration let us consider the other case, a rise in the propensity to save $s$. The explanation is best begun at the stage where *CGNP* has just increased as a result of previous saving and investment. The propensity to save increases. As a result, the level of saving is larger than it would otherwise have been. To clear output from the market a larger volume of investment is required; that is, the larger volume of investment is necessary in order to offset increased saving (reduced consumption). As a result of the fact that saving and investment are raised above levels they would otherwise have, the growth in *CGNP* is still larger in the following period, and so on.

In our standard illustration $p'$ is taken to be $1/3$, $s = S/GNP$, where $S$ is gross saving (investment), to be $1/8$ and $p's$ to be, therefore, $1/24 = 4.16\%$. Suppose the productivity ratio increased from $1/3$ to $2/5$, and the propensity to save remains at $1/8$; the growth rate then rises from $4.16\%$ to $2/5 \cdot 1/8 = 2/40 = 5\%$. On the other hand, a rise in the saving rate from $1/8 = 3/24 = 12.5\%$ to $3/20 = 15\%$ will cause the growth rate to rise from $4.16\%$ to $1/3 \cdot 3/20 = 1/20 = 5\%$. Of course, these substitutions merely illustrate the content of the model. Perhaps the key point is that an increase in $p'$ or $s$ will require investment to grow at a faster rate if *GNP* is to be maintained equal to *CGNP* at all times. In the appendix these cases are illustrated graphically.

Public action may be taken to bring about changes in $p'$ and $s$. On the one hand $p'$ can be increased by providing public services that are designed to increase the efficiency of such investment. It goes without saying that efficient police and fire protection, as well as just administration of the laws, favors the productivity of private investment. Even more clearly, a good educational system that provides efficient workers to staff the businessman's plant is going to help. A more direct measure is to provide funds for research and development that may provide products and equipment needed in common by business and government. A final and direct relationship consists in the taxes, such as corporation income taxes, levied on the business. Any reduction in these taxes will tend to stimulate the search for more productive forms of capital, as the fruits of its use are greater.

The saving rate may be altered by manipulating tax rates. Because corporations are proportionately big savers, an increase in corporate saving would probably result if the tax burden were shifted somewhat to individuals. Likewise, a shift in tax burdens from the less to the more well-to-do would probably increase saving out of a given income, because high-income recipients tend to save proportionately more. One might have qualms about such a policy on grounds that it ran counter to our ideas of social justice. The entire policy of raising $p'$ and $s$ raises questions about whether an accelerated growth of capacity will be counterbalanced by the necessary growth of investment that raises *GNP* to equal *CGNP*. We consider this point below.

**The Level of Saving and Investment.** Although the growth rate depends upon the productivity of investment and the long-run savings rate, capacity *GNP* is attained only if the level of saving and investment are equal. There is no guarantee that these variables will satisfy this requirement. Consider a level of savings sufficient to maintain a high growth rate. Investment must rise at the proper rate if *GNP* is to continue its growth. Opinion is divided as to the possibilities of a rise in investment. Two extreme views are offered in this connection: the first infers that limits on investment will not be reached for some time, and that an increase in saving will be sufficient, by itself, to induce an equal increase in investment. The second view suggests that the amount of investment firms are willing to undertake at any particular time—given the expectations with respect to the rate of return—is sharply limited. In effect, investment will remain close to, and often fall below, the normal supply of savings. According to this thesis an increase in the supply of savings cannot be expected to bring forth a comparable increase in investment.

There is little need for us to adopt either extreme view, because neither assumption is wholly acceptable. However, we need to recognize that policies should be implemented in such a way that long-run saving and investment will tend toward equality at a given rate of growth. At times investment will tend to outrun saving, causing inflationary pressure; at other times it will fall short, thus generating deflation. Temporary vicissitudes can be offset by appropriate public policies without destroying the long-run balance between saving and investment. We will not repeat here the various ways in which monetary and fiscal policies may be used to deal with short-run instability.

## PUBLIC SAVING AND GROWTH

Up to this point we have dealt with growth in terms of private sector saving and investment. On the last few pages we saw how a higher long-run saving ratio might permit a rise in the growth rate by providing additional funds for private investment. It was also suggested that a higher productivity of investment might bring about a higher growth rate.

Our discussion would be incomplete, however, if we failed to recognize the involvement of government in a growing society. Though a large part of the rising saving–investment needs of a mixed economy are provided by the private sector, government shares in satisfying these needs. In so doing, public capital contributes to output and influences the growth rate. Granting that both private and public investment are instrumental in increasing output, we know that they depend upon the total supply of savings. Investment cannot take place unless there exists a sufficient supply of savings, and given the availability of savings, the intentions to invest must be strong enough to absorb the flow of savings.[5]

To see more clearly how government facilitates growth of output we begin with an assumed equilibrium *GNP* condition for total saving and investment.[6] Thus

$$I + G = S + T, \tag{1}$$

where $I$ is private gross real investment, $G$ is government expenditure, $S$ is private gross real savings, and $T$ is taxes. Now we may consider the probable behavior of these variables.

First we assume that saving and taxes are each proportional to *GNP*. If we were to draw saving and tax lines separately, each would appear as a straight line through the origin, like the saving line in Figure 28–4. These assumptions seem to be borne out approximately by the facts. The saving–*GNP* relation has already been discussed. Our tax system is set up in such a way that taxes increase with income, the most striking illustration of this being the income tax. Furthermore, as a matter of record, the percentage of *GNP* taxed, $T/GNP$, does not seem to have been subject to much variation in recent years (leaving out of account the 1964–65 tax cut).

Investment is assumed to have a capacity creating role in this analysis marked by a productivity ratio, $p' = GNP/I$. Also investment has an income creating aspect that operates in a familiar way, as we shall see presently.

Finally, we come to government spending. For the sake of simplicity we are going to ignore the capacity creating aspects of government spending. Instead, we concentrate on the relationship to income, or *GNP*. Over a period of years it seems that government spending rises with income, or *GNP*. In fact, government spending has been referred to as collective consumption. As *GNP* rises, there is a tendency for new public wants to manifest themselves that ultimately tend to be met by government action and spending. This re-

[5] Intentions to invest refer to firms of the private sector. It was pointed out earlier in the text that government investment involves political rather than economic decisions. All we infer here is that total investment (private and public) must be equal to the total saving of the economy, if a given growth rate is to be maintained or a higher growth rate is to be achieved and maintained.

[6] For a short but excellent theoretical explanation of income growth refer to Kenneth K. Kurihara, *National Income and Economic Growth* (Chicago: Rand, McNally & Company, 1961), Ch. 11.

mark has especial validity when applied to state and local spending, which is directly tied to local and immediate public needs and income. If we look at the available data we find, indeed, that over a period of successive years government spending does actually vary in rather close relationship to *GNP*. This does not necessarily contradict the assumption that for short periods, such as a year, government spending tends to be constant. After all, budgets do sharply limit the variation of government spending. To summarize, we assume $G = g \cdot GNP$, where $G$ is government spending on output and $g$ is the constant fraction of *GNP* thus spent.

We can now reframe our equilibrium analysis to fit into the theory of growth. We may write our equation, as follows:

$$\begin{aligned} I &= S + T - G \\ &= S + (T - G)\,. \end{aligned} \tag{2}$$

We may regard the right-hand side as saving, supplemented by a surplus when taxes exceed government spending or reduced by a deficit when the opposite is true. In fact, we may interpret the equation as follows:

$$\begin{aligned} \text{investment} &= \text{saving plus government surplus} \\ &\qquad \text{(or minus the deficit)} \\ &= \text{net social saving.} \end{aligned} \tag{3}$$

We may refer to saving plus government surplus as net social saving. Actually, whenever government runs a surplus it has "savings" that it can make available to firms for investment. The opposite is true in case of a deficit. The sum of the two items constitutes net social saving, the sum available to investors to expand the capital stock. By our assumptions net social saving is tied to *GNP*. We have already explained the logic and factual basis of this assertion.

Let us now add a final bit of notation and we are ready to begin drawing conclusions. Let us designate net social saving by the letter $S'$ and note that $S' = S + (T - G)$. Then we can conclude by a few algebraic manipulations that $S' = s'GNP$, where $s' = s + (t - g)$.[7] At this point we can say that net social saving $S'$ plays the same role in this analysis that saving $S$ did in that of the preceding chapter. All we need to do is to relabel Figure 28–4, replacing the letter $S$ by $S'$ and interpreting the straight line through the origin as the net social saving at every level of *GNP*. In equilibrium, $S'$ is offset by corresponding investment, $I$. This determines a corresponding level of $GNP = CGNP$. The rest of the analysis is identical with that of Chapter 28.

[7] Here $s = S/GNP$, $t = T/GNP$, and $g = G/GNP$.

The rate of growth determined in an economic system which behaves in this way is expressed by:

$$p's', \text{ where } \quad s' = s + (t - g)\,. \tag{4}$$

Anything that increases $p'$ or $s'$ will increase the rate of growth of *GNP* and, equally, the required growth of investment. It is very easy to detect three kinds of policy actions for the government. First, suppose $t - g = 0$; the fraction of *GNP* spent and taxed is the same, the budget is balanced, and government fiscal operations do not affect net social saving $S'$ or the propensity to save socially $s'$. Then $s' = s$, and the rate of growth is not affected directly by fiscal operations. Here the government is fiscally neutral with respect to the rate of economic growth.

A second case occurs when the government acts to stimulate economic growth. If it believes that investment growth is being held back by inadequate social saving, it may attempt to run a budget surplus. It does this by raising $T$ relative to $G$ and $t$ relative to $g$. If $t$ exceeds $g$ so that $t - g$ is positive, the propensity to save socially is increased. This implies that the government, which is now running a surplus, makes these funds available to investing firms by, say, purchasing outstanding government bonds and retiring them. The former bondholders are now in a position to lend money to firms seeking to expand. If investment has been held back by a shortage of saving, this will increase the rate of investment and *GNP* in like measure.

A third case occurs when the government acts to slow down economic growth. It is possible that economic growth, spurred on by a high rate of investment, is too rapid to be sustained on a sound basis. For example, output may be outrunning resource supplies so that future expansion is at stake. Or capacity may be expanding at a more rapid rate than available supplies of labor. Here capacity output may have a tendency to exceed potential output. This tendency was noted in Western Germany during the 1950's. In this case the government may choose to reduce the supply of social saving by running a deficit. Then $t - g$ becomes negative, thus reducing $s' = s + (t - g)$. The government deficit absorbs part of the flow of available savings, leaving less for business firms to invest.

## LIMITATIONS ON THE ANALYSIS

**Investment Behavior.** The analysis we are following defines a common rate of growth for investment and *GNP*. The implication is that it is necessary for investment to grow at this rate if the condition $GNP = CGNP$ is to be satisfied in every time period. The nature of the model is that investment is restrained only by lack of adequate social saving. On the other hand, business firms do not resort to the banks for additional funds beyond that provided by social saving. If investment incentives are actually this strong and are satisfied only through social saving, the rate of economic growth can be altered by changing social saving. In turn, this may be modified by changing $t - g$ in the appropriate way.

From the qualifications we have put on the model it is going to be possible to apply it only under certain circumstances. Thus the analysis just outlined regarding the effects of government fiscal policy does not apply to an economy in which *GNP* tends to be less than *CGNP*. We have already noted that in the United States *GNP* has been less than potential *GNP* for some time. Also potential *GNP* is apparently less than *CGNP,* as the analysis of the last chapter suggested. Thus our *GNP* has apparently been less than *CGNP* for most of the last 10 years. Therefore the conclusions reached in the second and third cases are probably not relevant to recent behavior in the United States.

What policies are appropriate? Because demand is deficient, the government should raise government spending and hold down taxes. The results of such policies were outlined in some detail in Chapter 7. The student should not be disturbed by the fact that the policies outlined in this chapter are not applicable to the present situation in the United States. Actually, the elementary tools of fiscal policy turn out to be the relevant ones. If our economy should begin to approach capacity, we could then apply these tools.

At the present time the best application of this analysis is to be found in the Common Market countries of Western Europe. Here the pressure for economic expansion has been so great that there has been a labor shortage and, at times, a capital shortage. Consequently, the tools we have just discussed seem to apply rather well to this region.

**Monetary Behavior.** Implicit in the analysis is the assumption that banks do not contribute to the supply of funds available for investment. If the banks either added to or absorbed part of social saving, the funds available for investment would be modified. In turn, this would affect the rate of economic growth. This assumption is unrealistic, the quantity of money tending to expand with *GNP*.

## PUBLIC INVESTMENT AND GROWTH

In the preceding analysis we concentrated on the effects of fiscal policy in making possible a larger flow of funds for investment. There is another way in which government may stimulate growth, and this is by devoting part of government spending to public projects analogous to private investment. Such items as highways, school buildings, bridges, dams, harbors, public buildings, hospitals, and public housing fall into this category. In any early stage of economic development social capital of this kind is believed by economists to be one of the key elements in growth.

Let us assume that we divide our government budgets into a current account and a capital account, listing in the former sums spent to provide such services as defense and education and in the latter all sums spent for investment type activities. We may call the expenditure for current items government consumption $G_c$, and the latter may be called government investment $G_i$.

Let us assume that $G_c$ varies directly with *GNP* and that the tax yield also varies with *GNP*. Let us treat $G_i$ as similar in character to investment. Particular decisions at separated intervals have to be made before deciding on public investment projects. A definite public need usually has to be demonstrated before it will be undertaken.

We can now assimilate the analysis of government investment into the foregoing discussion of budgetary surpluses for growth. We now interpret investment as social investment, including private investment, $I$ and government investment $G_i$. The growth rate is

$$p'' s'' ,$$

where $p''$ is the productivity of social capital and $s'' = s + (t - g_c)$, where $g_c$ is the fraction of *GNP* spent on government consumption and $(t - g_c)$ represents the fractional surplus of taxes over government consumption. The latter fraction represents surplus taxes available for government investment.

More important than this algebra is the basic concept. Government may design a fiscal policy that brings in a surplus of taxes over government consumption. Such funds may be used to finance government investment. However, government investment may either fall short of or exceed these sums. In the first case, the excess of taxes, in addition to financing government investment, could be used to retire debt and thus to channel funds into private investment. In the second case government could tap private saving to add to the surplus government funds and thus finance the desired government investment.

What is the effect of government investment on the rate of economic growth? The strategy, as applied in France, and attempted in some of the less developed countries, is to reduce expenditure on government consumption as far as possible, raise taxes, and thus generate a surplus over government consumption that may be applied to government investment. This increases $s''$, the fraction of *GNP* consisting of social saving and available for social investment. Of course, the growth rate $p'' s''$ will increase and thus step up the rate of growth in the model.

Will this approach work? The answer depends in large part on the willingness of the public to accept the forced-saving program. France is an example of a country that has succeeded in expanding social savings in this way. The method is being applied with varying success in the less developed countries. Occasionally, there is an explosion when the deprived population makes its discontent known.

One feature of this approach that tends to make it workable is that the behavior of public investment is predictable. An increase in social saving without a corresponding increase in social investment causes *GNP* to fall short of *CGNP*. In part, this appears to account for the lagging rate of growth in the United States. Because social investment can be planned and executed firmly and definitely, the increased social saving can be matched with increased social investment.

A final word on the less-developed countries. These countries often lack well-developed financial institutions that channel individual bits of saving into investment. Also the traditions of these countries are frequently unfavorable to the development of an entrepreneurial class. There is no group prepared to undertake investment, weighing properly its attendant risks and costs against the prospective returns. For these and other reasons private saving and investment is apt to be low. Consequently, the need for government surpluses applied to public investment is all the greater.

## INCREASING EFFICIENCY IN PRODUCTION

Nearly everyone agrees that greater efficiency in production would have a favorable effect on a nation's rate of growth. Positive measures leading in this direction have been pointed out at various places in the text. In the following paragraphs we will review a few of the more important obstacles to efficiency that tend to restrict the long-run growth of output.

A host of laws and private restrictions have developed that prevent the most efficient allocation of resources among the various lines of production. Laws have been enacted granting subsidies to farmers and businesses; patents to protect individuals and firms; tariffs and other commercial and monetary restrictions to promote and protect domestic industry; laws to maintain retail prices; and many others. Private restrictions include monopolistic practices by firms and labor organizations.

Subsidies and tariffs result in an uneconomical use of domestic resources by discouraging submarginal producers from transferring resources to more economical employments consistent with the desires of consumers. Subsidies may be justified at times—for example, to channel necessary resources into war production—but their prolonged use leads to decreased output per unit of resources employed. Furthermore, subsidies create a form of forced saving on the part of consumers, because taxes and the prices of some goods rise. Earlier, it was indicated that tariffs may stimulate domestic investment. As a consequence, it is necessary for tariffs to assure businesses of a market so that the rising output can be sold. But this policy ignores the long-run effects of retaliatory restrictions abroad. In this sense, tariffs tend to restrict investment by confining the latter to the production of domestic goods only.[8] What amounts to a monopoly in the domestic market tends to result in a limited expansion of output and a rise in prices for the goods of protected firms.

Patents are granted to encourage technological advance by insuring individuals and firms a greater share of the gains from inventions. Nevertheless, patents discourage widespread use of new knowledge by providing protection to patent recipients for a series of years. Proponents of freer access to new knowledge question the degree of privilege afforded patent holders. Several proposals have been offered over the years that would alter the present patent system. One such scheme is to offer financial rewards, perhaps in the form of royalties, replacing—in whole or in part—the monopoly privilege now granted the holders of patents. For our purposes, this and other proposals are important in that they represent sound thinking devoted to finding better ways of maximizing output per unit of input.

The existence of a partially or wholly monopolistic situation in a market tends to reduce rather than encourage full use of resources. This is especially true of oligopoly, where existing firms resist the entry of new firms and thereby hope to limit output and to maintain a high price. (Recall the detailed explanation concerning monopoly imperfections back in Chapters 15, 16, and 17.) Even in those industries where economies of scale apply, diminishing returns set in when the scale is pushed too far. The result of overexpansion among a large number of competitive firms will spell losses or reduced profits and thereby cause a reduction of excess capacity. But where restrictions on the entry of firms exist, the fewer firms involved can reduce capacity and keep prices high.

Restricting the entry of new workers in various types of jobs, discriminating against minority races, lengthy strikes, promoting workers solely on the basis of seniority, and preventing the use of the most

[8] Obviously, this is an extreme case, implying that tariffs are sufficiently high to bring a halt to trade. The point is that tariffs are likely to act as a deterrent to rising investment because they limit the extent of the market.

recent tools and equipment on the job are examples of acts imposed by workers or workers and employers that set up barriers to efficient utilization of resources.

**An Omission.** We have not brought into the analysis the foreign trade sector. The reason for this is that imports and exports do not fit neatly into the pattern we have set up for the analysis of growth. Rather than undertaking these modifications here we defer them to the appendix that follows. The interested reader will find there how the foreign trade analysis broadens and modifies the theory of growth.

**Summary.** A constant rate of growth requires a fairly constant rate of increase in economic resources. The rate can be maintained only if the right proportion of current income is consumed and saved. Furthermore, aggregate saving must equal aggregate investment spending.

Discussion concerning the possibility of the higher rate of growth developed around five main points: (1) increasing the supplies of factors, (2) raising the productivity of capital and the saving rate, (3) public saving and growth, (4) public investment and growth, and (5) increasing efficiency in production.

A larger and more effective supply of labor is influenced by the extent of available technical skills, the determinants of the standard hours of work, the number of work hours lost each year because of labor disputes, illness and accidents, and the employment of certain groups, including part-time workers, the aged, and immigrants. The rise in the productivity of the growing labor supply will be greatly affected by the efficiency achieved by service industries.

A higher productivity of investment enhances the economy's ability to expand output at a higher rate. Assuming the economy is growing along an equilibrium growth path, a rise in the long-run saving ratio also makes possible a higher growth rate. Certain governmental policies may be instituted to bring about such changes. There are some reservations about whether investment will necessarily expand hand in hand with its income (*GNP*) creating capacity to absorb the output from the more rapidly growing capacity.

Beginning with an equilibrium *GNP* condition for total saving and investment, $I + G = S + T$, an assumed budgetary surplus, expressed in terms of ratio $t - g > 0$, can maintain a given rate of growth if the budgetary surplus offsets a smaller private saving ratio. A higher growth rate is possible where a small private saving ratio is more than offset by a large total saving. In both cases the public is being forced to save through fiscal policy and the accumulation of a treasury surplus.

Government surpluses of taxes over government consumption may be channeled into public investment. In cases where there are great needs for such investment there may result a faster growth rate. This approach has the advantage that investment can be directly matched with available saving.

Greater efficiency in producing output may be realized by reducing certain obstacles. Examples of such obstacles are found in laws granting subsidies and tariffs and in laws protecting patent rights and in private monopolies and monopsonies in product and resource markets.

In the aggregate sense successive levels of full-employment and capacity output (measuring aggregate supply) must be matched by actual spending on current output (measuring aggregate demand), if a given growth rate is to be continuously maintained. A higher level of full-employment and capacity *GNP* is realized as increased spending, acted upon by the multiplier, stimulates demand sufficiently to absorb into production the increment in productive capacity.

### QUESTIONS

1. How do the supplies of the several factors influence economic growth?
2. What are the effects of increases in $p'$ and $s$, respectively, on the rate of economic growth?
3. What important assumption must be made in order that the conclusions reached be true? Is this assumption valid?
4. How can government enlarge the flow of funds available for private investment by its fiscal policy? How do these funds become available to investing firms?
5. What is government investment? How may it be financed?
6. Is government investment productive? Cite some examples to prove your contention.
7. To what sort of countries does a program of government saving and investment seem most applicable?
8. How can government policies increase the productivity of private capital and the private savings rate?
9. Taxing, government consumption, and government investment are variables that behave in somewhat different ways. What assumptions are made in the text regarding the behavior of these variables?

## Appendix

### GRAPHS SHOWING CHANGES IN THE GROWTH RATE

In the text we described how an increase in the productivity ratio of capital or an increase in the propensity to save would increase the growth rate. Of course, this assumes that investment is strong enough to absorb the additional saving.

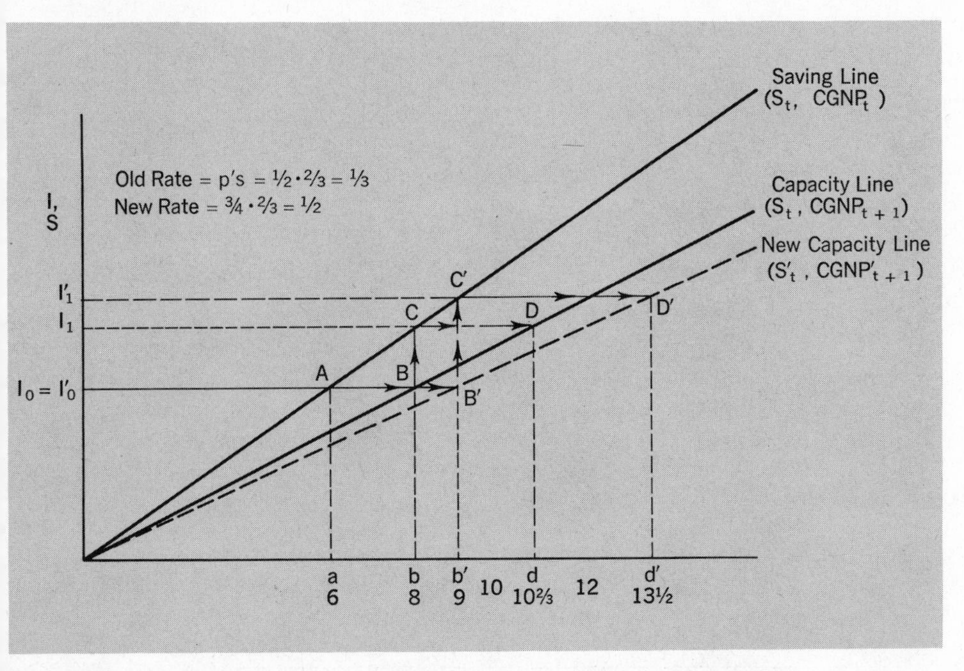


**Figure 29–1.** Effect of change in productivity ratio on the rate of growth.

**Change in Productivity Ratio.** In Figure 29–1 the productivity ratio is ½, initially, whereas the propensity to save is ⅔. This yields a growth rate of $p's = ½ \cdot ⅔ = ⅓$. As the expansion of *GNP* and $S = I$ follows the path *ABCD,* the successive values of *CGNP*—6, 8, 10⅔, and so on—are generated. Of course, this sequence illustrates the growth rate of ⅓. As the productivity ratio increases to ¾, the capacity line shifts to the right. The spread between the saving and capacity lines is now greater. So, as a result, are the successive increases in *CGNP* and $I = S$. Here the growth rate is $p's = ¾ \cdot ⅔ = ½$, as borne out by the sequence of *CGNP* values—6, 9, 13½, and so on.

**Increase in the Propensity To Save.** In Figure 29–2 an upward shift in the saving line is illustrated. Here the propensity to save is originally ⅗, the productivity ratio ½, leading to a growth rate of $p's = ½ \cdot ⅗ = \frac{3}{10}$. This leads to a sequence of *CGNP* values of 50, 65, 84½, and so on, which illustrates this growth rate.

In period zero, under the initial conditions, equilibrium of saving and investment is found at A. Now the propensity to save rises from ⅗ to ⅘, and with it the saving line. If equilibrium is to obtain at $CGNP = 50 = Oa$, investment must rise from $I_0$ to $I'_0$. Then a new equilibrium obtains at $A'$. The shift in the saving line also shifts the capacity line, because that line is a relationship between saving (= in-

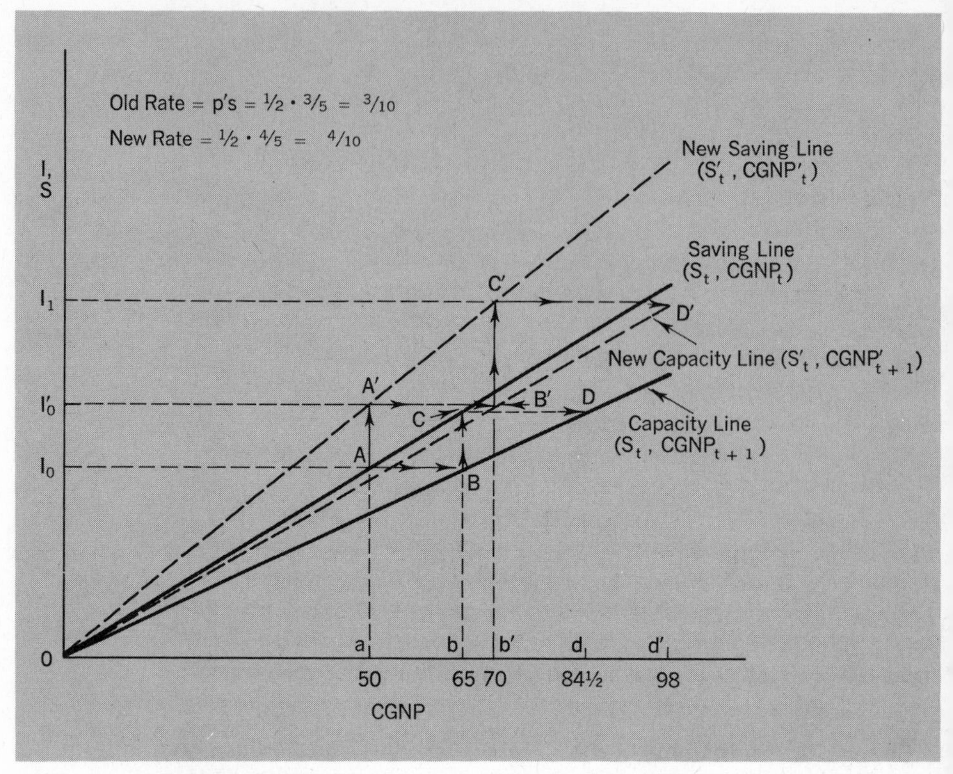


**Figure 29–2.** Effect of change in propensity to save on rate of growth.

vestment) and *CGNP* in the following period; the horizontal distance between the saving and capacity lines at a given level of saving remains unchanged.

As a result of this shift the growth rate rises from $p's = \frac{1}{2} \cdot \frac{3}{5} = \frac{3}{10}$ to $\frac{1}{2} \cdot \frac{4}{5} = \frac{4}{10}$. This is borne out by the sequence of values of *CGNP*, namely, 50, 70, 98, and so on.

## IMPORTS, EXPORTS, AND GROWTH

**Imports.** Though an economy may depend mainly on domestic forces to achieve and maintain a higher rate of growth, foreign trade exerts some influence on the growth of income. For example, the less-developed countries are likely to depend heavily on imports from the industrialized countries. Imports of capital and consumer goods tend to raise the rate of growth. Of course, imports of consumer goods have some effect on the rate of growth, increasing it if domestic resources can now be shifted to the production of capital goods. The more highly industrialized nations also depend upon imports, in varying degrees, to sustain a higher growth rate. It therefore seems worth while to give at least passing consideration to an open economy and to observe how imports may stimulate growth.

Before setting up a simple model to express the influence of imports on the growth of income, we pause long enough to examine the long-run import function. In shifting from a short-run equilibrium analysis to long-run growth equilibrium it is necessary to alter the import function to agree with people's long-run tendencies to import. Because we assume a constant marginal propensity to import in short-run analysis, changes in the amount of imports depend mainly on changes in the amount of income. Even at zero income society spends a certain amount; as income rises, more is spent on imports. However, society fails to spend for imports exactly proportional amounts out of its income.

The import pattern in the long run is somewhat different. Historically, the United States has tended to improve its level of living by increasing imports in proportion to a rise in real income. (Refer back to Figure 25–3, and note the relationship between imports and real income during the years 1929–64.) There are many reasons why the public acted in this manner. People had sufficient time to adjust their spending in accordance with changes in real income. "Keeping up with the Joneses" prompted the purchase of additional foreign goods, as well as domestic products, at higher levels of real income. As specialization became more widespread, output or real income rose. (Recall the gains in production and consumption that result from specialization and exchange in the theory of trade in Chapter 23!) Such gains implied larger real incomes and more consumption of foreign as well as domestic goods. Real savings were possible from importing goods produced more efficiently abroad. Of course, a part of total imports consisted of raw materials and capital goods. These imports helped to make possible a larger domestic output, higher income, and additional consumption, saving, and imports. These few observations should be sufficient to indicate that the long-run level of imports varies in direct proportion to real income.

Perhaps we can more readily understand the nature of the long-run import function if we momentarily revert to short-run analysis. Back in Chapter 25, it was explained that what is not spent for consumption or saved out of the open economy's income is necessarily spent on imports. (We are here ignoring the role of government.) Consequently, $M = NNP - (C + S)$. In a growing economy the relationship between consumption, saving, imports, and $GNP$ reveals similar properties—that is $C + S + M = GNP$. But since the level of consumption and the level of saving vary in direct proportion to *GNP,* the import function must also reveal this characteristic. A long-run import curve is therefore drawn as a straight line through the origin, as shown by the line labeled *M* in Figure 29–3. The slope of the *M* (propensity to import) line is less than 1 and lies below a 45-degree line through the origin (not shown), because imports are a proper fraction of real income.

The average propensity to import is the ratio between imports and *GNP,* or $M/GNP$. Because the long-run average propensity to import is constant with respect to *GNP,* the long-run marginal propensity to import $\Delta M/\Delta GNP$ is also constant, and, hence, equal to the long-run average propensity to import. Table 29–1 shows these relationships. Estimates of the long-run marginal (and average) propensity to import for the United States show that this magnitude amounts to approximately 0.030, or 3 per cent of *GNP* during the 15-year period 1950–64. Though the long-run marginal (and average) propensity to import for the United States is among the lowest in the world, we should not get the impression that the volume of imports is insignificant. Incidentally, the noticeable steepness in the progression of the average propensity to import between 1950–64 compared to the earlier period (see Figure 25–3) substantiates the notion that as a nation becomes richer it requires increased imports.

So much for the nature of the long-run import function. Now let us see how imports may influence growth. In the ensuing discussion

**Figure 29–3.** Long-run import line.

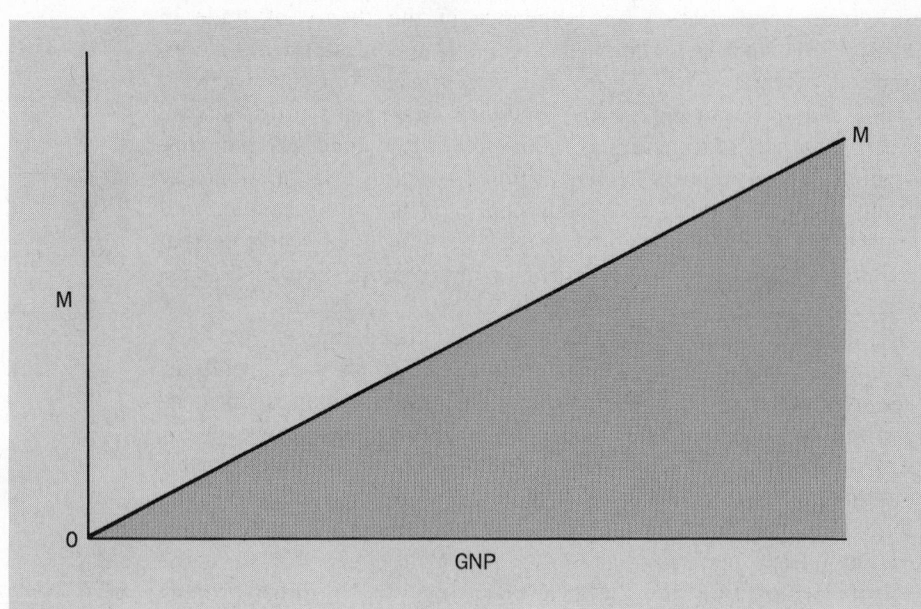

we will ignore the role of government in order to make the analysis as free from complications as possible. We begin with the saving and investment equilibrium condition for an open economy: Thus

$$I + E = S + M \, , \tag{5}$$

where $I$ is domestic gross real investment, $E$ real exports, $S$ domestic gross real saving, and $M$ real imports. Now we consider the functional relationships involved.

**TABLE 29-1**
**Average and Marginal Propensities to Import for the United States, 1950–64 (Billions of 1954 Dollars)**

| Year | GNP | Expenditures on Imports | Average Propensity to Import | Marginal Propensity to Import |
|---|---|---|---|---|
| 1949 | 292.7 | 7.5 | 0.026 | |
| 1950 | 318.1 | 9.9 | 0.031 | 0.093 |
| 1951 | 341.8 | 11.4 | 0.033 | 0.062 |
| 1952 | 353.5 | 10.9 | 0.031 | −0.044 |
| 1953 | 369.0 | 10.9 | 0.030 | 0.000 |
| 1954 | 363.1 | 10.2 | 0.028 | 0.118 |
| 1955 | 392.7 | 11.2 | 0.029 | 0.034 |
| 1956 | 400.9 | 12.0 | 0.030 | 0.097 |
| 1957 | 408.6 | 12.0 | 0.029 | 0.000 |
| 1958 | 401.3 | 11.6 | 0.029 | −0.056 |
| 1959 | 428.6 | 13.3 | 0.031 | 0.061 |
| 1960 | 439.9 | 12.8 | 0.029 | −0.045 |
| 1961 | 447.7 | 13.0 | 0.029 | 0.026 |
| 1962 | 474.8 | 14.9 | 0.031 | 0.069 |
| 1963 | 492.6 | 17.0 | 0.038 | 0.117 |
| 1964 | 516.0 | 18.6 | 0.036 | 0.067 |
| | | | 0.454 | 0.599 |

Average propensity to import = 0.454/15 = 0.032.
Marginal propensity to import = 0.599/15 = 0.039.

Saving and imports are assumed to be individually and jointly proportional to *GNP*. We can draw a saving plus import line through the origin to designate the value of $S + M$ at every level of *GNP*. As usual, investment, through its productivity, causes a rise in the subsequent *CGNP*. Exports stand in a separate position, as autonomous spending, neither functionally related to *GNP* like imports nor causing subsequent changes in capacity like investment.

Perhaps the easiest approach is geometrical. We start by drawing an $S + M$ line in Figure 29–4, showing the value of savings and imports at *CGNP*. From this we subtract the autonomous level of exports $MN$ vertically from the $S + M$ line, giving the $S + M - E$ line. This line gives the relation between $S + M - E$ and *CGNP* in the same period. We then follow our procedure of the appendix to the preceding chapter by expressing the productivity of investment as a horizontal distance laid off to the right of the $S+M-E\ (=I)$ line. Thus $AB = \Delta CGNP_t = CGNP_{t+1} - CGNP_t$ at $I\ (= S+M-E)$ of $OR$.

Suppose investment in period zero is $OR$. Then equilibrium is found at $A$ where $I_0 = S_0 + M_0 - E$, or $I_0 + E = S_0 + M_0$. Here $E$ bears no subscript, because it is autonomous and does not necessarily change from period to period. With investment of $OR$ there is an in-

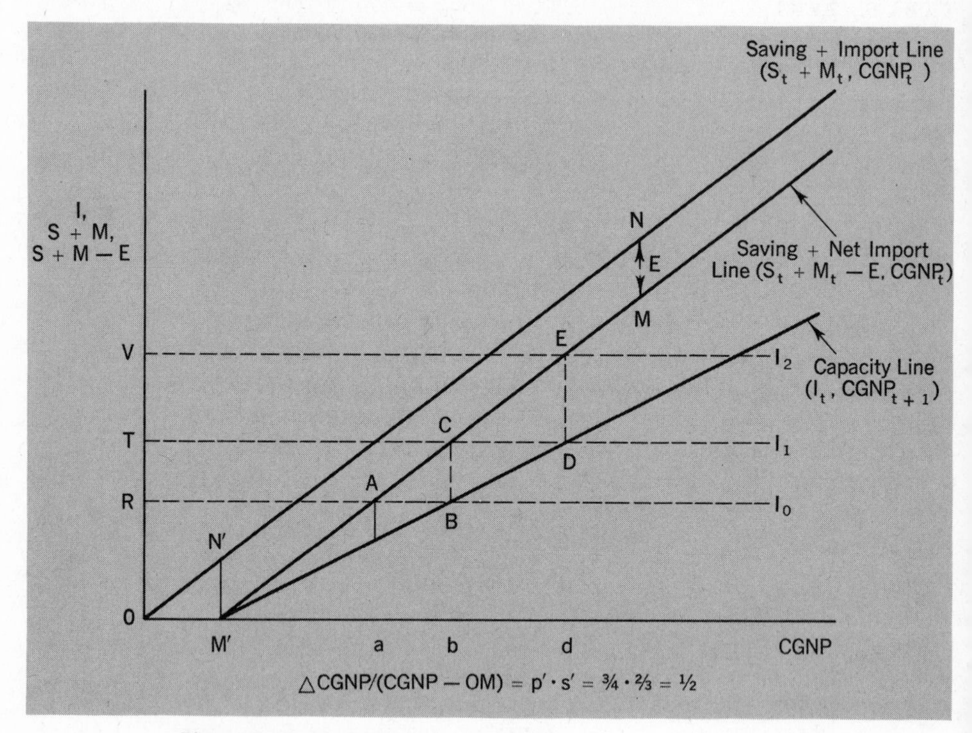


**Figure 29–4.** Foreign trade and growth.

crease in productive capacity of $AB$, and $CGNP$ increases to $RB$ in period one. With this larger $CGNP$, capacity $S+M-E$ rises to $OT$, found at point $C$. If $GNP$ is to equal $CGNP$, investment must rise to $OT$ in period one. Thus $CGNP$ (and $GNP$) follow the stair-step pattern $ABCDE$.

What can we say about the growth rate? Intuitively, it is clear that the growth rate, starting from an origin of $M'$, is a proportional one. The proof is exactly the same as in the last chapter. Here the slope of the Saving + Net Import line is $s+m$, where $s$ and $m$ are the (marginal and average) propensities to save and import. The growth rate of $CGNP$ measured from $M'$ is a constant percentage rate equal to

$$p'(s+m)\ ;$$

more precisely,

$$\frac{\Delta CGNP}{CGNP - OM'} = p'(s+m)\ . \tag{6}$$

Here

$$OM' = \frac{OM'}{M'N'} \cdot M'N' = \frac{GNP}{S+M} \cdot E$$
$$= E \div (S+M)/GNP = E \times \frac{1}{s+m} \cdot \tag{7}$$

The expression $1/(s+m)$ is the multiplier, and $E \times 1/(s+m)$ is the total effect of $E$ on $GNP$ operating through the multiplier.

We may derive the (varying) growth rate for $CGNP$ algebraically, as follows.

The equilibrium condition is:

$$S + M - E = I$$
$$sCGNP + mCGNP - E = I$$
$$(s+m)CGNP = I + E$$
$$CGNP = (I+E) \times 1/(s+m)\ . \tag{8}$$

Growth in $CGNP$ results from the productivity of investment. Thus,

$$\Delta CGNP = p'I\ . \tag{9}$$

Dividing equation (9) by (8), we get

$$\frac{\Delta CGNP}{CGNP} = \frac{p'I}{(I+E) \times 1/(s+m)}$$
$$= p'(s+m) \times \frac{I}{I+E} \cdot \tag{10}$$

As $I$ grows through time, $I/(I+E)$ apparently approaches 1, because $E$ is assumed to be autonomous and not to increase with time. Hence the growth rate seemingly approaches $p'(s+m)$ through time. This final condition is of more theoretical than practical interest, because $E$ actually does tend to increase, although quite irregularly, with the passage of time. Accordingly, it is better to reserve judgment on the possibility.

**Combining All Elements.** We may show the final synthesis graphically and simply. The equilibrium condition is that

$$I + G_i = S + M + (T - G_c) - E\ . \tag{11}$$

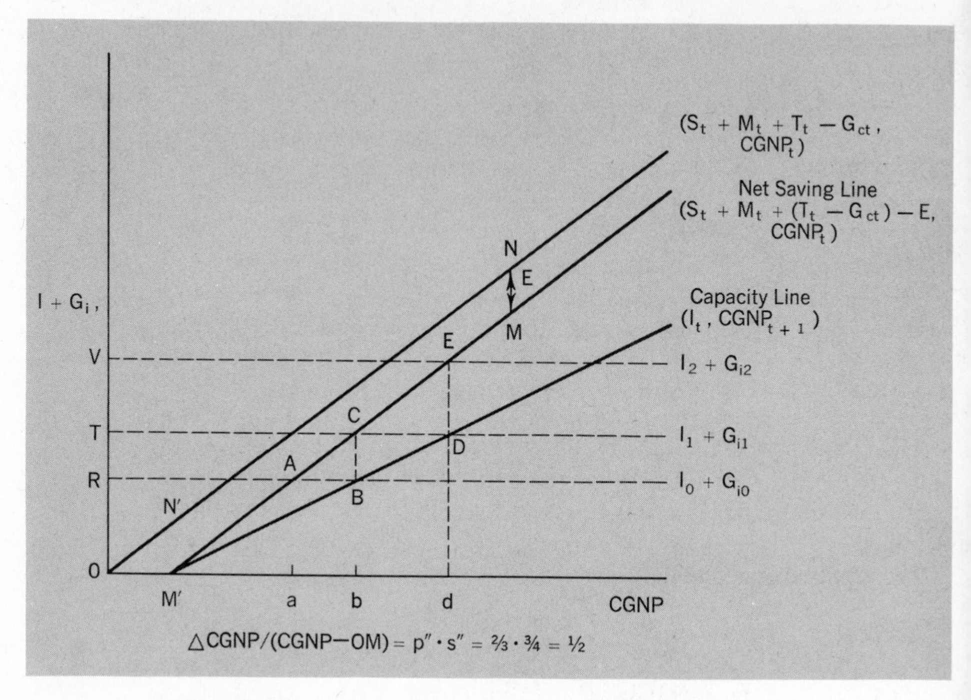


**Figure 29–5.** Summary diagram combining all elements.

We may call the right-hand side *net saving*. Here *S, M,* and $(T - G_c)$ are all proportional to *CGNP, E* is autonomous, and $I - G_i$ acts on *CGNP* in a proportion $p''$. We may relabel the preceding figure simply to indicate the formal relationships. The growth rates, as developed in the preceding note, can be written

$$\frac{\Delta CGNP}{CGNP - OM'} = p''(s + m + t - g) \tag{12}$$

$$\frac{\Delta CGNP}{CGNP} = p''(s + m + t - g) \times \frac{I + G_i}{I + G_i + E}\,. \tag{13}$$

We show the revised labeling in Figure 29–5 to picture the growth process. This seems to require no additional explanation.